D1807004

International Law and Power

Perspectives on Legal Order and Justice

International Law and Power

Perspectives on Legal Order and Justice

Essays in Honour of Colin Warbrick

Edited by

Kaiyan Homi Kaikobad and Michael Bohlander

MARTINUS

NIJHOFF

PUBLISHERS

LEIDEN • BOSTON
2009

This book is printed on acid-free paper.

Library of Congress Cataloging-in-Publication Data

International law and power : perspectives on legal order and justice : essays in honour of Colin Warbrick / edited by Kaiyan Homi Kaikobad and Michael Bohlander.
    p. cm.
  Includes index.
  ISBN 978-90-04-17587-7 (hardback : alk. paper)
  1. International law. 2. Human rights. I. Warbrick, Colin, 1943- II. Kaikobad, Kaiyan Homi.
III. Bohlander, Michael, 1962-

  KZ3410.I5783 2009
  341–dc22

2009020197

ISBN 978 90 04 17587 7

PRINTED IN THE NETHERLANDS

Foreword

Judge Rosalyn Higgins

President
International Court of Justice

I am extremely pleased that this *festschrift* has been prepared for Colin Warbrick. He is a colleague for whom I have the highest respect. He is also greatly liked by all who know him.

If there were a need to explain 'the essence' of Colin Warbrick, two things would immediately come to my mind. He is a top drawer international lawyer, and he is irretrievably a man of the north.

Colin Warbrick is an international lawyer who is at once a fine generalist and also a leading specialist in particular topics. He has, among other things, written about the use of force, diplomatic representation and protection, recognition, the Security Council and UN peacekeeping. But his reputation rests primarily on his great expertise in the fields of human rights and the European Convention on Human Rights in particular, international criminal law and associated themes such as extradition.

His annual case survey on the European Convention (sometimes in collaboration with others) in the *Yearbook of European Law* has been absolutely invaluable to the rest of us, as has his leadership on the project on United Kingdom Materials on International Law appearing annually in the *British Yearbook of International Law*. We can be in no doubt that the work entailed in these publications has been daunting in its volume and complexity. For the reader, there has been the comfort of knowing that everything has been presented with clarity, scrupulous fairness and meticulous attention to detail. But Warbrick's contribution has been more than that – it is that all of this knowledgeable imparting of information is buttressed by a trenchant and original analysis.

Although Professor Warbrick joined the University of Birmingham in 2006, he was associated for long years with the University of Durham. It is no exaggeration to say that the high profile in international law of the Law Department of the University of Durham is owed to Colin Warbrick's presence there. He worked tirelessly for the Department and the University, introduced and taught with great flair, in his indomitable style, LL.M. courses on *Human Rights* and *Select Problems in International Law* and looked after the undergraduate students learning international law. His stature, reputation and personality were such as to also attract other younger international lawyers to that department.

With his colleagues, whether at Durham and Birmingham or elsewhere, Colin Warbrick could always be relied on to be forthright and totally unpretentious. Whatever the occasion, however formal the rest of us might have felt it to be, there would be Colin in his shirtsleeves, calling a legal spade a spade. Not for him empty formalities or the passing fashions from which the world of international law is no more immune than other intellectual worlds. There has always been something deeply grounded in the character of Colin Warbrick.

He has felt it very important to spend most his academic life in the part of England he so knew and loved. This affinity to his surroundings and the intellectual comfort they provided him, was made clear to me when on one occasion I sought (unsuccessfully) to lure him away to pastures new. The North of England was where he wanted to be.

And thus it is that in Britain we are fortunate enough to have, throughout the Law Departments around the country, international lawyers of the highest quality. We may count ourselves lucky that the lure of Oxbridge, London and overseas has been entirely resistible for Colin Warbrick and some other our of eminent international law teachers.

At the same time, all international lawyers have to work in an international world. Although Professor Warbrick's northern roots and attachments have been important to him, he has fully engaged in important ventures that reflect his international standing. He has had longstanding contacts with the Council of Europe, where he became Consultant for human rights questions. He has lectured for the Council in Poland, Romania, Lithuania and Croatia. He gave a very successful course of lectures on international criminal law at the University of Thessaloniki and has also addressed the NATO staff college in Rome. His advice on human rights has been equally valued by the OSCE.

Nor has he shirked the burdens of a successful international lawyer closer to home. He has among other things, been a special adviser to the Select Committee on the Constitution of the House of Lords, assisted with training of the Judiciary, Lord Chancellor's Department, Home Office and Tribunal chairs when the Human Rights Act was introduced.

His services have been much sought after. Professor Warbrick has also been active in the International Law Association (including as a member of the Committee on Extradition and Human Rights) and as Chairman of the British Branch Committee on Theory and International Law. He was a member of the Council of Europe's Committee on Mutual Assistance and has been a valued member of the Advisory Board on Public International Law of the British Institute of International and Comparative Law.

A man of the north and an internationalist; a colleague of the utmost reliability; a forthright personality and a razor-sharp intellect and a warm companion. This volume is a tribute to the man and to his work, prepared by those who are at once his friends and his admirers.

Colin Warbrick: An Appreciation

Harvey Teff[*] and Bob Sullivan[**]

[*] Professor Emeritus, Department of Law, University of Durham (1969–2004).
[**] Professor of Law, University College London, former Professor of Law, Department of Law, University of Durham (1973–2006).

Few scholars can have made such a distinctive contribution to knowledge and understanding in their areas of expertise as Colin Warbrick. A formidable record of scholarly publication and public involvement in International Law, Human Rights and Constitutional Law, combined with a singular capacity to inspire generations of students, particularly postgraduates, are testimony to the extent of his influence. Colin has never been content to settle for the quiet academic life, even in the days when this was a relatively easy option. Because he has always been acutely conscious that his specialties have a key role to play beyond the confines of the academy, the quality of his scholarship and pedagogical skills has been enhanced by extensive personal engagement in national and international conferences, seminars and high level meetings with politicians, officials and their lawyers. He is as much at ease when acting as a Council of Europe 'Expert' on Human Rights; Adviser to the House of Lords Select Committee on the Constitution, or addressing delegates at major conferences on International Law, as when enlightening, when not berating, colleagues at University and Board of Studies meetings. Whatever the occasion, he will be alarmingly well-informed, quick-witted and highly persuasive. Most importantly, his forensic skills are underpinned by a consistent set of principles and a deeply-ingrained sense of fairness.

In 1966, on completing his legal studies at Cambridge, Colin was appointed as a Research Officer at the British Institute of International and Comparative Law. Throughout his career he has remained very actively involved in the affairs of the Institute. As well as his Editorship of Current Developments in the *International and Comparative Law Quarterly*, a position which he has held since 1985, he has been a member of the Institute's Public International Advisory Board since 1992, and was Chairman of its International Criminal Court Project (1993–1998). In 1968–1969, he was a Fulbright Scholar at the University of Michigan, and in the following year joined the handful of staff then at the Law Department of the University of Durham. There he would later become a Senior Lecturer (1981), Professor (1996) and Chairman of the Board of Studies in Law (1998–2001), before his departure to Birmingham University, in 2006, where he became Barber Professor of Jurisprudence, before retiring in 2009. It is in our capacity as longstanding friends and colleagues that we offer the following reflections.

It is impossible to think of Colin at Durham without evoking vivid memories of his room. Colin has always been most hospitable and gregarious, and one was always made very welcome. The door to his room was almost invariably open, well, as far as it could be. The problem for any visitor squeezing through it was to identify and then reach a chair not already occupied by assorted journals, articles, lecture notes, and sundry documents, in no discernible order. There must have been a time when this was not the case, but neither of us can recall it. The delicate ecological balance had several consequences. The obvious apparent difficulty for Colin himself, in finding the appropriate lecture notes, or minutes of the last meeting, was perhaps the least of his worries. He has always been more than ready to deliver the (or a) lecture, or address the meeting, extempore. More troubling was the predicament of the daily cleaners, who would occasionally ask us if anything could be done. As for the window cleaners, their task was beyond human endeavour. The target was simply way out of reach, surrounded by two bookcases, and a large desk, bulging with a further array of precariously balanced files and documents. Colin resolutely stood his ground, unabashed, not to say affronted, by any diplomatic inquiries about this state of affairs, dismissing outright the argument that it was incompatible with his official role as Departmental Health and Safety Officer.

What is most significant about all this, of course, is that Colin had volunteered for that role. When the familiar Board of Studies request for a volunteer elicited the predictable silence and lowering of heads, more often than not it was Colin who was first to respond, despite the numerous commitments that he already had. No department can flourish without a core of members who lead by example, not only by insisting on rigorous academic standards but by encouraging younger members of staff and contributing to administrative matters and the development of policy. In all these respects, Colin has been an exemplary leader. In the inevitable battles departments have with the Administration, no one, we would venture, has been quicker to discern any hidden agenda and identify the most appropriate strategy, just as, when the chips were down, no one could expose the threatened departures from principle and fairness more robustly and effectively, whatever the forum.

As can readily be imagined, Colin was in his element in the staff common room. On the subject of University policy, unerringly accurate predictions of dire consequences would be interspersed with a fund of stylishly delivered anecdotes and detailed information on a remarkably diverse range of topics, from worldwide events to the most esoteric minutiae of sporting achievement. On one occasion, what began as an innocuous inquiry about the number of States in the World ended with Colin purporting to name them all. Even when due allowance is made for unresolved disputes over juridical status, not to mention our own geographically-challenged status, we could not deny a sneaking admiration for the impressive if suspiciously large list.

An acknowledged authority in several areas of International Law, Colin developed particular expertise in the law of the sea, extradition, recognition and, latterly, International Criminal Courts. From the early 1980s onwards, his increasing involvement in Human Rights issues was to be reflected in numerous articles on the European Convention, culminating in co-authorship of the seminal text, *Law of the European Convention on Human Rights* (with D. Harris and M. O'Boyle) in 1995. Not long afterwards, he was to play an important part in providing training on the Human Rights Act, addressing senior officials from key bodies and institutions, including the Lord Chancellor's Department, Judicial Studies Board, Home Office and the Foreign and Commonwealth Office, as well as several leading barristers' chambers and solicitors' firms.

Colin has had the distinction of being appointed Director of Studies in Public International Law at the Hague Academy (1993), and a Council of Europe 'Expert' on Human Rights and Academic Freedom in several East European countries. He has also been much in demand on advisory and editorial boards; as an external examiner; assessor for senior appointments, and as a referee for numerous leading publishers and journals. Yet despite such copious demands, he has always found time for his students and, in particular, has devoted exceptional attention to the supervision and career prospects of the many postgraduates who have benefited from his tutelage.

Although, as is apparent, Colin has travelled far and wide in his academic career, he has always been immensely attached to Durham City, playing for the first XV rugby team for many years and now ruling over an ever expanding allotment. Consequently, many friends and colleagues would have been surprised and curious when Colin resigned his Chair at Durham to become a professor at the School of Law, University of Birmingham, in 2006. This is not the time and place for even the most anodyne account of the circumstances that led to his departure alongside so many other gifted staff from the Department of Law at Durham. Suffice it to say that Colin found the then prevailing stewardship of the Department, and the University's attitude towards the treatment of some of his colleagues, intolerable. Though he put all his considerable powers at their disposal, even his best efforts could not prevail. Typically, he entered the scholarly and social life of the School of Law at Birmingham with exceptional enthusiasm and commitment, to the great benefit of students and staff. We would not have expected anything else.

Colin is singularly indifferent to matters of formal recognition and external status. It took much persuasion by colleagues, over a period of years, to induce him to apply for promotion to a chair at Durham. This was not due to any diffidence on his part, far from it. It was simply that acquisition of a chair did not feature high on his priorities. Yet his ever increasing stature as an international lawyer made its absence all the more anomalous. Earlier mention of Colin's role as Adviser to the House of Lords Select Committee on the Constitution prompts another memory. It would seem to provide an apt tribute with which to conclude this brief sketch of a man who does not stand on ceremony and prides himself on not being a slave to sartorial etiquette. When he first arrived at the gates to discharge his role as Adviser, a factotum apparently insisted on his wearing a jacket and tie like the other participants. Despite his prolonged protestations, eventually, suitably attired by the powers-that-be, he took his place amongst the august members of the Committee. The first person to give evidence was another distinguished international lawyer. On entering the room, he was completely thrown, and was heard to mutter under his breath 'Blimey, they've made Warbrick a Lord.'

Contents

Acknowledgments

We would be remiss if we failed to acknowledge with gratitude the help and assistance we have received from various persons over the two years since the decision was first taken to produce this *festschrift*. In the first place, we wish to thank all the contributors without whom the project would not, of course, have reached fruition. In the second place, two sets of outstandingly competent persons need to be identified, the first of them being located in Durham and the other at Brunel. As far as the Durham set is concerned, we need emphatically to single out Ms. Joanne Emerson who, when approached with the idea and proposal to be the lead administrative official for the project, accepted the offer readily. Not only was her fortitude in this regard matched by the efficiency, promptness, patience and skill with which she undertook the task of administering the project, but Joanne's ready smile generated the buoyancy necessary for such a journey. Mr. Rupert Prudom, who came to the project as the expert in information technology, was a constant source of support, and it is true that we would never have been able to succeed had it not been for the expertise he brought in helping with sorting out various problems attending the gradual expansion of the book. Ms Rachel Tucker was also very helpful on a number of occasions.

Always willing to go the extra mile for the Law School and its former members, the Palace Green librarians have been truly magnificent in their support. Manifesting genuine enthusiasm for the project, Mrs. Anne Farrow and Mrs. Judy McKinnell's skill and patience in handling our requests with respect to the book and other materials must not go unacknowledged. A special word of thanks also goes out to two Palace Green Library antique book conservation experts, Ms Elizabeth Branigan and Ms Emma Lloyd-Jones, who helped us in connection with our enquiries regarding the production of a special pre-publication leather bound half-Morocco to be presented to Colin at his valedictory dinner at Birmingham.

We must also mention members of staff at Brunel Law School. Chief among the persons who gave us valuable help, advice and encouragement in managing and organising the chapters of the book from time to time was the information technology officer, Mr. Matthew Howells. Apart from regularly resolving computer-based problems, Mr. Howells, not unlike his counterpart at Durham, was unflappable and there would never have been a final and definitive printout for purposes of the special presentation copy at the Birmingham function for Colin had it not been for his support. We must give a special word of thanks to Ms Amanda Kunicki, Ms Jenny King and Ms Rahena Begum, all three of whom helped out in several ways on different occasions.

Our experience with the publishers, Brill, has been truly rewarding. Very professional and thorough in every way, the Acquisitions Editor, Ms Lindy Melman, showed great understanding, patience and cooperation. We need also to record our gratitude for all the help and advice provided throughout by three outstanding and highly supportive editors, namely Ms. Gera van Bedaf, Mrs. Renee Otto and Mrs. Marjolein Schaake, with respect to a large number of queries, requests and problems. Our sense of gratitude also extends to Ms Gaby van Rietschoten for her advice regarding the production of the *festschrift*. We must also say *hartelijk dank* to Ms. Celine Ostendorf who designed the very handsome cover for the book, a feature not to be underestimated by any means. *Heel erg bedankt!*

It is conventional for authors and editors to end their acknowledgements with a special word of thanks for close members of the family, especially their spouses. In our case, however, it is not a question of convention but more a veritable need to express our heartfelt sense of gratitude to our wives, Christine Bohlander and Dhun Kaikobad, both of whom have had to bear up with our absences, the prioritising of *festschrift* work, and of course, with the demands of writing our own contributions. We extend our sincerest sentiments of gratitude to both of them.

Preface by the Editors

Colin Warbrick's work over the long years of his distinguished career has spanned a wide range of legal fields. It is only fitting that the essays compiled below should seek also to address the wide-ranging areas of the law in which he has had great impact. The book is divided into three parts to reflect the doctrinal categories in order to which Colin, we feel, is particularly drawn.

In Part One, the *festschrift* looks at salient general principles of public international law and in particular international human rights. *Harris* assesses the impact of the collective complaints remedy under the European Social Charter after its first decade or so of operation. He examines the approach adopted by the European Committee of Social Rights with respect to the interpretation of the Charter in collective complaint cases. The approach taken by the Committee is in keeping with the human rights character of the Charter. It is especially noticeable for the dynamic interpretation of the Charter adopted by it and for its treatment of the problem of the justiciablity of economic and social rights by reference to the need to take some account of a Sate's 'available resources'. Overall, the experience of the first ten years of the Charter system is considered a positive development providing as it does an encouraging model for the (individual) right of petition under consideration for the International Covenant on Economic, Social and Cultural Rights.

Hartmann investigates the guidance provided by the European Convention on Human Rights (ECHR) on extradition following the decision of the European Court of Human Rights in the *Soering* case. Since then, the Court has heard a good number of complaints by individuals against their removal. Renewed interest in the subject is warranted given the burgeoning jurisprudence of the Court and the fact that several Member States of the Council of Europe may have been involved in the rendition of individuals by clandestine or irregular procedures, also known as 'extra-ordinary rendition'. This chapter looks at the removal of persons from the jurisdiction of a State in the context of the ECHR. It analyses how individuals' rights, in particular those that have been or are likely to be advanced as an obstacle to extradition, may influence removal in order to ascertain the weight to be attached to each right within its specific context. Examining the Convention from this perspective, this chapter seeks to identify how various rights within the Convention may affect the removal of a person from the jurisdiction of a Contracting State.

Neff raises the question of the possible existence of a *non liquet* in international law, a question which continues to provoke disagreement amongst scholars. The view that the International Court of Justice pronounced a *non liquet* in the *Nuclear Weapons* advisory opinion in 1996 is widespread. An important issue of concern discussed below is what is called a 'systemic' *non liquet*, referring to a gap in the fabric of international law itself. Hans Kelsen and Hersch Lauterpacht were strongly of the view that such a *non liquet* could not exist, though on very different grounds. Kelsen relied on the mechanical application of what he called the residuary negative principle to avoid a *non liquet*, while Lauterpacht placed his faith in judicial creativity. In opposition was Julius Stone, who maintained that a *non liquet* is possible. The Court's advisory opinion of 1996 did not in reality, as argued by Neff, pronounce a *non liquet*, since the Court's inability to reach a firm conclusion lay chiefly in the absence of the necessary factual basis rather than on a gap in the law itself. Moreover, six of the judges expressed in their individual opinions views on the *non liquet* question, two on the lines of Kelsen and two on the lines of Lauterpacht. Present evidence is against the possibility of a *non liquet*, but the issue remains an open one.

Wood takes a sceptical view of the notion of the 'constitutionalization' of international law. Most 'constitutionalist' approaches, including such ideas as 'global administrative law', are essentially policy prescripts, and have little bases in the realities of international affairs. They reflect, perhaps, a peculiarly European (or even Germanic) approach to international law, which may well be influenced by the fact that in some countries teachers of international law also teach constitutional law.

Cullen studies a number of measures which address issues of child labour and the imposition of new positive obligations on States. Whereas obligations under International Labour Organisation Conventions, up to and including Convention No. 138 of 1973, emphasised the creation of a legislative framework setting out minimum ages for employment, new treaties, including Convention No. 182 of 1999 which deals with the worst forms of child labour, require a wider range of actions by States parties. These include legislative changes, labour inspection, criminal prosecutions of violators and protective measures for persons caught up in exploitative child labour. Other recent legal initiatives, including the two Optional Protocols to the Convention on the Rights of the Child, certain treaties concerning people trafficking concluded under the aegis of the UN and the Council of Europe, and relevant European regional measures for purposes of combating the sexual exploitation of children, also impose obligations in relation to the areas identified by Convention No. 182 as the worst forms of child labour. However, States seem to have made a stronger commitment to addressing the criminal law aspects of child labour than the protective ones. This is reinforced primarily by the greater detail in which criminal law obligations are drafted in the relevant treaties, including treaties on trafficking in persons, commercial sexual exploitation of children and child soldiers. It has also been argued that the approach of international human rights law generally, and the European Court of Human Rights in particular, privileges criminal law responses to human rights violations. The highly detailed obligations in relation to the prosecution of those who exploit child labour may be contrasted with the vagueness of the obligations imposed on States to protect the victims of abusive child labour. These obligations are relatively under-developed, and States have demonstrated some resistance to such obligations, for example, by failing to provide residence rights for trafficked children. Arguably, protective measures for exploited children should come first, and the prosecution of offenders should follow, with protective measures in place for children involved in these criminal proceedings as victims and witnesses as an integral part of the proceedings. However, States seem to have begun with the need to prosecute and to have viewed protective measures as subsidiary. There are some notable exceptions in the practice of the International Criminal Court and in recent Council of Europe standards, but the trend is still to choose prosecution over protection as the number one priority in addressing exploitative child labour.

Lowe considers the different normative roles that might be played by a rule of international law and asks whether its role within English Law is necessarily the same as its role within international law. He sets out by examining the relationship between international law and English law. Viewing it as essentially a simple one, he reminds the reader that the connection between English law and international law is established not through the royal power but through the common law, as pointed out by Blackstone. The Crown does indeed have the prerogative to devise foreign policy and conduct the international relations of the State but it may do so only within the framework of international law. He asks whether the present traditional position that customary international law is a part of and is automatically incorporated into English law is a satisfactory one. His study of this problem leads him to the proposition that international law is in fact a source as opposed to being a part of English common law, a proposition which raises a number of implications and juridical problems. He does not neglect to point out the fact that difficulties may arise when there is a wholesale adoption of international law in the municipal sphere: one of the dangers is that when individuals seek to defend themselves against the actions of the State by relying on principles of international law, they also run the risk arising from the fact that the rules of international law may cut both ways and thereby jeopardise their defence.

McCorquodale asserts that many international organisations act in ways that infringe the protection of human rights. His contribution examines the extent to which international organisations have international legal responsibilities under international human rights law. He shows that the general principles of State responsibility can be applied to the international legal responsibility of international organisations. Accordingly, international organisations have international legal responsibility to act with due diligence and not to infringe international human rights law. Such an approach has the potential of broad application within the international legal system, and in particular in post-conflict situations where sovereign power can be held by more than one participant. It is, moreover, relevant in the context of globalisation where certain powers of States and international organisations (and other non-State actors) are often intertwined. By way of caution, it is to be noted that McCorquodale reminds the reader that all parts of the law of State responsibility cannot uniformly or symmetrically apply to international organisations, or apply without considerable change. It is pointed out that there is at present no coherent avenue within the international legal system to enforce compliance with this responsibility. Even so, the fact is that these obligations and responsibilities of international organisations do exist, and where there is such compliance it can be at the institutional, managerial and political levels, and this may lead to different kinds of legal impact.

Part Two, entitled International Criminal Law and Justice, addresses issues which have been brought to the fore as a result of the increasing significance of criminal justice at the international level. *Fox* argues that the functional immunity of State officials is separable and that it is not an automatic, inevitable consequence of the rule of imputability which attributes the act to the State responsible for appointing the relevant official. She demonstrates that the recognised 'asymmetry between the rules of liability and immunity' with respect to the consequences of an international crime should properly be extended to the civil consequences of grave violations of international law. Immunity goes to jurisdiction of the municipal court whereas imputability goes to responsibility and the attribution of the act to the State. A removal of immunity in respect of the commission of international crimes does not result in an automatic judgment against the State; it merely provides a national court with an opportunity to decide in accordance with conflict of law rules whether there is sufficient connection to assume jurisdiction; whether the issue is justiciable in municipal law, and if so, whether the alleged crime is attributable to the State.

Cryer argues that it is a commonplace that judicial decisions do not usually create general international law in a formal sense. This much is clear from Article 38(1)(d) of the Statute of the International Court of Justice. Nonetheless, it is a truism that case-law is frequently highly influential, either because it crystallises a nascent rule, or because it is referred to as a shorthand expression for the position maintained in international law. This piece evaluates the extent to which the jurisprudence of the international criminal tribunals has precedential effect, both in their own legal orders, in the international legal order more generally, and finally in the United Kingdom. It does so through an analysis of the system of precedent created by the International Criminal Tribunal for Yugoslavia and the International Criminal Tribunal for Rwanda, and the analogous rules in the Rome Statute of the International Criminal Court. It then proceeds to look at the jurisprudence of those tribunals in other international courts, concentrating in particular on the ICJ decision in the *Bosnian Genocide* case. Turning to the UK, Cryer evaluates the position in common law, where the *Furundžija* case has relatively speaking, been frequently cited. He goes on then to examine the status granted to international criminal case-law under the United Kingdom International Criminal Court Act of 2001.

Bohlander reflects on the fact that the modern discussion of the laws of war, both in the area of the *ius ad bellum* and naturally more so of the *ius in bello*, increasingly centres on issues such as asymmetrical warfare and collateral damage among the civilian population, and how traditional concepts can be adapted to the new exigencies in the theatres of battle. His contribution takes up the issue of collateral damage and asks the question whether it is not preferable to re-evaluate the ban on targeted assassinations of heads of State and other regime elites responsible for the outbreak of hostilities and the ensuing human suffering, rather than to allow warring parties to use weaponry, no matter how 'smart', that will inevitably have a devastating impact on the lives of civilians. After all, the protection and non-involvement of civilians in the hostilities is one of the axiomatic principles of the modern law of war.

In his chapter, *Sullivan* argues that voluntary conduct on the part of a defendant is a necessary conceptual element for all forms of criminal liability across all jurisdictions. Moreover, the conduct which constitutes the prohibitory norm of the offence at issue must also be proved at any trial for that offence. He argues that criminal liability without any form of responsibility is conceptually untenable. Compliance with these necessary conditions by the courts of England and Wales is then scrutinised. He concludes that English law does not insist on conduct as a necessary predicate for criminal liability. However, if Article 6 of the European Convention for the Protection of Human Rights is fully to be realised by the judiciary, then all offences would have to be construed as requiring conduct and proof of conduct to establish criminal liability. This would improve the normative and conceptual condition of English criminal law.

McGoldrick seeks to provide a detailed analysis of the *Bosnian Genocide* case decided by the International Court of Justice in February 2007. At the heart of the case were fundamental issues of State identity, the consensual nature of jurisdiction and the interpretation of the Convention on the Prevention and Punishment of the Crime of Genocide, 1948, and his contribution is concerned with providing extensive commentary and analysis on these issues of the case. His examination reveals a measure of inconsistency in the Court's judgments as compared with its decision affirming jurisdiction in 2007, which is in some ways a reflection of personnel changes stretching over a period of fourteen years. He is sceptical as regards the problem of membership status of the Former Republic of Serbia (FRY)/Serbia and questions whether or not it was indeed a Member of the United Nations between 1992 and 2000. As far as the acts of genocide are concerned, McGoldrick comments on the approach adopted by the Court and notes that while the *actus reus* of that crime may well be relatively easy to establish, the necessary *mens rea* in terms of the specific genocidal intent will always be relatively more difficult to demonstrate. He argues that resort to a pattern of conduct to evidence the existence of the necessary specific intent would have been a defensible and realistic alternative because States will almost never specifically instruct the commission of genocide. Even so he points out that the Court did find that FRY/Serbia had failed to carry out its obligation to prevent the Srebrenica genocide and that this importantly was an obligation of conduct rather than result. He concludes by looking at the legal and political legacy of the Court's judgment on the merits of the case.

Post's chapter seeks to shed light on the legal problems arising from the presence of explosive remnants of war arising out of the Eritrean-Ethiopian armed conflict of 1998–2000. It focuses on the nature, scope and effects of the rights and duties of States in international law in general, and international humanitarian law in particular with reference to this war. It begins by examining the basic legal framework associated with explosive remnants and the terminology employed in various international instruments. With a view to providing perspective, the study gives a detailed account of the devastating consequences of the war and the presence of such explosive remnants for the two belligerent Parties. While Post examines the responsibilities incurred by these two States in this regard, he also demonstrates the extent to which they have satisfied or have failed to satisfy their obligations with respect to casualties and survivor assistance. The study then turns its attention to the problem of the explosive remnants of war in the light of international humanitarian law. In particular, Post examines the prohibition not to cause superfluous injury or unnecessary suffering; the prohibition against the use of weapons which cause indiscriminate harm, especially anti-personnel land mines and anti-vehicle mines and booby traps; and the obligation to locate and register such weapons in an ongoing armed conflict. The author is careful to point out the distinction between *jus in bello* and *jus post bello*. Special focus is thus placed on the duty to remove and destroy, and the duty to provide assistance with a view to rendering harmless land mines, booby traps and the explosive remnants of war *after* the cessation of hostilities. The study demonstrates that although efforts were made by both Parties to carry out their obligations under the law of armed conflict, they both remain, to one degree or another, in breach of the relevant and applicable rules of international law.

In *Kritsiotis'* essay an attempt is made to explore the substance of the *jus ad bellum* and *jus in bello* from the specific perspective of the violence of non-State actors, awarding a broad berth of definition to that term. The idea pursued by the author here is to reconstruct the Statist focus of the law on the matter from both the historical and contemporary standpoints. He goes on to consider how the interpretation and application of the law might have been wider in scope than that which the formal positions or representations suggest. The author scrutinises how, over time, and within the separate trajectories of the *jus ad bellum* and *jus in bello*, the law has engaged questions dealing with the violence of non-State actors, and how these engagements have been allied to the law's commitment to its own relevance and effectiveness in the real world and to an evolving sense of fairness and justice on the matters upon which the law has deliberated.

Part Three is concerned with topics generally related to international order and security. *Anderson* begins by showing how, over the past fifty years, international law has expanded and diversified into new areas and how the International Law Commission and the Sixth Committee of the United Nations have played a coordinating role in these developments. Although international courts and tribunals have multiplied during the past twenty years, there has been no overall planning in this respect, and there exists no hierarchical structure of these courts and tribunals. The result is a 'disordered medley'. A measure of responsibility for maintaining the coherence of international law rests upon the members of the different courts and tribunals. The best approach is that of respectful co-existence and cooperation among all international courts and tribunals.

In her chapter, *Katselli* points out that the recent violence and human rights abuses against political opponents or specific ethnic groups, such as those in Zimbabwe under the regime of Robert Mugabe and in Sudan, bring to the fore not only questions regarding the role of the international community and individual States in situations like these, but also the significance of countermeasures taken in the collective interest, the so-called solidarity measures. While it has progressed in some respects by establishing the international criminal responsibility of perpetrators of atrocities amounting to war crimes and/or crimes against humanity, international law has remained under-developed in the area of State responsibility and the enforcement of international norms owed to the international community as a whole. The concept of countermeasures taken in the collective interest is one which has developed through the work of the International Law Commission (ILC) on the codification of the Law on State Responsibility, and also through State practice, especially where it is based in *opinio juris*. The growing recognition that certain principles and norms are owed to the international community as a whole has led to the understanding that the circle of States affected by a given infringement of a norm of this nature is necessarily wide, giving rise to the question whether States not directly affected by such an infringement may resort to countermeasures. The question has proved to be a controversial one with, on the one hand, some States expressing reservations over giving a carte blanche, as it were, to States to respond to violations of international obligations on the pretext of pursuing collective interests; and, on the other, with the ILC deciding not to incorporate a right to solidarity measures in its 2001 Final Articles on State Responsibility. Nevertheless, the likelihood of a future recognition of a right by States other than the injured to resort to countermeasures makes a study of the latter of continuous interest. After providing a brief analysis of how the concept of third-State countermeasures has evolved, Katselli embarks on a study of the legal parameters that should be attached to such a right. She concludes her study by looking into some examples of State practice not considered by the ILC which, in the author's view, re-enhance the existence of a right vested in third States to adopt solidarity measures.

Merrills' appraisal of recent developments with regard to the Optional Clause Declaration is set out in three parts. The first part compares the situation in 2006 with that in prevalent in 1993 as regards (a) the number of declarations in force under Article 36(2) of the Statute of the International Court of Justice; and (b) their geographical distribution. The second part considers the changing quality of those declarations, and the third part reviews recent and pending cases involving the Optional Clause. The author's conclusion is that whilst the culture shift that a general acceptance of compulsory jurisdiction would require has yet to occur, States continue to make declarations under Article 36(2) and to use them, and accordingly he believes that the Optional Clause still matters.

Williams' examination proceeds from the fact that recent years have witnessed the establishment of a number of so-called hybrid or internationalized tribunals. Such institutions comprise a blend of the national and the international, both in their structure and composition, and the applicable law. Despite the continued use of such internationalized tribunals, there is little or no discussion of the legal bases for such tribunals. Her chapter outlines the background to the establishment of seven tribunals: the Special Court for Sierra Leone; the Extraordinary Chambers in the Courts of Cambodia; the War Crimes Chamber in the State Court of Bosnia and Herzegovina; the Regulation 64 Panels in Kosovo; the Special Panels for Serious Crimes in East Timor; the Iraqi High Tribunal and the Special Tribunal for Lebanon. It then assesses the legal basis for each of these institutions, which, she argues, is essential for determining correctly various complex issues of immunity, amnesty and State cooperation.

White shows that the current manifestation of international intervention in Afghanistan, the NATO-led International Security Assistance Force (ISAF), is being undertaken under the authority of the United Nations Security Council. Since February 2006, Britain, as a member of the UN and NATO, has committed a significant number of troops to ISAF, and these troops have been engaged in heavy fighting with the Taliban. Though militarily extremely problematic, the international legal basis of the operation seems straightforward since the UN Charter recognises Security Council authority as one of the exceptions to the prohibition on the use of force, along with action taken in self-defence in response to an armed attack. However, Security Council authority tends to obscure the deeper justifications and arguments of politics, law and justice behind each State's decision to contribute to such a dangerous operation. In tracing the history of the *jus ad bellum* and Britain's attitude towards it, this essay seeks to give a more informed account of the arguments of law and justice behind the British military contribution to the current fight against the Taliban in Afghanistan.

Rounding off the collection, *Kaikobad* explains how the issue of non-consensual military activities in the exclusive economic zones of coastal States was a hard one to settle by Member States of the Second Committee of the Third United Nations Conference on the Law of the Sea. While the matter was indeed finally resolved by way of compromise in the UN Convention on the Law of the Sea, the debate regarding the lawful nature of such activities remains alive today and periodically rises to the surface. In this chapter an attempt is made to study the issue by reference to the debates held between participating States in the Second Committee with a view to determining the true nature and scope of the compromise reached in Article 58 of the UN Convention on the Law of the Sea. The conclusion he draws is that non-consensual military activities, including, more specifically, aerial surveillance for defence and military purposes of the relevant maritime State, is not, in fact, permitted under a strict reading of the terms of Article 58 of the Convention. These views are then tested and analysed in the light of other provisions of the Convention, including Articles 88, 300 and 301. The study then seeks to discover whether there is a divergence in the textual law of the Convention and the actual practice of States, that is, whether there is enough evidence to show the development of a new permissive norm of customary international law on the matter. The author concludes that no change in the initial conclusion is warranted.

We hope that this *liber amicorum* is a fitting tribute to the work of a true original and a giant in the field of public and international law – and that his professional retirement will not mean that Colin will lay down his pen entirely.

Kaiyan Homi Kaikobad
Michael Bohlander
London and Durham, November 2008

Part One

General Principles and
International Human Rights

Chapter One

Collective Complaints under the European Social Charter: Encouraging Progress?

David Harris[*]

I. Introduction

The right of collective complaint under the European Social Charter is one of the few international remedies for violations of economic, social and cultural rights. The intention in this chapter is to review the progress made in the first decade or so of its operation. In particular, the focus will be on the approach to the interpretation of the Charter that the European Committee of Social Rights (the Committee) has followed. The paper will then reflect upon what may be learnt from the Committee's practice that may be relevant to the adoption of a right of communication under the International Covenant on Economic, Social and Cultural Rights (ICESCR),[1] a matter currently under consideration.[2]

Before considering the Committee's decided cases, it may be helpful to outline the background to the collective complaints procedure. The European Social Charter[3] is the regional counterpart within the Council of Europe

---

[*] Professor Emeritus and Co-Director, Human Rights Law Centre, University of Nottingham.
[1] 999 *UNTS* 3.
[2] A Working Group established by the UN Human Rights Council is in the process of drafting an Optional Protocol providing for a right of communication. It held its 4th Session in July 2007. For the draft text under consideration and other information, see www.ohchr.org/english/issues/
escr/group4 .htm.
[3] *ETS* 35. The Charter was adopted in 1961. It was updated by the Revised European Social Charter 1996: *ETS* 163, which adds to the rights guaranteed. 16 Council of Europe members are parties to the 1961 Charter; 23 are parties to the Revised Charter, making a total of 39 Charter parties. Of the other Council members, Russia has yet to ratify either instrument, as have Switzerland, the mini States of Liechtenstein, Monaco and San Marino and the new Council members Bosnia and Herzegovina, Montenegro and Serbia. On the Charter, see

K.H. Kaikobad & M. Bohlander (eds.), *International Law and Power: Perspectives on Legal Order and Justice*. Essays in Honour of Colin Warbrick, pp. 3–24.
© 2009 Koninklijke Brill NV. Printed in the Netherlands.

human rights system to the ICESCR. It imposes obligations in respect of most economic and social rights; it extends to cultural rights only in so far as it applies to the cultural rights of minorities.[4] From the beginning, States have been obliged to report periodically under the Charter, but no complaints procedure was included when it was adopted in 1961. One was introduced only by the 1995 Additional Protocol to the Charter.[5]

The procedure provides for collective, not individual complaints.[6] It is collective in two senses. First, only certain categories of trades unions, employers' organisations and NGOs may bring complaints;[7] individual victims of a violation may not do so. Second, the complaint may concern only a general situation (for example, that education is not provided for autistic persons generally): 'individ-

---

Harris and Davey, *The European Social Charter* (Second edition), Ardsley, New York, 2001; and Samuel, *Fundamental Social Rights: Case Law of the European Social Charter* (Second edition), Strasbourg, 2002. In this chapter, 'Charter' refers to either or both instruments; 'Revised Charter' is used where its text differs from that of the 1961 Charter.

4   See *infra*, note 5.

5   Additional Protocol to the European Social Charter Providing for a System of Collective Complaints (Additional Protocol) 1995, *ETS* 158; 3 (1996) *IHRR* 2000; in force since 1998, the Protocol has 12 Parties. On the Protocol, see Birk, 'The Collective Complaint: A New Procedure in the European Social Charter'', in Engels and Weiss (eds.), *Labour Law and Industrial Relations at the Turn of the Century: Liber Amicorum in Honour of Roger Blanpain*, The Hague, 1998, p. 261; Brillat, 'A New Protocol to the European Social Charter Providing for Collective Complaints', 1 (1996) *EHRLR* 52; Churchill and Khaliq, 'The Collective Complaints System of the European Social Charter: An Effective Mechanism for Ensuring Compliance with Economic and Social Rights?', 15 (2004) *EJIL* 417; Cullen, 'The Collective Complaints Mechanism of the European Social Charter', 25 (2000) *ELRHR* 18; Harris, 'The Collective Complaints Procedure', in *The Social Charter of the 21st Century*, Council of Europe Publication, 1997, p. 113 *et seq.*; Jaeger, 'The Additional Protocol to the European Social Charter Providing for a System of Collective Complaints', 10 (1997) *Leiden JIL* 69; Novitz, 'Are Social Rights Necessarily Collective Rights? A Critical Analysis of the Collective Complaints Protocol to the European Social Charter', 5 (2002) *EHRLR* 50; and Sudre, 'Le Protocol Additionnel à la Charte Sociale Européenne prévoyant un système de réclamations collectives', 100 (1996) *RGDIP* 715.

6   The procedure was based on the collective complaints procedure of the ILO Freedom of Association Committee which allows trades unions and employers' organisations to bring complaints alleging violations of the right to freedom of association. The Council of Europe Parliamentary Assembly proposed the establishment of a working group to consider the introduction of a Charter right of individual petition: Recommendation 1795 (2007). It was adopted 24 May 2007. For text see www.assembly.coe.int

7   Article 1, Additional Protocol. The categories referred to above are (i) international organisations of employers and trades unions that have observer status with the Charter Governmental Committee; (ii) international NGOs with consultative status with the Council of Europe where they have been and put on a list for this purpose; and (iii) representative national employers and trade union organisations. A State may separately make a declaration allowing representative national NGOs to bring a complaint against it: Article 2, ibid. Only Finland has done so.

ual situations may not be submitted.'[8] The complaint must comply with certain admissibility criteria.[9] If satisfied that these are met, the Committee decides on the merits of the complaint. The Committee's decision, which is not legally binding, goes to the Committee of Ministers of the Council of Europe which must adopt a resolution closing the procedure. This resolution may include a recommendation, which again is not legally binding, to a State found in default calling upon it to take certain action.[10] By June 2007, 43 complaints had been registered against the 12 Charter parties that had accepted the Additional Protocol. The Committee had decided 30 of these on their merits, finding a breach of the Charter in 21 of them.[11]

Although the procedure has a number of limitations,[12] it has already proved its worth, to judge from the number of complaints that have been submitted from a limited number of possible complainants, the variety of the subject matter of the complaints, the contribution of some of the Committee's decisions to the substance of international human rights law and the precedent that they set as an example of a workable international system for the consideration of complaints concerning economic, social and cultural rights.

II. The Committee's Approach to the Interpretation of the Charter

1. *General Approach*

The Committee has established or confirmed a number of rules concerning the interpretation of the Charter in the course of considering collective complaints.[13] Its general approach was most fully spelt out in *International Federation of Human Rights Leagues (FIDH) v. France.*[14] There the Committee stated that, as a treaty, the Charter was to be interpreted on the basis of the Vienna Convention on the Law of Treaties 1969, Article 31(1) of which provides

[8] Explanatory Report, 3 (2006) *HRR* 204, paragraph 31.
[9] See Articles 3, 4 and 6, Additional Protocol; and see the Explanatory Report, ibid, paragraphs 29 to 33 and paragraph 35. There is no requirement to exhaust local remedies.
[10] Article 9, Additional Protocol.
[11] The other complaints had been admitted for consideration on the merits (6), declared inadmissible (4) or were awaiting an admissibility decision (3).
[12] See Churchill and Khaliq (note 5), p. 445 *et seq.*
[13] Much of the Committee's approach to interpretation had already been developed in the reporting process: see Harris (note 3), pp. 24–31.
[14] 12 (2005) *IHRR* 1153, paragraphs 27–29. All Committee decisions may also be found on the Council of Europe website www.coe.int

that a treaty is to be interpreted 'in accordance with the ordinary meaning to be given to the terms of the treaty in their context and in the light of its object and purpose'. The Committee continued:

> The Charter was envisaged as a human rights instrument to complement the European Convention on Human Rights. It is a living instrument dedicated to certain values which inspired it: dignity, autonomy, equality and solidarity. The rights guaranteed are not ends in themselves but they complete the rights enshrined in the European Convention on Human Rights. Indeed, according to the Vienna Declaration of 1993, all human rights are 'universal, indivisible and interdependent and interrelated (para 5)'. The Committee is therefore mindful of the complex interaction between the two sets of rights. Thus, the Charter must be interpreted so as to give life and meaning to fundamental social rights. It follows inter alia that restrictions on rights are to be read restrictively, i.e. understood in such a manner as to preserve intact the essence of the right and to achieve the overall purpose of the Charter.[15]

In the *FIDH* case, the Committee applied this approach as follows. The case concerned a restriction in French law by which illegal immigrants with very low incomes did not qualify for free medical assistance in the same way as others with very low incomes did. The Committee held that 'legislation or practice which denies entitlement to medical assistance to foreign nationals, within the territory of a State party, even if they are there illegally, is contrary to the Charter'.[16] The Committee reached this conclusion despite the fact that the Revised Charter guarantee extends generally *ratione personae* only to nationals of other contracting parties who are '*lawfully* resident' in the territory of a contracting party[17] or, in the case of the guarantee of the right to social assistance in Article 13 (4), to nationals of other contracting parties who are '*lawfully* within' the territory of a contracting party (italics added). Despite this clear wording, the Committee decided that Article 13 (4) and Article 17 (on the rights of children and young persons, to which the general *ratione personae* rule applies), did extent to persons illegally present in a State's territory. In taking this decision, the Committee relied upon its approach to interpretation whereby restrictions upon human rights (in this case *ratione personae* restrictions) should be interpreted narrowly and whereby respect for human dignity was central to the object and purpose of the Charter.

As to human dignity, the Committee stated that 'human dignity was the fundamental value and indeed the core of positive European human rights law' under both the Charter and the European Convention on Human Rights and

---

[15] Ibid, paragraphs 27, 28 and 29.
[16] *Supra* (note 14), paragraph 32.
[17] Appendix to the Revised Charter.

that 'health care is a prerequisite for the preservation of human dignity'.[18] It scarcely needs saying that this a very strong teleological and human rights minded interpretation of the Charter which reaches the limits of what a body whose role is to interpret a text may properly do.[19] But, having decided that illegal immigrants were protected by the Charter in respect of medical assistance, the Committee nonetheless found, by 9 votes to 4, no breach of Article 13 (4) because medical assistance was provided to illegal immigrants in cases of emergency or of life threatening conditions or where they had been resident for three months or more. It did, however, find, by just 7 votes to 6, a breach of Article 17: children and young persons who were illegal immigrants were entitled to medical assistance without such limits.

2. *Effective Guarantee of Rights*

In addition to its general approach spelt out in the FIDH case, the Committee has indicated its approach to interpretation in other particular respects in the FIDH and other cases. Thus it has stressed the need to look beyond the letter of the law to see how effectively it operates in practice. As stated in *International Commission of Jurists v. Portugal*,[20] 'the aim and purpose of the Charter, being a human rights protection instrument, is to protect rights not merely theoretically, but also in fact.' Accordingly, a State party may be found to be in breach of its obligations where its laws are in order, but in reality the position is unsatisfactory. In this case, the defendant State was found in breach of Article 7 (1) on this basis when a large number of under-age children were illegally employed contrary to Portuguese law in circumstances in which there was evidence that the Labour Inspectorate was not enforcing the law, which was satisfactory on its face, as efficiently as might have been expected. The Committee's insistence in *European Roma Rights Centre v. Italy*[21] on legal remedies and legal aid to challenge forced evictions as an aspect of the right to housing may also be seen as an element of the obligation to guarantee rights effectively.

---

[18] *Supra* (note 14), paragraph 31.
[19] For criticism of the Committee's approach to the matter, see the Dissenting Opinions of Mr. Evju, joined by Mrs. Koncar and Mr Francois, and Mr Birk.
[20] 7 (2000) *IHRR* 525, paragraph 32.
[21] 14 (2007) *IHRR* 239. The Committee has read a requirement of judicial or other national remedies into several provisions of the Charter in its reporting practice: see Harris (note 3), p. 30. See also *Marangopoulos Foundation for Human Rights v. Greece*, Council of Europe website www.coe.int: 2006, paragraph 207.

3. *Living Instrument*

As the Committee stated in the *FIDH* case, the Charter is a 'living instrument', the meaning of which may evolve with changing standards and values. This dynamic nature of the Charter was important in a series of cases concerning the corporal punishment of children.[22] Acting on the basis that the Charter absolutely prohibited all physical violence against children, the Committee held that the prohibition of corporal punishment that this demanded of States parties called for a legislative basis and appropriate sanctions. In doing so, the Committee stated that the Charter was 'a living instrument which must be interpreted in the light of developments in the national law of the member States of the Council of Europe as well as relevant international instruments',[23] which had clearly moved in this direction on the matter of corporal punishment of children. Similarly, in *Marangopoulos Foundation for Human Rights v. Greece*,[24] the Committee invoked the 'living instrument' doctrine as a justification, 'in the light of current conditions'[25] for interpreting the guarantee of the right to health in Article 11 of the Charter as including 'the right to a healthy environment'.[26]

4. *Reliance on National and International Standards*

The Committee has drawn upon national and international standards generally when determining what may be expected of States parties, not only in situations where these standards signal a change in standards or values. Thus in *Centrale générale des service public v. Belgium*,[27] the Committee rejected the applicant trade union's complaint that the absence of any proposal for consultation with trades unions on amendments to draft legislation in the course of parliamentary debate was a breach of Article 6 (1) (2) (the right to consultation and negotiation). In

---

[22] *World Organisation against Torture v. Ireland*, 13 (2006) IHRR 288; *World Organisation against Torture v. Greece*, 13 (2006) IHRR 274; *World Organisation against Torture v. Portugal*, 13 (2006) IHRR 299; *World Organisation against Torture v. Italy, Complaint No. 20/2003*, Council of Europe website *www.coe.int*; *World Organisation against Torture v. Belgium, Complaint No. 21/2003*, ibid; *World Organisation against Torture v. Portugal, Complaint No. 19/2003*, ibid.

[23] *World Organisation against Torture v. Ireland* (note 22), paragraph 63. As to international instruments, the Committee referred to Article 19, UN Convention on the Right of the Child; Article 3, European Convention on Human Rights and recommendations of the Committee of Ministers and the Parliamentary Assembly of the Council of Europe.

[24] Council of Europe website www.coe.int: 2006. See further on this case: text to notes 53 and 72.

[25] Ibid, paragraph 194.

[26] Ibid, paragraph 195.

[27] 13 (2006) IHRR 1181, paragraph 39. The Committee did not limit itself to European practice in this case, but presumably this would be particularly relevant.

doing so, it relied upon the absence of any such provision in States that provide for consultation prior to the initiation of legislation and the fact that it is 'traditional legal practice in democratic States' to regard parliamentary debate as negating the need for consultation. In other cases, the Committee has also referred to international standards in UN human rights treaties to support its conclusions.[28]

5. Margin of Appreciation

The Committee has applied a 'margin of appreciation' doctrine in its collective complaints decisions, though not as regularly as the European Court of Human Rights.[29] Thus the Committee has allowed States a certain discretion as to the manner in which an objective required by the Charter is realised, using 'margin of appreciation' language when doing so. For example, in *Syndicat des Agreges de l'Enseignment Superieur v. France*,[30] the Committee held, by 8 votes to 6, that whereas the right to form and join a trade union in Article 5 of the Charter includes for trades unions the possibility of membership of consultation bodies established by the government that are relevant to the protection of their members' interests, States parties had a 'wide margin of appreciation' in determining the composition of such bodies so that a trade union could not, as was claimed in the case, insist upon a particular election procedure.

The Committee has also used 'margin of appreciation' language in some cases of restrictions upon rights. For example, in *Quaker Council for European Affairs v. Greece*,[31] the question was whether alternative civilian service for conscientious objectors that was 18 months longer than the military service which they were unable to undertake gave rise to a breach of the prohibition of forced labour in Article 1 (2) of the Charter. Viewing this as a restriction on freedom to work voluntarily, the Committee acknowledged that the State enjoyed 'a certain margin of appreciation in this area' but concluded, by 6 votes to 3, that 'this additional duration, because of its excessive character, amounted to a 'disproportionate restriction' in breach of Article 1(2). To take another example, in *European Roma Rights Centre v. Bulgaria*,[32] provision was made by planning law for illegal housing to be legalised, but subject only to very strict conditions

---

[28] See, for example, the *FIDH* case (note 14), *supra*.

[29] Thus none was applied in *Confederation of Independent Trade Unions in Bulgaria et al v. Bulgaria*, Council of Europe website www.coe.int (2006); or in the *FIDH* case (note 14), paragraph 34.

[30] 13 (2006) *IHRR* 1188, paragraph 38.

[31] 8 (2001) *IHRR* 1158, paragraphs 24 and 25.

[32] Council of Europe website www.coe.int: 2006, paragraphs 54 and 55. See also *Marangopoulos Human Rights Foundation v. Greece*, *infra*, text to notes 53 and 72.

that were disadvantageous for those whose dwellings had been in existence and tolerated for a long time. The Committee found a breach of Article 16 (right to family life, including family housing) and Article E (non-discrimination) of the Revised Charter. Although States have a 'wide margin of appreciation' as to their planning law rules, they must strike a 'balance between the general interest and the fundamental rights of the individuals'. In this case, the Greek law on the legalisation of dwellings had affected the right to housing of Roma families in 'a disproportionate manner'.

6. Restrictions upon Rights

This 'proportionately' language echoes that of the European Court of Human Rights when that Court looks to see whether a restriction upon a Convention right is permitted. The Charter permits restrictions upon all Charter rights using the same formula as is found in some Convention articles. Article G of the Revised Charter permits restrictions to any Charter right where these are 'prescribed by law and are necessary in a democratic society' to protect specified heads of public interest. These are to be restrictively interpreted[33] and are also subject to a requirement of proportionality.

A case in which the Committee applied precisely the European Court's proportionality approach in assessing the compliance with the Charter of a restriction upon a right when applying Article G is *Confederation of Independent Trade Unions in Bulgaria et al v. Bulgaria*.[34] In that case, the Committee concluded that various prohibitions or restrictions in Bulgarian national law on the right to strike were in breach of the guarantee of that right in Article 6 (4). Thus the general prohibition by law of strikes in the electricity, communications and health care sectors was not 'necessary in a democratic society': although some limitation on the right of workers in such essential services might be proportionate to the legitimate purpose pursued, a general ban upon the withdrawal of their labour by all workers in these sectors was not. Similarly, the general prohibition of the right to strike of all civil servants 'irrespective of their duties and function' was disproportionate.[35] Finally, a restriction upon the right to strike by railway workers by which they had to ensure a satisfactory transport service while they were on strike of at least 50% of the normal service was held to be too vaguely worded to be 'prescribed by law' and had not been shown by

---

[33] See the *FIDH* case (note 14).
[34] *Supra* (note 29).
[35] Ibid, paragraph 46. Civil servants were only allowed to engage in symbolic action, by wearing arm bands, badges and the like without withdrawing their labour.

the defendant government to have a 'legitimate purpose'. What is interesting is that the Committee does not apply a 'margin of appreciation' approach in this case when assessing the legitimacy of the purpose being pursued or the proportionality of the restriction, as the European Court of Human Rights would almost certainly have done.[36]

7. *Financial Resources*

With regard to positive obligations involving public expenditure, when considering national reports that States make on their compliance with the Charter, the Committee has not used language suggesting that a State may claim lack of financial resources as a justification for not making the necessary provision.[37] However, it has taken a different stand in the context of collective complaints, where it has indicated its willingness to make some such allowance.

Before looking at the cases in which the Committee has taken this stand, it should be noted that no allowance for financial constraints is made in the text of the Charter. The structure of the Charter is different from that of the ICESCR in this regard. There is no article in the Charter by which States parties subject themselves to a general obligation to realise all of the rights in the Charter – an article which might be drafted so as to limit that obligation to 'available resources'. As is well known, the ICESCR has such an article and this article does contain such a limitation.[38] Instead, in each Charter article that guarantees a particular right, the State parties undertake to take appropriate or necessary measures or other action to realise that right. While the formula varies, no express allowance is made for financial resources, even in the case of expensive social rights such as health, social security and assistance, education and housing.[39] An exception is Article 12 (3) of the Charter. Whereas in Article 12 (2) States parties undertake 'to maintain the social security system at a satisfactory level at least equivalent to that required for ratification of International Labour Convention (No. 102) Concerning Minimum Standards of Social Security', in Article 12 (3) the obligation is only to 'endeavour to raise progressively the system of social security to a higher level' than that required by Convention No. 102. Clearly financial resources are relevant when deciding whether the required 'endeavour' has been forthcoming.[40] Otherwise,

---

[36]   See for example *Tüm Haber Sen and Çinar v. Turkey*, Judgment of 21 February 2006.
[37]   See Harris (note 3), p. 26.
[38]   Article 2 (1), ICESCR, as to which see text to notes 62 to 65, *infra*.
[39]   See Articles 11, 12, 13, 17 and 31 of the Revised Charter.
[40]   See also Article 31 (2), Revised Charter, by which States Parties undertake to take measures designed to 'reduce homelessness with a view to its gradual elimination'.

in accordance with the normal rule concerning treaty obligations,[41] the Charter imposes an immediate obligation upon States parties to adopt the required measures or other action to realise the right concerned, making no allowance for cost.

The reason why States agreed to this strict approach when drafting the Charter may have been because they were West European States which operated, when viewed in a world-wide context, at a level of relative affluence and anticipated that they would be judged by a common European standard of fulfilment of social rights which they would generally be able to satisfy as well as their neighbours could. This situation was, of course, never perfectly as just described in that the gross national products and the resulting ability to fund social rights has always varied markedly from the richest to the poorest West European States. In any event, it has changed dramatically with the arrival of States parties from other parts of Europe – first Turkey and then post Soviet States in Central and Eastern Europe – which has widened the range of financial resources available for social rights and other national purposes in Charter State parties as a whole. Some recognition of the cost issue may also have been an element in the process of drafting the Charter when it was decided that, in contrast with the ICESCR, parties to the Charter do not have to accept all of the articles of the Charter: they may instead become a party by accepting no more than approximately sixty per cent of them.[42]

However, as indicated, the Committee has deviated from the strict reading of the Charter just posited when deciding complaints. In particular, it has shown itself prepared to take financial resources into account, though seemingly not in all cases,[43] when assessing whether States have 'done enough' to meet their Charter obligations. At the same time, as will be seen, this dispensation has not proved important in practice, with no State as yet seemingly reliant upon it or benefiting from its application so as not to be found in breach of the Charter.

The Committee first spelt out its approach on this matter in *Autism-Europe v. France*.[44] In that case, the complainant organisation claimed that insufficient provision had been made by France for the education of autistic children

---

[41] See Aust, *Modern Treaty Law and Practice*, Cambridge, 2000, p. 144.

[42] See Article 20, Charter.

[43] There are cases involving public expenditure, as for example the *FIDH* case (note 14), in which the Committee does not refer to the 'available resources' dispensation even in the abstract. Cf. the UK case of *Szoma v. Secretary of State for Work and Pensions*, [2006] 1 AC 564, in which regulations concerning income support that were adopted in part to implement Article 13 (4) of the Charter were interpreted widely by the House of Lords without mention of the financial cost.

[44] 11 (2004) *IHRR* 843.

and adults in special or mainstream schools, in violation of Articles 15 and 17 of the Revised Charter, concerning the rights of disabled persons and of children respectively.[45] It asserted, *inter alia*, that only ten per cent of those in need of special education had places, and that the percentage of such children in mainstream schools was even less. On its calculation, government action would take many years to rectify the situation. The defendant government acknowledged that its 'catch up' plans had 'fallen short of real needs', but pointed to recent increases in resources. The Committee explained its approach to such a case as follows:

> When the achievement of one of the rights in question is exceptionally complex and particularly expensive to resolve, a State Party must take measures that allow it to achieve the objectives of the Charter within a reasonable time, with measurable progress and to an extent consistent with the maximum use of available resources.

It added that States parties must be 'particularly mindful' of the impact their choices had for vulnerable groups, such as autistic persons.

Applying this approach, the Committee decided, by 11 votes to 2, that the defendant State was in breach of both Articles 15 and 17, whether these were read alone or together with the non-discrimination guarantee in Article E of the Revised Charter. The Committee noted that, despite a national debate that had lasted over more than 20 years and the enactment of disabled persons legislation as long ago as 1975, France had 'failed to achieve sufficient progress in advancing the provision of education for persons with autism'.[46] As was acknowledged or not contested by the defendant State, the proportion of children with autism being educated either in general or specialised schools was 'much lower than in the case of other children, whether or not disabled' and there was 'a chronic shortage of care and support facilities for autistic adults'.[47] Clearly the Committee had in mind its 'reasonable time' dispensation when it took into consideration the (too) many years during which France had had the matter on its agenda as a pressing issue. Otherwise, as to the provision for autistic

---

[45] Article 15 (1) reads: '... the parties undertake ... to take the necessary measures to provide persons with disabilities with guidance, education and vocational training in the framework of general schemes wherever possible or, where this is not possible, through specialised bodies, public or private.' By Article 17 (1) (a), 'the parties undertake ... to take all appropriate and necessary measures designed ... to ensure that children and young persons ... have the ... education and the training they need'. The claim also relied on the non-discrimination guarantee in Article E, Revised Charter.

[46] *Supra* (note 44), paragraph 54.

[47] Ibid. In its Resolution closing the case, the Committee of Ministers took note of the French Government's undertaking to bring the situation into conformity with the Revised Charter and that measures were being taken in this respect (see Appendix to this Resolution): CM Res ChS (2004); and 11 (2004) *IHRR* 856.

persons the defendant State could be expected to make, the Committee did not spell out the criteria that it was applying, beyond its reference in the abstract to rights that are 'particularly expensive to achieve' and to 'available resources'. However, the defendant State did not argue lack of resources: instead it referred to the resources that it had put in place and that it had committed itself to providing in the future.

The Committee did not apply its 'available resources' criterion *proprio motu*, making no reference to priorities in State expenditure or the large cost of making provision for the education of autistic persons in particular. The Committee's approach basically would appear to have been a somewhat impressionistic one, taking into account (a) the large number of autistic children and adults for whom appropriate education was not provided on the evidence before it; (b) what a Contracting Party with the resources of a West European State could reasonably be expected to provide; and (c) the length of time during which the problem had been known and remained unsolved.

The issue of resources was next raised by the *Committee in European Roma Rights Centre v. Greece*.[48] In this case the Committee found, by 8 votes to 2, a violation of the obligation in Article 16 of the Charter to 'promote the economic, legal and social protection of family life by such means as … provision of family housing' in the arrangements made for the housing of members of the Roma community. The obligation had been infringed on three fronts, in respect of each of which there was a separate violation. First, there was insufficient provision of permanent housing for Roma. The allegation made by the complainant organisation, which the Committee found was supported by the concluding observations of more than one UN treaty monitoring body,[49] that approximately 100,000 Roma lived in sub-standard housing and had done so for many years was not denied by the defendant State. Noting that the 'overarching aim of the Charter is to achieve social inclusion', the Committee found a breach of Article 16 on the basis of these 'excessive numbers'. In so far as the defendant State argued that the problem was a lack of unwillingness on the part of local authorities to act, the Committee noted that the defendant State was required by Article 16 to take steps to cause them to act.

---

[48] 13 (2006) *IHRR* 895. See also *European Roma Rights Centre v. Italy* (note 21); and *European Roma Rights Centre v. Bulgaria* (note 32). For other non-Roma housing cases, see *International Movement ATD Fourth World v. France*, Council of Europe www.coe.int: 2006; ibid, and *European Federation of National Organisations Working with the Homeless v. France*, ibid; both cases are pending on merits.

[49] *Supra* (note 48), paragraph 40. The UN treaty monitoring bodies were the Committee on Economic, Social and Cultural Rights and the Committee against Torture.

Second, the Committee found that insufficient provision was made for temporary campsites for Roma to comply with Article 16. Third, the Committee found that the forced evictions of Roma from sites or dwellings which they had occupied illegally was in breach of Article 16. Whereas illegal occupants of land may be forcibly evicted, 'the criteria of illegal eviction must not be unduly wide, the eviction should take place in accordance with the applicable rules of procedure and these should be sufficiently protective of the rights of the persons concerned'.[50] The question of financial resources was relevant to the first two of these grounds of violation. The Committee quoted its statement in the *Autism-Europe* case requiring States to take measures to realise the aims of the Charter 'within a reasonable time, with measurable progress and to an extent consistent with the maximum use of available resources'.[51] However, as in the *Autism-Europe* case, the defendant Government did not argue lack of resources. Instead it sought to justify its position by reference to the funding it had put in to Roma housing and its adoption of an integrated action plan for them. The Committee found these arguments unconvincing on the basis that the situation had not improved despite the adoption of the State's integrated action plan as long ago as 2001: as in the *Autism-Europe* case, not enough had been done, as judged by the level of lack of housing provision on the evidence before the Committee.[52]

Resources were also relevant in the important environmental case of *Marangopoulos Foundation for Human Rights v. Greece*.[53] In this case the complainant organisation claimed a breach of Article 11 of the Charter, which guarantees the right to health. It was claimed that the defendant State had not done enough to counter the adverse environmental effects and risks to public health resulting from lignite mining on its territory. The defendant State countered by arguing that lignite mining was justified in the general interest as enabling the country to maintain its energy independence and providing electricity at reasonable cost for industry and the private consumer.[54] It argued further that it was following a coherent and progressive emissions reduction strategy in accordance with its obligations under EU environmental directives and the Kyoto Protocol. The Committee found a breach of Article 11, by 9 votes to 1.[55] It first noted that

---

[50] Ibid, paragraph 51.
[51] Ibid, paragraph 20.
[52] Cf. the approach and findings in *European Roma Rights Centre v. Bulgaria* (note 32), *supra*.
[53] *Supra* (note 24).
[54] As the Committee noted lignite had been the main form of fuel for energy production in Greece for 40 years and was likely to continue to be such in the near future: ibid, paragraph 197.
[55] It also found breaches of Article 2 (4) (reduced working hours for workers in dangerous occupations) and Article 3 (2) (health and safety at work).

Article 11 includes a right to a 'healthy environment'. As a 'living instrument', the Charter took account of the link that is now made by States and by other international human rights treaty bodies[56] between the 'protection of health and a healthy environment'. A consequence was that the obligation in Article 11 (1) 'to remove as far as possible the causes of ill health' included a requirement to reduce air and other pollution that could impair good health. As to how far this requirement went, the Committee again relied as a point of reference on its dictum in the *Autism-Europe* case. It stated:

> Admittedly, overcoming pollution is an objective that can only be achieved gradually. Nevertheless, states parties must strive to attain this objective within a reasonable time, by showing measurable progress and making best possible use of the resources at their disposal (see ... *Autism-Europe v. France* ...).[57]

Examining the defendant State's plans for emission reductions, the Committee concluded that 'they do not offer real evidence of Greece's commitment to improving the situation within a reasonable time or making such an outcome plausible.'[58] This conclusion was supported by the only recent introduction of an inspectorate to monitor operator compliance with environmental regulations, as well as the low number of inspectors and the limited fines imposed for non-compliance. Also relevant was the lack of proof by the defendant State of its commitment to the EU 'best available practice' requirement and its tolerance of the continued operation of power stations on the basis of temporary licences without prior approval of the environmental criteria. In addition, the Government acknowledged that very little had been done to organise systematic epidemiological monitoring to reveal the health implications of lignite mining on the population.

In conclusion, while acknowledging the general interest of the State in ensuring energy independence and economic progress, the Committee stressed that Article 11 required the government to 'strike a reasonable balance' between the right to health of persons living in the lignite mining area and that general interest, and this had not been done.[59] No express reference was made to the resource implications for the defendant State, which would have included the financial cost for the economy of having to resort to other more expensive forms of energy and/or the cost of reducing pollution from lignite mines.

---

[56] The treaty bodies identified by the Committee were the European Court of Human Rights, the Inter-American Court of Human Rights, the African Commission on Human and Peoples' Rights, the European Court of Justice and the UN Committee on Economic, Social and Cultural Rights.

[57] *Supra* (note 24), paragraph 204.

[58] Ibid, paragraph 207.

[59] Ibid, paragraph 221.

Considering the cases just discussed as a whole, what is interesting is that, with the possible exception of the 'general interest' argument by Greece in the *Marangopoulos* case, in none of the – as yet few – cases in which the Committee has referred to 'available resources' has a government relied upon this argument.[60] It was not to be expected that the French Government would do this in the *Autism-Europe* case, as the Committee's prior practice had given no sign of it making any such allowance. But no defendant Government has relied upon it since. Thus no such argument was put in the Roma housing cases. Nor has the Committee applied it *proprio motu* to the benefit of a State on the facts. Nonetheless, the 'available resources' dispensation is there, and brings the Charter into line with the ICESCR and provide thereby a precedent of relevance to the question of justiciability when assessing the feasibility of a right of communication under the Covenant.

As a final comment concerning the cost of social rights, it may be mentioned that some social rights cases[61] involve obligations that are no more expensive than those of a positive kind that are imposed upon States to enact and enforce legislation in respect of civil rights. For example, as noted above, there has been a series of cases in which the corporal punishment of children has been found (or in some cases not found) to be in breach of Article 17 of the Charter, which guarantees the rights of the child. The Committee in these cases takes the stand that Article 17 requires a clear, legislative prohibition of all forms of corporal punishment, whether within the family, in educational institutions, in residential care or otherwise, and sanctions that are adequate, dissuasive and proportionate. The positive obligation in such cases entails no cost other than that of legislation and enforcement.

III. Lessons for a Possible Right of Communication under the International Covenant on Economic and Political Rights

Rights of complaint concerning economic, social and cultural rights in international human rights treaties are scarce, much more so than for civil and political rights. A glaring absentee is a right of individual complaint under the ICESCR,

---

[60] In *FIDH v. France, supra* (note 14), the defendant Government argued that the *ratione personae* point strongly, but made no reference to the cost of providing medical assistance. The issue of resources will also be relevant in *International Movement ATD Fourth World v. France*, Council of Europe website www.coe.int, pending on the merits, concerning violations of the right to housing of persons in extreme poverty.

[61] Cf. the position concerning most economic rights cases, see below, Part III; and text to notes 74 *et seq.*

although this is a gap that may shortly be filled. The failure to provide for such a right at the outset when the ICESCR was adopted in 1966, whereas such a right was already established in the International Covenant on Civil and Political Rights (ICCPR), has been attributed to several causes.[62] One was the fact that States within the Soviet bloc, which were most supportive of international guarantees of economic, social and cultural rights, were generally opposed to any intrusion upon State sovereignty, and they saw a right of individual complaint as such an intrusion. Western States, however, which were more likely to favour a right of individual complaint, lacked enthusiasm for an international guarantee of such rights. Another was the 'programmatic nature' of the obligations of States under the ICESCR. According to Craven, not only was it considered that there was a lack of criteria to evaluate State compliance. It was also argued: 'Complaints relating to that Covenant could only refer to insufficient programmes in the attainment of certain goals and it would be impossible for the Committee to determine what rate of progress in any particular should be.'[63]

The first of these reasons has lost most of its force, although it is still the case that some Western States are strongly opposed to a right of individual communication under the ICESCR, or are at best neutral in their approach to the idea. The second has remained problematic, translated, as it has been, into an argument that economic, social and cultural rights are not justiciable.[64] In the context of the ICESCR, this argument has been linked to the wording of the basic obligation that States parties accept. By Article 2 (1), ICESCR, a State party undertakes to 'take steps ... *to the maximum of its available resources, with a view to achieving progressively* the full realisation of the rights recognised' in the ICESCR.[65] It is the allowance for resources (which include, above all, financial resources), together with the obligation to achieve only progressively the realisation of the rights recognised, that forms the basis for the claim that ICESCR rights are not justiciable.

---

[62] See Craven, *The International Covenant on Economic, Social and Cultural Rights: A Perspective on Its Development*, Oxford, 1995, p. 35.

[63] Ibid, p. 36. The quotation is from UN Doc A/2929, cited by Craven *supra* (note 62). Another argument was that a complaint procedure would overlap with existing ILO and UNESCO complaint procedures.

[64] For academic discussion of the argument, see Addo, 'Justiciability Re-Examined', in Hill and Beddard (eds.), *Economic, Social and Cultural Rights*, London, 1992, Chapter 5; Craven, 'The Justiciability of Economic, Social and Cultural Rights', in Burchill, Harris and Owers (eds.), *Economic, Social and Cultural Rights: Their Implementation in UK Law*, Nottingham, 1999, Chapter 1; Steiner and Alston, *International Human Rights in Context* (Second edition), Oxford, 2000, pp. 275 *et seq.*; Van Hoof, "The Legal Nature of Economic, Social and Cultural Rights: A Rebuttal of Some Traditional Views", in Alston and Tomaševski (eds.), *The Right to Food*, Boston, 1984, p. 97; and Vierdag, 'The Legal Nature of the Rights Granted by the International Covenant on Economic, Social and Cultural Rights', 9 (1978) NYIL 69.

[65] Emphasis added.

But recent developments have taken away much of the force of the non-justiciability argument. Cases concerning economic, social and cultural rights have proved justiciable before other UN[66] and regional treaty monitoring bodies,[67] including cases having financial implications, and awareness has grown from cases decided by national courts, particularly some high profile cases in the South African Constitutional Court.[68] These have shown that while the closeness or legal basis for judicial control of State action in fulfilment of positive obligations involving the large public expenditure associated with (particularly) social rights[69] might differ from that involving compliance with the typically negative obligations (or positive obligations with less, or less obvious, expenditure) associated with civil and political rights, and while the nature of the remedy may differ (in some cases a public law remedy declaring a programme illegal rather than a right to damages), there is a valuable role for

---

[66] See for example *Broeks v. Netherlands*, 2 (1987) *Selected Decisions HRC* 179 (ICCPR: discrimination in social security law); *Yilmaz Dogan v. Netherlands*, 2 (1988) *IHRR* 348; (CERD: discrimination in employment law); *AS v. Hungary*, (14 (2007) *IHRR* 997); (CEDAW: health care); and *Dung Thi Thuy Nguyen v. Netherlands*, (14 (2007) *IHRR* 987); (CEDAW: maternity benefits). The CERD and CEDAW decisions are on the UN website. On the controversial nature of the *Broeks* case, see Joseph, Schlutz and Castan, *The International Covenant on Civil and Political Rights* (Second edition), Oxford, 2004, p. 686.

[67] See the cases decided by the African Commission on Human and Peoples' Rights: *Purohit and Moore v. Gambia*, 11 (2004) *IHRR* 257 (right to health); and *Social and Economic Rights Action Centre and the Centre for Economic and Social Rights v. Nigeria*, 10 (2003) *IHRR* 282 (right to health, housing and food). On the relevant jurisprudence of the European Court of Human Rights, see Warbrick, 'Economic and Social Interests and the European Convention on Human Rights', in Baderin and McCorquodale (eds.), *Economic, Social and Cultural Rights in Action*, Oxford, 2007, Chapter 10. On economic and social rights claims before the Inter-American Commission on Human Rights and the right of petition under the 1988 Protocol on Economic, Social and Cultural Rights to the American Convention on Human Rights, see Craven, 'The Protection of Economic, Social and Cultural Rights under the Inter-American System of Human Rights', in Harris and Livingstone (eds.), *The Inter-American System of Human Rights*, Oxford, 1998, p. 289, at p. 305 and p. 307. There have long been ILO Freedom of Association Committee cases: see Valticos and Potobsky, *International Labour Law*, Deventer, 1995, pp. 295 *et seq*.

[68] See *Soobramoney v. Minister of Health, KwaZulu-Natal*, (1998) 1 S.A. 965; *Government of the Republic of South Africa v. Grootboom*, (2001) 1 S.A. 46; and *Minister of Health v. Treatment Action Campaign*, (2002) 5 S.A. 721; 13 B.H.R.C. 1. See Liebenberg, 'The Protection of Economic and Social Rights in Domestic Legal Systems', in Eide, Krause and Rosas (eds.), *Economic, Social and Cultural Rights: A Textbook* (Second edition), Dordrecht, 2001, p. 55.

[69] The argument was never strong or much relied upon in respect of economic rights. There have long been ILO Freedom of Association Committee cases: see Valticos and Potobsky (note 67), pp. 295 *et seq.*, and national courts are well used to adjudicating on individual or collective claims under employment or trade union law, see further, text to notes 75 to 86, *infra*. The argument has not focused upon cultural rights, either in the sense of Article 15 of the ICESCR or of the cultural rights of minorities.

adjudication in the protection of social rights and that this can be provided through a right of individual communication under the ICESCR,[70] perhaps supplemented by a public interest communication procedure such as that in the collective complaints system of the European Social Charter.[71]

This conclusion is supported by the experience of the collective complaints system of the European Social Charter. While the Charter system is one of collective complaints, a review of the cases that have been brought under it suggest that there is no reason why they could not have been presented as complaints alleging a breach of the Charter by individual applicants. For example, a complaint could have been lodged in the case of *Autism-Europe v. France* by an autistic person who could not obtain appropriate education. Among the cased decided by the Committee to date, the one possible exception is *Marangopoulos Foundation for Human Rights v. Greece*, in that it would have required a victim whose health had suffered from the pollution caused by lignite mining, who might not have been easy to find.[72] In such a case, a collective communications remedy such as that of the European Social Charter has its attractions.

As far as a right of individual communication under the ICESCR for *social* rights is concerned, the European Committee of Social Rights has, as noted, formulated an approach to evaluating compliance with the Charter that addresses the problem of justiciability. As articulated in the *Autism-Europe* case, the Committee requires a State party to 'take measures that that allow it to achieve the objectives of the Charter within a reasonable time, with measurable progress and to an extent consistent with the maximum available resources'. The 'within a reasonable time' and 'measurable progress' parts of this formula equate to the

---

[70] Most States now seem to accept this. They are, however, wary of a procedure that might result in adverse decisions with large financial implications which, although not legally binding, would bring pressure to bear upon them to act. There is also concern (i) as to whether the Committee on Economic, Social and Cultural Rights is the proper body to be entrusted with competence to rule upon what are seen essentially as budgetary matters within a State's discretion and (ii) about the reference to 'international assistance and cooperation' in Article 2 (1) of the ICESCR.

[71] Article 3 of the draft Protocol to the ICESCR, under consideration by the Working Group in 2007 included, controversially, in addition to the right of individual communication, a collective communications right for NGOs with ECOSOC consultative status comparable to the Charter collective right. It also includes an inter-state communications procedure (Article 9) and an inquiry procedure (Article 10). As the Charter collective complaints regime shows, there is a role for public interest litigation in the protection of economic and social rights.

[72] Cf. *Lopes Ostra v. Spain* A 303-C (1994); 20 *EHRR* 277 in which the nuisance, caused by pollution from a waste processing plant, effected the health of the applicant's daughter, forcing her to move away from her family home, and which thereby made her a victim of a breach of the right to respect one's home and private and family life as provided in Article 8 of the European Convention on Human Rights.

obligation in Article 2 (1) of the ICESCR to realise the rights recognised 'progressively'. The reference to the 'available resources' of the particular State in that formula then interprets the Charter obligation in social rights cases involving public expenditure so that it is identical to that in Article 2 (1) of the ICESCR. While both of these requirements may be seen as dispensations when set against a strict textual interpretation of the Charter, the result of the Committee's interpretation of the obligation of States parties to the Charter in (particularly) social rights cases is to equate it with that in the ICESCR, so that the cases decided under the Charter are an instructive precedent – one that leads to the positive conclusion that there should be no problem of justiciability should similar claims that be brought under a right of individual communication under the ICESCR.

More particularly, with regard to the 'progressive', or programmatic, character of the obligation in Article 2(1), the Committee's approach under the Charter of determining whether a programme or plan has been put in place and implemented within a reasonable time in order to resolve a serious and known problem would be relevant and transferable to the ICESCR. As to 'available resources', the Committee would, not unreasonably, appear to place the onus upon the State to raise this as a problem, and not to consider the matter if it does not do so, although there may be an implicit assumption that the defendant European State in question must have had the resources needed. In the cases decided to date, no State has raised the issue of resources, so that the Committee has decided the case essentially on the basis of the first requirement – enough has not been done way of planning and implementation within a reasonable time to tackle a serious and known deficiency in the guarantee of a social right.

A separate element of the Committee's approach to the Charter that would be relevant to social rights cases that might arise under the ICESCR is the indication that discrimination in the allocation of resources may in itself be a basis for a breach of the Charter. This was particularly noticeable in *European Roma Rights Centre v. Italy*[73] where the Committee decided that the defendant State's failure to show that its criteria for access to permanent social housing was not discriminatory towards the Roma and to take into account the particular housing needs of the Roma amounted to a breach of Articles 31 (housing) and E (non-discrimination) of the Revised Charter taken together. One can easily imagine such an approach being adopted without difficulty in an individual communication under the ICESCR.

If, next, one examines the Committee's practice in dealing with collective complaints concerning *economic* rights, there is certainly no indication of any

---

[73] *Supra* (note 21). See also *Autism-Europe v. France* (note 44) on discrimination against autistic persons.

problem of justiciability in such cases. These complaints have mostly raised issues concerning trade unions. They focus on the right to form and join a trade union (Article 5) and aspects of the right to bargain collectively (Article 6). Article 5 complaints have concerned the prohibition in national law of members of the armed forces joining a trade union;[74] restrictions on the right of members of police forces to do so;[75] and pre-entry closed shop requirements,[76] as well as limitations on the functioning of trades unions in the protection of the interests of their members.[77] Article 6 claims have concerned the entitlement of trade unions to take part in consultation and negotiation arrangements on behalf of their members,[78] and also the right to strike.[79]

Other economic rights complaints have mainly concerned the prohibition of forced labour or discrimination guarantees in Article 1 (2), or elements of the right to reasonable working hours in Article 2.[80] Breaches of the forced labour prohibition were found in respect of the length of time (25 years) a member of the armed forces could be made to remain in employment[81] and of penal sanctions preventing all merchant seamen from going on strike.[82] Such a breach was also found in respect of the length of time that a conscientious objector to military service had to serve in alternative civilian employment, thus restricting unduly his freedom to take employment of his own choice.[83] A breach of the non-discrimination guarantee in Article 1 (2) was found in respect of unjustified discrimination between different categories workers in respect of

---

[74] *European Federation of Employees in Public Service v. France*, 8 (2001) IHRR 564.

[75] *European Council of Police Trade Unions v. Portugal*, 10 (2003) IHRR 572.

[76] *Confederation of Swedish Enterprise v. Sweden*, 11 (2004) IHRR 832.

[77] *Syndicat Occitan de l'Education v. France*, 12 (2005) IHRR 1146; and *Syndicat des Agreges de l'Enseignment Superieur v. France* 13 (2006) IHHH 1188.

[78] *Autism-Europe v. France* (note 44); *Syndicat Occitan de l'Education v. France*, (note 77) and *Centrale Generale des Services Publics v. Belgium* 13 (2006) IHRR 1181.

[79] *European Trade Union Confederation et al v. Bulgaria*: Council of Europe website www.coe.int: 2006. See also *Confederation Francaise de l'Encadrement v. France*, 10 (2003) IHRR 559; and *Confederation Francaise de l'Encadrement v. France*, 12 (2005) IHRR 1164 (deductions from strikers' pay). On the right to strike in the Charter, see Kovács, 'The Right to Strike in the European Social Charter', 26 (2005) *Comparative Labor Law and Policy Journal* 445.

[80] Issues have also been raised in a few cases concerning the rights to safe and healthy working conditions (Article 3): see *Marangopoulos Foundation for Human Rights v. Greece* (note 24); for the right to fair remuneration (Article 4), see *Confederation Francaise de l'Encadrement v. France* (note 79); and *Confederation de l'Encadrement v. France* (note 79); for the prohibition of child labour, see *International Commission of Jurists v. Portugal*, 7 (2000) IHRR 525; and for the right to vocational training, *Syndicat National de Professions des Tourisme v. France*, 8 (2001) IHRR 554.

[81] *International Federation of Human Rights Leagues v. Greece*, 8 (2001) IHRR 1153.

[82] Ibid.

[83] *Quaker Council for European Affairs v. Greece: supra* (note 31).

vocational training.[84] As to the right to reasonable hours of work, the exclusion of managerial staff from the limit on the number of hours of work in French law was found to be a breach of Article 2(1) as read with Article E of the Revised Charter, which prohibits discrimination in respect of Charter rights.[85]

What is striking about all of these cases is that they echo claims that could be brought by trade unions (acting to defend their own legal rights, not on the collective complaint basis available to them in the Charter) or by individuals in national courts applying national trade union or employment law guarantees that are common to most national legal systems. What they confirm is that it perfectly possible to imagine them being brought under an international complaints procedure that allowed for individual complaints, as opposed to collective complaints in the Charter sense.

As far as a right of individual communication under the ICESCR for the economic rights in Articles 6–8 of the Covenant is concerned, which tend to be disregarded in the dialogue about the establishment of a Covenant right of individual communication, the allowances in Article 2 (1) ICESCR for 'available resources' and progressive implementation concerning 'resources' do not have much relevance for them. As the Charter cases demonstrate, the question of financial cost is generally not such a large issue in economic right cases as it is in cases concerning social rights and the time, if any, reasonably required for their realisation – not being dependent upon any or large scale financial resources – will expire within a few years of ratification. In some economic rights cases, there will be just a negative obligation on the part of the State not to intervene, as, for example, in the case of the obligations to allow workers to form and join trades unions and to permit those organisations to function in the interests of the members (subject to permissible basic registration requirements and the like).

In other cases, the State will have a direct obligation of a negative or a positive kind concerning its own employees (for example, to leave the armed forces within a reasonable time or to be protected by health and safety measures), which again will not raise large questions of cost or time. In many cases, it will be a positive obligation to provide and enforce a legal framework for private employment in which economic rights are respected, including the rights to reasonable working hours, safe and healthy working conditions, fair remuneration, protection from child labour and non-discrimination in employment. In all of these cases, the financial cost will be of a kind which exists for positive obligations in respect of many civil and political rights also (including legislation, inspections,

---

[84] *Syndicat National de Professions des Tourisme v. France, supra* (note 80).
[85] *Confederation Francaise de l'Encadrement v. France* and *Confederation Francaise de l'Encadrement v. France* (note 79); and *Confederation General du Travail v. France*, 13 (2006) *IHRR* 599.

investigation and court proceedings) and is not at the level that applies to the protection and fulfilment of social rights such as health, housing, education and social security:[86] it is the cost of social rights, coupled with the need for time to implement programmes to realise them, that is the source of most of the concerns for States in the dialogue about a system of complaints under the ICESCR.

iv. Conclusion

The practice of the European Committee of Social Rights under the Collective Complaints Protocol is encouraging for those who are concerned to see it stay the course. Despite the limited number of possible complainants, the disappointingly few States parties that have ratified the Protocol, the restrictions that flow from the collective nature of any complaint and the lack of enthusiasm shown so far by the Committee of Ministers to support the collective complaints procedure, the Committee has made considerable progress in having it take its allotted place. It is the common experience that international complaints procedures require time to take root, so that it is not surprising for this reason alone that the number of complaints has not yet been large. What is encouraging for the Charter complaint procedure is that the Committee has developed an approach to the interpretation of the Charter in a complaints context that is fully in keeping with the Charter's human rights character and generally establishes a sound basis for the Committee's future work. What is also welcome is the evidence that the Committee's practice provides that economic and social rights may be satisfactorily adjudicated before an international treaty monitoring body. This can only add force to the momentum now building for the introduction of a right of individual – and possibly collective – communication under the ICESCR.

Special Note

The 2008 Optional Protocol to the International Covenant on Economic, Social and Cultural Rights, which provides for a right of individual communication, was adopted after the completion of this chapter. For an analysis of the Protocol, see Mahon, 'Progress at the Front: The Draft Optional Protocol to the International Covenant on Economic, Social and Cultural Rights', 8 (2008) *Human Rights Law Review* 617.

---

[86] Some economic rights, such as vocational guidance and training, may also have large financial implications, not unlike the economic rights dimensions of the right to social security, as for example, maternity leave and industrial injury benefits.

Chapter Two

The European Convention on Human Rights and Extradition

Jacques Hartmann[*]

Much has been written about the European Convention on Human Rights (ECHR) and extradition following the decision of the European Court of Human Rights (ECtHR) in the *Soering* case.[1] Since then the Court has heard a considerable number of complaints brought by individuals against their extradition. Renewed interest, nonetheless, is warranted in the subject given the burgeoning jurisprudence and the fact that several Member States of the Council of Europe (CoE) may have been involved in the rendition of individuals by clandestine or irregular procedures, also known as 'extra-ordinary rendition'.[2] The principle established in the *Soering* case is equally applicable

[*] Jesus College, Cambridge. Perhaps more than any of his students, I owe an enormous debt of gratitude to Professor Colin Warbrick who has generously shared with me both his time and knowledge. For this and many other things, I am immensely grateful.

[1] ECtHR, *Soering v. The United Kingdom* (7 July 1989) Appl. No. 14038/88. For commentaries, see Breitenmoser and Wilms, 'Human Rights v. Extradition: The Soering Case', 11 (1989–1990) *Michigan Journal of International Law* 845; Warbrick, 'Coherence and the European Court of Human Rights: The Ajudicative Backgound of the Soering Case', 11 (1989–1990) *Michigan Journal of International Law* 1073; Van den Wyngaert, 'Applying the European Convention on Human Rights to Extradition: Opening Pandora's Box?', 39 (1990) *ICLQ* 757; Sudre, 'Extradition Et Peine De Mort: Arrêt Soering De La Cour Européenne Des Droits De L'homme Du 7 Juillet 1989', 94 (1990) *Revue Générale de Droit International Public* 103; Shea, 'Expanding Judicial Scrutiny of Human Rights in Extradition Cases After Soering', 17 (1992) *YJIL* 85; Allenweldt, 'Protection Against Expulsion Under Article 3 of the European Convention on Human Rights', 4 (1993) *EJIL* 360; Dugard and Van den Wyngaert, 'Reconciling Extradition With Human Rights', 92 (1998) *AJIL* 187; and Hailbronner, 'Art. 6 Emrk Als Hindernis Der Auslieferung Und Abschiebung', in Bröhmer, Bieber Calliess (eds.), *Internationale Gemeinschaft Und Menschenrechte, Festschrift Für G. Ress*, Cologne, 2005, pp. 997–1010.

[2] See Report by Marty, *Secret Detentions and Illegal Transfers of Detainees Involving Council of Europe Member States: Second Report*, 11 June 2006, CoE Doc. 11302 rev.

K.H. Kaikobad & M. Bohlander (eds.), *International Law and Power: Perspectives on Legal Order and Justice*. Essays in Honour of Colin Warbrick, pp. 25–62.
© 2009 Koninklijke Brill NV. Printed in the Netherlands.

to this form of disguised extradition as well as all other forms of removal, and the principles extracted from one form of removal apply *mutatis mutandis* to all others.[3] Examining the Convention from this perspective, this article will seek to identify how various rights within the Convention may effect the removal of a person from the jurisdiction of a Contracting State.

I. EXTRADITION OUTSIDE THE JURISDICTION OF THE CONVENTION

As a preliminary point, it should be noted that in its jurisprudence, the ECtHR has made a significant distinction between removal within and outside the jurisdiction of a Contracting State.[4] One reason for this is that, while a person may be moved from the territory of one State Party to another, such transfer does not remove him from the protection of the Convention. Thus after having been extradited, any affected person would be entitled to bring an application before the ECtHR.[5] This pragmatic approach has some merit in relation to minor infringements of some rights but the irreversible nature, for instance, of capital punishment or the lasting effects of torture preclude this line of argument. Accordingly, in the *Saadi* case the ECtHR rejected the argument that a distinction must be drawn under Article 3 between treatment inflicted directly by a signatory State and treatment inflicted by the authorities in a receiving State outside the jurisdiction of the Convention.[6] In addition to this, some Member States of the CoE have refused extradition requests from other Party States, citing potential human rights violations as the reason for their

---

[3] See e.g ECtHR, *D. v. The United Kingdom* (2 May 1997), Appl. No. 30240/96, paragraph 47; and ECtHR, *T. I. v. The United Kingdom (Admissibility)*, (7 March 2000) Appl. No. 43844/98, p. 12.

[4] See e.g. ECtHR, *K. and F. v. The Netherlands (Admissibility)*, (12 December 1986) Appl. No. 12543/86, p. 5; and ECtHR, *Tomic v. The United Kingdom (Admissibility)*, (14 October 2003), Appl. No. 17837/03, paragraph 1. See also decision of the German Federal Administrative Court, *BVerwG*, vol. 122, pp. 271–286.

[5] See ECtHR, *Altun v. The Federal Republic of Germany (Admissibility)*, (3 May 1983) Appl. No. 10308/83 where the Commission noted that Turkey had not yet signed up to the optional clause in Article 25 (now Article 34) of the individual petition: see paragraph 15; ECtHR, *G. D. v. Switzerland (Admissibility)*, (17 March 1989), Appl. No. 14514/89, paragraph 1.

[6] ECtHR, *Saadi v. Italy* (28 February 2008), Appl. No. 37201/06, paragraphs 137–138. This is in line with other human rights bodies and cases: see, for example, CAT, *Alan v. Switzerland* (8 May 1996), Comm. No. 21/1995.

refusal.[7] This, incidentally, also illustrates that the traditional principle of non-inquiry is of little consequence in today's extradition practice.[8]

II. THE HUMAN RIGHT OF NON-REMOVAL

Although in practical terms it is not the most important example, in terms of establishing the principles involved in a human rights-based approach to non-removal, the most significant authority is the judgment of the ECtHR in the *Soering* case.[9] While the facts of the case are well-known, for the purposes of this paper it is useful to state that Soering was a German national, detained in the United Kingdom facing extradition to the United States on a capital charge. Under the UK-US extradition treaty, the United Kingdom had a right to refuse extradition unless the United States provided assurances satisfactory to the United Kingdom that the death penalty would not be carried out. The British government pronounced itself so satisfied with the very limited assurances offered by the United States Federal Government.[10] Soering was not satisfied and he therefore petitioned against his removal under the ECHR. However, inasmuch as Article 2 clearly allows capital punishment, he could not complain that the imposition or even the carrying out of a capital sentence was contrary to the Convention. Instead, the Court accepted his argument that the ECHR obliged States not to extradite a person where there is substantial evidence that the fugitive would face a real risk of treatment which, if it

---

[7]   In 2002, for instance, the English High Court quashed a decision by the Home Secretary allowing extradition to France of Rachid Ramda on the basis of his inability to contest information allegedly obtained by torture: *Ramda v. The Secretary of State for the Home Department*, [2002] EWHC 1278 (Admin) (unreported). Ramda was eventually extradited on 1 December 2005. See also the case of *Moreno and Garcia*, mentioned by Dugard and Van den Wyngart (note 1), p. 201.

[8]   In this regard see the detailed assessment by the Special Immigration Appeals Commission of the guarantees offered by the Government of Jordan in relation to the surrender of Omar Othman (aka Abu Qatada), [2007] UKSIAC 15/2005.

[9]   *Supra* (note 1). The term 'human-rights based' is used rather than a more general principle of 'non-refoulement', such as that contained in Article 33 of the 1951 Convention Relating to the Status of Refugees since the protection afforded under the ECHR is substantially broader than that in the Refugee Convention. Cf. ECtHR, *Chahal v. The United Kingdom* (15 November 1996), Appl. No. 22414/93, paragraph 80; and ECtHR, *Ahmed v. Austria* (27 November 1996), Appl. No. 25964/94, paragraph 41.

[10] The Attorney for Bedford County, Virginia, swore in an affidavit that: '. . . [T]hat should . . . Soering be convicted of the offence of capital murder as charged in Bedford County, Virginia . . . a representation will be made in the name of The United Kingdom to the judge at the time of sentencing that it is the wish of The United Kingdom that the death penalty should not be imposed or carried out.' See *Soering* (note 1), paragraph 20.

occurred within the jurisdiction of a Contracting State, would breach Article 3. The Court found that there was sufficient evidence of a real risk that Soering would receive a capital sentence and that the resulting incarceration in oppressive conditions for a extended period before any sentence were carried out would be incompatible with Article 3, the so-called '*death row phenomenon*'. Referring to the abhorrence of torture, the Court stated that:

> It would hardly be compatible with the underlying values of the convention ... were a contracting state knowingly to surrender a fugitive to another state where there were substantial grounds for believing that he would be in danger of being subjected to torture, however heinous the crime allegedly committed. Extradition in such circumstances, while not explicitly referred to in the brief and general wording of article 3, would plainly be contrary to the spirit and intendment of the article, and in the court's view this inherent obligation not to extradite also extends to cases in which the fugitive would be faced in the receiving state by a real risk of exposure to inhuman or degrading treatment or punishment proscribed by that article.[11]

In its reasoning, the Court emphasised the absolute nature of the prohibition of torture and inhuman or degrading treatment. Not all rights are, however, absolute. Thus while the human rights of every person within the jurisdiction of the ECHR are protected,[12] not all rights offer the same level of protection in relation to extradition. In this regard the Court in *Soering* stated:

> Article 1 [of the ECHR] cannot be read as justifying a general principle to the effect that, notwithstanding its extradition obligations, a Contracting State may not surrender an individual unless satisfied that the conditions awaiting him in the country of destination are in full accord with each of the safeguards of the Convention. Indeed ... the beneficial purpose of extradition in preventing fugitive offenders from evading justice cannot be ignored in determining the scope of application of the Convention and of Article 3 in particular.[13]

It follows that not any violation of a right recognised within the ECHR will obstruct extradition and individual rights may have varying thresholds of application depending on specific circumstances and the inevitable tension between interests of the individual and those of society. A fundamental distinction must therefore be made between absolute rights that may not be restricted or derogated in any circumstances and other rights that may either be derogated in time of emergency or restricted for certain specific purposes.[14] This is so because in

---

[11]   *Soering* (note 1), paragraph 88.
[12]   Article 1, European Convention on Human Rights, 1950.
[13]   *Supra* (note 1), paragraph 86.
[14]   Cf. Van den Wyngaert (note 1), p. 764; and see also Dugard and C. Van den Wyngaert (note 1), p. 210.

the search for a requisite fair balance between community interests and the requirements of individual protection inherent within the Convention, non-derogable rights, by their very nature, take a special position. Compelling considerations that necessitate effective protection of absolute rights do not therefore automatically apply to other provisions.[15]

III. HUMAN RIGHTS THAT MAY OBSTRUCT EXTRADITION

It is a widely recognised principle that extradition should be refused where there are substantial grounds for believing that the extradited person would be at real risk of subjection to torture. Thus, as noted by Christine Van den Wyngaert, the problem lies not in acceptance of the principle but rather in the definition of its threshold of application.[16] This is true of other rights as well. The likelihood of the imposition of a death penalty or that someone will be forced into slavery might, for instance, *per se* bar extradition. The same, however, cannot be said of every ill-treatment, denial of fair trial or indeed most other rights within the Convention. Therefore, each case must individually be assessed; and hence where substantial grounds are shown to exist for believing that a person would, if extradited, face a 'real risk' of treatment contrary to the Convention, it is necessary to asses the conditions in the receiving State against the specific standard of the Convention. In this regard it is beneficial to draw a distinction between the distinct categories of human rights mentioned above, namely absolute and relative rights.

1. *Absolute Rights*

Although the concept of 'absolute rights' may not properly have been established in the jurisprudence of the ECtHR,[17] a special point of a distinction may be traced in relation to extradition. This was first established with respect to Article 3, but it is equally applicable to other so-called 'absolute rights'.

---

[15] See ECtHR, *Z and T v. The United Kingdom (Admissibility)*, (28 February 2006), Appl. No. 27034/05.

[16] *Supra* (note 1), p. 765.

[17] Cf. Addo and Grief, 'Does Article 3 of the European Convention on Human Rights Enshrine Absolute Rights?', 9 (1998) *EJIL* 510–524.

a. The Right to Life and Protection against Capital Punishment

According to the ECtHR, the right to life is an inalienable human attribute and as such is accorded supreme value in the hierarchy of human rights.[18] The right to life encompasses a wide range of issues which cannot satisfactorily be dealt with here.[19] It must, however, be emphasised that the right to life entails not only negative obligations against the intentional taking of life, but also encompasses positive obligations to take appropriate steps to safeguard it, including the protection against threats from non-State parties.[20]

Although the right to life is commonly included within the category of so-called 'absolute rights', this categorisation – at least from a strictly positivist perspective – is not self-evident.[21] The Convention only prescribes that the right to life shall be 'protected by law'.[22] While generally read as implying an obligation to ensure adequate protection of human life,[23] the wording of Article 2 does not convey an absolute quality. On the contrary, it may be read as confirming the proposition that not all taking of life is illegal. Capital punishment, for instance, is expressly permitted[24] and the right to self-defence may provide another example where intentional killing may be permissible. Article 15, furthermore, allows for derogation in times war,[25] a prospect which, seemingly, goes against the very definition of an 'absolute right'.[26] It follows that the substance of the 'right to

---

[18] ECtHR, *Streletz, Kessler and Krenz v. Germany* (22 March 2001), Appl. No. 34044/96, paragraphs 93–94.

[19] Cf. generally Mathieu, *The Right to Life in European Constitutional and International Case-Law*, Strasbourg, 2006.

[20] See e.g ECtHR, *Osman v. The United Kingdom* (28 October 1998), Appl. No. 23452/94, paragraph 115.

[21] See e.g. Shestack, 'The Jurisprudence of Human Rights', in Meron (ed.), *Human Rights in International Law: Legal and Policy Issues*, Oxford, 1984, p. 71.

[22] Article 2 (1) of the European Convention on Human Rights (1950).

[23] Harris, O'Boyle and Warbrick, *Law of the European Convention on Human Rights*, London, 1995, p. 38.

[24] The capital punishment exception is, however, conditional: it may only be imposed after a trial that is compliant with the standards of the ECHR. Thus while the risk of capital punishment *per se* would not violate the Convention, risk of violation of the conditions of the exception, i.e. of the right to a fair trial, might in itself be enough to bar extradition. Also the means of execution may cause a conflict with Article 3. See e.g. ECtHR, *Öcalan v. Turkey* [GC], (12 May 2005), Appl. No. 46221/99, paragraph 166; ECtHR, *Bader and Others v. Sweden* (8 November 2005), Appl. No. 13284/04, paragraph 42.

[25] Article 15 (2), European Convention on Human Rights, 1950. In addition to this, international humanitarian law, which is considered *lex specialis*, allows killing in armed conflict when it offers a definite military advantage.

[26] Cf. Addo and Grief (note 17), p. 512 *et seq.* See also Gewirth, 'Are There Any Absolute Rights?', 31 (1981) *The Philosophical Quarterly* 1.

life' is limited. Only deprivations of life, which are not in accordance with *law*, are prohibited. The mere fact, however, that the deprivation of life is 'lawful' in some national legal systems does not, by itself, prevent it from being considered 'arbitrary' under the Convention. The capital punishment exception to the right to life further necessitates a distinction between removal which may lead to deprivation of life as a result of a legal sanction and other situations that may result in loss of life, as for example, dangers arising from civil war, lack of food or medical treatment, persecution from non-State actors and so forth. In relation to capital punishment, the Convention requires that the most rigorous standards of fairness are observed in criminal proceedings but such abstract norms cannot be established in relation to other potentially lethal circumstances. Instead, these require individual assessment of the concrete threat to, and the specific circumstances of, the person being removed from the jurisdiction.

i. *Extradition and the Risk of Capital Punishment*

At the time of the *Soering* case, capital punishment was not completely forbidden either by the ECHR or by customary international law.[27] Neither could Article 3 be interpreted as prohibiting capital punishment since that would have nullified the clear wording of Article 2 (1). Consequently, the Court based its finding on the so-called '*death row phenomenon*' discussed below. Subsequently, in the *Öcalan* case, the Court refused to accept the argument to the effect that the second sentence of Article 2 (1), which explicitly permits capital punishment, had been abrogated by State practice so that the death penalty itself constituted inhuman and degrading treatment contrary to Article 3. On this point the Court stated:

> For the time being, the fact that there are still a large number of States who have yet to sign or ratify Protocol No. 13 [concerning the abolition of the death penalty in all circumstances] may prevent the Court from finding that it is the established practice of the Contracting States to regard the implementation of the death penalty as inhuman and degrading treatment contrary to Article 3 of the Convention, since no derogation may be made from that provision, even in times of war.[28]

The qualifying words 'for the time being' clearly indicate the unsettled nature of the matter.[29] However, the underlying premise – that that there are still a large number of States who have yet to sign or ratify Protocol No. 13 – no longer holds. Protocol 13 has by now been ratified or signed by all CoE Member

---

[27] Cf. Dugard and Van Den Wyngaert (note 1), p. 196.
[28] *Supra* (note 24), paragraph 165.
[29] See also *Bader* (note 24), paragraph 42.

States except two.[30] Nonetheless, this practice does not change the meaning and scope of Article 2 (1) for non-ratifying States as the Court specifically noted that Contracting States had chosen the 'traditional method of amendment' in pursuit of abolition.[31] The *'death row phenomenon'* is therefore still relevant. This does not mean that States that have not yet ratified Protocol No. 13 are prohibited *per se* from extraditing anyone who might have to endure the risk of capital punishment. It only means that these States are prohibited from extraditing persons facing a real risk due to mental, or other conditions, of inhumane suffering as a result of harsh conditions of internment and proximity to execution.[32] Those States, however, which have ratified Protocol No. 13 are prohibited from extraditing where there is a real risk of capital punishment.[33] Article 3 of Protocol No. 13 provides unequivocally that 'no one shall be condemned to such penalty [the death penalty] or executed'. Nor does it allow for any reservation or derogation. It follows that the prohibition instituted by Protocol No. 13 of capital punishment is as absolute as the prohibition of torture, inhuman or degrading treatment.[34] So far, however, the Court has focused on assurances that the death penalty would not be carried out and it has yet unequivocally to state the implications in relation to extradition.[35] It was in the admissibility decision, *Z and T*, that the Court made its most incontrovertible statement to date:

---

[30] As of May 2009, the two States which have not signed Protocol No. 13 are The Russian Federation and Azerbaijan. Those States which have signed but have yet to ratify are Armenia, Latvia, Moldova, Poland, and Spain. Refer to ⟨http://conventions.coe.int/⟩.

[31] Öcalan (note 24), paragraph 164. See also ECtHR, *Shamayev and Others v. Georgia and Russia* (12 April 2005), Appl. No. 36378/02, where it was stated that: 'A Contracting State which has not ratified Protocol No. 6 and has not acceded to Protocol No. 13 is authorised to apply the death penalty under certain conditions, in accordance with Article 2(2) of the Convention.' See paragraph 333. This presumably would also influence extradition.

[32] Cf. *Soering* (note 1); ECtHR, *Poltoratskiy v. Ukraine* (29 April 2003), Appl. No. 38812/97; ECtHR, *Iorgov v. Bulgaria* (11 March 2004), Appl. No. 40653/98; and ECtHR, *G. B. v. Bulgaria* (11 March 2004), Appl. No. 42346/98.

[33] It should be recalled that States which have not yet ratified are still obliged to refrain from acts which would defeat the object and purpose of the Protocol: *vide* Article 18 of the 1969 Vienna Convention on the Law of Treaties; even so, the effects of this provision should not be exaggerated.

[34] This has led the Council of Europe's Commissioner for Human Rights, T. Hammarberg, to state that the death penalty exception within Article 2(1) of the ECHR has now become 'redundant'. See 'Europe Should Remain a Death-Penalty Free Zone,' *Viewpoint*, www.coe.int/t/commissioner/Viewpoints/060821_en.asp, 21 August 2006.

[35] See *Soering* (note 1), paragraphs 97–98; ECtHR, *Mamatkulov v. Turkey* [GC], (4 February 2005), Appl. No. 46827/99, paragraphs 76–77; ECtHR, *Nivette v. France (Admissibility)*, (3 July 2001), Appl. No. 44190/98; and ECtHR, *Kordia v. Turkey (Admissibility)*, (4 July 2006), Appl. No. 6575/06.

The case-law that followed [*Soering*], and *which applies equally to the risk of violations of Article 2*, is based on the fundamental importance of these provisions, whose guarantees it is imperative to render effective in practice.[36]

This suggests that the protection against extradition applicable to Article 3 may be extended to Article 2, at least for Contracting Parties to Protocol No. 13.[37] The statement, however, came as mere *obiter dictum* in an admissibility decision relating to an Article 9 application and the Court has yet to make an uncontroversial assertion of its standpoint. There is, nonetheless, little doubt that Protocol No. 13 prevents Contracting Parties from extraditing suspects to countries where there is a real risk of capital punishment. This conclusion is compelled from the Court's reasoning in relation to Article 3 and the absolute nature of the prohibition of capital punishment in Protocol No. 13.[38]

ii. *Other Lethal Circumstances*
The indirect effect of the Convention, first attributed to Article 3 and which may find analogous application in Article 2, not only applies where an applicant may be deprived of his life as a result of the imposition of a death penalty but to all situations endangering the life of a person.[39] This greatly broadens the potential scope of Article 2 in relation to extradition. Often, however, issues relating to removal under Article 2 and 3 are considered 'indissociable' and are examined principally under the heading of Article 3.[40] Thus, for example, cases concerning the expulsion of the seriously ill, dependent on life-preserving medication, have all been considered and predominantly pleaded under Article 3.[41] One case has been decided conjointly under Articles 2 and 3. This was an admissibility case decided by the Commission before a restructuring of the Court took place and is thus possibly of limited precedent.[42] Nevertheless, *Mbunzu* is interesting as it is the only case (to the knowledge of the author) where a more general right

---

[36] *Supra* (note 15), p. 4. Emphasis added.

[37] The proposition that it may only be extended to Contracting Parties of Protocol No. 13 derives from the fact that Article 2 specifically allows for capital punishment.

[38] See *Soering* (note 1), paragraph 88; ECtHR, *Bello v. Sweden (Admissibility)*, (17 January 2006), Appl. No. 32213/04; ECtHR, *Gomes v. Sweden (Admissibility)*, (7 February 2006), Appl. No. 34566/04; and *Saadi* (note 6). Unfortunately, the Court has so far confused the issue. See on this *Bader* (note 24).

[39] See e.g. ECtHR, *Sinnarajah v. Switzerland (Admissibility)*, (11 May 1999), Appl. No. 45187/99; and ECtHR, *Dejbakhsh and Mahmoud Zadeh v. Sweden (Admissibility)*, (13 December 2005), Appl. No. 11682/04.

[40] See e.g., *N. v. The United Kingdom* (27 May 2008), Appl. No. 26565/05, paragraph 25; *Dejbakhsh and Mahmoud Zadeh* (note 39), p. 9; *Bello v. Sweden* (note 38), p. 9; and *Gomes v. Sweden* (note 38), p. 9.

[41] See e.g., *D.* (note 3); and ECtHR, *Bensaid v. The United Kingdom* (6 February 2001), Appl. No. 44599/98, paragraph 30.

[42] ECtHR, *Mbunzu v. The Netherlands (Admissibility)*, (10 May 1992), Appl. No. 17878/91.

to life was considered in relation to removal. The case concerned expulsion from the Netherlands to Angola, a country at that time devastated by civil war. The applicant argued that in view of the continuing violence in Angola and its general shortage of food, he would, if returned, certainly die as a result either of starvation or forced conscription.

The Commission considered that the general situation in Angola at the time of the applicant's requests was undoubtedly unstable but that the applicant had failed to substantiate as to how his personal situation was worse than that of the generality of other young Angolan men who were enlisted for active service. Consequently, the Commission held that Mbunzu had failed to disclose evidence sufficient to establish that he was personally at real risk of a violation. Notwithstanding the above, it did not find the claim to be unprotected by the Convention.[43] It is uncertain as to what may be inferred from this decision but it seemingly does not rule out that a lack of food in the receiving State or the threat of forced conscription therein may prevent removal, although the Commission did insist on the existence of an individualised threat.[44]

Decisions of domestic courts also confirm that the absence of accommodation, food or the means to obtain such essentials may also raise an issue in context of Article 3.[45] In this respect, it should also be noted that while the Court generally insists on applying special distinguishing features, that is, circumstances which make the situation of the applicant worse than those applicable to the generality of society, or special groups, the ECtHR has on one occasion found that the conditions prevalent in a specific group were sufficient to prevent removal.[46] This might also be relevant with regard to detainees.[47] Unlike other forms of removal, conditions of destitution would not normally pose a risk to a person facing extradition since he would be in the custody of the requesting State. Access to food may, nonetheless, be an issue in countries where detainees rely on relatives or acquaintances for these and other necessities. Indirectly, it might further be relevant if no arrangements were made in case of an acquittal.[48]

---

[43] See paragraph 1. Cf. Leach, *Taking a Case to the European Court of Human Rights*, Oxford, 2005, pp. 157–160.

[44] See paragraph 1. Cf. ECtHR, *Vilvarajah and Others v. the United Kingdom* (30 October 1991), Appl. No. 13163/87; ECtHR, *Cruz Varas and Others v. Sweden* (20 March 1991), Appl. No. 15576/89; and ECtHR, *Salah Sheekh v. The Netherlands* (11 January 2007), Appl. No. 1948/04.

[45] See in this respect *Secretary of State for the Home Department v. Limbuela and Others* [2004] EWCA Civ 540. See also *R (on the Application of Limbuela) v. Secretary of State for the Home Department* [2005] UKHL 66; [2007] 1 AER 951.

[46] *Salah Sheekh* (note 44), paragraph 148.

[47] See below 'Prison Conditions': subsection b (iii).

[48] See in this regard, the practice of Austria as reported by the Steering Committee for Human

b. The Prohibition of Torture and Inhuman or Degrading Treatment

There is little doubt that customary international law recognises the prohibition on torture.[49] Every major human rights convention prohibits such conduct, as do special conventions and the laws of many States.[50] Thus the example of torture presents no difficulty in relation to extradition: the prohibition is absolute and no balancing of other considerations, even national security, is allowed. The Court has repeatedly stressed in its line of authorities involving extradition, expulsion or deportation that: 'Article 3 prohibits in absolute terms torture or inhuman or degrading treatment or punishment and that its guarantees apply irrespective of the reprehensible nature of the conduct of the person in question.'[51] And while some governments have challenged this,[52] the wording of Article 3 does not allow any other interpretation.

The absolute ban applies equally to inhuman or degrading treatment or punishment. While, however, there is broad consensus that inhuman or degrading treatment is prohibited there is little common agreement on what constitutes this lesser form of ill treatment. In other words, there is no agreement with regard to the lower threshold for the application of Article 3. This means that whereas in theory no proportionality test may be applied, States may nevertheless

---

Rights, *Group of Specialist on Human Rights*, Council of Europe, (DH–S–TER (2006) 002BiL), p. 12, where reportedly it was made a condition of extradition that the person concerned would be allowed to leave the territory of the requesting State within 45 days in case of acquittal.

[49] For an examination of the status of torture in customary international law, see e.g. ECtHR, *Al-Adsani v. The United Kingdom* (21 November 2001), Appl. No. 35763/97, paragraphs 25–31.

[50] Article 17 of the International Covenant on Civil and Political Rights, 1966; the Convention Against Torture and Other Cruel, Inhuman or Degrading Treatment or Punishment (1984); Article 13 of the European Convention on Human Rights, 1950; European Convention for the Prevention of Torture and Inhuman and Degrading Treatment or Punishment, 1987; and the Inter-American Convention to Prevent and Punish Torture, 1985. Many of these instruments also oblige Contracting States to implement the prohibition in national law.

[51] See *D* (note 3), paragraph 47. See also ECtHR, *Ireland v. The United Kingdom* (18 January 1978), Appl. No. 5310/71, paragraph 163; *Chahal* (note 9), paragraphs 79–80; *Ahmed v. Austria* (note 9), paragraph 40; ECtHR, *H.L.R. v. France* (22 April 1997), Appl. No. 24573/94, paragraph 35; *Bensaid* (note 41), paragraph 32; ECtHR, *Indelicato v. Italy* (18 October 2001), Appl. No. 31143/96, paragraph 30; ECtHR, *Sanchez v. France* (4 July 2006), Appl. No. 5945/00, paragraphs 115–116; ECtHR, *N. v. Finland* (26 July 2005), Appl. No. 38885/02, paragraph 159; and *Saadi* (note 6), paragraph 127.

[52] See intervention by various States in the pending cases of ECtHR, *Ramzy v. The Netherlands*, Appl. No. 25424/05; see for example, the statement of the Foreign and Commonwealth Office before the House of Commons, 'United Kingdom Materials on International Law', Entry No. 6/82, in 77 (2006) *BYIL* 597, at p. 715; and see also *Saadi* (note 6), paragraphs 117–123.

use a proportionality test when settling the threshold for the application of the ban for removal;[53] that is to say, a State may argue that a risk of ill-treatment may be proportionate in view of the threat to national security.[54] Divergence in opinions as to the lower threshold of inhuman or degrading treatment is well illustrated in the current debate concerning the legitimate minimal protection applicable to terrorist suspects. In the context of the ECHR, any assessment of this minimum is, in the nature of things, relative, and depends on a variety of factors such as duration, physical or mental effects and in some cases, the sex, age and state of health of the victim.[55] Thus, depending on the specific circumstances of a given case, the entry threshold may be very low, especially in relation to vulnerable people, as for example, detainees.[56] The complexity of the case-law necessitates a distinction between various categories of ill-treatment that have been or are likely to be advanced as an obstacle to extradition in order to ascertain the weight to be attached to each form in that context.

i. *Life Imprisonment without Possibility of Release*
The Court has on many occasions affirmed that it is not its role to decide on what constitutes an appropriate term of detention for a particular offence.[57] Nonetheless, arbitrary or disproportionately lengthy sentences may, in some circumstances, raise an issue under the Convention.[58] In relation to extradition, this may mean that Article 3 prohibits transfer unless adequate assurances are

---

[53] Cf. ILA, 'Third Report of the Committee on Extradition and Human Rights', *ILA Report of the Sixty-Eighth Conference: Taipei 1998*, London, 1998, p. 132, at p. 138.

[54] See e.g., *Chahal* (note 9), paragraph 136; and *Saadi* (note 6), paragraphs 117–126.

[55] Cf. *Ireland* (note 51), paragraph 162; ECtHR, *Aksoy v. Turkey* (18 December 1996), Appl. No. 21987/93, paragraphs 63–64; and ECtHR, *Selmouni v. France*, (28 July 1999), Appl. No. 25803/94, paragraphs 96–105.

[56] See for instance ECtHR, *Yavuz v. Turkey* (10 January 2006), Appl. No. 67137/01, paragraphs 37–44, where the Court found a violation of Article 3 based on the absence of a plausible explanation as to the cause of the relatively minor injuries on the back and neck of the applicant, sustained while in custody; and also ECtHR, *Karakas and Yesilirmak v. Turkey*, (28 June 2005), Appl. No. 43925/98. In this case the applicants complained that they were, amongst other things, blindfolded, kept standing facing a wall and beaten on both hands (*el falakası*). A number of elements in the case raised doubts as to whether the applicants had indeed been subjected to such treatment. Nevertheless, as in *Yavuz*, in the absence of a plausible, satisfactory explanation with regard to the applicants' injuries, the Court found a violation of Article 3. In neither case did the Court make any distinction as to what form of mistreatment the applicants had suffered.

[57] See e.g. ECtHR, *Sawoniuk v. The United Kingdom (Admissibility)*, (29 May 2001), Appl. No. 63716/00, paragraph 3.

[58] See ECtHR, *V. v. The United Kingdom* (16 December 1999), Appl. No. 294888/94, paragraphs 97–101; and ECtHR, *Weeks v. The United Kingdom* (2 March 1987), Appl. No. 9787/82, paragraph 72.

obtained. The Court has not, so far, directly pronounced on the matter but it has explicitly kept open the possibility that extradition of an individual to a State where he runs a real risk of being sentenced to life imprisonment without possibility of early release may raise an issue under Article 3.[59] Here an important distinction must be made between a person who is sought for trial and an individual wanted to serve a custodial sentence.[60] This is so because unless an extradition request concerns a crime for which a mandatory life sentence is prescribed or the person has already been convicted, it would be difficult to substantiate a claim of a real risk of life imprisonment without the possibility of early release. The difficulty was well illustrated in the admissibility decision of *Kordia v. Turkey.*[61] Here the applicant argued that the risk of capital punishment and alternatively life imprisonment without the possibility of parole should bar his extradition. The Court, however, relied on a guarantee that the prosecution authorities would not seek capital punishment. The assurance explicitly left open the possibility of life imprisonment. In regard to the latter, the ECtHR stated that:

> Contrary to the applicant's submission, in view of the guarantees given by the US authorities, the Court considers it unlikely that, if he were convicted on several counts of murder, the possible sentences of life imprisonment would be converted to the death penalty. Moreover, *the Court is unable to speculate whether the applicant would receive a life sentence without the possibility of parole*, the conditions in which he might serve that sentence or the effect such a sentence might have on him.[62]

Thus while life imprisonment may theoretically prevent extradition, any such claim would be unlikely to succeed. It should also be noted that the possible

---

[59] See ECtHR, *Einhorn v. France* (16 October 2001), Appl. No. 71555/01 where the Court stated that it is not to be 'excluded that the extradition of an individual to a State in which he runs the risk of being sentenced to life imprisonment without any possibility of early release may raise an issue under Article 3 of the Convention': see paragraph 27. See also *Sawoniuk* (note 57); ECtHR, *Nivette* (note 35); ECtHR, *Partington v. The United Kingdom* (26 June 2003), Appl. No. 58853/00; and ECtHR, *Léger v. France* (11 April 2006), Appl. No. 19324/02.

[60] It should further be noted that the Convention for the Rights of the Child, which has been ratified by all States with the exception of Somalia and the United States of America, provides in Article 37(1) that: '[N]either capital punishment nor life imprisonment without possibility of release shall be imposed for offences committed by persons below eighteen years of age.' Thus almost all States are prohibited from sentencing children under the age of 18 to life imprisonment without possibility of early release. The broad consensus against the life imprisonment of juveniles might also affect some States' willingness to co-operate in regard to extradition.

[61] *Supra* (note 35).

[62] Ibid, pp. 4–5. Emphasis added. In contrast to *Soering*, there was little consideration here of whether the applicant would be convicted, and if so, whether he would be subject to life imprisonment: see *supra* (note 1), paragraphs 93–99.

evolution in the Court's jurisprudence, restricting extradition where the subject may face life imprisonment without early release, may significantly impede criminal co-operation outside the CoE because many States that make use of capital punishment often substitute this form of penalty with life without parole in order to enable extradition from abolitionist States.[63]

ii. *Harsh Interrogation Methods*
In *Ireland v. The United Kingdom*, the ECtHR held that intimidatory interrogation techniques constituted inhuman and degrading treatment, but not torture.[64] The Court took into consideration the so-called 'five techniques' of interrogation which comprised: wall-standing, stress positioning, hooding, subjection to 'white' noise and the deprivation of sleep, food and drink.[65] Since then the ECtHR has not had many occasions to consider the various interrogation methods which to some extent have been developed to avoid the constraints of the jurisprudence of various human rights bodies.[66] Importantly, the ECtHR has noted that reported conditions in detention facilities outside the United States, such as Guantanamo Bay, are at a variance with the standards of Article 3.[67] This assertion may provide some guidance with respect to the application threshold of Article 3, but it does not answer the question as to how harsh a requesting State's interrogation methods need to be in order to affect the requested State's decision on whether or not to grant extradition. Arguably the threshold is low. The ECtHR has consistently stressed that any use of physical force against a

---

[63] During the drafting of the Rome Statute, several States favouring capital punishment argued that life imprisonment was too timid a punishment. In contrast, various European and Latin American States were in principle opposed to life imprisonment, and, at any event, to its imposition without the possibility of parole or conditional release. Cf. Schabas, *An Introduction to the International Criminal Court*, Cambridge, (2001) 141.

[64] *Supra* (note 51), paragraphs 165–168.

[65] Ibid, at paragraph 96. Although the European Commission on Human Rights unanimously found that the combined use of the five techniques constituted torture, the Court held that the applicants 'did not occasion suffering of the particular intensity and cruelty implied by the word torture as so understood'. See paragraph 167. Thus the Court was clearly less impressed than the Commission by the psychological methods of interrogation, although a similar conclusion would in all likelihood not be reached today. Cf. Harris, O'Boyle and Warbrick (note 23), p. 61.

[66] Cf. Nowak, 'What Practices Constitute Torture? US and UN Standards', 28 (2006) *HRQ* 809. See also U.S. Department of Defence, *Working Group Report on Detainee Interrogations in the Global War on Terrorism* (March 2003), available at the Centre for Constitutional Rights ⟨www.ccr-ny.or⟩.

[67] See ECtHR, *Al-Moayad v. Germany (Admissibility)*, (20 February 2007), Appl. No. 35868/03, paragraph 69. A similar case, *Zayed v. Germany (Admissibility)*, (20 February 2007), Appl. No. 35866/03, was struck off the list. See also the pending case of *Ahmed and Aswat v. The United Kingdom* (lodged on 10 June 2007) Appl. No. 24027/07.

person deprived of his liberty which is not made strictly necessary as a result of the person's own conduct violates human dignity.[68] Evidently, the aim of obtaining information does not fall within this exception, especially since the purpose of extracting information often seems to be an aggravating factor when characterising treatment as 'torture'.[69] Acts affecting the dignity of detainees such as strip searches, forced shaving or handcuffing without specific justification may also breach Convention standards.[70] While the risk of such treatment has not yet in itself prevented extradition, it does give some indication of the seriousness with which the ECtHR regards the use of physical force against people in custody.[71] Implicit in the Court's reasoning is also the supposition that mental anguish alone may constitute torture or inhuman or degrading treatment.[72] In this respect, the common use of solitary confinement and sensory deprivation may especially give rise to issues in relation to Article 3.[73]

Thus while the Convention does not *per se* prevent extradition for purposes of interrogation, the absolute prohibition of torture, inhuman or degrading treatment and the particular vulnerability of persons in detention sets a low threshold against surrender where there is a real risk of coercive interrogation.

---

[68] First suggested by Judge De Meyer in ECtHR, *Tomasi v. France* (27 August 1992), Appl. No. 12850/87, paragraph 112 and subsequently endorsed by the Court in ECtHR, *Ribitsch v. Austria* (21 November 1995), Appl. No. 18896/91, paragraph 38; ECtHR, *Tenkin v. Turkey* (9 June 1998), Appl. No. 22496/93, paragraph 53; and *Selmouni* (note 55), paragraph 99.

[69] See ECtHR, *Egmez v. Cyprus* (21 December 2000), Appl. No. 20869/92, paragraph 78; ECtHR, *Denizci and Others v. Cyprus* (23 May 2001), Appl. No. 25316/94, paragraph 384; and ECtHR, *Corsacov v. Moldova* (4 April 2006), Appl. No. 18944/02, paragraphs 63–65.

[70] See e.g. ECtHR, *Van der Ven v. the Netherlands* (4 February 2003), Appl. No. 50901/99; ECtHR, *Yankov v. Bulgaria* (11 December 2003), Appl. No. 39084/97; and ECtHR, *Raininen v. Finland* (16 December 1997) Appl. No. 20972/92.

[71] In this regard, see Nowak, who, as Special Rapporteur on the Question of Torture, observes that '. . . a thorough analysis of the *travaux préparatoires* of Articles 1 and 16 of CAT as well as a systematic interpretation of both provisions in light of the practice of the Committee against Torture leads one to conclude that the decisive criterion for distinguishing torture from CIDT [cruel, inhuman or degrading treatment or punishment] may best be understood to be the purpose of the conduct and the powerlessness of the victim, rather than the intensity of the pain or suffering inflicted, as argued by the European Court of Human Rights and many scholars'. See 'Civil and Political Rights, Including the Question of Torture and Detention', UN Doc. E/CN. 4/2006/6, at p. 39.

[72] Harris, O'Boyle and Warbrick (note 23) p. 61.

[73] Solitary confinement does not in itself constitute breach of Article 3 and may serve legitimate purposes. On the other hand, it may also be used as a form of coercion to force co-operation from a suspect. The ECtHR has held that complete sensory deprivation coupled with total social isolation can destroy the personality and constitutes a form of inhuman treatment which cannot be justified by the requirements of security or for any other reason. See e.g., *Van der Ven* (note 70), paragraph 51. For an overview of the Courts case-law see *Sanchez v. France* (note 51) paragraphs 112–150. Mr Sanchez is better known by his alias: 'Carlos the Jackal'.

In contrast to other forms of removal, extra vigilance might also be warranted in regard to extradition since people are sure to be held in custody and experience shows that it is precisely in such circumstances that individuals are at risk of ill-treatment, especially if held *incommunicado*.[74] The legitimate exceptions to the right to liberty are moreover exhaustively listed in Article 5, and do not include interrogation. Thus while the Court has noted that it is unclear whether an issue could be raised in relation to extradition by the prospect of arbitrary detention under Article 5,[75] an individual could never legitimately be deprived of his liberty solely for the purpose of interrogation, which in itself would prevent extradition. In addition to the above, the *double criminality* principle, common to most extradition agreements, implies not only that conduct for which the person is sought must be a crime in both requesting and requested States, but also that the person must be requested for purposes of standing trial or to serve a sentence of imprisonment.[76] And while the *double criminality* principle is not a mandatory principle of international law, it does serve an important function in the protection of human rights.[77] The right to silence and the privilege against self-incrimination likewise provide protection against ill-treatment. They, *inter alia*, protect against improper compulsion, thereby contributing to the avoidance of a miscarriage of justice.[78] The right not to incriminate oneself in particular presupposes that the prosecution in a criminal case seeks to prove its case against the accused without resort to evidence obtained through any method of coercion. Any use of evidence obtained by torture would also raise an issue in relation to the right to a fair trial.[79]

---

[74] See e.g., UN Commission on Human Rights, Resolution 2003/32, paragraph 14.

[75] See *Tomic* (note 4), paragraph 3; and ECtHR, *F. v. The United Kingdom (Admissibility)*, (22 June 2004), Appl. No. 17341/03, paragraph 2. In relation to judicial review of extradition measures, see e.g., *Soering* (note 1), paragraphs 119–124; and ECtHR, *Garabayev v. Russia* (7 June 2007), Appl. No. 38411/02, paragraphs 89–102.

[76] See e.g., Article 2 of the UN Model Treaty on Extradition, 1990. Some extradition arrangements also allow for temporary transfer of detainees to provide assistance to investigations of prosecutions in another jurisdiction. See Article 13 of the International Convention for the Suppression of Terrorist Bombing, 1997; and Article 16 of the International Convention for the Suppression of the Financing of Terrorism, 1999.

[77] Cf. ILA, 'Third Report of the Committee on Extradition and Human Rights', *ILA Report of the Sixty-Eighth Conference* (note 53), pp. 148–149.

[78] Cf. ECtHR, *Jalloh v. Germany* (11 July 2006), Appl. No. 54810/00, paragraph 100. For the level of compulsion that is necessary to violate Article 6, see e.g., ECtHR, *Heaney and McGuinness* (21 December 2000), Appl. No. 34720/97, paragraphs 48–55. For the principle against self-incrimination, see generally Trechsel, *Human Rights in Criminal Proceedings*, Oxford, 2005, pp. 340–360.

[79] Article 15 of the Convention against Torture and Other Cruel, Inhuman or Degrading Treatment or Punishment, 1984, provides: 'Each State Party shall ensure that any statement which is established to have been made as a result of torture shall not be invoked as evidence

iii. *Prison Conditions*

Breach of Article 3 in relation to prison conditions was first established by the Commission in the *Greek* case.[80] It reached this conclusion on the basis of over-crowding, inadequate facilities for heating, sanitation, sleeping arrangements, food, recreation and contact with the outside world. The assessment is, as in all other cases, subjective and special circumstances of a victim may result in other-wise lawful conditions violating Article 3.[81] Thus while the Convention cannot be interpreted as laying down a general obligation to release a detainee on health grounds, it obliges States to ensure adequate facilities so that incarceration is compatible with human dignity.[82] Lack of proper sanitary or medical facilities may therefore prevent extradition where the subject's conditions require special treatment.[83] In general, relevant circumstances include elements such as available space, catering, sleeping, recreational facilities and sanitation, especially toilet and other sanitary conditions. Other factors such as lighting, heat and ventila-tion, although not in themselves capable of constituting a breach of Article 3, are relevant to the assessment of whether impugned conditions breach the threshold of the Convention. Some factors may be counterbalanced against others.[84] The

---

in any proceedings, except against a person accused of torture as evidence that the statement was made.' See also *A and Others v. Secretary of State for the Home Department* [2004] UKHL 56. See also *Othman (Jordan) v. Secretary of State for the Home Department* [2008] EWCA Civ 290.

[80] ECtHR, *Denmark, Norway, Sweden and the Netherlands v. Greece* (5 November 1969), Appl. No. 3321/67. See also ECtHR, *Dougoz v. Greece* (6 March 2001), Appl. No. 40907/98; ECtHR, *Peers v. Greece* (19 April 2001), Appl. No. 28524/95; ECtHR, *Kalashnikov v. Russia* (15 July 2002), Appl. No. 47095/99; and ECtHR, *Ilascu and Others v. Moldova and Russia* (8 July 2004), Appl. No. 48787/99.

[81] See e.g., ECtHR, *Price v. The United Kingdom* (10 July 2001), Appl. No. 33394/96; and ECtHR, *M. M. v. The United Kingdom (Admissibility)*, (8 January 2001), Appl. No. 58374/00.

[82] For example, in *D.*, the Court held that it would be incompatible with the obligations of The United Kingdom under Article 3 to deport a person in an advanced stage of a terminal illness to a place where medical treatment and social support was grievously inadequate: *supra* (note 3).

[83] Ibid; see also ECtHR, *Karara v. Findland (Inadmissible)*, (29 May 1998), Appl. No. 40900/98; ECtHR, *B.B. v. France (Struck off the list)*, (9 March 1998), Appl. No. 39030/96; *M. M. v. Switzerland (Inadmissible)*, (14 September 1998), Appl. No. 43348/98; and ECtHR, *S. C. C. v. Sweden (Inadmissible)*, (15 February 2002), Appl. No. 46553/99. See also *Ex parte Razgar v. Secretary of State for Home Department* [2004] UKHL 27; and *N. v. Secretary of State for the Home Department* [2005] UKHL 31. Further, refer also to the practice of Austria, reported by the Steering Committee for Human Rights, *Group of Specialist on Human Rights* (note 48), p. 15.

[84] Accordingly, in *Valasinas v. Lithuania*, no violation of Article 3 was found in view, *inter alia*, of the fact that the somewhat restricted sleeping facilities were counterbalanced by unlimited freedom of movement enjoyed by the detainees during the day: ECtHR, (24 October 2001), Appl. No. 44558/98, paragraphs 103 and 107.

length of incarceration is also of vital importance.[85] Since, however, the ECtHR has pronounced itself unlikely to speculate on the outcome of criminal trials, the time element may be of lesser importance in relation to extradition to stand trial.[86] This despite the increasingly common so-called 'eliminative method' of designating extraditable crimes by prescribing minimal terms of imprisonment – often one year or longer – means that those extradited would, if convicted, be expected to serve longer custodial sentences.[87] In addition to this, special problems may arise in relation to people extradited to foreign countries where food and other necessities are not provided by the State.

Thus, given the practical demands of imprisonment, States must ensure that individuals are detained in conditions that are compatible with respect for human dignity and that extradition does not subject prisoners to distress or hardship of an intensity exceeding the unavoidable level of suffering inherent in detention.[88] Until recently, however, the ECtHR has been reluctant to find a violation of Article 3 with respect to general conditions in detention facilities;[89] even more so in relation to establishing this as a bar to extradition.[90] In *Mamatkulov*, the Court decided that general conditions of detention in Uzbekistan, although below UN basic minimum standards for prisoners, were not in themselves enough to prevent extradition.[91] This finding is difficult to reconcile with the general principle that the Convention seeks to guarantee not rights that are theoretical or illusory, but practical and effective,[92] especially when viewed in the light of the fact that the applicants were extradited to Uzbekistan, that is to say, outside the jurisdiction of the Convention. Although the ECtHR did not find in this case that extradition had breached Article 3, its conclusion was based on specific evidence and it was not contested that prison conditions in themselves may bar extradition. In this respect, the finding must be contrasted with other findings where similar circumstances were found to violate Article 3.[93] The fact that prison con-

---

[85] Cf. ECtHR, *Sakkopoulos v. Greece* (15 January 2004), Appl. No. 61828/00, paragraph 32.

[86] Cf. *Kordia* (note 35), paragraph 1.

[87] Cf. Gilbert, *Transnational Fugitive Offenders in International Law: Extradition and Other Mechanisms*, The Hague, 1998, p. 86. As an example, see the UK-US Extradition Treaty of March 2003, Cm 5821, which, according to the Minister of State for the Home Office, 'reflects the best of modern practice': HL Deb 9 November 2004, vol. 666, col. 752.

[88] ECtHR, *Kudla v. Poland* (26 October 2000), Appl. No. 30210/96, paragraph 93.

[89] See e.g. ECtHR, *Zhu v. The United Kingdom (Admissibility)*, (12 August 2001), Appl. No. 36790/97.

[90] See *Mamatkulov* (note 35).

[91] Ibid.

[92] See e.g. ECtHR, *Airey v. Ireland* (9 October 1979), Appl. No. 6289/73, paragraph 24.

[93] In *Kalashnikov*, the applicant was detained in an overcrowded prison cell and forced to sleep in shifts, which was made even more difficult with constant light and a television set which was kept turned on for twenty fours a day. The conditions of hygiene were so bad that they led

ditions may in themselves breach Article 3, combined with the absolute nature of the provision, reinforces the conclusion that extradition should be excluded altogether to countries where general prisons conditions fall below Convention standards. The Court, however, has so far been reluctant to follow such a broad reading of the *Soering* precedent. This is so despite it having held that a lack of economic resources cannot justify harsh or inadequate prison facilities.[94]

iv. *Discrimination*

Discriminatory treatment has been found to infringe Article 3 and extradition to extreme oppressive regimes may therefore be prohibited.[95] The Court, however, has established a high threshold for the breach of Article 3 by way of discriminatory treatment. Thus only severe restrictions which in effect curtail the exercise of basic freedoms may be considered serious enough to bar extradition.[96] A lesser threshold may, however, apply to discrimination based on nationality.[97] That some States may be unwilling to extradite a person to a country that openly discriminates on grounds such as race was illustrated during the apartheid era when many States cancelled existing extradition arrangements with South Africa.[98]

Another form of discrimination which may be more relevant to normal extradition practice is where a request for extradition has been made for the purpose of prosecuting or punishing a person on account of his race, religion, nationality or other unjustified grounds. Most extradition treaties specifically state that extradition shall not be granted if such an ulterior motive lies behind a

---

to serious health problems and ultimately to the loss of finger- and toe-nails. In the light of this, and the fact that the applicant endured these conditions of detention for more than four years – two years if the period begins from the date of entry into force of the Convention – the Court found a violation of Article 3, thus maintaining the principle that prison conditions in themselves may violate Article 3 of the Convention: *supra* (note 80), paragraphs 96–103. See also ECtHR, *Trepashkin v. Russia* (19 July 2007), Appl. No. 36898/03, paragraph 85–95. The state of prison conditions was also considered in *Government of the Russian Federation v. Akhmed Zakayev* (13 November 2003) (unreported; Bow Street Magistrates' Court), ILDC 259 (UK 2003).

[94] *Poltoratskiy* (note 32), paragraph 148. While this statement concerned conditions within a Contracting State it is arguably relevant also to non-Contracting States since it concerns an absolute prohibition of ill-treatment. However, relatively inexpensive measures concerning prison facilities must be distinguished from more expensive health care facilities. Cf. *mutatis mutandis, Bensaid* (note 41), paragraph 38.

[95] Cf. ECtHR, *Cyprus v. Turkey* (10 May 2001), Appl. No. 25781/94.

[96] Cf. *Tomic* (note 4), paragraph 1.

[97] Cf. *East African Asians v. The United Kingdom* (14 December 1973), Appl. Nos. 4403/70; 4404/70; and 4405/70.

[98] Dugard, *International Law: A South African Perspective*, Cape Town, 2000, p. 156.

request,[99] thus reflecting a general principle of equality and non-discrimination that is fundamental to human rights law. Since most extradition treaties disallow requests on discriminatory grounds, such requests are unlikely to be compatible with the Convention. The fact that only a small number of applications have been made either under Article 14 in conjunction with another right or under the free-standing right of non-discrimination established in Protocol No. 12 is most likely owed to the immense difficulties in proving that reasons for a request do not relate to an alleged offence but to discrimination or persecution.[100]

c. Prohibition of Slavery and Forced Labour

Article 4 of the Convention provides an absolute prohibition of slavery and forced labour. The prohibition is unqualified in relation to slavery, whereas forced or compulsory labour is subject to four limitations. In the Court's reading these do not constitute limits to the exercise of the right guaranteed by Article 4, but simply delimit it's very content.[101] Slavery and servitude must therefore be distinguished from forced or compulsory labour. The first encompasses far-reaching control over an individual, which can never be permissible under the Convention; the second concerns a less serious form of involuntary work which, in certain circumstances, may be viewed as indispensable to the general interest of society.[102] A parallel might be drawn here with the vertical approach under Article 3 where different categories of ill-treatment represent a progression of seriousness. Not unlike Article 3 and 'torture', there is no problem in relation to Article 4 and 'slavery', whereas 'forced labour' suffers from the same vagueness as 'inhuman or degrading treatment'. States may therefore have differing views on the threshold of its application, which might be reflected in the ongoing tensions regarding the extent to which prisoners may be required to work not only as part of their rehabilitation programme but also for economic purposes.[103] According to the ECtHR, work during detention is generally permitted, but only in the 'ordinary course of detention'.[104]

---

[99] See Article 3 (2) of the European Convention on Extradition; and Article 3 (b), UN Model Treaty on Extradition, 1990.

[100] As stated by Judge Kennedy in *Serbeh v. Governor of Brixton Prison* [2002] EWHC 2356 (Admin): '[There is] a fundamental assumption that the requesting state is acting in good faith. If there is a reason in the particular case to call that assumption into question, then the reason can be examined, and if appropriate acted upon …': paragraph 40.

[101] ECtHR, *Van der Mussele v. Belgium* (23 November 1983), Appl. No. 8919/80, paragraph 83.

[102] Ibid.

[103] Cf. ILO, *A Global Alliance Against Forced Labour*, ILO/Geneva, 2005, 28–29.

[104] ECtHR, *De Wilde, Oms and Versyp v. Belgium* (18 June 1971), Appl. No. 2832/66, paragraphs 88–90.

To date, relatively few cases have been brought under Article 4. Moreover, most Article 4 claims have concerned convicted prisoners and have been pursued largely without success.[105] Thus work in prison will not in itself violate Article 4, although some form of work, especially if afflictive or exploitative in nature, would most likely contravene Convention standards.[106] In the admissibility decision of *Ould Barar v. Sweden*, the Court found that 'the expulsion of a person to a country where there is an officially recognised regime of slavery might, in certain circumstances, raise an issue under Article 3 of the Convention'.[107] This statement seems curiously timid. The absolute nature of the prohibition of slavery, coupled with the Court's reasoning in relation to Article 3, compels the conclusion that any real risk of a violation of Article 4 must prevent extradition. In the few cases where the Court had the opportunity to consider the relevance of Article 4 in a case of removal, it predominantly relied on Article 3 instead.[108] This is, however, in all likelihood owing to the fact that any violation of Article 4 would unavoidably also violate human dignity.

d. The Right to a Fair Trial

The right to a fair trial is of fundamental importance to the rule of law and functioning of a democratic society.[109] Even the legitimate aim of protecting the community as a whole from serious threat such as terrorism, cannot, according to the Court, justify measures which extinguish the very essence of a fair trial as guaranteed in Article 6.[110] Its importance may, *inter alia*, be inferred from the fact that it may only be derogated in times of emergency and thus, arguably, retains an absolute quality in times of peace.[111] It is also one of most complex of human rights in existence, and it is not possible within this article to give a comprehensive account of the various rights and obligations entailed within the

---

[105] Cf. Leach (note 43), pp. 218–225.

[106] In this respect, guidance maybe sought in the Standard Minimum Rules for the Treatment of Prisoners, UN Doc. E/3048 (1957), amended E.S.C. Res. 2076: 62 *UN ESCOR* Supp. (No. 1), at p. 35: UN Doc. E/5988 (1977), Article 71.

[107] ECtHR, *Ould Barar v. Sweden (Admissibility)*, (1 January 1999) Appl. No. 42367/98, p. 4.

[108] See *Ould Barar* (note 107); and ECtHR, *Siliadin v. France* (26 July 2005), Appl. No. 73316/01.

[109] See e.g. *Soering* (note 1), paragraph 113.

[110] See ECtHR, *Heany and McGuiness* (note 78), paragraphs 51–58; ECtHR, *Papon v. France (Admissibility)*, (7 June 2001), Appl. No. 64666/01, paragraph 98; and *Al-Moayad* (note 67), paragraph 101.

[111] European Convention on Human Rights (1950), Article 15. See also the Advisory Opinion of the Inter-American Court of Human Rights on judicial guarantees in states of emergency: OC-9/87 of October 6, 1987, *Series A*, No. 9; and Human Rights Committee, 'General Comment 29: States of Emergency (Article 4)', UN Doc. CCPR/C/21/Rev.1/Add.11 (2001).

notion of the right to a fair trial. The aim, instead, is to provide an overview of the most important aspects bearing on extradition.

With reference to extradition it should, in the first place, be noted that the determination of a criminal charge within Article 6 (1) concerns the full process of examination of an individual's guilt in relation to an offence, and not the process of determining whether or not a person may be extradited to a foreign country.[112] Complaints about fairness of extradition proceedings of the sending State are therefore incompatible *ratione materiae* with the Convention.[113] This means that the protection otherwise afforded by Article 6 is not directly applicable to extradition proceedings. In *Soering*, and numerous other cases, the Court, nevertheless, stated that:

> [It] . . . does not exclude that an issue might exceptionally be raised under Article 6 by an extradition decision in circumstances where the fugitive has suffered or risks suffering a flagrant denial of a fair trial in the requesting country.[114]

It follows that the right to a fair trial may indirectly affect extradition where the requested person has suffered or risks suffering a flagrant denial of the right to a fair trial in the receiving State. And whenever a Contracting Party to the Convention is required to enforce a judicial decision – such as an extradition request – of a country which is not a Contracting Party, the former must duly satisfy itself that the proceedings in the foreign jurisdiction have fulfilled the guarantees of Article 6.[115] The Convention, however, does not require Contracting Parties to impose its standards on third States since this, according to the Court, would thwart the current trend towards strengthening international co-operation in the administration of justice.[116] Instead, the Court has qualified the indirect applicability of Article 6 to extradition by stating that only a 'flagrant denial' may bar removal. This abstract standard is not easily quantifiable, although the adjective 'flagrant' evidently implies a higher threshold of application than

---

[112] See ECtHR, *Raf v. Spain* (21 November 2000), Appl. No. 53652/00, paragraph 1; ECtHR, *A. B. v. Poland* (18 October 2001), Appl. No. 33878/96, paragraph 2; and ECtHR, *Eid v. Italy (Admissibility)*, (22 January 2002) Appl. No. 53490/99, paragraph 93.

[113] See e.g., ECtHR, *Sarinas Albo v. Italy (Admissibility)*, (8 January 2004), Appl. No. 56271/00, paragraph 3; and *Al-Moayad* (note 67), paragraph 94. Similarly decisions regarding the entry, stay and deportation of aliens do not concern the determination of an applicant's civil rights or obligations or of a criminal charge against him, within the meaning of Article 6(1) of the Convention: ECtHR, *Maaouia v. France* [GC], (5 October 2000), Appl. No. 39652/98, paragraphs 33–41.

[114] *Supra* (note 1), paragraph 112.

[115] See, *mutatis mutandis*, ECtHR, *Pellegrini v. Italy* (20 July 2001), Appl. No. 30882/96, paragraph 40; and ECtHR, *Saccoccia v. Austria (Admissibility)*, (5 July 2007), Appl. No. 69978/01.

[116] ECtHR, *Drozd and Janousek v. France and Spain* (26 June 1992), Appl. No. 12747/87, paragraph 110.

the standard formulation in relation to absolute rights, which only refers to a real risk.[117] The threshold in relation to Article 6 is accordingly closer to so-called 'relative rights', as will be illustrated below.

Van Den Wyngaert has argued that the higher threshold associated with Article 6 is justified because applying fair trial rights to extradition has a different impact from applying those same rights in domestic trials, as it is relatively rare for States to prosecute persons whose extradition has been denied and consequently the requested person is likely to go untried.[118] While undoubtedly true, this is not a feature unique to fair trial claims. Nor does Article 6 allow such a balance to be struck. Other reasons must therefore hold to justify the apparently higher threshold. One obvious reason is that Article 6 is not a genuine 'absolute right', even though it is non-derogable in times of peace. The mere complexity of the right to a fair trial may also provide some explanation: it is arguably far more complicated to asses whether a person's right to a fair trial has been, or will be, violated compared, for instance, with the prohibition of torture, inhuman or degrading treatment. In the latter situation, it has 'only' to be assessed whether a there is a real risk of mistreatment and whether such treatment exceeds the limits of Article 3.

Thus the difficulty lies not so much in establishing the subjective threshold of Article 3 but rather in the probability of mistreatment. In contrast, Article 6 does not require a subjective test, as the right to a fair trial is impartial. Instead, difficulties relating to Article 6 lie in establishing when various factors, sometimes cumulatively, constitute a flagrant breach of Convention standards. Such assessment is easy where it can be proven that a defendant will not, or did not, have access to an independent and impartial tribunal.[119] Likewise, a deliberate or systematic refusal to provide access to a lawyer must, according to the Court, be considered a flagrant denial of the right to a fair trial.[120] However, it becomes less easy where a requested person is to be given a trial and is also to be provided a lawyer. Here, the fairness of the proceedings *as a whole* may still be questioned. Thus, while minor infringements may sometimes be overlooked especially where overall proceedings are fair, questions of unfairness may arise even where all formal requirements have been met.[121] It follows that the open-

---

[117] *Soering* (note 1), paragraph 91.

[118] *Supra* (note 1), p. 771.

[119] Cf. *Al-Moayad* (note 67), paragraph 101. See also ECtHR, *Assanidze v. Georgia* (8 April 2004), Appl. No. 71503/01, paragraph 8.

[120] ECtHR, *John Murray v. the United Kingdom* (25 January 1996), Appl. No. 18731/91, paragraph 66; ECtHR, *Öcalan* (note 24) paragraphs 131–137 and 148; and *Al-Moayad* (note 67), paragraph 101.

[121] Cf. Leach (note 43), p. 253.

ended nature and residual quality of Article 6 make it difficult to determine when procedural shortcomings may, in themselves, be considered a violation of the Convention.[122] In fact, it is often not possible to say in advance whether or not a person extradited will receive a fair trial.

It follows that unless there are systemic defects in the trial system of a requesting State – which might have been the case with the Diplock Courts in Northern Ireland and which certainly is the case with regard to the Turkish State Security Courts – it might not in all cases be possible to foresee a real risk of a flagrant denial of the right to a fair trial. Violation of the right to a trial within a reasonable period of time, for instance, which might prevent extradition, is inherently difficult to predict, since nobody can say in advance how long a trial will last. This uncertainty may warrant a higher threshold since not any prospect of a procedural failure should bar extradition. Another consideration is that unlike violation of the prohibition of torture or capital punishment, violations of the right to a fair trial are not irreparable and may easily be remedied, for example, by way of a new trial. Furthermore, individuals extradited within the CoE have the right to pursue a claim before the ECtHR.[123]

In relation to the assessment of extradition, a fundamental distinction must also be made between, on the one hand, a person who has already been convicted and who challenges his extradition by claiming that his right to a fair trial was violated in the course of the proceedings which led to his conviction and, on the other, an individual who, suspected of having committed a crime, is wanted for trial and who claims that he will not receive a fair trial in the requesting country.

In the first situation, it is simpler to determine whether the right has been violated and how it may be remedied. The Court has for instance held that a flagrant denial of justice occurs where a person tried *in absentia* is unable to obtain a new determination of the merits of the charge, in respect both of law and fact.[124] This is in line with established case-law confirming that the right of an accused to participate in person in criminal proceedings is a fundamental element of a fair trial.[125] The Court followed this reasoning in *Bader and Others*

---

[122] Cf. Harris, O'Boyle and Warbrick (note 23), p. 202. Uncertainty regarding the application of Article 6 to extradition is further exacerbated by the general vagueness of the provisions and reluctance of the ECtHR to establish clear guidance. This reluctance has, according to one commentator, left Article 6 in a 'cloud of ambiguity'. See Trechsel (note 78), p. 87.

[123] Cf. the decision of the German Federal Administrative Court (note 4), pp. 271–286.

[124] ECtHR, *Stoichkov v. Bulgaria* (24 March 2005), Appl. No. 9808/02, paragraph 55; and ECtHR, *Sejdovic v. Italy* [GC], (1 March 2006), Appl. No. 56581/00, paragraph 84.

[125] This is so since the right to appear in Court is of capital importance with respect to verification of the accuracy of the defendant's statements and their comparison with those of the victim

v. Sweden where the summary nature of proceedings *in absentia* resulting in a death sentence and the total disregard of the rights of the defence was considered a 'flagrant denial of a fair trial'.[126] The Court, moreover, considered that the imposition of the death penalty following an unfair trial would inevitably cause the applicants additional fear and anguish as to their future if they were forced to return to Syria, thereby establishing an unmistakable connection between the right to a fair trial and human dignity.

The situation is more complicated in the second scenario: when the violation has not yet occurred but exists as a mere potentiality. Not only is it inherently difficult to asses the outcome of a criminal trial, but the intricacies of the due process of law and differences between criminal systems make it difficult to predict the fairness of the outcome of a criminal trial in another jurisdiction.[127] Even within the CoE, with the common minimal standard enshrined in Article 6, there are significant differences in relation to matters such as the admissibility of evidence, acceptable length of criminal proceedings, the right to legal assistance and the availability of public subvention for this purpose. The latter was also at issue in the *Soering* case.[128] That fair trial rights vary between CoE Member States is evident *inter alia* from the large number of Article 6 applications brought before the ECtHR. Furthermore, the Commission of the European Union (EU) has addressed discrepancies within the EU.[129] This has further led the EU Commission to propose a framework decision covering the rights of suspects and defendants in criminal proceedings.[130] Thus not even within the EU do common standards exist.

Notwithstanding that the Court has consistently stated that Article 6 may exceptionally bar extradition, comparatively little case law has been generated on this point. Moreover, no successful claim has ever been made before the ECtHR

---

and of the witnesses. Cf. *Stoichkov* (note 124), paragraph 56; and *Sejdovic* (note 124), paragraph 84.

[126] *Supra* (note 24), paragraph 42.

[127] See comments of Lord CJ Wolf in *Government of the United States of America v. Montgomery (No. 2)*, [2003] 1 WLR 1916, paragraphs 25–26.

[128] The Commission rejected the claim that the respondent Government could be held responsible for the absence of legal aid; the Court did not directly address the issue: *supra* (note 1), paragraph 112.

[129] The formulation of a non-binding document was considered necessary in order to increase trust and confidence in EU Member States' judicial systems, thus furthering mutual judicial co-operation, e.g., *The European Arrest Warrant, Commission Green Paper on Criminal Proceedings*, COM (2003) 75 final.

[130] Notably the right to legal advice, interpretation and translation, medical attention and the right to seek consular assistance: see Proposal for Council Framework Decision on Certain Procedural Rights in Criminal Proceedings Throughout the European Union, COM (2004) 328 final.

in regard to removal under this provision. Some argue that the relative nature of Article 6, as opposed to the absolute nature of Article 3, makes it difficult to consider broadening the exception to general international law developed by the Court according to which Contracting States may be held responsible for acts occurring on the territory of another State under Article 3.[131] This, however, sits uncomfortably with the general trend of the Court and decisions by domestic authorities. Extradition to the United States, for instance, would undoubtedly raise an issue under Article 6 where there are substantial grounds for believing that the extradited person would not be tried by ordinary criminal courts.[132] Admissibility of evidence, especially where obtained by torture, might also bar extradition.[133]

2. Relative Rights

Some provisions of the ECHR specifically allow States a limited right to interfere with the enjoyment of Convention rights in the protection of some public interest or the rights of others.[134] These rights may be termed 'relative' because their enjoyment is conditional upon external factors, such as the interest of society.[135] Accordingly, these rights only provide attenuated protection against extradition, as they must be weighed against community interests. As a general premise, there are two essential requirements for extradition: first, interference with an individual's rights must be in accordance with the law and secondly, such interference must be necessary in a democratic society. With few exceptions, extradition – the formal process whereby a suspect or fugitive is surrendered to a requesting State – would always satisfy these requirements. Only if domestic law does not provide adequate protection against interference or if procedural rules are deliberately circumvented would extradition contravene the general legality requirement.[136] As to the second requirement, there is no doubt that extradition would normally be considered to be pursuing a legitimate aim, namely the prevention of disorder and crime.[137] It follows that unless extradition is sought with an ulterior motive, it would in most cases fall within the restriction clauses

---

[131] Cf. Hailbronner (note 1), p. 1007. See also *Regina v. Special Adjudicator ex parte Ullah (FC)*, [2004] UKHL 26.

[132] See *Al-Moayad* (note 67).

[133] See e.g., *Ramda* (note 7); and the case concerning *Moreno* and *Garcia* mentioned in Dugard and Van den Wyngaert (note 1), p. 201.

[134] See Articles 8, 9, 10 and 11 of the European Convention on Human Rights; as well as Article 2 of Protocol No. 4.

[135] Cf. Harris, O'Boyle and Warbrick (note 23), pp. 283–302.

[136] See ECtHR, *Bozano v. France* (18 December 1980), Appl. No. 9120/80, paragraphs 54–60.

[137] Cf. ECtHR, *Shkelzen v. Germany (Admissibility)*, (20 January 2000), Appl. No. 44770/98, p. 3.

contained within the Convention. This is so in relation to the right to respect for family life, which may influence the right of removal under the Convention.[138] Article 8 (2) explicitly permits interference when it is in accordance with law and necessary in a democratic society and falls within one of the legitimate aims. In this regard the Court stated in *Shkelzen v. Germany*:

> Assuming that the decision of the German authorities to grant the applicant's extradition to the United States constituted an interference with the applicant's rights under Article 8 (1) of the Convention, the Court finds that any such interference was justified under paragraph 2 of this provision. There is no doubt that the measure at issue was in accordance with the law and pursued a legitimate aim, namely the prevention of disorder and crime. Extradition being an indispensable means of international co-operation in the field of justice, the measure was also necessary in a democratic society.[139]

The Court further recalled that prisoners have no right, as such, under the Convention to choose the place of confinement, and that the separation of detainees from families constitutes an inevitable consequence of detention. Thus the decision by the German authorities to grant the applicant's extradition, although inevitably adversely affecting the applicant's family life, did not disclose any appearance of violation of the applicant's rights in accordance with Article 8 (1). Consequently, the case was declared manifestly ill-founded.[140] The majority of cases brought under Article 8 in relation to removal have concerned deportation orders following the conclusion of a prison sentence. These have had some success and the Court in *Boultif v. Switzerland* set out guiding principles by which to assess the proportionality of expulsion.[141] No such principle exists in relation to extradition. This may be explained by the fact that traditionally extradition only concerned the most serious crimes and therefore always would be considered proportional to the needs of society.

The right to freedom of thought, conscience and religion is another important element in a democratic society. Nevertheless, only a small number of applications have been made under this heading concerning removal, and few have been successful. Even fewer applications have been made in relation to extradition, and none of them successfully. The reason for this was clearly stated in *Z and T* where two Pakistani citizens claimed that their risk of religiously

---

[138] See e.g. ECtHR, *Boultif v. Switzerland* (2 August 2001), Appl. No. 54273/00.

[139] *Supra* (note 137), p. 3.

[140] See Article 35 (3) of the European Convention on Human Rights (1950).

[141] *Supra* (note 138), paragraph 48. See also Rogers, 'Immigration and the European Convention on Human Rights: Are New Principles Emerging?', 1 (2003) *EHRLR* 53.

motivated attacks should bar their deportation.[142] In this regard, the Court reiterated the importance of Article 9 noting that this, first and foremost, was a standard applied within Contracting States. In considering whether the protection afforded in relation to extradition under Articles 2 and 3 could be extended to cover Article 9, the Court emphasised not only the absolute nature, but also the international abhorrence of torture, and went on to state that:

> Such compelling considerations do not automatically apply under the other provisions of the Convention. On a purely pragmatic basis, it cannot be required that an expelling Contracting State only return an alien to a country where the conditions are in full and effective accord with each of the safeguards of the rights and freedoms set out in the Convention ... Where however an individual claims that on return to his own country he would be impeded in his religious worship in a manner which falls short of those proscribed levels, the Court considers that very limited assistance, if any, can be derived from Article 9 by itself. Otherwise it would be imposing an obligation on Contracting States effectively to act as indirect guarantors of freedom of worship for the rest of world ... While the Court would not rule out the possibility that the responsibility of the returning State might in exceptional circumstances be engaged under Article 9 of the Convention where the person concerned ran a real risk of flagrant violation of that Article in the receiving State, the Court shares the view of the House of Lords in the *Ullah* case that it would be difficult to visualise a case in which a sufficiently flagrant violation of Article 9 would not also involve treatment in violation of Article 3 of the Convention.[143]

Similarly in *Razaghi v. Sweden*, where the applicant who was fleeing Iran and feared return, *inter alia*, on the basis that his conversion to Christianity would put him at risk of suffering treatment contrary to Article 3, the Court noted that in so far as any alleged consequence of the applicant's conversion to Christianity attains the level of treatment prohibited by Article 3, it should be dealt with under that provision.[144] Thus it is clear from the Court's case-law that relative rights only provide limited protection against removal; even less so in relation to extradition as this is considered an indispensable tool of international co-operation and as such necessary in a democratic society. It is therefore difficult to envisage a situation where interference with a relative right may constitute a bar to extradition, unless the same infringement also violates Article 3.[145]

---

[142] *Supra* (note 15).
[143] Ibid, pp. 4–5.
[144] ECtHR, *Razaghi v. Sweden (Admissibility)*, (11 March 2003), Appl. No. 64599/01.
[145] See *Ullah* (note 131).

IV. RISK ASSESSMENT

It is settled case-law of the Court that extradition by a Contracting State may violate an individual's human rights and hence engage the responsibility of that State under the Convention. The establishment of such responsibility inevitably involves an assessment of conditions in the requesting State against the standards of the Convention. Nonetheless, there is no question of adjudicating or establishing the responsibility of the receiving State, whether under general international law, the Convention or otherwise.[146] To the extent that any liability is incurred by an extraditing State it is by reason of the latter having taken action the direct consequence of which is the exposure of an individual to proscribed ill-treatment.[147]

Any potential victim evoking the prohibition of removal has to satisfy the Court that there are 'substantial grounds' for believing that there is either 'real risk' of violation of an absolute right or 'flagrant denial' of a relative right.[148] Thus there are three parts to the '*Soering* test': first, there is an objective element according to which the applicant must state what might happen if he were to be extradited; secondly, there is an subjective element requiring the applicant to substantiate why he personally is likely to suffer the impugned treatment, and finally, both elements have to be proved in all their parts sufficiently to satisfy the real risk requirement, apparently beyond a reasonable doubt.

1. *Objective Element*

The objective element of the *Soering* test may be divided into two sub-categories, distinguishing between absolute and relative rights. This is so because absolute rights require relatively little to satisfy the objective element since any sufficient risk of a violation of an absolute right should bar extradition, although a potential applicant might have to explain why the risk of a relatively minor imposition in the particular circumstances breaches the threshold of, for instance, Article 3. In contrast, the bar on removal in regard to relative rights is qualified by the term 'flagrant'. The meaning of the term 'flagrant denial' has not been fully explained in the Court's jurisprudence. Nevertheless the use of the adjective is clearly intended to impose a more stringent test heightening the normal threshold of application for rights within the Convention.[149] In regard to Article 6, the House

---

[146] *Soering* (note 1), paragraphs 35–36 and 89–91; and *Mamatkulov* (note 35), paragraph 67.

[147] See e.g., *Garabayev* (note 75); *Ahmed* (note 9), paragraphs 38–41; and ECtHR, *Hilal v. United Kingdom* (6 March 2001), Appl. No. 45276/99, paragraph 59.

[148] On the potential victim requirement, see Leach (note 43), pp. 126–129.

[149] See the joint partly dissenting opinion of Judges Sir Nicolas Bratza, Bonello and Hedigan in

of Lords in the *Ullah* and *Razgar* cases spoke of a 'virtually complete denial or nullification' of the right to a fair trial.[150] Thus, after examining the Court's jurisprudence in both cases, the House of Lords found itself in agreement with the Immigration Appeal Tribunal in *Devaseelan v. Secretary of State for the Home Department*, where the Tribunal had stated that:

> The reason why flagrant denial or gross violation is to be taken into account is that it is only in such a case – where the right will be completely denied or nullified in the destination country – that it can be said that removal will breach the treaty obligations of the signatory state however those obligations might be interpreted or whatever might be said by or on behalf of the destination state.[151]

This suggests a very high threshold of application, at least in regard to relative rights. Consequently relative rights would rarely, if ever, be capable of preventing extradition unless the infringement were so serious as to nullify the very essence of the right in question.[152] Presumably, however, any such 'flagrant denial' would in itself be considered a violation of human dignity and hence a violation of Article 3.[153] Even so, a distinction must be drawn in relation to Article 6. There are two reasons for this: first, this provision evidently does not fit neatly within the category of 'relative rights' and, secondly, it has been suggested that the Court's case-law concerning indirect effect has evolved in relation to this provision.[154] The latter has been questioned.[155] Even so, it is clear that although the Court has yet to establish a breach either of Article 6 or any of the so-called relative rights in relation to extradition, concrete examples and comparative better guidance are available with regard to the former.[156]

Mamatkulov (note 35), paragraph 14. It is further evident from the fact that the Court does not wish to impose Convention standards or act as an indirect guarantor for the rest for the world. See *Drozd and Janousek* (note 116), paragraph 110; and *Z and T* (note 15), p. 5 respectively.

[150] See Lord Bingham of Cornhill at pp. 24–25 and Lord Carswell at pp. 69–70 in *Ullah* (note 131), and Lord Walker of Gestingthorpe in *Razgar* (note 83), p. 32.

[151] [2003] UKIAT Imm AR 1, paragraph 111. This passage was quoted in *Ullah* (note 131): first by Lord Bingham of Cornhill and then by Lord Carswell in paragraphs 24 and 69 respectively; and see *Razgar* (note 83), at p. 32, *per* Lord Walker of Gestingthorpe. Note that the ECtHR in *Z and T. v. The United Kingdom* (note 15), stated that it shared the view taken by the House of Lords in *Ullah*.

[152] Cf. *Ullah* (note 131).

[153] Cf., *mutatis mutandis*, *Cyprus* (note 95).

[154] Cf. Costa, 'Il Ragionamento Giuridico Della Corte Europea Dei Diritti Dell'uomo', 2 (2002) *Rivista internazionale dei diritti dell'uomo* 437.

[155] Cf. the opinion of Lord Carswell in *Government of the United States of America v. Barnet and Another*, [2004] UKHL 37, at p. 28.

[156] See especially, *Al-Moayad* (note 67), paragraphs 101–107; and for other cases concerning a flagrant denial of justice see: *Soering* (note 1), paragraph 113; *Drozd and Janousek* (note 116), paragraph 110; *Einhorn* (note 59); and *Mamatkulov* (note 35), paragraph 88. In *Brown (aka*

Furthermore, in his concurring opinions in *Drozd and Janousek*, Judge Matscher distinguished,[157] in keeping with various national judges,[158] between 'indirect' and 'direct' effect, implying, as confirmed by the Court itself,[159] that some Convention rights only have a reduced effect when applied outside Convention States. Importantly, in *Saadi*, the ECtHR rejected any distinction in relation to absolute rights, although it did not consider Article 6.[160] It follows that in relation to absolute rights the same standards apply, regardless of whether the applicant is being moved to a non-Contracting State. Thus even a real risk of forced shaving may prevent extradition. In contrast, applicants who object to removal on the basis of derogable rights may not be able fully to rely on the Court's case-law when establishing the lower threshold of treatment that may prevent removal. Instead, these applicants would have to satisfy the Court that the impugned ill-treatment is sufficiently serious to constitute a so-called 'flagrant denial'.

2. Subjective Element

In cases of removal, applicants must prove that their claims have special distinguishing features that could or ought to have enabled national authorities to foresee that they would be treated in a manner incompatible with the Convention. This was clearly stated in *Vilvarajah and Others v. the United Kingdom*, where although the Court found that there was a distinct possibility of ill-treatment in respect of young male Tamils returning to Sri Lanka, it nevertheless held that the applicants had failed to disclose enough evidence that

---

Bajinja) & Others v. The Government of Rwanda Secretary & Another [2009] EWHC 770 (*Admin*) (8 April 2009), the English High Court barred the extradition of four Rwandan men accused of taking part in the 1994 genocide on the basis that there was 'a real risk they would suffer a flagrant denial of justice'. In a similar case, the Swedish Supreme Court did not share this concrete assessment of the Rwandan courts, although it did not disagree with the Article 6 argument in principle.

[157] *Supra* (note 116), pp. 795–796.

[158] See Lord Bingham in *Ullah* (note 131), paragraph 9; and Lord Carswell in *Government of the United States of America v. Barnet* (note 155), paragraph 15. Both judges were referring to 'foreign' or 'domestic' cases. For the same distinction see also *Othman* (note 79).

[159] In relation to absolute rights, see *Soering* in which the Court held: 'Indeed … the beneficial purpose of extradition in preventing fugitive offenders from evading justice cannot be ignored in determining the scope of application of the Convention and of Article 3 in particular.' See *supra* (note 1), paragraph 86. In relation to relative rights, see *Z and T* (note 15) and specifically on Article 6, see, e.g., *Drozd and Janousek* (note 116), paragraph 110; and *Pellegrini* (note 115), paragraph 40.

[160] *Saadi* (note 6), paragraphs 137–138 and 160.

they were personally at real risk of violation.[161] Thus mere membership of a persecuted group was not enough to prevent removal.[162] Instead an applicant has to show that there is a real risk to him personally resulting from special distinguishing features. It follows that a consistent pattern of human rights violations is insufficient in itself for determining that an individual would be at sufficient risk upon return.[163] Neither, however, does the absence thereof mean that a person cannot be considered to be in sufficient danger in his or her specific circumstances. Thus it is usually of little importance whether general conditions are bad.[164] The personal position of the applicant has to be worse than for the generality of other members of society or specific group and the applicant has to show why he personally is at a heightened risk of ill-treatment.[165] The Court will therefore in each case seek to determine whether there are special distinguishing features that render it foreseeable that the applicant is at risk of treatment either prohibited absolutely or flagrantly contravening Convention standards.[166]

3. Real Risk

In relation to risk, the use of the qualifying adjective 'real' is somewhat unfortunate since it is unclear how its addition contributes to assessment of a putative threat.[167] The 'real risk' test is not, however, used solely in removal cases. On the contrary, the Court often makes use of similar terminology where national authorities are obliged to take preventive measures to ensure compliance with the Convention, i.e. so-called positive obligations.[168] In this regard it

---

[161] *Supra* (note 44), paragraph 111. In contrast, see *N.* (note 51), where the Court distinguishes its decision from *Vilvarajah* based on the applicant's prior activities: paragraph 162. See further *Tomic* (note 4), paragraph 1.

[162] See, however, *Salah Sheekh* (note 44) where the Court accepted that the applicant's belonging to a Somali minority group was, in itself, enough to prevent removal, paragraph 148. This approach was reaffirmed in *Saadi* (note 6), paragraph 132.

[163] Cf. e.g., *Vilvarajah* (note 44), paragraph 111; and *Shamayev* (note 31), paragraph 371.

[164] See e.g., *H.L.R.* (note 51), paragraph 41.

[165] See e.g., *Mbunzu* (note 42), p. 5; and *Vilvarajah* (note 44), paragraph 111; and ECtHR, *Narcisio v. The Netherlands (Admissibility)*, (27 January 2005), Appl. No. 47810/99, paragraph 3.

[166] *Soering* (note 1), paragraph 86; *Chahal* (note 9), paragraphs 98 and 106; *Vilvarajah* (note 44), paragraph 111; and *Shamayev* (note 31), paragraph 350.

[167] Other human rights bodies have adopted a similar test. See, for example, CAT, 'General Comment on the Implementation of Article 3 of the Convention in the Context of Article 22', UN Doc. A/53/44, Annex IX (21 November 1997); and Human Rights Committee, 'General Comment 31: Nature of the General Legal Obligation on States Parties to the Covenant', UN Doc. CCPR/C/21/Rev.1/Add. 13 (2004).

[168] For positive obligations to arise it must be established, for instance, that authorities knew or ought to have known *of a real and immediate risk* to life. See for example *Osman* (note 20), paragraph 116; and ECtHR, *Öneryildiz v. Turkey* (30 November 2004), Appl. No. 48939/99,

should be recalled that the Court in *Osman v. The United Kingdom* stated that not every risk claimed entails for the authorities a Convention requirement to take operational measures to prevent that risk from materialising.[169] A violation of the Convention only occurs where it is established that the authorities have failed to take measures within their powers which might have been expected to meet a real and immediate risk which they knew of, or ought to have known of, at the time of its existence. Moreover, in the same case, the Court explicitly rejected the claim that inaction must be tantamount to gross negligence or wilful disregard of the duty to protect life. Such a rigid standard was found to be incompatible with Article 1 of the Convention and the obligation to secure the practical and effective protection of the rights and freedoms laid down therein. Instead, it is sufficient for an applicant to show that the relevant authorities did not do all that could reasonably be expected of them to avoid a real and immediate risk to life of which they had or ought to have had knowledge. This was stated in relation to Article 2 and the right to life.

However, the positive duty, according to which States are obliged to protect individuals from violence by persons other than its own officials, resembles, in many ways, the human rights principle of non-removal, although the former is essentially a negative obligation.[170] In the first place, the human rights principle of non-removal protects – exactly as do positive obligations – against violations by third parties and secondly, it implies an obligation to investigate claims of a risk of a violation before it occurs.[171] Arguably, therefore, the 'real risk' test implies a degree of reasonableness similar to that applied in relation to positive obligations, which means that a sending State must take all reasonable measures to ensure that a requested person will not suffer any breach of applicable Convention standards in the receiving country, regardless of whether this risk emanates from a State or persons who are not public officials.[172] The question whether a sending State has complied with this obligation can only be answered in light of all the circumstances of a particular case with reference to the facts which were known or ought to have been known at the time of extradition.[173] Given the absolute nature of some provisions it is furthermore clear that it is impermissible to balance any potential threat posed by a person to be deported against his risk of ill-treatment in a foreign jurisdiction. In this respect the Court has stated:

---

paragraph 101. In relation to the right of access to health records connected with the exercise of dangerous activities, the Court has made use of the real risk test: see ECtHR, *L. B. C. v. the United Kingdom* (9 June 1998), Appl. No. 23413/94, paragraph 164.

[169] *Supra* (note 20), paragraph 116.

[170] See comments of Lord Justice Laws in *Limbuela* (note 45), at p. 64.

[171] In regard to the latter, see below 'Effective Remedy': this Part, section 5.

[172] See for example, *Chahal* (note 9); *H. L. R.* (note 51); *T. I.* (note 3); and *Salah Sheekh* (note 44).

[173] *Mamatkulov* (note 35), paragraphs 67–69.

> The concepts of "risk" and "dangerousness" in this context do not lend themselves to a balancing test because they are notions that can only be assessed independently of each other. Either the evidence adduced before the Court reveals that there is a substantial risk if the person is sent back or it does not. The prospect that he may pose a serious threat to the community if not returned does not reduce in any way the degree of risk of ill treatment that the person may be subject to on return. For that reason it would be incorrect to require a higher standard of proof … where the person is considered to represent a serious danger to the community, since assessment of the level of risk is independent of such a test.[174]

Even so, the assessment of risk is a complex problem and it is not possible to establish some convenient legal test. Mere possibility is not enough; neither, however, is considerable certainty required.[175] Any test should be strict because of its implications for third States. In *Shamayev*, the Court adopted the standard of proof 'beyond reasonable doubt' but added that such proof may follow from the coexistence of sufficiently strong, clear and concordant inferences or of similar unrebutted presumptions of fact.[176]

4. Evidence

The term 'substantial grounds' generally refers to the availability of reliable information that there may be a risk of ill-treatment. Such information may come from various sources, including the applicant himself, as long as the competent authorities are made sufficiently aware of the risk,[177] and allegations are supported by appropriate evidence.[178] Complete accuracy is not expected, especially of victims of torture, but allegations should be sufficiently substantiated and reliable.[179] Where such evidence is adduced, it is for the respondent

---

[174] *Saadi* (note 6), paragraph 139.

[175] See *Vilvarajah* (note 44), paragraph 111; and *Soering* (note 1), paragraph 94, respectively. Refer also to Warbrick, 'The Structure of Article 8', 32 (1998) *EHRLR* 37.

[176] *Supra* (note 31), paragraph 338. This is in line with previous case-law according to which 'a reasonable doubt is not a doubt based on a merely theoretical possibility or raised in order to avoid a disagreeable conclusion, but a doubt for which reasons can be drawn from the facts presented'. See ibid. See also *Garabayev* (note 75), paragraph 76. See also *AA and DD (Libya) v. Secretary of State for Home Affairs and Liberty* [2008] EWCA Civ 289.

[177] See e.g *Garabayev* (note 75), paragraph 78. The Court has further stated that it is incumbent on applicants to adduce, to the greatest extent practically possible, material and information allowing the authorities of the Contracting States concerned, as well as the Court, to assess the risk a removal may entail: *Said v. The Netherlands* (5 July 2002), Appl. No. 2345/02, paragraph 49.

[178] On evidence see, *mutatis mutandis*, ECtHR, *Klaas v. Germany* (22 September 1993), Appl. No. 15473/89, paragraphs 29–31; and *Mamatkulov* (note 35), paragraph 70.

[179] See e.g., ECtHR, *Nasimi v. Sweden (Admissibility)*, (16 March 2004), Appl. No. 38865/02; and *N.* (note 51).

Government to dispel any doubts concerning its validity.[180] In determining whether substantial grounds have been shown to exist, the Court will assess the issue in the light of all the material placed before it or, if necessary, obtained *proprio motu*, in particular where the applicant or a third party[181] provides reasoned grounds which cast doubt on the accuracy of the information relied on by the respondent Government.[182] In so doing, the Court will make a full *ex nunc* assessment of the situation in the receiving country taking into account any reliable source of information.[183] This may include decisions of other human rights bodies, although it will not find a violation in each and every case where such a body has expressed the view that general conditions fall below international standards.[184]

The presence of risk must be assessed primarily with reference to those facts which were known or ought to have been known to the Contracting State at the time of extradition, although the Court is not precluded from having regard to later information since this may be of value in confirming or refuting the well-foundedness of an applicant's fears.[185] If the applicant has not yet been extradited when the ECtHR examines the case, as a result, for instance, of an interim order, the relevant time will be that of the proceedings before the ECtHR.[186]

5. Effective Remedy

In addition to the above, the notion of an effective remedy in Article 13 requires that procedures exist that may prevent the execution of measures that are contrary to the Convention and whose effects are potentially irreversible. Consequently, it is inconsistent with Article 13 for removal to be executed before national authorities have examined whether it is compatible with the Convention.[187] The importance attached to absolute rights further requires

---

[180] *Saadi* (note 6), paragraph 129.

[181] European Convention on Human Rights (1950), Article 36.

[182] *Hilal* (note 147), paragraph 60; and *Salah Sheekh* (note 44), paragraph 136.

[183] Cf. *Cruz Varas* (note 44), paragraph 76; *Salah Sheekh* (note 44), paragraphs 135–137; and *Gordyeyev v. Poland (Admissibility)*, (3 May 2005), Appl. No. 43369/98.

[184] Cf. ECtHR, *Aert v. Belgium* (12 September 2000), Appl. No. 36790/97, paragraphs 65–67; *Mamatkulov* (note 35), paragraphs 72–73; and *Narcisio* (note 165). See also *Shamayev* (note 31), paragraph 367.

[185] See *Cruz Varas* (note 44), paragraphs 75–76; *Vilvarajah* (note 44), paragraph 107; ECtHR, *Venkadajalasarma v. the Netherlands* (17 February 2004), Appl. No. 58510/00, paragraph 63; and *Mamatkulov* (note 35), paragraph 69.

[186] *Chahal* (note 9), paragraphs 85–86.

[187] Contracting States, however, are afforded some discretion as to the manner in which they conform to their obligations under this provision. See ECtHR, *Conka v. Belgium* (5 May 2002), Appl. No. 51564/99, paragraph 79; and *Garabayev* (note 75), paragraph 105.

an independent and rigorous scrutiny of any claim that there exist substantial grounds for fearing a real risk of treatment contrary to the Convention, and the possibility of suspending the implementation of the measure impugned in accordance with Article 13.[188] Accordingly the victim requirement in Article 34 has been extended also to cover future violations, which requires Contracting States to refrain from any act or omission which, by destroying or removing the subject matter of an application, would make it pointless or otherwise prevent the Court from considering it under its normal procedure.[189]

6. *Diplomatic Assurances*

When assessing the risk that an applicant may face if extradited to a foreign jurisdiction, the Court will often take into consideration whether the sending State has obtained 'effective' assurances from the receiving jurisdiction that the requested person will not be at risk of violations of Convention standards.[190] The use of diplomatic assurances to facilitate extradition is not recent practice.[191] In the *Soering* case, for instance, the United Kingdom Government sought assurances from the United States' authorities that if the death penalty were to be imposed, it would not be carried out.[192] Human rights bodies have broadly approved such practice, provided that they meet certain qualitative requirements.[193] The Committee against Torture, for instance, has insisted on independent and effective verification of diplomatic guarantees.[194]

---

[188] See ECtHR, *Jabari v. Turkey* (11 July 2000), Appl. No. 40035/98.

[189] *Mamatkulov* (note 35), paragraph 102.

[190] *Soering* (note 1), paragraphs. 38–39; *Nivette* (note 35), p. 4; *Einhorn* (note 59), paragraph 26; and *Al-Moayad* (note 67), paragraphs 102–106.

[191] For an overview of practice within the CoE, see the compilation of replies to the questionnaire on the practice of States in the use of diplomatic assurances by the Steering Committee for Human Rights, *supra* (note 48); see also the Second and Third Reports of the ILA Committee on Extradition and Human Rights, *ILA Report of the Sixty-Seventh Conference: Helsinki 1996*, London, 1996, p. 214, at pp. 229–232 and *ILA Report of the Sixty-Eighth Conference* (note 53), pp. 141–145 respectively.

[192] *Supra* (note 1), paragraphs 15, 36 and 69. See also ECtHR, *Aylor-Davis v. France (Admissibility)*, (20 January 1994), Appl. No. 22742/93; *Nivette* (note 35); *Bader* (note 24); and *Kordia* (note 35).

[193] For criticism on this, see Reports of the Special Rapporteur on Torture to the General Assembly for 2004 (UN Doc. A/59/324) and 2005 (A/60/316), paragraphs 31–40 and 40–50 respectively; Report to the Commission on Human Rights by the Special Rapporteur on Torture 2005: UN Doc. E/CN.4/2006/6, paragraphs 28–33; and Human Rights Watch, 'Empty Promises: Diplomatic Assurances No Safeguard against Torture', April 2004; and 'Still at Risk – Diplomatic Assurances No Safeguard against Torture', April 2005.

[194] CAT, *Agiza v. Sweden* (24 May 2005), Comm. No. 233/2003. The CAT distinguished the case from the largely analogous communication, *Hanan Attia v. Sweden* (17 November 2003), Comm. No. 199/2002. In the former case, the CAT stated: 'The procurement of diplomatic

While the ECtHR has noted that arrangements for visits by the International Committee of the Red Cross might not be sufficient to exclude the risk of treatment contrary to Article 3, it has yet to make effective verification an absolute requirement.[195] In *Mamatkulov*, for instance, guarantees by the Republic of Uzbekistan that the applicants would 'not be subjected to acts of torture or sentenced to capital punishment' and reaffirmation that it would comply with its obligation under the Convention against Torture were a decisive factor in the Court's conclusion that the applicants did not face any real risk of treatment proscribed by Article 3.[196] No specific assurances were given that the applicants would not be subject to inhuman or degrading treatment in accordance with Article 3 of the ECHR.[197] Nor did the Court give much weight to the fact that general conditions of detention in Uzbekistan were below UN basic minimum standards. In regard to the specific threat of torture or other forms of ill-treatment the Court's assessment was exceedingly superficial making the 'real risk' test inconsequential. The Court made only a brief reference to the repressive policies of Uzbek authorities and little consideration was given to the alleged ill-treatment and torture by law-enforcement officials of banned Islamist opposition parties in Uzbekistan continually reported by human rights organisations.[198] Nor was there any consideration given to the claim that the police had sought out and tortured associates of the applicants.[199]

By contrast, the risk assessment in *Hilal v. United Kingdom* apparently intensified as a result of the fatal ill-treatment by members of the police of the applicant's brother, who was involved with the same political group as was the

---

assurances, which, moreover, provided no mechanism for their enforcement, did not suffice to protect against this manifest risk [of torture].' See Comm. No. 233/2003, paragraph 13.4. In the latter case, it found itself satisfied with the assurances provided. An important distinction between the two cases is that in *Agiza* the CAT took into account information obtained after the removal.

[195] *Saadi* (note 6), paragraph 145.

[196] *Supra* (note 35), paragraphs 28 and 34. See also *Saadi* (note 6), where the Court stated that the existence of domestic laws or accession to international treaties in itself was insufficient guarantee against risk of ill-treatment, paragraph 147.

[197] By stating that it would comply with the obligations of the Convention against Torture, Uzbekistan indirectly also undertook not to submit the applicant to inhuman or degrading treatment (cf. Article 15). However, the threshold of proscribed treatment is arguably lower in Article 3 of the ECHR than in the Convention against Torture. Thus it is doubtful whether the ECtHR should have accepted this guarantee even though standards may be different in 'indirect' cases. Cf. Evans, 'Getting to Grips With Torture', 51 (2002) *ICLQ* 365.

[198] See *Amicus Brief* submitted by Human Rights Watch and the AIRE Centre: on file with the author.

[199] Ibid.

applicant.[200] Moreover, in *Mamatkulov* the Court did not take into consideration the fact that no arrangements existed concerning verification of compliance. Independent verification, however, has been emphasised by the ECtHR in subsequent case-law, which might represent a welcome strengthening of its scrutiny of diplomatic guarantees.[201]

v. Conclusion

The foremost problem in relation to the human rights-based principle of non-removal is the assessment of risk.[202] The matter is fraught with difficulties as any consideration of risk will always contain an element of estimation not easily be expressed in abstract standards. The test of 'real risk' adopted by the Court does not, however, do much to counter this problem, and the lack of express consideration often leaves the reader guessing why a person might not be removed or otherwise. It is evident that in relation to absolute rights the Court primarily considers the risk of violation, whereas in relation to other rights the Court attaches greater emphasis to the proportionality of a contested removal. This invariably reflects the structure of the Convention and the importance attributed to some provisions, although the Court has yet satisfactorily to explain the special position of Article 6. Moreover, while the distinction between the 'direct' and 'indirect' application of Convention standards is reasonable in relation to so-called 'relative rights', a theory of absolute rights does not admit any aberration. Thus all rights that are considered absolute within the jurisdiction of the Convention should also prevent extradition to non-Contracting Parties. The effective protection of these rights would further imply that any uncertainty should to be resolved in favour of the applicant by a Court of law and not left to the tender conscience of diplomatic or political expediency.[203]

---

[200] *Supra* (note 147), paragraph 64.

[201] Cf. *Al-Moayad* (note 67). However, for the Court to ensure that the rights within the Convention are not just theoretical or illusory, it also needs to consider other elements. The latter implies that the sending State must be in a position to take immediate action upon suspicion of ill-treatment. See also

[202] See the concurring opinion of Judge Jupancic in *Saadi v. Italy* (note 6).

[203] See e.g., CAT, *Mutombo v. Switzerland* (27 April 1994), Comm. No. 13/1993, where the Committee stated that that even if there were doubts about certain facts adduced by an applicant, it must ensure that his security was not endangered.

Chapter Three

In Search of Clarity:
Non Liquet and International Law

Stephen C. Neff[*]

Non liquet means, literally, 'it is not clear' in Latin. More precisely, it is a pronouncement by a court to the effect that it is unable to render a decision in a particular matter because of the existence of a gap in the law, or the lack of a sufficient basis in law for reaching a decision one way or the other. It is not to be confused with declining to decide a case due to, say, an absence of jurisdiction on the court's part, or to the absence of an essential third party, or to a lack of standing on the part of the litigants, or because the handing down of a decision would serve no practical purpose, or because the case had become moot.[1] It refers, specifically, to failing to decide a case because of the absence of an applicable rule of law. There has been a great deal of debate amongst legal scholars as to whether a *non liquet* is really possible, namely, whether, either in practice or in principle, any gaps actually exist in the fabric of international law. This discussion is intended to shed some light on the 'misty Doubt' attending this question.[2]

---

[*] Reader in Public International Law, University of Edinburgh.
[1] For an example of a failure to decide a case because of the absence of jurisdiction, see the *Norwegian Loans Case (France v. Norway)*, ICJ Reports 1957, p. 9. For a notorious example of declining to decide because of the absence of standing on the part of the litigants, see the *South West Africa Cases, Second Phase (Ethiopia and Liberia v. South Africa)*, ICJ Reports 1966, p. 6. For an example of the non-rendering of a decision on the ground that the requesting body lacked competence to seek the decision, see *Legality of the Use by a State of Nuclear Weapons in Armed Conflict*, ICJ Reports 1996, p. 66. For examples of a failure to decide because of the absence of essential third parties, see the *Monetary Gold Case (Italy v. France, Great Britain and USA)*, ICJ Reports 1954, p. 19; and the *East Timor Case (Portugal v. Australia)*, ICJ Reports 1995, p. 90. For an example of a decision not rendered on the ground that no practical purpose would be served, see the *Northern Cameroons Case (Cameroon v. Great Britain)*, ICJ Reports 1963, p. 15. For an example of a failure to hand down a decision on the ground of mootness, see the *Nuclear Tests Case (Australia v. France)*, ICJ Reports 1974, p. 253. None of these was a case of *non liquet*.
[2] Samuel Johnson, 'The Vanity of Human Wishes', in Smith and McAdam (eds.), *The Poems of Samuel Johnson*, Oxford, 1974, p. 110, at p. 146.

K.H. Kaikobad & M. Bohlander (eds.), *International Law and Power: Perspectives on Legal Order and Justice*. Essays in Honour of Colin Warbrick, pp. 63–83.
© 2009 Koninklijke Brill NV. Printed in the Netherlands.

In a certain sense – which some would dismiss as being trivial – it is obvious that a gap in the law can exist. That is to say, that a situation might arise for which a legal system (whether international or domestic) does not have a 'ready-made' *specific* rule to apply. In the present discussion, this situation will be referred to as a 'provisional gap' or a 'provisional *non liquet*'. That such a provisional gap in a legal system can occur is, in the eyes of some, simply an indication of the trivially obvious fact that law-makers are not able to foresee all situations that will ever arise and to tailor precise rules for them in advance. This is not, however, a true *non liquet*. A true *non liquet* is a pronouncement by a tribunal not simply that such a provisional gap exists but also, and far more crucially, that no means are available for dealing with it, i.e., that it is not possible to devise any means of repairing the defect. The real issue regarding *non liquet* is therefore whether or not it is *always* possible, in practice or as a matter of principle, to find some way of filling any provisional gaps that happen to appear.

In dealing with this question, an important distinction should be made at the outset, concerning the nature of a true *non liquet* – specifically, with respect to whether the point at issue is about the ability of judges or arbitrators to arrive at and pronounce decisions in cases, or whether it is about the character of the underlying legal system itself. A *non liquet* in the first of these senses will be referred to as a 'decision-making *non liquet*'. A *non liquet* in the second of these senses will be referred to as a 'systemic *non liquet*'.

The first section of the discussion will deal with the question of a decision-making *non liquet*, in which it will be explained that such a *non liquet* does not exist. The second part will deal with the more important, and contentious, issue of a systemic *non liquet*. It will set out the various schools of thought on the subject, with brief comments on each. The third section will discuss what has sometimes been presented as the foremost example of an actual *non liquet*: the World Court's advisory opinion of 1996 on the threat and use of nuclear weapons.[3] It will be explained that the Court's holding in that opinion did not, in reality, comprise a *non liquet*. Finally, some general thoughts will be offered on the current state of the law in this area and on the broader issues that are at stake in the debate.

---

[3] See *Legality of the Threat or Use of Nuclear Weapons, ICJ Reports* 1996, p. 226; (hereinafter referred to as *Nuclear Weapons* Advisory Opinion (note 3).

I. Concerning a Decision-Making *Non Liquet*

A decision-making *non liquet* does not exist. The reason was pointed out, with characteristic clarity of thought and exposition, by Hans Kelsen.[4] It arises simply and directly from the fundamental principle that, in international (or, for that matter, domestic) litigation, a claimant is attempting to obtain something from a respondent on the basis of some proffered rule of law. In this process, the burden of proof lies on the claimant to establish the existence of a rule of law entitling it to relief. Either the claimant succeeds in discharging this duty of proof, or it does not. In the one case, it wins the litigation; in the other, it does not. Either way, there is a definitive outcome to the litigation. In a given case, to be sure, the judge may be wracked by the deepest anguish in attempting to decide whether the claimant has proved his/her case or not. But in such a situation, he or she must find for the respondent because the claimant's arguments have failed to convince.[5]

A few observations about this swift conclusion are in order. First of all, it will readily be appreciated how powerful it happens to be. It deals, with remorseless efficiency, with *all* possible cases of provisional gaps in the law. It will also be observed that this resolution of the problem of the provisional gap is essentially procedural in character. It relies wholly on the single principle of allocation of the burden of persuasion, and not at all on the discovery (or creation) of any substantive rule of law to resolve the problem. For this reason, it may also be characterised as a 'negative' approach to the matter, in the sense that the *non liquet* problem is dealt with entirely by the *inability* of a claimant to establish its case. It is not really a means of *filling* provisional gaps in the law, so much as it is a matter of learning to live with them – by means of the single and inflexible device of systematically and mechanically denying relief to claimants whose cases (so to speak) fall into the gaps.

The deeper question is whether this single-action, negative, all-purpose solution really solves the problem (or pseudo-problem) of *non liquet*. That is to say, is there any reason, in the light of this conclusion about the non-existence of a decision-making *non liquet*, even to bother considering the question of a systemic *non liquet*? Thus, is there any need to fill provisional gaps, in light of the fact that *not* filling them will never, under *any* circumstances, prevent courts from arriving at definitive results in cases?

---

[4]   Kelsen, *Principles of International Law* (Second edition, revised by R.W. Tucker), New York, 1966, at pp. 438–39; hereinafter referred to as *Principles* (note 4); and ibid, *General Theory of State and Law* (Translated by A. Wedberg), Cambridge, Mass., 1945, at pp. 146–49.

[5]   To this effect, see also Cassese, *International Law* (Second edition), Oxford, 2005, at p. 189, n. 3.

The answer to this question depends on the view that is taken of the very nature of a legal system. Some would take the view that law is primarily – or even wholly – a system for the adjudication of claims, that it is essentially, as it were, a dispute-resolution apparatus. On this thesis, a clear rule allocating burden of proof will suffice, always and necessarily, to ensure that the apparatus works effectively. And if no more is asked of a legal system than that, then the demonstrated impossibility of a decision-making *non liquet* would constitute a complete resolution of any problem that might be thought (erroneously) to exist.

There is, however, some palpable reluctance on the part of many international lawyers to leave the matter of *non liquet* at this point. Perhaps there is something like an innate human drive towards systematisation, or perhaps simply an intense curiosity as to whether it is possible to deal with provisional gaps in the law in a more 'positive' manner, by finding principled means of actually filling such gaps, rather than merely passively accepting them. Perhaps most importantly, some writers (such as, admittedly, the present one) take the view that a legal system is something importantly more than a dispute-resolution machine. It is (or should be), in addition, a means of discovering or creating substantive principles of right and justice, and then of effectually applying these rules across as broad a spectrum of social life as possible. There is no reason for supposing that substantive justice will result, always and necessarily, from a policy of simply and mechanically denying relief to claimants in situations where provisional gaps in the law occur. There is, instead, a necessity, where *specific* rules of law are absent, to search for more general principles to apply, in order to reach a maximally just result.

An apt illustration of the clash between these two positions is furnished by the famous *Lotus* case, decided by the World Court in 1927.[6] France was claiming against Turkey for the allegedly unlawful extension of its prescriptive criminal jurisdiction over a French national in the context of a collision on the high seas. France's claim failed. This result can be interpreted in (at least) two ways. One possibility is to see the ruling in procedural terms, as a rule about decision-making by courts, that is, as a statement about burdens of proof in lawsuits. This might be termed as the narrow or minimalist view of the *Lotus* judgment. As such, it illustrates the impossibility of a decision-making *non liquet*.

The other possibility is to see the ruling in substantive terms, as the pronouncement of a general principle of law, to the effect that anything which is not actually forbidden by an ascertained rule of law is, *ipso facto*, permissible.

---

[6]   See the *S.S. Lotus* case (*France v. Turkey*), *PCIJ Reports, Series A*, No. 10, Judgment No. 9 (1927), p. 4.

It must be admitted that the Court's judgment gave, or at least appeared to give, considerable support to this reading, since it spoke in terms of what it called a 'principle of freedom' in international law – meaning, in essence, a principle to the effect that anything that is not actually forbidden by a legal rule is positively lawful. This is clearly a much more sweeping interpretation of the *Lotus* judgment than the narrow, procedural view just identified.

Whichever of these views is taken, the immediate material result is the same: the French claim fails. But the implications for international law are vast. Few (if any) international lawyers would have any quarrel with the narrower view of the *Lotus* holding, that France simply failed to discharge the burden of persuasion that lay on it. Many international lawyers, however, are extremely wary of accepting the substantive interpretation of the decision, with its potentially vast implications over the entire field of international law. The root of the problem is the question of whether the *Lotus* decision stands naked (so to speak), as *merely* a statement of where the burden of persuasion lies, or whether, alternatively, that decision is the surface manifestation of a deeper substantive principle, namely, a 'principle of freedom' to which the Court referred in its judgment (perhaps too carelessly).

Another way of putting this same question is to ask whether resorting to a 'principle of freedom' is an effective way of filling a provisional gap in the underlying fabric of substantive law. If this is thought to be undesirable, then the question arises as to whether there might be some other, preferable way of filling provisional gaps. Yet another possibility is to hold that provisional gaps should be left unfilled, at least in some circumstances, that is to say, that the possibility of a systemic *non liquet* should be conceded. To these issues we shall now turn.

II. Concerning a Systemic *Non Liquet*

The question of whether a systemic *non liquet* can exist amounts, in essence, to asking whether it will *always* be possible to find some 'positive' (i.e., substantive) principle by which a provisional gap in the law can be, as it were, patched up. On this issue, there are rival positive and negative camps. More specifically, the proponents of the view that a systemic *non liquet* is *not* possible may readily be divided into two distinct viewpoints, the one articulated most clearly by Hans Kelsen and the other by Hersch Lauterpacht. The position that a systemic *non liquet* is possible is represented most prominently by Julius Stone. These rival points of view will be briefly summarised.

1. *Against the Possibility of a Systemic* Non Liquet: *Kelsen and Lauterpacht*

As a very broad generalisation, it may be said that the Kelsen position on the impossibility of a systemic *non liquet* is a doctrinaire one, primarily logical in nature. It is, in essence, the substantive counterpart of Kelsen's argument, given above, for the non-existence of a decision-making *non liquet*. The Lauterpacht view, in contrast, is more policy-oriented and pluralistic in character.[7]

Kelsen's position was that a systemic *non liquet* 'is logically not possible'.[8] The reason is, for all intents and purposes, the same as that given for the non-existence of a decision-making *non liquet*. That is to say, international law *always* possesses either a specific rule on a given subject, or else, in the absence of such a specific rule, a general rule – or, in modern parlance, a default principle. The default principle is the one that he infers from the *Lotus* case: that any action, which is not prohibited by some ascertained rule of law, is automatically lawful.[9] Kelsen, in other words, endorsed the view that the *Lotus* judgment was not simply a procedural statement of burden of persuasion but was also a substantive pronouncement of a 'principle of freedom.' Kelsen's own term was 'residual negative principle'. Specific rules, in combination with this residual negative principle, operate to guarantee that no substantive legal question can ever lack an answer.

Three points may be noted about this Kelsen position. The first is that it is a doctrinaire stance rooted entirely in logic and not at all in any empirical survey of the actual content or history of international law or adjudication. It is not the case, in the Kelsen view, that a *non liquet* simply *happens* not to exist in international law. Rather, the contention is that a *non liquet cannot* exist, by virtue of the sweeping character of the residual negative principle. That principle operates as a kind of universal, all-powerful panacea, automatically and mechanically filling any provisional gap in the law, wherever it might occur and in whatever substantive subject area.

The second point about Kelsen's theory is that there might be room for debating about whether to characterise it as, so to speak, a unitary or a binary approach. If seen in binary terms, it could be said to involve a two-step analysis. First is the identification of a provisional gap in the law, with the second step being the invocation of the residual negative principle, which would therefore function as a sort of repair device. If the Kelsen argument were put in unitary

---

[7] For a brief and lucid account of this conflict of views, see Weil, ' "The Court Cannot Conclude Definitively . . .": *Non Liquet* Revisited', 36 (1997) *Columbia Journal Transnational Law* 109 at pp. 110–14.

[8] Kelsen, *Principles* (note 4), at p. 438.

[9] Ibid, pp. 438–39.

terms, it would be said that the specific norms of international law and the residual negative principle are of equal standing, forming a single, seamless normative web – with the result that there can never be even a provisional gap in the law. Although the Kelsen position could be formulated in either of these ways, with identical final results, it is probable that Kelsen's own characterisation would be the unitary one.[10] That is to say, the residual negative principle is to be regarded not as a secondary, stop-gap device, to be used sparingly and even apologetically, but rather as a fully valid norm of international law entirely on a par with other norms, making up a single gapless system.

The third point about Kelsen's approach is that there is scope for disagreement as to when the residual negative principle really comes into play. If taken in its strictest and narrowest possible sense, it could be taken to mean that, in every single case in which a *specific* rule of law is absent, the residual negative principle must be automatically and immediately invoked. There would then be *no* resorting to such means as analogy or general principles of law to deal with the matter. Kelsen's position also lends itself, however, to a rather looser interpretation, which would allow at least some measure of use of general principles and the like – and that only when those failed in turn to resolve the matter would the residual negative principle be employed. In other words, the question of what to do about a potential or provisional *non liquet* is the easy part of Kelsen's system to apply. Just bring in the residual negative rule. The more difficult part is deciding exactly *when* a potential *non liquet* is really present, so as to trigger the application of that universal solution. Notwithstanding this difficulty, however, the general tenor of Kelsen's thought in this area is clear enough: that the *primary* (though not necessarily exclusive) stress in international law is on specific rules, and that, in the absence of specific or reasonably specific rules, the residual negative principle will be invoked as the all-encompassing remedy, to guarantee that a *non liquet* can never occur.

Hersch Lauterpacht, like Kelsen, also argued against the possibility of a systemic *non liquet* in international law, but on quite different grounds.[11] Unlike Kelsen, he did not rely on a single, unitary, catch-all device for ensuring against it. His approach, instead, was more pluralistic or even impressionistic. More specifically, he advanced a two-pronged argument against the existence of a *non*

---

[10] It is, admittedly, difficult to cite a single source for this conclusion. But a reading of Kelsen's *General Theory* reveals the presence of a fundamentally monistic turn of mind running strongly throughout his thought.

[11] See generally Hersch Lauterpacht, 'Some Observations on the Prohibition of "Non Liquet" and the Completeness of the Law,' in *Symbolae Verzijl présentées au Professeur J.H.W. Verzijl à l'occasion de son LXX-iéme anniversaire*, The Hague, 1958, p. 196 *et seq.*; hereinafter referred to as Lauterpacht, 'Observations' (note 11).

liquet. One of his prongs was an empirical claim: an appeal to '[t]he constancy of international judicial and arbitral practice', which reveal a complete lack of concrete evidence for a systemic *non liquet*. This argument, however, is clearly not conclusive on the question. Simply because a *non liquet* has not, thus far, turned up in international case-law is, logically, no guarantee that one might not come to light at some future point.[12]

Accordingly, Lauterpacht had a second prong to his argument against the existence of a *non liquet*. Like Kelsen, he believed that international law possesses means of guaranteeing that a provisional *non liquet* can always be filled whenever it arises. Unlike Kelsen, he did not rely on the residual negative principle (or 'principle of freedom' from the *Lotus* case) as the means of achieving this. Instead, he posited that international law possesses a rather more eclectic solution, in the form of a kind of juridical tool kit comprising, basically, three principal implements. One of these is the employment of analogy – the extension of established rules from one class of cases to the resolution of other relevantly similar situations. A second device is the resort to principles of a high level of generality, applying those general principles to novel situations. A third device is the resort to equity, that is, equity in the sense of a departure from normal rules of law, in the interest of achieving substantive justice. For present purposes, an exhaustive discussion of the merits and demerits of these strategies is not necessary; and they may safely be referred to, collectively, as general principles of law. The important point is that Lauterpacht contended that the application of these strategies (or broadly similar ones) would suffice to fill any and all provisional gaps in the law that might appear.[13]

An illustration of these strategies in action was offered by Lauterpacht, in the form of the *Eastern Extension, Australasia and China Telegraph Co. Ltd.* arbitration of 1923, between Great Britain and the United States.[14] It involved a claim by Britain for compensation for the American cutting of a British-owned submarine telegraph cable in the course of the Spanish-American War of 1898. The first issue to be resolved was the lawfulness of the cutting of the cable. On this question, the arbitral panel conceded that no 'specific provision of

---

[12] A point made forcefully by Stone, '*Non Liquet* and the Function of Law in the International Community', 35 (1959) *BYIL* 124, at pp. 138–39; hereinafter referred to as Stone, 'Non Liquet' (note 12).

[13] For a summary of Lauterpacht's views on this issue, see Scobbie, 'The Theorist as Judge: Hersch Lauterpacht's Concept of the International Judicial Function', 8 (1997) *EJIL* 264, at pp. 274–78. Supporting Lauterpacht's position is Corten: see *L'utilisation du 'raisonnable' par le juge international: Discours juridique, raison et contradictions*, Brussels, 1997. See also Ford, 'Judicial Discretion in International Jurisprudence Article 38 (1) (c) and "General Principles of Law"', 5 (1994) *Duke J. Comp. & Int'l Law* 35, at pp. 59–65.

[14] 6 *UN Reports of International Arbitral Awards* 112; reprinted in 18 (1924) *AJIL* 835.

law' existed, i.e., that there was a provisional *non liquet*. The problem was to be resolved, in the panel's view, by 'applying … the corollaries of general principles, and so to find – exactly as in the mathematical sciences – the solution of the problem'. This approach was confidently stated to be 'the method of jurisprudence' common to all countries. The particular general principle that was called into aid was the proposition that 'the legitimate object of sea warfare is to deprive the enemy of those means of communication, which the high seas … afford to every nation'.

On this basis, belligerent countries are clearly entitled to interfere with the trade of their enemies carried on by means of surface vessels (by such means as the capture and condemnation of enemy-owned merchant vessels and of contraband of war carried from neutral States to the enemy). The panel concluded that this general principle embraces communication by way of submarine cables as well as by way of surface traffic. The second issue in the arbitration was whether, even though the severing was lawful, there was a duty to compensate the owners of the cable, on the analogy of compensation owed for requisition of neutral property by belligerents in wartime. The panel considered the point and concluded that the proposed analogy was unsound, with the result that compensation was held not to be owing.

A sceptic might advance an immediate and obvious objection to the Lauterpacht view: that it appears to contain no absolute *guarantee*, as the Kelsen one does, that it will *always* work, that is to say, that the juridical tool-kit is guaranteed to be equal to the task of repairing any and every provisional gap in the law that would ever appear. Is there not the possibility that a provisional gap might turn up that will be too gaping, or too serious, to be repaired by the tools at hand? Lauterpacht was well aware of this potential objection, and he dealt with it by positing the existence of an *overriding* general principle of law to the effect that, whenever a provisional gap in the substantive law is identified, the judge *must* apply the various tools with whatever degree of vigour and energy are necessary in the circumstances to repair the hole. The upshot of this position, in Lauterpacht's view, is that 'the principle of the completeness of the legal order is in itself a general principle of law ….' He even went so far as to contend that the impermissibility of a systemic *non liquet* is 'perhaps the most general of the general principles of law', to the point that '[i]t is not easy to conceive of a rule or principle of international law to which the designation "positive" could be applied with greater justification than the prohibition of *non liquet*.'[15]

---

[15] Lauterpacht, 'Observations' (note 11), at p. 206. It appears that, by 'positive', Lauterpacht meant positive in the sense of incontrovertible or unquestionable, rather than positive in the sense of positive (i.e., man-made) law.

The existence of this overriding principle is what (in Lauterpacht's opinion) actually *compels* the tool kit to be adequate, in all cases, to the task of dealing with whatever repair work would ever be at hand. Fortified by this posited overriding principle, Lauterpacht inevitably had no difficulty in concluding that the resort to general principles of law (as authorised by the Statute of the World Court) 'made [it] certain that there would always be at hand, if necessary, a legal rule or principle for the legal solution of any controversy ....'[16] It would be fair to characterise this approach to the matter as being a system in which the basic device for guaranteeing that a *non liquet* would never appear is mandatory judicial creativity, under the rubric of the application of general principles of law.

Three points may be usefully noted about the broad features of the Lauterpacht approach. The first is that it is more pluralistic, flexible and policy-oriented than the Kelsen one. Where the Kelsen approach is mechanistic and doctrinaire in its application of one single solution to any and all cases of provisional (or potential) *non liquet*, the Lauterpacht one offers a variety of remedies, to be tailored to the particular needs of particular provisional gaps as and when they might arise. For precisely this reason, the Lauterpacht approach relies heavily, for better or worse, on judicial creativity and discretion.

The second point about Lauterpacht's stance on systemic *non liquet* is that, from the historical standpoint, there is much to be said for it. In the drafting of the Statute of the first World Court (that of the Permanent Court of International Justice) in 1920, the Advisory Committee of Jurists carefully considered the possibility that gaps in the law might prevent the Court from rendering a decision in particular cases. It was precisely to forestall such a possibility that the Committee authorised the Court to apply 'general principles of law', in addition to the more standard sources of customary law and treaty law.[17]

The third feature of the Lauterpacht approach is that, in its own way, it is every bit as doctrinaire as that of Kelsen. In a certain sense, Lauterpacht's approach is pluralistic, in that judges are left with a high degree of flexibility in applying general principles of law to provisional gaps. Advocates of the Kelsen approach need not necessarily have any great objection on that point. But the Kelsen system holds that this application of general principles will not necessarily be sufficient in all cases – and that, when general principles

---

[16] Ibid, at p. 205.

[17] See the Advisory Committee of Jurists, *Procès-verbaux of the Proceedings of the Committee June 16th – July 24th 1920*, The Hague, 1920, pp. 293–97; 307–21 and 331–38; hereinafter referred to as Advisory Committee of Jurists, *Procès-verbaux* (note 17).

fail, then the residual negative principle provides the resolution. Lauterpacht's position was that the application of general principles of law would *never* fail, so that the residual negative principle would never be required as a means of providing a substantive rule of law for the resolution of any dispute. But Lauterpacht could *only* be confident of this conclusion if there existed a high-level or overriding general principle, to the effect that the tools are legally *required* to suffice for any and all tasks. In the absence of such an exogenous or overriding general principle, the Lauterpacht repair kit could not be guaranteed to work in all cases; and the supposed impossibility of a *non liquet* in principle would become unsustainable. The Lauterpacht approach could also, therefore, be termed monistic, in the sense that it too, like that of Kelsen, relies crucially and ultimately on the application of a single residual general principle: that, whenever a provisional gap in the law occurs, the judge must employ whatever degree of creativity is necessary in order to fill it.

Nevertheless, it is true to say that, on the whole, the Lauterpacht approach is more open-ended and flexible than the Kelsen one, in that his guiding or overriding general principle is not substantive in character, but rather is an instruction to judges to be creative. The actual substantive rules that are applied in particular cases will be more varied, not reducible to a single sweeping formula. Lauterpacht therefore envisaged, in effect, a legal system that would, over the course of time, gradually become ever more detailed as case-law gradually grew larger, that would evolve along with the ever evolving system of international relations itself. To Lauterpacht, therefore, international law, as expressed through the judicial mechanism, would be a sort of ever-growing, self-enriching system. Organic imagery comes readily to mind in describing this outlook (although Lauterpacht himself may not have approved of that). The Kelsen approach, in contrast, is more starkly logical and static, more cut-and-dried.

The Lauterpacht approach is, however, open to criticism from the standpoint of persons who harbour suspicions of its crucial reliance on a dangerously high degree of judicial activism. One of Lauterpacht's principal critics, on just this ground, was Julius Stone, the most prominent spokesman for the view that a systemic *non liquet* is possible – and sometimes even desirable.

2. *For the Possibility of a Systemic* non liquet*: Stone*

For all of their differences, the Kelsen and Lauterpacht approaches share one important feature: both conclude that, ultimately and as a matter of principle, a systemic *non liquet* cannot occur. That conclusion has not gone unchallenged. The principal challenge that will be noted here is the one advanced by Julius

Stone.[18] Stone's position on the matter was mainly developed in opposition to that of Lauterpacht. As will be seen presently, it shares some important affinities with the stance of Kelsen.

Stone stated the basic problem at hand with clarity and simplicity: that courts, when faced by a provisional gap in the law, 'must either declare a *non liquet* or necessarily engage in the creation of law by a judicial act of choice ....'[19] Where Lauterpacht had pumped for the second of these two alternatives, Stone opted instead for the first. In effect, Stone's position was that the international legal system consists primarily (and perhaps even solely) of a 'menu' of specific rules, dealing with specific situations. Any provisional gap that appeared in the system must remain in place, because there are no overriding general or residual principles available to fill it. That is to say, there would be a *non liquet*.

In Stone's view, the heart of the question is the debate over 'the law-creative as distinct from the merely law-making competence of international courts'.[20] Stone maintained that Lauterpacht's solution for filling provisional gaps – reliance on a potentially high degree of judicial creativity and discretion – is too high a price to pay for any benefit that would be received. In particular, he doubted the existence of any overriding general principle of law, of the sort proffered by Lauterpacht, *requiring* judges to apply whatever degree of judicial creativity would be necessary, in any given case, to fill a provisional gap. Such a 'solution' to the *non liquet* problem amounted (Stone protested) to 'the imposition upon the court of a duty to develop new rules limited only by the novelty and range of the matters coming before it for decision'. In Stone's opinion, the Lauterpacht position has a natural-law flavour, in its heavy reliance on general principles of law as a means of filling provisional gaps, with these general principles constituting 'a kind of inexhaustible storehouse of potential law'.[21]

Stone's position, in essence, was that Lauterpacht's preferred 'cure' for the 'problem' of a *non liquet* was worse than the so-called disease itself. The existence of gaps in the law is nothing (in Stone's view) to be unduly alarmed about. On the contrary, a system which contains gaps is positively to be preferred to one which does not – or, more accurately, to a system in which provisional gaps

---

[18] See Stone, 'Non Liquet' (note 12), p. 124 *et seq.* Much along the lines of Stone's analysis is Lucien Siorat, in *Le problème des lacunes en droit international: Contribution à l'étude des sources du droit et de la fonction judiciaire*, Paris, 1958. See also Fastenrath, *Lücken im Völkerrecht: Zu Rechtscharakter, Quellen, Systemzusammenhang, Methodenlehre und Funktionen des Völkerrechts*, Berlin, 1991, which also supports the possibility of a *non liquet*.

[19] Stone, 'Non Liquet' (note 12), at p. 132. For an identical position voiced by Elihu Root during the drafting of the Statute of the Permanent Court of International Justice, see Advisory Committee, *Procès-verbaux* (note 17), pp. 308–10.

[20] Stone 'Non Liquet' (note 12), p. 127.

[21] Ibid, at p. 133.

must be filled in the Lauterpacht manner. Stone contended that, in situations for which the law makes no specific provision, it is actually better to leave the gaps to be filled in, over the course of time, by the evolution of state practice and of future treaty-making. This would be the best way of ensuring that substantive international law would evolve over time in line with the actual practice of States, which after all is ultimately the source of the whole of international law. The (unacceptable) alternative, favoured by Lauterpacht, carried the risk that, in cases of provisional gaps in the law, judges would impose artificial or overly theoretical or excessively idiosyncratic solutions, too far removed from the realities of international life.

It may be noted that Stone's position on the *non liquet* question bears a certain structural similarity to that of Kelsen. He, like Stone, was reluctant to grant any high degree of discretion to judges in dealing with the provisional gaps in the law. They differed only in their views of what the preferable alternative is. To Kelsen, the alternative is to fill the gaps (or, in the monistic manner of stating it, to prevent gaps from arising in the first place) by means of a single *non-discretionary* device: the residual negative principle. To Stone, the preferable alternative was to leave the gaps in place, and to let them be filled over the course of time through the normal law-making processes of State practice and treaty-making.

The contest between these various views about *non liquet* in international law raged (if that is the right word) primarily amongst scholars – as would be expected, given that, as noted above, there is no possibility for the emergence of a decision-making *non liquet*. The position changed, however, in 1996, when the possibility of determining the existence or non-existence of a systemic *non liquet* arose, in dramatic form: in the request by the UN General Assembly to the World Court for a determination of the lawfulness (or otherwise) of the threat or use of nuclear weapons.

III. Whether a *Non Liquet* Actually Occurred in the *Nuclear Weapons* Advisory Opinion

The advisory-opinion process of the World Court presents the best means in practice of finding enlightenment on the question of a systemic *non liquet*. Whenever there are parties contending in litigation, it will always be possible for a court to rely on the impossibility of a decision-making *non liquet* to avoid dealing with the more difficult theoretical question of the existence of a systemic *non liquet*. In advisory cases, in which there are no contending parties, this easy way out is not available. The Court is required to deal directly, as it were, with the law itself.[22] In 1996, in its advisory opinion on nuclear weapons, the World Court proceeded to do so, in an instructive (if not necessarily a satisfactory) manner.

1. *The Holding of the Court – and Whether it Was a* Non Liquet

In its 1996 advisory opinion on nuclear weapons, the World Court certainly identified a provisional *non liquet*, in that it held that no *specific* rule of international law exists prohibiting the use of nuclear weapons *per se*.[23] The question, then, was what to do next. What the Court, significantly, did *not* do was to pronounce a *non liquet* forthwith, as it might have done if it had taken the Stone approach in what might be termed its purest form. It also did not adopt the Kelsen solution of applying the residual negative principle straight away and thereby concluding that the use of nuclear weapons would be lawful. Instead, it took the course broadly outlined by Lauterpacht: of analysing a range of more general principles of international humanitarian law, to see if they would shed light on the matter.

These principles of humanitarian law include general rules against 'superfluous injury' and 'unnecessary suffering', as well as the law of neutrality.[24] On the basis of these considerations, the Court concluded that the use of nuclear weapons 'seems scarcely reconcilable' with that general body of law, that is to say, that the use of nuclear weapons 'would generally be contrary to the rules of international law applicable in armed conflict, and in particular the principles and rules of humanitarian law'.[25] At the same time, however, the Court stopped short of holding that it was absolutely impossible to employ nuclear weapons without violating international humanitarian law. Specifically, it held itself unable to reach a 'definitive conclusion' concerning the lawfulness of the use of nuclear weapons in one marginal situation: 'an extreme circumstance of self-defence' in which a State's 'very survival' was at stake.[26] As the Court put the matter in the *dispositif* at the conclusion of the opinion, by the narrowest possible margin (i.e., on the casting vote of the President of the Court):

> [I]n view of the current state of international law, and of the elements of fact at its disposal, the Court cannot conclude definitively whether the threat or use

---

[22] On this, see Punzhin and Wiles, 'Judge Vereschetin: A Russian Scholar at the International Court of Justice,' 19 (2002) *Leiden Journal of International Law* 719, at pp. 727–29.

[23] *Nuclear Weapons* Advisory Opinion (note 3), paragraphs 51 to 72.

[24] Ibid, paragraphs 74 to 97.

[25] Ibid, paragraphs 95 and 105.

[26] Ibid, paragraphs 95 to 97.

of nuclear weapons would be lawful or unlawful in an extreme circumstance of self-defence, in which the very survival of a State would be at stake.[27]

The Court did not explicitly state that it was here pronouncing a *non liquet*. Nevertheless, the overwhelming majority of commentators have contended that that was what the Court did in reality.[28] Several members of the Court also took this view (as will be discussed in more detail presently).[29] These commentators and judges, however, are incorrect.[30] The language quoted above, contrary to initial appearances, is not a true *non liquet*. It is important to appreciate why this is so.

---

[27] Ibid, paragraph 105.

[28] See, for example, Weiss, 'The World Court Tackles the Fate of the Earth: An Introduction to the ICJ Advisory Opinion on the Legality of the Threat and Use of Nuclear Weapons', 7 (1997) *Transnational Law and Contemporary Problems* 313, at p. 325; Weston, 'Nuclear Weapons and the World Court: Ambiguity's Consensus', ibid, at p. 388; Mendlovitz and Datan, 'Judge Weeramantry's Grotian Quest', ibid, pp. 405–406; McCormack, 'A Non Liquet on Nuclear Weapons – The ICJ Avoids the Application of General Principles of International Humanitarian Law', 316 (1997) *International Review of the Red Cross* 76; Weil (note 7), at pp. 117–18; Scobbie (note 12), at pp. 290–91; Kohen, 'L'avis consultative de la CIJ sur la Licéité de la menace ou de l'emploi d'armes nucléaires et de la function judiciaire,' 8 (1998) *EJIL* 336 at pp. 346–49; Koskenniemi, 'The Silence of Law/The Voice of Justice,' in Boisson de Chazournes and Sands (eds.), *International Law, the International Court of Justice and Nuclear Weapons*, Cambridge, 1999 at pp. 489–90; hereinafter referred to as Boisson and Sands; Heffernan, 'The Nuclear Weapons Opinions: Reflections on the Advisory Procedure of the International Court of Justice', 28 (1998) *Stetson Law Review* 133, at pp. 153–55; Ouchi, 'The Threat or Use of Nuclear Weapons: Discernable Legal Policies of the Judges of the International Court of Justice', 13 (1998) *Conn. J. Inernational Law* 107, at pp. 112–14; O'Daly, 'The Nuclear Age, a Threat to Humanity and a Threat to Law?', 1 (1998) *Trinity Coll. Law Review* 43, at pp. 52–53; Aznar-Gomez, 'The 1996 Nuclear Weapons Advisory Opinion and Non Liquet in International Law', 48 (1999) *ICLQ* 3, at p. 19; Dekker and Werner, 'The Completeness of International Law and Hamlet's Dilemma: Non Liquet, the Nuclear Weapons Case and Legal Theory', 68 (1999) *Nordic Journal of International Law* 225, at pp. 242–44; Skordas, '*Epilogomena* to a Silence: Nuclear Weapons, Terrorism and the Moment of Concern', 6 (2001) *JCSL* 191; and Searl, 'Natural Law, International Law and Nuclear Disarmament', 33 (2001–2002) *Ottawa Law Review* 271, at pp. 291–92.

[29] For a forthright contention that the Court pronounced a *non liquet*, see the Dissenting Opinion of Judge Higgins, *Nuclear Weapons* Advisory Opinion (note 3), p. 583, at paragraphs 2, 7 and 29 to 30 (pp. 583–84 and 590). For positions to the same effect by implication rather than by explicit statement, see the Dissenting Opinions of Judge Koroma, pp. 557–58; and of Judge Schwebel, at pp. 322–23.

[30] For commentators holding that the opinion did not pronounce a *non liquet*, see Perez, 'The Passive Virtues and the World Court: Pro-dialogic Abstention by the International Court of Justice,' 18 (1997) *Michigan Journal of International Law* 399, at pp. 429–36. Others, however, have refrained from taking a clear stand on the point, notwithstanding detailed treatment of the advisory opinion in other respects. See, for example, Falk, 'Nuclear Weapons, International Law and the World Court: A Historic Encounter', 91 (1997) *AJIL* 64, at p. 68; Nagan, 'Nuclear Arsenals, International Lawyers, and the Challenge of the Millennium', 24 (1999) *YJIL* 485, at pp. 523–24; and Bodansky, '*Non Liquet* and the Completeness of International Law', in Boisson and Sands (note 27), at pp. 153–70.

First of all, it should be noted that the actual wording used by the Court, both in the *dispositif* and in the text of the judgment, referred to its inability to pronounce on the question as arising from two quite distinct factors: first, from 'the present state of international law viewed as a whole'; and second, from 'the elements of fact at its disposal'.[31] The most reasonable reading of the opinion is that it was the factual, rather than the legal, consideration that stood most seriously in the way of a definitive pronouncement. The reference to 'the present state of international law' is most reasonably seen as referring to the absence of an *absolute* prohibition against nuclear weapons *per se*. But the absence of an absolute prohibition is not, as such, a bar to the Court's rendering a definitive decision in a particular case, as and when it might arise, based on the particular facts at hand. Moreover, the Court made it clear in its opinion what it would do in such a case: apply the norms of the general law of armed conflict. These include, most outstandingly, the general principle of proportionality in situations of self-defence, together with the general rules of humanitarian law.[32] There is no reason to suppose that, when the Court applied this general body of law to the specific facts of a case involving an employment of nuclear weapons, it would be unable to reach a definitive conclusion.

The problem in the 1996 advisory opinion was simply that there was no such situation before it, and hence no set of specific facts to which the general law of armed conflict could be applied. That is to say, it was the problem of 'the elements of fact at its disposal' – that is, the complete *absence* of any such facts – that prevented it from rendering a definitive pronouncement. This is readily apparent from the Court's discussion in the main body of the opinion. The Court noted that, although various States had contended that low-yield nuclear weapons could lawfully be employed in certain circumstances, none of those States had gone so far as to indicate 'the precise circumstances' in which this would be so. For that reason, the Court was not able to pronounce on the matter.[33] Nor, it is submitted, should this conclusion be regarded as particularly surprising. It is (or should be) patently obvious that the Court could not pronounce, in advance of the occurrence of any actual case, on the legal merits of every single possible situation of 'extreme ... self-defence' that would ever arise, in the entire future history of the world.[34]

---

[31] *Nuclear Weapons* Advisory Opinion (note 3), paragraphs 97 and 105.
[32] Ibid, paragraphs 40 to 43 (on self-defence) and 34, 79 to 89 (on general principles of international humanitarian law).
[33] Ibid, paragraph 94.
[34] See, to this effect, Lowe, 'Shock Verdict: Nuclear War May or May Not Be Unlawful', 55 (1996) *CLJ* 415.

This conclusion is reinforced by the Court's treatment of the contention that the use of nuclear weapons would entail a breach of the Genocide Convention of 1948. It accepted that, in a given specific case, there might be such a breach, but only if the necessary elements of intention for the crime of genocide were present in the particular situation. It is obviously impossible to state in advance, in the complete absence of facts relating to an actual use of nuclear weapons, whether such an intention would be present or not. Not only did the Court not suggest or imply that, once the facts of a given case were presented to it, it would be unable to reach a decision. It even went so far as to state the opposite: that it *would* be possible for it to reach a conclusion, though only 'after having taken due account of the circumstances specific to each case'.[35]

The position is, for all practical purposes, the same regarding the contention that there could be situations in which the employment of low-yield nuclear weapons would be lawful. As noted above, the Court stated that it did not have sufficient factual information to pronounce conclusively on the point. In the very same passage, however, it did indicate (if only briefly) the sort of information that it would need to have in order to give a comprehensive answer to the question. Specifically, information would be required on three points: (i) whether it is actually 'feasible' to employ 'low yield, tactical nuclear weapons' in a 'clean' manner; (ii) the 'precise circumstances' that would allegedly justify such a use; and (iii) the magnitude of the risk that the use of nuclear weapons in such a circumstances might 'tend to escalate into the all-out use of high yield nuclear weapons'.[36] These are, in essence, simply a statement of the *factual* information that would be necessary to enable the Court to arrive at a legal conclusion. There was no suggestion, express or implied, of any gap in the law itself – and consequently no *non liquet*.

2. *Various Judges on the General Question of a Systemic* Non Liquet

The fact that a *non liquet* was not pronounced by the Court in the particular opinion at hand does not, of course, dispose of the *general* question of whether a systemic *non liquet* is possible in principle or not. That question is still open.

It may be noted that four of the judges took clear stands on this *general* question of the possibility of a systemic *non liquet*. All four of them maintained that a systemic *non liquet* is *not* possible. Interestingly, two of them took the Kelsen view of the question, and two of them took the Lauterpacht view. In the Kelsen camp were Judges Guillaume and Shahabuddeen. Guillaume was the

---

[35] *Nuclear Weapons* Advisory Opinion (note 3), paragraph 26.
[36] Ibid, paragraph 94.

more forthright. Explicitly citing the *Lotus* judgment, he invoked the 'principle of freedom', contending that, in the absence of a specific rule of international law prohibiting the use of nuclear weapons, that use must be held not to be prohibited (although of course the strictures of international humanitarian law would have to be complied with). '[I]f the law is silent in [the particular] case', he maintained, 'States remain free to act as they intend'.[37] A more straightforward application of Kelsen's position could not be imagined.

Judge Shahabuddeen was also clearly in the Kelsen camp, although slightly less explicitly so. Agreeing with Kelsen, he contended that, in the absence of a specific rule of international law on the subject in question, a single default principle comes automatically into play to resolve the matter. Shahabuddeen parted company slightly with Kelsen, however, in carefully refraining to commit himself as to precisely what the default rule actually is. It could be, he opined, *either* Kelsen's residual negative rule (that anything not prohibited is permitted) *or* its mirror image (that anything not permitted is prohibited).[38] In either event, though, the reasoning employed was clearly that of Kelsen: that, in the absence of a specific rule on the subject in question, a single default principle kicks in automatically and mechanically to prevent a *non liquet* from appearing.

Interestingly, although Guillaume and Shahabuddeen both took the Kelsen position on the question of *non liquet*, neither one expressed a clear view that the Court had actually pronounced one in the case at hand. Guillaume went no further than to say, rather delphically, that the Court's wording in the relevant paragraph of the *dispositif* was 'not entirely satisfactory'.[39] Shahabuddeen, equally cautiously, merely stated that it was 'possible' that the Court's holding would be 'interpreted' by some commentators as being a *non liquet* – and that, *if* the holding did constitute a *non liquet*, then he would dissent.[40]

In the Lauterpacht camp on the question of *non liquet* were Judges Schwebel and Higgins. Both of them took the view (either expressly or by implication) that the Court had pronounced a *non liquet* – but that it had been wrong to do so, on the ground that a *non liquet* cannot exist in international law. Echoing Lauterpacht, Judge Higgins invoked 'an important and well-established principle that the concept of *non liquet* ... is no part of the Court's jurisprudence'. She also strongly implied that Kelsen's residual negative approach is unsuitable as a means of guaranteeing against a *non liquet*. This was evident in her insistence that, as a general matter, '[i]nternational law does not simply consist of total pro-

---

[37] Separate Opinion of Judge Guillaume, ibid, p. 287, at pp. 291–92; paragraphs 9–12.
[38] Dissenting Opinion of Judge Shahabuddeen, ibid, p. 375, at pp. 389–90.
[39] Separate Opinion of Judge Guillaume, ibid, p. 287, at pp. 290–91, paragraph 8.
[40] Dissenting Opinion of Judge Shahabuddeen, ibid, at 389.

hibitions', with freedom left unrestricted wherever prohibitions were lacking. In the spirit of Lauterpacht, she expressed confidence that 'norms indubitably exist' which would enable the Court to arrive at a decision on the lawfulness of the use of nuclear weapons in particular cases.[41]

Judge Schwebel's views on the *non liquet* issue were even more forthright. Explicitly invoking the authority of Lauterpacht, he contended that 'predominant legal theory', as well as the precedents of the World Court itself, precluded the pronouncing of a *non liquet*. He also maintained (though somewhat vaguely) that 'the legal progress of the twentieth century', combined with the principles of the UN Charter, suffice to ensure that a *non liquet* could never materialise.[42]

The position of Judge Koroma may be mentioned in passing. He was less sweeping in his stance on the general question of *non liquet* in international law, merely stating that a *non liquet* pronouncement was 'wholly unfounded in the present case'. His subsequent analysis, however, was much in the spirit of Lauterpacht, as it marshalled an immense amount of law and practice to reach the conclusion that the use of nuclear weapons must be held to be prohibited in all circumstances.[43]

IV. CONCLUDING REMARKS: WHERE THE LAW NOW STANDS ON *NON LIQUET*

The final position may be summed up briefly. The World Court in its 1996 advisory opinion on nuclear weapons did *not* pronounce a *non liquet*. Consequently, the broad question of whether a *non liquet* is possible in international litigation remains undecided. This much may be said with confidence. Beyond this point, speculation (more or less educated) must enter in. It would appear that, on balance, the prevailing view is that a systemic *non liquet* is not possible and, consequently, that the Stone position appears, on balance, to be disfavoured.[44] All four of the World Court judges who took a stand on this question were in agreement on this broad point. Here too, then, it would appear that a reasonably high degree of confidence is warranted.

---

[41] Dissenting Opinion of Judge Higgins, ibid, p. 583, at pp. 590–93; paragraphs 29 to 41.

[42] Dissenting Opinion of Judge Schwebel, ibid, p. 311, at pp. 322–23. In support for this position, see Kohen (note 27), at pp. 346–49.

[43] Dissenting Opinion of Judge Koroma, *Nuclear Weapons* Advisory Opinion (note 3), p. 429, at pp. 556–82.

[44] On this, see Jennings and Watts (eds.), *Oppenheim's International Law*, vol. i: *Peace* (Ninth edition), London, 1992, at 12–13.

If this conclusion is correct, then the remaining question to be determined is whether the Kelsen analysis or the Lauterpacht one more accurately states the reason for the impossibility of a systemic *non liquet*. On this question, the element of speculation becomes greater. On the whole, the tenor of the World Court's advisory opinion of 1996 was distinctly more in the spirit of Lauterpacht than of Kelsen. No reliance was placed in the opinion of the Court on the residual negative principle. Instead, the identification of the provisional gap in the law (i.e., of the absence of a specific rule dealing with the use of nuclear weapons *per se*) led the Court immediately to look further afield for substantive norms. Specifically, it led to the consideration of the general principles of international humanitarian law, which were found to be applicable to the situation in question. Although the matter cannot be considered to have been definitively determined, it seems safe to say that the analysis favoured by Lauterpacht is the one that was the most strongly in evidence in the 1996 advisory opinion.

In the light of this conclusion, some very tentative conclusions may be offered as to the current status of Kelsen's residual negative principle. There is no evidence from the Court's holding in the 1996 advisory opinion that it operates, in the manner posited by Kelsen (and Judge Guillaume), as a general all-purpose principle of substantive law. That a minimalist interpretation of the Lotus decision is the appropriate one, was suggested (persuasively, it is submitted) by Judge Bedjaoui in his separate opinion, in the following terms:

> The Court's decision in the '*Lotus*' case ... should be understood to be of very limited application ... It would be to exaggerate the importance of that decision of the Permanent Court and to distort its scope were it to be divorced from the particular context, both judicial and temporal, in which it was taken. No doubt this decision expressed *the spirit of the times*, the spirit of an international society which as yet had few institutions and was governed by an international law of strict co-existence, itself a reflection of the vigour of the principle of State sovereignty.[45]

The present-day world, Judge Bedjaoui continued, is 'markedly altered' from that one. The 'resolutely positivist' view of international law which was reflected in the *Lotus* judgment (chiefly in the form of the residual negative principle) must now be acknowledged to have given way to 'an objective conception of international law', which seeks 'to reflect a collective juridical conscience and respond to the social necessities of States organized as a community'.[46]

---

[45] Declaration of Judge Bedjoui in *Nuclear Weapons* Advisory Opinion (note 3), p. 268, at p. 270, paragraph 12. Emphasis in the original.

[46] Ibid, paragraph 13.

It would be difficult to imagine a pronouncement more squarely in the spirit of Lauterpacht's position than this one.

The matter, however, cannot be considered fully to be resolved, as there remains doubt about the validity of Lauterpacht's strongest contention: the existence of an overriding general principle of law actually *prohibiting* judges from *ever* pronouncing a *non liquet*, that is, requiring judges to exercise whatever degree of creativity is necessary to fill any provisional gap that arises. Judges Higgins and Schwebel were clearly of this persuasion, but they were both dissenters in the case. This proposition of Lauterpacht's must therefore be regarded as being very far from being established. The possibility must logically remain that concrete cases might arise in which Lauterpacht's general-principles tool-kit will not be adequate to the repair job at hand. If that were to prove to be so in any single case then − but only then − will we have incontrovertible evidence of a *non liquet* in international law. Stone's contention that such a *non liquet* is a real possibility appears to be out of favour on present evidence. But it cannot be altogether ruled out that he may yet have his day.

Chapter Four

'Constitutionalization' of International Law: A Sceptical Voice

Michael Wood*

On 14 March 2007, Colin and I took part in a conference at the Centre for International Governance, University of Leeds, entitled *The 'Constitutionaliza-tion' of International Law; Sceptical Voices*.[1] The present contribution draws on what I said on that occasion.

After some preliminary remarks, I look at certain 'constitutionalist' approaches to international law that are found in the literature. I then examine briefly the nature of the Charter of the United Nations and the Security Council. Is the Charter a world constitution? Is the Council an executive, a legislature, or quasi-judicial? At Leeds, I went on to offer some thoughts about Article 103 (priority of Charter obligations over other obligations), a provision of the Charter of the United Nations that may be considered to have a constitutional function within the international community; and about possible limits on the powers of the Council, deriving either from the Purposes and Principles of the United Nations (Articles 1 and 2 of the Charter) or from peremptory norms of international law (*jus cogens*) – but I shall not repeat those thoughts here.[2]

---

* Sir Michael Wood, KCMG; Former Legal Adviser, Foreign and Commonwealth Office; Senior Fellow, Lauterpacht Centre for International Law, University of Cambridge, and a member of the International Law Commission.

[1] The participants took part at the kind invitation of Steven Wheatley. Colin Warbrick spoke on 'Constitutionalism and European Court of Human Rights', David Anderson on '"Constitutionalization" and the Law of the Sea', while I spoke on 'The Security Council and the 'Constitutionalization' of International Law'. The three contributions at the conference are (as of May 2009) available on the website of the Centre for International Governance, University of Leeds.

[2] I have already set out some views on these matters in my 2006 Hersch Lauterpacht Memorial Lectures entitled 'The UN Security Council and International Law'. These are available on

K.H. Kaikobad & M. Bohlander (eds.), *International Law and Power: Perspectives on Legal Order and Justice*. Essays in Honour of Colin Warbrick, pp. 85–97.

1. Preliminary Remarks

When speaking to persons coming new to international law, particularly non-lawyers, I sometimes offer three 'health warnings.' Beware of idealists and cynics! Beware of single-issue lawyers![3] Beware of policy-driven lawyers![4] In the case of some friends and colleagues, all three warnings may be appropriate. None is needed in the case of Colin Warbrick.

I shall say just a few words about the first of these health warnings. Scepticism should not be confused with cynicism, though the two may overlap. The sceptics and the cynics were followers of different teachers in ancient Greece, and the latter may seem less admirable to the modern mind. A dictionary definition of 'sceptical' reads 'Inclined to suspend judgement, given to questioning truth of fact(s) and soundness of inference(s), critical, incredulous'; 'cynical', on the other hand, is defined as 'Like a cynic [one who sarcastically doubts human sincerity and merit], incredulous of human goodness; sneering.'[5] We all recognize the cynics when we come across them. 'Idealists', on the other hand, tend to act as though international law is a panacea that will save the planet (or at least the whale); stamp out human rights abuses; prevent war and terrorism; eliminate weapons of mass destruction; usher in an era of harmony in world trade; eliminate poverty, etc., etc. International law has, of course, a contribution to make towards each of these important aspirations, but their achievement is ultimately a matter for policy-makers. As Vaughan Lowe puts it in the concluding sentence of his *International Law*, '[t]here are many times when it is better to call upon a politician, or a priest, or a doctor, or a plumber'.[6] To overstate the role of international law can be as harmful as to understate it.

The 'idealist' approach has been around for a long time, and is not confined to (and not necessarily to be found in) those working for non-governmental organizations. Early in the twentieth century there was a strong movement among the foreign policy establishment in the United States, inspired in part by the success of the *Alabama* arbitration, that believed that war could replaced by international arbitration, that the establishment of an international court would

---

the website of the Lauterpacht Centre for International Law, University of Cambridge (and will be expanded and published as a book in due course).

3   That is, those specializing in a single field, such as the law of the sea, international environmental law, or international human rights law.

4   Such as those associated with a particular cause or the adherents of certain policy-oriented 'Schools', not least in the United States. For what seems to be a 'sceptical' view of these Schools, see J.-P. Cot, 'Tableau de la pensée juridique américaine', 110 (2006) *RGDIP* 537.

5   *Concise Oxford Dictionary.*

6   Oxford, 2007, p. 290.

herald an era of universal peace.[7] Such idealism was not confined to the New World. In 1904 the *Institut de Droit International* received the Nobel Peace Prize in recognition of its contribution to peaceful conflict resolution.

Perhaps the most influential international lawyers are the realists with a healthy dose of idealism. Sir Hersch Lauterpacht, for example, was undoubtedly imbued with a considerable degree of idealism, but at the same time was realistic as to what international law could achieve and hence not without influence in what were then such new fields as the punishment of war crimes and the prosecution of human rights.

There are two further points to make at the outset. First, the use of domestic law analogies in international law is often misleading. The 'international community' – itself a much misused term[8] – has little in common with society within a State. The Appeals Chamber of the Yugoslav Tribunal pointed out that:

> [D]omestic judicial views or approaches should be handled with the greatest caution at the international level, lest one should fail to make due allowance for the unique characteristics of international criminal proceedings,[9]

and, in rejecting a domestic judicial analogy, stated emphatically that:

> The setting is totally different in the international community. It is known *omnibus lippis et tonsoribus* that the international community lacks any central government with the attendant separation of powers and checks and balances. ... the transposition onto the international community of legal institutions, constructs

---

[7] The early movers of the American Society of International Law were mostly in this camp. See Kirgis, *The American Society of International Law's First Century 1906–2006*, Leiden, 2006, pp. 1–53. Kirgis recalls that 'the American peace movement ... gave birth to the American Society of International law' (at p. 1), and refers to '[a]rbitration as an instrument of peace – the motivating force behind the creation of the Society' (at p. 33).

[8] The ambiguous concept 'international community' appears in various contexts in international law: as 'the international community of States as a whole' in article 53 of the Vienna Convention on the Law of Treaties; and (following the language of the ICJ in *Barcelona Traction*) as 'the international community as a whole' in Articles 42 (b) and 48 (1) (b) of the ILC Articles on the Responsibility of States for Internationally Wrongful Acts: see Crawford, *The International Law Commission's Articles on State Responsibility*, Cambridge, 2002, pp. 276–280. The term is much used – or abused – by politicians, who invoke it to justify all kinds of actions: for the literature, see the works cited in the various contributions in: Byers and Nolte (eds.), *United States Hegemony and the Foundations of International Law*, Hart Publishing, Oxford/Portland, 2003; Warbrick and Tierney (eds.), *Towards an 'International Legal Community'? The Sovereignty of States and the Sovereignty of International Law*, London, 2006; and see ICJ President Guillaume's comment in his Separate Opinion in the *Arrest Warrant of 11 April 2000* case: *ICJ Reports 2002*, p. 3, at p. 43, paragraph 15.

[9] *Blaskić*, Judgment of the Appeals Chamber of 29 October 1997 on the Request of the Republic of Croatia for Review of the Decision of Trial Chamber II of 18 July 1997: IT-95-A, 110 *ILR* 688, at 697, paragraph 23.

or approaches prevailing in national law may be a source of great confusion and misapprehension.[10]

Second, it is important for international lawyers to distinguish clearly between law and policy. Lawyers may be well qualified to give views on policy in certain fields, not least on issues within the field now often referred to as 'governance', but if they do they are not advising on the law. It is obviously necessary to distinguish clearly between law and policy when facing litigation. Any court that is true to its nature will decide questions of fact and law, not policy. But even when litigation is not in prospect, an international lawyer needs to distinguish carefully (not least in his or her own mind) between the function of advising on the law and expressing views on policy. This is important for the credibility both of the lawyer and of the law. Policy advice is worth what it is worth; legal advice has a special authority precisely because it is advice on the law, and the law itself has authority.

II. 'CONSTITUTIONALISM' AND INTERNATIONAL LAW

There is an increasing literature on the 'constitutionalization' of international law.[11] By way of example, reference could be made to two recent articles focusing on the 'constitutionalization' of international law within the European Union. The first refers to three approaches to international law.[12] The Germans think of international law as a set of value norms, with the United Nations at its centre. The French model perceives it more as a means to safeguard national interests and to strengthen international influence. The British concept is shaped more by the common law approach that international law norms are developing, but do not necessarily constitute a complete system of

---

[10] Ibid, at 709–710, paragraph 40.
[11] See, for example, Walter, 'Constitutionalising (Inter)national Governance – Possibilities for and Limits to the Development of an International Criminal Law', 44 (2001) *GYIL* 192; Macdonald and Johnston (eds.), *Towards World Constitutionalism, Issues in the Legal Ordering of the World Community*, Leiden, 2005; Cass, *The Constitutionalization of the World Trade Organization; Legitimacy, Democracy, and Community in the International Trading System*, Oxford, 2005; Peters, 'Compensatory Constitutionalism: The Function and Potential of Fundamental International Norms and Structures', 19 (2006) *Leiden Journal of International Law* 579; de Wet, 'The Emergence of International and Regional Value Systems as a Manifestation of the Emerging International Constitutional Order', 19 (2006) *Leiden Journal of International Law* 611; Petersmann, 'Human Rights, Constitutionalism and the World Trade Organization: Challenges for World Trade Organization Jurisprudence and Civil Society', 19 (2006) *Leiden Journal of International Law* 633; and de Wet, 'The International Constitutional Order', 55 (2006) *ICLQ* 51.
[12] Gosalbo-Bono, 'Some Reflections on the CFSP Legal Order', 43 (2006) *CMLR* 337.

law. The second article adopts a somewhat similar approach.[13] Thus, the United Kingdom (and, according to the author, Denmark) closely follow the leading superpower. France (with support from Belgium, Luxembourg, Spain, Portugal and Greece) is more focused on building a unified Europe, thereby helping to shape international law in a more distinct European way. And a constitutionalist Germany[14] (followed by Austria, Sweden, Finland, together with The Netherlands) strives for a global legal community that frames and directs the power of all international actors alike. These are very broad generalisations, albeit perhaps not without a grain of truth – caricatures rather than reality. It seems improbable that the world can be divided up so simply, certainly not when it comes to the approaches of governments and their advisers.[15] Why, if this is true, has the United Kingdom accepted the compulsory jurisdiction of the International Court of Justice for decades,[16] whilst Germany has done so only in the last year?

Many international legal theories, including those that may be seen to fall under the heading of 'constitutionalism,' are essentially policy approaches.[17] As such they may be instructive, even at times useful, but they are policy constructs, not law. At the risk of oversimplifying, they might include the following:

(a) The idea of the *'constitutionalization'* of international law. This includes, but goes beyond, the concept of a hierarchy among international legal rules, deriving in part from widespread acceptance of the existence of *jus cogens* and the priority accorded to Charter obligations by the United Nations Charter – sometimes referred to as 'relative normativity'.[18] Constitutionalist approaches seem to be especially popular with those writing on the law of the World Trade Organisation and United Nations law. Those who adopt a 'constitutional perspective' towards the Charter, or indeed towards other areas of international law, seek to import into international affairs legal concepts from various domestic laws, while sometimes admitting that the analogy is imprecise, and that national constitu-

---

[13] von Bogdandy, 'Constitutionalism in International Law: Comment on Proposal from Germany', 47 (2006) *Harvard International Law Journal* 223.

[14] The explanation could be simply that academic international lawyers in Germany also teach constitutional law.

[15] Wood, 'A European Vision of International Law: To What End?', in Ruiz-Fabri, Jouannet and Tomkiewicz (eds.), *Proceedings of the Second Biennial Conference of the European Society of International Law*, Hart Publishing, Oxford/Portland, 2008.

[16] Wood, 'The United Kingdom's Acceptance of the Compulsory Jurisdiction of the International Court', in Fauchald, Jakhelln and Syse (eds.), *Festskrift til Carl August Fleischer Fred er ej det Bedste*, Oslo, 2006, p. 621.

[17] Scobbie, 'Wicked Heresies or Legitimate Perspectives? Theory and International Law', in Evans (ed.), *International Law* (Second edition), Oxford, 2006, p. 83.

[18] Weil, 'Towards Relative Normativity in International Law?', 77 (1983) *AJIL* 413; and Shelton, 'International Law and "Relative Normativity"', in Evans (note 17), p. 159.

tional concepts (which of course themselves vary from State to State and over time within each State) are not directly transferable to the international sphere. Often they fail to clarify in what sense they are using the word 'constitution'.[19]

(b) The less prescriptive idea of '*global administrative law*', or '*global public law*', or '*global governance.*'[20] This is a more modest approach than that of the 'constitutionalists'. 'Global administrative law ... asks whether and to what extent ideas from domestic administrative law can help us solve accountability problems in global governance. ... [i]n the circumstances of global governance, attempts at 'constitutionalising' the political order by forcing it into a coherent, unified framework are problematic as they tend to downplay the extent of legitimate diversity in the global polity. ... the shape of global administrative law is likely to be, and should be, essentially different from that of domestic administrative law.'[21]

What the proponents of this idea seem to be saying is that when international bodies engage in regulation they should (as a matter of policy) apply public law principles comparable to, though not necessarily identical to, those found in many domestic systems. And that if they do not, they may find their legitimacy lessened and run the risk that domestic courts are more ready to question what they have done.

(c) An '*international rule of law*' approach. The term 'rule of law' (*l'état de droit, Rechtsstaat*) has no fixed meaning, even at the domestic level.[22] At the international level, the term is used in a variety of contexts and with a range of meanings: see, for example, the Security Council's debates on the rule of law,[23] the numerous references in the 2005 World Summit Outcome[24] and the debate on the item 'The Rule of Law at the International and National Levels' in the Sixth (Legal) Committee of the General Assembly from 2006.[25]

---

[19] For a discussion of the term in the context of the United Nations Charter, see Crawford, 'Multilateral Rights and Obligations in International Law', 319 (2006) *RCADI* 325, at pp. 363–391; and Fox (ed.), *The Changing Constitution of the United Nations*, London, 1997.

[20] See Kingsbury, Krisch, Stewart and Wiener, 'The Emergence of Global Administrative Law', 68 (2005) *Law and Contemporary Problems* 1; (symposium with extensive bibliography); Krisch, 'The Pluralism of Global Administrative Law', 17 (2006) *EJIL* 247.

[21] Krisch (note 20), at p. 248.

[22] On the rule of law in the United Kingdom, see (with reference to the first incorporation of the concept into statute in section 1 of the Constitutional Reform Act, 2005) the Sixth Sir David Williams Lecture, entitled *The Rule of Law* given by Lord Bingham at the Law Faculty, University of Cambridge, on 17 November 2006. The annual meeting of the French Society for International Law in 2008 (Brussels/Louvain) was devoted to *L'Etat de droit en droit international*.

[23] Most recently, see the UN Secretary-General's Report, *Uniting our Strengths; Enhancing United Nations Support for the Rule of Law*, UN Doc. A/61/636-S/2006/980.

[24] UN General Assembly Resolution 60/1 of 16 September 2005.

[25] UN General Assembly Resolutions 61/39 of 4 December 2006; 62/70 of 6 December 2007 and 63/128 of 15 January 2009.

Expressions of support for 'the rule of law in international affairs' or 'the international rule of law' usually seem to mean little more than that States (and other international legal persons) should act in accordance with their obligations under international law. (This also appears to be the sense of the curious term, a 'rules-based' international society.) Sometimes 'rule of law' is used in the context of post-conflict institution-building, where it presumably has a domestic meaning. And occasionally (though largely in the literature) the term is used in its domestic sense but with reference to international bodies such as the UN Security Council.[26] Attempts have been made by some authors to see how far domestic notions of the rule of law might be applicable to international affairs, but these have not been particularly convincing – unsurprising, given the differences between society within a State and international society.

(d) And then there are a multitude of other '*values-based*' theories of international law, including those based on concepts such as 'legitimacy',[27] 'fairness'[28] 'legality'[29] and 'democracy',[30] or in the past 'world public order',[31] which likewise have but tenuous links to the actual practice of States.

At this point, it may be worth offering a word of caution about the use of language. The followers of particular theories have a tendency to create their own closed world, in which words are used with special meanings, understood only by the initiated. Terms such as 'international community'[32] and 'accountability'[33] are in vogue. Let us take, by way of example, the term 'global governance.' What does it mean, and why is it used? The word 'global' is apparently used in place of 'international' to signify that we are not only concerned with States. But then the word 'international' does not necessarily refer only to States, so

---

[26] For a critique, see H.E. (Former) Judge Rosalyn Higgins, 'The ICJ, the United Nations System, and the Rule of Law': a talk delivered at the London School of Economics, 13 November 2006 (available on the LSE website); and see her Grotius lecture delivered in Middle Temple Hall on 16 October 2007. See also Watts, 'The International Rule of Law', 36 (1993) GYIL 15.

[27] Franck, *The Power of Legitimacy Among Nations*, New York/Oxford, 1990; and see also ibid, 'The Power of Legitimacy and the Legitimacy of Power: International Law in an Age of Disequilibrium,' 100 (2006) AJIL 88.

[28] Franck, *Fairness in International Law and Institutions*, Oxford, 2005.

[29] Manusama, *The United Nations Security Council in the Post-Cold War Era Applying the Principle of Legality*, Leiden, 2006.

[30] Franck, 'The Emerging Right to Democratic Governance', 86 (1992) AJIL 46.

[31] That is to say, the New Haven School.

[32] As Warbrick has written, 'Although it is common to speak of States being members of "the international community", it is probably better to regard them as members of an international system ... which avoids misleading assumptions about quite what the values and processes of this international community might be': see 'States and Recognition in International Law', in Evans (note 17), p. 217, at p. 223.

[33] See 'Accountability of International Organizations, Final Report', in International Law Association, *Report of the Seventy-first Conference: Berlin 2004*, London, 2004, pp. 164–234.

why choose a different word? 'Governance' is a portmanteau word that is often intended to mean something more than 'government', but what?[34]

III. 'CONSTITUTIONALISM', THE UNITED NATIONS CHARTER AND THE SECURITY COUNCIL

Much of the literature on the 'constitutionalization' of international law concerns the United Nations Charter and Security Council. As examples of the 'constitutionalist' approach, one could mention Professors Fassbender[35] and de Wet.[36] Fassbender seeks to portray the United Nations Charter as 'the constitution of the international community'. De Wet, on the other and, in an article based on her inaugural lecture as Professor of International Constitutional Law at the University of Amsterdam, 'argues the case for an emerging constitutional order consisting of an international community, an international value system and rudimentary structures for its enforcement', and refers to 'an embryonic international constitutional order with the United Nations Charter as the main connecting factor'.[37] On the more sceptical (pragmatic and practical) side, mention should be made of Professor Szurek.[38] The 'constitutionalist' approach may even become damaging; it risks becoming part of what has been termed the 'demonisation' of the Security Council.[39] Much that is currently written about the Council is theoretical, negative, misleading or just plain wrong. The language is often intemperate.[40] Over

---

[34] The Centre for International Governance, University of Leeds, has happily retained the word 'international'; perhaps its use of the term 'governance' is forgivable. The term 'world government' may well be one to avoid.

[35] See 'The United Nations Charter As Constitution of The International Community', 36 (1998) *Columbia Journal of Transnational Law* 529; and *UN Security Council Reform and the Right of Veto A Constitutional Perspective*, The Hague, 1998.

[36] *The Chapter VII Powers of the UN Security Council*, Hart Publishing, Oxford/Portland, 2004.

[37] De Wet, The International Constitutional Order (note 11), p. 56.

[38] 'La Charte des Nations Unies: Constitution Mondiale?,' in Cot, Pellet and Forteau, *La Charte des Nations Unies: Commentaire article par article* (Third edition), Paris, 2005, at pp. 29–68; Crawford, 'Multilateral Rights and Obligations in International Law', 319 (2006) *RCADI* 325, at pp. 363–391; and generally see Fox (note 19).

[39] The title of my talk to the Swedish Branch of the International Law Association, Stockholm, on 10 May 2004.

[40] See, by way of recent examples (in an otherwise generally thoughtful piece), the reference to Security Council resolution 1540 (2004) as 'a legal travesty' and 'null and void of legal effect', and to its adoption as 'the dangerous exercise of power wielded by the Council, out of all step with both the spirit and letter of the Charter': see Joyner, 'Non-Proliferation Law and the United Nations System: Resolution 1540 and the Limits of the Power of the Security Council', 20 (2007) *Leiden Journal of International Law* 489, at p. 490, p. 515 and p. 518.

the longer term, this may tend to sap the Council's effectiveness as a central instrument of multilateralism. Among the criticisms are the following:

(a) It is said that the Council routinely exceeds its Charter powers and acts *ultra vires*. It determines threats to the peace where there are none, and is beginning to act like a 'super-legislature' or a world government. It pays no attention to the limitations on its powers laid down by the Charter. It does not act in accordance with the Purposes and Principles of the United Nations; it ignores *jus cogens*; it ignores human rights.

(b) It is said that the Council imposes impossible obligations on States, which run counter to their constitutional and/or legal traditions and the implementation of which gives rise to real internal difficulties (political, judicial, human rights).

(c) It is said that the Council is not subject to oversight or control (whether judicial or otherwise); it lacks accountability.

The *Charter of the United Nations* is a treaty between States, a multilateral treaty with (as of May 2009) 192 parties. The parties include virtually all States, a relatively recent state of affairs. It is the constituent instrument (that is to say, constitution) of the organisation known as the United Nations, and as such sets out the composition and powers of its principal organs. The International Court of Justice may have referred to the Charter of the United Nations as a constitution in the *Conditions of Admission* case.[41] But that does not mean that the Charter has the same characteristics as a national constitution.[42] The Charter also embodies certain principles of international law, including those on the peaceful settlement of disputes and the use of force, as well as the right of self-defence. And (and this may be its chief "constitutional" element) it provides in Article 103 that in the event of a conflict between obligations under the Charter and obligations under any other international agreement, the obligations under the Charter prevail.

---

[41] The Court said that '[t]o ascertain whether an organ has freedom of choice for its decisions, reference must be made to its constitution': see *Conditions of Admission of a State to Membership in the United Nations (Article 4 of the Charter)*, Advisory Opinion of 28 May 1948, *ICJ Reports 1948*, p. 56, at p. 64.

[42] The constituent instruments of some international organisations are entitled 'Constitution', but they are no different in nature from constituent instruments not so named. The debate over the title of the so-called European Constitution (now overtaken) was essentially political. It had little to do with law. In the end the document was formally called 'Treaty establishing a Constitution for Europe', but often referred to as the 'Constitutional Treaty' or 'European Constitution'. The word 'Constitution' has been studiously avoided in the new draft Treaty which was adopted at an Intergovernmental Conference meeting in Lisbon on 13 December 2007. This is entitled 'Treaty amending the Treaty on European Union and the Treaty establishing the European Community' (Document CIG 1/1/07, REV.1).

None of this makes the Charter a 'constitution of the international community'.[43] The word 'constitution' has no particular meaning in international law.[44] As Colin Warbrick expressed it in his contribution to the Leeds conference, 'We have to put up with a rather messy, plural international order.'[45]

It has occasionally been suggested that the Charter should be interpreted in the same way as a national constitution. Thus, in his essay on the interpretation of the Charter in the Simma Commentary (2002), Ress asserts that 'for the normative side of the founding treaty, the Charter and the organizational law derived from it (secondary law), the applicable parallelism can only be found in domestic public law, e.g. the constitutional and administrative law of the member States'. This must be done, he says, 'because of its similarity to national constitutional law. The general principles of law that are applied to the law of international organizations will therefore be primarily those originating in public law'. He cites in support Zemanek, 1964. And he later explains: 'Of special significance in the interpretation of the Charter [is] the object and purpose of this "constitution for the international society".'[46] Yet Conforti is surely right when he warns that 'extreme caution must be used in transferring onto the plane of the United Nations and international law doctrines that belong to domestic constitutional law'.[47]

I turn now to the *Security Council*, which is the principal organ of the United Nations upon which, in order to ensure prompt and effective action, the Members of the Organisation have conferred primary responsibility for the maintenance of international peace and security. Its powers and functions are those set out in the Charter, as developed in practice. It has, in particular, the power to make recommendations, and to adopt decisions binding on the Members of the United Nations.[48]

Some seek to analyse the Council in terms of the separation of powers at the national level, executive, legislative, or judicial. As already suggested, the use of domestic law analogies in international law is often misleading. It is not helpful

---

[43] Fassbender (note 35). As early as the 1940s, 'Pollux' referred to the UN Charter as 'the Constitution of a World Society': see 'The Interpretation of the Charter', 23 (1946) *BYIL* 54, at p. 63.

[44] In fact, even within a particular national legal system, the term is used in many different contexts: the basic document of a barristers' chambers or a golf club, for example.

[45] *Supra* (note 2).

[46] Simma (ed.), *The Charter of the United Nations: A Commentary* (Second edition), Oxford, 2002, pp. 13–32, at p. 15 and p. 30.

[47] Conforti, *The Law and Practice of the United Nations* (Third edition), The Hague, 2005, p. 13.

[48] For recent works on the Security Council see Malone (ed.), *The United Nations Security Council: From the Cold War to the 21st Century*, Boulder, Colorado; Matheson, *Council Unbound The Growth of UN Decision Making on Conflict and Postconflict Issues after the Cold War*, Washington, DC, 2006; and Luck, *UN Security Council: Practice and Promise*, London, 2006.

to seek to capture the nature of the Council in a single term, especially one derived from domestic systems. Those who seek to do so often go on to deduce further legal or political consequences: that as a legislature it lacks democratic legitimacy; and that as a quasi-judicial body it should follow certain 'rule of law' principles and be subject to judicial review. But each of these lines of argument starts from a false premise.

Especially in the early days, the Council was referred to as the 'executive organ' of the United Nations. Indeed, in early drafts it was referred to as the Executive Council. To the extent that the Council acts like an executive, this is in only one area of United Nations activity (albeit an important area), the maintenance of international peace and security. In this it is unlike organs of limited membership in some other international organisations, which do have general executive powers between meetings of the plenary organ.

A question often asked nowadays is whether the Council may act as a legislature or, as it has been put, as a 'global legislator'.[49] Here, too, the domestic law analogy is not helpful. The question itself is somewhat abstract. It all depends what is meant by 'legislature'.[50] When criticisms are made of the Council 'legislating' instead of taking specific decisions for specific situations, the real question is whether the mandatory decisions contained in Security Council resolution 1373 (2001) on terrorism, or those in Security Council resolution 1540 (2004) on non-proliferation, are within the powers of the Council, and thus lawfully adopted, or not?

Both resolution 1373 (2001) and resolution 1540 (2004) were, as it happens, adopted unanimously and have been repeatedly reaffirmed. No State has seriously suggested that resolution 1373 (2001) was not lawfully adopted. Such concern as was expressed about resolution 1540 (2004) seems mostly to have been concerned with policy question: 'Should the Council so act?', not, 'Is it within the Council's powers so to act?' In the case of both resolutions,

---

[49] Rosand, 'The Security Council as "Global Legislator": *Ultra Vires* or *Ultra* Innovative?', 28 (2005) *Fordham International Law Journal* 101.

[50] As Matheson says: '[T]he Council does exercise functions that are normally thought of as "legislative" in character, such as imposing legal obligations and creating subordinate bodies with legal authority. But the Council's jurisdiction is limited to actual threats to the peace, and while such threats can be generic in character rather than limited to specific situations, the Council does not have a mandate to address the broad range of international problems that do not pose such a threat. Nor would States accept that the Council should supersede the treaty-making process as the primary creator of legal obligations, as the debate over the Council's actions on WMD proliferation has shown. States will assent to the imposition of obligations where peace and security requires it, but they will otherwise insist on retaining the right to accept or reject such obligations and to participate in their formulation': *supra* (note 48), pp. 235–236.

virtually all States are doing their best to comply. In the General Assembly's Counter-Terrorism Strategy of 2006, the Members of the United Nations all resolved to 'implement all Security Council resolutions related to international terrorism and to cooperate fully with the counter-terrorism subsidiary bodies of the Security Council in the fulfilment of their tasks'.[51] There is no real support in State practice for those who have suggested that elements of these two resolutions were *ultra vires*, quite the contrary.

It has further been suggested that 'there have been a number of occasions on which ... the Security Council has framed its resolutions ... in language resembling a judicial determination of the law and of the legal consequences said to flow from the conduct of the State that is arraigned', and that there is a line to be drawn, 'admittedly imprecise', between 'prescriptions of conduct that are directly and immediately related to the termination of the impugned conduct ... and those findings that ... have a general and long-term legal impact that goes beyond the immediate needs of the situation'. The main conclusion drawn is to suggest that 'quasi-judicial decisions' should be subject to some kind of judicial review.[52]

Yet nothing in the practice of the Council suggests a distinction between two categories of decisions: prescriptions of conduct and findings with a general and long-term impact. The Council's action for the maintenance of international peace and security is no longer (if it ever was) confined to immediate or short- or medium-term steps to restore peace. Much of what it does today is long-term: dispute resolution; peace-keeping; peace-building. It may deploy a wide range of measures for the peaceful settlement of disputes and the investigation of situations. If it considers it necessary to pronounce upon a legal matter, there is no basis in the Charter for saying that to do so is not within its competence. This is reflected in the established practice of the Council, for example when it calls for the non-recognition of a situation in order to maintain or restore international peace and security, as in the cases of the South African 'homelands' and the 'Turkish Republic of Northern Cyprus.'

IV. CONCLUSION

What conclusion may be drawn as regards the approaches outlined earlier in this article: the idea of the 'constitutionalization' of international law; the less prescriptive idea of 'global administrative law'; an 'international rule of law'

---

[51] General Assembly Resolution 60/288 of 20 September 2006, Annex, paragraph 2(c).
[52] E. Lauterpacht, *Aspects of the Administration of International Justice*, Cambridge, 1991, pp. 37–48.

approach; and various other 'values-based' approaches, including those based on concepts such as fairness and democracy?

It is submitted that these are each in reality policy proscriptions, which may or may not be reflected in the practice of States and international organisations. Of course, from a policy viewpoint, there is no doubt much that international lawyers may learn from private (and public) law analogies. But it is a mistake, leading to something of a dead-end, to suppose that the various constitutional or public law doctrines found in particular domestic legal systems can be transposed directly into the international legal system. Only to the extent that express provision is made to this effect – and that is still rare – can it be said that international law has been 'constitutionalized'.

Chapter Five

The Nature of State Obligations in Relation to Child Labour: Choosing Prosecution over Protection

Holly Cullen[*]

I. INTRODUCTION

In the past decade, there has been a significant expansion of international legal measures designed to address the problems of exploitative child labour.[1] During that time, there has been a shift of emphasis,[2] with a move towards more complex and detailed standards. Whereas the International Labour Organisation (ILO) Convention No. 138 of 1973 focussed on the setting of minimum ages for entry into employment, more recent standards focus on removing children from harmful and exploitative labour. Not surprisingly, this change of focus has led to child labour issues being linked to a number of other children's rights issues, notably trafficking of children and the use of child soldiers.[3]

Most State obligations in relation to child labour are positive obligations.[4] Even the most basic obligation, to bring State law into line with international

---

[*] Reader in Law, School of Law, University of Durham.
[1] For a review of the international law measures on child labour, see Cullen, 'Child Labor Standards: From Treaties to Labels', in Weston, (ed.), *Child Labor and Human Rights: Making Children Matter*, Boulder, Colorado, 2005, pp. 87–115 (hereinafter referred to as Cullen, 'Treaties').
[2] This shift probably has its roots in the adoption of the Convention of the Rights of the Child in 1989, but can be seen most clearly with the ILO's establishment of the International Programme on the Elimination of Child Labour (IPEC) in 1992.
[3] See Cullen, 'Treaties' (note 1).
[4] The inspiration for this chapter lies in Professor Colin Warbrick's interest in the development of positive obligations under the ECHR for which see ibid, notably 'The Structure of Article 8', 1 (1998) *EHRLR* 32.

K.H. Kaikobad & M. Bohlander (eds.), *International Law and Power: Perspectives on Legal Order and Justice*. Essays in Honour of Colin Warbrick, pp. 99–123.

obligations, goes far beyond an obligation of non-interference. There are still examples of violations of negative obligations. States themselves still use child labour, most obviously where they recruit children under 18 as soldiers.[5] In some cases, as in Myanmar's use of forced labour, child labour of other kinds is used by States.[6] However, there is a much greater emphasis in recent developments in child labour on positive obligations.

New measures addressing issues of child labour have imposed new positive obligations on States. Whereas the obligations under ILO Conventions up to and including Convention No. 138 emphasised the creation of a legislative framework setting out minimum ages for employment, new treaties, including the ILO's Convention No. 182 of 1999 on the worst forms of child labour, require a wider range of actions by States parties. These include legislative changes, labour inspection, criminal prosecutions of violators and protective measures for children caught up in exploitative child labour. However, States seem to have made a stronger commitment to addressing the criminal law aspects of child labour than the protective ones. This is reinforced primarily by the greater detail in which the criminal law obligations are drafted in the relevant treaties, including treaties on trafficking in persons, commercial sexual exploitation of children and child soldiers. It has also been argued that the approach of international human rights law generally, and the European Court of Human Rights in particular, privileges criminal law responses to human rights violations.[7] The highly detailed obligations in relation to the prosecution of those who exploit child labour may be contrasted with the vagueness of the obligations of States to protect the victims of abusive child labour. These obligations are relatively under-developed, and States have demonstrated some resistance to such obligations, for example, to provide residence rights for trafficked children.[8] Arguably, protective measures for exploited children

---

[5] See Coalition to Stop the Use of Child Soldiers, *Global Report 2008*, London, pp. 389–409.

[6] Cullen, *The Role of International Law in the Elimination of Child Labour*, Leiden, 2007, pp. 26–29 (hereinafter referred to as Cullen, *International Law*).

[7] Pitea, 'Rape as a Human Rights Violation and a Criminal Offence: The European Court's Judgment in *M. C. v. Bulgaria*', 3 (2005) *Journal of International Criminal Justice* 447.

[8] The United Kingdom Government has only belatedly accepted the need for even limited residence rights. See 'Trafficking Victims to be Granted 30-day Stay', *The Guardian*, 23 March 2007: http://www.guardian.co.uk/society/2007/mar/23/asylum.humanrights. However, NGOs such as ECPAT UK continue to criticise the United Kingdom for refusing to grant trafficked children permanent residence rights. This policy is also reflected in its reservation to the CRC, which states that 'The United Kingdom reserves the right to apply such legislation, in so far as it relates to the entry into, stay in and departure from the United Kingdom of those who do not have the right under the law of the United Kingdom to enter and remain in the United Kingdom, and to the acquisition and possession of citizenship, as it may deem necessary from time to time.' See http://www.ohchr.org/english/bodies/ratification/11.htm#reservations.

should come first, and the prosecution of offenders should follow afterwards, with protective measures for children involved in these criminal proceedings as victims and witnesses as an integral part of proceedings. However, States seem to have begun with the need to prosecute and have seen protective measures as subsidiary. There are some notable exceptions in the practice of the International Criminal Court and in recent Council of Europe standards, but the trend is still to choose prosecution over protection as the number one priority in addressing exploitative child labour.

II. OVERVIEW OF INTERNATIONAL LEGAL MEASURES ON CHILD LABOUR

All norms in relation to child labour can be implied from the statement in Article 32(1) of the Convention on the Rights of the Child (CRC), repeating the provisions of Article 10(3) of the International Covenant on Economic, Social and Cultural Rights (ICESCR): 'States Parties recognize the right of the child to be protected from economic exploitation and from performing any work that is likely to be hazardous or to interfere with the child's education, or to be harmful to the child's health or physical, mental, spiritual, moral or social development.' The protection from economic exploitation is the essence of the right. All other formulations are elaborations of, or extrapolations, from this principle.

This raises the question of why there has been a proliferation of international legal standards relating to different aspects of child labour. One key reason is that the economic exploitation of child labour is often linked to other forms of exploitation and abuse experienced by children: slavery-like practices including bonded labour, child trafficking, commercial sexual and criminal exploitation of children, the use of child soldiers, health and environmental hazards faced by child workers. Many of these issues, it was decided by the ILO, amounted to the worst forms of child labour, and are directly prohibited by Convention No. 182. This is true of slavery-like practices, trafficking, commercial sexual and criminal exploitation and child soldiers, which are mentioned in Article 3, paragraphs (a), (b) and (c) of Convention No. 182:

> For the purposes of this Convention, the term "the worst forms of child labour" comprises:
>
> (a) all forms of slavery or practices similar to slavery, such as the sale and trafficking of children, debt bondage and serfdom and forced or compulsory labour, including forced or compulsory recruitment of children for use in armed conflict;
> (b) the use, procuring or offering of a child for prostitution, for the production of pornography or for pornographic performances;
> (c) the use, procuring or offering of a child for illicit activities, in particular for the production and trafficking of drugs as defined in the relevant international treaties.

Other abusive forms of child labour are arguably covered by Article 3(d), which includes as worst forms of child labour, 'work which, by its nature or the circumstances in which it is carried out, is likely to harm the health, safety or morals of children'. This could easily be understood as covering health and environmental hazards, and possibly developmental harms such as separation from families or denial of education.[9] Articles 3 and 4 of Recommendation No. 190 which accompanies Convention No. 182 support an interpretation of Article 3(d) of the Convention which would include physical and moral harms and at least some developmental harm such as separation from families.

The idea of child labour being an issue of exploitation or abuse rather than simply an issue of underage working emerged in the decade after the adoption of the CRC. Up to this point, despite the existence of Article 10(3) ICESCR which identifies the concept of economic exploitation, the most frequently-mentioned international law standards on child labour were those of the ILO, which concentrated on setting minimum ages for employment.[10] Convention No. 138 of 1973 was the crystallisation of the ILO's approach.[11] Its general rule, setting the minimum age for employment at around the school leaving age, was accompanied by two categories of exception. First was 'light work', which was permissible at a younger age if it did not interfere with education. Second was 'hazardous work', which was only permissible at an older minimum age, with appropriate safety precautions.

Article 32 CRC made the economic exploitation approach to child labour more prominent. The CRC has received near-universal ratification, and few States have entered reservations to Article 32.[12] Not long after the coming into force of the CRC, in 1992, the ILO established its International Programme on the Elimination of Child Labour (IPEC). Under the auspices of IPEC, better statistical research into child labour was conducted, and projects were undertaken in a wide range of countries with child labour problems. IPEC's approach to understanding child labour, by distinguishing between child work (benign) and child labour (harmful), is more consistent with Article 32 CRC's

---

[9] Cullen, *International Law* (note 6), p. 140 and pp. 149–152. On the difficulties in determining what Article 3(d) is meant to cover, see Ennew, Myers and Plateau, 'Defining Child Labor as if Human Rights Really Matter', in Weston (note 2), p. 27, at pp. 41–43.

[10] Cullen, Treaties (note 1).

[11] For an extended critique of this treaty as setting inappropriate and unrealistic standards, see Creighton, 'Combating Child Labor: The Role of International Labor Standards', 18 (1997) *Comparative Labor Law Journal* 362.

[12] All States except the United States of America and Somalia have ratified the CRC, which has 193 States parties: http://www.ohchr.org/english/bodies/ratification/11.htm. Although many States have ratified subject to wide-ranging reservations, few States have made reservations in relation to Article 32 CRC: see Cullen, *International Law* (note 6) p. 176.

emphasis on exploitation than with the then-existing body of ILO standards.[13] Child labour thereby became linked not merely with economic activity by children, but with economic activity where there was an additional element of abuse or exploitation. This thinking shaped the drafting of ILO Convention No. 182, which ultimately focussed on the worst forms of child labour, obliging States to eliminate these in respect of all children, defined, as in the CRC, as persons under 18.

While it is difficult to say exactly how much of the ILO's activities in the area of child labour have influenced the drafting of other international standards, or were themselves influenced by those processes,[14] it is striking how the priorities of Convention No. 182 reflect those of the international community at large at the turn of the millennium. In particular, the two Optional Protocols to the CRC elaborate on two of the worst forms of child labour set out in Article 3 of Convention No. 182. The Optional Protocol on Children in Armed Conflict goes beyond Convention No. 182 by addressing not only forced and compulsory recruitment, but also voluntary recruitment and recruitment by non-State armed forces. Under this Optional Protocol, States may not:

(a) allow children under 18 to take direct part in hostilities;[15]
(b) engage in forced or compulsory recruitment of children under 18;[16]
(c) allow non-state forces to use or recruit children under 18.[17]

They must also set a minimum age for voluntary recruitment which is higher than 15, the minimum age set by Article 38 CRC.[18] Where the minimum age is less than 18, there must be safeguards to ensure that recruitment is genuinely voluntary and subject to informed consent from parents.

The Optional Protocol on the Sale of Children, Child Prostitution and Child Pornography encompasses many of the issues addressed by the ILO, namely trafficking, slavery-like practices (in the context of sexual exploitation) and commercial sexual exploitation of children. It calls on States to prohibit the sale of children, the use of children in pornography and in prostitution. In particular, it is worth noting that the Optional Protocol prohibits the sale of children for a variety of purposes, not just for sexual exploitation. Sale for the purpose of sale of organs or for forced labour is also prohibited.[19]

---

[13] International Labour Organisation, *Child Labour: Targeting the Intolerable*, Geneva, 1996.
[14] Cullen, Treaties (note 1).
[15] Article 1 of the Optional Protocol on Children in Armed Conflict.
[16] Article 2, ibid.
[17] Article 4, ibid.
[18] Article 3, ibid.
[19] Article 3 of the Optional Protocol on the Sale of Children, Child Prostitution and Child Pornography.

The Council of Europe Convention on the Protection of Children Against Sexual Exploitation and Sexual Abuse, is intended to elaborate on the standards in the above-mentioned CRC Optional Protocol.[20] It deals with the prevention of sexual exploitation and abuse of children, the protection of victims and the definition and prosecution of offences. It goes beyond the CRC Optional Protocol or ILO Convention No. 182 as it calls on States to criminalise all forms of sexual abuse, even within families, without the link to some form of economic exploitation. As such, it addresses not only child labour issues but also other forms of human rights violations.

Trafficking of children is also addressed in certain new United Nations and regional treaties. The United Nations Protocol to Suppress and Punish Trafficking in Persons, Especially Women and Children, supplementing the United Nations Convention against Transnational Organized Crime[21] defines trafficking of children as including any act of 'recruitment, transportation, transfer, harbouring or receipt of a child for the purpose of exploitation', regardless of the presence of coercion, abuse or fraud, all of which are necessary to establish trafficking where the person trafficked is an adult. As with the CRC Optional Protocol, the forms of exploitation covered include prostitution, slavery-like practices (which arguably includes all forms of forced labour)[22] or the removal of organs.

Regional measures on trafficking have also been adopted, particularly in Europe.[23] The Council of Europe Convention on Action against Trafficking in Human Beings,[24] follows the broad outlines of the United Nations Trafficking

---

[20] CETS No. 201; opened for signature on 12 July 2007, Article 42. The Convention is not yet in force, as it needs five ratifications, of which at least three must be Council of Europe Member States (Article 45(3)). Article 45(1) states that the Convention is open for signature by Council of Europe Member States and by non-member States which participated in its drafting, and by the European Community.

[21] A/RES/55/25, Annex II, entered into force on 25 December 2003.

[22] See Cullen, *International Law* (note 6) pp. 23–26.

[23] Regional treaties outside Europe include: (1) the Inter-American Convention on International Traffic in Minors, adopted at Mexico City, 18 March 1994, at the Fifth Inter-American Specialized Conference on Private International Law, OAS Treaty Series, No. 79. The Convention entered into force on 15 August 1997. The text of the Convention is available at: http://www.oas.org/juridico/english/Treaties/b-57.html; (2) South Asian Association for Regional Cooperation Convention on Preventing and Combating Trafficking in Women and Children; opened for signature on 5 January 2002: published on the website of the Coalition Against Trafficking in Women: http://action.web.ca/home/catw/readingroom.shtml?sh_itm =996380b3c1b538862ddaacced30ea5f4.

[24] Council of Europe, Convention on Action against Trafficking in Human Beings, CETS 185. This treaty came into force on 1 February 2008: see Council of Europe, Opening Address by Maud de Boer-Buquicchio, Deputy Secretary General of the Council of Europe at the 28th Conference of European Ministers of Justice, 'Emerging Issues of Access to Justice for Vulnerable Groups, in Particular Migrants and Asylum Seekers and Children, including Children as

Protocol, but provides stronger protection to victims in several areas.[25] In 1997 and 2007, the EU adopted measures concerning trafficking.[26] The more recent measure (2007), like the Council of Europe Convention, follows the United Nations Trafficking Protocol, particularly in its definition of trafficking. The 1997 measure covers both trafficking and sexual exploitation of children and is still in force in respect of sexual exploitation issues. It was followed in 2003 by a Council Framework Decision to combat sexual exploitation of children and child pornography.[27] The Framework Decision was influenced by the CRC Optional Protocol on the Sale of Children, Child Prostitution and Child Pornography and follows the provisions of the Council of Europe's Cybercrime Convention.[28]

This overview of international standards demonstrates the consensus which has emerged concerning child labour. It is now associated with other forms of child abuse and exploitation. The types of child labour which States have united to prohibit primarily lie in the fields of slavery-like practices, trafficking, commercial sexual exploitation and the recruitment and use of child soldiers. It is not surprising that the nature of State obligations in this area has moved strongly towards positive obligations. However, it is important to evaluate the content of these positive obligations which are often set out in detail in the relevant international instruments. I will now proceed to discuss two key areas of State obligations. The first is the set of obligations which have effective criminal law measures, including obligations to establish jurisdiction over crimes committed outside the State's territory in some cases, and the obligation of international co-operation in the investigation and prosecution of crimes involving these forms of child labour. The second is the set of obligations to protect children

---

Perpetrators of Crime', 25 October 2007: http://www.coe.int/t/dc/press/news/20071025_sga
_EN.asp? For a review of the background and contents of the Convention, see Sembacher, 'The Council of Europe Convention on Action Against Trafficking in Human Beings', 14 (2005–2006) *Tulane Journal of International and Comparative Law* 435.

[25] Sembacher (note 24), p. 440.

[26] Council Joint Action 97/154/JHA of 24 February 1997 concerning action to combat trafficking in human beings and sexual exploitation of children: OJ 1997 No. L 63/2, 4 March 1997; and Council Framework Decision 2002/629/JHA of 19 July 2002: OJ 2002 No. L 203/1, 1 August 2002.

[27] 2004/68/JHA of 22 December 2003: OJ 2004 No. L 13/44, 20 January 2004. The implementation deadline was 20 January 2006. This supplements the earlier Decision to combat child pornography on the Internet: Council Decision 2000/375/JHA of 29 May 2000: OJ 2000 No. L 138/1, 9 June 2000.

[28] Convention on Cybercrime, CETS 185; adopted 23 November 2001; entered into force 1 July 2004. For a general review to the background and contents of the treaty, see Oddis, 'Combating Child Pornography on the Internet: The Council of Europe's Convention on Cybercrime', 16 (2002) *Temple Journal of International and Comparative Law* 477.

who have been victims of abusive child labour, including obligations to provide asylum or residence to such children, to provide rehabilitation measures and to provide compensation or civil remedies.

iii. The Obligation to Prosecute Crimes Involving Exploitative Child Labour

As is evident from the review of international law standards above, a major concern of the international community over the past decade has been the trafficking of children. This has been addressed largely through the elaboration of obligations to establish crimes in relation to trafficking and to investigate and prosecute these criminal offences. The same is true in relation to the recruitment and use of child soldiers and the commercial sexual exploitation of children. In addition to this, the European Court of Human Rights has read in *Siliadin v. France*[29] a positive obligation on States to take effective criminal law proceedings against those who use forced child labour.

1. *The Obligation to Create Offences in Domestic Law*

The following are the offences which States must create under national criminal law relating to child labour issues:

A. Child Prostitution:
  (i) Articles 3(b) and 7(1) of ILO Convention No. 182;
  (ii) Article 12(b) of Recommendation No. 190;
  (iii) Article 3(1)(b) of the CRC Optional Protocol;
  (iv) Article 19 of Council of Europe Convention on Sexual Exploitation and Abuse;
  (v) Article 7(1)(g) of the ICC Statute (measures not exclusively focussing on children which could also apply to child prostitution); and
  (vi) Article 2 of Council Framework Decision 2004/68/JHA.

B. Child Pornography
  (i) Articles 3(b) and 7(1) of ILO Convention No. 182;
  (ii) Article 12(b) of Recommendation No. 190;
  (iii) Article 3(1)(c) of the CRC Optional Protocol;
  (iv) Articles 20 and 21 (and some aspects of Articles 22, on the corruption of children, and Article 23, the solicitation of children for sexual purposes) of the Council of Europe Convention on Sexual Exploitation and Abuse;

---

[29] 43 (2006) *EHRR* 16; noted by Cullen: '*Siliadin v. France*: Positive Obligations under Article 4 of the European Convention on Human Rights', 6 (2006) *Human Rights Law Review* 585.

    (v) Article 9 of the Council of Europe Cybercrime Convention;[30] and
    (vi) Article 3 of Council Framework Decision 2004/68/JHA;

C. Trafficking of Children
    (i) Article 3(1)(b) of the CRC Optional Protocol;
    (ii) Articles 3 and 5 of the UN Trafficking Protocol;
    (iii) Articles 18 to 21 of the Council of Europe Trafficking Convention; and
    (iv) Articles 1 and 2 of Council Framework Decision 2002/629/JHA.

D. Recruitment and Use of Child Soldiers
    (i) Articles 3(a) and 7(1) of ILO Convention No. 182;
    (ii) Article 12(a) of Recommendation No. 190;
    (iii) Article 8(2)(b)(xxvi) and 8(2)(e)(vii) ICC Statute;[31]
    (iv) Articles 1, 2 and 4(1) and (2) of the CRC Optional Protocol;[32] and
    (v) the recruitment of children under 15 is also recognised as a crime at
        customary international law as confirmed by the Special Court for Sierra
        Leone in *Prosecutor v. Norman*.[33]

E. Child Slavery and Forced Labour
    (i) Articles 3(a) and 7(1) of ILO Convention No. 182
    (ii) Article 12(a) of Recommendation No. 190;
    (iii) Article 7(1)(c) of the ICC Statute; and
    (iv) Article 4 of the ECHR, as interpreted by the European Court of Human
        Rights in *Siliadin v. France*.

F. Use of Children in Illicit Activities
    (i) Article 3(c) and 7(1) of ILO Convention No. 182; and
    (ii) Article 12(c) of Recommendation No. 190.

---

[30] Although Article 42 of the Convention sets strict limits on which provisions may be the subject of reservations by States, under Article 9 (4) States may refuse to criminalise some behaviour covered by Article 9: see Oddis (note 28), p. 503, and pp. 505–507.

[31] The elements of these crimes were elaborated in the decision of the Pre-Trial Chamber in *Prosecutor v. Thomas Lubanga Dyilo*, ICC-01/04–01/06, 29 January 2007; appeal dismissed by the Appeals Chamber, ICC-01/04–01/06 0A8, 13 June 2007. See comment by Happold, '*Prosecutor v. Thomas Lubanga*, Decision of Pre-Trial Chamber I of the International Criminal Court, 29 January 2007', 56 (2007) *ICLQ* 713.

[32] Although only Article 4 specifically mentioned the need for criminal legislation, in relation to the recruitment of children under 18 by non-State forces, the Committee on the Rights of the Child requests information about the criminal legislation on the prohibitions in Articles 1 and 2 as well: see 'Revised Guidelines on Initial Reports to be Submitted by States Parties under Article 8, Paragraph 1 of the Optional Protocol to the Convention on the Rights of the Child on Involvement of Children in Armed Conflict', September 2007, http://www.ohchr.org/english/bodies/crc/docs/AdvanceVersions/guidelinesopac.doc.

[33] *Prosecutor v. Sam Hinga Norman, Decision on Preliminary Motion Based on Lack of Jurisdiction (Child Recruitment)*, Case No. SCSL-2004-14-AR72(E), 31 May 2004, paragraphs 17–24. This decision is extensively criticised by Happold, *Child Soldiers and International Law*, Manchester, 2005, particularly at pp. 131–132.

In general, international treaties depict children as victims to be protected, even where they may have committed offences themselves. Article 26 of the Council of Europe Trafficking Convention explicitly requires States to refrain from prosecuting victims of trafficking, although this applies to all victims, not just children. Article 26 of the ICC Statute excludes jurisdiction over offences committed by child soldiers, requiring that the accused must have been at least 18 at the time the offence was committed.[34] However, nothing in international law prevents States from prosecuting children for international crimes where the State in question can establish jurisdiction over the crime.[35]

The Council of Europe Trafficking Convention introduces a number of innovations, notably an explicit obligation to establish corporate liability for the offences contained therein.[36] It also goes into greater detail than most concerning sanctions,[37] and sets out that where children are trafficked, this is to be seen as an aggravating factor.[38]

As noted above, the European Court of Human Rights has interpreted Article 4 of ECHR, which prohibits slavery, servitude and forced labour, as imposing positive obligations on States to have effective criminal law to combat these human rights violations. In *Siliadin v. France*,[39] a girl had been brought from Togo to France under false pretences and was used for forced domestic labour. She had entered France on a tourist visa and the persons who employed her confiscated her passport and threatened to have her deported if she did not comply with their wishes. After escaping from her situation, and informing the authorities, the couple for whom she had been working were unsuccessfully prosecuted. The European Court of Human Rights determined that this was because of inadequate criminal legislation in France and thereby found that France had violated its positive obligations under Article 4, particularly because slavery and related acts were not explicitly made offences under the Criminal Code. The Court relied heavily on recent international developments to justify its finding, particularly the Council of Europe Trafficking Convention.

---

[34] On the other hand, both the Courts of Sierra Leone and Rwanda allow for the prosecution of older children, although in practice no prosecutions have occurred: Cullen, *International Law* (note 6), p. 110.

[35] Cullen, *International Law* (note 6), pp. 109–110, noting in particular the detention of children at Guantanamo Bay.

[36] Article 22. This is also followed in the other relevant Council of Europe treaties, the Cybercrime Convention and the Convention against Sexual Exploitation and Abuse of Children.

[37] Articles 23, 24 and 25.

[38] Article 24(b).

[39] *Supra* (note 29).

2. The Obligation to Establish Jurisdiction over Offences Involving Exploitative Child Labour

One of the most significant barriers to successful prosecution of offences relating to exploitative child labour is the establishment of jurisdiction where the offence did not occur in the State which seeks to prosecute. There is a need for extraterritorial jurisdiction, particularly in trafficking cases, sex tourism, and even in relation to recruitment of child soldiers, as former child soldiers will often end up in States other than that of the conflict in which they participated. Increasingly, States provide for jurisdiction based on the nationality of the accused as well as on the basis of the territory on which the offence was committed.[40] The Torture Convention probably represents the high water mark of obliging States to take jurisdiction over crimes outside their territory, but even more conservative treaties, such as the ICC Statute, provide for nationality jurisdiction,[41] and the majority of the treaties relating to child labour issues provide for the possibility of jurisdiction based on the nationality of the victim, which is increasingly seen as an orthodox ground of jurisdiction.[42] In addition to this, virtually all of the instruments discussed below include some version of the principle that where an extradition request is received in respect of a national of a State, that State should prosecute its national in its own courts if it is unwilling to comply with the extradition request on the ground of the accused holding its nationality (the 'prosecute or extradite' principle).

None of these treaties provide for universal jurisdiction over offences. Attempts to prosecute senior officials of foreign governments under a Belgian law asserting universal jurisdiction over war crimes and crimes against humanity was heavily criticised and its use faltered in the face of State immunity.[43] However, the application of such a law could be possible where the accused was a leader of non-State forces.[44] An example might be the case of Joseph Kony, one of the leaders of the Lord's Resistance Army (LRA) in Uganda. The LRA's activities, including the use of child soldiers, were referred to the International

---

[40] Arnell, 'The Case for Nationality Based Jurisdiction', 50 (2001) *ICLQ* 955.

[41] Article 12(2).

[42] *Case Concerning the Arrest Warrant of 11 April 2000 (Democratic Republic of the Congo v. Belgium)*, *ICJ Reports 2002*, p. 3; see the Joint Separate Opinion of Judges Higgins, Kooijmans and Buergenthal, paragraph 47.

[43] *Supra* (note 42). The judgment decided that the persons concerned could not be prosecuted by Belgium because they benefited from State immunity. The Separate Opinion of President Guillaume, and the Joint Separate Opinion of Judges Higgins, Kooijmans and Buergenthal agreed with the majority but added extensive critiques of the concept of universal jurisdiction.

[44] Cullen, *International Law* (note 6) p. 115.

Criminal Court in 2004, and a warrant was issued for his arrest in 2005.[45] However, the prospect of peace negotiations between the Ugandan Government and the LRA has led to pressure on the ICC to drop the prosecution of Kony.[46] If this were to happen, the only prospects for prosecution would be a State exercising either passive personality jurisdiction (where a former child soldier had taken up the nationality of the prosecuting State) or universal jurisdiction. Unless Kony became part of the Ugandan Government as a consequence of any peace settlement, he would not be able to rely on State immunity as a bar to prosecution. Even if Uganda were to grant him immunity from prosecution within its own judicial system, other States would not be obliged to recognise that amnesty, as it could only operate within the jurisdiction of Uganda.

Article 4 of the CRC Optional Protocol on the Sale of Children, Child Prostitution and Child Pornography obliges States to establish jurisdiction over the offences covered by the Optional Protocol on the basis of territory, nationality of accused, habitual residence of the accused or nationality of the victim. Article 5(5) of the Optional Protocol requires States parties to 'take suitable measures to submit the case to its competent authorities for the purpose of prosecution' where the reason for refusing extradition is the nationality of the offender.

The UN Trafficking Protocol does not deal with jurisdiction itself, but rather refers back to the Convention against Transnational Organised Crime.[47] Article 15 of the Convention against Transnational Organised Crime requires States to take jurisdiction where the crime was committed on the State party's territory, where the accused or the victim is a national of the State party or where the victim is a stateless person having habitual residence in the State party. It also requires States to adopt the necessary measures to take jurisdiction over an alleged offender who is within their respective territories where it will not extradite solely on the ground that the alleged offender is a national, and to coordinate action where several States are investigating or prosecuting the same conduct.

The UN Trafficking Protocol is partly implemented in Europe by the European Union's Council Framework Decision 2002/629/JHA of 19 July

---

[45] Doc. No. ICC-02/04–01/05, Warrant of Arrest for Joseph Kony issued on 8 July 2005 as amended on 27 September 2005.

[46] McGreal, 'African search for peace throws court into crisis', *The Guardian*, 9 January 2007: http://www.guardian.co.uk/frontpage/story/0,,1986047,00.html. Preliminary peace talks have begun without indictments being withdrawn, but Kony himself did not attend: Walker, 'Rebels Arrive in Uganda for Peace Talks with President', *The Guardian*, 1 November 2007: http://www.guardian.co.uk/international/story/0,,2203188,00.html.

[47] Article 1(2) of the Trafficking Protocol.

2002, which is designed to complement the Trafficking Protocol and to introduce many of its provisions into EU law.[48] Article 6 requires member States to take jurisdiction over trafficking offences on the basis of territory or on the nationality of the accused, but not on the basis of habitual residence of the accused or on the basis of nationality of the victim. States are required to apply the 'prosecute or extradite' principle. The same approach is followed in the Council's Framework Decision 2004/68/JHA of 22 December 2003 on the sexual exploitation of children and child pornography.[49]

The Council of Europe Trafficking Convention, calls on States in Article 31 to establish jurisdiction over trafficking offences where the offence was committed on its territory (including ships and aircraft), where the accused is a national or a stateless person with habitual residence in the State, or where the victim is a national of the State. However, States may enter reservations to the acceptance of jurisdiction based on nationality/habitual residence of the accused or the nationality of the victim.[50] The principle of prosecute or extradite is applied: States parties are obliged to take the necessary measures to take jurisdiction over offenders present in their territory where they decline to extradite on grounds of nationality.[51]

The Council of Europe Convention on Sexual Exploitation and Abuse contains provisions similar to the conventions relating to trafficking and the CRC Optional Protocols on jurisdiction. Article 25 provides that 'each party shall take the necessary legislative or other measures to establish jurisdiction over any offence established in accordance with this Convention' where the offence was committed on the State's territory (including on ships of aircraft), or where the accused is a national or habitual resident of the State party.[52] It therefore imposes a broader scope of jurisdiction based on the accused's connection with the State than does the Council of Europe Trafficking Convention. Furthermore, Article 25(7) sets out an obligation to prosecute or extradite in language similar to the Trafficking Convention. Like the Trafficking Convention, this Convention explicitly requires that States establish the criminal liability of corporations and other legal persons.[53] It also places a weaker obligation on States, that is, to 'endeavour to take' the necessary measures to take jurisdiction over offences

---

[48] OJ 2002 No. L 203/1, 1 August 2002 (2002/629/JHA of 19 July 2002).
[49] See Articles 8 and 9.
[50] Article 31(2). In other respects, Article 45 of the Convention precludes reservations.
[51] Article 31(3).
[52] Article 25(1). Paragraph 3 allows States to make a declaration limiting its acceptance of jurisdiction over offences where the accused is a habitual resident, as, by virtue of Article 48, no reservations to this treaty are permitted.
[53] Article 26. Article 12 of the Cybercrime Convention also provides for corporate liability.

covered by the Convention where a national or habitual resident is the victim of the crime, a disappointing weakness when compared with the Trafficking Convention.[54]

The Cybercrime Convention has less extensive grounds of jurisdiction, possibly reflecting the controversial nature of some of its subject matter, particularly in relation to child pornography.[55] Only the territory and nationality of the accused criteria are compulsory grounds of jurisdiction.[56] States are not even exhorted to consider jurisdiction based on the nationality of the victim, and they may refuse to accept any jurisdiction beyond the strictest version of territorial jurisdiction.[57] Nonetheless, a 'prosecute or extradite' principle does apply where the accused is a national of a State party and an extradition request is made.[58] The cautious approach to jurisdiction could be justified if it had the effect of attracting wide ratification of the treaty. If all the States, both within and outside the Council of Europe who are eligible to become States parties did so, a very large proportion of the world's data traffic would be covered.[59] However, there are only twenty-six States parties to this Convention, and only one of the non-Council of Europe States eligible to ratify, the United States, has done so.[60]

Although the extension of jurisdiction to offences outside the territory of the State, where the accused is a national of that State, is common to many of the treaties relating to child labour issues, in many cases it will only be possible to bring a prosecution if the act were also criminal not only in the State of the nationality of the accused, but also in the State where the alleged offence was committed. This rule, called the double criminality requirement, has been

---

[54] Article 25(2).
[55] Oddis (note 28), at pp. 479–480, noting the opposition from NGOs highlighting concerns about freedom of expression. There is also the problem of conflict between the approach of North American and European courts to freedom of expression issues involving child pornography. In *R. v. Sharpe*, [2001] 1 S.C.R. 45, the Supreme Court of Canada read an exception into the Canadian Criminal Code to permit possession of child pornography for personal use only. The United States Supreme Court declared part of the Child Pornography Prevention Act in violation of freedom of expression principles insofar as it covered representations of sexual acts involving persons who appeared to be children but were not: *Ashcroft v. The Free Speech Coalition* (2002), 122 S. Ct. 1389; discussed by Oddis (note 28) at pp. 512–518. The European Court of Human Rights, however, has allowed States to prohibit child pornography as part of their margin of appreciation: *Handyside v. United Kingdom*, (1979–1980) 1 *EHRR* 737.
[56] Article 22.
[57] Article 22(2). This is one of the few provisions of the treaty which may be accepted subject to reservations: see Article 42.
[58] Article 22(3).
[59] Oddis (note 28) p. 502.
[60] See Council of Europe Treaty database: http://conventions.coe.int/Treaty/Commun/ChercheSig.asp?NT=185&CM=1&DF=11/6/2007&CL=ENG.

criticised as a bar to successful prosecutions, particularly in the area of sexual exploitation of children.[61] States parties to the Council of Europe Convention on Sexual Exploitation and Abuse are obliged to remove the double criminality requirement by virtue of Article 25(4). States parties must also remove any requirement that jurisdiction over offences committed by nationals or habitual residents is subject to a 'report of the victim or a denunciation from the State of the place where the offence was committed', thereby eliminating a further procedural barrier to prosecution for offences committed outside the State's territory.[62]

It is worth comparing the obligations to take extraterritorial jurisdiction over offences relating to exploitative child labour with the more vague obligations of international co-operation in other areas.[63] ILO Convention No. 182 sets out one of the more precise obligations in Article 8, where it lists 'support for social and economic development, poverty eradication programmes and universal education' as examples of appropriate international cooperation.[64] However, in the Council of Europe Convention on Sexual Exploitation and Abuse, Article 38 sets out only general principles concerning international cooperation. These principles relate primarily to judicial cooperation. Obligations to cooperate in relation to the prevention of sexual exploitation and abuse of children and to provide protection and assistance to victims are stated simply as principles. In the only paragraph to address these issues more specifically concerning the integration of prevention activities and the combating of sexual exploitation and abuse into development assistance programmes, the obligation is only to 'endeavour' to integrate these concerns.[65] The CRC Optional Protocol on the Sale of Children, Child Prostitution and Child Pornography sets out only vague obligations in relation to international cooperation on prevention

---

[61] Van Bueren, 'Child Sexual Exploitation and the Law A Report on the International Legal Framework and Current National Legislative and Enforcement Responses, Theme Paper for the Second World Congress against the Commercial Sexual Exploitation of Children', Yokohama, 18 December 2001. Although Article 25(4) removes the double criminality requirement in principle, paragraph (5) allows States to declare that they will limit the application of paragraph (4) to nationals having their habitual residence in the State party's territory.

[62] Article 25(6).

[63] The Cybercrime Convention, however, has extensive obligations in relation to cooperation and information sharing in the context of investigating and prosecuting the offences contained within the Convention: see Articles 23 to 35.

[64] Article 8. See also Article 16 of Recommendation No. 190.

[65] Article 38(4). Compare this with Article 38(2), which obliges States to 'take the necessary legislative or other measures to ensure that victims of an offence established in accordance with this Convention in the territory of a Party other than the one where they reside may make a complaint before the competent authorities in their state of residence.'

and protection against sexual exploitation of children.[66] The CRC Optional Protocol on Children in Armed Conflict sets out more detail concerning the areas in which States are expected to cooperate, specifying both prevention of the recruitment and use of child soldiers and the rehabilitation of former child soldiers.[67] It also specifies that international cooperation should include technical cooperation and financial assistance.[68]

The Council of Europe's Trafficking Convention is somewhat more explicit in the obligations placed on State parties to cooperate beyond the taking of extraterritorial jurisdiction and ensuring that Convention offences are extraditable. States are obliged to share information, particularly where victims or potential victims are in danger.[69]

IV. PROTECTIVE OBLIGATIONS
TOWARDS VICTIMS OF EXPLOITATIVE CHILD LABOUR

1. *Obligations in the Context of the Criminal Justice Process*

This obligation overlaps between obligations in relation to prosecution and protective obligations in relation to victims of exploitative child labour. Supporting child victims in the criminal process enables them to be effective witnesses, but it also recognises at least some of their needs as victims of serious human rights violations. As a result, it is not surprising that while most treaties are vague on protective obligations more generally, they do impose obligations on States to protect children as victims and witnesses in the context of the prosecution.

Article 8(1) of the CRC Optional Protocol sets out detailed protective obligations in relation to child victims of sexual exploitation in the context of the criminal justice process, with an emphasis on the vulnerability of children, but it also recognises the need for the views of child victims to be presented in all proceedings. Article 8 is based on the best interests principle as contained in Article 3 of the CRC.

Article 6 of the UN Trafficking Protocol is reasonably detailed concerning support for victims in the criminal process. They are to be given information about the processes, protection of their privacy and assistance to present their views. States are to take into account the age of the victim in applying this article.

---

[66] Article 10.
[67] Article 7(1).
[68] Article 7(1) and (2).
[69] Articles 32 to 34.

The Council of Europe Trafficking Convention goes much further than the UN Trafficking Protocol in its protective measures for victims. States are obliged to ensure that Convention offences can be prosecuted without the requirement of a victim complaint.[70] Protection of victims and their families from retaliation,[71] and protection of their privacy during court proceedings are also required.[72] In both contexts, the Convention obliges States to take into account the special needs of child victims.

The Council of Europe Convention on the Protection of Children against Sexual Exploitation and Abuse emphasises both protection and meaningful participation of children in all areas of prevention and prosecution. In Article 9 it uses language similar to Article 12 of the CRC in calling for children to be involved 'according to their evolving capacity'.[73] In Article 30, dealing with the process of investigation and prosecution, it uses instead the language of Article 3, CRC, emphasising a protective approach, and requiring that such processes be conducted in accordance with the best interests principle. Article 31 goes on to specify the protective measures which States must take to safeguard the rights and interests of victims and witnesses, including protection from retaliation.[74]

In the Statute of the International Criminal Court, we can see how the issue of protection of the interests of victims applies in practice. Article 68 of the ICC Statute sets out the rights of victims and witnesses to protection and participation. The safety, well-being, dignity and privacy of victims and witnesses are to be safeguarded, with the age of the victim and the fact that a crime involves violence against children to be taken into account.[75] In addition, Article 68(3) obliges the Court to allow victims to present their views to the Court where their personal interests are affected, in a manner that respects the rights of the accused and the need for a fair and impartial trial. Article 15(3) attributes a similar right to victims in the pre-trial stage. In the *Prosecutor v. Kony* case,[76] the Chamber of the Court applied the Court's Rules that define victims as 'natural persons

---

[70] Article 27.

[71] Article 28.

[72] Article 30.

[73] Article 12(1) CRC calls on States to involve children in decisions affecting their interests in accordance with their level of development: 'States Parties shall assure to the child who is capable of forming his or her own views the right to express those views freely in all matters affecting the child, the views of the child being given due weight in accordance with the age and maturity of the child.'

[74] See also Article 35 on interviews with the child, and Article 36 on criminal court proceedings (including the possibility for proceedings to be held *in camera*).

[75] Furthermore, proceedings may be held *in camera* in the interests of protecting a victim or witness.

[76] Decision on victims' applications for participation of Pre-Trial Chamber II, 10 August 2007.

who have suffered harm as a result of the commission of any crime within the jurisdiction of the Court.' However, the child victims, as well as some of the adult applicants, had their applications deferred pending further evidence as to their identities. This difficulty of crossing even the most basic procedural hurdles is inevitable in conflict-ridden societies where authoritative documents are not easily available. As a result, we see that in practice it may be difficult for child victims to realise their rights to participate in the criminal justice process.

2. Obligations to Rehabilitate and Re-integrate Victims of Exploitative Child Labour

Since the CRC, the international community has begun to recognise the need to provide for the recovery of children who are victims of serious human rights violations, including exploitative child labour. Article 39, which follows a series of articles relating to children's rights to be free from abuse and exploitation (including Article 32 on child labour, Article 34 on sexual exploitation and Article 38 on child soldiers) states that:

> States Parties shall take all appropriate measures to promote physical and psycho-
> logical recovery and social reintegration of a child victim of: any form of neglect,
> exploitation, or abuse; torture or any other form of cruel, inhuman or degrad-
> ing treatment or punishment; or armed conflicts. Such recovery and reintegration
> shall take place in an environment which fosters the health, self-respect and dignity
> of the child.

Recent measures on forms of exploitative child labour reflect the idea that States have obligations to attend to the recovery of children who have experienced forms of exploitative child labour. However, when compared with the criminal law obligations, where States are explicitly obliged to create specific offences in their domestic law, the obligations to assist in the recovery of child victims are often unspecific. ILO Convention No. 182, although brief, is comparatively detailed. Article 7(2) calls on States to remove children from the worst forms of child labour, to provide for rehabilitation and social integration of child workers and to ensure access to vocational training and education.[77] Convention No. 182 is probably unique amongst recent treaties in setting out protective obligations (Article 7(2)) in greater detail than obligations to prosecute (Article 7(1)).[78]

---

[77] See also Article 15 of Recommendation No. 190, for further elaboration of the protective obligations.

[78] This fact would tend to undermine the argument advanced by Smolin, 'Strategic Choices in the International Campaign against Child Labor', 22 (2000) *HRQ* 942, that the ILO, in its approach to child labour in Convention No. 182, has unacceptably moved beyond its competence into international criminal law. See also, for some further elaboration of the criminal law obligations, Articles 13, 14 and 16 of Recommendation No. 190.

Other treaties have not followed suit. Only the Council of Europe Conventions on Trafficking and Sexual Exploitation and Abuse pay as much attention to the general protective obligations towards children.

The CRC Optional Protocol on the Sale of Children, Child Prostitution and Child Pornography is less detailed concerning State obligations in relation to rehabilitation of victims of sexual exploitation than it is on their rights in the criminal justice process. States are obliged 'in appropriate cases' to adopt general measures of protection and rehabilitation.[79]

The UN Trafficking Protocol is designed as a criminal law measure, being a protocol to a treaty addressing matters of organised crime. It therefore has little to say about protection and assistance to victims beyond the criminal process. Article 6 of the UN Trafficking Protocol only requires States to consider providing support for victims for their social and medical needs. Similarly, the EU's Framework Decision on Trafficking sets out only general obligations to provide assistance to victims.[80] Some of the gaps in the UN Trafficking Protocol are filled by soft law, particularly the guidelines prepared by the Office of the High Commissioner for Human Rights on the implementation of the Trafficking Protocol.[81] Paragraph 10 calls for assistance and protection for trafficked children, in accordance with the best interests principle. Guideline 8 sets out specific measures of special protection, including family reunification and the provision of appropriate physical, psychosocial, legal, educational, housing and health-care assistance.

As with the protection of victims in the criminal justice process, the provisions of the Council of Europe Trafficking Convention are far superior, and take greater account of the needs of child victims, including a general obligation to protect victims' privacy in Article 11. From the outset, when a trafficked child is identified, States must appoint a guardian for the child's interests.[82] Among the detailed provisions contained in Article 12 relative to meeting the victim's needs for assistance in relation to medical care, counselling, housing and other resources, are additional obligations with respect to children.[83] Children must be provided with access to education, whereas adults only have the right to

---

[79] Article 8.
[80] This is criticised by Askola, *Legal Responses to Trafficking in Women for Sexual Exploitation in the European Union*, Hart Publishing: Oxford/Portland, 2007, pp. 125–126.
[81] *Recommended Principles and Guidelines on Human Rights and Human Trafficking, Report of the United Nations High Commissioner for Human Rights to the Economic and Social Council*, E/2002/68/Add.1, 20 May 2002, especially Guideline 6 on protection and support for trafficked persons.
[82] Article 10(4).
[83] See Sembacher (note 24), pp. 447–449.

access to vocational training and education if they are lawfully resident in the State. In all areas, the special needs of children must be taken into account. Of particular relevance to children is Article 12(6), which provides that States may not make assistance conditional on acting as a witness, a practice which is currently followed in a number of European countries.[84]

The Council of Europe Convention on the Protection of Children Against Sexual Exploitation and Abuse contains extensive provisions on protection and assistance for victims of sexual exploitation or abuse. However, even in this treaty the obligations are not set out in as much detail as those relating to prosecution. Nonetheless, the basic obligation in this area does focus on the social needs of children as victims of a serious human rights violation. Article 11(1) sets out as a principle that each Party shall establish effective social programmes and set up multidisciplinary structures to provide the necessary support for victims, their close relatives and for any person who is responsible for their care. Article 14(1) is more specific, requiring States to 'take the necessary legislative or other measures to assist victims, in the short and long term, in their physical and psycho-social recovery'; and Article 14(4) extends this right to assistance, particularly therapeutic assistance, to those close to the victim. It is worth noting that, unlike the other treaties discussed above, this Convention places the obligations of assistance to victims before the criminal law obligations, rather than afterwards.

The CRC Optional Protocol on Children in Armed Conflict also sets out quite clearly, although still in fairly general terms, the protective obligations of States. Article 6 requires that States take 'all feasible measures'[85] to demobilise and rehabilitate child soldiers, including 'all appropriate assistance for their physical and psychological recovery and their social reintegration'.

Few treaties impose obligations on States to prevent children (and adults, in the case of instruments on trafficking) from becoming victims in the first place. Article 7(2)(a) of Convention No. 182 calls on States to take effective and time-bound measures to prevent the worst forms of child labour, although it leaves to States the determination of what measures should be taken, beyond, in subparagraphs (d) and (e), identifying children at special risk and taking into account the situation of girls.[86] Article 9 of the UN Trafficking Protocol

---

[84] Askola (note 80), pp. 108–120.
[85] There is some dispute between commentators as to the nature of this obligation. While it is clearly not an absolute obligation (or an obligation of result), but rather an obligation to take measures (an obligation of means), there is disagreement as to whether 'feasible' means all possible measures or all practical measures: see Vandewiele, *A Commentary on the United Nations Convention on the Rights of the Child: Optional Protocol on the Involvement of Children in Armed Conflict*, Leiden, 2006 at pp. 27–28. See also Cullen, *International Law* (note 6), p. 118.
[86] See also Article 2(b) of Recommendation No. 190.

obliges States to take preventive measures, but gives relatively little detail and where measures are specified; the obligation is only to 'endeavour' to introduce these measures. More explicit obligations in Article 10 relate to the exchange of information between State authorities. The Council of Europe Trafficking Convention, on the contrary, is specific and detailed.[87] The measures which States are expected to take range from technical (research and information programmes; international coordination) to redistributive (social and economic initiatives and training programmes)[88] to the providing adequate means of legal migration. The latter obligation is somewhat weakened by an emphasis on the provision of information concerning the avenues of legal migration.[89] Both the UN and Council of Europe instruments include more palatable obligations to strengthen border controls and to ensure the security and control of travel documents.[90]

3. Obligations to Repatriate Child Victims or to Given them Residence Rights

The UN Trafficking Protocol was the first instrument to address the issue of the right to remain for trafficking victims, including children, but only requires States to *consider* measures allowing victims to remain either temporarily or permanently.[91] However, it is the Council of Europe's Trafficking Convention which provides for the most extensive rights of trafficking victims to remain in the destination country. Where there are reasonable grounds to consider that a person is a trafficking victim, the person must be given a 30 day reflection period without threat of expulsion.[92] Thereafter, victims should be given a renewable residence permit where their personal circumstances merit it or (the more likely scenario) where they are cooperating with the police.[93] The European Union has adopted a Directive on temporary residence permits for trafficking victims,

---

[87] Articles 5 to 9. See discussion by Sembacher (note 24), pp. 443–445.
[88] The UN Trafficking Protocol uses similar language, but this is one of the areas where States need only 'endeavour' to act.
[89] Article 5(4).
[90] Articles 11 and 12 of the UN Trafficking Protocol, and Articles 7 and 8 of the Council of Europe Trafficking Convention.
[91] Article 7. Article 8 provides similarly for the right to be repatriated to one's home country.
[92] Article 13.
[93] Article 14. In the case of child victims, their best interests must be considered when granting or renewing a residence permit. Askola notes that in trafficking trials, defence lawyers have argued that the granting of residence permits to witnesses amounts to a bribe or payment for their testimony, and seek to undermine their credibility before the court on this basis: (note 80), at p. 111.

but this only covers those who cooperate with criminal justice procedures.[94] The Directive follows the Trafficking Convention in requiring States to provide a period of reflection and support during that time.[95] However, the application of the Directive to children is optional.[96]

States are, unsurprisingly, more willing to accept obligations to repatriate victims of exploitative child labour and these are found in the UN Trafficking Protocol,[97] and in the Council of Europe Trafficking Convention. Article 16 of the Trafficking Convention, however, provides that children should not be repatriated if it is not in their best interests.

The Deputy Secretary General of the Council of Europe has stated that it is necessary for States to take into account the risk of trafficking of children when dealing with child migrants and asylum seekers. More specifically, she expressed concern that children held in detention centres for asylum seekers disappear only to resurface as trafficked children.[98] She wants States, particularly in relation to the Council of Europe Trafficking Convention, to make a distinction between people trafficking and illegal immigration. However, States are often unwilling to go beyond the obligations set out in the Trafficking Convention which only require providing temporary residence rights. The United Kingdom still routinely deports trafficking victims.[99]

4. *Obligations to Provide Facilities to Seek Compensation*

There are few explicit obligations on Sates in any of the relevant treaties in relation to ensuring that children who are victims of exploitative child labour practices may obtain compensation or damages. Only the UN Trafficking Protocol[100] and the Council of Europe Trafficking Convention oblige States

---

[94] Council Directive 2004/81/EC of 29 April 2004 on the residence permit issued to third-country nationals who are victims of trafficking in human beings or who have been the subject of an action to facilitate illegal immigration, who cooperate with the competent authorities: OJ 2004 No. L 261/19, 6 August 2004.

[95] Ibid, Articles 6 and 7.

[96] Ibid, Articles 3(3) and 10.

[97] Article 8.

[98] Opening Address by Maud de Boer-Buquicchio (note 24).

[99] Andy Travis, 'Sex trafficking victims rescued by police may face deportation', *The Guardian*, 4 October 2007: http://www.guardian.co.uk/crime/article/0,2182973,00.html. On the situation of trafficked children in the UK, see Sillen and Beddoe, *Rights Here, Rights Now: Recommendations for Protecting Trafficked Children*, London/UNICEF/ECPAT UK, 2007.

[100] Article 6(6). Unlike some other provisions of Article 6 concerning assistance and protection for trafficking victims where States are only obliged to *consider* providing certain forms of assistance, this paragraph requires States to *ensure* that its legal system provides avenues to seek compensation.

to provide avenues for compensation, through civil redress.[101] This is, at least in part, because there are formidable practical and legal difficulties facing a civil claim for damages. Even in the simplest of cases, there may be difficulties in finding a legal base for a cause of action for this type of human rights violation. Cases are often further complicated by an international dimension. Most importantly, those responsible may not be in the same State as the child, rendering both suit and execution of judgment practically impossible. Even where there is a defendant who is present in the same State as the child, for example in the case of a transnational corporation, the acts which form the subject matter of the suit may have taken place outside the State whose courts are hearing the claim. This presents difficulties in relation to evidence. More fundamentally, the exercise of such extraterritorial jurisdiction is controversial.

Nonetheless, some States do provide a legal route for suing for human rights violations which occurred in other States. This is notably true of the United States, in relation to the Alien Tort Claims Act, which allows American courts to take jurisdiction over 'any civil action by an alien for a tort only … committed in violation of the law of nations'.[102] This legislation was used to sue the American oil company Unocal for alleged collusion with the Myanmar government in the use of forced labour.[103] The Act is currently being used to sue a number of Arab Sheikhs for the alleged abduction and trafficking of children as camel jockeys in the United Arab Emirates.[104]

The use of the Alien Tort Claims Act to sue in the United States over human rights violations which occur in other States is controversial. Some argue that the grant of jurisdiction in the statute has been wrongly interpreted as a cause of action in itself. The United States Supreme Court decision in *Sosa v. Alvarez-Machain*,[105] appeared to resolve the controversy in favour of a restricted reading which treated the statute as solely jurisdictional, but cases like *Doe I v. Unocal* continue to be brought before the lower courts. In addition to the case concerning child labour noted above, suits have been instituted against Chinese nationals or American companies working in China. The plaintiffs in

---

[101] Article 15.

[102] 28 U.S.C. § 1350.

[103] *Doe I v. Unocal Corp.*, 41 (2002) *ILM* 1367 (U.S. Court of Appeals for the Ninth Circuit). The case was settled before final judgment: see 'Settlement of UNOCAL Case, December 2004,' *at* http://www.laborrights.org/projects/corporate/unocal/settlement1204.htm.

[104] Press Release, 'Motley Rice Files Suit Against Arab Sheikhs for Alleged Kidnapping, Human Trafficking and Child Enslavement', http://www.motleyrice.com/ news/releases/Child_Slavery_Suit.asp. The ILO's Committee of Experts has issued Individual Observations concerning the UAE's use of children as camel jockeys in 2005 and 2006, finding this to be a violation of Article 3(d) of Convention No. 182: Cullen, *International Law* (note 6), p. 165.

[105] 542 US 692 (2004).

these cases argue that the ruling in *Sosa* preserves the possibility of claims under rules of international law that are 'specific, universal and obligatory'.[106] They further argue that in case where clear well-established norms of international law are in issue, the claim should not be balanced against federal foreign policy considerations.[107]

v. Conclusion

Given the priority areas within current international legal instruments concerning child labour, it is hardly surprising that these standards give rise to positive obligations upon States. Furthermore, it is in some respects inevitable that these obligations are primarily in the area of criminal law. However, there are a number of reasons to be wary of this emphasis. There is some scepticism about how effective criminal justice responses can be when faced with complex phenomena such as people trafficking.[108] A comparison can be made with the clamour for international trade responses to child labour in the 1990s, which was justifiably criticised for leading to the removal of children from comparatively safe working situations only for those children to end up in more hazardous forms of work.[109] Without a parallel emphasis on protecting children in situations of exploitative child labour, prosecution of people traffickers or non-State forces who use child soldiers is an inadequate response. An exclusive focus on criminal law responses reduces these issues to ones of security rather than justice.[110]

Child labour is now understood as a human rights issue rather than a question of labour regulation. Consequently, the focus of international legal measures concerning child labour should be on the rights of children who are victims of abusive and exploitative forms of child labour. While the prosecution of those

---

[106] *Supra* (note 105), p. 730. *Doe I v. Liu Qi*, Case C 02 0672 CW EMC, United States District Court, Northern District of California, Plaintiffs Response to Statement of Interest of the United States, 11 August 2004, p. 8; *Plaintiff A v. Xia Deren*, Case C 02 0695 CW, Plaintiffs' Responsive Brief to the United States' Statement of Interest Dealing with the Relevance of the United States Supreme Court's Decision in *Sosa v. Alvarez-Machain*, p. 2, arguing that the Supreme Court had left open the possibility of using the Act for a limited range of the most well-established treaty-based and customary international law.

[107] *Supra* (note 106) *Plaintiff A*, pp. 4–6.

[108] Askola (note 80), pp. 99–100, argues that ineffective criminal justice measures can even worsen the situation for victims.

[109] See, for example, Myers, 'The Right Rights? Child Labor in a Globalizing World', 2001 (575) *Annals of the Academy of Politics and Social Science* 42, and more generally, Cullen, 'The Limits of International Trade Mechanisms in Enforcing Human Rights: The Case of Child Labour', 7 (1999) *International Journal of Children's Rights* 1.

[110] Askola (note 80), p. 100.

responsible for such abuses is an appropriate response to acts such as trafficking in children or the use of children as soldiers or in prostitution, it is not a complete response to the needs of these children as victims of human rights violations. The relative under-development of protective obligations is therefore a cause for concern.

Chapter Six

Shadows in the Cave:
The Nature of International Law When it Appears before English Courts

Vaughan Lowe[*]

International lawyers come in many shapes and sizes. Earnest environmentalists and human rights lawyers; hard-bitten investment lawyers; masters and mistresses of the WTO labyrinth; and a few old-fashioned general practitioners, who take everything in their stride and rely as much on a robust common sense and feeling for what is morally and legally right as on the latest wrinkle in the case law or seminal shift in the discourse on the problematic of the law. Among this minority, a very few manage to maintain an existence as lawyers rooted in a municipal system, focusing on the level at which all laws are actually brought to bear upon the lives of men and women. Colin Warbrick is one, as much at home with English public law and the European Convention on Human Rights as with the intricacies of international law; and even more at home in an argument over what makes sense and will work in the world, and in poking holes in flabby doctrines and theories. It is one of the great fortunes of my life, professional and personal, to have him as a friend and as a colleague, as ready to deflate and debunk as he is to agree. This short paper is a wholly inadequate token of my esteem. Readers may view it as a somewhat inconsequential paper. Colin, I hope, will see it as another round of an argument pursued eight months ago, knee-deep in mud and over too much good wine in Herefordshire: I think more slowly than he does.

In this essay I will examine some aspects of the relationship between International Law and English Law. The coverage is neither systematic nor particularly profound, and my purpose is simply to open up the question of what should be the relationship between the two systems.

---

[*]   Chichele Professor of International Law, University of Oxford.

K.H. Kaikobad & M. Bohlander (eds.), *International Law and Power: Perspectives on Legal Order and Justice*. Essays in Honour of Colin Warbrick, pp. 125–139.

I. What the Law is

As every law student knows, the relationship between International Law and English Law is essentially simple. Treaties cannot create rights or duties in English law unless they are given effect by statute. This is a consequence of the principle, at the heart of the English Civil war in the seventeenth century, that is to say, the Crown cannot create rights or duties by the exercise of the prerogative; and treaties are made by exercise of the prerogative.[1]

Courts may refer to treaties in order to aid the construction of statutes; and there is a general principle that uncertainties in the law should be resolved where possible so as to fulfil rather than violate the United Kingdom's obligations under international law.[2] But treaties cannot themselves alter the law.

Customary international law, on the other hand, is part of the Law of England, and will be applied by English courts in appropriate cases. A consistent line of authority in cases in which such rules have been in issue establishes that customary international law is part of the law of England. The proposition is commonly expressed in the words of Lord Mansfield in *Triquet v. Bath*[3] that 'the law of nations, in its full extent was part of the law of England'. At around the same time, Blackstone commented that:

> In arbitrary states this law, wherever it contradicts, or is not provided for by the municipal law of the country, is enforced by the royal power: but since in England no royal power can introduce a new law, or suspend the execution of the old, therefore the law of nations (wherever any question arises which is properly the object of its jurisdiction) is here adopted in its full extent by the common law, and is held to be part of the law of the land.[4]

It is worth pausing here. This passage is frequently quoted, but less frequently given careful consideration. Blackstone does not make only the point that international law is a part of English law. He pins the status of international law within the English legal system to a precise constitutional point. It is *because* England is not (or at least in his eyes was not) an 'arbitrary State' that

---

[1] The scope of the prerogative was described in a Memorandum from the Treasury Solicitor's Department (MPP 09(a)), submitted to the House of Commons Select Committee on Public Administration and printed in its *Fourth Report Taming the Prerogative: Strengthening Ministerial Accountability to Parliament (HC 422)* on 16 March 2004.

[2] See, e.g., *Brind and Others v. Secretary of State for Home Department* [1991] 1 AC 696.

[3] (1764) 3 Burr 1478. Recalling and endorsing the opinion of Lord Talbot in *Barbuit's* Case (1736) Cases L. Talbot 281. This statement of Lord Talbot's is not in the report and Lord Mansfield relied on his own note of the case, in which he was counsel.

[4] Sir William Blackstone, *The Commentaries on the Laws of England* (Facsimile of the First Edition of 1765–1769, University of Chicago Press), vol. iv, 'Of Public Wrongs': Chapter the Fifth, 'Of Offences Against the Law of Nations', p. 67.

the connection between English law and international law is established not through 'the royal power' (even though foreign relations were and are matters to be conducted by the Crown) but through the common law. The point, made a century after the Civil War, was a sharp one. International law is real law; and compliance with it is not to be left to the whim of the monarch.[5] Therein lies the key to the maintenance of the Rule of Law.

The position reflected by Blackstone was the orthodoxy. The phrase, 'common law, of which the law of nations must be deemed a part', was used by the court in the case of the *Duke of Brunswick v. King of Hanover* (1844),[6] where it is attributed to Lord Tenterden. In that case, Lord Langdale MR had to decide upon a claim to sovereign immunity made on behalf of the King of Hanover, who was also an English peer and subject. Lord Langdale held that:

> The law of nations includes all regulations which have been adopted by the common consent of nations, in cases where such common consent is evidenced by usage or custom. In cases where no usage or custom can be found, we are compelled, amidst doubts and difficulties of every kind, to decide in particular cases, according to such light as may be afforded to us by natural reason, or the dictates of that which is thought to be the policy of the law.[7]

Again, that passage deserves careful attention. The reference to natural reason and the dictates of the policy of the law signals the latitude that may be left to those charged with decisions on questions of international law. Deciding in such circumstances is an essentially judicial skill and an essentially judicial responsibility. There is no suggestion that where no custom or usage can be found, the Crown is free to do as it chooses. The Crown may have the prerogative right to devise foreign policy and conduct the international relations of the State; but it does so within the framework of international law.

The principle extended beyond legal duties, such as the according of immunity by the courts, to rights. Thus, in the case of *Emperor of Austria v. Day and Kossuth* (1861),[8] Sir John Stuart V-C was asked to order that counterfeit Hungarian currency notes be delivered up at the suit of the Emperor of Austria. He said:

> If the question related merely to an affair of State it would be a question, not of law, but for mere political discussion. But the regulation of the coin and currency of every State is a great prerogative right of the sovereign power. It is not a mere

---

[5]   A forthright point. Blackstone was Solicitor-General to Queen Charlotte, Queen Consort of George III, on a salary of £180 per annum, whose loss he would have noticed.

[6]   6 Beavan 1 at 52, 49 ER 724 at 744. The case contains a classic discussion of the roles of international and comparative law before English courts.

[7]   6 Beavan 45–46, 49 ER p. 741.

[8]   2 Giff. 628, 66 ER 678.

municipal right, or a mere question of municipal law. Money is the medium of commerce between all civilized nations; therefore, the prerogative of each sovereign State as to money is but a great public right recognised and protected by the law of nations. A public right, recognised by the law of nations, is a legal right; because the law of nations is part of the common law of England.

The principle that customary international law is part of the law of England (or, as Lord Langdale said in the *Duke of Brunswick's* case, 'is deemed part of the common law of England')[9] has been upheld by the English courts in what is now a long and firmly established line of authority,[10] of which the classic statement appears in *Trendtex Trading Corporation v. Central Bank of Nigeria*, where Lord Denning MR[11] (referring to customary international law) set out the principle in the following terms:

> [T]he rules of international law are incorporated into English law automatically and considered to be part of English law unless they are in conflict with an Act of Parliament.[12]

There is, it is true, a persistent notion that this clear principle was long controversial, and that there was a doctrinal debate in English law between the 'incorporation' and 'transformation' doctrines, resolved only in 1977 by the Court of Appeal in the *Trendtex* case. The notion derives largely from a misconstruction of the *Franconia* case (*R v. Keyn*) in 1876. There the Court was invited to rule that because under international law States were entitled to a three-mile territorial sea, it followed that the UK had a three-mile territorial sea so that an act or omission that occurred within three miles of the coast and caused death would be triable as a crime under English law, in English courts.

The fault in that position is obvious. The argument before the Court in *Keyn* was that international law entitles each coastal State to a territorial sea: it was not argued that each coastal State was obliged to maintain a territorial sea and to extend the application of its laws to that territorial sea. If the UK were entitled, but not obliged, to claim a three-mile territorial sea, it obviously had a choice as to whether or not to claim one. There had been no act, legislative

---

9 6 Beavan 45–46, 49 ER p. 741.

10 See, e.g., *West Rand Central Gold Mining Company Ltd v. The King* [1905] 2 KB 391, *per* Lord Alverstone CJ at 406; *R v. Bow Street Metropolitan Stipendiary Magistrate, ex p. Pinochet (No. 1)* [1998] 3 WLR 1456, *per* Lord Slynn at p. 1471D–F (citing *Trendtex*), p. 1472C–D (citing the Nuremburg Tribunal), p. 1472G (citing the Rome Statute of the International Criminal Court.); *R (European Roma Rights Centre and others) v. Immigration Officer at Prague Airport and another* [2005] 2 AC 1, *per* Lord Bingham at paragraph 22 and following.

11 It is notable how many of the great decisions on points of public international law have been made by the Court of Appeal, often by a panel presided over by the Master of the Rolls.

12 [1977] QB 529, at p. 553B, and see p. 554C.

or prerogative, which purported to establish a British territorial sea. If neither Parliament nor the Crown had chosen to establish a British territorial sea, should the courts take it upon themselves to do so? Plainly not: they must await the decision of Parliament or the Crown (depending upon whether the definition of the limits of the territory, which include the territorial sea, is regarded as an act within the prerogative).[13] That was an inevitable result of the permissive nature of the rule that was before the Court. The issue before the Court in *Keyn* was clearly different from the issue in cases which concerned mandatory rules of customary international law. Mandatory rules have long been given effect by English courts without the need for legislation.

Customary international law is automatically incorporated into English law, and that position is clear in the authorities. *Keyn* is not an example of a ruling that customary international law has no effect in English law unless it is transformed into English law by legislation. *Keyn* is an example of the need to consider what nature of the putative rule is, and to recognize that where permissive (rather than mandatory) rules are concerned one must ask whether 'the UK' has chosen to exercise the right it is allowed by international law before one asks what the consequence of that exercise is in English law. And the critical question is, who chooses?

II. Is the Present Position Satisfactory?

This basic position, according to which treaties need to be transformed into English law and customary international law is automatically a part of English law, has attracted some criticism, suggesting that it demonstrates an inadequate regard for international law on the part of English Law. As yet, the English legal system has perhaps faced no dilemma quite as acute as that faced by the US courts and other US authorities in the context of the *La Grand* case,[14] in which Walter La Grand was executed in Arizona despite a provisional measures order from the International Court of Justice that the 'United States of America should take all measures at its disposal to ensure that Walter LaGrand is not executed pending the final decision of the Court'.[15] Nonetheless, there are cases which appear to show a certain reluctance on the part of English courts to give effect to international law.

---

[13] See Edeson, 'The Prerogative of the Crown to Delimit Britain's Maritime Boundary', 89 (1973) *LQR* 364.
[14] See *ICJ Reports 2001*, p. 466. Further, see Tams, 'Consular Assistance and Rights and Remedies: Comments on the ICJ's Judgment in the LaGrand Case', 13 (2002) *EJIL* 1257.
[15] *ICJ Reports 1999*, p. 9.

In the context of treaties, the best-known instance is the case of the *Arab Monetary Fund v. Hashim*.[16] The Arab Monetary Fund ('AMF' or 'the Fund') was established by twenty or so Arab States[17] by treaty in 1976 and Dr Hashim was its Director General. The Fund alleged that Dr Hashim had appropriated around $70 million of the Fund's assets and sued in the English courts to recover it. The Court of Appeal refused to recognize that the 1976 treaty (to which the United Kingdom was not a party), had created a 'person' that existed in the eyes of English law. Such personality could be conferred by Order in Council under the International Organizations Act 1968; but no such order had been made in respect of the Fund. Hence Lord Donaldson's much quoted remark:

> As I see it, absent an Order in Council, an international organisation is as much a fact as a tree, a road or a hill. But it is not a person and the law can only deal in the rights and liabilities of persons. Once it is touched by the magic wand of an Order in Council it becomes a person, but one which is quite unlike other persons. Self-evidently it is not a natural person. But equally it is not a United Kingdom juridical person; nor is it a foreign juridical person. It is a person sui generis, which has all the capacities of a United Kingdom juridical person, but is not subject to the controls to which such a person is subject under English law. It is not a native, but nor is it a visitor from abroad. It comes from the invisible depths of outer space.[18]

The House of Lords reached a different conclusion, but not on the ground that English courts should recognise an international organization created by treaty. The Fund's juridical personality was accepted because it had been given legal personality in law of the United Arab Emirates, one of its member States and the place where the Fund had its headquarters.[19]

That decision is sometimes thought to betray a certain insularity on the part of English courts. They refuse to accept the personality of an international organization created by twenty States under international law, but will accept its personality if it exists under the law of the UAE.[20] But the House of Lords was surely precisely right in the approach that it adopted. Not every international body that exists by virtue of a treaty has legal personality, even in international law. The GATT, for example, was not a legal person. And while the constitutions of most international organizations contain stipulations concerning their legal

---

[16] [1990] 2 All ER 769.

[17] Twenty States plus Palestine.

[18] [1990] 2 All ER 769 at p. 775. [On other aspects of the legal personality of international organisations, see Chapter Seven by R. McCorquodale. Eds.]

[19] [1991] 1 All ER 871 at p. 880.

[20] See, e.g., Dixon, *International Law*, London, 1996, pp. 85–86.

personality, not all do so. The Constitution of the Universal Postal Union,[21] for example, is silent on this point. If none of the Member States of an organization gives it legal personality in its own law, why should the English courts do so? Would the practice of the Member States not indicate the intentions of the parties as to the existence and the kind of personality possessed by the organization? It is a mistake to think that it is always desirable to transpose the position in international law straight into municipal law.

The House of Lords in the *Arab Monetary Fund* case, far from adopting a 'face-saving' solution,[22] in my view showed a very keen awareness of the precise relationship that should exist between international law and English law. The proper degree of deference to the role of international law was the acceptance by the House that the entity which had legal personality and capacity 'added' to it by its establishment as a legal person under the law of the UAE was the international body, the AMF. The legal entity was not a UAE corporation. Lord Lowry (dissenting, but not on this point) made the position clear. Having drawn a comparison with the treatment of the International Tin Council in earlier litigation,[23] he said:

> I think it is clear that both the ITC and the [Arab Monetary] fund, having started as international organizations created by agreements made under international law, continue as such with the addition of a legal personality and capacity which have been conferred on them by one or more member states. Like the ITC, the fund is not a new creation under the law of the headquarter State; it is still an international organization with a conferred capacity in that State.[24]

That point was taken up in the case of *Westland Helicopters Ltd v. Arab Organisation for Industrialisation*,[25] where it was held that the organization remained subject to international law as its proper law, and was not governed by the law of the State(s) in which it was accorded personality in the way that a domestic corporation incorporated in the State(s) would be governed by that law. The AMF was thus seen by the English courts rather like the shadows in Plato's cave. It was not the international legal person which appeared to their eyes; it was the shadow cast by it, in the form of the person that existed on the plane of municipal law – the personality conferred by the law of the UAE.

The *AMF* case is drawn from the realm of treaty law; but the position of rules of customary international law before English courts is essentially similar. The

---

[21] ⟨http://www.upu.int/acts/en/index.shtml⟩

[22] Reinisch, *International Organizations before Municipal Courts*, Cambridge, 2000, p. 68.

[23] *The International Tin Council* case [1990] 2 AC 418; [1989] 3 All ER 523.

[24] [1991] 1 All ER 871 at p. 892. Further, see Lord Templeman for the majority, at pp. 876–77.

[25] [1995] 2 QB 282 at p. 303.

point is illustrated by the case of *R v. Jones (Margaret)*,[26] itself a case sometimes seen as an instance of a reticence on the part of English courts to adopt rules of international law lock, stock and barrel. In that case the defendants were accused of causing criminal damage when they broke into the air base at Fairford, Gloucestershire, in an attempt to prevent aircraft taking off to bomb Iraq at the start of the 2003 invasion by the USA, the UK, and the States persuaded to participate in the curiously-named 'Coalition of the Willing'.[27] One element of their defence was the claim that they were acting to prevent the commission of a crime and were therefore entitled to rely upon s. 3 of the Criminal Law Act 1967 ('A person may use such force as is reasonable in the circumstances in the prevention of crime ...'), the crime in question being the international law crime of aggression.

The House of Lords accepted that aggression was a crime under international law.[28] As the United Kingdom had a hand in executing people for that crime fifty years ago after the Nuremburg trials, it would have been startling if it had reached any other conclusion. In the light of the clearly established principle that the rules of international law are incorporated into English law automatically and considered to be part of English law (as it was put in *Trendtex*), the House also accepted that crimes under international law may be assimilated into domestic criminal law and that some had become part of English law.[29] But the House refused to accept that crimes under international law automatically become *crimes* under English law.

It may appear paradoxical and profoundly unsatisfactory that a person may use reasonable force to prevent a shoplifter taking a packet of crisps from a sweetshop counter, but may not use reasonable force to prevent an unlawful act of aggression that may kill thousands of innocent people and inflict catastrophic damage. (And, at this stage of the analysis, it is to be assumed that the acts that the defendants sought to prevent would amount to aggression and a crime under international law.) We would regard as a hero someone who tried to blow up a railway track in order to prevent trains delivering victims to the gas chambers. We might even regard such action as a moral duty. So why, if someone seeks to prevent an internationally unlawful act of aggression, for which the perpetrator

---

[26] [2006] UKHL 16.

[27] Afghanistan, Albania, Australia, Azerbaijan, Bulgaria, Colombia, the Czech Republic, Denmark, El Salvador, Eritrea, Estonia, Ethiopia, Georgia, Hungary, Italy, Japan, South Korea, Latvia, Lithuania, Macedonia, the Netherlands, Nicaragua, the Philippines, Poland, Romania, Slovakia, Spain, Turkey, United Kingdom and Uzbekistan. See ⟨http://news.bbc.co.uk/1/hi/world/americas/2862343.stm⟩

[28] [2006] UKHL 16, paragraph 19.

[29] [2006] UKHL 16, paragraphs 20–22.

might subsequently be tried and punished for the international law crime of aggression, should that act not be excused using the defence under s. 3 of the Criminal Law Act? Does the House of Lords' position signify that English law encourages us to use reasonable force to prevent 'ordinary' crimes but not to prevent the very gravest crimes known to humankind, unless those crimes happen to have been brought into English law by legislation? And where does that leave the principle that customary international law is a part of English law?

These are powerful arguments, and many may wish that the House of Lords had upheld the right to act to prevent the international law crime of aggression.[30] But the House did not do so, and its approach to the issue is subtle. The ground was laid for it by Lord Bingham's statement that:

> There seems to be truth in JL Brierly's contention ('International Law in England' (1935 51 LQR 24 p. 31)) ... that international law is not a part, but is one of the sources, of English law.[31]

That distinction between customary international law as part, and customary international law as a source[32] of English law, is important.

If customary international law were a *part* of English law, the courts would apply the rule of customary international law itself. If the international law rule criminalises conduct, the conduct would be criminalised in English law because a rule that is *ex hypothesi* a part of English law would define the conduct as a crime. One would still have to deal with questions of venue – finding an English court with jurisdiction to try the offence;[33] but there could be no room for doubting that the conduct is criminal.

If, on the other hand, customary international law is simply a *source* of English law, the position is different. What the court applies is not the rule of customary international law as such, but rather the rule of English law whose source lies in international law. The position is analogous to the distinction drawn in the *AMF* case between the personality of international organizations on the plane of international law (the 'source') and their personality and capacity in municipal law (the juridical phenomenon that is handled by the English courts). Here there is no logical reason why the rule of English law should have the same juridical quality as the rule of customary international law.

---

[30] The defendants in the case were permitted to run the defence that they were acting to prevent the commission of war crimes, criminalised in English law by the International Criminal Court Act 2001. There could be no doubt that war crimes are crimes under English law, and within the scope of the defence under s. 3 of the Criminal Law Act 1967.

[31] [2006] UKHL 16, paragraph 11.

[32] Readers having difficulty with the distinction might contemplate the relative merits of holding the Oxford and Cambridge Boat Race on a part of the Thames and at the source of the Thames.

[33] See O'Keefe, 'Customary International Crimes in English Courts', 72 (2001) *BYIL* 293.

The point can be put slightly differently. A criminal law is a prohibition. But there are different kinds of prohibition. I have no right[34] to steal or to slander; but one is a crime and one a tort. Similarly, in international law, intervention in the internal affairs of another State is prohibited; but it is not in itself a crime against international law. One might say that the prohibition – do not steal, slander, intervene or whatever – is the essential, irreducible normative charge borne by the rule. The rule cannot exist if what it prohibits when applied in one context is permitted in another context. But the question whether the *nature* of the prohibition is one which sounds in criminal law or in tort may be said not to be an inherent and necessary aspect of the rule itself but rather a quality impressed upon it by the particular legal system within which it is applied.

If this distinction seems a little far-fetched it should be recalled that in private international law the rule in *Phillips v. Eyre*[35] originally[36] required that in order to be actionable in England an act done in a foreign country must both be (i) an act which would be tortious if done in England and (ii) 'not justifiable' in the law of the State where it was committed, and that an act was 'not justifiable' if it entailed either civil or criminal liability. The category of 'not justifiable' acts is precisely the kind of category that I have in mind as the proper designation of the class of norms to which international law prohibitions should be regarded as belonging when they serve as a source of English law rules. It includes the equivalents of crimes and torts and cognate norms, but is not limited to any one of those kinds of norms and does not distinguish between them.

On this basis, once English law (or any other municipal law) draws upon international law as a source of legal rules it is for the receiving legal system to decide whether or not to stamp the rule with the mark of a criminal law. Rather as in the case of EC directives, it is for each legal system to decide exactly how it will implement the rule. That seems to me to be correct. The essence of a crime is that it is something that is liable to be condemned, prosecuted and punished with the repressive power of the State. It is not a question of how serious or how trivial the offence is. Taking a tin of paint from one's employer is a crime: taking the jobs of a thousand employees by closing a factory in order to increase profitability is not. In some States adultery is generally tolerated: in others, it may result in stoning to death. Communities make their own public orders and decide what conduct warrants repression by the State, what conduct

---

[34] The relationship between prohibitions and categories of norms such as Hohfeld's 'no-rights', duties, disabilities, and liabilities is an important aspect of this question.

[35] (1870) LR 6 QB 1.

[36] The position was modified by *Boys v. Chaplin* [1971] AC 356. The modification did not affect the existence of the concept of a category of 'not justifiable' or 'prohibited' acts, some of which entail civil and some criminal liability (and some, both).

warrants civil liability at the instance of victims, and what conduct is to be regarded as innocuous or as part of the rough and tumble of human existence. And different States draw the lines in different places.

Viewed in this light one may say that there is no more reason for English law to treat a particular prohibition under international law as a crime simply because international law regards it as a crime[37] than there was for English courts applying the rule in *Phillips v. Eyre* to treat conduct as a crime simply because, say, Brazilian law treated it as a crime.

The question again is, Who decides? In *R v. Jones*, the House of Lords gave a clear answer. Lord Hoffman referred to:

> ... the democratic principle that it is nowadays for Parliament and Parliament alone to decide whether conduct not previously regarded as criminal should be made an offence.[38]

He continued:

> ... [N]ew domestic offences should in my opinion be debated in Parliament, defined in a statute and come into force on a prescribed date. They should not creep into existence as a result of an international consensus to which only the executive of this country is a party.[39]

Therein lies a powerful argument in support of the House of Lords' position. It is tempting for international lawyers to assume that international law is a benign, enlightened force for good in the world and that it is desirable that municipal courts should give effect to it wherever possible. In the nature of things, international law arguments are usually raised in domestic courts by individuals seeking to challenge or defend themselves against actions of the State. But the wholesale adoption of international law would cut both ways.

A recent example of the use of international law arguments by the State against the individual is to be found in *Al Jedda v. Secretary of State for Defence.*[40] There Mr Al Jedda, detained indefinitely by UK forces at a base in Iraq, sought to invoke his right to due process under Article 5 of the European Convention on Human Rights. The Government argued that Mr Al Jedda was interned

---

[37] Of course, if a treaty imposed a duty to criminalise certain conduct, States Parties would be bound to implement the treaty in that way. But there the duty arises not from the prohibition of the conduct under the treaty but from the distinct obligation relating to the manner in which the treaty is to be implemented.

[38] [2006] UKHL 16, paragraph 60. Lord Bingham, at paragraph 23, approved a similar point made by Sir Franklin Berman: see 'Jurisdiction: The State', in Capps, Evans and Konstadinidis (eds.), *Asserting Jurisdiction: International and European Legal Perspectives*, Hart Publishing/Oxford, 2003, p. 3 at 11.

[39] *Supra* (note 26), paragraph 62.

[40] [2006] EWCA Civ 327.

pursuant to Security Council resolution 1546, which was binding on the UK under Article 25 of the UN Charter and therefore prevailed over the European Convention by virtue of Article 103 of the Charter, with the result that Mr Al Jedda's Convention rights were suspended to the extent that they conflicted with the right to intern set out in the resolution. Because it has been held that 'a party unable to mount a successful claim in Strasbourg can never mount a successful claim under [the Human Rights Act 1998]',[41] the suspension of Mr Al Jedda's treaty right would be fatal to his claim. That is a classic example of the invocation of powers by the Executive, based on a source in international law. That argument succeeded before the Court of Appeal, and an appeal to the House of Lords is pending.

Whatever the fate of the appeal in *Al Jedda*, the factual situation in *Al Jedda* exemplifies some of the less desirable consequences of sweeping international law rules directly into English law. The Security Council resolution at issue in that case focuses upon particular measures such as internment in the specific context of Iraq. But the logic of the Government's position would extend to all Security Council resolutions, enabling it to override (for example) provisions in the European Convention on Human Rights. For example, in Security Council resolution 1373, the Security Council '*Decides* that all States shall (a) Prevent and suppress the financing of terrorist acts'. If a State decided that it was necessary to use degrading treatment to obtain information on terrorist financing it would, on this view, be entitled to invoke Articles 25 and 103 of the UN Charter to override its human rights obligations. Few would regard that as a desirable development.

There is a common thread that links the *AMF* and *Jones* cases. It is a certain wariness of the Executive and a reluctance to give determinative legal effect to putative rules of law that are generated in the corridors where only the members and officials of the Executive tread, their acts not receiving even the lightest brushing of legitimacy through being touched by an Order in Council or approval under the Ponsonby Rule[42] or any of the other fig-leaves which modern governments and their whips slap on to their more exposed parts to preserve the illusion of democratic assent.[43] This leads the English courts to

---

[41] *Regina v. Secretary of State for Foreign and Commonwealth Affairs, ex parte Quark Fishing Limited* [2005] UKHL 57, paragraph 25.

[42] See ⟨www.fco.gov.uk/Files/kfile/ponsonbyrule,0.pdf⟩

[43] *Festschriften* invite an element of personal reflection. Mine is that when Colin Warbrick and I first propped up the bar at legal conferences the judiciary were generally seen among academics as painted with the brush, so ably wielded by John Griffith in *The Politics of the Judiciary*, (London/Fontana, 1977), as reactionary, middle-class, middle-aged, right-wing, white males. Now the judiciary seems to be the only institution standing between Everyman

view attempts to modify rights and duties established by 'English' (i.e., non-international) law by reference to rules of international law with a degree of circumspection and a careful attention to the precise manner in which the international law rules are to be accommodated within the English legal system.

Sensible as a profound mistrust of governments may be as a rule of thumb, it must not be supposed that they are invariably bent on mischief or incapable of reaching reasoned and reasonable conclusions on international law issues. The practice in the English courts of accepting Executive certificates on certain matters, for example, is a wise one. The matters properly covered by certificates are what Dr Mann called 'facts of State', which are:

> facts, circumstances and events which lie at the root of foreign affairs … These are facts which are peculiarly within the cognisance of the Executive.[44]

Some such 'facts' are the subject of statutory provisions which provide for the issuance of certificates by the Foreign Secretary. Certification of the status of persons as (accredited) diplomats, under the Diplomatic Privileges Act 1964, and of the diplomatic status of premises under s. 9 of the Criminal Law Act 1977 are examples. These 'facts' are, of course, not strictly factual. They are determinations of the legal character, in the two examples given, of persons and of premises. But no one could seriously doubt the appropriateness of permitting the Foreign Office to have the last word on the whether persons or places in the United Kingdom qualify for diplomatic immunity.

Other matters certified by the Foreign Secretary may be even more overtly legal and extend into the area of discretion in the making of foreign policy, but still lie within the area where deference to the Foreign Office is appropriate. The provision in the State Immunity Act 1978 for the certification of the status of an entity as a State or a component of a State for the purposes of the Act is an example. Certification there is plainly an expression of the Government's policy on the recognition of the entity; and it appears reasonable to leave it to the Foreign Office to determine such matters. If, for example, the courts were free to decide, for example, whether the 'Turkish Republic of Northern Cyprus' or Taiwan or Palestine is a State, a decision could cause severe difficulties for the conduct of foreign policy. The entity would have a claim to a right to immunity, and to accede to treaties of which the United Kingdom is a depository, and so on. One can understand the decision to leave questions of the recognition of States to the Executive.

and the smothering benevolence of an overbearing paternalistic State, for whose authoritarian obesity the grossly and pointlessly inflated waistlines of my generation seem only the most pallid metaphor.

[44] Mann, *Foreign Affairs in English Courts*, Oxford, 1986, p. 23.

What is plainly not appropriate is for the Executive to make binding determinations on questions of law. As Dr. Mann said:

> It is ... not for the Executive to pronounce upon any question of either English or international law.[45]

The courts have taken the same view. In *Carl Zeiss Stiftung v. Rayner & Keeler Ltd.*, the House of Lords refused to accede to the respondent's proposal that the Government be asked what matters fell within the scope of an international instrument (the Declaration of 19 September 1950 in which the Western Allies declared that they considered the Government of the Federal Republic of Germany to be the only government entitled to represent the German people internationally). Lord Upjohn said: 'It has never been the practice of Her Majesty's Secretaries of State to express any views upon the law';[46] and Lord Wilberforce said, 'The questions, which it was suggested should be asked, were questions of law which it is the function of the courts to determine ...'[47]

The central issue is, I think, that which precipitated the Civil War. To what extent may the Crown change the law by the exercise of prerogative powers? The answer should be that it cannot – or at least, that it cannot do so beyond the limits of the constitutional settlement that defines the scope of the prerogative. As was memorably said in *BBC v. Johns*:

> [I]t is 350 years and a civil war too late for the Queen's courts to broaden the prerogative. The limits within which the executive government may impose obligations or restraints upon citizens of the United Kingdom without any statutory authority are now well settled and incapable of extension.[48]

That salutary principle entails limitations upon the extent and nature of the reception of international law into English law which to some may seem to smack of insularity, but which are in my view essential to the effective implementation of the Rule of Law.

If governments in this country disregard their international obligations, and people are denied rights to which they are entitled under international law, that is, shameful. But the most effective remedy does not lie in the wholesale incorporation of international law rights and duties into municipal law. That would serve only to increase the scope and power of the prerogative. The answer lies in forcing change in English law by bringing pressure to bear on those who can change the law and those who have the power to choose how to apply it.

---

[45] Ibid, p. 51.
[46] [1967] 1 AC 853, at p. 950.
[47] [ibid, p. 974.
[48] [1965] Ch. 32, at p. 79, *per* Diplock, LJ.

Individuals in the United Kingdom, and in other States, are in practice incapable of exercising any significant influence in the short term over the development of international law: such influence is, perhaps inevitably, the exclusive preserve of governments. They can, and do, exercise real pressure upon the national government, whether it is acting as Executive or as Legislature.

One of the great provisions of the European legal order appears at the end of the Greek Constitution. Entitled 'The Right to Resist' it provides that:

> Observance of the Constitution shall be committed to the patriotism of the Greeks who shall have the right and the obligation to resist by any means anybody who tries to subvert it violently.[49]

That admirably Byronic provision exemplifies an important political truth. The Rule of Law in a State has, ultimately, to be maintained and secured by those within that State. It cannot be imposed from outside. For those of us who believe that international law is indeed a source of enlightened and useful rules and procedures, the best course is generally to press for it to be adopted, consciously and formally, by the legislature. The judicial oath requires the courts to uphold the domestic legal order, and it is on that order that their focus should remain, even when they are applying principles of international law.

---

[49] Article 120 (4).

Chapter Seven

International Organisations and International Human Rights Law: One Giant Leap for Humankind

Robert McCorquodale[*]

[A]n international organisation ... is not a native, but nor is it a visitor from abroad. It comes from the invisible depths of outer space.[1]

International organisations are not aliens, despite the above comment by a senior judge. Yet they are often treated as strange, or even invisible, and hence outside much of the international legal system. Despite the significant growth of international organisations over the past century, some significant international legal decisions and the increasing literature about the law of international organisations,[2] there are aspects of their activities that remain unclear in terms of their legal effect. In particular, the international legal responsibility of international organisations for violations of international human rights law is still contentious.

[*] Director of the British Institute of International and Comparative Law; Professor of International Law and Human Rights at the University of Nottingham. I am very grateful for the research work of Gwyneth Williams. It is my pleasure to be part of the volume in honour of Professor Colin Warbrick. He has been a wonderful example of an international lawyer who is unafraid to challenge current ways of thinking, of whatever philosophical persuasion. This chapter was completed in early 2008.
[1] *Per* Lord Donaldson MR in *Arab Monetary Fund v. Hashim (No. 3)* [1990] 2 All ER 769, at p. 775.
[2] See, for example, Klabbers (ed.), *International Organizations*, Aldershot, 2005; Alvarez, *International Organizations as Law-Makers*, Oxford, 2005; Amerasinghe, *Principles of the Institutional Law of International Organizations* (Second edition), Cambridge, 2005; Blokker and Schermers, *International Institutional Law* (Fourth edition), Leiden, 2003; Klabbers, *An Introduction to International Institutional Law*, Cambridge, 2002; Sands and Klein, *Bowett's Law of International Institutions* (Fifth edition), London, 2001; White, *The Law of International Organisations*, Manchester, 1996; Bekker, *The Legal Position of Intergovernmental Organizations A Functional Necessity Analysis of Their Legal Status and Immunities*, Dordrecht, 1994; and Kirgis, *International Organizations in their Legal Setting* (Second edition), St. Paul, 1993.

K.H. Kaikobad & M. Bohlander (eds.), *International Law and Power: Perspectives on Legal Order and Justice*. Essays in Honour of Colin Warbrick, pp. 141–162.
© 2009 Koninklijke Brill NV. Printed in the Netherlands.

This chapter aims to consider the extent to which international organisations have international legal responsibilities under international human rights law. It will demonstrate the link between international legal personality rights with international legal responsibilities, and then examine the extent of those responsibilities of international organisations in regard to human rights. It is evident that international organisations have for many years acted in ways that impact very negatively on human rights in a range of their activities, from peace-keeping and refugee action, to economic assistance.[3] Yet, mainly due to the nature of an international legal system, which is essentially State-focused especially within international human rights law, there has been no coherent response to this impact of international organisations on human rights in terms of international legal responsibility.

In this chapter, the term 'international organisation' (or 'organization') is used to refer to intergovernmental organisations[4] with the following characteristics:

(a) its membership must be composed of States and/or other international organizations;
(b) it must be established by treaty;
(c) it must have an autonomous will distinct from that of its members and be vested with legal personality; and
(d) it must be capable of adopting norms addressed to its members.[5]

Others expand on these characteristics of an international organisation, such as the need to possess a constitution and have organs separate from its member States.[6] The examples that will be used here in relation to international human rights law will generally relate to those international organisations that have a global membership, such as the United Nations (UN) and its agencies, and the major international financial institutions, being the World Bank and International Monetary Fund (IMF),[7] with some occasional reflection in relation

---

[3] See, for example, Abraham, 'The Sins of the Savior: Holding the United Nations Accountable to International Human Rights Standards for Executive Order Detentions in its Mission in Kosovo', 52 (2002–2003) *American University Law Review* 1291; Verdirame, 'Testing the Effectiveness of International Norms: UN Humanitarian Assistance and Sexual Apartheid in Afghanistan', 23 (2001) *HRQ* 733; and ibid, 'Human Rights and Refugees: The Case of Kenya', 12 (1999) *J Refugee Studies* 54; and Sadasivam, 'The Impact of Structural Adjustment on Women: A Governance and Human Rights Agenda', 19 (1997) *HRQ* 630.

[4] See Article 2 (1) (i) of the Vienna Convention on the Law of Treaties between States and International Organizations or between International Organizations, 1986.

[5] Sands and Klein (note 2), p. 16.

[6] See the Final Report of the Committee on the Accountability of International Organisations in the *Report of the Seventy-first International Law Association Conference Berlin 2004*, London, 2004, available www.ila-hq.org/pdf/Accountability/Final/%20Report%20200.pdf (hereinafter referred to as the ILA Report).

[7] See discussion of the link of the UN with the International Monetary Fund (IMF) and

to those international organisations where there has been judicial consideration of human rights responsibilities.

I. INTERNATIONAL LEGAL PERSONALITY

An entity has international legal personality if it has direct international rights and responsibilities, can bring international claims, and is able to participate in the creation, development, and enforcement of international law.[8] This is still sometimes referred to as an entity being a 'subject' of the international legal system, though the terminology of 'subject' and 'object' (and its consequent binary opposition) has been rightly criticized,[9] with the concept of 'participants' in the international legal system being much preferred.[10] In particular, for the purposes of considering international organisations, the use of 'participation' as a framework for considering their activities is flexible and open enough to deal with developments in the international legal system over the centuries and is not constricted to a State-based concept of that system or limited to appearances before international bodies. This is consistent with the concept of international legal personality as it 'was born from a confrontation between moral idealism and political realism and emerged as a concept intimately linking the responsibility to pursue justice with the right of international participation'.[11] Indeed, the International Court of Justice (ICJ) has noted that:

> Throughout its history, the development of international law has been influenced by the requirements of international life, and the progressive increase in the collective activities of States has already given rise to instances of action upon the international plane by certain entities which are not States.[12]

---

the World Bank in Gianviti, 'Economic, Social and Cultural Rights and the International Monetary Fund', in Alston (ed.), *Non-State Actors and Human Rights*, Oxford, 2005, p. 113.

[8] For a discussion of the history and concepts of international legal personality, see Nijman, *The Concept of International Legal Personality*, The Hague, 2004.

[9] Rosalyn Higgins comments that 'the whole notion of "subjects" and "objects" has no credible reality, and, in my view, no functional purpose. We have erected an intellectual prison of our own choosing and then declared it to be an unalterable constraint'. See *Problems and Process: International Law and How We Use It*, Oxford, 1994, p. 49. See also Koskenniemi, *From Apology to Utopia: The Structure of International Legal Argument*, Helsinki, 1989; and Charlesworth and Chinkin, *The Boundaries of International Law: A Feminist Analysis*, Manchester, 2000.

[10] See, for example, Knop, *Diversity and Self-Determination in International Law*, Cambridge, 2002; and Schreuer, 'The Waning of the Sovereign State: Towards a New Paradigm for International Law', 4 (1993) EJIL 447, at p. 453.

[11] Nijman (note 8), p. 457.

[12] *Reparation for Injuries Suffered in the Service of the United Nations*, Advisory Opinion, *ICJ Reports 1949*, p. 174, at p. 178.

By this statement, the ICJ is acknowledging that the international legal system does change over time due to the 'requirements of international life' and this is reflected in the ability of different non-State entities to participate ('take action') upon the international plane.

The classic statement of the position of international organisations in relation to the rights and responsibilities that arise from having international legal personality is that of the ICJ in the *Reparations for Injuries Suffered in the Services of the United Nations* Advisory Opinion:

> The subjects of law in any legal system are not necessarily identical in their nature or in the extent of their rights, and their nature depends on the needs of the community ... In the opinion of the Court, the [UN] Organisation was intended to exercise and enjoy, and is in fact exercising and enjoying, functions and rights which can only be explained on the basis of the possession of a large measure of international personality and the capacity to operate upon an international plane ... That is not the same thing as saying that it is a State, which it certainly is not, or that its legal personality and rights and duties are the same as those of a State ... It does not even imply that all its rights and duties must be upon the international plane, any more than all the rights and duties of a State must be upon that plane. What it does mean is that it is a subject of international law and capable of possessing international rights and duties, and that it has capacity to maintain its rights by bringing international claims.[13]

It is clear from this Opinion that not all those with international legal personality have the same rights and duties (responsibilities) as States. While some international organisations have a limited range of rights and responsibilities others, such as when the UN administers territory, could be considered to have almost all the rights and responsibilities of a State.[14] However, it is also clear that there are some rights and some responsibilities that arise from having any degree of international legal personality.[15] In particular it is certain that international organisations, which have international personality by definition, have some international rights and responsibilities. The importance of this here is that it confirms the legal personality of an international organisation as being distinct from its members.[16]

---

[13] Ibid, pp. 178–179.

[14] See Wilde, 'From Danzig to East Timor and Beyond: The Role of International Territorial Administration', 95 (2001) *AJIL* 583; and Chesterman, *You, The People: The United Nations, Transitional Administration and State-Building*, Oxford, 2004.

[15] See also Suzuki and Nanwani, 'Responsibility of International Organizations: The Accountability Mechanisms of Multilateral Development Banks', 27 (2005) *Michigan Journal of International Law* 177.

[16] This was confirmed by the Swiss Supreme Court in *Arab Organisation for Industrialisation*, Judgment of 19 July 1988, 80 *ILR* 658.

What the ICJ does not assert in its Opinion is that having international legal personality means that an international organisation automatically has certain powers. Each international organisation will have different powers and capacities (express and implied) depending on the organisation's objects, purposes and functions, which are usually set out in its constitutive instrument. This was clarified by the ICJ in a later Opinion:

> The Court need hardly point out that international organizations are subjects of international law which do not, unlike States, possess a general competence. International organizations are governed by the 'principle of speciality', that is to say, they are invested by the States which create them with powers, the limits of which are a function of the common interests whose promotion those States entrusts to them .... The powers conferred on international organizations are normally the subject of an express statement in their constituent instruments. Nevertheless, the necessities of international life may point to the need for organizations, in order to achieve their objectives, to possess subsidiary powers which are not expressly provided for in the basic instruments which govern their activities. It is generally accepted that international organizations can exercise such powers, known as 'implied' powers.[17]

This Opinion confirmed that an implied power was not linked to an express power but was linked to the international organisation's purposes, and hence was broader in scope. Yet it was not unlimited. Whilst the final view of the ICJ in this particular Opinion can be criticised as unduly functionalist and ignoring the reality of the impact of nuclear weapons,[18] it nevertheless highlights the need to be clear about the purposes and functions of each international organisation in order to determine its own rights and responsibilities within the international legal system. However, there may be some general principles of international legal responsibility that can apply to most international organisations.

II. INTERNATIONAL LEGAL RESPONSIBILITY

The International Law Commission (ILC) has been in the process of drafting articles on the Responsibility of International Organizations since 2002 and had

---

[17] *Legality of the Threat or Use of Nuclear Weapons Opinion (WHO Advisory Opinion)*, *ICJ Reports 1996*, p. 66.

[18] See Klein, 'Reflections on the Principle of Speciality Revisited and the "Politicisation" of Specialised Agencies', in Boisson de Chazournes and Sands (eds.), *International Law, The International Court of Justice and Nuclear Weapons*, Cambridge, 1999, p. 78.

drafted fifty-three articles by its 2008 session.[19] Vested with the task of formulating draft Articles, the Special Rapporteur of the Working Group of the ILC, indicated that

> [T]he draft Articles had a level of generality which made them appropriate for most, if not all, international organizations; this did not exclude, if the particular features of certain organizations so warranted, the application of special rules.[20]

It is, therefore, assumed by the ILC that there can be general principles of international legal responsibility that apply to most international organisations. These general principles expressed in the draft Articles in most key respects replicate the final ILC Articles on Responsibility of States for Internationally Wrongful Acts (ILC Articles on State Responsibility).[21] In particular, the key general principles are set out in Article 3:

1. Every internationally wrongful act of an international organization entails the international responsibility of the international organization.
2. There is an internationally wrongful act of an international organization when conduct consisting of an action or omission:
    (a) Is attributable to the international organization under international law; and
    (b) Constitutes a breach of an international obligation of that international organization.[22]

This draft Article establishes that there is international responsibility for an internationally wrongful act where that act is attributable to the international organisation and it is a breach of an international obligation of the international organisation. This is based on the equivalent position in regard to States, where it is generally considered to represent customary international law.[23]

The position as regards the international legal responsibility of States is that a State is responsible for the actions of their officials and organs, even where those actions are committed outside the scope of the State official's or organ's apparent authority if they 'acted, at least apparently, as authorised officials or organs, or

---

[19] See the homepage of the International Law Commission (ILC), especially the summary of its work in this area: http://untreaty.un.org/ilc/summaries/9_11.htm (last viewed 30.08.08).

[20] See the Fifth Report of the Special Rapporteur at: http://untreaty.un.org/ilc/reports/2007/2007report.htm (last viewed 30.10.07). The Draft Articles referred to in this chapter are set out in that Report (hereinafter 'ILC Draft Articles').

[21] International Law Commission, Articles on Responsibility of States for Internationally Wrongful Acts, *Report of the International Law Commission on the Work of its Fifty-third Session*, UNGAOR, 56th Session, Supp. No. 10, UN Doc. A/56/10 (2001); hereinafter referred to as 'ILC Articles on State Responsibility'.

[22] Draft Article 3, ILC Draft Articles (note 20).

[23] See, for example, *Factory at Chorzów* (*Claim for Indemnity*) (*Germany v. Poland*) (*Merits*) PCIJ *Reports, Series A*, No. 17 (1928), p. 4.

that, in so acting, they ... used powers or measures appropriate to their official character'.[24] In addition, the general law of State responsibility provides for the possibility of attribution to a State where a State empowers an entity to exercise elements of public authority (including in the absence of default of the State);[25] where an entity acts on the 'instructions of, or under the direction or control of' a State;[26] and where the State, through aiding and assisting the entity is complicit in the commission of an internationally wrongful act committed by another State or by the entity itself.[27] In all of these cases, such acts will be attributable to the State even where they are committed outside the territory of that State.[28]

On the basis of equivalence of State responsibility and international organisation responsibility, the ILC has considered that the actions and omissions of officials, agents and organs of international organisations are attributable to those organisations,[29] which must include where those actions are committed outside the scope of the official's apparent authority.[30] There is also attribution to international organisations of actions by entities under the effective control of international organisations, including in the situations referred to above.[31]

In relying on the direct application of these general principles of State responsibility to international organisations,[32] the ILC quotes a report on UN peacekeeping operations, where the UN Secretary-General stated:

> The international responsibility of the United Nations for the activities of United Nations forces is an attribute of its international legal personality and its capacity to bear international rights and obligations. It is also a reflection of the principle of State responsibility – widely accepted to be applicable to international organizations – that damage caused in breach of an international

---

[24] *Caire Claim (France v. Mexico)* 5 *UN Reports of International Arbitral Awards* 516. However, 'much depends on the type of activity and the related consequences in the particular case'. See Brownlie, *Principles of Public International Law* (Fifth edition), Oxford, 1998, at p. 454.

[25] Articles 5 and 9, ILC Articles on State Responsibility (note 21).

[26] Ibid, Article 8.

[27] Ibid, Article 16.

[28] For a detailed discussion see McCorquodale and Simons, 'Responsibility Beyond Borders: State Responsibility for Extraterritorial Violations by Corporations of International Human Rights Law', 70 (2007) *MLR* 598.

[29] Draft Article 4, ILC Draft Articles (note 20).

[30] Ibid, Draft Article 6.

[31] Ibid, Draft Articles 5 and 12–15. See also the decision of the European Court of Human Rights in *Behrami v. France* [GC], (2 May 2007), Appl. No. 71412/01.

[32] International Law Commission, *Report of the International Law Commission on the Work of its Fifty-fifth Session*, UNGAOR, 58th Session, Supp. No. 10, UN Doc. A/58/10 (2003): see Chapter IV, available at: http://untreaty.un.org/ilc/reports/2003/english/chp4.pdf; (hereafter referred to as *ILC Commentaries on Responsibility of International Organisations*). The ILC also notes that 'damage does not appear to be an element necessary for international responsibility of an international organization to arise': see p. 46.

obligation and which is attributable to the State (or to the Organization), entails the international responsibility of the State (or of the Organization) and its liability in compensation.[33]

The ILC also notes the ICJ's views:

> [T]he Court wishes to point out that the question of immunity from legal process is distinct from the issue of compensation for any damages incurred as a result of acts performed by the United Nations or by its agents acting in their official capacity. The United Nations may be required to bear responsibility for the damage arising from such acts .... Furthermore, it need hardly be said that all agents of the United Nations, in whatever official capacity they act, must take care not to exceed the scope of their functions, and should so comport themselves as to avoid claims against the United Nations.[34]

Beyond this, there is no substantial evidence provided by the ILC of State practice or international documents to support its view that the general principles of State responsibility are applicable automatically to international organisations. This is a pity, as there is other support for this position, both by writers[35] and in UN practice, with the UN accepting responsibility for injuries to State's nationals during some UN peace-keeping operations.[36]

Yet the ILC's view is open to some criticism. First, it assumes that the international law of State responsibility as set out in the ILC Articles on State Responsibility is both universally accepted and generally uncontroversial.[37] Second, the ILC assumes that an international law developed to deal with State actions and omissions, and which developed through State practice and State views, is applicable to entities that are not States (even if created by States).[38] The law on State responsibility is a law in which States themselves have determined their own obligations for certain acts in relation to other States and when a State

---

[33] Report of the Secretary-General, Financing of the United Nations Protection Force, the United Nations Confidence Restoration Operation in Croatia, the United Nations Preventive Deployment Force and the United Nations Peace Forces Headquarters: Administrative and Budgetary Aspects of the Financing of the United Nations Peacekeeping Operations, General Assembly, UN Doc. A/51/389 (1996), paragraph 6.

[34] *Difference Relating to Immunity from Legal Process of a Special Rapporteur of the Commission on Human Rights*, Advisory Opinion, *ICJ Reports 1999*, p. 62, at paragraph 66.

[35] See, for example, Sarooshi, *International Organizations and their Exercise of Sovereign Powers*, Oxford, 2005.

[36] See the discussion in Amerasinghe (note 2), pp. 399–406, especially in regard to the Congo and Egypt.

[37] See, for example, the strong critique by Allott: 'State Responsibility and the Unmaking of International Law', 29 (1988) *Harvard International Law Journal* 1.

[38] For a detailed discussion of the State-focussed nature of the international legal system, see McCorquodale, 'An Inclusive International Legal System' 17 (2004) *Leiden Journal of International Law* 477.

can enforce these obligations against other States i.e. it is a law by States limiting when States are legally responsible to other States. Therefore, it is arguable that all or parts of the law of State responsibility cannot apply – or apply with considerable differences – to international organisations. Third, the creation of an international organisation is by a treaty and this can be a constitutive part of international law (such as the United Nations Charter), and so the institutional practices of international organisations may constitute part of international law. The ILC did recognize this concern, as it noted that the usual rule for States that an internal law of a State cannot justify a breach of international law may not be directly applicable to international organisations:

> The difficulty in transposing this principle to international organizations depends on the fact that the internal law of an international organization cannot be sharply differentiated from international law. At least the constituent instrument of the international organization is a treaty or another instrument governed by international law; some further parts of the internal law of the organization may be viewed as belonging to international law. One important distinction is whether the relevant obligation exists towards a member or a non-member State, although this distinction is not necessarily conclusive, because it would be questionable to say that the internal law of the organization always prevails over the obligation that the organization has under international law towards a member State. On the other hand, with regard to non-member States, Article 103 of the United Nations Charter may provide a justification for the organization's conduct in breach of an obligation under a treaty with a non-member State. Thus, the relations between international law and the internal law of an international organization appear too complex to be expressed in a general principle.[39]

Despite acknowledging this difficulty, the ILC Draft Articles provide that there is a breach of an international obligation by an international organisation when an act by it is contrary to international law 'regardless of its origin or character … [and includes a] breach of an obligation under international law established by a rule of the international organization.'[40] This implies that, in a similar way to States, an international organisation can act in conformity with its own rules and yet be acting in breach of international law. Finally, there is the continuing problem of primary and secondary rules in relation to international responsibility,[41]

---

[39] *ILC Commentaries on Responsibility of International Organisations* (note 32): see commentary on Article 3, paragraph 10, pp. 48–49.
[40] Draft Article 8, ILC Draft Articles (note 20).
[41] The rules set out in the ILC Articles on State Responsibility are considered by the ILC to be secondary rules of international law, that 'indicate the consequences of a breach of an applicable primary obligation': see Crawford, *The International Law Commission's Articles on State Responsibility: Introduction, Text and Commentaries*, Cambridge, 2002, p. 74; (hereafter referred to as *ILC Commentaries on State Responsibility*).

as '[a]rticulating secondary rules of [an international organisation's] obligation without clarifying which primary rules of obligation apply (and to what extent) appears, in light of these realities, to be a surreal exercise'.[42] Indeed, it could be that, especially in light of the issues of legitimacy of international organisations,[43] the 'relatively unaccountable nature of international organizations may be a key structural feature ... [and] not something that has come about by accident'.[44]

These concerns are allayed to some extent by the expectation of the ILC that the international legal responsibility of an international organisation can be considered as separate to State responsibility. It notes that:

> The fact that an international organization is responsible for an internationally wrongful act does not exclude the existence of parallel responsibility of other subjects of international law in the same set of circumstances. For instance, an international organization may have cooperated with a State in the breach of an obligation imposed on both.[45]

This view is consistent with the position that having international legal personality does not mean that international organisations have exactly the same rights and responsibilities as States (as noted above). It is also clear that a State is not able to hide behind an international organisation in order to avoid its own international responsibility. The Grand Chamber of the European Court of Human Rights has held:

> The Court is of the opinion that where States establish international organisations in order to pursue or strengthen their cooperation in certain fields of activities, and where they attribute to these organisations certain competences and accord them immunities, there may be implications as to the protection of fundamental rights. It would be incompatible with the purpose and object of the [European Convention on Human Rights], however, if Contracting States were thereby absolved from their responsibility under the Convention in relation to the field of activity covered by such attribution. It should be recalled that the Convention is intended to guarantee not theoretical or illusory rights, but rights that are practical and effective.[46]

---

[42] See Alvarez's comments in his review of D. Sarooshi, *International Organisations and Their Exercise of Sovereign Powers* in 101 (2007) *AJIL* 674, at p. 677.

[43] See, for example, some of the work by international relations scholars in this area: Keohane, 'Global Governance and Democratic Accountability', in Held and Koenig-Archibugi (eds.), *Taming Globalization: Frontiers of Governance*, Polity Press, Oxford, 2003, p. 130; and Grant and Keohane, 'Accountability and Abuses of Power in World Politics', 99 (2005) *American Political Science Review* 23.

[44] Wilde, 'Enhancing Accountability at the International Level; The Tension between International Organization and Member State Responsibility and the Underlying Issues at Stake', 12 (2006) *ILSA Journal of International and Comparative Law* 396, at p. 402.

[45] *ILC Commentaries on Responsibility of International Organisations* (note 32), p. 47, at paragraph 8.

[46] ECtHR, *Waite and Kennedy v. Germany* [GC], (18 February 1999), Appl. No. 26083/94, at paragraph 67.

The Court is confirming that States have their own responsibility under international law and that this responsibility 'continues even after such a transfer' of competences to an international organisation.[47] It is also possible that a State may be responsible within national law for actions of an international organisation even where that international organisation has immunity.[48] At the same time it necessary to acknowledge that States create international organisations for a variety of purposes, which include taking action that a State cannot, such as to reduce significantly inter-State trade barriers or to provide large financial aid, and taking action that a State would not want to do in its own name, such as to undertake peace-keeping operations.[49] Therefore, it is coherent that the international legal responsibility of international organisations must be separate from that of States.

Above all, as it is uniformly accepted that international organisations have international legal personality, by which they participate in the international legal system, then they must have international rights and responsibilities. Even if these international legal responsibilities are not exactly the same as those of States, international organisations must have some legal responsibilities arising from their participation in the international legal system. At the very least, this responsibility means that actions by officials of international organisations are attributable to those organisations and that when international organisations breach international law they are internationally legally responsible. The fact that it may be difficult to enforce that responsibility is not a key factor in the international legal system, as, for example, it was accepted that genocide was a breach of customary international law for many decades before there was a means to enforce this within the international legal system.[50] On this basis it is possible to examine the extent to which international legal responsibility for international organisations arises in the area of international human rights law.

---

[47] ECtHR, *Matthews v. United Kingdom*, [GC], (18 February 1999), Appl. No. 24833, at paragraph 32.

[48] See Wickremasinghe and Verdirame, 'Responsibility and Liability for Violations of Human Rights in the Course of UN Field Operations', in Scott (ed.), *Torture as Tort*, Hart Publishing, Oxford/Portland, 2001, at p. 465 and p. 485, who claim that a host State of an international organisation can be responsible under its national law even where the international organisation has immunity. See also Nollkaemper, 'Internationally Wrongful Acts in Domestic Courts', 101 (2007) *AJIL* 760.

[49] See the discussion about the role of the European Union in Menon and Weatherill, 'Democratic Politics in a Globalising World: Supranationalism and Legitimacy in the European Union', 13 (2007) *LSE Law, Society and Economy Working Papers* (www.lse.ac.uk/collections/law/wps/wps.htm; last visited 30.10.07).

[50] See, for example, van Zyl Smit, 'Punishment and Human Rights in International Criminal Law', 2 (2002) *Human Rights Law Review* 1; and Schabas, *Introduction to the International Criminal Court*, Cambridge, 2001.

III. INTERNATIONAL HUMAN RIGHTS LAW

1. *Applicability*

Before it is possible to examine the extent to which international legal responsibility for international organisations arises in the area of international human rights law, it is necessary to determine if the general principles of international legal responsibility can be applied to international human rights law at all. After all, the focus of international human rights law is the protection of the human person and not about actions between States, and '[t]he law of State responsibility distinguishes "public" actions for which the State is accountable from those 'private' ones for which it does not have to answer internationally'.[51] Indeed, it is Andrew Clapham's view that 'human rights law has developed a set of State obligations that cannot be understood by the application of the primary rules of diplomatic protection of foreigners and the secondary rules of State responsibility'.[52] Further, at a time when international human rights law is being strongly criticized for its lack of direct responsibility on non-State actors for violations of human rights,[53] the adoption by it of general State-focused international responsibility principles could be problematic.

The narrow focus of human rights law on State responsibility is not only out of step with current power relations, but also tends to obscure them. The exclusive concern with national governments not only distorts the reality of the growing weakness of national-level authority, but also shields other actors from greater responsibility. The focus on State responsibility also creates a false sense of rigidity or inevitability about social and political hierarchies and existing inequities.[54]

Despite these concerns, it is clear that the ILC itself considered that the general provisions about State responsibility applied to international human rights law. In the ILC's Commentary on its Articles on State Responsibility, it notes that these principles are to be applied to all areas within the international legal system, though there may be different compliance mechanisms for its

---

[51] Charlesworth and Chinkin (note 9), p. 148.

[52] See *Human Rights Obligations of Non-State Actors*, Oxford, 2006, p. 318. See also the critiques of Mazzechi, 'The Marginal Role of the Individual in the ILC's Articles on State Responsibility', 14 (2004) *Italian YBIL* 39, at p. 47; Bodansky, Crook and Brown Weiss, 'Invoking State Responsibility in the Twenty-First Century', 96 (2002) *AJIL* 798, at p. 809; and Charlesworth and Chinkin (note 9), p. 148.

[53] See, for example, McCorquodale (note 38).

[54] Jochnick, 'Confronting the Impunity of Non-State Actors: New Fields for the Promotion of Human Rights', 21 (1999) *HRQ* 56, at p. 59.

enforcement in parts of that system, such as with human rights treaty monitoring bodies.[55] Whilst there is an exclusion of the application of the Articles on State Responsibility where the existence, content or implementation of State responsibility is governed by special rules (*lex specialis*) of international law[56] – and international human rights law clearly has special rules and procedures – the ILC has considered that areas of international law such as human rights are 'special regimes' and are not outside the framework of general international law.[57] Indeed, the ILC has commented that these Articles are generally applicable to 'the whole field of the international responsibility of States, whether the obligation is owed to one or several States, to an individual or a group, or to the international community as a whole,'[58] and there is often reference in the Commentaries on State Responsibility to human rights examples and cases.[59] There is no reason to suppose that this position does not apply equally to the ILC's Draft Articles on Responsibility of International Organisations in light of its general linking of those Draft Articles to the Articles on State Responsibility, as discussed above.

In fact, the human rights treaty monitoring bodies have applied the general law of State responsibility to key aspects of human rights matters before them. Sometimes they have done this explicitly, for example, the Inter-American Court of Human Rights has stated that:

> According to the rules of law pertaining to the international responsibility of the State and applicable under international human rights law, actions or omissions by any public authority, whatever its hierarchic position, are chargeable to the State which is responsible under the terms set forth in the American Convention [on Human Rights].[60]

The Grand Chamber of the European Court of Human Rights has added:

> [The Court] must also take into account relevant rules of international law when examining questions concerning jurisdiction and, consequently, determine State responsibility in conformity and harmony with the governing principles of

---

[55] See *ILC Commentaries on State Responsibility*, in relation to Parts II and III of the ILC Articles on State Responsibility: *supra* (note 21).

[56] Article 55, ILC Articles on State Responsibility (note 21).

[57] See ILC Study Group on Fragmentation of International Law, 'First Report: Study on the Function and Scope of Lex Specialis Rule and the Question of "Self-Contained Regimes"', UN Doc. ILC (LVI)/SG/FIL/CRD.1/Add.1 (2004), at paragraph 134.

[58] *ILC Commentaries on State Responsibility* (note 40), p. 76.

[59] See, for example, *ILC Commentaries on State Responsibility* (note 41), p. 129.

[60] *The Mayagua Awas Tingni Community v. Nicaragua*: Inter-American Court of Human Rights, 10 (2003) *IHRR* 758, paragraph 154.

international law of which [the European Convention] forms a part, although it must remain mindful of the Convention's special character as a human rights treaty.[61]

More often, the human rights treaty monitoring bodies have applied the general law of State responsibility implicitly.[62] Yet it should be noted that, in the development of jurisprudence in this area, these bodies have not always distinguished clearly between the concepts of attribution, the scope of a State's obligations and State responsibility.[63] Nevertheless, this chapter will continue on the basis that the general principles of State responsibility are applicable to international human rights law and, accordingly, the general principles of international legal responsibility of international organisations are applicable.

2. *International Obligations*

The core issue, though, is whether there exist international obligations of international organisations in relation to human rights. If there are no such obligations then there can be no breach of them under the general principles of international responsibility, as there is no 'conduct consisting of an action or omission by it that constitutes a breach of an international obligation'.[64] This section will look at three approaches to considering whether there are such international obligations: the international organisation must not act contrary to its member State's obligations; international organisations are bound by customary international law (which includes some human rights obligations) as are all international legal persons; and the nature of human rights obligations extends to international organisations.

The approach that an international organisation has international human rights obligations because it must not act contrary to its member State's obligations arises because of the position, noted above, that a State cannot hide

---

[61] *Behrami* (note 31); and ECtHR, *Saramati v. France, Germany and Norway* [GC], (Admissibility), (31 May 2001), Appl. No. 78166, paragraph 122.

[62] Lawson, 'Out of Control. State Responsibility and Human Rights: Will the ILC's Definition of the "Act of State" Meet the Challenges of the 21st Century?', in Castermans, van Hoof and Smith (eds.), *The Role of the Nation-State in the 21st Century, Human Rights, International Organisations, and Foreign Policy: Essays in Honour of Peter Baehr*, Cambridge, MA, 1999, p. 91, who notes that 'the European Court of Human Rights has consistently applied the principles articulated in the ILC Draft Articles on State Responsibility, without, however, referring expressly to the Draft Articles': p. 115.

[63] See Cerone, *Out of Bounds? Considering the Reach of International Human Rights Law*, Center for Human Rights and Global Justice, Working Paper Number 5, 2006: at http://www.chrgj.org/publications/docs/wp/WPS_NYU_CHRGJ_Cerone_Final.pdf (last visited 05.02.08).

[64] Draft Article 3(2)(b), ILC Draft Articles (note 20).

behind an international organisation to avoid its own international obligations. Hence, the Committee on Economic, Social and Cultural Rights (CESCR) has stated:

> State parties [to the International Covenant on Economic, Social and Cultural Rights (ICESCR)] should ensure that their actions as members of international organizations take due account of the right to water. Accordingly, States parties that are members of international financial institutions, notably the International Monetary Fund, the World Bank, and regional development banks, should take steps to ensure that the right to water is taken into account in their lending policies, credit agreements and other international measures.[65]

The UN High Commissioner for Human Rights has made a similar statement with regard to the obligations of member States under the World Trade Organisation (WTO).[66] On this basis, this approach argues that the international organisation must ensure that it acts in such a way that member States do not breach their international human rights obligations (whether arising from customary international law or treaties).[67] After all, every State is a party to at least one of the major global human rights treaties,[68] and each of these treaties place an obligation on a State to adopt legislation or other measures to 'ensure' or 'realise' the rights in the human rights treaty, whether immediately or progressively.[69] This approach to international responsibility of international organisations for human rights reinforces the broad obligations of States to respect, protect and fulfil human rights in all their activities. However, this approach seems merely to reinforce the position that a State cannot avoid its obligations by becoming a member of an international organisation and that a State's obligations (and hence responsibility under international law) is separate from that of an international organisation. It does not resolve whether an international organisation has its own international human rights obligations, especially as international organisations are not party to any of the major global

---

[65] Committee on Economic, Social and Cultural Rights (CESCR), 'General Comment 15: The Right to Water', UN Doc. E/C.12/2002/11 (2002), paragraph 36.

[66] UN High Commissioner for Human Rights, *Liberalization of Trade in Services and Human Rights*, UN Doc. E/C.4/Sub.2/2002/9, paragraph 5.

[67] See, for example, Künneman, 'Extraterritorial Application of the International Covenant on Economic, Social and Cultural Rights', in Coomans and Kamminga (eds.), *Extraterritorial Application of Human Rights Treaties*, Antwerp, 2004, p. 214.

[68] The issue of reservations is not considered here because no State has argued that it has no obligation to adopt any measures to comply with its international human rights treaty obligations.

[69] See, for example, Article 2 of both the International Covenant on Economic, Social and Cultural Rights (ICESCR) and the International Covenant on Civil and Political Rights (ICCPR).

human rights treaties. It also does not take account of the fact that the role of each individual State within an international organisation, in terms of a State's ability to direct or control the actions of that organisation, will vary considerably.[70]

The second approach is to argue that international organisations have direct human rights obligations arising from customary international law and respect for the UN Charter.[71] The ICJ's view is clear:

> International organisations are subjects of international law and, as such, are bound by any obligations incumbent upon them under general rules of international law, under their constitutions or under international agreements to which they are parties.[72]

This approach focuses especially on the UN and UN agencies because the UN Charter mandates the creation of UN specialised agencies 'required for the accomplishment of the purposes set forth in Article 55',[73] which includes 'the promotion of ... universal respect for, and observance of, human rights and fundamental freedoms for all without distinction as to race, sex, language, or religion'.[74] Therefore,

> A reasonable inference would be that the purposes set forth in Article 55 are the raison d'être of any specialised agency created under Article 57 or Article 59. Interpreted in this manner, the IMF [and other UN specialised agencies] is under an obligation to fulfil the human rights purposes set forth in Article 55 of the United Nations Charter.[75]

---

[70] See Coomans, 'Some Remarks on the Extraterritorial Application of the International Covenant on Economic, Social and Cultural Rights', in Coomans and Kamminga (note 67), who writes: '[I]nternational organisations yield control to the States that contribute financially to the organisation, while at the same time States yield control to the organisation to execute its mandate. Therefore, in a way, there is a vacuum in the sphere of controlling the execution of the decisions of these organisations and a vacuum also in the sphere of accountability and responsibility': p. 194. See also Broude, *International Governance in the WTO: Judicial Boundaries and Political Capitulation*, London, 2004.

[71] See, for example, Blokker and Schermers (note 2), pp. 1002–1010; and Reinisch, 'Securing the Accountability of International Organizations', 7 (2001) *Global Governance* 131.

[72] *Interpretation of the Agreement of March 25 1951 between the WHO and Egypt*: Advisory Opinion, *ICJ Reports 1980*, p. 73, at pp. 89–90. Similar views are expressed by other international tribunals considering these issues: see Sands and Klein (note 2), p. 457 and WTO Appellate Body, *United States – Standards for Reformulated and Conventional Gasoline*: WTO Doc WT/DS2/AB/R (May 1996), p. 16. See also the Final Report of the ILA Committee on the Accountability of International Organisations where it is stated that 'international organisations are subjects of international law and, as such, are bound by any obligations incumbent upon them under general rules of international law in carrying out their functions and in exercising the powers attributed to them': *supra* (note 6), p. 20.

[73] See Article 50, UN Charter.

[74] See ibid, Article 55.

[75] Rajagopal, 'Crossing the Rubicon: Synthesising the Soft International Law of the IMF and

In addition to this, the Vienna Declaration and Programme of Action on Human Rights 1993, agreed by all States, expressly stated:

> The World Conference on Human Rights recognises that relevant specialised agencies … play a vital role in the formulation, promotion and implementation of human rights standards, within their respective mandates, and should take into account the outcome of the World Conference on Human Rights within their fields of competence.[76]

Therefore this approach considers that an international organisation is subject to customary international law in its activities and these include those aspects of international human rights law, such as the prohibition on discrimination, that form part of customary international law.[77] Whilst this approach has the appeal of linking UN organisations with the human rights purposes of the UN, and human rights can be a valuable tool in decision-making by these organisations,[78] it does not conclusively show that there are direct human rights obligations on these UN agencies. The obligations on the UN agencies are couched in terms of 'promotion' of human rights, with failure to do so being contrary to the UN agencies own purposes and not directly a violation of international human rights law by those international organisations.

The third approach begins with the nature of international human rights law obligations and examines the extent to which they are appropriately applied to international organisations. Whilst international human rights law places the core legal obligations on States, the international human rights treaty monitoring bodies have extended these obligations to include actions that fall within the broad sovereignty of a State. Thus international human rights law

---

Human Rights', 11 (1993) *Boston University International Law Journal* 81, at p. 94. Although the IMF (and the World Bank) were created before the UN Charter was concluded, they are now specialised agencies of the UN. For a discussion of the link of the UN with the International Monetary Fund (IMF) and the World Bank see Gianviti (note 7), p. 113.

[76] See Part II, paragraph 3 of the Declaration adopted at the UN World Conference on Human Rights, Vienna, 1993: 32 (1993) *ILM* 1661.

[77] See also UN Commission on Human Rights, *Question of the Realization in All Countries of the Economic, Social and Cultural Rights Contained in the Universal Declaration of Human Rights*, UN Doc. E/CN.4/1996/22 (1996), especially paragraph 50, and UN Commission on Human Rights, *The Realization of Economic, Social and Cultural Rights, Second Progress Report by Special Rapporteur, UNESCOR*, UN Doc. E/CN.4/Sub.2/1991/17 (1991), especially paragraphs 52–54. This is supported by Sands and Klein (note 2), especially at pp. 458–459.

[78] See the excellent analysis of the World Bank and the IMF in terms of their human rights obligations in Darrow, *Between Light and Shadow, The World Bank, The International Monetary Fund and International Human Rights Law*, Hart Publishing, Oxford/Portland, 2003. Also note the role of the International Labour Organisation in human rights protections: see, for example, Rodríguez-Piñero, *Indigenous Peoples, Postcolonialism, and International Law: The ILO Regime*, Oxford, 2005.

obliges a State to take measures – such as by legislation and administrative practices – to control, regulate, investigate and prosecute actions by non-State actors that violate the human rights of those within the territory of that State, even when that action is not by a State official. For example, in *Velásquez Rodriguez v. Honduras*,[79] the Inter-American Court of Human Rights held that the international responsibility of a State may arise

> [N]ot because of the act itself, but because of a lack of due diligence to prevent the violation or to respond to it as required by [the human rights treaty] ... The State is obligated to investigate every situation involving a violation of rights under the Convention. If the State apparatus acts in such a way that the violation goes unpunished and the victim's full enjoyment of such rights is not restored as soon as possible, the State has failed to comply with its duty to ensure the free and full exercise of those rights to persons within its jurisdiction. The same is true when the State allows private persons or groups to act freely and with impunity to the detriment of the rights recognised in the Convention.[80]

This position has been followed by the various international human rights treaty monitoring bodies, including the UN Human Rights Committee[81] and the European Court of Human Rights.[82] So a State is considered to have a positive obligation to exercise due diligence to prevent human rights violations by all persons within that jurisdiction.[83] Therefore, even where a State is not directly responsible for the actual violation of international human rights law, the State can still be held responsible for a lack of positive action in responding to, or preventing, the violation.[84]

---

[79] 28 (1989) *ILM* 294.

[80] Ibid at paragraphs 172 and 176.

[81] *Herra Rubio v. Colombia* (161/1983), *HRC Report*, UNGAOR, 43rd Session, Supp. 40 (A/43/40), 1988, p. 190, paragraph 11.

[82] For example, ECtHR, *Ergi v. Turkey* (28 July 1998), Appl. No. 23818/94; and ECtHR, *Timurtas v. Turkey* (13 June 2000), Appl. No. 23531/94. See also the further extension of this obligation in *A v. UK*, 27 (1999) *EHRR* 611.

[83] See, for example, ECtHR, *Jordan v. UK* (4 May 2001), Appl. No. 24746/94, at paragraph 143, where the ECtHR held that the conduct of the investigation, the coroner's inquest, delay, the lack of both legal aid for the victim's family and the lack of public scrutiny of the reasons of the Director of Public Prosecutions not to prosecute, constituted a violation of Article 2 of the ECHR. See also *Halimi-Nedzibi v. Austria* (8/1991), UN Committee Against Torture: 1 (1994) *IHRR* 190 at paragraph 13.5; ECtHR, *Z v. UK* (10 May 2001), Appl. No. 29392/95, at paragraph 109; and ECtHR, *Keenan v. UK* (3 April 2001), Appl. No. 27229/95. See also Rhot-Arriaza, 'State Responsibility to Investigate and Prosecute Grave Human Rights Violations in International Law', 78 (1990) *California Law Review* 449; and Mendez, 'Accountability for Past Abuses', 19 (1997) *HRQ* 261.

[84] See Sornarajah, 'Linking State Responsibility for Certain Harms Caused by Corporate Nationals Abroad to Civil Recourse in the Legal Systems of Home States', in Scott (note 48); and see Alston (note 7).

This development in the scope of the obligations of States under human rights law has relevance for international organisations in that these broader obligations arise under international human rights law wherever there is an exercise of sovereignty within a State's jurisdiction. Yet that exercise of sovereignty need not be limited to State sovereignty. Sovereignty in international law has always changed with changed relationships. At the beginning of the development in the international legal system of the concept of sovereignty, the relevant relationship was one of princes or feudal lords,[85] but it has developed considerably since then. Sovereignty is relational and not static.[86] Being relational, sovereignty changes over time with changes in the relationship and there is no requirement within the concept of sovereignty itself that means that it can only be applied between States.[87] In fact, it is evident that international organisations are increasingly acting like sovereigns.[88] Indeed,

> [T]he United Nations assumption of powers akin to those of sovereign States allows the conceptual leap toward a vision of the United Nations as not merely a benign promoter, but as a potential guarantor of human rights in places like Kosovo or East Timor .... Both UNTAET and UNMIK in turn emphatically proclaimed the 'applicability' of human rights standards by stipulating that '[i]n exercising their functions, all persona undertaking public duties or holding public office [in the respective territories] shall observe internationally recognised human rights standards'.[89]

On this basis, the Ombudsperson in Kosovo considered that the UN had created UNMIK as a 'surrogate State [which imposed] all ensuing obligations, including affirmative obligations to secure human rights to everyone within

---

[85] Brierly, *The Law of Nations: An Introduction to the International Law of Peace* (Sixth edition edited by Humphrey Waldock), Oxford, 1963, pp. 1–2.

[86] See the view of the Permanent Court of International Justice in *Tunis-Morocco Nationality Decrees* Advisory Opinion: 'The question whether a certain matter is or is not solely within the jurisdiction of a State is an essentially relative question; it depends upon the development of international relations'. See *PCIJ Reports, Series B, No. 4* (1923), p. 7, at p. 24.

[87] For a full discussion, see McCorquodale, 'International Community and State Sovereignty: An Uneasy Symbiotic Relationship', in Warbrick and Tierney (eds.), *Towards an 'International Legal Community'? The Sovereignty of States and the Sovereignty of International Law*, London, 2006, p. 241.

[88] See, for example the series of articles on international administration in 10 (2004) *Global Governance*; and in Wilde, *International Territorial Administration*, Oxford, 2008. Note the view that 'to replace absolute sovereigns with absolute supra-sovereigns in the form of institutions is hardly the solution': see Rajagopal, *International Law from Below*, Cambridge, 2003, p. 294.

[89] Mégret and Hoffmann, 'The UN as a Human Rights Violator? Some Reflections on the United Nations Changing Human Rights Responsibilities', 25 (2003) *HRQ* 314 at pp. 333–334.

UNMIK's jurisdiction'.[90] It is, therefore, possible to consider that an international organisation that is acting as a sovereign is subject to international human rights law obligations. In fact, there are instances where international organisations have acknowledged this, with the 'abundance of official training manual and courses on the duty of UN personnel to protect and respect human rights [making] it quite clear that the UN itself sees that it, and its personnel, must respect international human rights'.[91] Further, in relation to the exercise of sovereignty, the ILC Draft Articles show, as noted above, that actions by non-State actors can be attributed to an international organisation where they are acting under the effective control of those organisations, and this can be where those organisations are exercising sovereignty.

Therefore, an approach that examines the nature of obligations under international human rights law, leads to the conclusion that international organisations can have human rights obligations, at least when exercising sovereign powers. As these powers arise from these organisations participating in the international legal system and thus having international legal personality, this is consistent with the position that there are rights and responsibilities that arise from all forms of international legal personality, including that of international organisations.

IV. CONCLUSIONS

International organisations are increasingly acting in ways that can infringe human rights. This can even occur when one of their functions is to protect human rights:

> UNMIK is not structured according to democratic principles, does not function in accordance with the rule of law, and does not respect important international human rights norms. The people of Kosovo are therefore deprived of protection of their basic rights and freedoms three years after the end of the conflict by the very entity set up to guarantee them.[92]

At the same time, it is accepted that international organisations have international legal personality, which acknowledges that they are participants in the international legal system, and have both rights and responsibilities within that

---

[90] Ompudsperson Institution in Kosovo, Special Report No. 2 (27 October 2000): see www.ombudspersonkosovo.org (last visited 30.10.07).

[91] Clapham (note 52), p. 127. See also the project on human rights field officers: O'Flaherty (ed.), *The Human Rights Field Operation: Law, Theory and Practice*, Aldershot, 2007.

[92] Ompudsperson Institution in Kosovo, Second Annual Report 2001–2002 (10 July 2002): see www.ombudspersonkosovo.org (last visited 30.10.07).

system. Yet there has been no agreement as to the nature of this international responsibility or how it relates to international human rights law.

As has been shown, the general principles of State responsibility have been, and can be, applied to the international legal responsibility of international organisations. These general principles apply to most international organisations and mean that actions by officials and those acting under the effective control of international organisations can be attributed to international organisations. State members of international organisations have individual obligations under international human rights law but these apply independently of the international organisation. International organisations have general obligations to comply with customary international law and the development of international human rights legal obligations can be understood to extend to those international legal persons exercising sovereign power.

Accordingly, international organisations have international legal responsibility to act with due diligence not to infringe international human rights law. Such a victim-centred approach has the possibility of broad application within the international legal system,[93] including to post-conflict situations where sovereign power can be held by more than one participant,[94] and is relevant in the context of globalisation where powers of States and international organisations (and other non-States) are often intertwined.

Enforcing compliance by international organisations with human rights obligations is not impossible. The European Union has the ability to check compliance within its system[95] and the European Court of Human Rights accepts that it can review compliance by the European Union organisations with the European Convention on Human Rights.[96] Beyond this, and statements by the human rights treaty monitoring bodies in General Comments and when considering State's periodic reports, there is at present no coherent avenue within the international legal system to enforce compliance with

---

[93] The acceptance of such a 'victim-oriented perspective' is found in the (former) UN Commission on Human Rights Resolution 2005/35: 'Convinced that, in adopting a victim-oriented perspective, the international community affirms its human solidarity with victims of violations of international law, including violations of international human rights law and international humanitarian law, as well as with humanity at large': see Preamble, UN Doc E/CN.4/2005/L.10/Add.11.

[94] See Verdirame, 'UN Accountability for Human Rights Violations in Post-Conflict Situations', in White and Klaasen (eds.), *The UN, Human Rights and Post-Conflict Situations*, Manchester, 2005, p. 79.

[95] See the discussion in Reinisch (note 70), *supra*.

[96] See the consideration of these issues by the European Court of Human Rights in *Bosphorus Airways v. Ireland* [GC], (30 June 2005), Appl. No. 45036/98, and *Behrami* (note 31).

this responsibility.[97] Yet the obligations and responsibilities of international organisations do exist, and compliance can be at the institutional, managerial and political levels. The lack of means of enforcement is not crucial, as it took many years for an international criminal law monitoring body to be created, even though there was little doubt that all international legal persons had obligations in relation to genocide and war crimes. In the same way that it took decades before humans took steps on the Moon, it will take years for the international legal responsibility of international organisations in relation to international human rights law to be universally accepted and enforced. Yet, to do so, will be a giant leap for the protection of humankind.

[97] For some suggested ways forward, see Hoffmann and Mégret, 'Fostering Human Rights Accountability: An Ombudsperson for the United Nations?', 11 (2005) *Global Governance* 43, who propose the appointment of an ompudsperson; and Reinisch, 'Developing Human Rights and Humanitarian Accountability of the Security Council for the Imposition of Economic Sanctions', 95 (2001) *AJIL* 851, who suggests that special mechanisms or procedures be created.

Part Two

International Criminal
Law and Justice

Chapter Eight

Imputability and Immunity as Separate Concepts: The Removal of Immunity from Civil Proceedings Relating to the Commission of an International Crime

Hazel Fox[*]

In this paper I plan to examine the rule of imputability of the acts of officials to the State as it affects reparation for violations of fundamental human rights constituting international crimes. The imputability rule serves in current law to enable the artificial entity of the State to act effectively as a legal person; acts performed by an official are treated as the acts of the State. Immunity is currently conceived as a companion rule which exempts the official from any personal liability for the acts he or she performs on the State's behalf and further secures the independence of the State by barring its subordination to another State indirectly by means of proceedings brought against the individual official. It is my intention to suggest that such a rule of immunity is not an automatic inevitable consequence of the rule of imputability which attributes the act to the State which appoints the official. My goal in writing is to assert and establish the separability of the plea of immunity from that of imputability.

I hope Colin Warbrick will approve of this endeavour. He has never been content to accept a proposition of law at face value. As a person and in all his writings, teaching, expositions of the law and friendly cross-questioning he has conducted a ceaseless and enjoyable pursuit of the right formulation of international law and its implementation in national laws, particularly in English

---

[*] CMG QC; Former Director of the British Institute of International and Comparative Law: 1982 to 1990.

K.H. Kaikobad & M. Bohlander (eds.), *International Law and Power: Perspectives on Legal Order and Justice*. Essays in Honour of Colin Warbrick, pp. 165–181.
© 2009 Koninklijke Brill NV. Printed in the Netherlands.

law. I know no one who in the examination of an area of law can better by a brief comment strip away false trappings and expose the hard kernel which gives a rule of law its vitality and moral force.

I, along with a number of others, am troubled that international law under the principle of universal jurisdiction now accepts that a national court, and even one neither of the State of the nationality of the alleged wrongdoer nor the State of the territory where the act was committed, can prosecute and punish an individual for committing the international crime of torture but the same international law bars such national courts from inquiring into who, whether the individual or the State which appoints him as its official, should pay reparation in respect of that crime. In this paper I first address the notion of severability and the reasons for removal of immunity in respect of criminal but not civil proceedings in a national court where proof of the commission of an international crime is established. I then discuss in general terms the two concepts of imputability and immunity and seek to show that they are distinguishable and independent concepts. In the final part I set out the manner in which this separation may properly be given effect by the exercise by the national courts of civil jurisdiction over the consequences of the commission of international crime.

At the outset I should make plain the limited scope of my proposals. My revision of the contemporary position is solely directed to functional immunity *ratione materiae*, and not to personal immunity; and further they relate to the removal of functional immunity solely in respect of the commission of international crimes which the State by treaty or international custom is under obligation not to commit itself or to permit their commission by its officials. Personal immunity *ratione personae* which is enjoyed by Heads of State and diplomats is in no way affected. On the authority of the decision of the International Court of Justice in the *Arrest Warrant* case, a similar personal immunity extends to the serving head of government and Minister for Foreign Affairs when in office. Such personal immunity exists during the holding of office and covers all acts including the commission of international crimes. On termination of office such persons lose their personal immunity but under current law they enjoy functional immunity in respect of their official acts performed while in office. My proposal would leave that position unchanged save as to any functional immunity after vacating office which they might claim as to the commission of an international crime. I would thus treat as *obiter dicta* and not binding in law the International Court of Justice's statement that the removal of immunity is confined to acts performed in a personal capacity; the words used by the Court being: '... after a person ceases to hold the office of Minister for Foreign Affairs, ... a court of one State may try a former Minister for Foreign Affairs of another State in respect of acts committed prior or subsequent to his or her period of office, as well as in respect of acts committed during that period of office in a private capacity'.[1]

As regards other officials or persons acting on the State's behalf, in accordance with the existing position functional immunity protects them in respect of official acts performed during or after the period in which they are in service but not, on the authority of *Pinochet*, in respect of criminal proceedings for the commission of an international crime for which universal jurisdiction exists. My proposals are narrowly directed to an extension of the removal of functional immunity to civil proceedings in respect of the commission of such an international crime and by that removal enabling civil proceedings to be brought against both the individual official and the State for reparation. The determination of any question of the attribution of such conduct to the State would, however, remain an independent issue; only immunity is removed. Whether with immunity removed the national court will exercise jurisdiction may depend on the presence of a sufficient jurisdictional connection and the exhaustion of local remedies. And as to the substantive claim the national courts' adjudication will depend on the international obligations which the defendant State has undertaken, proof of their violation and any reparation made.

I. The Separability of Immunity from the Attribution of the Act

In *Jones v. Saudi Arabia* the House of Lords ruled that no civil proceedings for reparation may be brought in English law for the commission of the international crime of torture either against the individual official who committed the crime or against the State who placed him in office. In that case four claimants, three of British and the fourth of Canadian nationality, alleged systematic torture in a Saudi Arabian prison over a period of two months from March to May 2001. Their applications came before Master Whitaker who dismissed Jones' claim against the Kingdom of Saudi Arabia as barred by State immunity and refused leave to serve out of the jurisdiction on the individual defendants on the ground that 'the immunity afforded to the State under the State Immunity Act 1978 clearly extends to [the individual defendants] as part of the Saudi Arabian State under section 14(1)' of that Act. On appeal, the Court of Appeal followed its previous decision in *Al-Adsani*[2] and ruled that State immunity barred civil proceedings against a foreign State for a claim for compensation in respect of systematic torture. But it held there to be no bar of immunity from

---

[1]　*ICJ Reports 2002*, p. 4; 41 (2002) *ILM* 536, paragraph 61.
[2]　*Al-Adsani v. UK*, 34 (2002) *EHRR* 111.

civil proceedings brought against three officials in the service of Saudi Arabia, a captain and lieutenant in the Saudi Arabian police, and a colonel, deputy governor of the prison where the torture was alleged to have occurred. The House of Lords, with Lords Bingham and Hoffmann giving opinions, reversed this second ruling holding that the immunity which barred proceedings against the State of Saudi Arabia also barred any claim against its officials.[3]

In the reasoning supporting this ruling it was necessary for the Law Lords to distinguish its prior decision in *Pinochet*.[4] Pinochet, a former head of the Republic of Chile, whilst receiving medical treatment in London, was placed under arrest on the request of the Spanish government to extradite him to Spain to stand trial for crimes including torture against Spanish nationals. His plea of immunity from extradition proceedings for the international crime of torture was rejected by a majority of six to one. Lord Bingham in *Jones* explained that decision as follows:

> The essential ratio of the decision, as I understand it, was that international law could not without absurdity require criminal jurisdiction to be assumed and exercised where the Torture Convention conditions were satisfied and, at the same time, require immunity to be granted to those properly charged. The Torture Convention was the mainspring of the decision ...[5]

Lord Bingham thus considered the absence of immunity in the proceedings brought against Pinochet turned on the proper construction of the terms of the UN Torture Convention. Adopting a narrow view, Lord Hoffmann explained the *ratio decidendi* of *Pinochet* as a construction of the Vienna Convention on Diplomatic Relations 1961 Article 39 as incorporated into English law by the UK State Immunity section 20(1):

> Section 20(1) of the SIA therefore gave rise to the question of whether torturing people could be an exercise of the functions of a head of State, which is a very different question from whether it could be an official act for the purpose of common law immunity ratione personae. It is in this context that one must read some of the dicta on which the Court of Appeal relied.[6]

But more significantly, building on the distinction between the substantive law of prohibition with the jurisdictional requirement of immunity Lord Hoffmann

---

[3] *Jones v. Minister of the Interior of the Kingdom of Saudi Arabia and another (Secretary of State for Constitutional Affairs and Others Intervening) Mitchell and Others v. Al-Dali* [2006] UKHL 26; [2006] 2 WLR 1424.

[4] *Ex parte Pinochet R v. Bow Street Metropolitan Stipendiary Magistrate, ex parte Pinochet Ugarte (Amnesty International Intervening), (No. 3)* [2000] I AC 147; [1999] 2 All ER 97.

[5] *Supra* (note 3), paragraph 19.

[6] Ibid, paragraph 87.

took a broader approach. He stressed the difficulty in which the applicants were placed by their reliance on the Torture Convention:

> To produce a conflict with State immunity, it is therefore necessary to show that the prohibition on torture has generated an ancillary procedural rule which, by way of exception to state immunity, entitles or perhaps requires states to assume civil jurisdiction over other states in cases in which torture is alleged. Such a rule may be desirable, and since international law changes, may have developed. But it is not *entailed* by the prohibition of torture.[7]

He then explains the ruling of no-immunity in *Pinochet* on the general ground as a situation where there is, in his phrase, 'an asymmetry between the rules of liability and immunity'.[8] Thus Lord Hoffmann explains the Lords' decision in that case as follows: 'The reason why General Pinochet did not enjoy immunity ratione materiae was not because he was deemed not to have acted in an official capacity; that would have removed his acts from the [2004 UN] Convention [on Torture] definition of torture. It was because, by necessary implication, international law had removed the immunity.'[9]

Clearly, then, here is a situation of the separability of immunity from the attribution of the act of a State official to the State. Yet, on the authority of *Jones* and the earlier decision of the European Court of Human Rights in *Al Adsani*, such removal of immunity only occurs in respect of the criminal consequences of the commission of the international crime of torture. Why? Is this to be explained as an exception, an anomaly, as a minor qualification, solely in respect of the criminal consequences of an international crime, of the general rule of immunity ratione materiae that protects an official of the State even when out of office? Or does it not point to the true position, namely that the concepts of attribution and the responsibility that results are separate and independent of the concept of immunity?

II. As an Exception to Immunity with Regard to Criminal Proceedings Against the Official

Those who support the restriction of the exception to the removal of immunity solely in respect of criminal proceedings do so on a number of somewhat conflicting grounds. Some rely on the peremptory nature of the *jus cogens* prohibitions relating to international crimes as overriding immunity. But if the

---

[7] Ibid, paragraph 45. Emphasis original.
[8] Ibid, paragraph 78.
[9] Ibid, paragraph 81.

peremptory nature of the *jus cogens* norm requires the setting aside of immunity for criminal proceedings why does it not also set aside immunity for civil proceedings so that reparation for the violation of the peremptory norm can be effected? Others categorise the commission of an international crime as a private act. The commission of an international crime, it is said, cannot be a function of the State in international law and consequently the criminal prosecution of an international crime relates to a private act. This position is well summarised in the Joint Separate Opinion of Judges Higgins, Kooijmans and Buergenthal in the *Arrest Warrant* case:

> It is now increasingly claimed in the literature ... that serious international crimes cannot be regarded as official acts because they are neither normal State functions nor functions that a State alone can perform ... This view is underscored by the increasing realization that State-related motives are not the proper test for determining what constitutes public State acts ...[10]

Akande challenges both these approaches.[11] To describe such acts as private acts is a legal fiction. Factually it is unrealistic where the act is performed on the orders or with the means or in a place provided by the State. Legally it contradicts the very ground on which the individual is made criminally liable. That ground is that his official position provides no defence. He is made personally liable because the defence of official status is removed. As the Nuremberg Tribunal stated in the *Trial of the Major War Criminals*:

> The principle of international law, which in certain circumstances, protects the representatives of a State cannot be applied to acts which are condemned as criminal by international law. The authors of these acts cannot shelter themselves behind their official position to be freed from punishment in appropriate proceedings.[12]

If the 'shelter' is removed in respect of acts which are condemned as criminal by international law how does it continue to apply in respect of civil proceedings brought in respect of the same acts? The recognition in the Nuremberg Charter, the Statutes of the International Criminal Tribunals for former Yugoslavia and Rwanda and now the Rome Statute of the International Criminal Court that official status is no defence to proceedings is treated as relevant to the personal liability of individuals both as regards proceedings in an international tribunal

---

[10] *Supra* (note 1), paragraph 74. References omitted.

[11] See 'The Jurisdiction of the ICC Over Nationals of Non Parties: Legal Basis and limits', 1 (2003) *JICJ* 618 at pp. 638–39; and see also 'The Application of International Law Immunities in Prosecutions of International Crimes', in Harrington, Milde and Vernon (eds.), *Bringing Power to Justice? The Prospects of the International Criminal Court*, Montreal, 2006, p. 47; and Cassese, *International Criminal Law*, Oxford, Chapter 14.

[12] 41 (1947) *AJIL* 172, at p. 221.

and before a national court, but not to the position of the State even though the offence may have been committed on its orders.

Under municipal law, the loss of immunity to permit his prosecution is declared to be without effect on the State's position. 'A State is not criminally responsible in international or English law, and therefore, cannot be indirectly impleaded for an act of torture.'[13] The loss of immunity of the official is accepted as not constituting too serious a concession or loss of protection because criminal proceedings only may be instituted by and at the discretion of the forum State who consequently retains political control of the process. But there is a hidden illogicality here. For the purposes of indictment of the individual both before an international tribunal and a national court the question of whether he acted on State orders is treated as an irrelevance. But as regards the State which gave the orders that irrelevancy is disregarded; the act is assumed to retain its quality as a State act sufficient to confer immunity for any consequences which the State might incur.

III. THE SEPARABILITY OF RESPONSIBILITY AND IMMUNITY

On the basis, then, that the removal of immunity solely in respect of criminal proceedings is an illogical distinction to maintain where the commission of an international crime is in issue, one can consider the problem more broadly. Here a moment's reflection surely assents to the separation of the two concepts. Responsibility and its companion in municipal law of liability relates to a substantive rule of international or municipal law, autonomous and usually preceding in time any consequence it may produce in respect of immunity from the jurisdiction of a national court. The basis of State immunity lies not in a concept of responsibility but in the concept of jurisdiction, of the permissibility of a national court of one State exercising jurisdiction over the acts of another State. That concept coupled with the artificial nature of the legal personality of the State gives rise to immunity by which international law defines the circumstances in which a territorial State may not exercise jurisdiction through its courts over another State. The International Court of Justice in the *Arrest Warrant* case recognised the distinct nature of the two concepts when it stated: 'Immunity from criminal jurisdiction and individual criminal responsibility are quite separate concepts. While jurisdictional immunity is procedural in nature, criminal responsibility is a question of substantive law'.[14]

---

[13] *Jones v. Saudi Arabia* (note 3), *per* Lord Bingham paragraph 31.
[14] *Supra* (note 1), paragraph 60.

Furthermore, the rule reflects a different direction in the legal consequence afforded to the performance of an act. In the rules of attribution the consequence of the act is moved from the actual performer to the person to whom the law attributes responsibility. In immunity the movement is in the opposite direction; the immunity of the State is extended, 'passed down' to protect the official. The State can only act by means of physical persons. In consequence writers explain immunity as extending to cover those who act in the State's name and on its behalf, and this explanation has grown up into a general presumption that the official also enjoys immunity for such acts as are imputed to the State. As stated by Leggatt LJ in *Propend Finance Party Ltd v. Sing* (1997), and approved by Hoffmann in *Jones*,[15] State immunity affords individual employees or officers of a foreign State 'protection under the same cloak as protects the State itself'.[16] Watts in describing this general rule recognises the two stages of the attribution of the act upwards to the State and downwards of the immunity of the State when returned to the protection of the official:

> States as artificial persons can only act through individuals and from this comes the general rule in international law by which an act of an individual performed with the authority and in the name of the State becomes the act of the State. Such an act is solely the act of the State; the individual is not a party nor incurs liability in respect of the act. On this account any jurisdictional immunity available to the State in respect of the act is extended to the individual who performed the act on the State's behalf. Any other rule would permit indirect avoidance of the State's own jurisdictional immunity.[17]

This extension of the State's immunity has been applied by several national courts in terms of according immunity to State officials when performing acts in the course of their official functions, namely, *Church of Scientology*;[18] *Holland v. Lampen-Wolfe*;[19] *Propend Finance Pty Ltd v. Sing*;[20] *Jaffe v. Miller*[21] and *Herbage v. Meese*.[22]

The separability of the two concepts is clearly demonstrated by reference to a situation where the State itself enjoys no immunity. Thus, in a situation where an official signs the order for office supplies on behalf of the State, assuming a restrictive rule of immunity applies in the country where the unpaid supplier

---

[15] *Supra* (note 3), paragraph 68.
[16] III *ILR* 611, at paragraph 669.
[17] 'Legal Position in International Law of Heads of States, Heads of Governments and Foreign Ministers', 247 (1994-III) *Hague Recueil des cours* 9 at p. 82.
[18] 65 ILR 193: BGH, German Supreme Court (1978).
[19] [2000] 3 AER 833: House of Lords.
[20] *Supra* (note 16); Court of Appeal (1997).
[21] 95 *ILR* 446; Ontario Court of Appeal, Canada (1993).
[22] 747 F Supp. 60: District of Columbia Circuit (1990).

sues for the price, the sale as one of a commercial nature attracts no immunity from the jurisdiction of the local court. That court may exercise jurisdiction and give judgment against the State but not the official who gave the order for the supplies. It cannot do so, not because the official is immune – there being no applicable immunity for this type of transaction – but because the law attributes responsibility to the State and not to the official. Kelsen, who is often cited in support of the doctrine of Act of State, observes:

> No State is allowed to exercise through its own courts jurisdiction over another State unless the other State expressly consents … Since a State manifests its legal existence only through acts performed by human beings in their capacity as organs of the State, that is to say, through acts of State, the principle that no State has jurisdiction over another State must mean that a State must not exercise jurisdiction through its courts over acts of another State unless the other State consents. Hence the principle applies not only in case a State as such is sued in a court of another State but also in case an individual is the defendant or the accused and the civil or criminal delict for which the individual is prosecuted has the character of an act of State.[23]

This passage comes from his discussion of the exercise of jurisdiction and is concerned not with responsibility but the inability of one State to bring proceedings against another. In so far as Kelsen here expands the rule of imputability into one of immunity – it was possibly as a permissible expansion at a time when an absolute rule of immunity for all acts of the State operated – but as shown above inapplicable when a restrictive doctrine is in place. In addition to moving the imputation of the act from the individual to the State, Kelsen goes the further stage to there invest it with the immunity of the State and return it to the individual as a non-immune act.

Attribution or imputability is an aspect of responsibility which applies rules of law to assess the manner and circumstances of the commission of the factual act in order to determine the person, natural or legal, who should answer for it. Here one should note Brownlie's view that, 'Imputability would seem to be a superfluous notion, since the major issue in a given situation is whether there has been a breach of duty; the content of "imputability" will vary according to the particular duty, the nature of the breach and so on. Imputability implies a fiction where there is none, and conjures up the idea of vicarious liability where it cannot apply.'[24] He criticises the distinction made by Oppenheim in earlier editions between original and vicarious liability. Jennings and Watts,

---

[23] Kelsen, *Principles of International law* (Second edition), New York, 1966, p. 358.
[24] *Principles of International Law* (Seventh edition), Oxford, 2008, p. 436

the editors of the ninth edition of *Oppenheim*, agree with that criticism and explain away that distinction as follows:

> 'Original' responsibility is borne by a state for acts which are directly imputable to it, such as acts of its government, or those of its officials or private individuals performed at the government's command or with its authorisation. 'Vicarious' responsibility, on the other hand, arises out of certain internationally injurious acts of private individuals (whether nationals, or aliens in a state's territory), and of officials acting without authorisation. It is apparent that the essential difference between original and vicarious responsibility in this sense is that whereas the former involves a state being in direct breach of legal obligations on it, and is accordingly a particularly serious matter, with the latter the state's responsibility is at one remove from the injurious conduct complained of: in such cases the state's responsibility calls for it to take certain preventive measures and requires it to secure that as far as possible the wrongdoer makes suitable reparation, and if necessary to punish him. But these preventive and remedial obligations of the state in cases of 'vicarious' responsibility are themselves obligations for the breach of which (as by refusing to take the remedial action which is required) the state bears direct responsibility.[25]

As Brownlie sums up, 'the legal consequences of the two categories may not be the same, but there is no fundamental difference between the two categories'.[26] On this basis, then, imputability becomes little more than an enquiry as to the precise nature of the obligation which the State is alleged to have breached.

However, this common law approach is not one which civil law adopts. Civil law treats the consequences of violation of a primary obligation as giving rise to general secondary rules of responsibility and this approach is adopted in the International Law Commission's Articles on State Responsibility. According to this formulation the content of the primary obligation supplies the 'objective' element and attribution is the 'subjective' element relating to the knowledge or intent of the State;[27] and in Part II of the ILC Articles, the rules of attribution spell out how that element may be supplied and hence be 'attributed' to the State by its organs or agents. Pursuant to Articles 5 and 6 of that Part, the conduct of a State organ or of a person empowered to exercise elements of the governmental authority are to be considered as acts of the State.

A general discussion of responsibility is thus shown in no way to require any consideration of immunity. In addition to the rules of attribution referred to above, Part II of the ILC Articles also set out principles relative to the various

---

[25] Jennings and Watts (eds.), *Oppenheim's International Law vol. i: Peace* (Ninth edition), London, 1992, pp. 501–502. Footnote references omitted.

[26] *Supra* (note 24), p. 436.

[27] ILC Articles on State Responsibility: see Article 2. There is an internationally wrongful act of a State when conduct consisting of an act or omission: (a) is attributable to the State under international law; and (b) constitutes a breach of an international obligation of the State.

degrees of responsibility and the manner by which the acts of an organ or official may be attributed to a State; but these rules say nothing as to the *availability* of immunity. Similarly, the 1995 Resolution of the Institut de Droit International on the Legal Consequences for Member States of the Non-Performance by International Organisations of their Obligations to Third States sets out with much qualification the circumstances in which Member States may be held responsible for the acts of an international organisation but nothing is said about either the organisation or the State obtaining immunity by reason of its proposed rules.[28]

Thus, in *Bosphorus Hava Yollari Turizm v. Ireland*,[29] Ireland implemented an EC Regulation giving legal force to UN Security Resolution 820 (1993) by impounding a Turkish registered aircraft as evading the UN sanctions against the Federal Republic of Yugoslavia (FRY). The Turkish airline charter company sought judicial review and the Irish Supreme Court referred the issue to the ECJ which upheld the legality of the impounding. The applicant then resorted to the European Court of Human Rights claiming that Ireland by its seizure of the aircraft had violated its right of property contrary to Article 1 of Protocol 1 of the European Convention, Ireland, supported by Italy, the UK and the European Commission, argued that Ireland had no discretion with regard to it acting as the EC Regulation required and that responsibility, if any for the impounding, should rest with the European Union. In effect they argued that responsibility was with the legal entity that authorised the act and that Ireland was a mere instrument in its execution. The Court dismissed the claim as not constituting a violation of the Convention right and on the issue of responsibility held 'State action taken in compliance with such legal obligations is justified as long as the relevant organisation is considered to protect fundamental human rights …'[30]

Thus, the European Court side-stepped the issue of responsibility by finding no violation of the right of property but at no time was any question of immunity raised. The *Caroline* incident and *Rainbow Warrior* case provide further illustration of these principles when the act complained of is committed not by a separate legal entity but by a component of the State or a non-State actor. In the first instance, British force despatched by way of self-defence an American ship, the *Caroline* over the Niagara Falls causing loss of life. The Law Officers of Her Majesty's Government stated their opinion which was subsequently assented to by the US representative Mr. Webster:

---

[28] 66 (1995) *Annuaire de l'Institut de droit international* 455.
[29] 42 (2006) *EHRR* 1; ECtHR (Grand Chamber), 30 June 2005; see Hoffmeister, Case Note, in 100 (2006) *AJIL* 442; and Kuiper *et al*, Case Note, 1 (2004) *Int. Org L Rev* 111, at pp. 113–16.
[30] 42 (2006) *EHRR* 1, paragraph 155.

> The principle of international law that an individual doing a hostile act authorized and ratified by the government of which he is a member cannot be held individually answerable as a private trespasser or malefactor but that the act becomes one for which the State to which he belongs is in such a case alone responsible is a principle too well established to be now controverted and indeed is distinctly admitted by Mr Webster in his instructions to the Attorney-General of the United States on March 15, 1841.[31]

Here attribution is discussed in terms of State responsibility, though it is to be noted that the US court in fact treated the individual as responsible by prosecuting MacLeod whose punishment was waived by executive pardon. In the case of the *Rainbow Warrior*,[32] New Zealand treated the death of a crewman resulting from two French agents' sabotage in a New Zealand harbour of a ship chartered by Greenpeace as giving rise to personal criminal liability on the part of the French agents as well as State responsibility of the French State who commissioned them.[33] This case, some years before *Pinochet*, illustrates a situation where issues of responsibility and immunity were treated separately. New Zealand had challenged the orthodox assumption concerning immunity by prosecuting the individual actors as well as demanding compensation from France.[34]

In *Blaskić*,[35] a case concerning the power to enforce disclosure of documents by a State official, the International Criminal Tribunal for Former Yugoslavia had occasion to consider the *Rainbow Warrior* case; in its judgment, the Yugoslav Tribunal took the view that the imprisonment of the two French agents following that incident was not justified 'taking into account in particular the fact that they acted under military orders and that France [was] ready to give an apology and to pay compensation to New Zealand for the damage suffered'.[36] In doing so, the Tribunal went further and treated as inseparable the concepts of responsibility and immunity. It was, on the one hand, correct to state that in respect of the State officials who withheld the required official documents,

---

[31] *MacLeod*, 20 November 1854: FO 83. 2209: reprinted in McNair, *International Law Opinions* vol. ii: *Peace*, Cambridge, 1956, p. 229; for full controversy, see pp. 221–30; and see generally 29 *BFSP* 1139; and also Jennings, 'The Caroline and McLeod Cases', 32 (1938) *AJIL* 82.

[32] 74 *ILR* 241.

[33] The two French agents were tried and convicted for manslaughter and for causing wilful damage and sentenced to ten and seven years respectively: see the ruling of the High Court of New Zealand: ibid, pp. 243–56.

[34] See the Memorandum of the Government of New Zealand, ibid, pp. 258–59.

[35] *Prosecutor v. Blaskic (Sub-Poenae)* Case IT-95-14, for which see Decisions of 29 July and 12 August 1997; and the Judgment of 29 October 1997 of the Appeals Chamber: 110 *ILR* 607.

[36] Ibid, see note 51 on p. 708. For the ruling of the Secretary-General of the United Nations, 6 July 1986, see 74 *ILR* 256; 19 *UN Reports of International Arbitral Awards* 213.

'Such officials cannot suffer the consequence of wrongful acts which are not attributable to them personally but to the State on whose behalf they act'.[37] However, the Tribunal was in error to explain this ruling on the ground that:

> [T]hey [that is the two French agents] enjoy so-called "functional immunity". This is a well established rule of customary international law going back to the eighteenth and nineteenth centuries, restated many times since.[38]

The Tribunal's ruling was based not on immunity but on imputability. The individual could not properly be sued by reason of the wrong attribution of the act to him. He was the wrong defendant; the State was the person in law to whom the responsibility for the withholding of the documents was to be attributed.

My conclusion, then, on the basis of the arguments put forward above, is that immunity is a separate concept from attribution and that there would seem no good reason why such functional immunity serves as no bar to criminal proceedings but continues to bar proceedings relating to the civil consequences of an international crime. Indeed, on the contrary there would seem good reason to remove immunity from all proceedings relation to the commission of an international crime.

IV. The Independent Issue of Imputability

As already stated, the removal of the bar of immunity leaves any question of the attribution of such conduct to the State as an independent issue for determination by either an international tribunal or by the national court before which civil proceedings are brought. The first question for such a national court, freed of the bar of immunity, will be to determine whether there is sufficient jurisdictional connection for it to assume jurisdiction; as the International Court has declared 'the rules governing the jurisdiction of national courts must be carefully distinguished from those governing jurisdictional immunities: jurisdiction does not imply absence of immunity, while absence of immunity does not imply jurisdiction'.[39] Determination of the territory where the crime was committed and the nationality of the accused official or the victim may indicate a stronger jurisdictional connection with another State.

Again there must be 'no reasonably available local remedies to provide effective redress,' or such local remedies as are available 'to provide no reasonable

---

[37] *Supra* (note 35), p. 707.
[38] Ibid.
[39] Arrest Warrant case, *supra* (note 1), paragraph 59.

possibility of such a redress'.[40] If 'the municipal system of the respondent State is reasonably capable of providing effective relief,'[41] it will clearly not be a case where the forum court should assume jurisdiction. Where, on investigation of these issues, the national court is satisfied that it may take jurisdiction it will then address the substantive issues including the question of imputability of the international crime to the respondent State. Obviously, here, any determination of the State's participation and responsibility by an international body will be of relevance, since the national court will have to be satisfied that the respondent State is under obligation to prevent the commission of the alleged international crime, is in violation of that obligation and has failed to provide reparation.

All these are weighty matters which the national court will have to address and in many cases the outcome, namely dismissal of the claim, may be no different, from that if the plea of immunity had succeeded. But this in my view is no argument for the retention of the immunity bar. Immunity at present constitutes a total bar on the reasons, many of which may be well founded but others totally spurious, why reparation should not be awarded for the consequences of the commission of or failure to prevent the commission of an international crime by a State. On this count attention is drawn to one scheme to put these proposals into effect.

IV. THE PROPOSALS OF THE THIRD COMMITTEE
OF THE INSTITUT DE DROIT INTERNATIONAL

The line of thinking developed in this paper has been taken forward by the Third Committee of the *Institute de droit international* of which I have the privilege of being Rapporteur. That Committee in discussions has decided to put forward a resolution for adoption by the Institut which recommends the removal of functional immunity for international crimes for which there exists universal jurisdiction in treaty and custom, that is for violations in consequence of a crime recognised by the international community as particularly grave, such as crimes under the 1984 UN Convention against Torture, crimes against humanity, grave breaches of the 1949 Geneva Conventions for the protection of war victims or other grave violations of international humanitarian law committed in international or non-international armed conflict, and genocide. In doing so, the

---

[40] See Article 15 (a) of the ILC Draft Articles on Diplomatic Protection, 2006: Report of the International Law Commission on its 58th Session: UN *GAOR*, 61st Session, Supp. No. 10 (A/61/10), p. 78, paragraph 3.

[41] Ibid, p. 79, paragraph 4.

Commission relies on existing international conventions imposing obligations on States parties to make certain defined international crimes offences within their domestic orders, to arrest alleged offenders found on national territory and then extradite or prosecute them. The Commission maintains that these obligations give rise to an implied commitment to afford reparation for the consequences of the commission of an international crime; the effect of such removal will be to permit the exercise of jurisdiction by national courts in respect of civil proceedings as well as criminal. Further support for its position is found in the absence in these conventions of any reservation of the State's immunity with regard to the prohibition of various international crimes in respect of which the State Parties undertake obligations. The absence of any reservation permits the customary rule of international law to operate by which reparation is required for breach of international law. Although recognising an element in its proposals may be *de lege ferenda* the Committee relies broadly on general principles of international law.

The first principle here is to stress that proceedings relating to violation of fundamental human rights are not solely of concern to the individual victim and the alleged offending State but also, and in particular where no effective remedy was available, of concern to all other States and the international community. Accordingly this first principle acknowledges the primary obligation of a State, pursuant to UN and regional human rights conventions and to international customary law, to afford the protection of human rights; and when a State fails in fulfilling that obligation, this principle affirms the existence of a legitimate interest of other States, acting in the interests of the international community, to seek to remedy its default. This principle was precisely summarised by Theodor Meron who stated that 'there has been a growing acceptance in contemporary international law of the principle that ... all states have a legitimate interest in and the right to protest against significant human rights violations, wherever they may occur, regardless of the nationality of the victims ...'[42] It is a principle founded on Articles 42 (b) and 48 (1) of the ILC Articles on State Responsibility.[43]

---

[42] See 'On a Hierarchy of International Human Rights', 80 (1986) *AJIL* 1 at p. 11.

[43] Article 42 stipulates: 'A state is entitled as an injured State to invoke the responsibility of another State if the obligation breached is owed to ... (b) ..., the international community as a whole and the breach of the obligation: ... (ii) is of such a character as radically to change the position of all other States to which the obligation is owed with respect to the further performance of the obligation.' Article 48, paragraph 1 stipulates: 'Any State other than an injured State is entitled to invoke the responsibility of another State in accordance with paragraph 2 if: ... (b) the obligation breached is owed to the international community as a whole.'

The second principle adopted by the Committee serves to acknowledge the function of immunity as a means for the allocation of jurisdictions between States and of ensuring respect for equality and independence as regards its internal administration, and gives effect to that value as expressly acknowledged in the Joint Separate Opinion of Judges Higgins, Kooijmans and Buergenthal in the Arrest Warrant case:

> The law of privileges and immunities retains its importance since immunities are granted to high State officials to guarantee the proper functioning of the network of mutual inter-State relations, which is of paramount importance for a well-ordered and harmonious international system.[44]

The third principle of the Committee's resolution requires a balance to be achieved between the first two principles; and the rules, which would then follow, are designed to achieve that balance. Put concisely, in reliance on these three principles the Committee's proposals are confined to the modification of the immunities of the State and its officials in respect of proceedings in national courts for acts constituting a violation of fundamental human rights as defined in the Resolution. They, thus, conform to the narrow modification suggested in the earlier part of this paper.

Article 3 of Part III implements that modification in relation to State immunity. Having regard to the accepted precedence of territorial jurisdiction, a distinction is made as regards the removal of immunity and the exercise of jurisdiction by reference to where the acts, constituting a violation of the fundamental human right, were alleged to have occurred. If such acts (including omissions) occurred within the territory of the forum State, the European Court of Human Rights will take into consideration 'a trend in international and comparative law in limiting State immunity in respect of personal injury caused by an act or omission within the forum State, but that this practice is by no means universal'.[45] The territorial link, together with the obligation on the forum State itself to secure human rights within its territory including the right of access to court,[46] provides additional ground for the removal of the foreign State's immunity.

Article 12 of the 2004 UN Convention on the Jurisdictional Immunities of States and their Property provides for an exception to State immunity where death or injury to the person or damage or loss to tangible property is caused

---

[44] *Supra* (note 1), paragraph 75.

[45] *McElhinney v. Ireland and UK*, 34 (2002) *EHRR* 13, at paragraph 38: Judgment 21 November 2001.

[46] See Articles 14 and 26: UN International Covenant on Civil and Political Rights, 1966; and Article 6 (1): European Convention of Human Rights, 1952.

by an act or omission attributable to the State if the act or omission occurred in whole or in part in the territory of the forum State, and if the author of the act or omission was present in the territory of the forum State at the time of the act or omission. To remove immunity from civil proceedings for reparation for an international crime committed on the territory of the forum State the Committee considers that an extension of the tort exception to the violation of fundamental human rights as defined in Article 1 would be a permissible innovation, not out of line with currently accepted international standards, and would bring jurisdictional immunities of States in line with the third principle above stated of achieving a balance between competing values.

With regard to the violation of fundamental human rights where the acts occurred outside the jurisdiction of the forum State, the exclusive jurisdiction accorded by international law to a State with regard to its internal administration provides a stronger restraint on the removal of immunity and consequently the competing jurisdiction of the forum State is based on weaker grounds. On this count a *de lege ferenda* proposal is put forward by the Committee that in respect of violations of the fundamental rights of the person as defined in the Resolution *wherever committed* outside the territory of the forum State, a State may not enjoy immunity from the civil jurisdiction of the national courts of another State unless it is established that the State has performed its obligations to make reparation in accordance with the applicable international convention or customary international law.

The resolution also provides for the restriction of functional immunity in respect of persons who, in the course of their functions, perform acts on behalf of the State. Here the recognised distinction in international law relating to personal and functional immunity (immunity *ratione personae* and *ratione materiae*) is applied. Part I of the resolution relates to the personal immunity of heads of State and government and certain other high ranking State officials and makes no change to existing law. This part also deals with functional immunity; here, as with the States immunity from civil jurisdiction, a modification to existing law is made in that functional immunity is removed for proceedings brought against officials for acts constituting a violation of fundamental human rights as defined in the Resolution.

These proposals offer one route by which the present illogical state of the law relating to functional immunity with regard to international crimes might be modified without too great an erosion of the protection of the lines of communication between international States and the effective performance of their functions by State officials. One must await the deliberations of the Institut to see whether they will gain the approval of all the members. But whatever the outcome it seems unlikely that the present unstable situation can long continue to prevail.

Chapter Nine

Neither Here Nor There?
The Status of International Criminal
Jurisprudence in the International and
UK Legal Orders[†]

Robert Cryer[*]

I. INTRODUCTION

Most international lawyers are familiar with at least one embarrassing conversation with their national law colleagues. This is one in which the name of a doyen or doyenne of international law is dropped, and is met with a resounding 'Who?' There are three ways of avoiding this blush-inducing moment. The first is to not shamelessly drop the names of the great and good of international law in conversation. The second is to only do so with international lawyers. The third, and best, way of averting such an academic *faux pas* is to mention Colin Warbrick. The reason for this is simple. Awareness of his standing is not the arcane lore of international lawyers, but something that we can share with our municipally focused colleagues. Colin's reputation is not merely that of a celebrated international lawyer, but of being an excellent lawyer *per se*.

Part of this relates to his personal approach to law which, whilst sympathetic to theoretical and conceptual analysis,[1] is one based in a very practical appre-

---

[†] With apologies to Karen Knop, see Knop, 'Here and There: International Law in Domestic Courts', 32 (1999–2000) *New York University Journal of International Law and Politics* 501.

[*] Professor of International and Criminal Law, School of Law, University of Birmingham. Thanks to Sangeeta Shah and Sandesh Sivakumaran for their very helpful comments on earlier drafts.

[1] See, for example Warbrick, 'Introduction' in Allott, Warbrick and Carty (eds.), *Theory and International Law: An Introduction*, London, 1991, p. 1; and Warbrick, 'Brownlie's *Principles of Public International Law*: An Assessment', 11 (2000) *EJIL* 621.

K.H. Kaikobad & M. Bohlander (eds.), *International Law and Power: Perspectives on Legal Order and Justice*. Essays in Honour of Colin Warbrick, pp. 183–206.

ciation of the importance of ensuring that international law has enforcement mechanisms,[2] including domestic courts.[3] Colin is also an exceptionally warm and kind person, always willing to give of his time, and to offer kind and honest advice and support. In depth discussion of that, however, would not really be appropriate, even in a *festschrift*. Therefore I will concentrate on a topic which relates to other aspects of Colin's work, in particular international criminal law, and elements of its application in domestic legal orders: The subject this chapter will seek to investigate is the normative status of the decisions of international criminal tribunals in the international legal order, and in the UK.[4]

II. The Status of Jurisprudence in International Law

It is a commonplace that judicial decisions do not usually create general international law. This much is clear from Article 38(1)(d) of the Statute of the International Court of Justice.[5] Nonetheless, it is a truism (because it is true) that case-law is frequently highly influential, either because it crystallises a nascent rule, or because it is referred to as shorthand for the position in international law.[6] After all, where cases contain a detailed review of State practice and/or *opinio juris*, it is far simpler to refer to the relevant case than repeat the discussion it contains.[7]

Such considerations hardly exhaust the debate though. There is also, for instance, the question of the status of a court's case-law in its own legal system,

---

[2]   See, for example, Warbick, 'The United Nations System: A Place for International Criminal Courts?', 5 (1995) *Transnational Law and Contemporary Problems* 237.

[3]   Hence his focus on international law as applied in domestic courts, see Warbick, 'Extradition Aspects of *Pinochet 3*', 48 (1999) *ICLQ* 958; and Warbick, Martin Salgado and Goodwin, 'The Pinochet Cases in the United Kingdom', 2 (1999) *Yearbook of International Humanitarian Law* 91.

[4]   For reasons of space, this piece will limit itself, for the most part, to a discussion of the jurisprudence of the ICTY, ICTR and ICC.

[5]   See generally Shahabuddeen, *Precedent in the World Court*, Cambridge, 1996; Jennings, 'The Judiciary, National and International, and the Development of International Law', 45 (1996) *ICLQ* 1; Hersch Lauterpacht, *The Development of International Law by the International Court*, London, 1958; and Schwarzenberger, *International Law as Applied By International Courts and Tribunals: vol. i* (Third edition), London, 1957.

[6]   The extent to which, for example, the *Tadić* case is referred in support of the position that individual liability exists in non-international armed conflict is not simply because of the inherent authority of ICTY decisions outside its own internal legal order. *Tadić*, despite the fact that it was a bold decision, is also authoritative because it was 'carefully made': see Warbick (note 2), p. 257.

[7]   There is also the small matter of the entirely understandable temptation to locate the authority for a position externally.

which is not as simple as is sometimes thought. To take the most well-known case, Article 59 of the ICJ Statute expressly rejects the idea of the ICJ binding itself: 'The decision of the Court has no binding force except between the parties and in respect of that particular case'.[8] However, it is also true that in practice the ICJ often refers to its earlier case-law as if they were precedents,[9] and in practical terms, what it has said is the law will almost always be taken as being the law as far as the ICJ is concerned.[10] As John Jackson has said, 'Too often some observers ... have tended to discuss the use of precedent in judicial decision-making as involving a dichotomous choice. They talk about it in terms of whether there is the principle of *stare decisis*, or not .... Actually ... it is quickly apparent that there are a number of different approaches to the underlying problem. That underlying problem is the question of how much influence a prior decision of a judicial body should have when considering new cases.'[11]

Hence, to extrapolate from Article 59 that '[i]nternational law does not recognize a binding force of precedents or the principle of *stare decisis*',[12] is to overstate the position, not least because the ICJ does not have an appellate structure. Where there is such a structure in an international tribunal, forms of precedent frequently arise, albeit at various levels of formality. For example, in the European human rights system, although there is nothing in the European Convention about the status of the decisions of the Grand Chamber of the European Court of Human Rights, it is generally accepted (including by the Chambers themselves) that other Chambers of the Court would be extremely ill-advised to ignore them.[13] This is particularly the case given that there is a right of appeal from other Chambers to the Grand Chamber.[14] The same considerations apply in the WTO system.[15]

---

[8] See generally Bernhardt, 'Article 59' in Zimmermann, Tomuschat and Oellers-Frahm (eds.), *The Statute of the International Court of Justice: A Commentary*, Oxford, 2006, p. 1231.
[9] See especially Shahabuddeen (note 5).
[10] Ibid, pp. 29–33.
[11] See Jackson, *Sovereignty, the WTO and the Changing Structure of International Law*, Cambridge, 2006, p. 173.
[12] Bernhardt, (note 8), p. 1244.
[13] For the pre-reform position, see *Cossey v. UK* 27 September 1990, Series A, vol. 184, paragraph 35.
[14] European Convention for the Protection of Human Rights and Fundamental Freedoms, Article 43.
[15] Jackson (note 11), pp. 175–177.

1. *The Ad Hoc Tribunals*

a. At Home

Probably the most notable example of a formal system of precedent in international law, however, is one of the most relevant to this chapter. That is the legal system(s?) of the ICTY and ICTR.[16] Although the statute of neither tribunal creates a strict set of rules relating to precedent, the Tribunals have created them. The joint Appeals Chamber[17] in the *Aleksovski* Appeal set the rules out as follows:

> the *ratio decidendi* of its decisions is binding on Trial Chambers for the following reasons:
>
> (i) the Statute establishes a hierarchical structure in which the Appeals Chamber is given the function of settling definitively certain questions of law and fact arising from decisions of the Trial Chambers. …;
> (ii) the fundamental mandate of the Tribunal to prosecute persons responsible for serious violations of international humanitarian law cannot be achieved if the accused and the Prosecution do not have the assurance of certainty and predictability in the application of the applicable law; and
> (iii) the right of appeal is … a component of the fair trial requirement … and gives rise to the right of the accused to have like cases treated alike. This will not be achieved if each Trial Chamber is free to disregard decisions of law made by the Appeals Chamber …. In such a system, it would be possible to have four statements of the law from the Tribunal on a single legal issue – one from the Appeals Chamber and one from each of the three Trial Chambers …. This would be inconsistent with … applying a single, unified, coherent and rational corpus of law. The need for coherence is particularly acute in the context in which the Tribunal operates, where the norms of international humanitarian law and international criminal law are developing ….[18]

However, the fact that the ICTY took the view that this was necessary was leavened with an understanding of the limitations of the statement, restatement or development of international criminal law through individual cases, when

---

[16] For general reviews, see Harris, 'Precedent in the Practice of the ICTY', in May, Tolbert, Hocking and Roberts (eds.), *Essays on ICTY Procedure and Evidence In Honour of Gabrielle Kirk McDonald*, The Hague, 2001, p. 341; and Tracol, 'The Precedent of Appeals Chambers Decision in the International Criminal Tribunals', 17 (2004) *Leiden Journal of International Law* 67.

[17] The reason for creating a joint appeals chamber was that there should be consistency between the jurisprudence of the two Tribunals, see e.g., Morris and Scharf, *The International Criminal Tribunal for Rwanda*, New York, 1998, p. 354.

[18] *Prosecutor v. Aleksovski*, Judgment, IT-95-14/1-A, 24 March 2000, paragraph 113.

the facts can have, at least, a reflexive relationship with the statement of the law. Hence its statement in *Aleksovski* that

> The fundamental purpose of the Tribunal is the prosecution of persons responsible for serious violations of international humanitarian law. The Appeals Chamber considers that this purpose is best served by an approach which, while recognising the need for certainty, stability and predictability in criminal law, also recognises that there may be instances in which the strict, absolute application of that principle may lead to injustice .... The principle of the continuity of judicial decisions must be balanced by a residual principle that ensures that justice is done in all cases.[19]

Having looked at the situation of the highest courts in common and civil law jurisdictions, as well as the practice of the ICJ, the ICTY decided that

> in the interests of certainty and predictability, the Appeals Chamber should follow its previous decisions, but should be free to depart from them for cogent reasons in the interests of justice ... What is followed in previous decisions is the legal principle (*ratio decidendi*) ... There is no obligation to follow previous decisions which may be distinguished for one reason or another from the case before the court.[20]

This, in itself is sensible. After all, as Lon Fuller said,[21] and Herbert Hart would have agreed,[22] clarity and certainty are important aspects of any legal system, let alone a system of criminal law, in which the *nullum crimen sine lege* principle has an extremely important role to play.[23] Nonetheless, owing to the somewhat fledgling nature of international criminal law, it may be ill-advised to have pronouncements entirely set in stone.[24] What is perhaps most notable about the approach of the Appeals Chamber in developing its jurisprudence on precedent is that it drew considerable weight from the point regarding the importance of consistency in criminal law, and the implications of having an appellate jurisdiction. Although there are risks in assuming normative natures, the Appeals Chamber was almost certainly correct; there is little reason for providing for appeals on points of law unless those decisions serve to guide

---

[19] Ibid, paragraphs 101–102.
[20] Ibid., paragraphs 107 and 110.
[21] Fuller, *The Morality of Law*, (Revised edition), New Haven, 1969, pp. 63–65.
[22] Hart, *The Concept of Law*, (Second edition), Oxford, 1994, pp. 124–133.
[23] Protected, e.g., in Article 15 of the International Covenant on Civil and Political Rights, 999 UNTS 171 (1966). See generally Boot, *Genocide, Crimes Against Humanity, War Crimes: Nullum Crimen Sine Lege and the Subject Matter Jurisdiction of the International Criminal Court*, Antwerp, 2002, pp. 127–178.
[24] On the ICTY acting as a laboratory, rather than a mouthpiece of an *a priori* universal law, see Rowe, 'Duress as a Defence to War Crimes After *Erdemović*: A Laboratory for a Permanent Court?', 1 (1998) *Yearbook of International Humanitarian Law* 210.

other Chambers and provide a level of certainty. Equally, in practice, Trial Chambers have occasionally ignored binding Appeals Chamber decisions,[25] and the Appeals Chamber has vacillated on certain points, whilst denying it has done so.[26] On occasion, however, the Appeals Chamber has been candid, and disavowed its earlier holdings in the interests of justice.[27]

b. Abroad

Leaving their own legal systems aside, the Tribunals' decisions have some formal status as persuasive authorities in other courts and tribunals. The most important of these is in the Special Court for Sierra Leone. By virtue of Article 20 (3) of the Special Court's Statute its decisions are to be 'guided' by decisions of the joint ICTY/ICTR Appeals Chamber. This provision was included in the Special Court's Statute in order to promote consistency in international criminal law, and represents an extraordinary decision to provide for an (admittedly persuasive rather than binding) status for the decisions of a court outside of its internal legal order.[28] Similarly, although less strongly, Article 17 (b) of the Iraq High Tribunal Statute provides that where that tribunal is interpreting international crimes they 'may resort to the relevant decisions of international courts of tribunals as persuasive authority for their decisions'.[29]

Other than by virtue of these provisions, however, the status of such case-law is formally the same as that of any other decision arising from an international

---

[25] *Prosecutor v. Vasiljević,* Judgment, IT-98-32-T, 29 November 2002, paragraph 197; this implicitly departed from *Prosecutor v. Tadić, Decision on Interlocutory Appeal on Jurisdiction,* IT-94-1-AR72, 10 October 1995, paragraph 94.

[26] *Prosecutor v. Multinović, Šainović and Odjanić,* Decision on Draganljub Odjanić's Motion Denying Jurisdiction – Joint Criminal Enterprise, IT-99-37-AR72 (hereinafter *Odjanić*), 21 May 2003, paragraph 9. See also *Prosecutor v. Hadžihasanović Alagić and Kubura, Decision on Interlocutory Appeal Concerning Jurisdiction: Command Responsibility,* IT-01-47-AR72, 16 July 2004, paragraph 35; *Prosecutor v. Blaškić,* Judgment, IT-94-14-A, 29 July 2004, paragraph 141; *Prosecutor v. Kordić and Čerkez,* Judgment, IT-96-14/2-A, 14 December 2004, paragraph 46; *Prosecutor v. Galić,* Judgment, IT-98-29-A, 30 November 2006, paragraph 85; see the Separate Opinion of Judge Shahabuddeen, paragraph 2.

[27] *Prosecutor v. Erdemović,* Judgment, IT-96-22-A, 7 October 1997, paragraph 20; and see the Separate Opinion of Judges McDonald and Vohrah, paragraphs 20–27; disapproved in *Prosecutor v. Tadić,* Judgment in Sentencing Appeal, IT-94-1-A, 26 January 2000, paragraph 69; and *Prosecutor v. Krstić,* Judgment, IT-98-33-A, 19 April 2004, expressly departed from in *Kordić and Čerkez* (note 26), paragraph 140.

[28] The Special Court has made use of ICTY decisions, see, for example, *Prosecutor v. Norman, Decision on Preliminary Motion on Jurisdiction: Child Recruitment,* SCSL-2004-14-AR72, 31 May 2004, paragraphs 25–26.

[29] See Bantekas, 'The Iraqi Special Tribunal for Crimes Against Humanity', 54 (2005) *ICLQ* 237, at p. 243.

court or tribunal, i.e. a subsidiary means of determining the law. Furthermore, one international court with analogous material jurisdiction to the ICTY, the European Court of Human Rights, has been somewhat chary of referring to the jurisprudence of the ICTY. There have been references, for example, to the *Furundžija* Trial Chamber decision's determination that torture was contrary to *jus cogens*, and to the fact that rape can amount to torture in a few cases,[30] but otherwise, the European Court has not, until recently, made much use of the ICTY's case-law.[31]

The European Court, however, may prove to be the outlier on point, at least if the International Court of Justice is any guide. The ICJ has recently granted an extraordinary degree of authority to the decisions of the ICTY, at least insofar as it has dealt with international criminal law *stricto sensu*. In the *Bosnian Genocide* case[32] the ICJ accepted that there was a considerable overlap of both fact and law between the issues before the ICTY and the Court in the case. The ICJ decided that it had to make factual findings itself,[33] but accepted that the ICTY had a greater opportunity to evaluate, and to have cross-examined evidence than it had, and thus: 'the Court ... should in principle accept as highly persuasive relevant findings of fact made by the Tribunal at trial, unless of course they have been upset on appeal. For the same reasons, any evaluation by the Tribunal based on the facts as so found for instance about the existence of the required intent, is also entitled to due weight.'[34]

In practice, the factual sections of the ICJ's judgment are replete with references to the findings of the ICTY, amply supporting Judge Tomka's comment who observed: 'The Court has given serious consideration to the ICTY's judgments and to the evidence produced in the trials before its Chambers to which the Parties referred. Without the work accomplished by the ICTY, it would have been much more difficult for the Court to discharge its role in the

---

[30] See, e.g. *Al-Adsani v. UK*, 21 November 2001, paragraphs 30–31; and *M.C. v. Bulgaria* Judgment, 4 December 2003, paragraphs 102–107. It is probable that the ICTY's jurisprudence influenced the discussion in *Aydin v. Turkey*, Judgment, 25 September 1997, paragraphs 51; and 80–86. There is also a reference to the ICTY in the concurring opinion of Judge Louciades in *Streletz, Kessler and Krenz v. Germany*, Appl. Nos. 34044/96, 35532/97 and 44801/98; Judgment of 22 March 2001, 33 EHRR 31, p. 789, at p. 790, note 78. For a more substantial use, see *Jorgic v. Germany*, Appl. No. 74613/01; Judgment of 12 July 2007, paragraphs 42–44 and 50–51, and paragraph 59.

[31] Conversely, as far as the respect ICTY has shown to the output of the European Court, see for example, *Prosecutor v. Kunarać*, Judgment, IT-96-23-T, 2 February 2001, paragraphs 465–497.

[32] *Case Concerning the Application of the Convention Concerning the Prevention and Punishment of the Crime of Genocide (Bosnia and Herzegovina v. Serbia and Montenegro)*, 26 February 2006, ICJ General List 91. [For extensive discussion of this case, see Chapter 12: 'State Identity and Genocide: The *Bosnian Genocide* Case' by D. McGoldrick. Eds.]

[33] Ibid, paragraph 212; and see the Declaration of Judge Skotnikov, pp. 6–7.

[34] Ibid, paragraph 223.

present case.'[35] Indeed, the majority judgment comes close to simply adopting the ICTY's view of the facts, and does not dispute any finding of the ICTY, much to the chagrin of Judge *ad hoc* Kreća.[36]

Turning to its discussion of international criminal law, the ICJ also essentially agreed with the ICTY, and drew heavily upon it. For example, when looking at the definition of protected groups under the Genocide Convention, the ICJ rejected the possibility of a negative definition of a group, stating that '[t]he Court observes that the ICTY Appeals Chamber in the *Stakić* case ... also came to the conclusion that the group must be defined positively, essentially for the same reasons as the Court has given'.[37] Furthermore, when dealing with the question of the substantial nature of the targeted part of a group, the Court, having stated its agreement with the relevant decisions of the ICTY and ICTR on point, concluded, 'The above list of criteria is not exhaustive, but, as just indicated, the substantiality criterion is critical. They are essentially those stated by the Appeals Chamber in the *Krstić* case, although the Court does give this first criterion priority.'[38] Again, as with the facts, on questions of international criminal law, the majority did not disagree with anything said by the ICTY.[39]

One of the dissenting judges, Vice-President al-Khasawneh, was prepared to go as far as to prefer the ICTY's formulation of the relevant test for State responsibility for international crimes, that is the *Tadić* case, to the ICJ's *Nicaragua* decision.[40] The majority, perhaps unsurprisingly, were not willing to go so far, and criticised the Appeals Chamber for having strayed beyond what the Court saw as the Chamber's mandate and applied general international law (and implicitly, for having dared to doubt *Nicaragua*):

---

[35] Ibid, Separate Opinion of Judge Tomka, paragraph 72.

[36] Ibid, Separate Opinion of Judge *ad hoc* Kreća paragraph 109. Judge Skotnikov was also unhappy with aspects of this: *supra* (note 33), pp. 7–9.

[37] *Bosnia Genocide* case (note 32), paragraph 195. It might be noted that the framing of the paragraph implies that the ICTY had followed the lead established by the ICJ rather than the other way around.

[38] Ibid, paragraph 201.

[39] Two judges, Judge Skotnikov and Judge *ad hoc* Kreća, disputed the relevance of ICTY judgments on the ground that they were based on the applicable customary law, rather than the Genocide Convention (which was the basis of jurisdiction in the case): *supra* (note 32), pp. 6–8 and paragraph 109 respectively. This appears to misunderstand the way in which both Tribunals have, in essence, taken the view that the treaty and customary law of genocide are identical. It also appears to reflect a fairly negative view of the ICTY by Judge *ad hoc* Kreća (see, for example, paragraph 130), who, nonetheless, was happy enough to cite ICTY judgments in support of his position, on which see, paragraph 104.

[40] See his Dissenting Opinion (note 32), paragraphs 37–39. On the difference, see Meron, 'Classification of Conflicts in Former Yugoslavia, *Nicaragua's* Fallout', in Meron, *War Crimes Law Comes of Age*, Oxford, 1998, p. 286.

The Court has given careful consideration to the Appeals Chamber's reasoning in support of the foregoing conclusion, but finds itself unable to subscribe to the Chamber's view. First, the Court observes that the ICTY was not called upon in the *Tadić* case, nor is it in general called upon, to rule on questions of State responsibility, since its jurisdiction is criminal and extends over persons only. Thus, in that Judgment the Tribunal addressed an issue which was not indispensable for the exercise of its jurisdiction. *As stated above, the Court attaches the utmost importance to the factual and legal findings made by the ICTY in ruling on the criminal liability of the accused before it and, in the present case, the Court takes fullest account of the ICTY's trial and appellate judgments dealing with the events underlying the dispute.* The situation is not the same for positions adopted by the ICTY on issues of general international law which do not lie within the specific purview of its jurisdiction and, moreover, the resolution of which is not always necessary for deciding the criminal cases before it.[41]

As the emphasised part shows, however, the level of respect given to the ICTY's jurisprudence on international criminal law (as opposed to general international law) is quite extraordinary, and shows the validity of the view that the absence of a formal system of precedent is very different to that of granting cases no weight. It is difficult to imagine the ICJ having taken a stronger view on the import of ICTY case-law on international criminal law than it did, other than by asserting that it was bound by its output, and that would have been outside the realms of international legal possibility.

2. *The ICC Statute*

Unlike the statutes of the *ad hoc* tribunals, the Rome Statute deals expressly with the status of its case-law. Article 21 sets out the law which is to be applied by the ICC.[42] It reads

   1. The Court shall apply:
      (a) In the first place, this Statute, Elements of Crimes and its Rules of Procedure and Evidence; (b) In the second place, where appropriate, applicable treaties and the principles and rules of international law . . .; (c) Failing that, general principles of law derived by the Court from national laws of legal systems of the world . . .;

---

[41] The *Bosnian Genocide* case (note 32), paragraph 403. Emphasis added. However, as Al-Khasawneh noted, on the reasoning of the ICTY, the State responsibility point was crucial to the exercise of its primary, criminal, jurisdiction over grave breaches of the Geneva Conventions.

[42] See generally de Guzman, 'Article 21', in Triffterer (ed.), *Commentary on the Rome Statute of the International Criminal Court*, Baden-Baden, 1999, p. 435. The drafting history of this article is usefully reproduced in Bassiouni, *The Legislative History of the International Criminal Court, vol. ii: An Article-by-Article Evolution of the Statute*, New York, 2005, pp. 171–181.

2. The Court may apply principles and rules of law as interpreted in its previous decisions.

As can be seen, the ICC is required to apply, in order, its Statue and Rules, then relevant treaties and 'principles and rules of international law', then in third place, general principles. Its case-law does not even gain a tertiary position in the Rome Statute. The ICC is not required to apply its own previous decisions, it is only, by virtue of Article 21(2), given the right to do so.[43] Interestingly, Article 21 does not set up any system of precedent between the Trial and Appeals Chambers, referring only to 'decisions'. Given that appeals lie against mistakes of law in Trial Chamber decisions,[44] it would nonetheless be a brave/foolhardy Trial Chamber that ignored Appeals Chamber decisions. Still, the formal status of case-law in the ICC would appear to be quite lowly in the Rome Statute, Article 21 doing just a little more than restating the traditional formal position of judicial decisions in international law. Time, of course, will tell if the practice of the ICC grants a greater *de facto* authority to its own earlier pronouncements. Still, it would be surprising if the considerations that led the ICTY to pronounce as it did in *Aleksovski* did not have a similar practical impact in the ICC, even if they are unlikely to lead the ICC to formally grant its decisions a greater role than that granted to them in the Statute.

In the international legal system as a whole, decisions of the ICC have the same formal authority as any other international case-law, i.e. they are a subsidiary means of determining the law. As we have seen though, the jurisprudence of international criminal tribunals has had considerable impact on the way many entities have seen and interpreted international (criminal) law, and it is likely that the output of the ICC, given that it is 'the' permanent international criminal court, will have considerable influence in the international legal order.[45] Were the ICJ to pronounce on aspects of international criminal law upon which the ICC had already made its views known, it is unlikely that the ICJ would not grant its statements a similar level of respect to that it granted the ICTY's *oeuvre* on genocide.

---

[43] Pellet, 'Applicable Law' in Cassese, Gaeta and Jones (eds.), *The Rome Statute of the International Criminal Court: A Commentary*, Oxford, 2002, p. 1051 and p. 1066.

[44] Rome Statute, Articles 81 (1) (a) (iii) and 81 (1) (b) (iii).

[45] Although see below on the question of the Rome Statute, the main source of law for the ICC, and general international law.

III. The Status of the Case-Law in the UK: The Common Law

Having spent some time explaining the status of the jurisprudence of the various international criminal courts in the international legal system, it is now time to look, comparatively, at the role it plays in the UK legal order. There are two ways in which the Tribunals' decisions may be relevant to UK proceedings, the first, more general, way is through the common law, the second is by virtue of statute.

The first way, the common law, is related to the status of customary law in the UK. This is a matter which, until recently, was thought to be fairly simple.[46] 'The dominant principle ... is that customary rules are to be considered part of the law of the land enforced as such, with the qualification that they are incorporated only so far as is not inconsistent with Acts of Parliament or prior judicial decisions of final authority.'[47] The fact that customary international law is to be applied unless it is conflicts with a prior authoritative judicial pronouncement might be thought to raise an additional problem. International law may change, whilst, under the traditional doctrine of precedent, the adoption by the House of Lords (or the Court of Appeal) of a statement about the relevant rule of international law might be thought to be binding on inferior courts, even against convincing evidence of a change in customary law.

This is not the prevailing wisdom in UK Courts. The seminal decision is the *Trendtex* case, in which Lord Denning expressed himself in no uncertain terms: 'international law knows no doctrine of *stare decisis*. If this court today is satisfied that the rule of international law on a subject has changed from what it was 50 or 60 years ago, it can give effect to that change, and apply the change in our English law, without waiting for the House of Lords to do it.'[48] Although this case is only from the Court of Appeal, Lord Slynn, in the House of Lords first decision in the *Pinochet* case was clear that this was now the accepted position.[49]

---

[46] See Brownlie, *Principles of International Law* (Sixth edition), 2003, pp. 41–45; and Thomas, 'The Changing Status of International Law in English Domestic Law', 53 (2006) *Netherlands International Law Review* 371. On the other hand, see Collier, 'Is International Law Really Part of the Law of England?', 38 (1989) *ICLQ* 924. One of the few works on international court decisions in the UK legal order is C. Wilfred Jenks, for which see 'The Authority in English Courts of Decisions of the Permanent Court of International Justice', 20 (1939) *BYIL* 1.

[47] Brownlie (note 46), p. 41.

[48] *Trendtex Trading Corp v. Central Bank of Nigeria* [1977] 1 All ER 881, at p. 890; see also p. 910: per Shaw, LJ.

[49] *R v. Bow Street Stipendiary Magistrate, ex parte Pinochet Ugarte (Amnesty International and Others Intervening)* [1998] 4 All ER 897, at p. 911.

The upshot of this is that, where case-law evidences, reflects, or perhaps crystallises, customary law, at least in civil law cases, the decisions of the international criminal tribunals can have an effect in the UK. Such a possibility is not simply speculative; the House of Lords has, on a number of occasions, relied quite heavily on ICTY jurisprudence. For example in the *Pinochet* litigation (the first time the House of Lords had cause to discuss the jurisprudence of the international tribunals)[50] Lord Slynn simply said:

> until *Prosecutor v. Tadic* … after years of discussion and perhaps even later there was a feeling that crimes against humanity were committed only in connection with armed conflict even if that did not have to be international armed conflict.[51]

Given that Lord Slynn goes some way to asserting that *Tadić* settled the position in international law it is surprising that such a statement is not prefaced with any discussion at all of normative status of such judgments in the UK. In the third *Pinochet* decision, again some (not, it must be noted, all) of their Lordships referred to ICTY jurisprudence, this time *Prosecutor v. Furundžija*, again with no explanation of the status of the case-law of the ICTY in the UK legal order.[52] It appears that they referred to it as a reflection of the existing custom on the point, and took it as such. This was, nonetheless, in the context of a case in which the House relied on a number of different sources for their proposition, including the case-law of foreign jurisdictions, scholarly writings, General Assembly Resolutions, the Statutes of the *ad hoc* tribunals, and those of the Nuremberg IMT and the (then unincorporated) Rome Statute of the ICC without any exposition of the relative status each enjoyed in the law of England and Wales.[53] Hence it can be argued, with some justification, that in this case the House was only relying on *Furundžija* in a crowd of authorities, and not placing particularly strong weight on it alone.

The same cannot be said for the next time *Furundžija* popped its head around the door of the common law. This was in the *Torture Evidence* case.[54] In the course of explaining the strong disapprobation of the House for the practice of torture, Lord Bingham, who gave the lead judgment, and on which point no

---

[50] Admittedly, in the quasi-criminal context of extradition proceedings.

[51] *Supra* (note 49), p. 915.

[52] *R v. Bow Street Stipendiary Magistrate, ex parte Pinochet Ugarte (Amnesty International and Others Intervening) [No. 3]* [1999] 2 All ER 97, at pp. 108–109, *per* Lord Browne-Wilkinson; and *per* Lord Millett, p. 177.

[53] With the exception of Lord Phillips who observed (p. 185) that he did not find writings of scholars cited before them 'unsupported as they are by any reference to precedent or practice, a compelling foundation for the immunity' suggested; and note his comment that a number of the US cases cited to them related to statutory immunities (p. 187).

[54] *A (FC) and Others v. Secretary of State for the Home Department* [2005] UKHL 71.

other member of the panel of seven expressed disagreement,[55] relied heavily on the ICTY's pronouncement in *Furundžija* and observed:

> It is common ground in these proceedings that the international prohibition of the use of torture enjoys the enhanced status of a *jus cogens* or peremptory norm of general international law ... The implications of this ... were *fully and authoritatively* explained by the International Criminal Tribunal for the Former Yugoslavia ... in a passage which, despite its length, calls for citation ...[56]

Lord Bingham then proceeds to cite, *verbatim*, eleven paragraphs from the case. To say that the ICTY 'fully and authoritatively' set down the law on point could be an extraordinary assertion of the authority of (a Trial Chamber of) the ICTY to set down international law, and the effect that Tribunal could have on the law of England and Wales. Equally, a more limited interpretation of Lord Bingham's statement could be that he was simply asserting that he found the reasoning in the case convincing, and thus that the relevant parts of *Furundžija* were 'authoritative' only in that sense, which would be more consistent with the status of judicial decisions in international law. It seems unlikely that Lord Bingham was seeking to argue that all ICTY decisions were 'authoritative' in international law, and *a fortiori* in domestic law.

Perhaps inevitably, however, owing to this reliance on *Furundžija* in the *Torture Evidence* case, the impact of the status of the prohibition of torture came before the House of Lords again without any great delay, in *Jones v. Saudi Arabia*.[57] Lord Bingham sought to clarify (or resile from) his extensive citation of *Furundžija*, which included a statement which might be interpreted as implying that immunities might not apply to civil actions for torture in a third State. He asserted that although

> the passage quoted included ... [a statement that might be taken as implying the above] ... I do not understand the tribunal to have been addressing the issue of State immunity in civil proceedings; but if it was, its observations, being those of a criminal tribunal trying a criminal case in which no such issue arose, were, on that issue, plainly obiter, as was my citation of them.[58]

Lord Hoffmann did not go as far, simply noting that the relevant 'interesting discussion' of the ICTY was 'not directed to the question of State immunity'.[59]

---

[55] See e.g. ibid, paragraph 67, *per* Lord Nicholls.

[56] Ibid, paragraph 33. Emphasis added.

[57] [2006] UKHL 26.

[58] Ibid, paragraph 21. Interestingly, Lord Bingham does elsewhere (paragraph 10) cite, without similar caveat, the decision of the ICTY Appeals Chamber in *Prosecutor v. Blaškić, Decision on the Request of the Republic of Croatia for Review of the Decision of Trial Chamber II* of 18 July 1997, IT-95-14-AR108 *bis*, 29 October 1997.

[59] *Jones* (note 57), paragraphs 51 and 54.

Like Lord Bingham, however, he was happy to rely on the *Blaškić* decision
for another point, and noted also that the case was 'presided over by the
distinguished international lawyer Professor Antonio Cassese'.[60] At no point
did either of their Lordships rely on the expedient of denying the precedential
value of the *Furundžija* case, although owing to the earlier use Lord Bingham had
made of it in the *Torture Evidence* case, this could not be considered unexpected.

In relation to criminal law the position has recently been clarified or,
depending on the point of view taken, muddied or altered, by the House
of Lords in the case of *R v. Jones, Milling, Olditch et al.*[61] In this case, which
related to protesters against the Iraq war of 2003, it became necessary to
determine whether or not the crime of aggression was, by virtue of the UK's
incorporationist stance towards custom, a crime in UK law. The House of
Lords, in a judgment that is not simple to follow on point, determined that
it is not.[62] The House decided that nowadays, Parliament is practically always
to be considered the sole creator of new crimes, via statute.[63] What is not
clear, however, is what the House meant by 'new' crimes. This is relevant in
particular owing to the practice of the UK in the aftermath of World War
II, when it asserted that crimes against peace were a pre-existing category of
crime in international law,[64] and the apparent acceptance by their Lordships of
the proposition in that case that war crimes were directly criminalised in the
UK legal order by virtue of customary law at that time.[65] As a result, it would
appear that using the case-law of international tribunals to try to argue that
new crimes had entered the UK legal system by virtue of custom would be a
difficult proposition to accept, although one to which the door may have been
left open especially in relation to war crimes.[66]

---

[60] Ibid, paragraph 66. Professor Cassese also gets another nod, as an eminent authority 'who
presided over the Appeals Chamber of the International Criminal Tribunal for the Former
Yugoslavia', ibid, paragraph 84.

[61] *R v. Jones, Milling, Olditch, Pritchard, Ayliffe and Others, and Swain* [2006] UKHL 16.

[62] The relation between this case and the earlier findings in *In re Piracy Jure Gentium* [1934]
AC 586 is not made clear by their Lordships.

[63] *R v. Jones* (note 61), paragraph 62, *per* Lord Hoffmann; paragraph 102, *per* Lord Mance. See
further, Rowe, 'The Effect on National Law of the Customary International Humanitarian
Law Study', 11 (2006) *JCSL* 165, at pp. 169–172. The earlier *Pinochet [No. 3]* decision appeared
very sceptical about the question of liability being directly based on customary law in the UK,
but see O'Keefe, 'Customary Crimes in English Courts', 72 (2001) *BYIL* 293.

[64] A point with which the Lords did not deal in the *R v. Jones* decision (note 61).

[65] *R v. Jones* (note 61), paragraphs 22 to 23, *per* Lord Bingham.

[66] Defences might be a different matter. The same areas of concern about legality and the (near)
exclusive authority of Parliament in the UK in relation to the development of crimes, do
not apply in the same way to the recognition of defences: see Smith, 'Judicial Law-Making

The statements in *Jones* also raise another issue, that of the status of statements of the ICTY (or other international tribunals) when they are incorporated into decisions of the House of Lords (or other Courts). After all, owing to the traditional law of precedent in England and Wales the *ratio decidendi* of a decision (especially one of the House of Lords) binds lower courts dealing with the matter. As a matter of basic UK law, the system of precedent would require a lower court to follow the decision of a higher court (including the part of the international tribunal's jurisprudence that it incorporated). As a result of this, and subject to *Trendtex*, a decision of one of the Tribunals, as quoted in a UK decision, could be a significant source of domestic law for England and Wales, not by virtue of its own authority, but by virtue of the precedential value of the decision that adopts the reasoning and/or, the conclusions of other international tribunals. Those members of the House of Lords that discussed the matter seemed, for whatever reason, to show deference to Lord Bingham's use of ICTY cases, albeit against the background of other decisions that had to be drawn into some form of coherent narrative structure.[67]

IV. The Status of the Case-Law in The UK: The Statutory Position

The common law is not the only way in which the jurisprudence of international tribunals may have a role in the UK legal order. The ICC Act 2001 grants the jurisprudence of international criminal tribunals at times a role when courts are interpreting genocide, war crimes and crimes against humanity for the purposes of that Act. Section 50(5) of the ICC Act provides: 'In interpreting and applying the provisions of the articles referred to in subsection (1) ... [war crimes, crimes against humanity and genocide] ... the court shall take into account any relevant judgment or decision of the ICC. Account may also be taken of any other relevant international jurisprudence'. Section 65 (5) (which

---

in the Criminal Law', 100 (1984) *LQR* 46, pp. 63–67. Thus, it might be possible to argue for the direct reception of customary international law into the criminal law of England and Wales here, and in doing so, the case law of the tribunals may be of use. On the other hand, their jurisprudence on point is not especially satisfactory, and the provisions of the Rome Statute may prove more useful. Particularly relevant in this regard would be Article 33 on superior orders, although the customary status of that provision is hotly contested: see Gaeta, 'The Defence of Superior Orders: The Statute of the International Criminal Court Versus Customary International Law', 10 (1999) *EJIL* 172; *contra*, see Garraway, 'Superior Orders and the International Criminal Court: Justice Delivered or Justice Denied?', 81 (No. 833; 1999) *International Review of the Red Cross* 785.

[67] See for example, Dworkin, *Law's Empire*, Hart Publishing, Oxford/Portland, 1998.

deals with command responsibility) is, in all material respects, the same. Section 66 (4), on the mental element provided for in Article 30 of the Rome Statute (which is to be used in prosecutions under the Act in the UK) on the other hand, is similar, rather than identical, as will be seen in due course.

The reason for much of this is entirely understandable. The UK is a party to the Rome Statute. The International Criminal Court works on the principle of complementarity. In other words, that Court only steps in when a State is determined to be 'unwilling or unable' to prosecute international crimes itself.[68] The UK fully intends to take appropriate advantage of this principle, and to ensure that no UK national is prosecuted by the ICC, by prosecuting them effectively at the domestic level.[69] To do so, it is advisable that UK courts calibrate their understandings of genocide, war crimes and crimes against humanity as far as possible to those held by the ICC.[70]

The explanatory notes to section 50(5) make aspects of this provision a little clearer and show that consonance with the ICC, and international criminal law more generally, was an aim of the Act: '*Subsection (5)* provides that in trying offences, domestic courts must take into account any relevant jurisprudence or decision of the ICC and may also take into account any relevant international jurisprudence.'[71] This statement brings out the difference between the status of the jurisprudence of the ICC and other international tribunals in section 50(5) (and section 65(5)). A court is obliged to take into account the relevant ICC case-law, whilst it is merely entitled to do so for the other case-law. There are a number of reasons why this difference is created.[72]

The first relates to the purpose of the crime-creating provisions of the ICC Act. As mentioned above, it is advisable for a State, should it wish to ensure that it may successfully invoke its complementarity rights, to ensure that its interpretations of international crimes are consonant with the ICC's. Hence the requirement that the ICC's case-law is taken into account. As other international courts do not play the superintending role the ICC has over the way in which States prosecute international crimes,[73] and their jurisprudence will involve their application and interpretation of their own definitions of the crimes (which are

---

[68] Holmes, 'Complementarity: National Courts *versus* the ICC', in Cassese, Gaeta and Jones (note 43), p. 667.

[69] Garraway, 'Military Excesses: Is There a Right Way of Dealing?', 2 (2004) *JICJ* 981, at p. 982.

[70] Interestingly, other than for command responsibility, the ICC Act requires courts in England and Wales to use the UK domestic principles of liability: see ICC Act, section 56(1).

[71] Explanatory notes, paragraph 89. Emphasis original.

[72] Although see below, text to notes 90–94 and accompanying text.

[73] See Cryer, *Prosecuting International Crimes: Selectivity and the International Criminal Law Regime*, Cambridge, 2005, pp. 160–167.

not necessarily the same as those in the Rome Statute), courts in the UK are, by virtue of the Act pointed towards them, but they do not even have to take them into account.

Secondly, the jurisdictional provisions of the International Criminal Court Act also make it necessary to ensure that UK determinations of the ambit of international crimes remain acceptable under international law. This is because in one instance, the International Criminal Court Act permits a broad form of extraterritorial jurisdiction. Jurisdiction over international crimes is asserted over 'a person who commits ... [ICC crimes] ... outside the United Kingdom ... and who subsequently becomes a resident in the United Kingdom' so long as the person is a UK resident when the proceedings are brought and the acts would have been an offence had they occurred in the UK.[74] The most convincing explanation of the lawfulness of this assertion of jurisdiction is that universal jurisdiction applies to such offences.[75] In addition, the ICC Act permits the extradition of suspects to States prosecuting international crimes on the basis of universal jurisdiction.[76] As a result of the fact that universal jurisdiction is a type of jurisdiction which may be asserted over certain forms of conduct defined by international law, rather than being a type of jurisdiction subject to the plenary authority of States, it is necessary to ensure that UK interpretations of that conduct are consonant with those accepted at the international level. The case law of the various courts and tribunals are often good evidence of this, hence the provisions in the Act.[77]

These provisions do, however, beg the question about what is meant by 'international jurisprudence'. The explanatory notes provide some, albeit tantalisingly vague, assistance, referring to international jurisprudence, as 'includ[ing] any relevant jurisprudence of the International Criminal Tribunals and the International Court of Justice'. There are two different interesting issues raised by this statement. The first is the question-begging term 'the International Criminal

---

[74] ICC Act, sections 68 (1) to (2).
[75] O'Keefe is a little less certain that this is the basis of this part of the Act: see ibid, 'Universal Jurisdiction: Clarifying the Basic Concept', 2 (2004) *JICJ* 735, at p. 747.
[76] ICC Act, section 72.
[77] There is one exception to this. It is in relation to the interpretation of intention, pursuant to section 66 of the ICC Act, sub-section (4) of which directs courts towards ICC decisions. It provides, 'In interpreting and applying the provisions of this section (which corresponds to article 30) the court shall take into account any relevant judgment or decision of the ICC.' There is no pointer for the courts to relevant decisions of other tribunals. This probably reflects the fact that there is little case-law from the tribunals on intention, rather than *mens rea* in general, and the decisions that have emanated from the tribunals have not applied anything like the Article 30 standard. See Cryer, Friman, Robinson and Wilmshurst, *An Introduction to International Criminal Law and Procedure*, Cambridge, 2007, pp. 318–320.

Tribunals'. The definite article implies that this includes the most well-known modern international criminal tribunals, the ICTY and ICTR. It is not quite so clear whether this is also intended to include the International Military Tribunals (i.e. Nuremberg and Tokyo), although the House of Lords has cited the Nuremberg IMT Charter and judgment, and the Tokyo IMT Charter (and General Assembly Resolution 95(I), which affirmed these three) as authority in the past without the necessity of a statutory poke in their direction.[78] More difficult to decide is whether or not 'internationalised courts', such as the Special Court for Sierra Leone,[79] or perhaps the chambers in East Timor or Kosovo or, at the furthest reaches, the Cambodian or Iraqi Special Tribunal are covered by this.[80] It might be questioned if other countries' case-law on international crimes could be brought under this provision, especially where it applies provisions of the Rome Statute or their domestic analogues, although there seems no reason why they could not look at such jurisprudence.

The second aspect of this, brought about by virtue of the comment that the decisions of the ICJ may be taken into account, shows that the provision is not limited to the output of criminal courts.[81] The decisions of the ICJ are clearly covered, but what, for example of the Eritrea-Ethiopia Claims Commission,[82] or other non-criminal tribunals that discuss humanitarian law?[83]

In practice, the question is unlikely to cause difficulty. Courts in England and Wales seem happy to cite the jurisprudence of non-UK courts on points of international law without a statutory mandate.[84] The *a contrario* argument that

---

[78] *Pinochet* (note 49), p. 930, *per* Lord Lloyd, p. 940, *per* Lord Nicholls; see also *R v. Jones* (note 61), paragraph 14; and *R v. Howe* [1987] AC 417, at p. 427, *per* Lord Hailsham. Similarly, the Crown Court used ICTY jurisprudence in the *Zardad* case, for which see Cryer, 'Zardad', in Cassese, Acquaviva, Akande and Baig (eds.), *The Oxford Companion to International Criminal Justice*, Oxford, 2009, p. 978, at pp. 978–979.

[79] Which is not quite the international tribunal it thinks it is.

[80] See generally Romano, Nollkaemper and Kleffner (eds.), *Sierra Leone, East Timor, Kosovo and Cambodia*, Oxford, 2004. Whether UK courts would be well advised to follow the findings of the much-criticised Iraqi High Tribunal can be rightly questioned. See in this context, Heller, 'A Poisoned Chalice: The Substantive and Procedural Defects of the Iraqi High Tribunal', 39 (2007) *Case Western Reserve Journal of International Law* 216. [With respect to international tribunals, see Chapter 18: 'Internationalized Tribunals: A Search for Their Legal Bases', by Sarah Williams. Eds.]

[81] The decision in the *Bosnia Genocide Case* would be an example of a relevant decision on point.

[82] See Aldrich, 'The Work of the Eritrea-Ethiopia Commission', 6 (2003) *Yearbook of International Humanitarian Law* 438.

[83] One example of which would be the Inter-American Court of Human Rights, which has, on occasion, applied humanitarian law, see for example, Moir, 'Decommissioned? International Humanitarian Law in the Inter-American Human Rights System', 25 (2003) *HRQ* 182.

[84] See, for example, the *Pinochet* case (note 49), above.

would have to be made, that the only time courts were permitted to refer to cases from outside the UK was when they were expressly permitted to do so, seems strained. As a result, a strong case can be made that, rather than altering the general practice of the courts in relation to citation of non-UK cases on point, the provisions merely serve as a reminder that these decisions may prove useful. This argument is made stronger by the fact that courts only 'may' rather than 'shall' take account of those decisions.

1. *Accounting for Cases: The Pounds, Shillings and Pence of Jurisprudence*

This raises the issue, though, of what 'take into account' means. The wording, of the relevant provisions of the Act, especially when compared to that of section 50(4)[85] is clear enough that it does not require courts to follow those decisions. What 'take into account' means is that the courts (may, or must, depending on the specific provision) consider the relevant jurisprudence when coming to their decision, rather than treat it as binding. It is notable that the terminology of 'take into account' is taken from the 1998 Human Rights Act's approach to the authority of the European Court of Human Rights' decisions in UK courts when they are interpreting the rights enshrined in the European Convention on Human Rights.[86] There is sense in this. Both the Human Rights Act and the ICC Act are attempting to ensure a reasonable correlation between the way the relevant norms are interpreted in the UK and in the international tribunal that oversees their implementation and enforcement.[87] In both systems genuine and reasonable domestic approaches to (at least some of) the relevant norms are given some form of deference. In the European Human Rights system this takes the form of the doctrine of the margin of appreciation,[88] in the ICC system, complementarity performs an analogous (although by no means identical) practical function.[89] This is, in a general sense, one of giving domestic jurisdictions the first bite of the cherry, whilst retaining the right for the ICC to refuse to swallow the stone.

That said, the ICC Act does not create a clear normative hierarchy between the authority of the output of the different tribunals or, indeed between them

---

[85]   On which, see text to notes 95–98.

[86]   Human Rights Act, section 2.

[87]   For a discussion of the approach of the courts with respect to the European Court of Human Rights cases, see Bonner, Fenwick and Harris-Short, 'Judicial Approaches to the Human Rights Act,' 52 (2003) *ICLQ* 549, at pp. 552–553.

[88]   See Yourow, *The Margin of Appreciation Doctrine in the Dynamics of European Human Rights Jurisprudence*, Dordrecht, 1996.

[89]   And legally, the concepts are not identical.

and the Elements of Crimes adopted by the Assembly of States Parties to the Rome Statute[90] over and above that in the distinction between the mandatory 'shall' and 'may' take account (or that account ... be taken) of the relevant statement. In other words, once the decision to look at the relevant case or other document has been taken (whether that decision was statutorily required or not) the Act, on its own terms gives them the same weight (i.e. that they are to be 'taken into account').

The possible difficulties that could arise from this can be shown by showing two conflicting sources, both of which (should the court decide to look at them both) fall under the standard of being taken into account. The Elements of Crimes provide that in relation to genocide '[t]he conduct took place in the context of a manifest pattern of similar conduct directed against that group or was conduct that could itself effect such destruction.'[91] The ICTY Appeals Chamber, however, has stated that

> The Trial Chamber's reliance on the definition of genocide given in the ICC's Elements of Crimes is inapposite ... Because the definition adopted by the Elements of Crimes did not reflect customary law as it existed at the time Krstić committed his crimes, it cannot be used to support the Trial Chamber's conclusion.[92]

Although there is the caveat that the elements did not reflect the law in 1995 (which might lead to an argument that the ICTY implicitly accepted that this is no longer the case),[93] a clear conflict can be seen between the relevant international jurisprudence and the Elements of Crimes. It is true that the Elements of Crimes, unlike the jurisprudence of the Tribunals, were created to be applied by the ICC. However, such an argument runs up against the fact that the Elements (a drafting slip in Article 21 aside) were only intended to assist the ICC in interpreting its Statute, rather than bind it, and there have been calls

---

[90] Section 50 (2) of the ICC Act provides that 'in interpreting and applying the provisions of ... [Articles 6–8 (2) of the Rome Statute] ... the court shall take into account: ... Any relevant Elements of Crimes adopted in accordance with Article 9[of the Rome Statute] ...'.

[91] See Oosterveld and Garraway, 'The Elements of Genocide' in Lee, Lee and Hakan Friman (eds.), *The International Criminal Court: Elements of Crimes and Rules of Procedure and Evidence*, New York, 2001, p. 41, at pp. 44–45.

[92] *Prosecutor v. Krstić*, Judgment, IT-98-33-A, 19 April 2004, paragraph 224.

[93] Any such argument could be countered by the claim that the ICTY was simply engaging in appropriate parsimony in reasoning, inasmuch as the question of what constituted custom in 2004 was irrelevant. Equally, the *lex mitior* principle would imply that if there were a change in favour of the accused, he or she ought to be entitled to benefit from it. To suggest, however, that the ICTY engaged in this analysis, and yet took the view, *sub silentio*, that the law had not changed, is to cross the line into pure speculation.

for the ICC to ignore this particular element.[94] The point is also more broadly applicable though. It is possible that UK courts will be inclined to apply the Elements of Crimes (in which the UK has had a hand in drafting, and will have input into any future amendments) over case-law of the Tribunals (including the ICC). Equally, there are countervailing considerations. The first of these is that at times, case-law may post-date the Elements, in which case, the view of the ICC on the relevant substantive provision might be given deference (not least as the ICC is the body that determines complementarity).

It might also be noted that an *a contrario* argument can be brought with respect to the Act itself, where it seeks to provide primacy for UK views, the Act expressly says so. Section 50 (4) of the ICC Act provides that Articles 6–8 of the Rome Statute 'shall … be construed subject to and in accordance with any relevant reservation or declaration made by the United Kingdom when ratifying any treaty or arrangement relevant to the interpretation of those articles'. The most important of these are probably the UK reservations and interpretative understandings submitted alongside the UK's ratification of Additional Protocol I.[95] That ratification was accompanied by a number of understandings and reservations, relating in part, although not exclusively, to reprisals.[96] Hence, if a UK court had to choose between that reservation and, e.g. the ICTY decision in *Kupreškić*,[97] it is required to choose the former, but this only applies with respect to questions covered by those reservations and statements. The extent to which the *a contrario* argument is convincing depends upon the extent to which section 50 (4) is taken as reflecting an exemption from the general trend of the Act (which is to respect decisions of international tribunals) or as the foundation of a contrary trend, to prefer, where it is important, UK views.[98]

---

[94] Triffterer, 'Genocide: Its Particular Intent to Destroy in Whole or in Part the Group as Such', 14 (2001) *Leiden Journal of International Law* 399; *contra*, Schabas, 'The *Jelesić* Case and the *Mens Rea* of the Crime of Genocide', 14 (2001) *Leiden Journal of International Law* 125.

[95] See Roberts and Guellf, *Documents on the Law of War* (Third edition), Oxford, 1999, pp. 510–512.

[96] Text available at: http://untreaty.un.org/ENGLISH/bible/englishinternetbible/partI/chapter XVIII/treaty10.

[97] Judgment, *Kupreškić*, Trial Chamber II, IT-95-16-T, 14 January 2000, paragraphs 521–536. The view of the UK is that the case is wrong on this point: see Ministry of Defence, *Manual of the Law of Armed Conflict*, Oxford, 2004, p. 421.

[98] See next sub-section, No. 2, *infra*.

2. *When Minds Are Changed, Who's First in Line?*

The questions of relative normativity are only made more complex by the issues of precedent referred to above. It is, if the practice of the ICTY and ICTR mentioned above are indicative of the possibility of the ICC changing its mind,[99] quite possible that its jurisprudence will change, (or 'develop') over time, and also that in response to decisions of the ICC, the Elements of Crimes might also alter.[100] If UK courts have not dealt with the question themselves, then the considerations in the previous sections, and the uncertainties they flag up, apply equally here. If, on the other hand, there have been authoritative UK decisions on point, the difficulty discussed in relation to *Trendtex* also comes into play.[101] For example, what if, to build upon the example mentioned above, the House of Lords, in interpreting genocide in the context of a prosecution in England and Wales originally preferred the Elements of Crimes, but, a subsequent judgment a Chamber of the ICC adopted the view that the Element was not an accurate reflection of international law (including the Rome Statute) and thus was not to be applied by the ICC? There is a further complication, whether the House did so as a matter of the *ratio decidendi* or whether its comments were simply *obiter dicta*, but, for the purpose of argument, it may be simpler to take the stronger case, when the question has arisen as an aspect of the *ratio*.[102]

Trendtex would imply that the question turns upon whether or not the relevant *ratio* was that the relevant international rule was the rule to be applied by a UK court, or whether the decision was that the specific rule accepted by

---

[99] And there are those who argue that some of its early jurisprudence is worthy of something of a rethink, see Schabas, 'First Prosecutions at the International Criminal Court', 25 (2006) *Human Rights Law Journal* 25.

[100] ICTY jurisprudence certainly had an effect on the debates on the Elements of Crimes, and some elements are a reaction to ICTY jurisprudence.

[101] The relevance of *Trendtex* might be questioned; after all, it dealt with the status of international law in the common law, rather than the status of international law (and 'international jurisprudence') where a UK statute gives express guidance as to the approach to be taken by a UK court in dealing with such questions in domestic law. This is especially so where there is an international tribunal which has a superintending role to which the UK has consented. However, as was seen above, the ICC Act is itself somewhat unclear regarding the relative normative status to be granted to the various pieces of evidence of international law, and even less so does it make clear the relation between those evidences and domestic decisions. This is reflective of a greater tension in the ICC Act more generally, and between UK views and the necessity of conforming those views to general international law.

[102] The question of whether or not the UK or ICC (or other international jurisprudence) may be preferred might turn on the wording of the House of Lords decision.

the UK was that to be applied in the UK. This throws us back to the question of whether the Act is intended to give precedence to UK views on international law as a matter of general principle, or whether it is to ensure that the UK is entitled to use complementarity, or something else. Given that the Act also gives the right to the UK to prosecute those who commit international crimes abroad and who later become UK residents, it might gently be suggested that the ambit of international law, as interpreted by the ICC ought to be given some respect, and that section 50(4) of the ICC Act is a specific exemption from this general principle, designed to preserve specific UK reservations.[103]

V. CONCLUSION

A broader version of the tension alluded to above is one of the reasons that the approach to international law taken by domestic courts is of perennial interest to scholars.[104] Domestic courts are one of the most important mechanisms for the enforcement of international law, and in doing so, such courts fulfil the double role (*dédoublement fonctionelle*) Georges Scelle identified back in the mid twentieth century.[105] Still, as this implies, they are also national, as well as international actors, and as such, can undermine (or supplement) international norms in the course of their domestication.[106] This piece has, *inter alia*, sought to show how the UK, in a limited instance has treated, and intends to treat, statements of international law by international courts, and the extent to which this differs from how those courts view their own jurisprudence, and the interplay between those cases and other statements of international law. The UK ICC Act attempts, genuinely, if not always perfectly clearly, to deal with such questions, whilst, in the final analysis, leaving it, as might be expected, to interpretation in individual cases. Civilian lawyers, alongside their common-criminal-lawyer colleagues may

---

[103] Interestingly, there is nothing in the Act about whether UK reservations and/or statements are to be applied if a person were to be prosecuted with respect to a conflict to which the UK was not a party. This matter is made more complex by the fact that the UK's reservations could be cited against it (but, *quaere*, does/ought this to apply where they involve the assertion of jurisdiction over a conflict to which those reservations did not apply?).

[104] See for example, Benvenisti, 'Judicial Misgivings Regarding the Application of International Law, An Analysis of Attitudes of National Courts', 4 (1993) *EJIL* 159; and Sadat-Wexler, 'The Interpretation of the Nuremberg Principles by the French Court of Cassation From Touvier to Barbie to Back Again', 32 (1994) *Columbia Journal of Transnational Law* 289.

[105] Cassese, 'Remarks on Scelle's Theory of "Role Splitting" ' (*dédoublement fonctionelle*) in International Law', 1 (1990) *EJIL* 210.

[106] See *supra* (note 104).

join hands in expressing some concern over this, even if such an approach does not violate the principle of legality as it is protected at the international level.[107]

This latter aspect also implicates another issue much beloved of international lawyers of late, the possibility of conflicting decisions of international courts. For the first time international lawyers may be faced with an embarrassment of international jurisprudence on point, and the possibility of contradictory statements of the relevant international law. The possibility has always existed, but has been practically limited by the number of (relatively) authoritative interpreters of international law. That is no longer the case,[108] and the difficulties in determining international law in a decentralised system are, ironically brought into rather sharp relief by the increasing number of international tribunals. Nowhere is this more notable than in international criminal law, where there are a plethora of tribunals passing judgment not only on individuals, but also on the state of international criminal law.

The creation of the ICC has, to some extent catalysed a degree of harmonisation of international criminal proscriptions, and in spite of Article 10 of the Rome Statute, caused some to treat it as a codification of international criminal law.[109] Although the UK ICC Act accepts that international criminal law does not begin and end with the Rome Statute, perhaps the most notable flaw it contains is that, whilst accepting this, it does not go beyond the Rome Statute in the identification of international crimes.[110] Nonetheless, at the end of this overview of international and UK practice, what can clearly be said is that both at home and abroad, the jurisprudence of the international criminal tribunals is a significant source of evidence of international criminal law,[111] and has quite often been treated as more.

---

[107] Shahabuddeen, 'Does the Principle of Legality Stand in the Way of Progressive Development of the Law?', 2 (2004) *JICJ* 1007.

[108] See, for example, Higgins, 'A Babel of Voices? Ruminations From the Bench', 55 (2006) *ICLQ* 791.

[109] See Zegveld, *Accountability of Armed Opposition Groups in International Law*, Cambridge, 2002, p. 102.

[110] Although there are also, for example, the Geneva Conventions Act 1957, and the Chemical Weapons Act 1996 which cover similar areas.

[111] On which see Parry, *The Sources and Evidences of International Law*, Manchester, 1965.

Chapter Ten

Killing Many to Save a Few?
Preliminary Thoughts about Avoiding
Collateral Civilian Damage by
Assassination of Regime Elites

Michael Bohlander[*]

The godly and merciful prince will also be influenced by seeing that the greatest part of all the great evils which every war entails falls upon people unconnected with the war, who least deserve to suffer these calamities.
Erasmus of Rotterdam, *The Education of a Christian Prince* (1516)

I open my books about rights and morals. I listen to scholars and legal experts, and inspired by their suggestive discourses, I deplore the miseries of nature, admire the peace and justice established by the civil order, bless the wisdom of public institutions and find consolation for being a man by seeing myself as a citizen. Well instructed as to my duties and my happiness, I close the books, leave the lecture room, and look around me. There I see a miserable people groaning under an iron yoke, the whole human race crushed by a handful of oppressors, and an enraged mob overwhelmed by pain and hunger whose blood and tears the rich drink in peace. And everywhere the strong are armed against the weak with the formidable power of the law. Jean-Jacques Rousseau, *The State of War* (1756–1758; unfinished fragment)

I. Introduction

When I was a child, I loved to read the comic books about the Gaul warrior Asterix by René Goscinny and Albert Uderzo. One of my favourites was a volume called 'Asterix and the Big Fight',[1] in which the chieftain of the village

---

[*] Professor of Law, School of Law, Durham University. I would like to thank the audience at the University of Northern Iowa for their stimulating comments during my lecture on the topic on 9 April 2008, especially Professor James Robinson for his intriguing reference to the Rules of Chess and the fact that the King can never be taken, but only immobilised.

[1] Original title: *Le combat des chefs*, 1964.

K.H. Kaikobad & M. Bohlander (eds.), *International Law and Power: Perspectives on Legal Order and Justice*. Essays in Honour of Colin Warbrick, pp. 207–233.

of Asterix is formally challenged to a duel by another chieftain, who is under the influence of the Roman occupying forces. The Gallic tradition, or so it is said, demanded that the tribe of the loser accept the winner as its new leader. After a wild goose chase and many complications, the good guy wins, but the Romans will not accept defeat and attack Asterix's village anyway but, of course, they are resoundingly beaten by the newly invigorated Gaul tribe. I do not profess to have read Asterix for its potential subliminal messages in political science then (or now), yet at that time the tradition struck me as a very sensible one: Why should the mere members of two tribes have to slug it out between themselves when it is their bosses who want more power and influence? It was only fair that *they* should be the ones to slug it out. Rather than drag many families into chaos by fighting in an all-out full-scale tribal war that the tribes-people themselves may have had no real interest in, it appeared preferable that, if there was a conflict about territory and power, that conflict should be solved with as little bloodshed as possible, and that submission to a new ruler was better than death and mayhem for the whole tribe.

Of course, that approach immediately evokes the memory of the famous anti-communist slogan from the Cold War era 'Better Dead than Red' and its communist comeback version of 'Better Red than Dead'. It is very simplistic and avoids many issues, such as, for example, the question of how political dissidents in the conquered tribe would be treated by the new chief, and it does not sit well with our modern individualistic approach to life choices, either. However, after all those years since I first read the comic book, I still found myself going back to this somehow very attractive idea. It resurfaced for good on my now hopefully matured research agenda during and since the US-led aggression against Iraq in 2003. I wondered why it was that innocent Iraqi civilians would have to die in their tens of thousands[2] because the Americans and their Allies thought it prudent to bomb the country's cities to rubble before they risked the lives of their own ground troops, and gambled on the very real dangers of destabilisation and ensuing sectarian violence, not to speak of the effects a destabilised Iraq would have on the whole region. None of these civilians had given any cause to be so treated. More to the point, I wondered why the cities had to be bombed at all. Could not the all-powerful United States have employed the services of its so-called 'black-ops' specialists and simply assassinated Saddam Hussein and his top henchmen as the real (or perceived) root of the problem? Surely that was better than making all those innocent and helpless people suffer? I am not

---

[2]   The estimates of Iraqi deaths resulting from the occupation after 2003 by some, as of June 2007, rank from roughly 65,000–71,000. See the Iraq Body Count website at www.iraqbodycount.net/database.

here going to address the discrepancy between the (several) professed and true reasons for that war, and how that may impact on the question of whether it is justifiable to sacrifice so many human lives.

Many will accuse me of being naïve: Saddam Hussein and his regime were too well-protected, with Hussein allegedly using doppelgangers and always being on the move between several palaces; it would have been next to impossible to infiltrate the circles in which they moved with secret agents and assassins, and so on. Others will say that even if it could have been done, who would have guaranteed that killing the regime would have resulted in a more peaceful and stable Iraq. You cannot just eradicate a government and then simply leave a leaderless people to its own devices; there needs to be a strategy of institution-building and pacification for the time after the change, too. Finally, yet others will accuse me of proposing the unthinkable by tinkering with a fundamental legal principle that generally prohibits the assassination of Heads of State by other States, thereby allowing the use of the crime of murder to become an acceptable, if *ultima ratio*, instrument of international politics.

These objections carry a lot of weight and must be taken very seriously. The first and second are factual, based on operative capability, political circumstances and prognostic difficulty. I cannot say anything with authority on them, at least not in the short space of a chapter. What one can say, however, is that intentional killing by black-ops missions *has* been used throughout history by many States, in recent history over the last 120 years often by the United States, as a means for regime change when it suited the interest of that State or its business community.[3] Considerations of the wider consequences have very often been notoriously absent in the decision-making process. The third objection is a legal issue, and that is the one I wish to address in this contribution. The legal issue does not go away simply because the factual issues may be unclear. The question we have to ask ourselves is: What if we could give affirmative answers about operative capability for a black-ops strike and a positive prognosis for the wider societal consequences of such a course of action? In short, if we could do it, would we be allowed to do it, or even more drastically: Would we have to do it?

This chapter is going to take a look at traditional ethical and legal positions on the issue of assassination, yet it will for reasons of space not address the use of assassination by the State against non-State-related actors, such as for example, the targeted killing practice of Israel vis-à-vis Palestinian resistance group leaders,

---

[3] See, for example, the recent popular account by Kinzer, *Overthrow: America's Century of Regime Change from Hawaii to Iraq*, New York, 2007, and his earlier book, *All the Shah's Men: An American Coup and the Roots of Middle East Terror*, Hoboken, N.J., 2004. The CIA has recently disclosed a number of its previous operations the 1950s to the 1970s, the so-called 'Family Jewels' and other documents; they are available online at www.foia.cia.gov/, last accessed 3 July 2007.

recently and succinctly circumscribed and analysed by the Supreme Court of Israel, sitting as the High Court of Justice, in the case of *The Public Committee against Torture in Israel and others v. The Government of Israel and others*, decided on 11 December 2005.[4] It will look merely at the assassination of foreign Heads of State by the forces of another State. It will then set out the results of a pilot study for a questionnaire that was done with the support of some of the Durham students in my international criminal law course, and which is meant to find out the attitudes of law students from universities in different countries to some of the underlying ethical questions. This is very much a work in progress and I do not presume to be able to present anything but musings and initial ruminations.

II. The Issues Defined

I remember that when I first told Colin Warbrick about my intention to research the use of assassinations in order to avoid massive civilian collateral damage, he looked at me as if I might be in need of psychological treatment for even thinking up such a topic. I vividly recall his written comment on the brief exposé I had given him, stating that I appeared to 'consider moving from theory to practice'. I could almost physically feel his discomfort at such an idea emanating from the page. However, for me it was a question of logical stringency arising from another study I had just finished at the time, namely the domestic use of military force against civilian airplanes that had been hijacked by terrorists in 9/11 scenarios.[5] My (utilitarian) conclusion was that under an argument based in substance on the principle of necessity, shooting down the planes was justified, even if there were hundreds of innocent passengers on board, as long as that served to save a greater number of innocent lives on the ground. Taken together with the State's duty to protect its citizens, one might even arrive at a duty of the State, or an individual for that matter, to choose a course of action that is made legitimate, and even lawful, by a defence of necessity or prevention of crime under section 3 of the Criminal Law Act 1967, in combination with the principle of collateral damage. Similar considerations return on the international law level under the headings of discrimination and proportionality.

If killing a Head of State can put a definite end to a serious danger to international peace and security caused by that Head of State, how can it be proportionate to respect international comity towards him[6] but to prefer killing

---

[4] Case No. HCJ 769/02, available online from the search engine of the Israeli Supreme Court at http://elyon1.court.gov.il/eng/home/index.html.

[5] '*In Extremis* – Hijacked Airplanes, "Collateral Damage" and the Limits of Criminal Law', (2006) *Criminal Law Review* 579.

[6] Generic language using the male gender includes the female.

thousands of his innocent subjects to achieve the same aim? Does it really make a decisive difference whether he is a part of the operational chain of command, as, for example, Thomas Wingfield[7] has suggested, or is it not enough that he holds de facto political power over the military? Do the actual circumstances of the assassination matter, i.e. whether it was done openly or treacherously or in a situation that did not (yet) warrant the initiation of hostilities in the conventional military[8] sense?[9] Are the traditional aversions against clandestine targeted operations not based on an outmoded code of chivalry from a time when the use of highly destructive weapons and the risk-free means of their delivery were not as widespread as they are today? Can, for example, national resistance movements, legitimately following the right to self-determination, be held at all to conventional methods of fighting, if by doing so they have to engage a superior enemy on a vastly uneven playing field? If certain States use methods such as extraordinary renditions and highly orchestrated transnational torture networks based on an interpretation of operative necessity to counter Islamist terrorism, what claim do these countries have to expect chivalry from others? Do we not foster resentment among the have–nots of the latest military technology and gadgetry, based on the double standards created by the haves?

In the age of the often bemoaned asymmetric warfare and the war on terror, is there not a much more immediate moral asymmetry: If murdering a dangerous Head of State by using stealth or deception is unacceptable under international law, does that not leave us with the cynical conclusion that the people whom a lot of the humanitarian law of war is meant to protect in the first place, the civilians, are at the end of the day the ones who have to suffer the consequences after all? Does this not apply especially in scenarios where weapons of such immense destructive force are used, such as, for example, the bunker-breaking bombs used in the 2003 Iraq war, that any talk about surgical targeting and unintended collateral damage becomes absurd? Is it really better that thousands of innocent citizens die for the sake of one person, who may even be oppressing them, and are we really right to worry in such a context about the 'innocent

---

[7] 'Taking Aim at Regime Elites: Assassination, Tyrannicide, and the Clancy Doctrine', 22 (1998) *Maryland Journal of International Law of Trade* 287 at p. 294.

[8] Wingfield (note 7), at pp. 295 *et seq*, with a concise historical overview of the development of the positions.

[9] Michael N. Schmitt, in his incisive article 'State-Sponsored Assassination in International and Domestic Law', 17 (1992) *Yale Journal of International Law* 609, makes this distinction, stating that under existing principles peacetime assassinations are forbidden if they happen for political reasons, in armed conflict if they are committed by treacherous means; he acknowledges, however, that other rules of international law may forbid acts of intentional homicide even if they meet the threshold for assassinations as such.

daughter, the uninvolved wife or mistress'[10] of the dictator? If the very people whom to 'liberate' is the aim of a humanitarian intervention can become the victims of the ideology of collateral damage in a campaign of area bombing, how much more can it be justified to risk collateral damage to the family and friends of the dictator by a direct attack on his home or office? Is it not time[11] that the war was brought, pre-emptively or not, home to those who *cause* it rather than those who merely have to *fight* it or cannot escape the theatre of operations?

Again, while some will be able to develop some sympathy for these emotionally charged questions, most will probably say that this is the way of the world. If, for example, the United States assassinates the Head of State of a small Latin American country because his policies conflict with the economic or geo-political interests of the United States, there will be diplomatic protests and then there will most likely be silence. If, however, a small Latin American country whose resources are being squandered by American business companies under the protection of the armed forces of the United States with the express approval of the President, and whose citizens were being held in abject poverty leading to a high death toll, had the chance to remove that President by assassination and did so, there would be massive diplomatic protests *and* the United States would retaliate with its far superior military power. Had the hijackers on 9/11 succeeded in crashing one of the planes on the White House, as had apparently been the plan, we might have had that situation, and look what happened to Afghanistan anyway without such an attack having been successful. What purpose would it serve if we allowed assassination? Would it not again be one of those international rules that apply to a multitude of smaller, weaker, poorer, or to put it bluntly: inconsequential countries, but not to the few big ones, and even among those not to each in equal measure? *Homo homini lupus – Hobbes locutus, causa finita?*

III. The Development of the law and ethics of assassination – A brief overview

The history of the ethics of war and especially the question of the suffering of non-combatants or civilians fills entire libraries. I will only attempt a very brief chronological outline of the ideas professed through the centuries. We

---

[10] Wingfield (note 7), at p. 311.

[11] This seems to be supported by Wingfield (note 7), at p. 316, with reference to Schmitt (note 9) at p. 679.

are moving in an area of overlap of the *ius ad bellum* (when may a State attack another one by using force, or by proxy, its Head of State) and more to the point, the question of pre-emptive self-defence, and the *ius in bello* (which methods can a State use in an otherwise lawful attack, that is to say, may the Head of State be targeted at all). The whole question rests on the acceptance of some form of just war theory;[12] the idea that the formula *inter arma silent leges* is no longer representative of common international opinion. In the age of asymmetrical warfare with resistance movements, insurgents and terrorist groups intentionally using the civilian population as cover, so-called 'concealment warfare', this consensus is being called into question by one side to the conflict. It is becoming more and more difficult to maintain the traditional just war standards and be effective in reaching a military goal against groups using such deplorable methods.[13] Not least, the reason for this is that those rules were drafted and pronounced with a classical war between sovereign States in mind.

Those have become more the exception than the rule, leaving aside the attendant issue that hardly ever are attacks by States accompanied or even preceded by a declaration of war. Often the conflicts are internal. Generally, the law is still not quite as clear-cut as one might expect after many centuries of warfare and attempts to restrain it. A look at the Bush Doctrine on pre-emptive strikes and the rather lukewarm criticism by the international community may serve as an example.[14] The guerrilla tactics used by resistance groups against their government's troops and occupying armies exact a high death toll among the regular troops and consequently States embarking on such an enterprise will have to weigh the need to protect their own soldiers from harm on the one hand, and the compliance with proportionality as well as targeting requirements, on the other. As the recent campaigns by the United States and its coalitions of allies since the first Gulf War in 1991 have shown, the approach tends to be 'better safe than sorry', or as a German proverb, literally translated, would say: 'Caution is the mother of the porcelain chest.' Almost every campaign has begun with the massive use of cruise missiles, extensive and prolonged aerial bombing and heavy artillery shelling.

When one talks about just war theory, the references are almost exclusively to schools of thought developed by thinkers in Western, and more to the point,

---

[12] See only the exceptional analysis by Walzer, *Just and Unjust Wars* (Fourth edition), New York, 2006.

[13] Reynolds, 'Collateral Damage on the 21st Century Battlefield: Enemy Exploitation of the Law of Armed Conflict, and the Struggle for a Moral High Ground', 56 (2005) *Air Force Law Review* 1.

[14] See, e.g., Hofmeister, 'Neither the "Caroline Formula" Nor the "Bush Doctrine" – An Alternative Framework to Assess the Legality of Pre-Emptive Strikes', 2 (2005) *UNELJ* 31.

Christian value systems. In some parts of the world, the use of, for example, treacherous surprise tactics and targeting of individuals were part of the code of warfare and expected of successful warlords. Karl Friday has shown that the medieval Japanese warrior's codex or *Bushido* had little time for ideas of chivalry as we would understand them; in fact, he states that while *bushi* did sometimes announce certain times and places for battles, 'such promises were honored far more often in the breach than in the event'.[15]

The sources that deal with tyrannicide and its attendant problems do not always distinguish between internal resistance (sedition) and external attack, although very often they will be seen in the context of an armed conflict, but the underlying ethical approaches are at the end of the day similar. They all centre around the issues of chivalry vis-à-vis the use of treacherous means, and the avoidance of casualties among the innocent population, namely of collateral damage. Cicero, for example, said after the assassination of Caesar:

> [T]here can be no fellowship between us and tyrants – on the contrary there is a complete estrangement – and it is not contrary to nature to rob a man, if you are able, whom it is honourable to kill. Indeed, the whole pestilential and irreverent class ought to be expelled from the community of mankind.[16]

St. Augustine, whilst emphasising that promises given to an enemy must be kept and the victor should show mercy to the vanquished enemy,[17] made it clear that he did not view it as illegitimate to use ruses and ambushes, as long as the war they were meant to further was legitimate:

> Such things as ambushes are legitimate for those who engage in a just war. In these matters the only thing a righteous man has to worry about is that the war is waged by someone who has the right to do so because not all men have that right. Once an individual has undertaken that kind of war, it does not matter at all, as far as justice is concerned, whether he wins victory in open combat or though ruses.[18]

This view of St Augustine was adopted by Gratian and the decretists in the *Decretum Divi Gratiani* and the glosses thereto after the 12th century.[19] Another writer of the 12th century, John of Salisbury, in his treatise *Policraticus* addressed the issue of tyrannicide at length. Although he, too, noted that promises under an

---

[15] Friday, 'Might Makes Right – Just War and Just Warfare in Early Medieval Japan', in Brekke (ed.), *The Ethics of War in Asian Civilizations A Comparative Study*, London & New York, 2006, 159 at p. 169.

[16] *On Duties, Book III*, section 32; cited in Reichberg, Syse and Begby (eds.), *The Ethics of War*, Blackwell Publishing, Maldon/Oxford/Carlton, 2006, p. 59. Hereinafter referred to as RSB.

[17] Letter 189 to Boniface, cited in RSB (note 16), p. 79.

[18] *Questions on the Heptateuch*, Book VI, Chapter 10, cited in RSB (note 16), p. 83.

[19] *Decretum Divi Gratiani*, Part II, Causa 23, Question II, Canon 2, cited in RSB (note 16), p. 113.

oath or an obligation of fealty must be honoured even when made to a tyrant,[20] that the use of poison was deplorable and not permitted[21] and that he was somewhat wary about leaving the decision in the hands of just any individual,[22] he was fairly straightforward as to what fate should generally befall a tyrant:

> To kill a tyrant is not merely lawful, but right and just. ... [T]he tyrant, the likeness of wickedness, is generally to be even killed. The origin of tyranny is iniquity, and springing from a poisonous root, it is a tree which grows and sprouts into a baleful pestilent growth, and to which the axe must by all means be laid. ... [I]t has always been lawful to flatter tyrants and to deceive them, and ... it has always been an honourable thing to slay them if they can be curbed in no other way.[23]

The view that promises and certain conventions must be honoured even against the worst and cruellest enemy can also be found in medieval Muslim war tradition; a telling example is the famous incident related to Saladin's treatment of Reynald de Châtillon, Lord of Karak and a ruthless crusader bent on destroying the fragile peace previously kept until the death of King Baldwin IV of leprosy in 1185 and that of his six-year-old nephew Baldwin V in 1186, and of the new King of Jerusalem, Guy de Lusignan, after their defeat at the battle of Hittin on July 4, 1187. As the biography of Saladin written by his confidant and *qadi al-'askar* (army judge-advocate) from 1188–1193, Ibn Shaddad, tells us, Saladin had offered Guy a cup of water, which Guy passed on to Reynald without the consent of Saladin. Saladin, who had previously vowed to kill Reynald and later did, is reported to have said to his interpreter, or *dragoman*:

> Say to the king, 'You are the one who gave him the drink. I give him no drink, nor any of my food'. What he meant was 'If anyone eats my food, chivalry would demand that I harm him not'.[24]

Saladin allegedly also told Guy that 'kings do no kill each other'.[25] Killing their subordinates was, however, apparently acceptable.

---

[20] *Policraticus*, Book VIII, Chapter 20, cited in RSB (note 16), p. 130.

[21] *Policraticus*, ibid, p. 130.

[22] Ibid, Chapter 18, cited in RSB (note 16), pp. 129–30.

[23] Ibid, Chapters 17 to 20, cited in RSB (note 16), pp. 129–30.

[24] Baha' al-Din Ibn Shaddad, *The Rare and Excellent History of Saladin* (Translated by D.S. Richards), Aldershot, 2002, pp. 37–38. See also the account given by Amin Maalouf, *The Crusades through Arab Eyes*, London, 2006, pp. 193–200, on the events after the Battle of Hittin and the re-conquest of Jerusalem by Saladin. This account also highlights the historical inaccuracies of popular films such as 'The Kingdom of Heaven', despite their apparent, and historically mostly justified, well-meaning intention of painting the Muslim leader in a very positive light.

[25] Ahmmad Shalabi, *Encyclopedia of Islamic History, Crusade Wars* (*Mawsoat Al-Tareekh Al-Islami, Al Horoob Alsalibiyat*) (Sixth edition), vol. vi, Cairo, 1983, p. 28; Al Kadi Salah Al-din Ibn Shamah (Ibn Shadad), *Tale of Salah Al-din, Al Kadi* (*Sirat Salah Al-din, Maktabat Al-Thakafat*

St Thomas Aquinas, writing in the 13th century in his *Summa Theologiae* made a distinction between an ambush based on false pretences and breach of a promise, which he declared illicit, and the mere concealment of one's intentions, which was a legitimate tactic of war in his view,[26] an approach which has survived to this day as the so-called 'ruse-perfidy' distinction.[27] He also approved of sedition against a tyrannical government unless such a course of conduct brought about even greater suffering for the people.[28] According to his *Commentaries on Lombard*, obedience to tyrants or rulers in general was based on the question of whether lawfully acquired authority was merely abused (presumption in favour of obedience), or whether authority was not even lawfully acquired (no obedience owed).[29] As far as tyrannicide was concerned, St Thomas Aquinas, in his *On the Governance of Rulers*, entertained the possibility of tyrannicide but warned at the same time against the dangers arising from unsuccessful attempts or from the ensuing power vacuum, which may be usurped by even worse people, resulting in deteriorating circumstances. In general, he appeared to favour a presumption against action by force.[30]

The ruse-perfidy distinction is again clearly mirrored in the writings of Christine de Pizan from the 14th and 15th centuries, which in part refer to the teachings of her mentor, Honoré Bonet[31] and are structured as a kind of dialogue between Christine and him. She also advocated the keeping of promises, for example, of safe-conduct to 'Saracens', as Muslims were called at the time, and which apparently was not a uniformly accepted custom in her days.[32]

Niccoló Machiavelli appeared to disagree with the evolving ideology of making moral judgments the basis for political decisions in peace or wartime. Accordingly, the ruse-perfidy rule meant nothing to him in moral terms. Famously, in his *Discourses*, he presents necessity and political expedience as the main factors of his approach:

> For when the safety of one's country wholly depends on the decision to be taken, no attention should be paid to either justice or injustice, to kindness or cruelty, or to its being praiseworthy or ignominious. On the contrary, every other

---

Al Diniat) (First edition), Port Saïd, 2000, p. 62. I wish to thank Judge Professor Adel Ibrahim Maged, Cairo/Abu Dhabi, for providing me with the original sources.

[26] *Summa Theologiae*, Part II–II, Question 40, Article 3, cited in RSB (note 16), pp. 180–81.

[27] See Schmitt (note 9), at p. 614, who credits Ayala with this.

[28] *Summa Theologiae* (note 26), Question 42, Article 2, cited in RSB (note 16), p. 186.

[29] *Scripta super libros sententiarum*, Article 2, cited in RSB (note 16), pp. 194–95.

[30] *De Regimine Principium*, cited in RSB (note 16), pp. 195–98.

[31] *Le livre des fais d'armes et de la chevalerie* (*The Book of Deeds of Arms and of Chivalry*), Part III, Chapter 13, cited in RSB (note 16), pp. 219–20.

[32] *Supra* (note 31), Part IV, Chapter 3, cited in RSB (note 16), p. 225.

consideration being set aside, that alternative should be wholeheartedly adopted which will save the life and preserve the freedom of one's country.[33]

Thomas More, a contemporary of Machiavelli, would seem to have agreed with the latter on a rather pragmatic view of warfare, although his attitude was driven by an almost economic cost-benefit analysis combined with just war ideas of proportionality. In *Utopia*, he explains how the inhabitants of his perfect world set about the business of going to war:

> And so, immediately after declaring war, they see to it that many notices certified by their official seal are put up secretly and simultaneously in the most conspicuous places in the enemy's territory promising a huge reward to anyone who does away with the enemy's prince; they also assign lesser, but still very substantial, sums for the deaths of those individuals they list in the same notices. These are the persons who, apart from the prince himself, were responsible for the plotting against the Utopians. ... Other nations condemn this practice of bidding for and buying off an enemy as a barbarous, degenerate crime, but the Utopians think it does them great credit: it shows them to be wise, since in this way they win great wars without fighting at all, and also humane and compassionate, since by killing a few malefactors they spare the lives of many innocent persons who would have fallen in battle, both their own soldiers and those of the enemy; for they pity the rank-and-file of the enemy's soldiers almost as much as their own citizens because they know they do not go to war of their own accord but are driven to it by the madness of princes. ... They offer amnesty to cities that surrender and even those taken by siege they do not sack; instead they execute those who prevented the surrender; they enslave the rest of the defenders, but the civilian populace they leave unharmed.[34]

The ideology espoused by Thomas More's perfect civilisation in theory comes close to what caused this chapter to be written in the first place: A desire to hold only those accountable, to differing degrees that are responsible. However, as we will see, this idea – maybe not surprisingly – was not successful in the course of history, and as later philosophers such as Alberico Gentili pointed out (see below), the expected result may also have been far from certain.

Martin Luther, the great Protestant reformer, seemed to recognise the appeal of a concept that allowed oppressed people, or by proxy those bent on humanitarian intervention, to depose or even kill a tyrant; yet he warned against the dangers of the slippery slope:

> Furthermore, such conduct has bad results or sets a bad example. If it is considered right to murder or depose tyrants, the practice spreads and it becomes a commonplace thing arbitrarily to call men tyrants who are not tyrants, and even

---

[33] *Discourses on the First Decade of Livy, Book II*, Chapter 41, cited in RSB (note 16), p. 257.
[34] *Utopia*, Book II, cited in RSB (note 16), pp. 262–64.

to kill them if the mob takes a notion to do so. The history of the Roman people shows us how this can happen. They killed many a fine emperor simply because they did not like him or he did not do what they wanted, that is, let them be lords and make him their fool. This happened to Galba, Pertinax, Gordian, Alexander, and others ...[35]

The other great Protestant reformer, Jean Calvin, would appear to have altogether rejected the idea of any aggressive action against tyrants from a Christian point of view that postulated obedience, even to those who blatantly abused their God-given office, to the point where obedience would have meant disobeying the commands of God. Calvin took a very individualistic Christian view by referring to the example of Christ who preferred unjust suffering to righteous resistance.[36] Calvin's approach brings out in sharp contrast the question of whether the Christian faith can be made the basis of any aggressive course of conduct at all. Both Luther and Calvin, the former famously by his motto '*sola scriptura*', did not put any similar weight on non-Christian philosophers as the protagonists of scholasticism and Catholicism had previously done.

The doubts about deposing, let alone assassinating princes were shared by Francisco de Vitoria. He appeared to allow such a course of action only in circumstance when the prince had been a tyrant, causing enormous suffering or harm, or if security and peace could not otherwise be restored.[37]

Balthazar Ayala, in his *Three Books on the Law of War* of 1582, approved of St Augustine's view that the use of trickery was as such irrelevant for deciding on the justice of military operations, but made it clear that he, like St Thomas Aquinas, wanted to distinguish treacherous means, which he called 'fraud and snares' from mere trickery.[38] Francisco Suárez, whose writings had a large influence on the course of modern philosophy, in reference to St Thomas Aquinas also supported the ruse-perfidy distinction as to which sort of tricks a party to a conflict is allowed to employ to further its own cause.[39]

Alberico Gentili, while approving of the actions of Pepin, the father of Charlemagne, who slew one of his enemies in his sleep, criticised the approach taken by Thomas More by calling the use of assassinations shameful, contrary to justice and honour and in contravention of the laws of nature and God. He also thought that More's hopes of keeping the casualties down to a minimum by

---

[35] *Whether Soldiers, Too, Can be Saved*, cited in RSB (note 16), p. 270.

[36] *Institutio Christianae Religionis*, Book IV, 20, paras. 22–32.

[37] *On the Law of War*, Question 3, Article 9, cited in RSB (note 16), p. 331.

[38] *Three Books on the Law of War and on the Duties Connected with War and on Military Discipline* (Translation by John P. Bate), New York, 1912, pp. 84–87.

[39] *Metaphysical Disputations, Disputation XIII (On War)*, Section VII, 23, cited in RSB (note 16), p. 367.

targeting those who carried the greatest responsibility and power were mistaken, as the use of treacherous means could have the unwanted effect of strengthening the solidarity the enemy's troops or even of the whole population.[40] However, Gentili was more progressive on the idea of pre-emptive attacks which he accepted were a reasonable course of action of anticipatory defence before surrounding States became too[41] powerful.[42] Johannes Althusius, writing in the 17th century in his *Politica*, reluctantly approved of killing a tyrant

> [W]hen his tyranny has been publicly acknowledged and is incurable: when he madly scorns all laws, brings about the ruin and destruction of the realm, overthrows civil society among men as far as he is able, and rages violently: and when there are no other remedies available.[43]

Hugo Grotius in his monumental work *De iure belli ac pacis* joined Gentili in his positive view of the course of action taken by Pepin, saying that

> Not merely by the law of nature but also by the law of nations … it is in fact permissible to kill an enemy in any place whatsoever; and it does not matter how many there are that do the deed, or who suffer. … According to the law of nations not only those who do such deeds, but also others who instigate others who do them, are considered free from blame.[44]

Grotius did, however, also adhere to the distinction between treachery and mere ruses, saying that treacherous killings may result in reprisals:

> In general a distinction must be made between assassins who violate an express or tacit obligation of good faith, as subjects resorting to violence against a king, vassals against a lord, soldiers against him whom they serve, those also who have been received as suppliants or strangers or deserters, against those who have received them; and such as are held by no bond of good faith.[45]

He also disagreed with any ideology that allowed a war to be waged for the mere purpose of regime change, even with the best of intentions such as, for example, the promotion of democracy and human rights.[46]

Returning to the issue of stealth and trickery, Samuel von Pufendorf in 1673 tried to push the envelope of the ruse category by stating:

---

[40] *De iure belli libri tres, The Classics of International Law*, No. 16 (Translation by John C. Rolfe), Oxford, 1933, pp. 167–68.
[41] With which Hugo Grotius strongly disagreed; see *De iure belli ac pacis*, Book II, Chapter I, XVII, cited in RSB (note 16), p. 405.
[42] *Supra* (note 40), pp. 61–66.
[43] *Politica*, Chapter XXXVIII, cited in RSB (note 16), p. 384.
[44] Cited by Schmitt (note 9), at p. 614.
[45] Schmitt (note 9), p. 615.
[46] De iure belli ac pacis, Book II, Chapter XXII, XII, cited in RSB (note 16), p. 411.

The most proper form of action in war are force and terror. But one has equal right to use fraud and deceit against an enemy, provided one does not violate one's pledged faith. Hence one may deceive an enemy by false statements or fictitious stories, but never by promises or agreements.[47]

Emmerich de Vattel, the Swiss scholar, despised any ideas that favoured the use of assassinations, but restricted the meaning of the word to situations of treachery:

> But in order to reason clearly on this question we must first of all avoid confusing assassination with surprises, which are, doubtless, perfectly lawful in warfare. When a resolute soldier steals into the enemy's camp at night and makes his way to the general's tent and stabs him, he does nothing contrary to the natural laws of war, nothing, indeed, but what is commendable in a just and necessary war ... If anyone has absolutely condemned such bold strokes it was only done with the object of flattering those in high position who would wish to leave to soldiers and subordinates all the danger of the war ... Hence I mean by assassination a murder committed by means of treachery, whether the deed be done by persons who are subjects of him who is assassinated, or of his sovereign, and who are therefore traitors, or whether it be done by any other agent who makes his way in as a suppliant or refugee, or as a turncoat, or even as an alien; and I assert that the deed is a shameful and revolting one, both on the part of him who executes it and of him who commands it.[48]

He further argued on the respect due to a Head of State:

> In former times he who succeeded in killing the King or general of the enemy was commended and rewarded; we know the honours attending the *spolia opima*. Nothing could have been more natural than such an attitude; for the ancients almost always fought for the very existence of the State, and frequently the death of the leader put an end to the war. At the present day a soldier would not dare, ordinarily at least, to boast of having killed the enemy's King. *It is thus tacitly agreed among sovereigns that their persons shall be held sacred.* It must be admitted that where the war is not a violent one, and where the safety of the State is not at stake, such respect for the person of the sovereign is entirely commendable and in accordance with the mutual duties of Nations. In such a war, to take away the life of the sovereign of the hostile Nation, when it could be spared, would be to do a greater injury to that Nation than is, perhaps, necessary for the successful settlement of the dispute. But it is not a law of war that the person of the enemy's King must be spared on every occasion, and the obligation to do so exists only when he can easily be made prisoner.[49]

---

[47] *On the Duty of Man and Citizen*, Book II, Chapter 16, § 155, cited in RSB (note 16), p. 458.
[48] *The Law of Nations or the Principles of Natural Law*, § 155 (Translation by Charles Fenwick), New York, 1916, at pp. 287–88.
[49] Ibid, § 159, at p. 290; emphasis added.

Immanuel Kant, the German philosopher, took a very clear stance on assassination in his treatise on *Perpetual Peace*:

> No state at war with another shall permit such acts of hostility as would make mutual confidence impossible during a future time of peace. Such acts would include the employment of assassins ... or ... poisoners ..., breach of capitulation, the instigation of treason within the enemy state.[50]

From the context it would appear clear that Kant also subscribed to the ruse-perfidy divide; yet it is curious why the excessive suffering inflicted on the civilian population does not merit explicit mention, too. One might safely assume, that with the pervasive public dissatisfaction with the political class in a vast majority of countries and the horrendous potential for severe civilian collateral damage, the people of almost any given nation would prefer to see their leaders killed rather than see them spared and their own children slaughtered. De Vattel came very close to the real reason for the ubiquitous aversion to aiming higher up the chain of command.

This is not really surprising and it becomes especially clear if one looks at the whole issue in the light of von Clausewitz's famous dictum, commonly rendered as 'war is the continuation of politics by other means', whereas the accurate quote is:

> We see, therefore, that war is not merely an act of policy but a true political instrument, a continuation of political intercourse, carried on with other means. ... The political object is the goal, war is the purpose of reaching it, and means can never be considered in isolation from their purpose.[51]

Moving into more recent times, we see the first attempt at codifying the rejection of assassinations in Article 148 of the so-called Lieber Code of 1863:

> The law of war does not allow proclaiming either an individual belonging to the hostile army, or a citizen, or a subject of the hostile government, an outlaw, who may be slain without trial by any captor, any more than the modern law of peace allows such intentional outlawry; on the contrary, it abhors such outrage. The sternest retaliation should follow the murder committed in consequence of such proclamation, made by whatever authority. Civilized nations look with horror upon offers of rewards for the assassination of enemies as relapses into barbarism.[52]

---

[50] *Perpetual Peace*, cited in RSB (note 16), p. 521.

[51] *On War*, Chapter 1, p. 24, cited in RSB (note 16), p. 556. The common form of the quote refers to the heading of paragraph 24, which appears, however, to be better translated by 'policy'.

[52] See the full text on the Avalon Project website of Yale Law School, at www.yale.edu/lawweb/avalon/lieber.htm#sec9, last accessed on 5 July 2007.

This has very much been the stance in the international community ever since, at least as far as the law was concerned and has become part of customary international law. I content myself, for reasons of space, regarding the further development, especially the Hague Regulations, Additional Protocols, military manuals and peacetime treaties such as, for example, the 1973 New York Convention, to referring to the perceptive article by Michael N. Schmitt[53] and the more recent and comprehensive ICRC study on customary international humanitarian law, especially Chapter 18 on deception.[54] Rule 65 of that Study states that 'killing, injuring or capturing and adversary by resort to perfidy is prohibited'. Perfidy is defined in the Study, using the language of Additional Protocol I, Article 37 (1), as

> acts inviting the confidence of an adversary to lead him to believe that he is entitled to, or obliged to accord, protection under the rules of international law applicable in armed conflict, with intent to betray that confidence.[55]

This does, of course, leave the interesting question open of whether it is perfidious to exploit a misunderstanding one has not invited or at least not with an intent to betray it at the time the invitation was made.

IV. THE DURHAM PILOT STUDY

The online[56] questionnaire that forms part of the underlying research is meant to capture the views of law students from universities in such diverse countries as the UK, Germany, the United Arab Emirates, the United States and China, on the ethical principles underlying the legal questions surrounding the issue of assassinations of regime elites and collateral civilian damage. Out of the 29 students of my module in International Criminal Law in 2006/2007, 7 replied to the pilot questionnaire that was meant to test the usefulness and intelligibility of the questionnaire. Statistically, this exercise is irrelevant, of course, but it nevertheless brought up some answers which it will be interesting to compare to the wider study. The answers were divided into the three categories of Yes, No and Don't Know, with requests for reasons after each of these. The questionnaire is attached as Annex A.

---

[53] *Supra* (note 9).

[54] Henckaerts and Doswald-Beck (eds.), *Customary International Humanitarian Law, Rules*, vol. i, Cambridge, 2005, p. 203 *et seq.*

[55] Ibid, p. 223.

[56] The form was available for students of selected universities at the website of the Durham Centre for Criminal Law and Criminal Justice from July 2007 to June 2008. The evaluation of the answers is still ongoing at the time of writing.

The first substantial question that was asked, was, 'Do you think that it is ethically justifiable for one country to attack another country in order to depose its current government?' 6 students answered with Yes, 1 with 'Don't know'. The reasons they gave for their answer were as follows:

> If obvious genocide is taking place, there is a moral obligation to intervene.

> Depends on the reason for disposal – must be for the accepted greater good.

> But only if it is done in order to remove threats to the international community.

> It can be justifiable where the attacking country fears a genuine threat from country B and is acting in citizens' best interests.

> A difficult question, which depends on many factors such as the harm the current government is doing, the benefits of attacking, the likely outcome, likelihood of protracted civil war etc. May be ethical if civilians are suffering unnecessarily and attack would not cause excessive harm.

> This would depend on motive, and the method by which the country was 'attacked'. It would also depend if every diplomatic avenue had been exhausted. If no human life was lost, then yes, if for the right motives. If less life was lost in invasion than would have been lost under an oppressive regime, it would not necessarily be ethically justifiable but pragmatically right to do so. If the motive was money, then no. If the motive was to stop genocide, then yes. There are so many variables that giving an absolute answer is difficult.

This question was meant to test the general attitude towards aggressive regime change in general. The question had no further specifics as far as particular reasons are concerned. It is interesting to note that all answers were given under ethical or moral qualifiers based on necessity and partly, chivalry arguments. But still, a full-scale attack with the express purpose of regime change appears acceptable to the large majority of the students.

The second question, 'Do you think it is ethically justifiable for country A to attack country B because country A feels threatened by B, when country B has not attacked country A?', was answered with Yes by 2, and with No by 5 students. The reasons given were the following:

> There are again so many variables. Type of force, degree of force, honesty in belief of being threatened. I do wonder whether I am considering ethics or utility. The implication of 'feels threatened' is that it may not be actually threatened. But even if a nation acts honestly and reasonably, this may still operate outside of what is considered ethically correct. Strictly speaking, it is not ethical for pre-emptive force on a global scale due to the large number of stakeholders in the situation. This is what separates it from the pre-emptive force condoned in criminal law (Bird), which usually involves small numbers of individuals.

> We have to draw a line somewhere, and pre-emptive force falls on the wrong side of it. Attacks ideally should be in self-defence only.

Mere tensions alone not a sufficient basis to begin a conflict, a peaceful solution should be sought.

Dependant on how serious the threat is.

Feeling threatened is not the same as actually being pushed into action.

This question tried to draw the students to answer about the general idea of preventive or pre-emptive attacks based on impressions of being threatened. Interestingly, 5 students who had answered the first question with Yes, switched to No on this one, despite the fact that they had included their own ethical qualifiers in that answer already. Apparently the mere feeling of being threatened is not perceived as a sufficient reason for the use of pre-emptive force, and students again try to qualify the answer by referring to the degree of threat and force.

The third question addressed directly the typical necessity situation of killing one person in order to save many: 'Do you think it is generally ethically justifiable to kill one person in order to save the lives of a larger number of people?' 6 students answered with Yes, 1 with Don't know. The following explanations were given:

> Again, a difficult issue – from a pure utilitarian view, yes. However we must consider the rights of the victim and whether he has placed himself knowingly in the position where he stands to be assassinated. What if he is under duress?

> Necessity should be delineated from morality. Utility undermines universal human rights, although that is not to say I wouldn't sanction a plane to be shot down to save the lives of thousands. I would be pragmatically right, but ethically wrong. Since ethics are the progeny of religion, they are not necessarily the product of logical thought, instead operating it would seem, at times, in a 'utopian vacuum.' Is there such a thing as majoritarian ethics? i.e. killing 4 to save 10 is relatively justifiable, therefore justifiable overall? I do not know, and I don't think such a scenario lends itself well to ethical analysis. According to absolute ethics, the life of a single person is infinitely valuable, therefore balancing this against a million other people still yields the same sum. A very difficult question to answer.

> The greater number of lives must be prioritised.

> The ends justify the means in some circumstances as some states led by one individual who could cause war.

> If that person poses a threat to more people.

> Utilitarian ethics – weigh the interests of one against another, interests are quantifiable.

The tendency in these answers, which given the introduction to the question-naire puts the students clearly on the path to the substantial question about assassinations, is a utilitarian one of counting numbers and degree of threat, but they also contain moral qualifiers such as the reference to duress and absolute ethics.

The next set of questions addressed the relationship between discrimination, necessity and several scenarios in a hypothetical case: 'Imagine the following: Country A attacks country B. The aim of the attack by country A is to remove the government of country B, because B's government is viewed as a threat to country A. No imminent attack has been threatened or carried out by country B.' It is not difficult to gauge that this refers to the attack on Iraq in 2003 by the so-called Coalition of the Willing but as seen from the point of view of the sceptics.

The first of the sub-questions was 'Do you think it is ethically justifiable in this case for country A to cause the death of an unknown number of members of the military forces of B?' 2 students answered Yes, 5 with No. They gave the following reasons:

> We elect governments to protect our interests as citizens; they must have the power to act on behalf of such interests where there is a genuine threat. Killing military members is a protection tactic. Military figures will present the greatest threat.

> The attack in itself is not justified.

> The threat must be suitably serious to warrant an attack. Military attacks are justified.

> Military means should not be pursued in the face of mere tensions or fear of another State.

> I would view military troops as innocent agents despite being agents of a (perhaps guilty by the standards of some) state.

> Soldiers are humans too, and as such, the death of one is as morally wrong as the death of a civilian baby. Although one may point to a choice argument, would the soldier choose to be in the army if he were born a millionaire? Choice can be an illusion.

The next question moved to a different victim group, asking whether it would be acceptable to cause the death of an unknown number of civilians in country B. All 7 students answered in the negative, giving the following reasons:

> See above. The death of anyone is not morally right. That is not to say that I wouldn't understand or condone the killing of a mass murderer.

> No imminent attack has been threatened or carried out by country B. Also, the chances are that killing civilians will not prevent an attack on country A, rather it would tend to invite attacks upon country A.

> See above.

Civilian deaths in no way reduce threat to other country.

Innocent civilians should not be harmed in armed conflicts.

Civilians are not necessarily responsible for the actions/choices of their govern-ments and shouldn't be punished if possible.

The students were then led to consider the idea of taking out government figures in different scenarios. The first of those asked whether it was legitimate to assassinate the *legitimate* head of State of country B, if he is the commander-in-chief of B's military forces, in order to avoid a full-scale attack on country B. 2 answered Yes, 5 with No:

Again, necessity, and the 'lesser of two evils', although pragmatically right, is morally wrong. It should be appreciated that there is no perfect solution to every situation, and sometimes any possible outcome is reprehensible. Therefore, although morally wrong in an absolute sense, the lesser of two evils is, relatively, morally right.

How do you define legitimate? Being nervous is no excuse for killing an innocent person. No action would have been taken, so it would be an aggressive action rather than a reaction in self-defence.

Utilitarian moral theory.

He has not necessarily done anything wrong.

Dependant on who likely to replace head of state.

No, a peaceful solution should be sought. There would be anarchy if one allowed the assassination of legitimate heads of state.

The next question altered the scenario to the head of state not being the commander-in chief. Now 1 answered Yes, 5 No and 1 with Don't Know:

Same reason as above, The fact he is in charge of the army is irrelevant. Absolute human rights and ethics would not foster such an argument. Again, that is not to say that I wouldn't act in such a way if in that position. That merely indicates that I would act unethically.

How do you define legitimate? Being nervous is no excuse for killing an innocent person. No action would have been taken, so it would be an aggressive action rather than a reaction in self-defence.

See above.

I have trouble saying yes as it is not ethical as legitimate head of state but would avoid many more casualties.

Possibly. Utilitarian moral theory.

The following question extended the scenario to the entire legitimate government, regardless of their standing in the military chain of command. The answers were: 5 No, 2 Don't Know:

> See reasons above.

> Seems like (pardon the awful pun) overkill. Same reasons as above – aggressive act rather than defence.

> May be different if B had attacked, but still shouldn't be a solution which comes first on the list.

> Although I advocate avoiding greater casualties I recognise this would be improper state practice.

> See above.

The questionnaire then tried to find out if the students' views shifted in a scenario where the head of state was an illegitimate head, a usurper and the like, and also the military commander-in-chief. 4 answered Yes, 3 No:

> An absolute human rights argument would resist such actions.

> Illegitimate or not – there is no threat. The head of state could be plucked randomly out of the nearest mental ward, but it shouldn't concern country A, as there would be no threatening actions.

> The repercussions are still too high; a peaceful solution should be sought.

> He is not a legitimate head of state plus would avoid many more casualties.

> If his actions as an illegitimate leader are threatening.

> Utilitarian moral theory.

> Like with a legitimate head, the question was also asked related to the case when the illegitimate head was not in the military chain of command. There was a slight shift in the evaluation in that 3 said Yes, 4 No, but a number did not give any reasons anymore:

> Ibid.

> Same reasons as previous response.

> See above.

The last question in this subset related to the entire illegitimate government, as above. The answers were 2 Yes, 3 No, 1 Don't Know. Again, few gave reasons:

> See above.

> It is improper state practice but would avoid war.

The final overall control question was 'Do you think it generally makes an ethical difference if civilian deaths caused in a conflict are accidental to a legitimate attack on a military target (so-called 'collateral damage')?' The answers were 2 Yes and 4 No:

> Recklessness would still give rise to liability in law, so why not ethically. Recklessness is merely a lower threshold of intention, and if a country was reckless they are morally accountable.

> Yes, as often collateral damage cannot be avoided yet not justifiable to attack civilians as they did not choose to fight for their country.

> There is no justification for the loss of innocent civilian lives.

> Utilitarian moral theory.

> Whilst regrettable, if the attack is legitimate, collateral damage is a fact of armed conflict.

The students were given an opportunity to add any comments of their own. One wrote:

> These questions are probing and interesting. They are hard to answer because there are so many variables. Although I do not think any taking of human life is ethical, I do think that it may be legitimate to do so on a logical basis. It would thus seem that utility is the new ethics. I would shoot down a plane in a 9/11 scenario, although I would appreciate that what I was doing was ethically wrong in an absolute sense. Sometimes circumstances compel a response that can only be categorised as the lesser of two evils, yet it is still evil nonetheless.

v. Conclusion

In the context of discussing terrorism and the targeting of State elites by terrorists – not quite our scenario – Michael Walzer has astutely pointed out:

> Characteristically (and not foolishly), lawyers have frowned on assassination, and political officials have been assigned to the class of nonmilitary persons, who are never the legitimate objects of attack. But this assignment only partially represents our common moral judgments. For we judge the assassin by his victim, and when the victim is Hitler-like in character, we are likely to praise the assassin's work ...[57]

The answers given by some students regarding the distinction between legitimate and illegitimate rulers would appear to betray similar moral attitudes. Would we all agree that replacing Hitler with Saddam Hussein in the above-mentioned quote would not have been such a big moral step to take? Possibly. What, other than the tacit and mutual agreement of the lords of this world who after all

---

[57] *Supra* (note 12), p. 199.

are the ones who sign and ratify such conventions and who make international law, can justify the existing absolute ban on assassination and the comparatively easy acceptance of collateral damage among those who have no choice or say? Possibly the objection that the use of such methods will result in much worse conditions, that we would set foot on a slippery slope. Yet are we sure that such an outcome would be the foreseeable result in any given case?

The existing power relations would make sure that no State would try to assassinate the Presidents of the United States or of Russia or China, because the retaliation would be massive. So we grudgingly accept that in international law, some States are more equal than others. However, by doing this, we have to agree with Rousseau who said:

> As for what is called the law of nations, it is clear that without any real sanction these laws are only illusions that are more tenuous even than the notion of natural law. The latter at least addresses itself to the hearts of individuals, whereas decisions based on the law of nations, having no other guarantee than the utility of the one who submits to them, are respected only as long as those decisions confirm one's own self-interest.[58]

It has become common currency to point out that this is no longer a true depiction of the state of affairs, and that with the advent of the United Nations and organisations such as the European Union, things have changed. I am not convinced. The Russian Duma on 7 November 2007 decided to suspend the CFE Treaty because of the US plans to build a missile defence in Eastern Europe. That and the US-led attack on Iraq in 2003, its policy of negotiating bilateral non-surrender agreements with States Parties to the ICC Statute, the motivation behind the American Service Members Protection Act of 2002, also called the 'Hague Invasion Act', and more obviously the fact that the five permanent members of the Security Council still cling to their veto power, are the best examples for the assertion that Rousseau is still right.

The five permanent members all are among the top traders in small arms,[59] one of the main scourges of the Third World. The evidence also shows that despite the ubiquitous protestations about the employment of 'surgical weaponry', 90% of the four million war-related deaths in the 1990s were civilians, 80% of which – in absolute numbers, 2,880,000 – were women and children.

---

[58] *The State of War*, cited in RSB (note 16), pp. 482–83.
[59] See www.guardian.co.uk/armstrade/graphic/0,,519667,00.html, last accessed on 23 July 2009.

So where does that leave us, with regard to avoiding unnecessary civilian deaths by targeting those who are politically responsible, and killing them if nothing else will help? The answer has to be very sceptical. Yet, even if we accept the difference in importance and power of States, is it such an unthinkable idea that if the heavyweights *have* to go after the weaker countries, then they should at least go after the people who are to blame, rather than leave them alone in the interests of possible future re-establishment of commerce, and bomb their innocent citizens to death instead?[60]

90% of the war-dead are civilians – and we call that 'collateral' damage?

---

[60] See also the discussion in Nils Melzer, *Targeted Killing in International Law*, Oxford, 2008, pp. 47–50. Melzer queries whether there is actually an international consensus on the definition of assassination in the wartime context and whether treachery is always a required element.

ANNEX A

RESEARCH QUESTIONNAIRE

The international law rule against the assassination of regime collateral damage
Genesis of the present law, practice in modern times and
consequences for the criminal evaluation of collateral civilian damage

Thank you for taking the time to have a look at this questionnaire!

The above-mentioned project is a mixed international law/criminal law/legal ethics topic dealing with the doctrine that (inter)national law traditionally forbids the assassination of heads of State or entire regime elites by the forces of another State, even when they sponsor serious criminal activities or terrorism.

The study will try to describe the origins and development of the doctrine and look at whether and to which extent it has been followed in recent times, particularly in the context of attempts at regime change and the so-called war on terrorism. A central issue will be whether the doctrine can still stand today given the huge potential for so-called 'collateral damage' through the means of modern warfare, and whether it stands to reason that is it more acceptable to kill tens of thousands of innocent civilians rather than go after the source of the evil directly.

The attached questionnaire intends to find out about the attitude of law students at universities in different countries, who will become persons in policy-making and leadership positions, to some of the underlying ethical questions.

ANONYMITY AND DATA PROTECTION; VOLUNTARY PARTICIPATION

Any personal data that may be gathered in the process will not be stored. The questionnaire is structured in a way to keep such data gathering to a minimum.

Answers will be treated, processed and published in strictest anonymity.

Although your university may have encouraged you to participate in the study by filling in the questionnaire, please be aware that there is no obligation whatsoever to do so.

Best wishes
Professor Michael Bohlander
Durham University
www.dur.ac.uk/law

A. About you

1. Which university do you belong to? Durham / Jena / Sharjah / Cairo Northern Iowa/USA / Northwest/China

2. Are you
a) an undergraduate student? YES / NO
b) a postgraduate student? YES / NO

3. What is your sex and age?
a) Sex: Male / Female
b) Age: 18–21 / 22–25 / 25–30 other:

4. Are you
a) a national of the country of your university? YES / NO
b) a foreign student? YES / NO Nationality: . . .

B. Questions

5. Do you think that it is ethically justifiable for one country to attack another country in order to depose its current government? Yes / No / Don't know
Please give a brief summary of the reasons for your answer:

7. Do you think it is ethically justifiable for country A to attack country B because country A feels threatened by B, when country B has not attacked country A? Yes / No / Don't know
Please give a brief summary of the reasons for your answer:

8. Do you think it is generally ethically justifiable to kill one person in order to save the lives of a larger number of people? Yes / No / Don't know
Please give a brief summary of the reasons for your answer:

9. Imagine the following: Country A attacks country B. The aim of the attack by country A is to remove the government of country B, because B's government is viewed as a threat to country A. No imminent attack has been threatened or carried out by country B.

Do you think it is ethically justifiable in this case for country A:

a) To cause the death of an unknown number of members of the military forces of B:
Yes / no / don't know

Please give a brief summary of the reasons for your answer:

b) To cause the death of an unknown number of civilians in country B? Yes / no / don't know
Please give a brief summary of the reasons for your answer:

*c) To assassinate the **legitimate** head of State of country B, if he is the commander-in-chief of B's military forces, in order to avoid a full-scale attack on country B?* Yes / no / don't know
Please give a brief summary of the reasons for your answer:

*d) To assassinate the **legitimate** head of State of country B, if he is NOT the commander-in-chief of B's military forces, in order to avoid a full-scale attack on country B?* Yes / no / don't know
Please give a brief summary of the reasons for your answer:

*e) To assassinate the entire **legitimate** government of country B, in order to avoid a full-scale attack on country B?* Yes / no / don't know
Please give a brief summary of the reasons for your answer:

*f) To assassinate the **illegitimate** head of State of country B, if he is the commander-in-chief of B's military forces, in order to avoid a full-scale attack on country B?* Yes / no / don't know
Please give a brief summary of the reasons for your answer:

*g) To assassinate the **illegitimate** head of State of country B, if he is NOT the commander-in-chief of B's military forces, in order to avoid a full-scale attack on country B?* Yes / no / don't know
Please give a brief summary of the reasons for your answer:

*h) To assassinate the entire **illegitimate** government of country B, in order to avoid a full-scale attack on country B?* Yes / no / don't know
Please give a brief summary of the reasons for your answer:

10. Do you think it generally makes an ethical difference if civilian deaths caused in a conflict are accidental to a legitimate attack on a military target (so-called "collateral damage")?
Yes / no / don't know
Please give a brief summary of the reasons for your answer:

11. If you have any other comments, please make them here:

Chapter Eleven

Conduct and Proof of Conduct – Two Fundamental Conditions for the Imposition of Criminal Liability

G.R. Sullivan[*]

It will be argued that two fundamental conditions – a conduct requirement and a proof of conduct requirement – must be satisfied as a prerequisite for any criminal conviction. If one or other of these conditions is not met, D will lack even the most basic responsibility for the commission of the offence. It will be argued that criminal liability without any form of responsibility is conceptually untenable. While compliance with these two conditions is compatible with a harsh and human rights insensitive criminal law, consistent observance of these conditions is essential if the criminal law is to constitute a distinctive domain distinguishable from other forms of coercion that a State may deploy against its citizens.[1]

While these conditions are conceptual requirements, there are also normative consequences arising from the breach of these conditions. While meeting these conditions can co-exist with many forms of injustice associated with the imposition of criminal liability,[2] compliance with these conditions will preclude

---

[*] Professor of Law, University College London, University of London.
[1] A State may make coercive interventions in its citizens' lives through its taxation, military and health systems and so forth without imposing liability for anything deemed to be a wrong. Where liability is imposed for a designated wrong our conditions should apply.
[2] Our conditions impose little by way of substantive constraints on what can be made criminal. Our subject is the basis of responsibility for outcomes or states of affairs. The fact that one is responsible for φ does not entail one should be criminally liable for causing or allowing φ. There may be all manner of objections to criminal liability premised merely on responsibility. Our point is that there must be responsibility before there can be liability. On the priority of responsibility to liability, see Duff, *Answering for Crime: Responsibility and Liability in the Criminal Law*, Hart Publishing: Oxford and Portland, 2007, especially chapters 1–5.

K.H. Kaikobad & M. Bohlander (eds.), *International Law and Power: Perspectives on Legal Order and Justice*. Essays in Honour of Colin Warbrick, pp. 235–253.

certain grave forms of injustice.[3] English criminal law broadly complies with these conditions but, as we shall see, by no means invariably. The central claim to be argued for here is that a judge presiding over a criminal trial or appeal should interpret any offence at issue in the proceedings in a manner compatible with these conditions even if the enactment in question seemingly departs from either or both of them. Judges in other Anglophone jurisdictions have been readier than their English counterparts to ensure compliance with these fundamental conditions even when faced with statutory provisions at variance with them. They have shown a greater awareness of what may be termed the constitutional implications of imposing criminal liability in circumstances where one or more of these conditions is not met.[4] It is to be hoped that the incorporation of the European Convention for Human Rights will assist in cultivating a greater receptiveness to the fundamental/constitutional issues we are about to discuss.[5]

We turn first to the conduct requirement. Criminal liability must be in respect of some act or omission attributable to the agency or within the agency competence of D. In other words, criminal liability must be based on at least one episode of conduct within the control of D.[6] Take away the need for conduct within the control of D, then liability is imposed on the basis of some event or state of affairs unrelated to any exercise of D's agency. As will be argued at greater length below, the imposition of criminal liability in the absence of anything done or omitted by D defies the most basic assumptions of the criminal law, assumptions clustered around the foundational concept of responsibility.[7]

---

[3]   Most fundamentally, the first condition will preclude liability for events or states of affairs wholly beyond the control of D and the second condition will preclude liability for things unproved.

[4]   See note 34 and associated text.

[5]   Human Rights Act 1998, Schedule 1.

[6]   The notion of agency comprehends the element of control. In terms of an act, this element would be present when D pushes V but not when D falls against V because he has tripped. In terms of omissions, when we claim that D has omitted to do φ we claim that, all things considered, that D could and should have done φ. If that condition holds, omissions are properly things within the domain of conduct, but not otherwise. See further Husak, 'Does Criminal Liability Require an Act?', in Duff (ed.), *Philosophy and the Criminal Law*, Cambridge, 1998, p. 60. The same condition should hold for crimes of possession: D should only be convicted of an offence based on possessing some controlled or proscribed item if he were able to control the circumstances in which possession was obtained or was in a position to divest himself of possession when he should have become aware that he was in possession of the item in question. Arguably, crimes for which D can be vicariously liable dispense with any agency requirement on the part of D but at least liability is triggered by the agency of another such as an employee or agent who was acting in the course of D's employment or on his behalf.

[7]   As Duff (note 2) cogently argues the grounds of responsibility must be present before questions of liability can be engaged. For offences of strict liability bare responsibility may suffice for

The conduct condition is most obviously satisfied when the actus reus of the offence requires as a definitional element some voluntary act or omission. To be more than a vacuous requirement, the act or omission must constitute the prohibitory norm of the offence.[8] What are called status offences – liability imposed on the basis of implication in a state of affairs[9] – may yet be compliant with the act/omission requirement provided some voluntary act or omission on the part of D gave rise to the proscribed state of affairs. It need not be the case that the ensuing proscribed state of affairs arises was entailed by the earlier act or omission. It suffices that it was a predictable, not necessarily a virtually certain upshot, of a voluntary act or omission on the part of D. It is unfortunately the case, however, that polities may impose criminal liability on D for states of affairs not attributable or connected to any act or omission on his part.

For instance, a theocratic State of a certain stripe may require, on pain of conviction and punishment, all adult males to grow beards of a certain shape and size. It may be that it will convict and punish D for this offence, despite a congenital inability to grow a beard of the required kind. His conviction may well be based on the suppositions of the ruling elite. For them, certain failings or absences may be due to matters much deeper and more significant than mere human agency, more reliable indicators of states of ill-being warranting the most severe denunciation and punishment. The claim to be enforcing the criminal law against D may be made in the utmost good faith by the prosecutors and judges involved in the case. But they were not enforcing criminal law, properly so called, or so it will be argued.[10]

Turning to our second condition, proof of conduct, it may be that D was capable of growing a beard meeting State specifications but an ill wisher shaved off his beard while he was in a deep sleep. He is now before the court with facial hair woefully short of the official requirements. Under the terms of the

---

liability as when, say, the selling of food unfit for human consumption is made an offence notwithstanding that the seller may have been blameless in the matter of the unfitness of the food as in *Hobbes v. Winchester Corporation* [1910] 2 KB 471. The fact that D did sell food that was unfit of itself establishes a basic responsibility for that event. A legislature may decide that something beyond basic responsibility is necessary for liability by for example providing for proof of lack of due care in respect of the fitness of the food.

[8] The 'prohibitory norm' is the external aspect of the proscription such as the sale of unfit food. If the conduct element for an offence of selling unfit food was simply the selling of food which D then had to prove was in fact fit the conduct requirement would be vacuous in terms of the prohibitory norm.

[9] See Glazebrook, 'Situational Liability', in Glazebrook (ed.), *Reshaping the Criminal Law Essays in Honour of Glanville Williams*, London, 1978, p. 108.

[10] There is no implication that systems of criminal law must be based on secular principles but merely to assert that states of being, damned or otherwise, cannot be the subject of criminal proscription unless they can be linked to some exercise of D's agency.

enactment applicable to his case, he will be convicted of the offence unless he is able to prove his beard was of the right size and shape prior to its removal. But no-one will come forward to testify to this effect on his behalf and so he is convicted. If it had been proved against him that the beard removed fell short of requirements for reasons within his control, his conviction for the offence could not be objected to as infringing either condition that is the subject of this paper. But if he is convicted without such proof, his conviction is not grounded within the basic suppositions of the criminal law, or so it will be argued.

So what was conceptually remiss in this second case? If a criminal offence is defined or interpreted to require some conduct attributable to D which constitutes the prohibitory norm (thereby observing our first conduct condition) the criminal justice system must have some touchstone to judge when an attribution of conduct can be made. It will be argued that the minimum standard is a formal finding to the effect that *it was more likely than not* that D engaged in conduct that led to breaking the prohibitory norm. Ideally perhaps, the standard to be employed should be proof beyond reasonable doubt. That might be better from the perspective of avoiding injustice to D and enhance the general quality of civic life.[11] But proof to such a standard is not a *conceptual* necessity. What is necessary is that a finding based at least on the balance of probabilities be made against D in respect of the conduct requirement. If such a finding is not a prerequisite for a conviction, in substance any conduct requirement will be negated. A legislature cannot coherently enact an offence requiring conduct yet waive any need for proof of that conduct. Were it to do so, the State would in effect licensing its officials to inflict punishment in the absence of proof of any breach of a prohibitory norm, a perfectly feasible state of affairs[12] but not compatible with imposing punishment within a system of criminal law. At the risk of undue emphasis, the condition is conceptual. The State cannot logically set down the actus reus of an offence whilst waiving the need for proof that D's conduct had brought about the actus reus.

It may be objected that these examples are exotic and far fetched (though, alas, they are not). But we will come up with examples from current English criminal law which are essentially in the same case. As we will discover, English criminal law does not require that there be conduct on the part of D as a predicate for his conviction for a crime. Furthermore, even for the more standard case where some form of conduct is a definitional requirement of the crime, it need not

---

[11] See Roberts, 'Taking the Burden of Proof Seriously', [1995] *Criminal Law Review* 783.

[12] There are many examples too notorious to list from the practices of totalitarian States. It is not the purpose here to test the absolute legality of State punitive measures which transgress the most basic of human rights. The more limited task here is to set the limits of what can be punished within a system of criminal law.

follow that the prosecution is required to prove that the conduct element of the offence is attributable to D. It may suffice for a conviction that D is unable to prove otherwise. This lamentable state of affairs has existed for many years. We will, among other matters, question whether certain provisions of the European Convention for Human Rights may remedy or at least improve this situation.

I. CRIMINAL LIABILITY AND THE CONDUCT REQUIREMENT

We return to D, the follicly challenged man incapable of growing a full beard. As we know, he is the subject of a State organised along theocratic lines where one may be punished for not sporting a growth compliant with State requirements. We envisaged a situation where he would be found liable and punished for the beard related offence, despite the fact that he was incapable by dint of natural and unalterable causes from growing such a beard.

Let us say something purporting to be a criminal trial was held and thereafter he served a term of imprisonment following the verdict of guilty as charged. Why *purporting* to be a criminal trial? Assuredly, the officials, from prosecutors through to jailors, may have entertained no doubts that they were engaged in enforcing the criminal law of their country. And their assurance may be well founded. For instance, the applicable law may have provided that an adult male incapable from natural causes of complying with the law could none the less be in conformity with it by donning in public places a false beard of the requisite dimensions. It is perfectly coherent to make a voluntary omission the subject of a criminal charge as omissions may be regarded as conduct provided the act required of D fell within his agency competence.[13] Or it may be that under the theocratic principles underpinning this law, the lack of capacity to grow a beard is taken as infallible proof that he has participated in forms of conduct that make for apostasy. This is very troubling from the possibility of grave injustices arising from non empirical ways of proving facts. Yet in terms of the letter, the conduct requirement is met.[14] Just as likely, however, is a more Calvinistic dispensation that takes a hairless condition to be indicative of a lack of grace as from D's very conception. It may be that this insufficiency *per se* is the target

---

[13] See note 6, *supra.*

[14] Many pre-modern and early modern systems of criminal law had faith-based ways of finding facts and many countries relied heavily on confessions obtained through torture: Langbein, 'The Legal History of Torture', in Levinson (ed.), *Torture: A Collection*, Oxford, 2004, chapter 5. Subject to the assumption of good faith, (even in systems using such methods we should differentiate genuine attempts to uncover the truth from the fabrication of criminal convictions) such 'fact finding' is compatible with a system of criminal law.

of this law, a failing or absence which is declared criminal and punished even if arising from whatever cause. Even then, the assurance of officials (and the general populace perhaps) that *criminal* law is being applied and enforced may be just as strong and held in good faith as in the previous instances. But the assumption is wrong; it rests on a category error about what criminal liability can be for.

Criminal liability must be in respect of *something*. To designate someone as a criminal is not to place the person in classes such as the short, the attractive or even the dangerous. In the very recent past, the UK government came exceedingly close to passing legislation which would have allowed the indeterminate detention of persons not convicted of any crime on the basis of an assessment that they were likely to perpetrate acts of violence. The detention envisaged was purely to serve public safety: it would not have been necessary to show any benefit (such as effective therapy for the dangerous condition) to the person detained.[15] Excessive though these contemplated provisions were, one excess at least was not entertained. It was never proposed that an adverse risk assessment for acts of violence should of itself constitute a crime warranting conviction and punishment. To do so would have constituted a civic wrong. Additionally, and this is the focus of our interest, it would have been incoherent, something not possible to accommodate within the conception of a crime.

As stated, a crime must be based on some externality for which one is responsible. Sometimes the bare conditions that establish 'outcome responsibility'[16] for some event or state of affairs – say causing, even blamelessly, the death of V – may also determine our criminal liability. A harsh penal law may apply severe penal sanctions to any conduct of D that causes the death of V whereas more enlightened systems may require proof of further matters as conditions of criminal liability. However liability for homicide based merely on the brute fact of causation satisfies our first condition, conduct which establishes an external outcome for which D is responsible. What a system of criminal law cannot do, however harsh it aspires to be, is make it criminal to be such things as ugly, short or humourless, conditions beyond our agency. The limits of our agency are difficult to state. We may allow that we are responsible for some of our thoughts, so crimes based on the content of our thoughts, though highly objectionable in principle from a liberal perspective, and likely to be oppressive in practice, cannot be ruled out as incoherent.[17] If we may be allowed to put to one side

---

[15] Home Office: *Managing Dangerous People with Severe Personality Disorder*, 1999.

[16] The phrase is Honoré's who regarded civil and criminal liability based purely on causation as defensible, indeed primary: see *Responsibility and Fault*, Hart Publishing: Oxford/Portland, 1999, chapter 2.

[17] See Duff (note 2), at pp. 60–63.

the question of liability for thoughts,[18] the extent of our criminal liability is limited to states of affairs attributable to our voluntary acts and omissions, in other words to conduct based on agency.

English Law and the Conduct Requirement

There is one extreme form of strict liability long permitted in English law, a form of absolute liability known as the status offence. These are offences where all that is required is that the defendant should fit a particular statutory description. It will frequently be the case that a voluntary act or omission on the part of D will foreseeably bring about the state of affairs that meets the statutory description. But, under English law, that is not a formal requirement of liability. Take the well known case of *Larsonneur*.[19] Cutting through the rather complex background to the case,[20] from the court record it seems that D found herself in police custody in Wales by way of *force majeure* after having taken herself to what is now called the Republic of Ireland, following a refusal of entry into the United Kingdom. The unpredictability of her subsequent entry into the United Kingdom, and her powerlessness to prevent it, were raised as grounds of appeal from the conviction for the offence of being an alien, present in the United Kingdom, after leave to land had been refused. The appeal failed. According to Lord Hewart CJ, 'the circumstances of her entry are perfectly immaterial',[21] reasoning castigated by Professor Jerome Hall as 'the acme of strict injustice'.[22]

Status offences have, of course, been associated with some of the worst perversions of the criminal process. They are rightly to be regarded with great circumspection. And yet they are indispensable to certain forms of legitimate regulation.[23] All the more important then that minimum conditions for their appropriate deployment are set and observed. It will be argued that minimum

---

[18] There are of course many crimes ostensibly requiring conduct which are essentially thought crimes, for instance the offence of engaging in *any conduct* (emphasis supplied) for or in connection with the preparation of acts of terrorism contrary to s. 5 (1) (a) of the Terrorism Act 2006. So choosing fruit instead of confectionary in a supermarket in order to be fitter for *jihad* training is a serious criminal offence. Where the conduct is so remote in time and substance from the wrong implicated in the offence (perpetrating or assisting terrorist acts) the conduct requirement is essentially vacuous.

[19] (1933) 24 Cr App R 74.

[20] See Lanham, '*Larsonneur* Revisited', [1976] *Criminal Law Review* 276. It seems historically possible that Mme Larsonneur may not have been the complete victim of circumstance that she appears to be from the report but the ruling in the case is based on the facts as reported.

[21] *Supra* (note 19), at p. 75.

[22] Hall, *General Principles of Criminal Law* (Second edition), Indianapolis, 1960, p. 329.

[23] For instance, it is difficult to see how the regulation of the right to reside within a given jurisdiction could be effectively done without resort to such offences.

conditions for the use of this form of liability are attainable and enforceable. The minimum conditions are that the proscribed status is attributable to some antecedent, voluntary act or omission on the part of D and that the acquisition of the status was a foreseeable consequence of that antecedent act or omission.[24] Where that is the case, the responsibility condition is met providing sufficient subject matter for the holding of a criminal trial. But if liability can be imposed in the absence of any ground establishing D's responsibility, the trial resembles a diagnostic rather than a forensic process. A criminal trial properly so called requires some issue relating to responsibility to be resolved, otherwise the very language and process of the trial rings false.

Status liability based on an excessively literal interpretation of statutory terms is still alive and well in England and Wales notwithstanding the incorporation of the European Convention for Human Rights Convention. In *Alison Barnfather v. London Borough of Islington, Secretary of State for Education and Skills*,[25] the appellant claimed that her conviction for an offence under section 441 of the Education Act 1996 infringed the presumption of innocence guaranteed by Article 6(2) of the Convention. Section 441(1) provides:

> If a child of compulsory school age who is a registered pupil at a school fails to attend regularly at the school, his parent is guilty of an offence.

The Divisional Court felt bound by previous authority to interpret this offence in the most literal of terms.[26] It accepted that a parent would be guilty if wholly unaware that his child was truanting and if wholly blameless in respect of the child's truancy. For instance, the court accepted that a father denied access to the child on a permanent basis would none the less be guilty of the offence should his child not be attending school regularly. It was argued on behalf of D that the imposition of criminal liability for matters blamelessly beyond her control, contravened the presumption of innocence by Article 6(2) of the European Convention for Human Rights. The court ruled that Article 6(2) had no bearing on a case such as this. As the article was solely concerned with the process of proof; it followed that it had no bearing on establishing the minimum grounds of liability for an offence. Kay J was relatively content to dismiss the appeal. He considered that prosecutors would typically use this

---

[24] Without the forseeability condition the conduct requirement is essentially empty as the status will invariably be linked to some earlier conduct of some kind such as Mme Larsonneur's decision to go to Ireland.

[25] [2003] 1 WLR 2318.

[26] For a searching and critical account of the jurisprudence of this offence, see Horder, 'Whose Values Should Determine When Liability is Strict?', in Simester (ed.), *Appraising Strict Liability*, Oxford, 2005, p. 105.

offence sensibly and not pursue defendants at the outer limits,[27] a complacent estimate confounded by the facts of the recent *New Forest* case discussed below. Elias J was far less content. He thought prosecutors should be constrained by law and not merely by their sense of what was reasonable. He was concerned about the stigma attached to this offence of strict liability which carried implications of, 'an indifference to one's children, or incompetence at parenting, which in the case of a blameless parent would be unwarranted'.[28] If he had been able to, he would have given a ruling that the offence was disproportionate to the objectives it sought to achieve. Yet he did not think that this could be achieved by the route of Article 6(2).

It is to be regretted that more basic questions relating to the very nature of criminal offences and criminal proceedings were not addressed. To be sure, the presumption of innocence guaranteed by Article 6(2) is a matter of evidential process rather than substantive law, a concern with the burden of proof rather than with the substance and content of the offence.[29] And yet the very engagement with the concept of innocence should raise a query whether the issue of guilt and innocence is in any real sense implicated if liability for a state of affairs can be imposed in the absence of proof of any act or omission falling within the control of the defendant. If the court had concerned itself with the foundational suppositions of criminal liability, it could have ruled that responsibility on the part of D for the truanting behaviour was a necessary condition for proof of the offence.[30] Guilt imposed without responsibility should have been castigated as a breach of Article 6 (2).

This deeper line of inquiry would also pose questions about the very applicability of the trial process, leading to a consideration of Article 6(1), the guarantee of fair trial. We have argued that a criminal trial is of necessity a determination of responsibility for some act or omission of D. If liability for an offence does not require D to have done or omitted to do anything there is no possibility of holding a trial properly so called to determine any matter for which D is responsible. Of course, the facts constituting the proscribed status may require proof but if the process of proof makes no connection with

---

[27] *Supra* (note 25), at p. 2331.

[28] Ibid, p. 2338.

[29] *Concannon*, [2002] *Criminal Law Review* 213; and *Gemmel*, [2003] 1 Cr App R 343.

[30] In practice this would frequently involve circumstances that establish some degree of fault on the part of D but not invariably. For instance, the conduct requirement would be met where, say, D could not give enough attention to her child's attendance because of work commitments but be not in any sense at fault. Such a regime is harsh but compliant with the conduct condition. An argument that fault is required takes us beyond the conduct requirement. For an argument that Article 6(2) does require proof of fault for this offence, see Tadros and Tierney, 'The Presumption of Innocence and the Human Rights Act', 64 (2004) *Modern Law Review* 402.

anything done or not done by D within the competence of his agency, he is in a very real sense uninvolved, a spectator to his own fate. We are confronted with the simulacrum of a trial, not the real thing. Such a fact-finding process, by whatever name called, should be ruled incompatible with Article 6(1), if used to determine criminal guilt.[31]

Of course, even if accepting of these arguments, one would not anticipate that an English court would refuse to exercise jurisdiction in such a case. What should be a realistic expectation is that following the lead given in other common law jurisdictions, status offences should be construed in a manner compatible with the minimum form of responsibility that any form of criminal liability requires.[32] Courts should insist that acquisition of the proscribed status must be a natural and foreseeable consequence of some voluntary act or omission. This requirement should be read into all status offences to ensure compliance with Articles 6(1) and 6(2). A substantive sense of the minimum conditions for responsibility necessary to constitute a criminal offence and the convening of a trial which is realistically engaged in resolving D's guilt or innocence, should inform readings of the notions of guilt, innocence and fair trial.

A recent case, *New Forest Local Education Authority v. E*,[33] shows how necessary such an approach is (it was not advocated in the case itself). Again, it was a prosecution under s. 441 (1) of the Education Act 1996. The Divisional Court accepted that D had fully cooperated with the relevant local authority and was not in any way at fault in failing to ensure the regular school attendance of her violent, drug-taking, 15 year old son. Her efforts were inhibited by the fear that if she was too persistent she and her daughter might be killed or seriously injured by the boy. She was none the less guilty of the offence. The defence of duress was not in point. The Divisional Court confirmed that the offence looked not to the conduct of the parent but simply to whether the child was attending school regularly. It follows from this conceptually impoverished and ludicrously harsh approach that it would not avail if say a parent was quite incapable of any influence because she had been taken hostage and detained by members of some illegal organisation. Other jurisdictions with a better sense of constitutional proprieties and limits would not countenance these ersatz forms of criminal guilt.[34]

---

[31] An argument similar to that in the text succeeded in the Sherriff's Court in *O'Hagan v. Rea* [2001] 1 SLT 30.

[32] For a full recognition of the fundamental importance of a conduct element as a prerequisite of criminal liability, see Moore, *Act and Crime The Philosophy of Action and Its Implications of Criminal Law*, Oxford, 1993, chapter 2.

[33] [2007] EWHC 2584 (Admin.)

[34] Some far from exhaustive examples include refusal to impose criminal liability for a state of

II. PROOF OF CONDUCT

We have argued that criminal liability as properly understood requires some act or omission assignable to the agency of D. It follows that there must also be proof of that act or omission. Imagine if proof were not required. Take the offence of selling food unfit for human consumption.[35] If the offence were amended to dispense with proof of selling food that was in fact unfit, providing instead that a prosecutor's decision to prosecute the offence was deemed to be proof that the offence had occurred, we would clearly be confronted with a colourable device and not in any legitimate sense a criminal offence. Recourse to such a device is most unlikely in a liberal democracy yet we may be met with essentially the same situation in less obvious form. It may be that a person charged with an offence of selling unfit food under such a deeming provision can clear himself by proving that all the food he has sold was fit for consumption.[36] Less objectionable still may be liability triggered by the prosecution establishing a reasonable suspicion that D sold unfit food with liability for any offence avoided if D can prove the food sold was safe. But even then, it is submitted, we are still in the realm of mere devices rather than the realm of criminal offences.

It is important to remind ourselves that we are making a conceptual argument and not an argument based on justice. To be sure, it can be cogently argued that the interests of justice would be better served if the prosecution had an unvarying burden to prove beyond reasonable doubt all elements of any offence that it charged. But that is not the argument here. The argument is essentially the same argument made in the first section. Any cogent conception of criminal liability implies accountability for something attributable to the agency of D. Accountability in this sense cannot be conjectural; it must rest on some facts that are in some sense established. And the facts established must constitute the prohibitory norm that informs the offence.[37] Even if the prosecution can raise a reasonable suspicion that D may have brought about the actus reus of the

---

addiction (*Robinson v. California* (1962) 370 US 660); for being a vagrant (*Papachristou v. City of Jacksonville* (1972) 405 US 156); and for remaining within a jurisdiction when airlines refused to carry because of late term pregnancy (*Finau v. Department of Labour* [1984] 2 NZLR 396).

[35] Contrary to the Food Safety Act 1990. The offence in reality is unobjectionable in that it requires proof that the food D sold was in fact unfit.

[36] Unfortunately such a conjecture is not fanciful: take the Prevention of Bribery Ordinance 1980 (Hong Kong), s. 10(1): 'Any person who being or having being a Crown Servant – (a) maintains a standard of living above that which is commensurate with his present or past official emoluments .... shall unless he gives a satisfactory explanation to the court as to how he was able to maintain such a standard of living ... be guilty of an offence'.

[37] So if an offence is, say, concerned with the selling of food unfit for human consumption the conduct element cannot simply be the selling of food.

offence, there is no logical ground for holding that he has done so. That only follows if it can be demonstrated that it is more likely than not that D was responsible for the actus reus.[38]

It is a serious offence under English law for D to possess an article in circumstances which give rise to a reasonable suspicion that his possession was for a purpose connected with the commission, preparation or instigation of an act of terrorism.[39] This offence has been defended as a conceptually defensible criminal offence on the basis that the actus reus is possession which gives rise to the reasonable suspicion. Apparently, all is well, at least in conceptual terms, provided the prosecution has the burden of proving the possession and the presence of a reasonable suspicion.[40] It is submitted that this is a flawed analysis if we insist that minimum standards of responsibility must be satisfied in respect of criminal liability. Conduct giving rise to mere suspicion cannot be characterised as the wrong with which the offence is engaged. It may (or may not) indicate that we are on our way to proving the commission of that wrong by D but semantically and substantively, a suspicion is a state short of proof. But until the wrong that is implicated in the offence is proved, there is nothing on which to rest the accountability of D. For instance, he may share the same household, a similar manner of dress, and worship at the same mosque as his brother E, with whom he has a close relationship. If E should be convicted of a terrorist offence and should, say, a large number of stolen credit cards be found in the possession of D, a perfectly reasonable suspicion may arise against D that these cards were obtained in order to generate funds for terrorist activity.[41] But how, logically, can he be held to account as a terrorist or instigator of terrorism? It is not an answer, even on the conceptual plane, to say he is being held to account not as a terrorist or terrorist instigator but for creating a situation where he can reasonably be suspected of such activities. The response carries its own contradiction. At the reasonable suspicion stage there may be any number of countervailing explanations in play: until the terrorist connection is established there is no basis for convicting D of the terrorist related offence.

---

[38] Of course we are dealing with probabilities rather than certainties even when the standard of proof is proof beyond reasonable doubt. But unless, under our conventions of proof, we can assign a probability of + .5 as to the instantiation of a past or concurrent event or state of affairs, we have no warrant for asserting within our conventions the proved fact of the event or state of affairs.

[39] Terrorism Act 2000, s. 57.

[40] See Roberts, 'The Presumption of Innocence Brought Home? *Kebilene* Deconstructed', 118 (2002) *LQR* 41.

[41] We may note that under the terms of s. 57 a rebuttable presumption arises that D is in possession of any items found in premises that he has access to.

In the *Kebilene* litigation, the majority of the judges were of the view that this possession for a terrorist purpose offence established on the basis of reasonable suspicion contravened the presumption of innocence guaranteed by Article 6(2) of the European Convention for Human Rights.[42] Although there are *dicta* supportive of the argument put above, the basis of their conclusion was somewhat obscured by their misgivings not only about the definition of the offence itself but also by further reservations concerning a provision which provided a defence for D if he could prove his possession of the article was not for a purpose connected with the commission, preparation or instigation of an act of terrorism.

The legislative response to *Kebilene* was to leave the substantive definition of the possession offence unchanged – establishing a reasonable suspicion of possession for a terrorist purpose sufficed – but changing the defence provision. As a consequence of the change D need no longer prove his possession of the article was not for a terrorist purpose but simply adduce evidence sufficient to raise an issue as to what the purpose was. If he does, his defence will succeed unless, 'the prosecution prove beyond reasonable doubt that it should not'.[43]

The danger is that subsequent courts may take the view that this improvement in the terms of the defence removes the objections identified in *Kebilene*. But the underlying conceptual vice remains. If D exercises his right not to give evidence he can straightforwardly be convicted on the basis of reasonable suspicion.[44] Even if he gives evidence sufficient to raise an issue as to the true purpose, it should still follow that the prosecution will win the case if they succeed in reinstating the reasonable suspicion. So a conviction may be sustained without proof of breach of the prohibitory norm.

It will be argued in the next section that this legislative change does not remove the fundamental objection to offences based on reasonable suspicion. It will be argued that a full reading of *Kebilene* and subsequent authority, together with consideration of the jurisprudence of Article 6 (2) establishes that offences which purport to convict on the basis of a reasonable suspicion must be read so as to require proof of the wrong underlying the offence. We will argue for a basic and unyielding principle that the conduct which constitutes the underlying wrong must be proved. This falls short of establishing a rich version of the presumption of innocence. It is quite compatible with placing a burden of proof of, say, lack of *mens rea* on D.[45] But the presumption of innocence is not

---

[42] [2000] 2 AC 326.

[43] Terrorism Act 2000, s. 118(2).

[44] Criminal Justice and Public Order Act 1994, s. 35.

[45] As in *Johnstone* [2003] UKHL 28 where it was held not disproportionate for D to prove a reasonable belief that an offending sign was not in breach of a registered trademark on proof

our theme. Our theme is the need to define crimes in a manner which requires conduct associated with the wrong with which the offence is concerned and to require proof of conduct associated with that wrong.

Proof of Conduct as an Entailment of the Presumption of Innocence

On the face of it, Article 6 (2) of the European Convention for Human Rights provides an unqualified guarantee of the presumption of innocence. Any person 'charged with a criminal offence shall be presumed innocent unless proved guilty according to law'. The briefest acquaintance with the English jurisprudence on the article will disabuse the reader of any sense of unqualified protection.[46] Since the receiving of the Convention into English law as from 2 October 2000,[47] Article 6 (2) has proved to be one of the most contentiously litigated areas of Convention protection.[48] The only matter on which there is complete certainty is that some derogations from the presumption of innocence in the form of reverse burdens of proof and presumptions of guilt are considered incompatible with Article 6(2) whereas other derogations taking those forms have been found in compliance. Valiant and learned attempts have been made to reconcile what, on the face of it, seem to be sharp conflicts in this jurisprudence.[49] With the best will in the world towards the respective authors, the sharp conflicts remain unresolved.[50]

---

that D possessed goods with signs that did breach registered trade marks. Whether this decision comports with the best reading of the presumption of innocence is not our concern. What matters for us is that the conviction of D rested on a wrong attributable to the conduct of D which had been proved against him. Of course, there can be argument as to when the presumption of innocence as properly understood should require proof by the prosecution of *mens rea*. That question is beyond our present concerns which are limited to the minimum conditions of criminal liability.

[46] See Emmerson and Ashworth, *Human Rights and Criminal Justice* (Second edition), London, 2007, chapter 9.

[47] The commencement date for the Human Rights Act 1998.

[48] There have been numerous appellate decisions including four decisions of the House of Lords: *Attorney-General's Reference (No. 4 of 2002)* [2005] 1 AC 264 a combined appeal with *Sheldrake v. DPP* [2005] 1 AC 264; *Johnstone* [2003] UKHL 28; *Lambert* [2002] 2 AC 545; and *R v. DPP Ex p Kebilene* [2000] 2 AC 206.

[49] See Dennis, 'Reverse Onuses and the Presumption of Innocence: In Search of Principle', [2005] *Criminal Law Review* 901; and Hamer, 'The Presumption of Innocence and Reverse Burdens: A Balancing Act', 66 (2007) *CLJ* 142.

[50] Dennis concludes his analysis of the leading cases with the general principle that the prosecution has the burden of persuasion where liability requires judgments of moral blameworthiness subject to an exception permitting a reverse burden based on voluntary assumption of risk. There is a further 'pragmatic exception' relating to proof of formal qualifications. However, consideration of the compatibility of a reverse burden may be required outside this framework

It is far beyond the scope and ambition of this paper to revisit in any substance the Article 6(2) jurisprudence. But one matter at the heart of that corpus of law is vital for our concerns. As indicated, Article 6 (2) has not been construed in its most obvious sense as an absolute barrier to any derogation from the presumption of innocence. Certain derogations are taken to be permissible in the light of the nature of the wrong and the public interest in its suppression and the ease of proof for the respective parties in relation to the matter to be proved or refuted. In some circumstances an onus of proof on D is said to be a proportionate measure by Parliament and thus not a contravention of Article 6 (2).[51]

On the face of it this seems to amount to an obvious category error. If we place for the moment Article 6(2) to one side, it is a comprehensible proposition to claim the public interest in the effective suppression of a particular form of wrong warrants some departure from the presumption of innocence. But it makes no sense at all to say that the public interest in the suppression of the particular wrong entails that there has been no departure from the presumption of innocence when there clearly has been a derogation from the presumption in the interests of effectiveness of prohibition.

But putting back Article 6(2) into the analysis, we seem to encounter just that contradiction when courts say that there has been no breach of the Convention – no departure from the presumption of innocence – because the derogation is a proportionate response by the legislature in the light of the public interest in suppressing the wrong. To achieve coherence these cases must be read as resting on findings (sometimes unarticulated) that in substance the presumption of innocence was sustained. And this must imply that the conduct at the core of the prohibitory norm has been proved and that the matters on which a burden of proof placed on D, such as refuting a presumption of *mens rea*, relate to matters going beyond the conduct element of the offence.

---

if an offence is drafted so widely as to include defendants who are not blameworthy. In such cases, a reverse burden is unjustified if the defendant is required to prove his lack of culpability but a reverse burden may be justified in the matter of demonstrating that the conduct of the defendant fell beyond the rationale of the offence. Dennis recognises that the state of the authorities still leaves considerable scope for argument and judgment in future cases even should his analysis be accepted as the baseline for further discussion. Hamer considers that his rationalisation of the authorities is more straightforward and clear by comparison with that of Dennis' but his conclusion is that '... the compatibility of reverse burdens with Article 6 (2) is ultimately a matter of judgment'. One can only concur and note that the scope for the exercise of judgment in future cases is not noticeably narrowed by Hamer's analysis. It should be added that the respective articles by Dennis and Hamer are learned and insightful. The arbitrary nature of the English case law on the compatibility of reverse burdens with the Convention withstands the most sophisticated attempts to bring it to order.

[51] For example, *Johnstone, supra* (note 45).

There is a baseline where the presumption of innocence and the minimum conditions for the imposition of criminal liability meet. We have argued, first, that the imposition of criminal liability requires some form of conduct within the control of D. Secondly, there must be more than a mere allegation that D has perpetrated conduct. At the very least it must be established by some formal process that it was more likely than not that D perpetrated the relevant conduct. As we have been at pains to make clear, these are formal constraints with no normative bite on the content of the prohibitory norms of the criminal law. An eccentric, despotic ruler could create a criminal offence consisting of stepping on the cracks between paving stones. What he could not do, faithful with a system of criminal law, is stipulate that anyone found walking the pavements falls under a reasonable suspicion of stepping on the cracks and will be convicted of the offence unless he can prove that he has not transgressed.

But, it might be argued this provision does satisfy our constraints. There has to be conduct in the sense there must be proof of walking the pavements. Yet the conduct requirement is completely vacuous unless it establishes the prohibitory norm. And there must be proof that the prohibitory norm has been violated. A reasonable suspicion still leaves the slate clean.

Does the English jurisprudence on the burden of proof require that the prosecution prove violation of the prohibitory norm? The prohibitory norm is the primary wrong of the offence. Proof of violation need not entail any moral wrongdoing, merely that D was responsible for the act, omission or state of affairs that is the subject of the proscription. Matters of exemption and excuse are not part of the prohibitory norm even if the may be part of the gravamen of the offence.[52] Happily, it does seem that the predominant position

---

[52] To illustrate, s. 5 (1) of the Misuse of Drugs Act 1971 makes it an offence for D to possess a controlled drug. The prohibitory norm of that offence is possession of an item that is proved to be a controlled drug. If that is proved by the prosecution there is no contravention of Article 6(2) on the position argued for above. Of course, English courts may provide greater protection to D than is strictly required by the presumption of innocence. In *Lambert* [2002] 2 AC 326, the House of Lords considered that for the more serious offence of possession with intent to supply the gravamen of the crime would be missing unless there were proof that D knew or should have reasonably suspected that the item he possessed was a controlled drug. The burden imposed on D to prove that he did not know nor have reasonable grounds to suspect that the item he possessed was a controlled drug by s. 28 of the 1971 Act was reduced to an onus to produce evidence that he need not do more than raise the issue. The decision by the House that the prosecution must prove the gravamen of the offence may be welcomed in terms of justice to the accused but *pace* the opinion of the House of Lords, such a ruling was not necessitated by Article 6 (2). So if a court in a case involving the less serious offence established by mere possession of a controlled drug were to read s. 28 literally, there would be no breach of Article 6 (2), at least in terms of the position taken here. Whether the court's

under English law is that the conduct constituting the prohibitory norm must be proved by the prosecution.

An example will assist. Take the offence of belonging to a proscribed organisation.[53] The prohibitory norm is belonging to an organisation that is in fact proscribed albeit that a fairer version of the offence might require knowledge of the proscription. But what if the organisation was not proscribed at the time that D joined it? If D is taken to have committed the offence the instant it is proscribed then both our conditions are breached. The initial conduct of joining is not linked to breach of any prohibitory norm. It follows categorically that there cannot be proof of any conduct linked to breach of the prohibitory norm. Unsurprisingly then, the House of Lords has ruled that the 'defence' of joining before proscription and not playing any part in the organisation post proscription is in effect an essential ingredient of the offence. It was for the prosecution to prove that D was active post proscription.[54] In the light of two in-depth studies of the burden of proof in English law,[55] it may be said that save for two exceptions, the prosecution will have the burden to prove the prohibitory norm. The first exception is well established and concerns activities essentially lawful but which require some form of licence or official permission such as driving on the highway. It would be strained to claim that the essence of the offence was driving per se. The illegality is based on the lack of a licence to drive on the highway. Yet in cases of this kind a burden is typically placed on D to prove that he has a valid licence for the activity in question.[56] This may be accepted as a pragmatic and acceptable departure from the general principle if it is the case that a holder of the licence has the wherewithal to reliably and straightforwardly establish his credentials.

The second exception is far more questionable and our purpose here is to undermine its existence. We return to offences defined in term of 'reasonable suspicion', most notoriously what is now section 57 of the Terrorism Act 2000 which provides:

> A person commits an offence if he possesses an article in circumstances that give rise to a reasonable suspicion that his possession is for a purpose connected with the commission, preparation or instigation of an act of terrorism.

---

decision would be compatible with a broad reading of the decision in *Lambert* is another matter.

[53] Contrary to s. 11(2) of the Terrorism Act 2000.

[54] *Attorney-General's Reference (No. 4 of 2002)* [2005] 1 AC 264.

[55] See the articles by Dennis and Hamer (note 49), and see also Ashworth and Blake, 'The Presumption of Innocence in English Law', [1996] *Criminal Law Review* 306.

[56] For a typical example see *DPP v. Barker* [2004] EWHC 2502 (burden of proof imposed on D to prove he held a provisional driving licence: upheld as proportionate).

Offences based on reasonable suspicion rather than proof of the facts constituting the prohibitory norm have not been unequivocally condemned as contravening Article 6(2) by English courts. It is fair to say that they have been treated with great circumspection. It is noteworthy that in *Kebilene* a majority of the judges of the Divisional Courts and the House of Lords took the gravamen of s. 57[57] to be possession with an intent to use for a terrorist purpose rather than mere suspicion of such an intent. But the matter is more fundamental than the gravamen of the offence. As we have argued, there can be no assertion of breach of a prohibitory norm on the basis of mere suspicion. The conduct constituting the wrong has not been shown to exist. It is of great significance that in the recent case of *Zafar and Others v. R*,[58] the Court of Appeal were of the view that if D were successfully to raise any doubt about his purpose, the prosecution would have to prove possession for a terrorist purpose. At the time of the *Kebilene* litigation, should the prosecution establish a reasonable suspicion, a burden of persuasion was imposed on D regarding a lack of any terrorist purpose. Because of a change in the law nowadays, D need merely adduce some evidence suggestive of a lack of terrorist purpose.[59] On the face of it, the prosecution would win their case within the terms of s. 57, were they to refute D's evidence to the extent of re-instating grounds for reasonable suspicion. But the Court of Appeal thought that the prosecution must do more:

> [T]he effect of section 118 of the 2000 Act is that, if a defendant adduces evidence that raises an issue as to whether his possession of the article in question was for a purpose connected with the commission, preparation or instigation of an act of terrorism, the burden shifts to the prosecution of proving beyond reasonable doubt *that the possession of the article was held for such purpose*.[60]

The decision must not be overworked in terms of supporting the rejection of mere suspicion as the ground for a criminal conviction. The grounds of appeal in *Zafar* did not concern this point. Yet the decision itself is of considerable interest. The Court clearly disliked the nebulous and all embracing terms of s. 57 and considered that they did not satisfy the principle of legality. It took the unusual and radical step of redrafting s. 57 in clearer and substantially narrower

---

[57] At the time of the litigation the offence was to be found in s. 16A(3) of the Prevention of Terrorism (Temporary Provisions) Act 1989.

[58] [2008] EWCA Crim 184.

[59] Terrorism Act 2000, s. 118.

[60] *Supra* (note 58), paragraph 15. Emphasis added. It is noteworthy too that at paragraph 24 the prosecution's task is explained not in terms of establishing reasonable suspicion of a terrorist purpose but rather, 'to prove first the purpose for which each appellant held the stored material and then to prove that this purpose was "connected with the commission, preparation or instigation" of the prospective acts of terrorism . . .'.

terms[61] and then quashing the convictions on the ground that the conduct of the appellants fell beyond the newly minted terms of the provision. In this context the passages requiring proof of a terrorist purpose rather than a reasonable suspicion of a terrorist purpose have great resonance. It is most unlikely that the Court of Appeal would have been satisfied with mere suspicion as the basis for criminal convictions. *Zafar* gives us substantial reasons to think that courts will insist on proof of the underlying prohibitory norm and not deal in the false coinage of suspicion. A suspicion, however reasonable, establishes nothing.

CONCLUSION

We have argued that criminal liability when properly understood must be based on some voluntary conduct on the part of D. Unfortunately English law does not insist on conduct as a predicate for criminal liability. If an offence does require proof of some conduct we can be reasonably content that English law will require the conduct element to be proved by the prosecution. If the potential of Article 6 of the European Convention – fair trial and the presumption of innocence – were to be fully realised by the judiciary, all offences would be construed as requiring a conduct element and proof of the conduct element by the prosecution. This would improve the conceptual and to some extent the normative condition of English criminal law.

---

[61] Ibid at paragraph 29.

Chapter Twelve

State Identity and Genocide: The *Bosnian Genocide* Case

Dominic McGoldrick*

I. Introduction

On 26 February 2007, after fourteen years, the International Court of Justice delivered its decision on the merits in the *Bosnian Genocide Case*.[1] It was its first judgment on the merits in a case in which allegations of genocide had been made by one State against another. Bosnia sought, 'to establish the responsibilities of a State which, through its leadership, through its organs, committed the most brutal violations of one of the most sacred instruments of international law'.[2] The progress of the case was marked by extensive factual and evidential disputes, the most extensive written pleadings in the court's history, procedural wrangling, applications for interim measures and counter-claims.[3] At the heart of the case

---

* Professor of Public International Law, University of Liverpool.

[1] *Application of the Convention on the Prevention and Punishment of the Crime of Genocide* (*Bosnia and Herzegovina v. Serbia and Montenegro*), ICJ General List No. 91, Judgment of 26 February 2007: ⟨http://www.icj-cij.org⟩; 46 (2007) *ILM* 188. Hereinafter the main judgment is referred to as '*Judgment*', while the Separate and Dissenting Opinions, and the Declarations are referred to as 'note 1'. On this case, see Sivakumaran, Case Note, 56 (2007) *ICLQ* 695; and the commentaries in 28 (2008) *Leiden Journal of International Law* 63 *et seq.*

[2] Cited in *Judgment*, paragraph 155. See Milanovic, 'State Responsibility for Genocide', 17 (2006) *EJIL* 553 and also 'Follow-Up', ibid, p. 669.

[3] See paragraphs 1 to 66 of the *Judgment*. The counterclaims were withdrawn. The Court had a mass of factual information presented to it. The pleadings and transcripts are published on the Court's website. The hearings lasted for two and a half months, witnesses were examined and cross-examined, and the Parties each submitted thousands of pages of documentary evidence (some of which had portions redacted). The public hearings on the merits in the case concluded in May 2006. See Riddell, 'Report on the Oral Proceedings in the *Application of the Convention on the Prevention and Punishment of the Crime of Genocide (Bosnia and Herzegovina v. Serbia and Montenegro)*: Selected Procedural Aspects', 20 (2007) *Leiden Journal of International*

K.H. Kaikobad & M. Bohlander (eds.), *International Law and Power: Perspectives on Legal Order and Justice*. Essays in Honour of Colin Warbrick, pp. 255–304.
© 2009 Koninklijke Brill NV. Printed in the Netherlands.

were fundamental issues of State identity, the consensual nature of jurisdiction and the interpretation of the Convention on the Prevention and Punishment of the Crime of Genocide (1948).[4] This article focuses on these central issues.

Part 2 outlines the history of the case and addresses the issue of State identity. Part 3 examines the Court's interpretation of the Genocide Convention. Part 4 deals specifically with the massacre at Srebrenica. Parts 5–6 deal respectively with the responsibility for breach of the obligations to prevent and punish genocide. Parts 7–8 deal briefly with responsibility for breach of the Court's orders indicating provisional measures and the question of reparation. Finally, Part 9 seeks to identify the likely legacy of the Judgment.

II. State Identity

1. *The History of the Case*

The 2007 Judgement forms part of the long and complicated legal and political consequences of the dissolution of the Socialist Federal Republic of Yugoslavia (SFRY).[5] In May 1992, Bosnia and Herzegovina, Croatia and Slovenia were admitted as Members to the United Nations, as was the Former Yugoslav Republic of Macedonia on 8 April 1993. The Federal Republic of Yugoslavia (FRY) (Serbia and Macedonia) claimed to be a continuation of the SFRY but this claim was not generally accepted.[6] In Resolution 777 (1992) the

---

Law 405. In her Separate Opinion, Judge Higgins argued that the FRY/ Serbia's approach to the issues was such that the Court should have discontinued the case from its list so as to protect the integrity of the judicial process.

4   78 UNTS 277 (1951). 140 State parties as at 18 July 2007. See Robinson, *The Genocide Convention: A Commentary*, New York, 1960; Whitaker, 'Revised and Updated Report on the Question of the Prevention and Punishment of the Crime of Genocide', UN Doc. E/CN. 4/Sub. 2/1985/6 (2 July 1985); Shaw, 'Genocide and International Law', in Dinstein (ed.) *International Law At a Time of Perplexity*, Dordrecht, 1989, p. 797; Schabas, *Genocide in International Law: The Crime of Crimes*, Cambridge, 2000; Kress, 'The Crime of Genocide Under International Law', 6 (2004) *International Criminal Law Review* 461; Kalere 'Genocide in the African Great Lakes States', 5 (2005) *International Criminal Law Review* 463; and Shelton (ed.), *Encyclopaedia of Genocide and Crimes Against Humanity*, Detroit, MI., 2005. Dimitrijevic and Milanovic submit that genocide is not the crime of crimes and labelling it as such trivialises crimes against humanity in public discourse: see 'The Strange Story of the Bosnian *Genocide* Case', 21 (2008) *Leiden Journal of International Law* 65, at p. 93.

5   See McGoldrick, 'The Tale of Yugoslavia: Lessons for Accommodating National Identity in National and International Law', in Tierney (ed.), *Accommodating National Identity*, The Hague, 2000, pp. 13–64; and Rich, 'Recognition of States: The Collapse of Yugoslavia and the Soviet Union', 4 (1993) *EJIL* 36.

6   See Scharf, 'Musical Chairs: The Dissolution of States and Membership in the United Nations', 28 (1995) *Cornell International Law Journal* 29.

Security Council recommended to the General Assembly (GA) that the FRY should apply for membership of the UN.[7] The GA followed that recommendation.[8] The FRY could not participate in the work of the GA or the Economic and Social Council,[9] but its membership of the UN was neither terminated nor suspended.[10] In 2000 the FRY, in the light of SC Resolution 777, requested admission to the UN. It was admitted on 1 November 2000. It kept the same name (the FRY), flag and national anthem.

The ICJ proceedings were instituted in 1993 by the Republic of Bosnia and Herzegovina (with effect from 14 December 1995 'Bosnia and Herzegovina') against the Federal Republic of Yugoslavia (FRY).[11] As noted, Bosnia and the FRY were among the State entities that emerged from the dissolution of the SFRY. The FRY was the name of Serbia and Montenegro between 27 April 1992 (adoption of its Constitution) and 3 February 2003. From 4 February 2003 it went under the name 'Serbia and Montenegro' and with effect from 3 June 2006, the 'Republic of Serbia'. The name of the respondent in the official title of the case is 'Serbia and Montenegro'. When discussing the evidence and the issues the 2007 Judgment refers to the respondent State as the 'FRY' but in the operative paragraphs it then refers to 'Serbia'. For convenience, and in order to avoid confusing name changes, I will henceforth refer to the entity in the various proceedings as FRY/ Serbia.

A short time after the close of the oral hearings in the case in May 2006, Montenegro declared its independence based on the results of a referendum. This raised the question of who was now the Respondent party in the case. The Court answered by saying that at the date of this Judgment, Serbia was the only respondent.[12] However, it noted that any responsibility for *past* events involved at the relevant time the composite State of Serbia and Montenegro.[13]

---

[7]   See Security Council (SC) Resolutions Nos. 757 and 777 (1992).

[8]   General Assembly Resolution 47/1 (1992).

[9]   See SC Resolution No. 821 (1993) and GA Resolution 47/229.

[10]   Wood, 'Participation of Former Yugoslav States in the United Nations and in Multilateral Treaties', 1 (1997) *Max Planck Yearbook of United Nations Law* 231. It continued to be assessed by the General Assembly for its financial contributions.

[11]   This is an astonishing period given the subject matter. It has been argued that Bosnia brought the case as part of its strategy against Security Council resolutions undermining its right of self-defence and proposals in international negotiations that it objected to. It continued so as to challenge the Dayton Peace Agreement and to present the Republika Srpska as an illegitimate, genocidal creation. See Szasz, 'Comment on the Genocide Case (Preliminary Objections)', 10 (1997) *Leiden Journal of International Law* 163. On the litigation strategies and storytelling of the two parties, see Dimitrijevic and Milanovic (note 4).

[12]   *Judgment*, paragraphs 67–79.

[13]   *Judgment*, paragraph 78.

2. Interim Measures

In April 1993, the Court indicated certain provisional measures with a view to the protection of rights under the Genocide Convention, viz., that: the Government of the FRY/ Serbia (i) should immediately, in pursuance of its undertaking in the Convention, take all measures within its power to prevent commission of the crime of genocide; and (ii) should in particular ensure that any military, paramilitary or irregular armed units which may be directed or supported by it, as well as any organizations and persons which may be subject to its control, direction or influence, do not commit any acts of genocide, of conspiracy to commit genocide, of direct and public incitement to commit genocide, or of complicity in genocide, whether directed against the Muslim population of Bosnia and Herzegovina or against any other national, ethnical, racial or religious group. In addition, the Government of the FRY/ Serbia and the Government of the Republic of Bosnia and Herzegovina should not take any action and should ensure that no action is taken which may aggravate or extend the existing dispute over the prevention or punishment of the crime of genocide, or render it more difficult of solution.[14] The interim measures were re-affirmed in September 1993. Interestingly, the only judge from the 1993 interim measures decision that was still on the Court at the merits stage in 2007 was Judge Ranjeva.

3. Jurisdiction Ratione Personae: *Judgment on Jurisdiction (1996)*

There were fundamental jurisdictional objections from the FRY/ Serbia. In July 1996, the Court rejected these preliminary objections.[15] The most difficult issue was that of jurisdiction *ratione personae*.[16] At the time of the proclamation of the Federal Republic of Yugoslavia, on 27 April 1992, a formal declaration was adopted on its behalf that expressed the intention of Yugoslavia to remain bound by the international treaties to which the former Yugoslavia was party. Thus, FRY/ Serbia did not contest that it was party to the Genocide Convention when the application was brought against it in 1993. The Court held:

> [T]he former Socialist Federal Republic of Yugoslavia ... signed the Genocide Convention on 11 December 1948 and deposited its instrument of ratification, without reservation, on 29 August 1950. At the time of the proclamation of

---

[14] Order of 8 April 1993.

[15] See Gray, Case Note, 46 (1997) *ICLQ* 688; and Szasz (note 11), above.

[16] *Application of the Convention on the Prevention and Punishment of the Crime of Genocide (Bosnia and Herzegovina v. Yugoslavia) Preliminary Objections, ICJ Reports 1996*, p. 595 at paragraphs 16–26. Hereinafter referred to as *Judgment on Jurisdiction*.

the Federal Republic of Yugoslavia, on 27 April 1992, a formal declaration was adopted on its behalf to the effect that: 'The Federal Republic of Yugoslavia, continuing the State, international legal and political personality of the Socialist Federal Republic of Yugoslavia, shall strictly abide by all the commitments that the Socialist Federal Republic of Yugoslavia assumed internationally.' This intention thus expressed by Yugoslavia to remain bound by the international treaties to which the former Yugoslavia was party was confirmed in an official Note of 27 April 1992 from the Permanent Mission of Yugoslavia to the United Nations, addressed to the Secretary-General. The Court observes, furthermore, that it has not been contested that Yugoslavia was party to the Genocide Convention. Thus, Yugoslavia was bound by the provisions of the Convention on the date of the filing of the Application in the present case, namely, on 20 March 1993.[17]

Neither party raised the issue of FRY/ Serbia capacity to be a respondent. Bosnia and Herzegovina as Applicant, while denying that the FRY/ Serbia was a Member of the United Nations as the continuator of the SFRY, was asserting that the FRY/ Serbia was nevertheless a party to the ICJ Statute, either under Article 35(2) of the ICJ Statute[18] or on the basis of the declaration of 27 April 1992. For the FRY/ Serbia to have raised the issue of capacity would have involved undermining or abandoning its claim to be the continuator of the SFRY as the basis for continuing membership of the United Nations.

In 29 December 1992, Bosnia-Herzegovina had transmitted to the Secretary-General of the United Nations, as depositary of the Genocide Convention, a Notice of Succession. Yugoslavia contested the validity and legal effect of that Notice, as, in its view, Bosnia-Herzegovina was not qualified to become a party to the Convention. The Court rejected that view. Bosnia-Herzegovina had become a Member of the United Nations and Article XI of the Genocide Convention opened it to 'any Member of the United Nations'. Thus Bosnia-Herzegovina could become a party to the Convention through the mechanism of State succession. The Court did not consider it necessary, in order to decide on its jurisdiction in this case, to make a determination on the legal issues concerning State succession in respect to treaties which had been raised by the Parties. Whether Bosnia-Herzegovina automatically became party to the Genocide Convention on the date of its accession to independence on 6 March 1992, or whether it became a party as a result – retroactive or not – of its Notice

---

[17] Ibid, paragraph 17.

[18] Article 35 provides that '(1) The Court shall be open to the States Parties to the present Statute. (2) The conditions under which the Court shall be open to other States shall, subject to the special provisions contained in *treaties in force* ...'. Emphasis added.

of Succession of 29 December 1992, at all events it was a party to it on the date of the filing of its Application on 20 March 1993.[19]

As for jurisdiction *ratione materiae* the Court found that it had jurisdiction to deal with the case on the basis of Article IX of the Convention on the Prevention and Punishment of the Crime of Genocide.[20] This provides that, 'Disputes between the Contracting Parties relating to the interpretation, application or fulfillment of the present Convention, including those relating to the responsibility of a State for genocide or for any of the other acts enumerated in article III, shall be submitted to the International Court of Justice at the request of any of the parties to the dispute'. The Court dismissed the additional bases of jurisdiction invoked by Bosnia-Herzegovina. It further found that the Application filed by Bosnia-Herzegovina was admissible. The Court only found jurisdiction under the Genocide Convention. It had no jurisdiction to determine whether particular atrocities could amount to war crimes and crimes against humanity.[21] For the Court it was genocide or nothing.

Only four of the judges from the 1996 Judgment on Jurisdiction were still on the Court at the merits stage in 2007, namely Judges Ranjeva, Shi, Koroma and Judge *ad hoc* Kreća.[22]

4. *Jurisdiction* Ratione Personae *Continued: The Application for Revision (2003)*

The FRY/Serbia persisted with its argument that the Court did not have jurisdiction *ratione personae*. In April 2001, it filed an Application instituting proceedings under Article 61 of the ICJ Statute, requesting the Court to revise the 1996 Judgment on Preliminary Objections and a separate 'Initiative to the Court to Reconsider *ex officio* Jurisdiction over Yugoslavia' to substantially the same

---

[19] *Judgment on Jurisdiction*, paragraph 23. Issues relating to mutual non-recognition had been cured by their mutual recognition under Article X of the Dayton-Paris Agreement (1995), ibid, paragraphs 25–26. On the Dissenting Opinion of Judge Kreća on Jurisdiction, see Grant, 'Territorial Status, Recognition, and Statehood: Some Aspects of the Genocide Case', 33 (1997) *Stanford Journal of International Law* 305.

[20] *Judgment on Jurisdiction*, paragraphs 27–33.

[21] The peremptory status (*jus cogens*) of the prohibition on genocide, accepted by the ICJ in *Armed Activities on the Territory of the Congo (New Application: 2002) (Democratic Republic of the Congo v. Rwanda)*, General List No. 126, 3 February 2006, paragraph 64, is also irrelevant to jurisdiction: *Judgment*, paragraph 147. See Wouters and Verhoeven, 'The Prohibition of Genocide as a Norm of Ius Cogens and its Implications for the Enforcement of the Law of Genocide', 5 (2005) *International Criminal Law Review* 401.

[22] There would have been six, but Judge Parra-Aranguren did not take part in the case pursuant to Article 24(1) of the Statute of the ICJ (he had been ill) and Judge Higgins recused herself (as did Judge Fleischhauer who had been UN Legal Counsel). Judge *ad hoc* Lauterpacht had resigned and been replaced by Judge *ad hoc* Mahiou.

effect.[23] FRY/ Serbia contended that it had not been a party to the Statute of the Court until its admission to the United Nations on 1 November 2000, that it had not been and still was not a party to the Genocide Convention until it acceded to it. Moreover, its notification of accession to that Convention of 8 March 2001 (received on 12 March 2001) contained a reservation to Article IX thereof.[24]

In February 2003, in the *Application for Revision* case, the Court found, by ten votes to three, that the FRY/ Serbia's Application for revision was inadmissible under the terms of Article 61 of the ICJ Statute.[25] An application for revision of a judgment can only be made only when it is 'based upon the discovery' of some fact which, 'when the judgment was given', was unknown. Such a fact must have been in existence prior to the Judgment and have been discovered subsequently. A fact that occurred several years after a judgment had been given was not a 'new' fact within the meaning of Article 61. This remained the case irrespective of the legal consequences that such a fact might have. The admission of the FRY/ Serbia to the UN had occurred on 1 November 2000, well after the 1996 Judgment. Thus the admission could not be regarded as a new fact within the meaning of Article 61.

The FRY/ Serbia had claimed that its admission to the UN and a letter of December 2000 from the Organization's Legal Counsel simply 'revealed' two facts which had existed in 1996 but had been unknown at the time: namely, that it was not then a party to the Statute of the Court and that it was not bound by the Genocide Convention. On this point, the Court considered that the FRY/ Serbia did not rely on facts that existed in 1996 but that, in reality, it based its Application for revision on the legal consequences that it sought to draw from facts subsequent to the Judgment that it was asking to have revised. The Court concluded that those consequences, even supposing them to be established, could not be regarded as facts within the meaning of Article 61.

---

[23] See Craven, 'The Bosnia Case Revisited and the "New" Yugoslavia', 15 (2002) *Leiden Journal of International Law* 323–343.

[24] On the validity of reservations to Article XI, see *Congo v. Rwanda* (note 21), paragraphs 65–68. See also the Dissenting Opinion of Judge Koroma who considered that Rwanda's reservation was invalid as contrary to the object and purpose of the Convention: see paragraph 11 *et seq.*; and the Joint Separate Opinion of Judges Higgins, Koojmans, Elarby, Owada and Simma who held that a reservation to a specific 'procedural' provision in a certain convention could be contrary to the object and purpose of that convention: see ibid, paragraph 21; and that the Court needed to revisit the issue: see paragraph 21. See 'Comment' by Orakhelashvili, 55 (2006) *ICLQ* 753 who notes, *inter alia*, that the UK has consistently maintained that reservations to Article XI are impermissible.

[25] *Application for Revision of the Judgment of 11 July 1996 in the Case Concerning Application of the Convention on the Prevention and Punishment of the Crime of Genocide (Bosnia and Herzegovina v. Yugoslavia), Preliminary Objections (Yugoslavia vs. Bosnia and Herzegovina), ICJ Reports 2003*, p. 7; for commentary, see Tsagourias, 'Comment', 53 (2004) *ICLQ* 731.

The Court observed that, at the time when the Judgment of 1996 was given, the situation obtaining was that created by General Assembly resolution 47/1. The Court observed that

> [T]he difficulties which arose regarding the FRY's status between the adoption of that resolution and its admission to the United Nations on 1 November 2000 resulted from the fact that, although the FRY's claim to continue the international legal personality of the Former Yugoslavia was not 'generally accepted' ..., the precise consequences of this situation were determined on a case-by-case basis (for example, non-participation in the work of the General Assembly and ECOSOC and in the meetings of States parties to the International Covenant on Civil and Political Rights, etc.).[26]

The Court found that, 'resolution 47/1 did not *inter alia* affect the FRY/ Serbia's right to appear before the Court or to be a party to a dispute before the Court under the conditions laid down by the Statute. Nor did it affect the position of the FRY in relation to the Genocide Convention'.[27] It further stated that resolution 55/12 of 1 November 2000 (by which the GA decided to admit the FRY/ Serbia to membership of the United Nations) could not have changed retroactively the *sui generis* position which the FRY/ Serbia found itself in vis-à-vis the UN over the period 1992 to 2000, or its position in relation to the Statute of the Court and the Genocide Convention.

The Court concluded that it had not been established that the request of the FRY/ Serbia was based upon the discovery of 'some fact' that was, 'when the judgment was given, unknown to the Court and also to the party claiming revision'. Six of the judges from the 2003 *Revision* Judgment were still on the Court at the 2007 merits stage, namely Judges Al-Khasawneh, Buergenthal, Ranjeva, Shi, Koroma and Judge *ad hoc* Mahiou.[28] All six voted with the majority in 2003.

5. *Jurisdiction* Ratione Personae *Again – Or Capacity*

Notwithstanding its *Judgment on Jurisdiction* in 1993, and its rejection of the *Application for Revision* in 2003, the Court accepted that an 'important issue of a jurisdictional character' had been raised by Serbia's 'Initiative to the Court to Reconsider *ex officio* Jurisdiction over Yugoslavia' of 2001, and that it had been asked to rule upon it. The central question raised was whether at the time of the filing of the Application instituting the proceedings in 1993 the FRY/ Serbia

---

[26] *Application for Revision* case (note 25), paragraph 70.
[27] Ibid.
[28] See note 22 above (on Judge Parra-Aranguren) who voted with the majority.

was or was not the continuator of the SFRY. FRY/ Serbia now contended that it was not a continuator State, and that therefore not only was it not a party to the Genocide Convention when the proceedings were instituted, but it was not then a party to the Statute of the Court by virtue of membership in the UN.[29] Not being such a party, it did not have access to the Court, with the consequence that the Court had no jurisdiction *ratione personae* over it.

FRY/ Serbia prayed in aid the decisions of the Court itself in 2004 in eight cases brought by Serbia and Montenegro against Member States of NATO (cases concerning the *Legality of Use of Force*).[30] The Applications instituting proceedings in those cases had been filed on 29 April 1999, that is to say prior to the admission of Serbia and Montenegro (then known as the FRY) to the UN on 1 November 2000. In each of these cases, the Court had unanimously held that it had no jurisdiction to entertain the claims made in the Application. However, the unanimity is deceptive. A bare majority of eight[31] to seven found no jurisdiction on the basis that FRY/ Serbia did not, at the time of the institution of the proceedings in 1999, have access to the Court under either Article 35 (1) or (2) of the Statute.[32] They held that, in light of the legal consequences of the new development since 1 November 2000, 'Serbia and Montenegro was not a Member of the UN, and in that capacity a State party to the Statute of the ICJ, at the time of filing its Application …'.[33] No finding was made in the judgments in the *Legality of Use of Force* cases on the question whether or not FRY/Serbia was a party to the Genocide Convention at the relevant time.[34] However, the judgments gave FRY/ Serbia a strong argument about capacity under the ICJ Statute to be a party to proceedings. The Court described FRY/Serbia's position during the period 1992–2000 as 'highly

---

[29] The ICJ's statute is annexed to the UN Charter of which it forms an integral part.

[30] See Olleson, ' "Killing Three Birds With One Stone"? The Preliminary Objections Judgments of the International Court of Justice in the Legality of Use of Force Cases', 18 (2005) *Leiden Journal of International Law* 237; Vitucci, 'Has Pandora's Box Been Closed?: The Decision on the Legality of Use of Force Cases in Relation to the Status of the Federal Republic of Yugoslavia (Serbia and Montenegro) within the United Nations', 19 (2006) *Leiden Journal of International Law* 114. Parallel applications against Spain and the US were declared inadmissible on the basis of the fact that the Court manifestly lacked jurisdiction on any of the bases relied upon.

[31] Then President Shi; Judges Koroma, Vereshchetin, Parra-Aranguren, Rezek, Owada and Tomka; and Judge *ad hoc* Kreća.

[32] See e.g., *Legality of Use of Force (Serbia and Montenegro* vs. *Belgium), Preliminary Objections, ICJ Reports 2004*, p. 279, at p. 328, paragraph 129. See also Brown, 'Access to International Justice in the Legality of Use of Force Cases', 64 (2005) *CLJ* 267.

[33] *Legality of Use of Force* (note 32), paragraph 79.

[34] FRY/ Serbia had alleged, *inter alia*, violations of the Genocide Convention.

complex', 'ambiguous' and 'open to different interpretations'.[35] It specifically stated that with FRY/ Serbia's admission to the UN in 2000, it 'became clear that the *sui generis* position of the Applicant could not have amounted to its membership in the Organization'.[36] Quite how admission of the FRY/ Serbia in 2000 made the pre-existing position 'clear' is not explained. But in any event, if FRY/ Serbia could not be an applicant in 1999, because it was not a member of the UN and therefore not a State party to the Statute of the Court, how could it have been a respondent in 1993 or any time thereafter (until its admission to the UN in 2000)?[37]

In a Joint Declaration seven judges – Vice-President Judge Ranjeva and Judges Guillaume, Higgins, Kooijmans, Al-Khasawneh, Buergenthal and Elaraby – 'profoundly disagree[d] with the reasoning adopted by the Court'.[38] They considered that contrary to its position in 1999 at the interim measures stage of the *Legality of the Use of Force* cases, the Court had preferred to rule on its jurisdiction *ratione personae*, without even examining the questions of jurisdiction *ratione temporis* and *ratione materiae* on which it had previously pronounced *prima facie*. Moreover, they considered that the majority's solution was at odds with a number of previous decisions of the Court, in particular the 1993 and 2003 Judgments in the *Bosnian Genocide Case*. It had found that FRY/ Serbia could appear before the Court between 1992 and 2000 and that this position had not been changed by its admission to the United Nations in 2002. Lastly, they regretted that the Judgment left some doubt as to whether Yugoslavia was a party, between 1992 and 2000, to the UN Genocide Convention and thus could call into question the solutions adopted by the Court in the *Bosnian Genocide Case*.

---

[35] *Legality of Use of Force* (note 32), paragraph 64.

[36] Ibid, paragraph 78. In its 2003 *Revision Judgment*, the Court had referred to the '*sui generis* position which the FRY found itself in' during the period between 1992 to 2000: *supra* (note 25), paragraph 71.

[37] As explained in Part II (7) below, this was the view taken in the Joint Dissenting Opinion in the *Bosnian Genocide* case (note 1) of Judges Ranjeva, Shi and Koroma. If FRY/ Serbia was not a UN Member in 1999, then it also must not have been a Member when the Application in that case was filed in March 1993 and it was thus ineligible to accede to the Genocide Convention pursuant to one of the two means specified in its Article XI (as a member of the UN or as a State invited by the General Assembly to sign the relevant instrument).

[38] Joint Declaration (note 32), paragraph 1. They also disagreed with the majority opinion interpretation of Article 35(2) of the Statute. They considered that it contradicted the 1993 Judgment that 'proceedings may validly be instituted by a State against a State which is a party to such a special provision in a treaty in force, but is not party to the Statute, and independently of the conditions laid down by the Security Council in its resolution 9 of 1946' (*Application of the Convention on the Prevention and Punishment of the Crime of Genocide (Bosnia and Herzegovina v. Yugoslavia (Serbia and Montenegro))*, *Provisional Measures*, Order of 8 April 1993, *ICJ Reports 1993*, p. 14, paragraph 19.

Some of the difficulties for the Court may be explained its changing membership. Of the eight judges in the majority in 2004 *Legality of Use of Force* case, only five participated in the 2007 *Bosnian Genocide* case. Two of the five, Judges Owada and Tomka, voted with the majority in favour of jurisdiction. Judge Owada followed the *res judicata* approach adopted by the majority.[39] Judge Tomka rejected that approach but found jurisdiction on a different basis. The other three, Judges Shi, Koroma, and Judge *ad hoc* Kreća, dissented on the issue of jurisdiction. Of the seven judges who signed the Joint Declaration in 2004, four were on the Court in 2007. Judge Higgins, by then President, and Judge Buergenthal went with the majority's *res judicata* approach. Judge Al-Khasawneh, who became Vice President in February 2006, agreed that the Court's jurisdiction was established, but had serious doubts whether the already settled question of jurisdiction should have been re-examined. Judge Ranjeva dissented, following the logic of the *Legality of the Use of Force* cases – if Serbia and Montenegro were not a United Nations Member in 1999, then it also must not have been a Member in 1993.

The Court in 2007 accepted that the question whether a State had the 'capacity' under the Statute to be a party to proceedings might be regarded as an issue prior to that of jurisdiction *ratione personae*, or as one constitutive element within the concept of jurisdiction *ratione personae*. Either way, unlike the majority of questions of jurisdiction, it was not a matter of consent of the parties.[40] Similarly, arguments relating to acquiescence, estoppel and good faith were also irrelevant. However, the key focus for the Court was whether the question of the application of Article 35 of the Statute had already been resolved as a matter of *res judicata*, and that if the Court were to go back on its 1996 Judgment on Jurisdiction, it would disregard certain fundamental rules of law.[41] Under Article 60 of the Statute a 'judgment is final and without appeal'. Did that cover the 1993 Judgment on Preliminary Objections and, if so, what elements of it?

6. Res Judicata

The Court identified two purposes underlying the principle of *res judicata*.[42] First, the stability of legal relations required that litigation should come to an

---

[39] See Part II (6) below.

[40] *Judgment*, paragraph 102, citing *Legality of Use of Force* (note 31), paragraph 36.

[41] *Judgment*, paragraph 104.

[42] See generally Reinisch, 'The Use and Limits of *res judicata* and *lis pendens* as Procedural Tools to Avoid Conflicting Dispute Settlement Outcomes', 3 (2004) *The Law and Practice of International Courts and Tribunals* 33; and Scobbie, '*Res judicata*, Precedent and the International Court: A Preliminary Sketch', 20 (1999) *Australian Yearbook of International Law* 299.

end. Secondly, it was in the interest of each party that an issue which had already been adjudicated in favour of that party not be argued again.[43] Apart from the possibility of Article 61 proceedings (for revision), *res judicata* was the applicable principle. The principle applied to judgments on jurisdiction and on the merits. Thus, 'the findings of a judgment are, for the purposes of the case and between the parties, to be taken as correct, and may not be reopened on the basis of claims that doubt has been thrown on them by subsequent events'.[44] The Court then applied the principle of *res judicata* to the 1996 Judgment on Jurisdiction.[45] As noted, neither party had raised the issue in 1996 for obvious reasons. However, the Court stressed that the question whether a State may properly come before the Court, on the basis of the provisions of the Statute, whether it be classified as a matter of capacity to be a party to the proceedings or as an aspect of jurisdiction *ratione personae*, was a matter which preceded that of jurisdiction *ratione materiae*, that is, whether that State had consented to the settlement by the Court of the specific dispute brought before it. The question was in fact one which the Court was bound to raise and examine, if necessary, *ex officio*, and if appropriate after notification to the parties. If the conditions concerning the capacity of the parties to appear before it were not satisfied, the Court could not have jurisdiction to decide the merits.[46]

The Court considered that its 1996 findings that 'Yugoslavia was bound by the provisions of the [Genocide] Convention on the date of the filing of the Application in the present case' and that 'on the basis of Article IX of the Convention on the Prevention and Punishment of the Crime of Genocide, it has jurisdiction to adjudicate upon the dispute' must, as a 'matter of construction be understood, by necessary implication, to mean that the Court at that time perceived the Respondent as being in a position to participate in cases before the Court'.[47] On that basis, it had proceeded to make a finding on jurisdiction which had the force of *res judicata*. The Court considered that it did not need, for the purpose of the present proceedings, to go behind that finding and consider on what basis it had been able to satisfy itself on the point. Whether the Parties classified the matter as one of 'access to the Court' or of 'jurisdiction *ratione personae*', the fact remained that the Court could not have proceeded to determine the merits unless the Respondent had had the capacity under the Statute to be

---

[43] *Judgment*, paragraph 116.
[44] Ibid, paragraph 120.
[45] The Court accepted that the judgments on interim measures in 1993 and on revision in 2003 did not constitute *res judicata* on the issue of capacity because it was not concerned with that issue: see ibid, paragraphs 105–113.
[46] Ibid, paragraph 122.
[47] Ibid, paragraph 132. See also the Separate Opinion of Judge Owada (note 1).

a party to proceedings before the Court.[48] The Court's express finding in the 1996 Judgment that it had jurisdiction in the case *ratione materiae*, on the basis of Article IX of the Genocide Convention, seen in its context, was a finding which was only consistent, in law and logic, with the proposition that, in relation to both Parties, it had jurisdiction *ratione personae* in its comprehensive sense, that is to say, that the status of each of them was such as to comply with the provisions of the Statute concerning the capacity of States to be parties before the Court.[49]

As regards the FRY/ Serbia, Court had taken took note of the declaration made by it on 27 April 1992, whereby the FRY/ Serbia, 'continuing the State, international legal and political personality' of the SFRY, declared that it would 'strictly abide by' the international commitments of the SFRY. That the FRY/ Serbia had the capacity to appear before the Court in accordance with the Statute was an element in the reasoning of the 1996 Judgment which 'can – and indeed must – be read into the Judgment as a matter of logical construction'.[50] That element was not one that could at any time be reopened and re-examined. Finally, the Court reasoned that, as a 'matter of law', there was no possibility that the Court might render its final decision with respect to a party over which it could not exercise its judicial function, because the question whether a State was or was not a party subject to the jurisdiction of the Court was one which was reserved for the sole and authoritative decision of the Court.[51] The law was what the Court decided. Similarly, no question of *ultra vires* action by the Court could arise because the operation of the 'mandatory requirements of the Statute' fell to be determined by the Court in each case before it. Once the Court has determined, with the force of *res judicata*, that it had jurisdiction, then for the purposes of that case no question of *ultra vires* action could arise, the Court having sole competence to determine such matters under the Statute:

> For the Court *res judicata pro veritate habetur*, and the judicial truth within the context of a case is as the Court has determined it, subject only to the provision in the Statute for revision of judgments.[52]

This result was said to be required by the nature of the judicial function, and the universally recognized need for stability of legal relations.

Finally, the same reasoning was applied to reject the FRY/ Serbia's contention that it was not, and could not have been, a party to the Genocide Convention at

---

[48]   Ibid.
[49]   Ibid, paragraph 133.
[50]   Ibid, paragraph 135.
[51]   Ibid, paragraph 139.
[52]   Ibid. A broad translation is that 'a thing adjudged must be taken for truth'.

the time of the institution of proceedings.[53] Indeed, the Court considered that it had been 'quite specific' on this issue in 1996. By deciding the issue via the *res judicata* route the Court did not find it necessary to consider the questions of the status of the FRY/Serbia under the UN Charter and the ICJ Statute, and its position in relation to the Genocide Convention at the time of the filing of the Application.

On the basis of the above arguments the majority of the Court, (ten votes to five) rejected the objections of FRY/Serbia that it had no jurisdiction. They affirmed that, as stated in the 1996 Judgment, the Court had jurisdiction on the basis of Article IX of the Genocide Convention.[54] However, of the majority of ten, three disagreed with the Court's approach or reasoning. Vice President Judge Al-Khasawneh had serious doubts whether, in terms of the proper administration of justice, the already settled question of jurisdiction should have been re-examined in the Judgment. FRY/Serbia's United Nations membership could only have been suspended or terminated pursuant to Articles 5 or 6 of the Charter. Security Council and General Assembly resolutions had not had the effect of terminating the FRY/Serbia's United Nations membership. The FRY/ Serbia's admission to the United Nations in 2000 did not retroactively change its position *vis-à-vis* the United Nations between 1992 and 2000. Between 1992 and 2000, the FRY/Serbia was the continuator of the SFRY, and after its admission to the United Nations, the FRY/Serbia was the SFRY's successor. The Court's Judgment in the *Legality of Use of Force* cases on the question of access and 'treaties in force' was not convincing and had led to confusion and contradictions within the Court's own jurisprudence. The Court should not have entertained the Respondent's highly irregular 2001 'Initiative' on access to the Court, nor should it have invited the Respondent to renew its jurisdictional arguments at the merits phase. He described the Court as having taken, 'refuge in the formalism of *res judicata*'.[55]

Jude Tomka supported the decision that the Court had jurisdiction but he also disagreed with the basis for it. For him the issue could not be resolved on the basis of *res judicata*. The Court in its 1996 Judgment did not deal with the issue of the FRY/ Serbia's access to the Court, either explicitly or implicitly. The majority opinion sought to operate a distinction between 'judicial truth' and reality. In his view, as the FRY/ Serbia was not a party to the Statute until 1 November 2000, the Court should not have exercised, in 1993 or in 1996, its judicial function in relation to it. However, he found an alternative route to satisfying the Court's requirements. This was based on (i) the FRY/ Serbia being a member of the

---

[53] Ibid, paragraph 140.
[54] Ibid, operative paragraph 1.
[55] Dissent of Judge Al-Khasawneh (note 1), paragraph 29.

UN, and *ipso facto* party to the Statute of the Court, since 1 November 2000 and (ii) its automatic succession to the Genocide Convention in 1992. The fact that FRY/ Serbia did not have access to the Court when the Application was filed was a remediable defect that did not, once remedied, preclude the exercise of jurisdiction.[56] Finally, Judge Bennouna pointed out that the admission of Serbia and Montenegro to the United Nations on 1 November 2000 was effective only prospectively and did not undo its previous status, or that of the FRY/ Serbia, within the Organization. It was on that basis that the State was able to appear before the Court in 1993 and to answer for its acts before the Security Council.[57]

7. *The Dissenting Judges*

The five dissenting judges on the jurisdiction issue in 2007 considered that the Court was quite simply wrong. In their Joint Dissenting Opinion, Judges Ranjeva, Shi and Koroma – the three full time members of the Court who had been part of the 1996 decision – (and the 2003 Revision Judgment) were strongly critical of the Court's resort to *res judicata* in relation to the 1996 Judgment, describing it as untenable and unsustainable. They rejected what the Court had described as the 'necessary implication' of the 1996 Judgment. For them the issue of access was not even addressed, let alone decided, in either the reasoning or the *dispositif* of the 1996 Judgment. The issue was neither raised at any time by any of the Parties to the proceedings nor discussed directly or indirectly in the text of the 1996 Judgment.[58] Moreover, 'necessary implication' was inadequate. The Court was required to state the legal principles on which it based a finding, and how it understood and applied the relevant principles and provisions of the law. The 1996 Judgment stated neither the legal principles on which the issue of access was decided nor how those principles were applied. For them the Court's decision in 1996 appeared to be based on estoppel but that principle was distinguishable from *res judicata* and in any event could not replace the requirements of the United Nations Charter or the Statute of the Court. In 1996 the Court had considered that Article IX of the Genocide Convention could be regarded *prima facie* as a special provision in a treaty in force within the meaning of Article 35(2) of the Statute. However, in its Judgment in the *Legality*

---

[56] The Court had studiously avoided the issue of automatic succession to treaties in general, and human rights treaties in particular. See *Judgment on Jurisdiction* (note 32), paragraph 23. Judge Weeramantry had supported automatic succession. See Rasulov, 'Revisiting State Succession to Humanitarian Treaties: Is There a Case for Automaticity?', 14 (2003) *EJIL* 141.

[57] See Declaration of Judge Bennouna (note 1).

[58] Joint Dissenting Opinion of Judges Ranjeva, Shi and Koroma (note 1), paragraph 3. For criticism similar to this, see Wittich, 'Permissible Derogation from Mandatory Rules? The Problem of Party Status in the Genocide Case', 17 (2007) *EJIL* 591.

of Use of Force (Serbia and Montenegro v. *Belgium)* case the Court had concluded that 'the special provisions contained in treaties in force' to which Article 35(2) applied were only those 'in force at the date of the entry into force of the new Statute'.[59] That condition excluded the Genocide Convention, which only entered into force on 12 January 1951.[60]

Judge Skotnikov considered that the Court's judgments had created 'parallel realities'. The Court had jurisdiction over FRY/Serbia in cases filed before 1 November 2001 (*per* the 2007 *Bosnian Genocide* case) except that it did not have jurisdiction (*per* the 2004 *Legality of Use of Force* cases).[61] The 1996 Judgment had not dealt with the issue of access. The part of the 1996 Judgment dealing with jurisdiction *ratione personae* concerned only the question whether Bosnia and the FRY/Serbia were parties to the Genocide Convention, and the assumption of that Judgment was that the Convention satisfied the requirement of Article 35(2) of the Statute, and thus represented an independent and sufficient basis for the FRY/Serbia's access to the Court. This was in line with the provisional view that the Court had taken in the 1993 Order indicating provisional measures. That was why the Court did not address the uncertain and contradictory issue of the FRY/Serbia's access to the Court under Article 35(1) either in 1993 or in 1996. However, in the 2004 *Legality of Use of Force* Judgments the Court addressed the issue of access under both Article 35(1) and (2) and stated that the 'treaty in force' clause in Article 35(2) concerned only the treaties which were in force at the date of the entry into force of the Statute. Moreover, the Court's position was based on the interpretation of the *res judicata* principle in incidental proceedings as absolute and exhaustive. That interpretation was a sharp departure from its previous more cautious and nuanced position on this subject. It came into conflict with the 'non-exhaustive character of preliminary objection proceedings' and limited the right and the duty of the Court to act *proprio motu* to ensure that at all stages of the proceedings jurisdiction had indeed existed.

Finally, unsurprisingly, the *ad-hoc* Judge for the FRY/Serbia, Judge Kreća, was very strongly critical of the decision on jurisdiction.[62] The majority's position on the application of *res judicata* to the 1996 Judgment suffered from two basic weaknesses: (*a*) a narrow and fetishist perception of the *res judicata* rule; and (*b*) an erroneous assessment of the relevant conditions for its application *in casu*. As a consequence, the perception of the *res judicata* rule as well as its application

---

[59] *Supra* (note 32), p. 324, paragraph 113.
[60] Joint Dissenting Opinion of Judges Ranjeva, Shi and Koroma (note 1), paragraph 15. See further *Legality of Use of Force (Serbia and Montenegro v. Belgium)*, *supra* (note 32), pp. 323–324, paragraph 113.
[61] See his Declaration *supra* (note 1).
[62] His Separate Opinion is mainly a dissenting one.

to the 1996 Judgment was completely misguided. Its assessment of standing (*jus standi*) was somewhat confused and significantly self-contradictory, mostly because it sought to reconcile the irreconcilable. The Court had maintained a judicial fiction in preference to proven facts. The 2004 Judgments in the *Legality of the Use of Force* cases were decisive and determinative of the issue of standing. For Judge Kreća, the critical question was whether the FRY/ Serbia was a member of the UN at the material point in time and, as such, a party to the Statute of the Court? The Court had said no in the 2004 *Legality of Use of Force* cases and that answer should have been followed. The Court's reasoning in 2007 reflected the anachronistic and totally unacceptable idea that the Court was not the guardian but the creator of legality and, in fact, that the Court made decisions independently from objective law established by its Statute. The Court had created its own, judicial reality in contrast to the objective legal one, and had produced a judicial illusion (*judicium illusorum*).

8. *Comments*

For the last decade or so, the ICJ has been relatively cohesive with clear majorities in most cases. However, close examination of the *Bosnian Genocide* decision affirming jurisdiction in 2007 reveals some clear inconsistencies between judgments. The decision on jurisdiction is thus much closer than the ten to five majority suggests. Only seven of the judges actually supported the reasoning of the majority based on *res judicata*. The dissenting judges were strongly critical. Consistency in the Court's jurisprudence has not been aided by the length of the case, some fourteen years. One consequence of this was that there were very significant changes in personnel between the relevant judgments in 1993, 1996, 2003, 2004 and 2007. A total of thirty judges were involved.

In 2007, the majority's position was that in 1996 the Court had, by necessary implication, decided that the FRY/ Serbia could participate in the case and on that basis it had then proceeded to decide that it had jurisdiction to decide the case. As noted above, it did not consider it necessary to 'go behind that finding and consider on what basis the Court was able to satisfy itself on that point'. In response it can be argued that it is important for the parties to the proceedings and for other parties to the Statute to know on what basis the Court has satisfied itself that it had jurisdiction. Applying the *res judicata* principle to a judgment when the determination of the implied findings of that judgment is deeply contested seems somewhat problematic.[63] In retrospect, perhaps, the Court

---

[63] See *Judgment*, paragraph 132; and see Sivakumaran (note 1), pp. 696–697, and Blum, 'Was Yugoslavia a Member of the United Nations in the Years 1992–2000?', 101 (2008) *AJIL* 800

should have expressly dealt with the issue even if it suited the parties not to have it examined. To be fair though the status of FRY/Serbia from 1992–2000 was unprecedented.[64] Moreover, the force of the majority's reliance on a *res judicata* approach is greatly weakened when it was a subsequent decision of the same Court in 2004 in the *Legality of Use of Force* that raised grave doubts about the consistency of the Court's judgments on standing with respect to FRY/ Serbia.

So the issue remains – was the FRY/Serbia a member of the UN between 1992 and 2000 (and thus automatically be a party to the ICJ Statute by virtue of Article 93(1) of the UN Charter) or not? Its membership was never suspended or terminated. In 1997, Szasz wrote that 'with almost general consent, the FRY has continued to be treated as a member for all significant purposes except for participation in ECOSOC and in the General Assembly'.[65] In retrospect it may be that the most accurate and plausible explanation is that the FRY was a member of the UN but was effectively subject to sanctions that had an impact on its membership rights by reducing particular aspects of its participation, but not its participation in proceedings before the ICJ, the principal judicial organ of the UN.[66] However, the Judgments in the *Legality of Use of Force* cases seem to contradict this view by denying that the FRY/Serbia was a member before 2000. As noted above, the Court specifically stated that with FRY/ Serbia's admission to the UN in 2000, it 'became clear that the *sui generis* position of the Applicant could not have amounted to its membership in the Organization'.[67]

The issue of FRY/Serbia's membership of the UN presents itself again in the separate case at the ICJ brought by Croatia against Serbia and Montenegro for

---

who comments: 'The 2007 judgment has also brought about the curious result that the Court's *explicit* finding in the Legality of Use of Force cases that FRY-I was *not* a member of the United Nations in the 1992–2000 period was set aside in the 2007 judgment by virtue of the Court's reliance on an *implicit* assumption affirming such membership': see at p. 813.

[64] For criticism of the Court's approach to mandatory rules on party status see Wittich (note 58) *supra*. Academic opinion has differed on the correct legal position on membership. See Blum, 'UN Membership of the "New" Yugoslavia: Continuity or Break', 86 (1992) *AJIL* 830; and see 'Correspondents' Agora: UN Membership of the Former Yugoslavia', 87 (1993) *AJIL* 240; *supra* (note 63); see also Scharf (note 6), and Szasz (note 11). See also the important 'Letter dated 29 September 1992 from the Under-Secretary-General, the Legal Counsel, addressed to the Permanent Representatives of Bosnia and Herzegovina and Croatia to the UN', UN Doc. A/47/485, Annex (30 September 1992).

[65] Szasz (note 11), p. 166.

[66] Analogies could be drawn with measures taken against Israel and South Africa that had similar effects on their participation for which see White, *The Law of International Organisations* (Second edition), Manchester, 2005, pp. 118–124.

[67] *Legality of Use of Force* (note 32), paragraph 78. In its judgment of 2003 in the *Application for Revision* case, the Court had referred to the '*sui generis* position which the FRY found itself in' during the period between 1992 to 2000: *supra* (note 25), paragraph 71.

violations of the Genocide Convention.[68] The proceedings were instituted on
2 July 1999, that is, before Serbia's admission to the UN. The ICJ could not
resort to *res judicata*, as it had not then given any judgment on Jurisdiction
with respect to Croatia's Application. But if it followed the precedent (in a
non technical sense) of the *Bosnian Genocide* case, as Croatia argued it should,
then it would have jurisdiction against the FRY/Serbia and could rule on the
merits. As expected, the FRY/ Serbia submitted that the Court did not have
jurisdiction because it lacked the capacity to be a party to the case. It was not
a State party to the Statute in July 1999 and hence had no access to the Court
under Article 35(1) of the Statute. It had invited the Court to follow its decision
in the *Legality of Use of Force* case in which the Application had been made a few
weeks before, on 29 April 1999. If Serbia could not have instituted proceedings
on 29 April 1999, because it was not then a member of the UN, and therefore
not a party to the ICJ Statute, then it was still not a Member on 2 July 1999 and
so could not be a respondent State either. FRY/ Serbia also submitted that in the
absence of continuity it could not remain bound by Article XI of the Genocide
Convention. It had subsequently acceded to the Genocide Convention with a
reservation to Article XI. It rejected as a matter of principle any argument based
on automatic succession.

Croatia responded that it was difficult to see how the Court could sensibly
explain how it was able to find jurisdiction in one genocide case against FRY/
Serbia (the *Bosnian Genocide* case) but not in another (the *Croatian Genocide*
case). It sought to rely on the reasoning of the Court's decision on preliminary
objections in 1996. It submitted that FRY/ Serbia's *sui generis* status in the UN
was sufficient to give it access to the Court and that it was at all relevant times
bound by the Genocide Convention, including Article XI. In November 2008,
the Court found that it had jurisdiction in the *Croatian Genocide* case, relying
on its flexible approach in the *Mavrommatis* Case (1924).

In addition, there was the issue of Article 35(2) of the Statute. FRY/ Serbia
submitted that the Court should follow its specific decisions in the *Legality of
Use of Force* that it could not have jurisdiction under Article 35(2) of the Statute
because the Genocide Convention was not a 'treaty in force' at the relevant time.
However, as noted, that decision was strongly attacked by seven of the judges in
that case.[69] Interpreting Article 35(2) to refer to treaties already in force at the
time of the application, rather than to the time of the adoption of the Statute,

---

[68] The oral hearings in the case took place in May 2008, Docs. CR 2008/8–13, and can be
     accessed at ⟨http://www.icj-cij.org⟩. See also Vitucci (note 30).
[69] See Part II (5) and text to note 38 above.

has much to commend it.[70] Croatia had specifically argued that the Court's interpretation of Article 35(2) of the Statute in the *Legality of Use of Force* cases was wrong. It noted that the Article 35(2) point was not argued by any of the States in the NATO cases nor even by Serbia itself. It remains to note that the decision on the interpretation of Article 35(2) in the *Legality of Use of Force* cases is obviously not *res judicata* in the *Croatian Genocide* Case. The Court had the opportunity to reverse the approach of the small majority and it is submitted that it should have done so. It did not do so. However, in its judgment on preliminary objections in November 2008 it managed to avoid having to reconsider Article 35(2).

III. INTERPRETATION OF THE CONVENTION ON
THE PREVENTION AND PUNISHMENT OF THE CRIME OF GENOCIDE (1948)

There had been limited discussion of the Genocide Convention in the *Reservations* case (1951)[71] and the *Nuclear Weapons* case (1996)[72] but, after nearly sixty years, this was the first opportunity for a major judicial examination of the scope of an instrument devised on a holocaust model.[73]

1. *Obligations on States*

In most other contexts in which the Convention has been judicially considered, the attention has focused on interpreting the definition of Genocide in Article II.[74] However, in the 2007 Judgment, the Court had to decide some fundamental questions of interpretation on the meaning and scope of most of the substantive articles of the Convention. Under Article I, '[t]he Contracting

---

[70] Indeed, this was the approach of the Court at the provisional measures stage of the *Bosnian Genocide* Case: see *Provisional Measures* (note 38), paragraph 19. See also Vitucci (note 30), pp. 117–118.

[71] *Reservations to the Convention on the Prevention and Punishment of the Crime of Genocide* advisory opinion, *ICJ Reports 1951*, p. 15.

[72] *Legality of the Threat or Use of Nuclear Weapons* advisory opinion, *ICJ Reports 1996*, p. 226. See Gowland-Debbas, 'The Right to Life and Genocide: The Court and International Public Policy', in Sands and Boisson de Chazournes (eds.), *International Law, the International Court of Justice and Nuclear Weapons*, Cambridge, 1999, pp. 315–337.

[73] Genocide had been alleged in *Trial of Pakistani Prisoners of War* (Pakistan v. India), Order of 13 July 1973, *ICJ Reports 1973*, p. 328; but Pakistan decided not to proceed with the case.

[74] For example, in the context of the ICTY, ICTR and ICC. See Byron, 'The Crime of Genocide,' in McGoldrick, Rowe and Donnelly (eds.), *The Permanent International Criminal Court*, Hart Publishing: Oxford/Portland, 2004, pp. 143–177; and Jorgensen, 'The Definition of Genocide: Joining the Dots in the Light of Recent Practice', 1 (2001) *International Criminal Law Review* 285.

Parties confirm that genocide, whether committed in time of peace or in time of war, is a crime under international law which they undertake to prevent and to punish'. The Court held, first, that the 'ordinary meaning of the word "undertake" [used in Article 1] is to give a formal promise, to bind or engage oneself, to give a pledge or promise, to agree, to accept an obligation'.[75] It was not merely hortatory or purposive. The undertaking was unqualified (a matter considered later in relation to the scope of the obligation of prevention) and was not to be read merely as an introduction to later express references to legislation, prosecution and extradition. Article I, in particular its undertaking to prevent, created obligations distinct from those which appeared in subsequent articles. That conclusion was also supported by the purely humanitarian and civilizing purpose of the Convention and the preparatory work.[76] Thus, the Contracting Parties had a direct obligation to prevent genocide.

Secondly, although Article I did not expressly require States to refrain from themselves committing genocide, taking into account the established purpose of the Convention, the effect of Article I was to prohibit States from themselves committing genocide.[77] This prohibition followed from the fact that the Article categorized genocide as 'a crime under international law'. By agreeing to such a categorization, the States parties must logically have been undertaking not to commit the act so described. The prohibition also followed from the expressly stated obligation to prevent the commission of acts of genocide:

> That obligation requires the States parties, *inter alia*, to employ the means at their disposal, in circumstances to be described more specifically later in this Judgment, to prevent persons or groups not directly under their authority from committing an act of genocide or any of the other acts mentioned in Article III. It would be paradoxical if States were thus under an obligation to prevent, so far as within their power, commission of genocide by persons over whom they have a certain influence, but were not forbidden to commit such acts through their own organs, or persons over whom they have such firm control that their conduct is attributable to the State concerned under international law. In short, the obligation to prevent genocide necessarily implies the prohibition of the commission of genocide.[78]

Thus Contracting Parties to the Convention were bound not to commit genocide, through the actions of their organs or persons or groups whose acts are attributable to them. That conclusion also applied to the other acts enumerated in Article III (conspiracy, incitement, attempt and complicity). A

---

[75] *Judgment*, paragraph 162.

[76] Ibid, paragraphs 162–163. On the drafting of the Convention, see Schabas (note 4), pp. 51–101 and pp. 553–568.

[77] For discussions during the drafting, see Schabas (note 4), pp. 418–446.

[78] *Judgment*, paragraph 166.

supporting argument for the Court was that under Article IX the responsibility contemplated was responsibility 'for genocide' (in French, '*responsabilité ... en matière de génocide*'), not merely responsibility 'for failing to prevent or punish genocide'.[79] The Court's conclusion, that States must themselves refrain from committing genocide, may seem obvious but the FRY/ Serbia had argued that the Convention was only concerned with States' obligations with respect to the prevention and punishment of crimes by individuals. The Court accepted that this was a possible reading of the Convention (and indeed six Judges accepted it) but the majority rejected it as the proper interpretation of it. The Court also made it clear that responsibilities of States that would arise from breach of obligations under the Convention were obligations and responsibilities under international law. They were not of a 'criminal nature'.[80] It was untroubled by the duality of State and individual responsibility which it described as a 'constant feature of international law'.[81] The Court had the capacity to find that genocide or the other acts enumerated in Article III had been committed by a State, while applying the standard of proof appropriate to charges of exceptional gravity.[82] State responsibility could arise under the Convention for genocide and complicity, without an individual being convicted of the crime or an associated one.[83] Finally, the substantive obligations arising from Articles I and III were not on their face limited by territory.[84] They applied to a State wherever it may be acting or may be able to act in ways appropriate to meeting the obligations in question.[85] The extent of that ability in law and fact was considered, so far as the obligation to prevent the crime of genocide was concerned, in the section of the Judgment concerned with that obligation.[86] The significant relevant condition concerning the obligation not to commit genocide and the other acts enumerated in Article III was provided by the rules on attribution.[87]

---

[79] Ibid, paragraph 169.

[80] Ibid, paragraph 170. The ILC eventually deleted its famous draft Article 19 on the criminal responsibility of States: see Crawford, *The ILC's Articles on State Responsibility – Introduction, Text and Commentaries*, Cambridge, 2002, pp. 16–20; Weiler, Cassese and Spinedi (eds.), *International Crimes of State: A Critical Analysis of the ILC's Draft Article 19 on State Responsibility*, Berlin, 1989; and Jorgensen, *The Responsibility of States for International Crimes*, Oxford, 2000. The US and the UK had been heavily critical of the idea of criminal responsibility.

[81] *Judgment*, paragraph 173. For criticism of the Court's interpretation of Article I, see Gaeta, 'On What Conditions Can A State Be Held Responsible For Genocide?', 17 (2007) *EJIL* 631.

[82] Ibid, paragraph 181.

[83] Ibid, paragraph 182.

[84] On the territorial application of human rights treaties, see Coomans and Kamminga, *Extraterritorial Application of Human Rights Treaties*, Antwerp, 2004.

[85] *Judgment*, paragraph 183, cross-referring to paragraphs 373 and 430.

[86] See Part V below.

[87] See *Judgment*, paragraphs 379 ff. For favourable comments on this approach, see Lowenstein

As noted six judges – Shi, Koroma, Owada, Skotnikov, Tomka, and Judge *ad hoc* Kreća – rejected this interpretation of Article I. Judges Shi and Koroma rejected the interpretation reached by implication from Article I and considered it to be contrary to the plain meaning of the treaty. Nonetheless these two judges voted in favour of the findings regarding the prevention of genocide in Srebrenica in July 1995,[88] as they believed in the intrinsic humanitarian value of the conclusion reached by the Court and recognized the overriding legal imperative established by Article I of the Convention, namely the duty of a State to do what it properly could, within its means and the law, to try to prevent genocide when there was a serious danger of its occurrence of which the State was or should have been aware.[89]

For Judge Skotnikov there was no implied obligation in the Genocide Convention for States not to commit genocide. Such an unstated obligation was unnecessary to engage State responsibility for genocide because this was engaged when an individual, whose acts were attributable to the State, committed the crime of genocide. The Court lacked the criminal jurisdiction necessary to establish whether individuals had committed genocide. Determination by courts and tribunals with such criminal jurisdiction could provide a basis for State responsibility for genocide if they were consistent with the requirements of the Genocide Convention.[90]

For Judge Tomka, the Convention was intended as an instrument for the prevention and punishment of the crime of genocide. Genocide, as a crime under international law, was construed in the Convention as a criminal offence whose perpetrators bore individual criminal responsibility and should be punished irrespective of their position. The Convention did not conceive of genocide as a criminal act of a State. The failure of a State to comply with its obligations under the Convention constituted an unlawful act and entailed its international responsibility. The jurisdiction of the Court, as a consequence of the addition of the words 'including those [disputes] relating to the responsibility of a State for genocide or for any of the other acts enumerated in Article III' into the compromissory clause in Article IX, was broader and it included the power of the Court to determine the international 'responsibility of a State for genocide' on the basis of attribution to the State of the criminal act of genocide perpetrated by a person. The Court, however, was not the proper forum in which to make

and Kostas, 'Divergent Approaches to Determining Responsibility for Genocide', 5 (2007) *Journal of International Criminal Justice* 839.

[88] See Part IV below.
[89] See Joint Declaration of Judges Shi and Koroma (note 1).
[90] See Declaration of Judge Skotnikov, ibid.

a legally binding pronouncement that a *crime* of genocide had been committed. Such a finding was to be made within the framework of a criminal procedure that also provided for a right of appeal. The Court had no criminal jurisdiction and its procedure was *not* a criminal one.[91] Judge *ad hoc* Kreća fundamentally disagreed with the Court's interpretation of the duties under the Genocide Convention and its understanding of State responsibility under it.

2. *Intent to Commit Genocide*

The Court stressed the prohibited acts must be done with the necessary special or specific intent or *dolus specialis*, namely the 'intent to destroy, in whole or in part, ... [the protected] group, as such'. This specific intent had to be distinguished from other reasons or motives which the perpetrator might have. Moreover, great care had to be taken in finding in the facts a sufficiently clear manifestation of that intent.[92] Ethnic cleansing could only be genocide if it corresponded to or fell within one of the categories of acts prohibited by Article II of the Convention.[93]

3. *Group Identity – The Protected Group*

Bosnia had followed what was termed the 'negative approach' to the definition of the group in question. In its final submission it referred to 'the non-Serb national, ethnical or religious group within, but not limited to, the territory of Bosnia and Herzegovina, including in particular the Muslim population'. The Court rejected this approach. The protected group had to have positive characteristics – national, ethnical, racial or religious – and not the lack of them.[94] The intent also had to relate to the group 'as such'. The crime required an intent to destroy a collection of people who had a particular group identity. It is a matter of who those people were, not who they were not.[95] This positive definition was supported by the preparatory work and the Appeals Chamber of the ICTY.[96] The Court's interpretation was crucial to how it then proceeded with the case. As Bosnia had made only very limited reference to the non-Serb

---

[91] See Separate Opinion of Judge Tomka, ibid.

[92] *Judgment*, paragraph 189. See on this Kress, 'The ICJ and the Elements of the Crime of Genocide' 17 (2007) *EJIL* 619.

[93] See Schabas (note 4), pp. 189–201.

[94] On protected groups, see ibid, pp. 102–150.

[95] *Judgment*, paragraph 193.

[96] Citing the Appeals Chamber in the *Stakić* case, IT-97-24-A, Judgment, 22 March 2006, paragraphs 20–28.

populations of Bosnia and Herzegovina other than the Bosnian Muslims, e.g. the Croats, the Court decided that it would examine the facts of the case on the basis that genocide might be found to have been committed if an intent to destroy the Bosnian Muslims, as a group, in whole or in part, could be established.[97]

4. Intent of Destruction of a Group in Whole or in a Part

The Court responded to a specific question raised by the Parties relating to the impact of geographic criteria on the group as identified positively. The question concerned in particular the atrocities committed in and around Srebrenica in July 1995, and whether in the circumstances of that situation the definition of genocide in Article II was satisfied so far as the intent of destruction of the 'group' 'in whole or in part' requirement was concerned. The Court had to interpret what was 'part' of a group for the purposes of Article II. It gave three non-exhaustive criteria. The first, described as a 'critical' and 'essential' factor was that the intent had to be to destroy at least a substantial part of the particular group.[98] The part targeted had to be significant enough to have an impact on the group as a whole. Secondly, genocide could be found to have been committed where the intent was to destroy the group within a geographically limited area. The opportunity available to the perpetrators was significant but this criterion had to be weighed against that of substantiality. Thirdly, there could be a qualitative element. It cited with approval the ICTY's Appeal Chambers statement, that is to say, 'If a specific part of the group is emblematic of the overall group, or is essential to its survival, that may support a finding that the part qualifies as substantial …'[99]

Finally, it is notable that in that part of the Court's Judgment which dealt with genocide, there are a number of references to the jurisprudence of the ICTY and the ICTR.[100] The Court cited the ICTY's decisions in *Kupreškić et al*,[101] *Krstić*,[102] *Stakić*[103] and the ICTR's decisions in *Kayishema, Byilishema, and Semanza*.[104]

---

[97] *Judgment*, paragraph 196.

[98] Ibid, paragraphs 198–201. See Kress (note 92) *supra.*

[99] *Judgment*, paragraphs 200.

[100] See Higgins, 'A Babel of Judicial Voices: Ruminations From The Bench', 55 (2006) *ICLQ* 791; Sivakumaran (note 1), pp. 706–708; and Riddell (note 3), pp. 628–634.

[101] IT-95-16-T, Trial Chamber Judgment, 14 January 2000; and Appeal Chamber of 19 April 2004.

[102] IT-98-33-T, Trial Chamber Judgment, 2 August 2001.

[103] IT-97-24-T, Trial Chamber Judgment, 31 July 2003.

[104] Referred to in *Krstić*, ICTY, IT-98-33-A, Appeals Chamber Judgment, 19 April 2004, paragraphs 8–11. See also Akhavan, 'The Crime of Genocide in the ICTR Jurisprudence', 3 (2005) *Journal of International Criminal Justice* 989.

5. Questions of Proof

The Court addressed a number of issues relating to proof but two are of particular interest. First, as regards the standard of proof, claims against a State involving charges of exceptional gravity had be proved by evidence that was 'fully conclusive'.[105] The Court required that it be 'fully convinced' that allegations made in the proceedings, that the crime of genocide or the other acts enumerated in Article III had been committed, had been clearly established. The same standard applied to the proof of attribution for such acts. In respect of Bosnia's claim that FRY/ Serbia had breached its undertakings to prevent genocide and to punish and extradite persons charged with genocide, the Court required 'proof at a high level of certainty appropriate to the seriousness of the allegation'.[106]

Secondly, in the context of methods of proof, the Court considered the processes and decisions of the ICTY because many of the allegations before the Court had already been the subject of those processes and decisions.[107] Because the judge or the Chamber did not make definitive findings at any of the pre-trial stages, the Court could not give weight to those rulings. The standard of proof that the Court required in this case would not be met. For example, as a general proposition, the inclusion of charges in an indictment could not be given weight. What might, however, be significant was the decision of the Prosecutor, either initially or in an amendment to an indictment, not to include or to exclude a charge of genocide. However, the Court concluded that it should in principle accept as 'highly persuasive' relevant findings of fact made by the Tribunal at trial, unless they hade been upset on appeal. For the same reasons, any evaluation

---

[105] *Judgment*, paragraphs 209–210: citing *Corfu Channel (United Kingdom v. Albania)*, *ICJ Reports 1949*, p. 17. In his Dissenting Opinion, Judge *ad hoc* for Bosnia, Judge Mahiou, was criticial of the Court's role in the evidentiary process (note 1), paragraphs 50–63. Similarly see Gattini, 'Evidentiary Issues in the ICJ's Genocide Judgment', 17 (2007) *EJIL* 889.

[106] *Judgment*, paragraph 210.

[107] On concerns regarding the Courts's reliance on ICTY jurisprudence in accomplishing its mission, see Judge *ad hoc* for Bosnia, Judge Mahiou, (note 1), paragraphs 50–63. See also the criticisms of Judge *ad hoc* Kreća, (note 1), paragraphs 107–110. For academic criticism of the ICJ's drawing of inferences from the practice of the ICTY, see Goldstone and Hamilton, 'Bosnia v Serbia: Lessons from the Encounter of the ICJ with the ICTY', 21 (2008) *Leiden Journal of International Law* 95 at pp. 103–108. They also criticise the Court's refusal to request unredacted versions of documents from Serbia and its refusal to draw any inferences from Serbia's failure to provide unredacted versions of those documents. The documents were in the possession of the ICTY but were the subject of a confidentiality order at Serbia's request. The documents were of the FRY/ Serbia's Supreme Defence Council. Bosnia believed that they were probative that the FRY/ Serbia had exercised effective control over the Army of the Republika Srpska (VRS). For a report on alleged contents of the documents, see Simons, 'Genocide Court Ruled for Serbia Without Seeing Full War Archive', *New York Times*, 9 April 2007, ⟨http://www.nytimes.com⟩. See also Milanovic, 'Follow-up' (note 2), pp. 677–80.

by the Tribunal based on the facts as so found, for instance about the existence of the required intent, was also entitled to due weight.[108] Sentencing judgments given following a guilty plea based on a statement of agreed facts could, when relevant, be given a certain weight.[109]

6. *The Factual Evidence*

On the basis of the approach in Part III, section 5 above, the Court then proceeded to assess at length the factual materials and evidence presented to it that were alleged to prove violations of Articles II of the Convention.[110] The Court found it established that the FRY / Serbia had made considerable military and financial support available to the Republika Srpska (formerly the Republic of the Serb People of Bosnia and Herzegovina), and that had it withdrawn that support, this would have greatly constrained the options that were available to the Republika Srpska authorities.[111] However, applying its strict standards, and relying heavily on decisions of the ICTY, the Court concluded that, the necessary intent required to constitute genocide had not been conclusively shown in relation to each specific incident.[112] The same conclusion was reached in relation to the events of July 1995 at Srebrenica.[113] The Court's precise findings in relation to Article II were as follows:

a. Article II (a) of the Convention: Killing of Members of the Protected Group

The Court found that it that was established by overwhelming evidence that massive killings in specific areas and detention camps throughout the territory of Bosnia and Herzegovina were perpetrated during the conflict. The evidence showed that the victims were in large majority members of the protected group, which suggested that they might have been systematically targeted by the killings. However, the Court was not convinced that it had been conclusively established that the massive killings of members of the protected group were

---

[108] *Judgment*, paragraph 223.

[109] Ibid, paragraph 224.

[110] Ibid, paragraphs 231–376.

[111] Ibid, paragraph 241. Historically, many States have provided and continue to provide financing of this kind.

[112] The operative clause finding that Serbia had not committed genocide was adopted by thirteen votes to two, namely Vice-President Al-Khasawneh and Judge *ad hoc* Mahiou. On the Court's methodology, see Loewenstein and Kostas, 'Divergent Approaches to Determining Responsibility for Genocide', 5 (2007) *Journal of International Criminal Justice* 839.

[113] See Part IV below.

committed with the specific intent (*dolus specialis*) on the part of the perpetrators to destroy, in whole or in part, the group as such. The Court highlighted the fact that of none of those convicted in the ICTY were found to have acted with specific intent (*dolus specialis*). Thus it had not been established by Bosnia that the killings amounted to acts of genocide.[114]

b. Article II (b) of the Convention: Causing Serious Bodily Harm to Members of the Protected Group

Similarly, the Court considered that it had been established by fully conclusive evidence that members of the protected group were systematically victims of massive mistreatment, beatings, rape and torture causing serious bodily and mental harm, during the conflict and, in particular, in the detention camps. Again though it had not been conclusively established that those atrocities were committed with the specific intent (*dolus specialis*) to destroy the protected group, in whole or in part, required for a finding that genocide had been perpetrated.[115]

c. Deliberately Inflicting on the Group Conditions of Life Calculated to Bring About its Physical Destruction in Whole or in Part

The Court concluded that Serb forces in Sarajevo and other cities had deliberately targeted civilian members of the protected group. However, reserving the question whether such acts were in principle capable of falling within the scope of Article II, paragraph (*c*), the Court did not find sufficient evidence that the alleged acts were committed with the specific intent to destroy the protected group in whole or in part.[116] There was persuasive and conclusive evidence that deportations and expulsions of members of the protected group occurred in Bosnia and Herzegovina. However, even assuming that deportations and expulsions could be categorized as falling within Article II, paragraph (*c*), the Court could not find that it was conclusively established that such deportations and expulsions were accompanied by the intent to destroy the protected group in whole or in part.[117] There was convincing and persuasive evidence that terrible conditions were inflicted upon detainees of the camps. However, the evidence had not enabled the Court to find that those acts were accompanied by specific

---

[114] *Judgment*, paragraphs 245–277.
[115] Ibid, paragraphs 298–319.
[116] Ibid, paragraph 323–338.
[117] Ibid, paragraphs 329–334.

intent (*dolus specialis*) to destroy the protected group, in whole or in part. In that regard, the Court observed that, in none of the ICTY cases concerning camps, had the Tribunal found that the accused acted with such specific intent (*dolus specialis*). Finally, there was conclusive evidence of the deliberate destruction of the historical, cultural and religious heritage of the protected group but the destruction of such heritage could not be considered to constitute the deliberate infliction of conditions of life calculated to bring about the physical destruction of the group.[118]

d. Article II (d): Imposing Measures to Prevent Births within the Protected Group

On the evidence the Court was unable to conclude that Bosnian Serb forces committed acts that could be qualified as imposing measures to prevent births in the protected group within the meaning of Article II (*d*).[119]

e. Article II (e): Forcibly Transferring Children of the Protected Group to Another Group

Similarly, it had not been established that there was any form of policy of forced pregnancy, nor that there was any aim to transfer children of the protected group to another group within the meaning of Article II (*e*).[120]

f. Pattern of Acts

As noted, the Court found that the necessary intent required to constitute genocide had not been conclusively shown in relation to each specific incident. Bosnia also relied on the alleged existence of an overall plan to commit genocide, indicated by the 'pattern of genocidal or potentially [*sic*] acts of genocide committed throughout the territory', against persons identified everywhere and in each case on the basis of their belonging to a specified group.[121] The Court found that a 'Decision on Strategic Goals' issued on 12 May 1992 by Momčilo Krajišnik as the President of the National Assembly of Republika Srpska, and published in the *Official Gazette* of the Republika Srpska, did not establish the necessary specific intent.[122] Moreover, it rejected the broad proposition that

---

[118] Ibid, paragraphs 335–344.
[119] Ibid, paragraphs 355–361.
[120] Ibid, paragraphs 362–367.
[121] Ibid, paragraph 370.
[122] Ibid, paragraphs 370–372.

the very pattern of the atrocities committed over many communities, over a lengthy period, focused on Bosnian Muslims and also Croats, demonstrated the necessary intent:

> The *dolus specialis*, the specific intent to destroy the group in whole or in part, has to be convincingly shown by reference to particular circumstances, unless a general plan to that end can be convincingly demonstrated to exist; and for a pattern of conduct to be accepted as evidence of its existence, it would have to be such that it could *only* point to the existence of such intent.[123]

The Court highlighted that this proposition was not consistent with the findings of the ICTY relating to genocide or with the actions of the Prosecutor, including decisions not to charge genocide offences in possibly relevant indictments, and to enter into plea agreements by which the genocide-related charges were withdrawn.[124] The Court found that Bosnia had not established the existence of that intent on the part of FRY/ Serbia, either on the basis of a concerted plan, or on the basis that the events reviewed by the Court revealed a consistent pattern of conduct which could only point to the existence of such intent.

IV. THE MASSACRE AT SREBRENICA

1. *Genocide*

What turned out to be the one provable case was the massacre at Srebrenica in which some 7,000 Bosnian male Muslims were detained and executed.[125] The Court concluded, again with heavy reliance on ICTY decisions,[126] that the acts committed at Srebrenica falling within Article II (*a*) and (*b*) of the Convention

---

[123] Ibid, paragraph 373. Emphasis added.

[124] Ibid, paragraph 374.

[125] The Court referred to the Report of the UN Secretary-General, *The Fall of Srebrenica*, UN Doc. A/54/549 (1999): see ⟨www.un.org⟩; Rohde, *Endgame: The Betrayal and Fall of Srebrenica, Europe's Worst Massacre Since World War II*, Boulder, Colo., 1997; and Herman, 'The Approved Narrative of the Srebrenica Massacre', 19 (2006) *International Journal for the Semiotics of Law* 409: challenging the evidence and media and official accounts and describing the 'Srebrenica massacre' as the 'greatest triumph of propaganda to emerge from the Balkan wars': p. 431.

[126] In particular, the Court relied on the decision of the Appeal Chamber in *Krstić* rejecting the appeal against the Trial Chamber's finding that genocide had occurred in Srebrenica (IT-98-33-A, Judgment, 19 April 2004). It also relied on the decision of the Trial Chamber I in *Blagojević and Jokić* (IT-02-60-T) 17 January 2005, paragraphs 293–296 of the latter. In May 2007, the Appeals Chamber reversed Blagojevic's conviction for complicity in genocide. It held that the Blagojevic's knowledge of the forcible transfer operation, the separations, and the mistreatment and murders in Bratunac town was insufficient, without knowledge of the mass killings, to allow a reasonable trier of fact to find genocidal intent beyond reasonable doubt.

were committed with the specific intent to destroy in part the group of the Muslims of Bosnia and Herzegovina as such; and accordingly that these were acts of genocide, committed by members of the army of the Republika Srpska (VRS) in and around Srebrenica from about 13 July 1995.[127] However, the Court's conclusion, fortified by the Judgments of the ICTY Trial Chambers in the *Krstić* and *Blagojević* cases, was that the necessary intent was not established until after the change in the military objective from 'reducing the enclave to the urban area' to taking over Srebrenica town and the enclave as a whole, and after the takeover of Srebrenica, on about 12 or 13 July. This proved to be significant for the application of the obligations of the FRY/ Serbia under the Convention but the Court had no reason to depart from the Tribunal's determination that the necessary specific intent (*dolus specialis*) was established and that it was not established until that time.[128]

Judge Skotnikov considered that the ICTY decisions relied upon by the Court were not consistent with the Genocide Convention and that therefore it had not been not been sufficiently established that the massacre in Srebrenica could be qualified as genocide.[129] For Judge *ad hoc* Kreća the determination of the tragic massacre in Srebrenica as genocide was, both in the formal and the substantive sense, well beyond the real meaning of the provisions of the Genocide Convention as applicable law *in casu*. Hardly any of the components of the special intent as *a sine qua non* of the crime of genocide as established by the Convention were satisfied in the relevant judgments of the ICTY as regards the massacre in Srebrenica. He was of the opinion that the massacre in Srebrenica, according to its characteristics, rather fitted in the frame of crimes against humanity and war crimes committed in the fratricidal war in Bosnia and Herzegovina.[130]

2. The Basis of Responsibility for the Events at Srebrenica: Effective Control or Overall Control?

On the evidence, the Court found that the acts of genocide at Srebrenica could not be attributed to FRY/ Serbia as having been committed by its organs (*de*

For discussion of the Chamber's decision, see Karnavas, '*Prosecutor v. Vidoje Blagojevic, Dragan Jokic*', 5 (2005) *International Criminal Law Review* 609. On reliance on the ICTY jurisprudence, see Gattini (note 105) *supra*.

[127] *Judgment*, paragraphs 278–297.

[128] Ibid, paragraph 295.

[129] See Declaration of Judge Skotnikov (note 1).

[130] See the Separate Opinion of Judge *ad hoc* Kreca (note 1), paragraphs 137–153.

jure) or by persons or entities wholly dependent upon it (*de facto*),[131] and thus did not on this basis entail its international responsibility. It had not been shown that the FRY/ Serbia army took part in the massacres, nor that the political leaders of the FRY/ Serbia had a hand in preparing, planning or in any way carrying out the massacres. Neither the Republika Srpska, the VRS, the 'Scorpions'[132] or other paramilitary units were *de jure* organs of the FRY/ Serbia, since none of them had the status of an organ of that State under its internal law.[133] Nor were any of them wholly or completely dependent on the FRY/ Serbia.

The 'whole' or 'complete dependence' test is a very stringent one and difficult to satisfy. Political and military entities will almost always display what the Court referred to as a 'qualified, but real, margin of independence'.[134] The more likely route of attribution will be on the basis of direction or control. The question identified by the Court was whether, in the specific circumstances surrounding the events at Srebrenica the perpetrators of genocide were acting on the Respondent's instructions, or under its direction or control. For the applicable rules the Court referred to Article 8 of the ILC Articles on State Responsibility.[135] That provision had to be understood in the light of the Court's jurisprudence on the

---

[131] Following its approach in *Military and Paramilitary Activities in and against Nicaragua* (*Nicaragua v. United States of America*), *Merits, ICJ Reports 1986*, p. 14, at pp. 62–64. See also De Hoogh, 'Articles 4 and 8 of the 2001 ILC Articles on State Responsibility – The *Tadić* Case and Attribution of Acts of Bosnian Serb Authorities to the Federal Republic of Yugoslavia', 72 (1998) *BYIL* 255; and Ziegler, 'In re G', 92 (1998) *AJIL* 78.

[132] During the oral proceedings, Bosnia presented a video to the Court showing the execution by paramilitaries of six Bosnian Muslims in Trnovo, an area near Srebrenica, in July 1995. This video had previously been shown on Serbian television and during the Milošević trial at the ICTY. See LeBor, '"Scorpions" Jailed for Massacre of Muslims Seen on Video', *The Times*, 11 April 2007.

[133] Vice President Judge Al-Khasawneh, dissenting, considered that the Court should have treated the Scorpions as a *de jure* organ of the FRY/ Serbia. The statement by the Serbian Council of Ministers in response to the massacre of Muslim men by the Scorpions amounted to an admission of responsibility. The Court failed to appreciate the definitional complexity of the crime of genocide and to assess the facts before it accordingly: *Judgment*, paragraphs 52–55. The relationships of dependence or control between the FRY/ Serbia and various special units, including the Scorpions, is due to be examined in *The Prosecutor v. Stanišić and Simatović* (IT-03-69). Stanišić and Simatović are accused of having directed, organized, equipped, trained, armed and financed secret units of the Serbian State Security which murdered, persecuted and deported Croats, Bosnian Muslims, Bosnian Croats and other non-Serb civilians from Bosnia and Herzegovina and Croatia between 1991 and 1995. After delay on health grounds, the trial recommenced in August 2009. See ⟨http://www.un.org/icty/cases-e/cis/simatovic/stanisicsimatovic.pdf⟩

[134] *Judgment*, paragraph 394.

[135] This provides: 'The conduct of a person or group of persons shall be considered an act of a State under international law if the person or group of persons is in fact acting on the instructions of, or under the direction or control of, that State in carrying out the conduct.'

subject, particularly that of the 1986 Judgment in the case concerning *Military and Paramilitary Activities in and against Nicaragua (Nicaragua v. United States of America), Merits*. The test applied there by the Court was whether the United States had 'effective control' of the military or paramilitary operations in the course of which the alleged violations were committed. The Court maintained that this was the correct test and rejected the alternative test of 'overall control' applied by the ICTY Appeal Chamber in the *Tadić* case.[136] As it had followed so much of the ICTY's finding elsewhere in the Judgment, the Court perhaps felt obliged to explain in detail why it did not agree with the test in *Tadić*.[137]

First, the ICTY was not called upon in the *Tadić* case, nor was it in general called upon, to rule on questions of State responsibility, since its jurisdiction was criminal and extended over persons only. Thus, the ICTY had addressed an issue that was not indispensable for the exercise of its jurisdiction. While the Court attached the utmost importance to the factual and legal findings made by the ICTY in ruling on the criminal liability the situation was not the same for positions adopted by the ICTY on issues of general international law which did not lie within the specific purview of its jurisdiction and, moreover, the resolution of which was not always necessary for deciding the criminal cases before it. The Court appeared to be putting down a marker here that it is 'the' Court with jurisdiction on general issues of international law.

Secondly, the arguments in favour of that test were unpersuasive. Logic did not require the same test to be adopted in resolving the two issues, which were very different in nature: the degree and nature of a State's involvement in an armed conflict on another State's territory which was required for the conflict to be characterized as international, could very well, and without logical inconsistency, differ from the degree and nature of involvement required to give rise to that State's responsibility for a specific act committed in the course of the conflict.

Thirdly, that the 'overall control' test had the major drawback of broadening the scope of State responsibility well beyond the fundamental principle governing the law of international responsibility, namely that a State was responsible only for its own conduct, that is to say the conduct of persons acting, on whatever basis, on its behalf. That was true of acts carried out by its official organs, by persons or entities in a relationship of complete dependence on the State, or where an organ of the State gave the instructions or provided the direction pursuant to which the perpetrators of the wrongful act acted or where it

---

[136] IT-94-1-A, Judgment, 15 July 1999: see 38 (1999) *ILM* 1518. Further, see Sivakumaran (note 1), pp. 701–703 for support for the Court's approach.

[137] *Judgment*, paragraphs 402–407.

exercised effective control over the action during which the wrong was committed. In this regard the 'overall control' test was unsuitable, because it 'stretched too far, almost to breaking point, the connection which must exist between the conduct of a State's organs and its international responsibility'.[138]

The differences between the two tests is often cited by those concerned with the fragmentation of international law.[139] The Court's response reflects academic critiques of the ICTY's approach and, although it has been criticised,[140] it is submitted that it is both principled and pragmatic. As Goldstone and Hamilton observed,

> The final outcome of the interplay between the ICJ and the ICTY on this question of attribution suggests that the ICJ will continue to use its *Nicaragua* test in assessing questions of state responsibility that come before it, and that the ICTY will continue to use its 'overall control test' in characterizing whether a conflict is internal or international for the purposes of applying the 'grave breaches' regime of IHL.[141]

Applying its settled and re-affirmed jurisprudence on 'effective control',[142] the Court found that the evidence did not establish that the massacres were committed on the instructions, or under the direction of organs of the FRY/ Serbia, nor that it had exercised effective control over the operations in the course of which those massacres, which constituted the crime of genocide, were perpetrated. Bosnia had not proved that instructions were issued by the federal authorities in Belgrade, or by any other organ of the FRY/ Serbia, to commit the massacres, still less that any such instructions were given with the specific intent (*dolus specialis*) characterizing the crime of genocide, which would have had to be present in order for the FRY/ Serbia to be held responsible on this basis. Indeed, all indications were that the decision to kill the adult male population of the Muslim community in Srebrenica was taken by some members of the VRS (the army of the Republika Srpska) Main Staff, but without instructions from or effective control by the FRY/ Serbia.[143] In conclusion the Court found that

---

[138] *Judgment*, paragraph 406.

[139] See the discussion in Higgins (note 100).

[140] See Cassese, 'The *Nicaragua* and *Tadic* Tests Revisited in the Light of the ICJ Judgment on Genocide in Bosnia', 18 (2007) *EJIL* 649, arguing that the ICJ had not proved the alleged inconsistency of the 'effective control' test with State practice and judicial precedent.

[141] *Supra* (note 107), at 102. They stress the importance of jurisprudential consistency within international judicial bodies. For the future this will particularly concern the ICJ and the International Criminal Court.

[142] The Court had also applied the 'effective control' test in *Case Concerning Armed Activities on the Territory of the Congo (Democratic Republic of the Congo v. Uganda)*, General List No. 116, Judgment of 19 December 2005: ⟨http://www.icj-cij.org⟩. See Okawa, Case Note, 55 (2006) *ICLQ* 742–753.

[143] *Judgment*, paragraph 413.

the acts of those who committed genocide at Srebrenica could not be attributed to the FRY/ Serbia under the rules of international law of State responsibility and thus, its international responsibility was not engaged on this basis.[144]

3. *Other Grounds of Responsibility*

The remaining questions concerned possible responsibility under Article III (b) to (e) of the Convention, viz., conspiracy to commit genocide (Art. III, paragraph (*b*)), direct and public incitement to commit genocide (Art. III, paragraph (*c*)), attempt to commit genocide (Art. III, paragraph (*d*)) and complicity in genocide (Art. III, paragraph (*e*)). Only the latter was given close attention. The Court analysed it in terms of whether organs of the FRY/ Serbia, or persons acting on its instructions or under its direction or effective control, furnished 'aid or assistance' in the commission of the genocide in Srebrenica, in a sense not significantly different from that of those concepts in the general law of international responsibility. It stated that the conduct of an organ or a person furnishing aid or assistance to a perpetrator of the crime of genocide could not be treated as complicity in genocide unless at the least that organ or person acted knowingly, that is to say, in particular, was aware of the specific intent (*dolus specialis*) of the principal perpetrator.

The evidence furnished by Bosnia that this condition was met did not convince the Court.[145] It had not been established beyond any doubt that the authorities of the FRY/ Serbia supplied, and continued to supply, the VRS leaders who decided upon and carried out those acts of genocide with their aid and assistance, at a time when those authorities were clearly aware that genocide was about to take place or was under way; in other words that not only were massacres about to be carried out or already under way, but that their perpetrators had the specific intent characterizing genocide, namely, the intent to destroy, in whole or in part, a human group, as such.[146] A decisive point was that it was not conclusively shown that the decision to eliminate physically the adult male population of the Muslim community from Srebrenica was brought to the attention of the FRY/ Serbia authorities when it was taken. The Court found that that decision was taken shortly before it was actually carried out, a process that took a very short time (essentially between 13 and 16 July 1995), despite the exceptionally high number of victims. It had therefore not been

---

[144] Ibid, paragraph 415.

[145] By eleven votes to four, namely, Vice President Judge Al-Khasawneh; Judges Keith, Bennouna and Judge *ad hoc* Mahiou.

[146] *Judgment*, paragraph 422.

conclusively established that, at the crucial time, the FRY/ Serbia supplied aid to the perpetrators of the genocide in full awareness that the aid supplied would be used to commit genocide.[147]

4. The Dissenting Judges with Respect to Genocide

Vice President Judge Al-Khasawneh, dissenting, considered that the question of Serbia's involvement, as a principal actor or an accomplice, in the genocide that took place in Bosnia and Herzegovina, was supported by massive and compelling evidence. In particular, he stressed that when the shared objective was the commission of international crimes, to require both control over the non-State actors and the specific operations in the context of which international crimes were committed was too high a threshold. The inherent danger in such an approach was that it gave States the opportunity to carry out criminal policies through non-State actors or surrogates without incurring direct responsibility therefor.[148]

Vice President Judge Al-Khasawneh held that the Court's refusal to infer genocidal intent from a consistent pattern of conduct in Bosnia and Herzegovina was inconsistent with the established jurisprudence of the ICTY and the ICTR.[149] For him, the FRY/ Serbia's knowledge of the genocide set to unfold in Srebrenica was clearly established.[150] Judge Keith considered that FRY/ Serbia, an alleged accomplice, must be proved to have knowledge of the genocidal intent of the principal perpetrator (but need not share that intent) and, with that knowledge, to have provided aid and assistance to the perpetrator. On the facts those two elements were proved to the necessary standard.[151] Specifically, he observed: 'Given President Milošević's overall role in the Balkan wars and his knowledge, his specific relationship with General Mladić, and his involvement in the detail of the negotiations of 14 and 15 July 1995, by that time he must have known of the change in plans made by the VRS command on 12 or 13 July and consequently he must have known that they had formed the intent to destroy in part the protected group.'[152] Judge Bennouna held that all the elements were present to justify a finding by the Court of complicity on the part of the authorities in Belgrade. Not only did they provide various forms of assistance to Republika Srpska and its army, the authorities in Belgrade

---

[147] Ibid, paragraph 423.
[148] Dissent of Vice President Judge Al-Khasawneh, (note 1), paragraph 39.
[149] See his Dissenting Opinion, ibid, paragraphs 40–47. See also the Dissenting Opinion of Judge *ad-hoc* Mahiou: ibid, Parts III–IV; and the criticisms of Sivakumaran (note 1), pp. 697–701.
[150] Dissenting Opinion (note 1), paragraphs 48–61.
[151] See Declaration of Judge Keith, (note 1), paragraph 1.
[152] Ibid, paragraph 15.

had the knowledge or should have had knowledge of the genocidal intention of the principal perpetrator of the massacre at Srebrenica. Finally, Judge *ad hoc* Mahiou considered that the evidence before the Court appeared sufficiently strong and convincing to have at the very least justified a finding of complicity in the crime of genocide.

5. *Comments*

A person familiar with the relevant history and events in Bosnia might have been surprised that, at this point of the case, the FRY/Serbia had not been found to have violated any of its obligations under the Genocide Convention with respect to the events in Bosnia in general or with respect to the massacre at Srebrenica in particular.[153] The approach of the Court makes it clear that while the *actus rea* of genocide may well be established, it will always be extremely difficult to conclusively establish the necessary *mens rea* in terms of the specific intent (*dolus specialis*). Resort to a pattern of conduct to evidence the existence of the necessary intent would have been a defensible and realistic alternative route because States will almost never specifically instruct the commission of genocide. However, but this was largely foreclosed because of the Court's requirement that it would have to be such that it could *only* point to the existence of such intent. That is an extremely demanding standard. The high standards of proof and the need for conclusive evidence in relation to the most serious of violations may be comprehensible to the legal profession, but the result is that establishing State liability for genocide is close to impossible because it is almost, but not quite, unprovable.[154] We now turn to the situations where the Court did establish liability under the Convention.

---

[153] See Shaw, 'The ICJ: Serbia, Bosnia and Genocide', in ⟨www.opendemocracy.net⟩: (28 February 2007) criticising the decision as an exercise in denial of the Bosnian genocide. See also the response by Dworkin (2 March 2007) and the further response from Shaw (6 March 2007): ibid. In his Dissenting Opinion, Vice President Judge Al-Khasawneh described the majority decision as achieving an 'extraordinary result in the face of vast and compelling evidence to the contrary': (note 1), paragraph 62.

[154] See Gibney, 'Genocide and State Responsibility', 7 (2007) *Human Rights Law Review* 760 who criticises the Court's failure to consider degrees of State involvement and degrees of State responsibility: ibid, p. 771. For doubts that the ICJ will ever hold a State responsible for genocide outside the parameters of the prior criminal convictions of individual perpetrators, see Goldstone and Hamilton (note 107).

v. Responsibility for Breach
of the Obligations to Prevent Genocide

1. *The Obligation to Prevent*

The Court then considered whether the FRY/Serbia had complied with its obligations to prevent and punish genocide under Article I of the Convention. As for prevention, the Court stressed, *inter alia*, that the obligation was one of conduct and not one of result. The obligation of States parties was to employ *all means reasonably available to them*, so as to prevent genocide *so far as possible*.[155] Responsibility was incurred if the State manifestly failed to take all measures to prevent genocide which were within its power, and which might have contributed to preventing the genocide. In this area the notion of 'due diligence', which called for an assessment *in concreto*, was of critical importance. In assessing whether a State had duly discharged the obligation the first parameter, which varied greatly from one State to another, was the capacity to influence effectively the action of persons likely to commit, or already committing, genocide.[156]

Significantly, a State could be held responsible for breaching the obligation to prevent genocide only if genocide were actually committed. Given its findings on genocide, the Court had to consider FRY/Serbia's conduct, in the light of its duty of prevention, solely in connection with the massacres at Srebrenica, because these were the only acts in respect of which the Court had concluded that genocide was committed. A State's obligation to prevent, and the corresponding duty to act, arose at the instant that the State learned of, or should normally have learned of, the existence of a serious risk that genocide would be committed.

Finally, the Court stressed the differences between the requirements to be met before a State could be held to have violated the obligation to prevent genocide (Article I of the Convention) and those to be satisfied in order for a State to be held responsible for 'complicity in genocide' (Article III, paragraph (e)). The ban on genocide and the other acts listed in Article III, including complicity, placed States under a negative obligation, the obligation not to commit the prohibited acts, while the duty to prevent placed States under positive obligations, to do their best to ensure that such acts did not occur. In particular, a State could be found to have violated its obligation to prevent even though it had no certainty, at the time when it should have acted, but failed to do so, that genocide was

---

[155] *Judgment*, paragraph 430. Emphasis added.
[156] Ibid.

about to be committed or was under way. For it to incur responsibility on this basis it is enough that the State was aware, or should normally have been aware, of the serious danger that acts of genocide would be committed. As the Court noted, this proved decisive in determining the responsibility incurred by the FRY/Serbia.[157]

2. Application of the Obligation to Prevent Events at Srebrenica

On the evidence the Court found that FRY/Serbia had violated its obligation to prevent the Srebrenica genocide in such a manner as to engage its international responsibility. It had been in a unique position of influence over the Bosnian Serbs who devised and implemented the genocide in Srebrenica. It had been bound by very specific obligations by virtue of the ICJ's two Orders in 1993 indicating provisional measures. Although the information available to the FRY/Serbia authorities did not indicate, as a matter of certainty, that genocide was imminent, they could hardly have been unaware of the serious risk of it once the VRS forces had decided to occupy the Srebrenica enclave. Documentary evidence supported this awareness. In view of undeniable influence and the information in their possession, the Yugoslav federal authorities should have made the best efforts within their power to try and prevent the tragic events then taking shape, whose scale, though it could not have been foreseen with certainty, might at least have been surmised.

The FRY/Serbia leadership, and President Milošević, were fully aware of the climate of deep-seated hatred which reigned between the Bosnian Serbs and the Muslims in the Srebrenica region. Although it had not been shown that the decision to eliminate physically the whole of the adult male population of the Muslim community of Srebrenica had been brought to the attention of the FRY/Serbia authorities, nevertheless, given all the international concern about what looked likely to happen at Srebrenica, and given the observations made by President Milošević which made it clear that the dangers were known and that these dangers seemed to be of an order that could suggest an intent to commit genocide unless brought under control, it must have been clear that there was a serious risk of genocide in Srebrenica. Yet the FRY/Serbia had not shown that it took any initiative to prevent what happened, or any action on its part to avert the atrocities which were committed. The organs of the FRY/Serbia did nothing to prevent the Srebrenica massacres, claiming that they were powerless to do so, but this hardly tallies with their known influence over the VRS. For a State to be held responsible for breaching its obligation of prevention, it did not need

---

[157] Ibid, paragraph 432.

to be proven that the State concerned definitely had the power to prevent the genocide. It was sufficient that it had the means to do so and that it manifestly refrained from using them. That was the case here.[158]

Judges Shi and Koroma voted with majority in connection with the prevention obligation but argued that the conclusion reached by the Court would have been legally secure had it been anchored on the relevant Security Council resolutions, instead of the various hypotheses put forward by the Court in the Judgment. Those formulations did not clearly specify what opportunities the FRY/Serbia had to prevent the genocide, while the Security Council had in fact very clearly warned of the imminent and serious humanitarian risk posed by any advance of Bosnian Serb paramilitary units on Srebrenica and its surroundings.[159] There is force in this argument. The judgment is quite vague in terms of what FRY/Serbia could and should have done. What were the means that it had to prevent the genocide and which it had manifestly refrained from using? It was obliged to make the best efforts within its power to try and prevent the tragic events then taking shape. Relatively minimal steps on its part could have satisfied that test or at least have made it difficult to find a clear violation of the obligation. What seems to have undone FRY/ Serbia was the argument that it did nothing.

3. *The Dissenting Judges on the Obligation to Prevent*

Three judges voted against the finding of a violation of the obligation to prevent genocide. For Judge Tomka it had not been established that the FRY/Serbia exercised jurisdiction in the areas surrounding Srebrenica where atrocious mass killings took place. Nor had it been established that it exercised control over the perpetrators who conducted these killings outside the territory of the FRY/Serbia. The plan to execute as many as possible of the military aged Bosnian Muslim men present in the Srebrenica enclave was devised and implemented by the Bosnian Serbs following the takeover of Srebrenica in July 1995. That was the factual finding of the ICTY in *Prosecutor v. Krstić*.[160] It had not been established as a matter of fact before the Court that the FRY/ Serbia authorities knew in advance of this plan. In such a situation they could not have prevented the terrible massacres in Srebrenica.[161] The effect of Judge Tomka's approach is to treat the obligation as one of result rather than conduct.

---

[158] Ibid, paragraph 438.
[159] See their Joint Declaration (note 1), paragraph 6. They expressly refer to Council Resolutions 819 (16 April 1993) and 1004 (12 July 1995).
[160] *Supra* (note 102).
[161] See Separate Opinion of Judge Tomka (note 1), paragraph 68.

Judge Skotnikov held that the Court's treatment of the obligation to prevent was 'extraordinarily expansive'. The content that the Court provided for the obligation to prevent represented a political statement that was clearly outside the specific scope of the Convention. It had introduced a politically appealing, but legally vague, indeed, hardly measurable at all in legal terms, concept of a duty to prevent with the essential element of control being replaced with a highly subjective notion of influence. For Judge *ad hoc* Kreća, the majority's understanding of the duty appeared to be highly innovative, transcending not only in degree but also in kind the standards generally accepted in the *genus* of laws regulating criminal matters.[162] Moreover, even if it existed, its application had been erroneous.[163]

VI. RESPONSIBILITY FOR BREACH
OF THE OBLIGATIONS TO PUNISH GENOCIDE

The Court focused on Article VI of the Convention which provides that, 'Persons charged with genocide or any of the other acts enumerated in Article III shall be tried by a competent tribunal of the State in the territory of which the act was committed, or by such international penal tribunal as may have jurisdiction with respect to those Contracting Parties which shall have accepted its jurisdiction'. It held that the ICTY was an 'international penal tribunal' within the meaning of Article VI.

The nature of the legal instrument by which such a Court was established was without importance in this respect.[164] The second issue was whether the FRY/Serbia was to be regarded as having 'accepted the jurisdiction' of the tribunal. The Court reformulated this question as being whether the FRY/Serbia was obliged to accept the jurisdiction of the ICTY, and to co-operate with the Tribunal by virtue of the Security Council resolution which established it, or of some other rule of international law? The Court followed a simple route by finding that the FRY/ Serbia was under an obligation to co-operate with the ICTY from 14 December 1995 at the latest, the date of the signing and entry into force of the Dayton Agreement between Bosnia and Herzegovina, Croatia and the FRY/ Serbia.[165] Annex 1A of that treaty, made

---

[162] See Separate Opinion of Judge *ad hoc* Kreća (note 1), paragraphs 113–122.

[163] Ibid, paragraphs 123–125.

[164] *Judgment*, paragraph 445.

[165] For a more complex analysis of the possible interpretations of the duty to punish, see Ben-Naftali and Sharon, 'What the ICJ Did not Say About the Duty to Punish Genocide', 5 (2007) *Journal of International Criminal Justice* 859.

binding on the parties by virtue of its Article II, provided that they must fully co-operate, notably with the ICTY.

On the facts the Court found that FRY/Serbia had failed in its duty to co-operate fully with the ICTY, in particular by arresting and handing over to the Tribunal any persons accused of genocide as a result of the Srebrenica genocide and finding themselves on its territory. It considered that FRY/Serbia had implicitly admitted that it had not been co-operating prior to the regime change in 2000. The Court also attached a certain weight to the plentiful, and mutually corroborative, information suggesting that General Mladić, indicted by the ICTY for genocide, as one of those principally responsible for the Srebrenica massacres, was on the territory of FRY/ Serbia at least on several occasions and for substantial periods during the last few years and was still there now, without the Serb authorities doing what they could reasonably do to ascertain exactly where he was living and arrest him.[166] The failure to transfer Mladić to the ICTY violated FRY/ Serbia's obligations under the Convention.[167]

VII. The Question of Responsibility
for Breach of the Court's Order

The Court found that from its own Judgment in the case it was clear that, in respect of the massacres at Srebrenica in July 1995, the FRY/ Serbia had failed to fulfil its obligation indicated in paragraph 52 A (1) of the Order of 8 April 1993 and reaffirmed in the Order of 13 September 1993 to 'take all measures within its power to prevent commission of the crime of genocide'. Nor did it comply with the measure indicated in paragraph 52 A (2) of the Order of 8 April 1993, reaffirmed in the Order of 13 September 1993, insofar as that measure required it to 'ensure that any ... organizations and persons which may be subject to its ... influence ... do not commit any acts of genocide'.[168]

---

[166] *Judgment*, paragraph 448.

[167] Under Article 9 of the ICTY Statute, the ICTY has primary jurisdiction and hence Serbia could not have avoided the obligation by prosecuting Mladić itself. Such primacy is exceptional in international law. Under the Statute of the International Criminal Court, the Court is complementary to a State's jurisdiction and a State would be complying with its obligations to cooperate by prosecuting the accused individual.

[168] *Judgment*, paragraph 456.

VIII. THE QUESTION OF REPARATION

The Court considered that the appropriate satisfaction was a declaration in the Judgment that FRY/ Serbia had failed to comply with the obligation imposed by the Convention to prevent the crime of genocide. Financial compensation was not the appropriate form of reparation for the breach of the obligation to prevent genocide because a causal nexus between the FRY/ Serbia's violation of its obligation of prevention and the damage resulting from the genocide at Srebrenica had not been proven. The standard for such a nexus was high. It could be established only if the Court were able to conclude from the case as a whole and with a sufficient degree of certainty that the genocide at Srebrenica would in fact have been averted if the FRY/ Serbia had acted in compliance with its legal obligations. The Court could not do this.[169] Similarly, the appropriate reparation for the breach of the obligation to punish acts of genocide was a declaration in the Judgment that FRY/ Serbia had outstanding obligations as regards the transfer to the ICTY of persons accused of genocide, in order to comply with its obligations under Articles I and VI of the Genocide Convention, in particular in respect of General Ratko Mladić. That declaration was sufficient as regards its continuing duty of punishment.[170] Finally, there was also a declaration that that the FRY/Serbia had failed to comply with the Court's Orders indicating provisional measures.[171]

IX. THE LEGACY OF THE JUDGMENT

1. *The Legal Legacy*

A proper assessment of the legacy of a legal judgment can only be made with some historical perspective.[172] However, some aspects of the likely legacy of the *Bosnian Genocide Case* can be identified. It is a long complex judgment and there

---

[169] Ibid, paragraphs 459–463. For criticism of the Court's approach to reparations, see Tomuschat, 'Reparation in Cases of Genocide', 5 (2008) *Journal of International Criminal Justice* 905; see also Milanovic, 'Follow-up' (note 2), pp. 688–692.

[170] Ibid, paragraphs 464–465.

[171] Ibid, paragraph 469.

[172] There continues to be discussion over the legacy of the Nuremberg judgment: see Bloxham, *Genocide on Trial: War Crimes Trials and the Formation of Holocaust History and Memory*, Oxford, 2003; Ratner and Abrams, *Accountability for Human Rights Atrocities in International Law: Beyond the Nuremberg Legacy* (Second edition), Oxford/New York, 2001, pp. 26–45; and McGoldrick, 'Criminal Trials Before International Tribunals: Legality and Legitimacy', in McGoldrick, Rowe and Donnelly (note 74), pp. 9–46.

were eleven dissenting, joint or separate opinions. Much of it is lawyer's law. In a Press Statement, President Higgins noted that the mixed findings did not completely satisfy either side but made a point of denying that the Court had been, 'seeking a political compromise, still less any predetermined outcome'.[173] However, there are serious inconsistencies in the Court's jurisprudence with respect to the standing of FRY/ Serbia.[174] These were still unresolved by the Judgment on *Preliminary Objections* in the *Croatian Genocide* case in November 2008. In the Court's defence, the issues of the FRY/ Serbia's State identity and succession were left ambiguous by the UN's political bodies. There was no authoritative determination by the competent organs of the UN defining clearly the legal status of the FRY/ Serbia vis-à-vis the United Nations.[175] Presumably, it suited the political organs not to have such a determination.[176] With hindsight one can argue that the Court's avoidance of the issue did it no service in the long term. In a future case it might decide to tackle the issue head on and force the UN's political bodies to clarify their respective positions if they disagree with the Court's analysis. In addition to this, changes in the judicial composition of the ICJ because the case took so long – fourteen years – allowed some thirty judges to take very different views in a series of cases.

As for the Genocide Convention, the legal possibility of State liability for committing genocide is clearly established. This is of major legal importance but in practice establishing a violation will be very difficult because the Court (i) has set a high standard for conclusive evidence of the necessary specific intent; and (ii) has held that for a pattern of conduct to be accepted as evidence of the existence of the necessary intent, it would have to be such that it could *only* point to the existence of such intent. The Court's findings on genocide with respect to FRY/ Serbia suggest that former President Milošević would not have been convicted on the counts of genocide or complicity in genocide with which he was charged.[177] The Genocide Convention is perhaps approaching a symbolic status. It signifies the moral disgust of the international community at certain kinds

---

[173] Statement to the Press by H.E. Judge Rosalyn Higgins, 26 February 2007, ⟨http://www.icj-cij.org⟩

[174] See Part II above.

[175] On the general legal complexities, see Craven, 'The Problem of State Succession and the Identity of States under International Law', 9 (1998) *EJIL* 142; and ibid, 'The Genocide Case, the Law of Treaties and State Succession', 68 (1997) *BYIL* 127.

[176] See Scharf (note 6), pp. 63–64. In her separate opinion Judge Higgins observed that in the period 1992–2000, the General Assembly and Security Council had 'in all deliberation felt the objectives of the United Nations were best met by legal ambiguity': see paragraph 20.

[177] See Wedgwood, 'Slobodan Milošević's Last Waltz', *New York Times*, 12 March 2007; McGoldrick, 'The Trial of Slobodan Milošević: A Twenty-First Century Trial?', in Melikan (ed.), *Domestic and International Trials 1700–2000*, Manchester, 2003, pp. 179–194.

of events. But, perhaps because they are so disgusting, the legal definitions and evidential thresholds are set so high that they are becoming almost impracticable and leave States very significant room for manoeuvre without fear of being liable for genocide. Cassese has argued for lower standards. He writes:

> The fundamental problem with the ICJ's decision is its unrealistically high standard of proof for finding Serbia to have been legally complicit in genocide. After all, one can also be guilty of complicity in a crime by not stopping it while having both the duty and the power to do so, and when, through one's inaction, one decisively contributes to the creation of conditions that enable the crime to take place.[178]

The situation in Darfur has similarly revealed difficulties in determining whether genocide has taken place.[179] The International Commission on Inquiry on Darfur concluded that the Government of Sudan had not pursued a policy of genocide, although a number of individuals might have acted with genocidal intent.[180] In contrast, in September 2004, the United States' administration had characterized the events in Darfur as amounting to genocide. The downside of the obsessive focus on genocide is that it diverts legal and political attention away from strategies to stop horrific events or punish the perpetrators of them even if they are 'only' war crimes or crimes against humanity.[181]

It took until 31 July 2007 for the Security Council to approve the creation of a hybrid United Nations-African Union peacekeeping force (UNAMID) to quell the violence and instability in the Darfur region where hundreds of thousands of people have been killed and two million others forced to flee their homes.[182]

---

[178] Refer to 'A Judicial Massacre', *The Guardian*, 27 February 2007, where he asks: 'Why was it not enough to prove that the Bosnian Serb military leadership was financed and paid by Serbia and that it was tightly connected to Serbia's political and military leadership?' Similarly, see Griebel and Plucken, 'New Developments Regarding the Rules of Attribution? The ICJ's Decision in Bosnia v. Serbia', 28 (2008) *Leiden Journal of International Law* 601. For a broader methodological criticisms of the use of the concept of criminal conspiracy, see ibid, 'On the Use of Criminal Law in Determining State Responsibility for Genocide', 5 (2007) *Journal of International Criminal Justice* 875.

[179] See Happold, 'Darfur, the Security Council and the International Criminal Court', 55 (2006) *ICLQ* 226; Symposium, 'Commission on Inquiry on Darfur and its Follow-Up: A Critical View', 3 (2005) *Journal of International Criminal Justice* 539. In May 2007, the ICC issued arrest warrants in respect of Mr. Ahmad Muhammad Harun, former Minister of State for the Interior of the Government of Sudan, and Mr Ali Muhammad Ali Abd-Al-Rahman, alleged militia leader also known as Ali Kushayb. See ⟨http://www.icc-cpi.int/cases/Darfur/c0205/c0205_all.html/⟩.

[180] See Kress, 'The Darfur Report and Genocidal Intent', 3 (2005) *Journal of International Criminal Justice* 562. See Brunk, 'Dissecting Darfur: Anatomy of a Genocide Debate', 22 (2008) *International Relations* 25.

[181] There is also the point that the ICJ may have jurisdiction over genocide but not over war crimes or crimes against humanity.

[182] See SC Resolution 1769 (2007): see ⟨http://www.un.org/Docs/sc/⟩.

The realist would argue that the end result suits States. There have been no official proposals to revise or amend the Genocide Convention to expand the scope of the protected groups or the other elements of the definition.[183]

The Court's approach to relying on the evidence and practice of an international criminal tribunal, the ICTY, in certain circumstances is sensible, realistic and pragmatic. The critical point is that the Court makes its own careful assessment of the weight of that evidence in the context of all of the other evidence before it. This will allow it to take account of evidential problems that arise in particular cases, as for example, redacted evidence. However, there is a risk that evidence will come to light in the future (for example when Karadic is tried, and if Mladić is ever tried) that undermines the Court's decision that there was no conclusive evidence of genocide or complicity in genocide and the ICTY decisions on which it placed such reliance. Similarly, ICTY decisions may be overturned on appeal. While according the ICTY a lot of respect for its work in relation to criminal prosecutions as such, the Court asserted a strong role for itself as having the more dominant jurisdiction on general issues of international law. Particularly striking in this respect is its rejection of the test of 'overall control' applied by the ICTY Appeal Chamber in the *Tadić* case in favour of its own 'effective control' test.[184]

In practical terms the more significant obligations under the Convention will continue to be the ones to prevent and punish. Although not binding on them as such, the *Bosnian Genocide* case thus has implications for all 140 States parties to the Convention.[185] Where a State party is aware or could not have been unaware of the grave risk of genocide, and where it has influence over the events and means of action by which it could seek to prevent genocide, then it will be liable if it manifestly refrains from employing those means of action. In addition to this, any country sheltering or failing to apprehend General Mladic or other alleged perpetrators of genocide, will be in violation of the Convention. As of June 2009, Karadic had been transferred to the ICTY but the whereabouts of General Mladic remained unknown.[186] There was no indication from Serbia that its authorities would do what they reasonably could do to ascertain exactly where

---

[183] The definition of Genocide in the ICC Statute 1998 follows that of the Geneva Convention. See Byron (note 74), above. See also Shaw, 'Genocide: Rethinking the Concept', 1 February 2007: ⟨www.opendemocracy.net⟩. Dimitrijevic and Milanovic observe that the ordinary, lay notion of genocide is significantly wider than the legal notion of genocide. This leaves it open to political manipulation. See *supra* (note 11).

[184] See Part IV (2), above.

[185] As of 18 June 2008.

[186] There are some reports that Mladic is living in the Serb part of Bosnia, while others claim that he is in Serbia. On Karadzic, see Milanovic, 'The Arrest and Impending Trial of Radovan Karadzic', 58 (2009) *ICLQ* 212.

he was living and to arrest him. On a more positive note, in June 2008, Stojan Župljanin, indicted for persecutions, murders, extermination, deportation and other crimes committed in northwestern Bosnia and Herzegovina in 1992, was arrested in Serbia by the Serbian War Crimes Prosecutor Vladimir Vukčević in close coordination with other agencies that form part of Serbia's Action Team in charge of tracking fugitives and surrendering them to the ICTY. He was one of the ICTY's four outstanding indictees.

2. *The Political Legacy*

As for the broader political context in the Balkans, the fear for Serbia and Bosnian Serbs was a ruling that the whole nation could be described as genocidal. As this was avoided they largely welcomed the judgment.[187] Immediate reporting of the Judgment stressed that Serbia had been 'cleared' or 'found not guilty of genocide', that the Court had drawn a clear distinction between Serbia proper and Bosnian Serbs (even in relation to Srebrenica), that Serbia owed no financial compensation or war damages to Bosnia, and that the Judgment would ease pressures on it to deal with its role in the recent wars.[188] It was argued that along with the Serbs, a lot of foreign diplomats and others who dealt with the region would welcome this ruling because, '[t]he ramifications within Bosnian politics would have been huge if it had gone the other way. Bosnian leaders, for example, would have said that the verdict proved that the Serb part of Bosnia, the Republika Srpska, was based on genocide and thus should be abolished'.[189] Milorad Dodik, Prime Minister of the Republic of Srpska, was reported as saying that individuals must be held responsible for the crimes committed in

---

[187] Hawton, 'Relief Sweeps Country After Hague Verdict', *The Times*, 27 February 2007: ⟨http://www.timesonline.co.uk⟩; and refer to 'Court Clears Serbia of Genocide', BBC News, 26 February 2007: ⟨http://news.bbc.co.uk/1/hi/world/europe/6395791.stm⟩. See also Dimitrijevic and Milanovic (note 11), *supra*.

[188] 'Serbia Held Not Guilty of Genocide', *Human Rights Tribune* (Geneva), 27 February 2007; Simons, 'World Court Absolves Serbia of Genocide Charge', *International Herald Tribune*, 26 February 2007: ⟨http://www.iht.com⟩; D. Byers, 'Court Clears Serbia of Srebrenica Genocide': *The Times*, 26 February 2007: ⟨http://www.timesonline.co.uk⟩; Charter, 'Serbia Cleared of Genocide Charge over Killing of 8,000 at Srebrenica', *The Times*, 27 February 2007: ⟨http://www.timesonline.co.uk⟩; Oliver and Tran, 'Serbia Cleared of Genocide', *The Guardian*, 26 February 2007, ⟨http://www.guardian.co.uk⟩; and 'International Court Clears Serbia of Genocide', Radio Australia News ⟨http://www.radioaustralia.net.au/news/stories/s1857852.htm⟩.

[189] Jovanic, 'International Court Clears Serbia of Genocide', ABC News, ⟨http://abcnews.go.com/International/story?id=2906051&page=1⟩. On the case as an intra-Bosnia dispute in the sense that the Applicant State included both the alleged perpetrators and the alleged victims of genocide for which see Dimitrijevic and Milanovic (note 11), *supra*.

Srebrenica and not the institutions or the people of Serbia as a whole.[190] The Bosnian Muslim member of the country's tripartite presidency, Haris Siladzic, expressed disappointment at the outcome but welcomed the violations found by the Court.[191] The Serbian legal team reportedly hailed the Judgment as a possible step towards reconciliation in the Balkans.[192] Alain Pellet, a member of the Bosnian legal team reportedly stated that, 'This is a moral victory, certainly, but less of a legal victory'.[193] The response of the regional media was split.[194]

The fact that it was not found responsible for the most serious violations (including the massacre at Srebrenica) and the fact that it was not ordered to pay any massive financial reparations may help the Serbian government to maintain its fragile reform process. It may assist the development of political forces that accept their responsibility for Srebrenica and favour greater cooperation with the ICTY as in its long-term interests.[195] In 2006, NATO invited Serbia to join its Partnership for Peace venture and some European Union countries want to start membership talks with Belgrade, but first require it to hand over Ratko Mladic, the Bosnian Serb military commander at the time of the Bosnian war. He has been charged with genocide at the ICTY. As of June 2009 the ICTY was only seeking two Serbs indicted for war crimes, including General Mladic (Radovan Karadzic, the Bosnian Serb wartime leader having been arrested in Serbia and transferred to the ICTY in July 2008). In February 2007, the German presidency of the European Union urged Serbia, 'to use today's Judgment as a further opportunity to distance itself from the crimes committed by the Milošević regime'.[196] European integration is one of Serbia's strategic priorities. Continued non-cooperation with the ICTY is a significant obstacle to better relations with the EU and any possibility of future membership. EU–Serbia negotiations on a stabilization and association agreement (SAA) have been stalled over Serbia's failure to hand over war crimes suspects for trial.

---

[190] Ibid.
[191] Cited in BBC News Report (note 187).
[192] Cited in Charter (note 188).
[193] Cited in Simons (note 188). On the *Bosnian Genocide* case as a 'political strategy' and as a 'cultural object', rather than merely a 'juridical and procedural entity', see Rajkovic, 'On "Bad" Law and "Good Politics"': The Politics of the ICJ Genocide Case and Its Interpretation', 21 (2008) *Leiden Journal of International Law* 885, at p. 908.
[194] 'Bosnia Genocide Ruling Splits Regional Media': BBC News, 28 February 2007: ⟨http://news.bbc.co.uk/1/hi/world/europe/6401583.stm⟩.
[195] See Simons, 'Mixed Ruling on Genocide Still Puts Pressure on Serbia', *New York Times*, 6 March 2006: ⟨http://www.nytimes.com⟩.
[196] 'EU Presidency Statement on the International Court of Justice's Judgment', 26 February 2007: ⟨http://www.eu2007.de/en/News/CFSP_Statements/February/0226Serbien.html⟩.

In February 2007, EU Commissioner Rehn said that a new government could make a fresh start on this. This would require a firm commitment to full cooperation with the International Criminal Tribunal for the Former Yugoslavia. Concrete steps in this direction had to be taken.[197] Simons has observed: '... [T]he ruling, even if strictly based on the law, hews close to the political wishes of Western countries that want to pull Serbia into a wider Western European community, rather than seeing it isolated as a pariah State with extreme nationalists growing in strength'.[198] After a new coalition government was formed in Serbia in May 2007, the European Commission resumed negotiations with Serbia in June 2007 with respect to the Stabilization and Association Agreement. The Agreement was signed in April 2008. That Serbia assumed the Presidency of the Council of Europe in May 2006 was further evidence of the strategy of bringing it within the European institutional fold.[199]

Another key political matter for Serbia is the resolution of the Kosovo status issue. In 2007, the UN envoy for Kosovo, Martti Ahtisaari, warned that if the UN Security Council failed to impose a solution for the contested province, it could lead to a return to violence there. He proposed to confer internationally supervised independence on Kosovo.[200] The plan was rejected by Serbia, which sees the province as the cradle of its culture.[201] After consultations with the parties, Ahtisaari's final report on Kosovo's future was sent to United Nations Security Council in March 2007.[202] The limited finding against it in the *Bosnian Genocide* case did not appear to have dealt a fatal blow to Serbia's claims to keep Kosovo as part of its territory. However, it may have strengthened the hand of Kosovo. On 17 February 2008, the Assembly of Kosovo issued its 'Declaration of Independence', in which it declared that the Republic of Kosovo was an 'independent and sovereign State'.[203] It accepted the principles of the Ahtisaari Plan and welcomed the continued support of the international community on the basis of Security Council Resolution 1244. Kosovo's claim to statehood was recognized by approximately thirty States. The claim to statehood was

---

[197] 'Trip by the European Union Troika to Serbia', 8 February 2007: ⟨http://www.eu2007.de/en⟩
[198] Simons (note 188). Similarly see Shaw (note 153).
[199] See Monbiot, 'The Price of Being Left Alone Has Been the Tolerance of Mass Murder', *The Guardian*, 8 May 2007.
[200] See 'UN Plan Calls for Kosovo Constitution', *The Guardian*, 2 February 2007.
[201] See Borger, 'Ahtisaari Warns UN: Find Kosovo Solution or Risk Return to Violence', *The Guardian*, 6 February 2007.
[202] See 'Report of the Special Envoy of the Secretary-General on Kosovo's Future Status', UN Doc. S/2007/168 and 'Comprehensive Proposal for the Kosovo Status Settlement', UN Doc. S/2007/168, Add.1 (both dated 26 March 2007). Draft resolutions were withdrawn in July 2007.
[203] See Warbrick, 'Kosovo: the Declaration of Independence', 57 (2008) *ICLQ* 675.

rejected by a smaller number, including Serbia. On 8 October 2008, the General Assembly of the United Nations adopted resolution A/RES/63/3 in which, referring to Article 65 of the Statute of the Court, it requested the International Court of Justice to 'render an advisory opinion on the following question: Is the unilateral declaration of independence by the Provisional Institutions of Self-Government of Kosovo in accordance with international law?' Securing the referral was a major diplomatic victory for Serbia. Seventy-seven States voted in favour, with six against and seventy-four abstentions. The Court will have to consider again some fundamental issues concerning statehood and State identity.

Chapter Thirteen

Explosive Remnants of the War between Eritrea and Ethiopia[†]

Harry H.G. Post[*]

The guns may stop firing and the soldiers return to base, but for many civilians the legacy of war will haunt them long after the conflict has ended. Millions of unexploded munitions in all shapes and sizes are left behind and all too often these Explosive Remnants of War (ERW) claim the lives or the limbs of innocent civilians.

(International Committee of the Red Cross)

Landmines, booby traps and other munitions left on the battlefields are one of the most devastating problems which modern armed conflicts tend to create. The magnitude of the problem has increased dramatically over the last two decades, to the extent that thousands of people have been killed and horrendously maimed and large areas of land have become wasteland. The problem is particularly serious in Africa and parts of Asia insofar as the explosive remnants of war (ERW) have become one of the main barriers to development in substantial parts of these continents. The Eritrea-Ethiopia war of 1998–2000 led to a considerable increase in ERW in these two countries both of which already had a massive problem with landmines, booby traps and other explosive devices from previous conflicts: the Italian invasion of 1935–1936, the 1963–1993 Eritrean War of Independence, and for Ethiopia, the 1980 Ogaden War with Somalia. This essay focuses on the international legal side of ERW: it focuses on the rights and duties

---

[†] It is a great pleasure to contribute to this volume in honour of Colin Warbrick. I admire his multi-faceted work in several areas of the law, in particular with respect to human rights and recognition. I am also most grateful to him for his wise advice and support ever since we met in 1995 at a memorable event in the city of Nijmegen, The Netherlands. This is a slightly modified version of 'Explosive Remnants of War'; in Andrea De Guttry, Harry Post and Gabriella Venturini (eds.), *The Armed Conflict between Eritrea and Ethiopia*, TMC Asser Press/Cambridge University Press, 2009.

[*] Professor of International Law, University of Modena and Reggio Emilia, Italy.

K.H. Kaikobad & M. Bohlander (eds.), *International Law and Power: Perspectives on Legal Order and Justice*. Essays in Honour of Colin Warbrick, pp. 305–341.

which exist in general international law and on international humanitarian law in particular with special reference to the ERW situation in Eritrea and Ethiopia.

Part I introduces the main legal terminology on landmines, booby traps and other explosive ordnance producing ERW. Here we will employ the terminology used in the four international instruments (see below) explicitly addressing the munitions and devices that produce ERW. Part II introduces the magnitude of the problem of ERW in Eritrea and Ethiopia in general and in particular as a consequence of the Eritrean-Ethiopian armed conflict which raged between 1998 to 2000. It thereby also provides a picture of the devastating effects of the war and the presence of ERW on these poor countries. This Part also provides an initial assessment of the policies of both States insofar as is relevant to and affected by the explosives of war. As indicated above, this essay undertakes to put the subject matter of explosive remnants of war in the larger perspective of international humanitarian law. In keeping with the approach adopted by the Eritrea Ethiopia Claims Commission (also referred to as EECC and the Claims Commission) this will be done primarily by assessing the state of the relevant rules of international customary law, as at the time of the war, neither Eritrea nor Ethiopia were parties to any of the three international legal instruments then in force that explicitly regulate the kind of weaponry here examined.[1] Since the end of the war, both States have become parties to the 1997 Ottawa Convention on the Prohibition of the Use, Stockpiling, Production and Transfer of Anti-Personnel Mines and on their Destruction (hereinafter referred to as the Ottawa Convention). For Eritrea, the Convention entered into force in 2002 upon its accession in 2001. Ethiopia signed the treaty in December 1997 and ratified it in June 2005 and thus became a party thereto. The two States, however, are not parties to the following:

(a) the 1980 Protocol on Prohibitions or Restrictions on the Use of Mines, Booby-Traps and Other Devices (hereinafter referred to as the 1980 Protocol II);

(b) the 1980 Geneva Convention on Prohibitions or Restrictions on the Use of Certain Conventional Weapons which may be deemed to be Excessively Injurious or to have Indiscriminate Effects, or the Conventional Weapons Convention (hereinafter referred to as CCW);

(c) the 1996 Amended Protocol II to the 1980 CCW (hereinafter referred to as Amended Protocol II); and

(d) the 2003 Protocol on Explosive Remnants of War to the 1980 CCW (hereinafter referred to as Protocol V).

These four instruments entered into force in 1999, 1983, 1998 and 2006, respectively.

---

[1]   See EECC Partial Award-Central Front, Ethiopia's Claim 2, paragraph 18. The three instruments are those identified in paragraphs (a), (b) and (c) above.

In Part III, the analysis will focus on the application of some of the 'cardinal' principles of international humanitarian law. The use of land mines, booby traps and other explosive devices will be examined in light of the duty not to cause superfluous injury or unnecessary suffering, and the prohibition of weapons which have indiscriminate effects. This Part will be concluded with an assessment of a possible duty to locate and register. In Part IV, the discussion will move away from the *ius in bello* and focus on the *ius post bellum*. Central here is the question of responsibility with respect, *inter alia*, to the period after the cessation of hostilities and, in particular, with respect to responsibility for making the explosive remnants of war harmless. What is the responsibility of the user of landmines, etc., in particular, if the user is a State no longer controlling the area where they are located? The Ottawa Convention, now binding on both States, gives an answer to that question. It contains various rules important for the peoples of both countries in this *post bellum* period of recovery, like those dealing with international co-operation and assistance. A brief excursion into these provisions of the Ottawa Convention will end Part IV. Finally, Part V contains some conclusions and suggestions.

I. EXPLOSIVE REMNANTS OF WAR: THE BASIC LEGAL FRAMEWORK

By way of orientation and for purposes of the legal analysis that follows, some terms and basic definitions will at first be introduced. Although they may now be basic to the relevant part of modern humanitarian law, the terms and definitions taken from the 2003 Protocol V did, of course, not exist at the time of the Eritrean-Ethiopian War. 'Explosive remnants of war' was not yet the term used for the cause of continuing casualties of the war and the inaccessibility of areas years afterwards. The terms and definitions introduced here are not necessarily the best nor are they even the most adequate but they do provide some order to the complicated subject matter here to be discussed. They are also indispensable to and will facilitate the legal analysis. Article 2 (4) of the 2003 Protocol V defines explosive remnants of war as: '... unexploded ordnance and abandoned explosive ordnance.' In Article 2 (3), *abandoned** explosive ordnance is defined as:

> [E]xplosive ordnance that has not been used during an armed conflict, that has been left behind or dumped by a party to an armed conflict, and which is no longer under control of the party that left it behind or dumped it. Abandoned explosive ordnance may or may not have been primed, fused, armed or otherwise prepared for use.

---

* Emphasis added.

According to Article 2 (2) of the Protocol, 'unexploded ordnance' or UXO, means:

> [E]xplosive ordnance that has been primed, fused, armed, or otherwise prepared for use and used in an armed conflict. It may have been fired, dropped, launched or projected and should have exploded but failed to do so.

For the purposes of the Protocol 'explosive ordnance' is to mean:

> [C]onventional munitions containing explosives, with the exception of mines, booby traps and other devices as defined in Protocol II of this Convention [namely, the 1980 CCW] as amended on 3 May 1996.

While 'mines, booby traps and other devices' are excluded, they, are, of course, like explosive ordnance, 'conventional munitions containing explosives'. However, the use, location, removal, etc. of mines and these other weapons have been already regulated elsewhere. Occasionally, in the following pages ERW will also be used for mines, booby traps and other devices. Article 2 makes a 'legal' distinction between ERW and *existing*** ERW. Existing explosive remnants of war, according to Article 2 (4), are:

> unexploded ordnance and abandoned explosive ordnance that existed prior to the entry into force of this Protocol for the High Contracting Party on whose territory it exists.

Neither Ethiopia nor Eritrea is a party to Protocol V. If they were to become parties to the Protocol in the near future, a rather limited number of its provisions would apply to the ERW in their respective territories, as 'existing' ERW (see *infra*). Here we will predominantly use the modern terminology of the Protocol, with the exception of ERW itself which is used more generally to include mines, booby traps and 'other devices' as causing ERW.

1. *Mines and 'some other devices'*

Article 2 (1) of Protocol V refers to the definition provided in the 1996 Amended Protocol II to the CCW for 'mines, booby-traps and other devices'. The definition of mines in Amended Protocol II and in the 1997 Ottawa Convention is almost the same. Article 2 (2) of the latter provides

> A munition placed under, on or near the ground or other surface area and to be exploded by the presence, proximity or contact of a person or vehicle.[2]

** Ibid.

[2] In both the original 1980 treaty and in the amended version, Protocol II qualifies mines as 'designed' to be exploded, etc. This addition was considered unhelpful and was thus deleted in

An 'anti-personnel mine' is defined in almost similar terms in both Amended Protocol II and the Convention as:

> [A] mine designed to be exploded by the presence, proximity or contact of a person and that will incapacitate, injure or kill one or more persons.[3]

An 'anti-vehicle mine' is defined in the Ottawa Convention in Article 2 (1) 'as opposed' to an 'anti-personnel' mine:

> Mines designed to be detonated by the presence, proximity or contact of a vehicle as opposed to a person ...

'Booby-trap' is defined in Article 2 (4) of Amended Protocol II as:

> [A]ny device or material which is designed, constructed, or adapted to kill or injure, and which functions unexpectedly when a person disturbs or approaches an apparently harmless object or performs an apparently safe act.[4]

Finally, the residual category of 'other devices' to which reference is made in Article 2 (1) of Protocol V is defined in Amended Protocol II as

> manually-emplaced munitions and devices including improvised explosive devices designed to kill, injure or damage and which are actuated manually, by remote control or automatically after a lapse of time.[5]

As all of these 'means of warfare' have (extensively) been used in the 1998–2000 Eritrean-Ethiopian armed conflict, we will address the duties and rights which international law attaches to their use and presence.

II. THE MAGNITUDE OF THE PROBLEM OF EXPLOSIVE REMNANTS OF WAR

It appears that during the 1998–2000 Border War between Eritrea and Ethiopia tens of thousands of new mines were used. There have been allegations that more than 100, 000 mines were laid in the disputed border area. This new use multiplies what were already difficult problems with respect to the explosive remnants of war arising from the previous armed conflict between Eritrea and Ethiopia. Landmines were used extensively during the 30 years conflict from 1963 until Eritrea's independence in 1993 when Ethiopia battled with the

---

   the Oslo process leading to the conclusion of the Ottawa Convention; the original Protocol II uses the terms 'designed to be detonated or exploded'.
[3] Ottawa Convention, Article 2 (1). The definition in Article 2 (3) of Amended Protocol II differs only in that the Article uses 'primarily' designed.
[4] This definition is the same as in the original 1980 version of Protocol II.
[5] Article 2 (5) of Amended Protocol II.

EPLF, the Eritrean People's Liberation Front. So even before the war, the border regions between Eritrea and Ethiopia were already heavily mined. At the time of the 1998–2000 war neither Ethiopia nor Eritrea was a party to any of the three basic instruments which had entered into force, or were about to enter into force, although Ethiopia had signed the 1997 Ottawa Convention in 1997. Both States had voted in favour of all three Resolutions adopted by the General Assembly of the UN in 1997, 1998 and 1999 favouring a ban on anti-personnel mines. By way of abundant caution, it must be emphasised that the account below is based on information which is not necessarily complete, definite, or even completely reliable. It has been collected from different independent sources and attempts to provide an adequate picture of the situation in Eritrea and Ethiopia within considerable practical restrictions.

1. *Ethiopia*

The Ethiopian Government estimates the total number of un-cleared mines in Ethiopia to be at more than 1.4 million; the US State Department puts the number of existing mines at 500,000.[6] In a statement issued at the signing ceremony of the Ottawa Convention on 3 December 1997, the Ethiopian Government re-affirmed its commitment to the treaty and urged the international community to adhere to the articles dealing with assistance to mine clearance and mine victims.[7] The Government of Ethiopia has denied on several occasions that it used anti-personnel mines in the conflict with Eritrea (or elsewhere) after signing the Ottawa Treaty. The use of such mines by a signatory State to the Convention can be considered a violation of international law under Article 18 of the 1969 Vienna Convention on the Law of Treaties insofar as it obliges signatory States to a treaty to refrain from acts which would defeat the object and purpose of that treaty.[8]

In April 2002, Ethiopia provided the United Nations with detailed maps of mines laid by its armed forces during the Border War, presumably all anti-vehicle mines. Since 2000 there have been no reports of newly laid anti-personnel mines. Even so, there have been numerous reports of incidents regarding victims

---

[6] See 'Ethiopia Report', 2000 *Landmine Monitor Report*, at p. 3; the rather wide divergence in these numbers also indicates the notorious difficulty of estimating numbers of landmines emplaced.

[7] Statement made by Dr. Fecadu Gadarmu, Ethiopia's Ambassador to Canada, on 3 December 1997, as reported in 'Ethiopia Report', 2000 *Landmine Monitor Report*, p. 1.

[8] Ethiopia is not a Party to the 1969 Vienna Convention. However, it must be noted that by 1998 Article 18 was generally considered to reflect international customary law. See further, Part III, section 2 (1) (a) below.

of existing landmines.[9] Since 2003, several incidents concerning newly laid anti-vehicle mines have taken place in the Temporary Security Zone (TSZ) which separates Eritrea and Ethiopia (see section 2, *infra*, on Eritrea).[10] Ethiopia is required by virtue of Article 7 to submit its 'so-called' annual transparency reports, but it has not done so as yet. Under Article 5 of the Ottawa Treaty, Ethiopia must as soon as possible destroy all anti-personnel mines in areas under its jurisdiction, and by 1 June 2015 at the latest.[11]

The size of Ethiopia's stockpile of anti-personnel mines is not officially known. No steps have been reported so far indicating the implementation of the Treaty in domestic law including the imposition of penal sanctions as required under Article 9 of the Treaty. Ethiopia has declared that it does not produce anti-personnel mines, and that it has not imported such mines since the fall of the Menghistu regime in 1991. The UN reported in 2005 that the war led, in particular, to ERW in the regions bordering Eritrea, in Tigray and, to a lesser extent, in Afar. About 364,000 people were displaced as a consequence of this war.[12] De-mining in Ethiopia is largely co-ordinated and executed at the regional level, but a national mine action centre, the Ethiopian Mine Action Office (EMAO), was created in 2001 as the successor to the Ethiopian De-mining Project (EDP) operated by the Ethiopian Ministry of Defence whose work was disrupted by the war.[13] In 2005, EMAO submitted a

---

9   Much of the information on Eritrea discussed in this section and in the next is based in UN reports and in the sections on Ethiopia and Eritrea in the *Landmine Monitor Reports* of the period 1999–2007.

10 The TSZ consists of a 25 km. demilitarised buffer zone within Eritrea running along the length of the disputed border with Ethiopia, as agreed in the Algiers Agreement on Cessation of Hostilities of 18 June 2000, *vide* Article 7.

11 The first annual Ethiopian report, submitted pursuant to Article 7, was due on 28 November 2005. In April 2007, the Ethiopian Government declared that by 2010 all high priority areas would be cleared; the rest would follow before the 2015 deadline. The *Landmine Monitor Report* of 2007 estimates the likelihood of Ethiopia meeting its 2015 deadline as 'high': see 'Ethiopia Report', p. 1.

12 According to the nation-wide Landmine Impact Survey (LIS) for the whole of Ethiopia, completed in 2004, 1,492 communities, where 1. 9 million people live, have been identified as being contaminated with landmines and UXO (Unexploded Ordnance). The LIS has shortcomings though, and has not been certified: see the 2006 and 2007 *Landmine Monitor Reports* on its status and use. Apart from the Eritrea-Ethiopia War, the ERW on Ethiopian territory are the result of (a) the Italian invasion and occupation of 1935–1936; (b) the Ogaden War with Somalia (1980); and (c) the period of grave internal conflict from 1975 to 1991.

13 In 1993, Ethiopian de-mining capacity was still deemed 'extremely limited'. However, from that year onwards, the situation began considerably to change in a positive way with foreign, primarily US, aid. From 1993 up to the end of 1997, EDP is reported to have cleared 17 sq. km. of land of some 74,850 mines: 'Ethiopia Report', 1999 *Landmine Monitor Report*, p. 3. The US Department of Defence estimates that by 1999, approximately 37,000 mines and

draft strategic plan which is still awaiting finalization (February 2008).[14] Apart from some non-governmental organisations – primarily the Norwegian People's Aid (NPA) – it is the UN Development Programme (UNDP) which is assisting and channelling funds for de-mining activity to Ethiopian agencies, including funds from the European Union.[15] In 2005, more than $2.6 million were donated for mine action funding, a sum which was slightly more than the funding provided in 2004. The World Bank provided a loan of over $4.7 million for the expansion of the operational capability of EMAO. In 2006, UNDP and the EU announced that they would provide about $10 million over a period of three years specifically for mine action in the Tigray and Afar regions. International mine action funding for 2006 is reported to have been over $7.8 million, a considerable increase over 2005.[16] In 2005, the EMAO reported the clearance of 4,365, 710 square meters, of 184 anti-personnel mines, 98 anti-vehicle mines and 6,607 UXO. The figures for 2006, according to Ethiopia, were 6.66 sq. km cleared, and the destruction of 1,725 antipersonnel mines, 52 anti-vehicle mines and 35,555 items of UXO.[17] Under Article 8 of the Algiers Agreement on Cessation of Hostilities of 2000, both Eritrea and Ethiopia are obliged to de-mine the TSZ to allow UN peacekeeping forces and humanitarian agencies safe access (see section 2 *infra*).

Casualties and Survivor Assistance

No systematic data collection on landmine and UXO casualties has taken place in Ethiopia, neither are there many reliable separate figures available for the Afar and Tigray regions, the regions bordering Eritrea and the areas most likely to have suffered hugely from ERW as a result of the war.[18] It is nevertheless

---

364,000 pieces of UXO were cleared. The Ethiopian Government claimed the removal of no less than 30,375 mines in 1999 and 40,000 in 2000 in the northern conflict zones which had been occupied by Eritrea since May 1998: 'Ethiopia Report', 2000 *Land Monitor Report*, p. 4. Estimates of the latter kind seem rather unlikely when compared to more recent clearance figures: see further text below and footnote 17, *infra*.

[14] See 'Ethiopia Report', 2007 *Landmine Monitor Report*, p. 5.

[15] Several evaluations of the de-mining activities in and by Ethiopia have been undertaken and of which the outcomes were very positive: ibid. p. 5.

[16] Ethiopia received 91% of a UN portfolio appeal; no national contributions were reported in 'Ethiopia Report', 2007 *Landmine Monitor Report*, p. 2.

[17] The figures with respect to the areas cleared and the number of devices destroyed tend to differ. In 2005, UNDP reported that over 6 sq. km. were returned to civilian use in Ethiopia: 'Ethiopia Report', 2006 *Landmine Monitor Report*, p. 7. In 2006, according to UNDP, 1,692 antipersonnel mines, 55 anti-vehicle mines and 16,734 ERW were cleared.

[18] Limited information sharing between stakeholders and a lack of political will to improve the situation are mentioned as additional reasons for this unsatisfactory state of affairs: 2006

clear that ever since 2000 numerous incidents have taken, and continue to take place, owing to the presence of mines and other ERW. As a result, the number of deaths and maimed is considerable and although less than in Angola or Cambodia, it is still very serious and tragic.[19] The Landmine Impact Survey (LIS) of 2004 provided the following figures for the period 2000–2004: 16,616 landmine and UXO casualties; and 9,314 people killed and 7,275 injured. The report stated that in 2004 more than 1.9 million people lived in landmine impacted communities. According to a UN survey, out of those communities, a total of 1,492 were positively identified as contaminated with landmines and UXO.[20] A UNICEF/EMAO survey conducted in 2004 of the Tigray, Afar and Somali regions shows that in Tigray about 34% of the casualties were children and 23% were in the Afar region (while 32% were in the Somali region).[21] The Ethiopian De-mining Project and later EMAO, certain UN organisations and several NGOs have all carried out mine awareness and education programmes in Ethiopia. Since 2005, these efforts have increased in, *inter alia*, the Afar and Tigray regions with financial and technical support from UNICEF. The programmes in Tigray and Afar have now officially been handed over to the local authorities and are hence conducted at the community level.[22]

After it announced its ratification of the 1997 Ottawa Convention, Ethiopia (as well as Eritrea), was identified as one of the 24 States Parties with significant numbers of mine survivors, and with 'the greatest responsibility to act, but also the greatest needs and expectations for assistance' in providing adequate services

---

Landmine Monitor Report, p. 10. Apart form the unreliability of the technical information, it is difficult to determine whether the ERW are from one conflict or another. It is true that the Border War was the latest armed conflict; it is also true that the armed conflict, which mainly involved Tigray and Afar, was very intense and it was thus likely to have been responsible for its most explosive remnants, and in particular in Tigray; yet it is also the case that preceding conflicts have left a considerable mark on the two countries.

[19] Before the 1998–2000 war, there were already an estimated 4,200 to 4,600 amputee mine victims in Ethiopia as a whole: 'Ethiopia Report', 2000 *Landmine Monitor Report*, p. 4.

[20] See 2004 *Landmine Monitor Report*, pp. 895–896; and the UN 2004 'Country Profile: Ethiopia'. The number of casualties in 2005 were at least 31, of whom 11 were caused by exploding mines; the rest were caused by other ERW. In 2006, there were at least 34 casualties, 12 of which were caused by mines: see 'Ethiopia Report' in 2006 and 2007 *Landmine Monitor Reports*, p. 10 and p. 8, respectively.

[21] UNICEF/EMAO, 'Landmines and Unexploded Ordnance Needs Assessment Survey: Findings and Recommendations Afar, Somali and Tigray Regions', June 2004, p. 9.

[22] A March 2005 evaluation of the mine risk education in Ethiopia concluded that it was one of the world's 'more mature mine risk education [programmes]': refer to 'An Evaluation of the Mine Risk Education Program in Ethiopia', Geneva International Centre for Humanitarian De-mining (GICHD), Geneva, July 2005.

and care for the survivors.[23] As mentioned above, Ethiopia has not yet provided its transparency report under Article 7 of the Ottawa Convention, a report which could also include more information on victim assistance. Ethiopia did prepare some of its victim assistance objectives for the period 2005–2009 for the Zagreb Meeting of the Ottawa Convention State Parties in 2005.[24] In a country like Ethiopia, where health services are generally still at a basic level and then primarily near urban centres, or are outright inadequate or non-existent, this is a very substantial task. According to the Landmine Survivors Network (LSN), only 10% of mine casualties have access to basic health care and rehabilitation, 'and access to more complex post-trauma care is even lower as there are only two orthopaedic surgeons in the country'.[25] A grant of $215 million by the World Bank in 2006 aimed to improve the situation. The grant is to support local authorities to provide essential services, including health care and education.[26]

2. Eritrea

In 1998 the number of mines and other ERW present in Eritrea was (very) roughly estimated at between 500,000 and 1 million, in addition to some 3 million UXO.[27] As estimated by UNMEE, during the Border War at least 240,000 mines were added to these numbers. Eritrea acceded to the 1997 Ottawa Treaty on 27 August 2001. The Convention entered into force for Eritrea on 1 February 2002. Eritrea has submitted three transparency reports under Article 7; the first two collectively covering the period from 1 February 2002 up to 30 April 2005. The third belated report covered the successive period up to 25 December 2006. No steps have been taken as yet to enact domestic legislation to implement the Ottawa Convention as required by Article 9.

---

[23] UN, Final Report, First Review Conference of the States Parties to the 1997 Ottawa Convention, Nairobi, 2004; in APLC/CONF/2004/2005, 9 February 2005, p. 33.

[24] These objectives include: establishing a continuous surveillance system for accurate data collection and for conducting a needs assessment of survivors, making medical treatment available by informing people of the services available, and developing a strategic plan for mine victim assistance in co-operation with relevant organisations: see Final Report of the Meeting of State Parties/Zagreb Progress Report, Part II, Annex V, Zagreb, 28 November, 2 December 2005, pp. 161–164.

[25] 'Ethiopia Report', 2006 *Landmine Monitor Report*, p. 12; and for a detailed report of survivor assistance, including a survey of the activities relevant for the survivors of ERW incidents assistance by the most important NGOs present in Ethiopia, see pp. 12–16; also see ibid, 2007 *Landmine Monitor Report*, p. 8 *et seq.*

[26] World Bank Press Release: 'World Bank Group Approves Plan to Protect Basic Services, Improve Governance': Press Release of 25 May 2006.

[27] See 'Hidden Killers', US Department of State, 1998: see p. 86 for mines and p. 25 for UXO.

Eritrea is affected by mines and other remnants of war as a result primarily of its long war of independence from Ethiopia, stretching from 1963 to 1993; it is also a result of the Border War and its aftermath.[28] According to the 2004 Eritrea Landmine Impact Survey (ELIS), some 914 areas spread all over the country are regarded as being hazardous. The total area covers over 129 square kilometres. About 10% of Eritrea's 4,176 communities with a population of some 650,000 are affected by the presence of mines and UXO.[29] According to the ELIS, 33 communities were highly affected, 100 communities suffered medium impact and 348 endured low impact. Eritrea has a population of 4,401,000 (2005 estimate) and covers an area of 117,600 square km.

In its Award of 2004, the EECC stated with respect to the use of anti-personnel mines during the 1998–2000 war: 'As with other *weredas*, the evidence indicates that Eritrea made extensive use of anti-personnel landmines ....'[30] There have been no reports of newly laid antipersonnel mines since 2000. But the Mine Action Co-ordination Centre (MACC) of the UN Mission in Ethiopia and Eritrea (UNMEE) has reported that since 2003 anti-vehicle mines have been laid and have caused incidents in the Temporary Security Zone (TSZ). It is unknown who planted these mines, but planting new mines in the TSZ is clearly in violation of Article 8 of the Algiers Agreement on Cessation of Hostilities signed on 18 June 2000 by Eritrea and Ethiopia. Article 8 obliges both States to de-mine the TSZ in order to allow UN peacekeeping forces and humanitarian agencies safe access.[31] Eritrea has declared that it no longer has a stockpile of anti-personnel mines. In its Article 7 transparency reports, the Eritrean Government maintains that all of the about 450,000 mines it acquired during the 30 year war of independence against Ethiopia were subsequently laid during the Border War, except for 40,000 mines that were destroyed. MACC estimates that Eritrea had laid about 240,000 mines during the Border War.[32]

---

[28] As in Ethiopia, the Italian invasion of Eritrea in 1935–1936 left its marks on that country.

[29] Data collected from 'Eritrea's National Plan to implement Article 5 of the [1997 Ottawa] Convention', p. 1.

[30] The EECC added '[B]ut it does not demonstrate a pattern of their unlawful use. For liability, the Commission would have to conclude that landmines were used in ways that intentionally targeted civilians or were indiscriminate.' See 2004 Partial Award-Central Front, Ethiopia's Claim 2, paragraph 95: PCA website.

[31] Several reports of the UN Secretary General to the Security Council on the situation between Eritrea and Ethiopia refer to incidents with newly laid anti-tank mines, most recently S/2008/40 of 23 January 2008: at p. 7. The 'Eritrea Report' of 2005 *Landmine Monitor Report* takes note of 10 incidents in 2005: p. 4; and see p. 8 in 2006 ibid. See, further Part III, section 2, subsection 2, *infra*.

[32] See 'Eritrea Report', 2006 *Landmine Monitor Report*, p. 13, footnote 10 where it is also reported that UNMEE MACC could not confirm the figures provided by the Eritrean Government mentioned above in the main text.

The Eritrean De-mining Authority (EDA) was established in 2002 and it is responsible for policy, planning and co-ordination of mine action. EDA has instructed all international mine clearance organisations to cease operations.[33] It is not responsible for mine action in support of UNMEE or the Eritrean-Ethiopian Boundary Commission.[34] Under its authority operates Eritrean De-mining Operations (EDO) which implements national mine action. In 2005 and 2006, Eritrean teams were carrying out de-mining operations supervised by RONCO, a US commercial company, and the civilian contractor Mechem. UNMEE's MACC was established in August 2000 with a mandate to provide de-mining support to UNMEE in the TSZ. In 2005, as a result of the impounding of mine action vehicles by Eritrean Government authorities, the UN-supported mine action capacity-building programme was suspended and it was later ended upon the request of the Eritrean Government which indicated its wish for national ownership of mine action. In the course of 2005, a number of UN personnel, who advised on various forms of mine action, left the country. Even so, from November of that year, sound de-mining operations did recommence in the TSZ and adjacent areas.[35]

Eritrea has developed a national plan based on the ELIS data to implement Article 5 of the Ottawa Convention. Article 5 requires the destruction of all anti-personnel mines in all mined areas in Eritrea by 1 February 2012. The national plan does not explicitly refer to intentions to meet the 2012 deadline. A Review Conference or other meeting of Sates Parties to the Ottawa Convention may grant a time-extension under Articles 5 (3) and 12 (2).[36] According to the Eritrean National Plan submitted under Article 5 of the Ottawa Convention, Eritrea has 64,000 displaced persons living in camps. 'Strategic Objective 1' of the Plan is to permit the return of these people by the end of 2006. This would

---

[33] One of them is still operating in Eritrea: see 'Eritrea Report', 2006 *Landmine Monitor Report*, p. 3.

[34] As established under Article 5 of the 2000 Algiers Peace Agreement.

[35] Report of the UN Secretary General on Ethiopia and Eritrea, S/2006/1, 3 January 2006, paragraph 35. From September 2006 to January 2008, UNMEE cleared about 3.2 sq. km. in the TSZ (against about 0.7 sq. km. from September 2005 to September 2006); 13 landmines and 2,028 UXO were destroyed. GICHD has evaluated the UNMEE MACC de-mining activities and concluded that although there were important achievements, structural and organisational factors had prevented effective co-ordination of mine action: see 'Eritrea Report', 2006 *Landmine Monitor Report*, p. 4. The results of UNMAS evaluation conducted in May 2006 have not yet (as of January 2008) been made public.

[36] The plan refers to 129 sq. km. of contaminated land (see, *supra*, in the text) and a current clearance rate of about 3.9 sq. km., and adds: '... this will have to be increased at least three fold in order to respond to the problem in a reasonable timeframe'. See Eritrea's 'National Plan to Implement Article 5 of the Convention', p. 2. The 'Eritrea Report' in 2007 *Landmine Monitor Report* estimates the likelihood of Eritrea meeting the 2012 deadline as 'low': see p. 1.

require clearance of about 6.8 sq. km of territory and an integrated effort by Mine Risk Education and Victims Assistance. In 2006, RONCO reported the clearance of 508,661 square meters of land where 285 anti-personnel mines and 411 items of UXO were destroyed, much less than the cleared area reported in 2005 (2.2 sq. km.). For both years no full clearance results are available.

The National Plan includes a detailed budget to obtain the desired result. In 2005, $4.85 million were internationally donated, slightly less than in 2004. In 2006, international funding decreased dramatically to $657,000. In the period 2002–2006, the Eritrean Government contributed $2.3 million, mainly in salaries for EDA and EDO.[37] 'Strategic Objective 2' requires the clearance of 48 sq. km and integrated MRE and victims assistance in order to eliminate the impact of mines and UXO in a further 116 communities defined in the ELIS as 'high and medium impact communities'. This objective is to be achieved by the end of 2009, but no detailed implementation (budget) has yet been submitted.[38]

Casualties and Survivor Assistance

The ELIS presents the most comprehensive data available on landmine casualties in Eritrea. The survey identified a total of 5,385 mine casualties, including 3,152 people killed and 2,233 injured. Of these, 295 incidents happened from 2002–2004. 77 people were killed, 218 injured (only 2 casualties were military personnel). The other 5,090 casualties, of which 3,075 people were killed and another 2,015 injured, occurred before 2002.[39] Every year since 2003, the UN has reported incidents in the TSZ by anti-vehicle mines: 15 in 2003, 2 in 2004, 6 in 2005 and 6 in 2006, leading to the killing and maiming of (mainly) civilians. For 2000–2004, UNMEE MACC has provided figures of the total number of victims of mine incidents in the UNMEE mission area of the TSZ.

---

[37] International funding for Eritrea in 2006 is featured in 'Eritrea Report', 2007 *Landmine Monitor Report*, p. 2. UNMAS reports in its Portfolio End-Year review (January 2007) that Eritrea received $7,899,895, which was 122% of the funds requested through the appeal process in 2006. However, all this funding was for UNMEE and 'the Eritrean Mine Action Centre', with an estimated budget of $1,163,340. These funds came in large part from the peacekeeping assessed budget. Other Portfolio projects for Eritrea, totalling over $5.3 million, received no funding. To this, UNMAS added that continued funding for UNMEE and the MACC was 'contingent on future developments in the field, particularly the resumption of the demarcation process with related mine clearance operations'. The budget in the national plan mentions total costs for 2005 and 2006 at $8.38 million. For each year the budget envisions a national contribution of $420,000: see Eritrea's National Plan (note 36), p. 5.

[38] 'Strategic objectives 3 and 4' are listed as 'Low impact communities and MRE/marking' and 'victim assistance', respectively, but are not yet elaborated upon.

[39] See 2004 *Landmine Monitor Report*, pp. 429–430. Further, see www.mineaction.org on Eritrea and Ethiopia. The precise starting year for the Eritrea Landmine Impact Survey is not clear.

In this period, there occurred 261 mine incidents in which 114 Ethiopians and Eritreans were killed and 293 injured. In 2006, a total of 32 mine and other UXO casualties were reported: 9 people were killed and 23 injured (21 of the victims were children).[40] A 2004–2005 national survey concluded that Eritrea has about 84,000 known landmine survivors among its people with disabilities – of whom 34,000 are younger than 18 years old – 'making landmines the most important cause of physical disability in the country'.[41] With UNICEF technical and financial support, mine risk education (MRE) has been provided by EDO/EDA teams in the wider Eritrea, including schools and in the form of teacher training. During 2005, close to 100,000 people received MRE, for many the first time in 30 years. In the same year UNMEE MACC teams provided MRE to some 28,000 people in the TSZ, focusing on the most heavily affected areas. In 2005 and 2006, MACC and the EDO/EDA teams continued to co-operate and to co-ordinate their activities.

Eritrea's medical and social infrastructure cannot provide adequate services for the care, rehabilitation and re-integration of large numbers of its war victims.[42] According to the ELIS, 94 percent of all mine survivors received some form of emergency care; however, 60 percent of casualties that took place more than two years ago died as a result of the mine incident. Only three percent of survivors reported receiving rehabilitation assistance. Since 1999, the International Committee for the Red Cross (ICRC) has tried to improve medical support by providing medical supplies, equipment, medicines, etc. In November 2001, the ICRC signed a Memorandum of Understanding on a physical rehabilitation programme to address the unmet demand for services. The Eritrean Government, in co-operation with the UNDP, has tried to improve the quality of care for landmine amongst other survivors, but decades of armed conflict and the poverty of Eritrea has made progress painstakingly slow.[43] Eritrea's transparency reports submitted under Article 7 of the Ottawa Convention did not provide

---

[40] The UNMEE mission area of the TSZ covers the 25 km. border area. These UNMEE figures are from the 'Eritrea Report' of 2006 and ibid, 2007 *Landmine Monitor Reports*, p. 11 and p. 12 respectively. Data collection in Eritrea is considered rather deficient though, for which see the 2006 *Landmine Monitor Report*, p. 19, note 118.

[41] See 'Eritrea Report', 2006 *Landmine Monitor Report*, p. 9 which also says that the actual number of mine survivors is likely to be higher. The quality of landmine survivor assistance in Eritrea is of grave concern (see ibid, 2007 *Landmine Monitor Report*, p. 12 and p. 13). Further see text.

[42] Owing to the normally long distance between the location of mine incident and the relevant health centre; and the general lack of transport, nearly half of landmine casualties reportedly die before reaching a centre. The embargo placed on helicopter evacuations by the Eritrean Government from the TSZ has not helped; there have been 40 such evacuations since 2000: ibid, 2006 *Landmine Monitor Report*, p. 10.

[43] See ibid, pp. 10–12.

updated information on improvement in victim assistance. But it was reported that Eritrea links survivor assistance with its Millennium Development Goals until 2015, and it has formulated a 'Strategic Objective 4' on victim assistance as part of its National Plan to implement Article 5 of the Convention (see *supra*). The UN capacity-building programme for mine action in Eritrea includes a mandate for victim assistance claims brought either by Ethiopia or Eritrea in respect of landmines and other explosives (that turn into explosive remnants of war). The claims submitted have not been honoured by the Eritrea Ethiopia Claims Commission which did not find that the devices were used in any way which violated the relevant rules of international law (see *supra*).

III. INTERNATIONAL HUMANITARIAN LAW

In this Part the major rules in international humanitarian law on the use of landmines, booby traps and other devices will be discussed. As in the Awards of the EECC, customary international humanitarian law must be centre stage. As noted above, during the Border War, neither Eritrea nor Ethiopia was a party to any of the three core international instruments then in force, namely the CCW, 1980 Protocol II and Amended Protocol II. The EECC does not give much space in its decisions to the legal issues here at stake, although it does pay some attention to situations during the war where landmines in particular played a specific role.[44] No claims were granted on the basis of illegal use of landmines, booby traps and other explosive devices, mostly owing to a lack of evidence. However, the Claims Commission said:

> Both Parties presented numerous claims alleging improper use of anti-personnel landmines and booby traps, but there was limited discussion of the law relevant to the use of these weapons in international armed conflict.

The Claims Commission, however, cannot be accused of contributing hugely to such a discussion. It considers that the two Protocols and the Ottawa Convention

---

[44] In the EECC Partial Award on the Central Front in the context of Ethiopia's Claim 2 of 28 April 2004, the Commission discusses, *inter alia*, Eritrea's use of anti-personnel landmines but states that it lacks evidence on such matters as to whether the mines were used with reasonable precautions, for which see Klein, 'State Responsibility for International Humanitarian Law Violations and the Work of the Eritrea Ethiopia Claims Commission So Far', 47 (2004) *GYIL* 214, at p. 234. The EECC has no doubt that there is enough evidence to argue 'that Eritrea made extensive use of anti-personnel landmines, but it does not demonstrate a pattern of their unlawful use'.

have been concluded so recently and the practice of States has been so varied and episodic that it is impossible to hold that any of the resulting treaties constituted an expression of customary international humanitarian law ....[45]

Certain aspects of State practice are undoubtedly somewhat 'varied and episodic'. An attempt, nevertheless, will be made here to assess some relevant features of this practice and legal opinion in the hope perhaps of identifying some more customary rules than the Claims Commission needed for its purposes. It provides an 'opening' to that effect when the Claims Commission added to its previous statement:

> Nevertheless, there are elements in Protocol II of 1980, such as those concerning recording of mine fields and prohibition of indiscriminate use, that express customary international law.

The Commission does not say why that would be so (State practice?), but adds:

> Those rules reflect fundamental humanitarian law obligations of discrimination and protection of civilians.[46]

Thus examined below are some of the 'cardinal' principles of international humanitarian law regarding the use of mines, booby traps and other devices. The duty to locate and register the presence of these weapons in international humanitarian law will then be discussed.

1. *The Duty not to Cause Superfluous Injury or Unnecessary Suffering*

Article 35 (1) of Protocol I Additional to the 1949 Geneva Conventions provides that:

1. In any armed conflict, the right of the Parties to the conflict to choose methods or means of warfare is not unlimited.
2. It is prohibited to employ weapons, projectiles and material and methods of warfare of a nature to cause superfluous injury or unnecessary suffering.

Article 35 (2) reflects Article 23 (e) of the 1899 and 1907 Regulations which prohibit the employment of means of warfare calculated to cause unnecessary suffering. In various ways, these instruments are central to this examination. The 1980 Protocol II refers only to booby traps in this way. Article 6 (2) of this Protocol states:

---

[45] EECC Partial Award (note 44), paragraph 18.
[46] Ibid. I wholeheartedly agree with this last-mentioned view of the Commission. However, although the Commission is not an academic *corpus* which must provide lengthy arguments for its opinions, I respectfully submit that as regards to the law on the use of landmines, booby traps and other devices, the Claims Commission has perhaps been somewhat too concise.

It is prohibited in all circumstances to use any booby-trap which is designed to cause superfluous injury or unnecessary suffering.[47]

In Article 3 (3) of the amended 1996 Protocol this prohibition is extended to cover all the addressed munitions and devices: 'It is prohibited in all circumstances to use any mine, booby-trap or other device which is designed or of a nature to cause superfluous injury or unnecessary suffering.' The Ottawa Convention is most explicit in its Preamble where the States Parties declare, *inter alia*, that:

> *Basing* themselves on the principle of international humanitarian law that the right of the parties to an armed conflict is not unlimited, on the principle that prohibits the employment in armed conflicts of weapons, projectiles and materials and methods of warfare of a nature to cause superfluous injury or unnecessary suffering ...[*]

Article 3 the Statute of the International Criminal Tribunal for Yugoslavia (ICTY) stipulates:

> The International Tribunal shall have the power to prosecute persons violating the laws or customs of war. Such violations shall include, but not be limited to:
>
> (a) employment of poisonous weapons or other weapons calculated to cause unnecessary suffering ...[48]

The International Criminal Court (ICC) Statute also refers to this principle, but in a 'conditional' form.[49] According to Article 8: 'The Court shall have jurisdiction in respect of war crimes in particular when committed as part of a

---

[47] The CCW itself includes a De Martens clause in the Preamble: 'The High Contracting Parties ... [c]onfirming their determination that in cases not covered by this Convention and its annexed Protocols or by other international agreements, the civilian population and the combatants shall at all times remain under the protection and authority of the principles of international law derived from established custom, from the principles of humanity and from the dictates of public conscience ...' See also the 1977 Additional Protocol I, Article 1 (2); and, more generally, on the De Martens clause, see, for example, see Roberts and Guelff, *Documents on the Laws of War* (Third edition), Oxford, 2000, pp. 8–9.

[*] Emphasis original.

[48] This particular formulation brings up the question of the difference between the criteria of 'unnecessary suffering' and 'superfluous injury'. As the distinction is not immediately relevant for the argument presented, it will not be further discussed here. The Principle of Article 3 is included in the indictments of many ICTY cases, including *The Prosecutor v. Krstić; Kupreškić; Kunarać; and Kordic*: IT-98-33-T, 2 August 2001; IT-95-16-T, 26 February 1999; IT-96-23-T, 22 February 2001; and IT-95-14/2-T, 26 February 2001 respectively.

[49] On 1 July 2002, the 1998 Rome Statute of the International Criminal Court entered into force; 105 States are parties, and 139 have signed (correct as of October 2007). Eritrea signed the ICC Statute on 7 October 1998, but did not become a party. Ethiopia did not sign the Statute, nor has it acceded to it.

plan or policy or as part of a large-scale commission of such crimes.' According to Article 8 (2) (b) (xx) 'War crimes' means, *inter alia*, such acts as:

> Employing weapons, projectiles and material and methods of warfare which are of a nature to cause superfluous injury or unnecessary suffering or which are inherently indiscriminate in violation of the international law of armed conflict, provided that such weapons, projectiles and material and methods of warfare are the subject of a comprehensive prohibition and are included in an annex to this Statute, by an amendment in accordance with the relevant provisions set forth in articles 121 and 123. ...

This condition has not yet been brought to the test by a proposal to add such an annex to the Statute, as, for example, for anti-personnel mines. Is the principle prohibiting the causing of unnecessary suffering or superfluous injury part of customary international (humanitarian) law? There is general consensus that it is.[50] State practice provides overwhelming evidence that this was already so by 1998.[51] Some States, like Australia, Canada and Germany, link the principle to the rule of proportionality, and so does the US Government as seen in the 1976 US Air Force Pamphlet. The Canadian Code of Conduct defines it as: 'the infliction of injuries or suffering beyond what is required to achieve the military aim.'[52] Other States just stress the inhumane nature or excessive traumatic effect, or just state that the principle is a rule of customary international law.[53] The ICRC Study produced by Doswald-Beck and Henckaerts on customary international humanitarian Law provides a wide-ranging sample of national legislation punishing the use of such weapons and munitions.[54]

Are any of the munitions and devices producing ERW such means of warfare? This is a difficult question to answer. I would submit that in the end an answer to this question will involve not only law but also medical science, which, subsequently, may transform itself into a legal criterion. In treaties

---

[50] Both in international and in non-international armed conflict. See, for example, Doswald-Beck and Henckaerts, *Customary International Humanitarian Law*, vol. i: *Rules*, International Committee of the Red Cross/ Cambridge, 2005, p. 237. Hereinafter referred to as *ICRC Study, vol. i*.

[51] Most military manuals are from before 1998.

[52] Canada, *Code of Conduct*, 2001, Rule 3, paragraphs 1, 5 and 6; Australia, *Defence Force Manual*, 1994, paragraph 402; and the *Germany Military Manual*, 1992, paragraphs 401–402 and 406–407.

[53] The French *LOAC Teaching Note 2000* and the *LOAC Manual 2001* both include anti-personnel mines as examples of such weapons; the US Air Force Pamphlet, 1976, says in paragraph 6–3 (b) (1): 'This rule is a matter of customary international law.' For more examples, see Doswald-Beck and Henckaerts, *Customary International Humanitarian Law*, vol. ii: *Practice*, Part 1, International Committee of the Red Cross/ Cambridge, 2005, paragraphs 56 and 88, pp. 1513–1518. Hereinafter referred to as *ICRC Study, vol. ii*.

[54] *ICRC Study, vol. ii* (note 53), paragraphs 95 to 118, pp. 1520–1523.

and in State practice, all kind of examples of means of warfare which cause unnecessary suffering or superfluous injury are mentioned or referred to, some controversial, others less so. Those not controversial are: the use of poison or poisonous weapons (international customary law), weapons that injure by non-detectable fragments (Protocol I to the CCW) or dum-dum bullets (the 1899 Hague Declaration) and light explosive or inflammable projectiles (the 1868 Declaration of St Petersburg). Controversy is soon reached in this area: for some, even a form of analogy is out of the question as only specifically prohibited weapons are unlawful.[55] Notwithstanding such regrettable points of view, there exist many examples of weapons which, although not proscribed by way of an international treaty, are nevertheless prohibited in manuals and other similar instruments. These include, for example, the use of shotguns (since a shot causes similar suffering unjustified from the military point of view), serrated-edged bayonets, and lances with a barbed head.[56] Some munitions and devices producing ERW are also specifically mentioned in military manuals, amongst other materials, as causing unnecessary suffering or superfluous injury: these are certain kinds of booby-traps[57] and anti-personnel mines.[58] Although it is likely that express references to anti-personnel mines in particular will considerably increase now that the number of State parties to the 1997 Ottawa Convention stands in excess of 150, the fact is that mere, albeit express, State practice is

---

[55] High-velocity rifle ammunition provides an almost classic example. Insofar as such ammunition is characterised by a 'tumbling end over end on striking its target and thereby producing a large, jagged wound', it is quite similar to the dum-dum bullet. But even at the 1979–1980 UN Weapons Conference in Geneva, several participants maintained that that analogy was out of the question in general and in respect to this type of ammunition in particular: see Roberts and Guelph (note 47), p. 63. The consequences of such a rigid position are most unfortunate and unacceptable and can in my view not legally be sustained within international humanitarian law. It would, for example, make the De Martens Clause void of any legal meaning. The application of analogy of effect of weapons or of the 'cardinal' principles and criteria here discussed should of course only be employed with great prudence, but that is an entirely different matter.

[56] The prohibition on shotguns is provided in Germany's *Military Manual*: paragraph 407. Quite a number of manuals or other codes of conduct mention shotguns: see *UK Military Manual*, *US Field Manual*, *New Zealand's Military Manual*, *Military Handbook of The Netherlands*, amongst others. One of the most controversial examples is perhaps provided by nuclear weapons, and this is amply demonstrated by many statements made by States before the International Court of Justice in 1995 in the context of the two *Legality of Nuclear Weapons* cases: see *ICRC Study*, vol. ii (note 53), paragraph 310 *et seq.*, p. 1563.

[57] '... [D]esigned to cause unnecessary suffering ...': for which see *Australia Defence Force Manual* (note 52), paragraph 428; 'explosive traps, when used in the form of an apparently harmless portable object, e.g., disguised as children's toys ...': for which see Germany, *1996 IHL Manual*, paragraph 305.

[58] France *LOAC Manual 2001*, p. 54 and *LOAC Teaching Note 2000*, p. 6.

legally not sufficient for a prohibition under customary law.[59] A national or international tribunal (other than the ICC perhaps) faced with the question whether such devices would be legal in view of the rule prohibiting weapons that cause superfluous injury or unnecessary suffering may decide the issue with reference to medical science and legal analogy. Since the 1990s much more is known about the impact of landmines than was known during the cold war period from which era the relevant State practice, including military manuals and other instruments, dates. It is worthwhile citing at some length the observations of a surgeon with considerable experience in the treatment of mine casualties. He observed:

> Buried or 'point-detonating' anti-personnel mines are the only weapons in widespread use which cause specific and severe injury resulting in specific and permanent disability. The treatment of the injury requires, on average, twice as many operations and four times as many blood transfusions as an injury from other weapons.[60]

Coupland urges us not to loose sight of the nature of the injuries caused by such weapons as a basis for deeming a weapon illegal, whilst recognising at the same time that the basic argument might be that these weapons kill or injure both combatants and civilians without being able to distinguish between them. Mines belong to this category and, moreover, unless they are equipped with de-activation devices, they remain active long after the armed conflict has ended.

2. *The Prohibition of Weapons Which are Indiscriminate*

The main argument against weapons producing ERW may, indeed, be that they are by nature indiscriminate in terms of effects. The use of weapons which are by nature indiscriminate in terms of effects is prohibited under customary international law, a prohibition supported by the general prohibition, also part of customary law, of indiscriminate attacks.[61] According to Article 51 (4) of Additional Protocol I expressing this rule, indiscriminate attacks are:

---

[59]   Most military manuals and comparable instructions of States are more than 10 years old and not always regularly updated. This is one of the problems being faced in assessing the state of customary international law with respect to a rather dynamic area which ERW producing weaponry happens to be.

[60]   Coupland, 'Review of the Legality of Weapons: A New Approach The SIrUS Project', 835 (1999) *International Review of the Red Cross* 583. The SIrUS project is a multi-disciplinary project endorsed by an important sector of the international medical community attempting to bring objectivity to the legal notion of 'superfluous injury or unnecessary suffering'.

[61]   The prohibition of the use of indiscriminate weapons applies to both international and non-international armed conflict: see *ICRC Study*, *vol. i* (note 50), p. 244 *et seq*. The prohibition of indiscriminate attacks has been the subject of several ICTY decisions and judgements, as,

(a) ...

(b) those which employ a method or means of combat which cannot be directed at a specific military objective; or

(c) those which employ a method or means of combat the effects of which cannot be limited as required by this Protocol;

> And consequently, in each such case, are of a nature to strike military objectives and civilians or civilian objects without distinction.[62]

The rule prohibiting the use of indiscriminate weapons is amply expressed in State practice, in particular in military manuals and other military codes of conduct. In its Advisory Opinion in the *Nuclear Weapons* case, the International Court of Justice referred to this prohibition as one of the 'cardinal principles' of international humanitarian law.[63] As cited *supra*, the EECC also held that the prohibition of an indiscriminate use of mines in Protocol II is declaratory of customary international law. Their use could be judged a war crime, following its inclusion in Article 8 (2) (b) (xx) of the ICC Statute.[64] Violations of the rule constitute an offence under the national legislation of many States.[65]

The two defining criteria, as found in Article 51 (4) (b) and (c), are: Is a weapon capable of being targeted at a military objective;[66] and, Can the effects of the weapon be limited, as required by international law? They are both 'part of the definition of indiscriminate attacks under customary international law'.[67] Examples of weapons which States deem do not to fulfil the first criterion include 'drifting armed contact naval mines', V-1 and V-2 rockets, Scud missiles and Katyusha rockets.[68] Many weapons can be used indiscriminately. In that

---

for example, the *Tadić (Interlocutory Appeal)*: IT-94-1-AR72, 2 October 1995; *Kordić and Čerkez (Decision on a Joint Defence Motion)* cases: IT-95-14/2-PT, 2 March 1999; and the judgement in the *Kupreškić* case: *supra* (note 48).

[62] The item 'Employing weapons, projectiles and material and methods of warfare ... which are inherently indiscriminate in violation of the international law of armed conflict ...' is listed in Article 8 (2) (b) (xx) of the 1998 ICC Statute as a war crime in respect of which the Court has jurisdiction, provided that such weapons are the subject of a comprehensive prohibition and are – unfortunately – included in an annex to the Statute.

[63] *Legality of the Threat or Use of Nuclear Weapons* advisory opinion, *ICJ Reports 1996*, p. 226, at p. 257, paragraph 78.

[64] *ICRC Study*, vol. ii (note 53), paragraph 408 ff., p. 1583 *et seq.*; and see with respect to the ICC Statute, *supra*, note 58.

[65] See the survey of State practice provided in *ICRC Study*, vol. ii (note 53), paragraph 170, p. 271 *et seq.*

[66] This is the only criterion Judge Rosalyn Higgins uses in her Dissenting Opinion in the *Nuclear Weapons* advisory opinion, *supra* (note 63), p. 588, paragraph 24.

[67] *ICRC Study*, vol. i (note 50), p. 247: as defined in Rule 12 of customary international humanitarian law, ibid, p. 40.

[68] Ibid, p. 250. The ICJ in the *Nuclear Weapons* advisory opinion was persuaded by arguments

sense the legality of the use of weapons depends also upon the manner in which they are employed.[69] But some are (virtually) incapable of being directed at military objectives only (see the examples just given).

For the kind of weapons and munitions which are the subject of this essay, the second criterion, that is whether the effects of the weapon can be limited, is of the greatest relevance. This criterion is largely the factor motivating the prohibition of some of these weapons in the 1980 Protocol II and the 1996 Amended Protocol II, and of anti-personnel mines altogether in the Ottawa Convention.[70]

a. Anti-Personnel Mines

Both Eritrea and Ethiopia are parties to the Ottawa Convention since 2001 and 2005 respectively. Neither State is a party to the two versions of Protocol II, nor to the new CCW Protocol V on Explosive Remnants of War. With the exception of the legal effect of Ethiopia's status as a signatory to the Ottawa Convention (see *infra*, this sub-section), these instruments did not directly impose obligations on either State in the period before 2001. At any rate, the first three of these treaties are highly relevant in order to assess the state of customary international humanitarian law with respect to the weapons and munitions here discussed.

The 1980 Protocol II imposes no restrictions specifically for anti-personnel mines; it stipulates only limited general restrictions on the use of mines that are not remotely delivered.[71] The restrictions on certain kinds of booby traps (see

---

presented by the UK and the US that modern nuclear weapons are capable of precise targeting against specific military objectives without indiscriminate effects on the civilian population: see *ICRC Study*, vol. ii (note 53), paragraphs 358, p. 1573; and paragraph 364, p. 1574; there is no assessment of the second criterion in this respect (see also, for example Judge Higgins' Dissenting Opinion, paragraphs 23 and 24, or, for example Meron, *The Humanization of International Law*, Leiden, 2006, pp. 83–84); cf. the ICRC's scrutiny on the Nuclear Weapons advisory opinion: *ICRC Study*, vol. ii (note 53), paragraph 400.

[69] Attributed to Hans Blix, this observation was utilised by the Russian Federation in its written statement in the *Nuclear Weapons* advisory opinion, 19 June 1995: see *ICRC Study*, vol. ii (note 53), paragraph 344, p. 1570.

[70] It is remarkable that this second criterion is not even mentioned in later texts on mines, as, for example, in Article 5 (6) defining 'indiscriminate use of MOTAPM', in the most recent US draft text for a new Protocol on anti-vehicle mines: see 'Set of provisions on the use of MOTAPM', and, in particular, Article 5 (6) of the text which is available at: http://www.ccwtreaty.com/usdanishproposal.html. MOTAPM stands for 'Mines Other than Anti-Personnel Mines'.

[71] Article 4 (2) applies to mines as well as to booby-traps and other devices. It is prohibited to use such weapons '... in any city, town, village or other area containing a similar [*sic*] concentration of civilians in which combat between ground forces is not taking place or does not appear imminent, unless either they are (a) placed on or in the close vicinity of a military objective

infra) and remotely delivered mines – thus here including anti-personnel mines – laid down in Article 5 are more detailed. The use of remotely delivered mines is prohibited unless such mines are only used within an area 'which is itself a military objective or which contains military objectives (Article 5 (1))...'. Furthermore, according to Article 5 (1) (a), the location of such mines should either be accurately recorded, or in the absence of such a record, an effective neutralising mechanism must be used, as further detailed in Article 5 (1) (b).

According to Article 6 (2) of the Amended Protocol II, remotely-delivered anti-personnel mines which are not in compliance with the self-destruction and self-deactivation standard set in its Technical Annex, are prohibited. Furthermore, the use of *all* remotely delivered mines is prohibited under Article 6 (1) unless such mines are recorded according to the standard set in the Technical Annex. Article 4 of Amended Protocol II prohibits the use of anti-personnel mines which are not detectable according to a specification stipulated in the Technical Annex. Article 5 of the Amended Protocol severely restricts the use of anti-personnel mines which are not of the 'Article 4 kind' and which are not remotely delivered: they are only to be used in strictly perimeter-marked areas under Article 5 (2) (b). These rather complicated provisions of Amended Protocol II in respect of anti-personnel mines[72] have now become largely irrelevant as almost all State Parties to Amended Protocol II – and quite a number more – have become parties to the Ottawa Convention of which Article 1 states:

1. Each State Party undertakes never under any circumstances:
   (a) To use anti-personnel mines;
   (b) To develop, produce, otherwise acquire, stockpile, retain or transfer to anyone, directly or indirectly, anti-personnel mines;
   (c) To assist, encourage or induce, in any way, anyone to engage in any activity prohibited to a State Party under this Convention.[73]

Ethiopia was a signatory to the Ottawa Convention during the war with Eritrea. Article 18 of the 1969 Vienna Convention on the Law of Treaties states that in such a situation '[a] State is obliged to refrain from acts which would defeat the

---

...; or (b) measures are taken to protect civilians ...' This is followed by some examples, like warning signs and fences. Probably due to the incomplete repetition of the text of Article 51 (5) (a) of the 1977 Additional Protocol, this formulation is rather odd, if not incorrect.

[72] Kalshoven and Zegveld, *Constraints on the Waging of War*, International Committee of the Red Cross, Geneva (Third edition), 2001, p. 166.

[73] Notable exceptions are the United States, China and the Russian Federation. However, the US Government has declared that it did not ratify only because of its treaty obligations to Korea, but that it fully supports the Convention. From 2010 onwards, the US position with respect to Korea is expected to change. See 'New US Policy on Landmines' at: http://www.ccwtreaty.com/022704landmines.htm.

object and purpose of a treaty ...' Had Ethiopia planted anti-personnel mines during the war that would have constituted an act defeating the object and purpose of the Ottawa Convention. By doing so, it would also have violated a well-established customary rule of international law.[74] Ethiopia has denied having used anti-personnel mines (see *supra*). The relevant decisions of the Eritrea-Ethiopia Claims Commission do not provide other information.

With respect to all States whether bound or otherwise by the Ottawa Convention, the following can be argued. Without effective neutralising and self-destructive mechanisms, no mine passes the 'indiscriminate weapon' test (criterion 2). Therefore, and this also applies to States not parties to Protocol II (old or new), the use of mines, whether remotely or otherwise delivered, without self-deactivation and self-destruction mechanisms is in violation of international humanitarian law, an act in principle constituting a war crime. Such an act would also violate what has been formulated in broader and more careful terms in Rule 81 in the ICRC Study, on customary international humanitarian law, a rule convincingly based on State practice: 'When landmines are used, particular care must be taken to minimise their indiscriminate effects.'

This rule, the Study argues, applies to the use of both anti-vehicle and anti-personnel mines. The authors do not argue that the use of anti-personnel mines is totally prohibited under customary international humanitarian law.[75] They do say: 'All the practice cited above appears to indicate that an obligation to eliminate anti-personnel landmines is emerging.'[76] I agree with the ICRC Study as far as its assessment of State practice at the end of last century is concerned. However, I submit that at least for the period 1998–2000 and thereafter, the use of anti-personnel mines was already prohibited under the indiscriminate weapons prohibition, notably according to criterion 2 (see *supra*).[77] The few important States, which at that time (and later) maintained that they were entitled to use anti- personnel mines, were at best in the (temporary) position of being 'persistent objectors' to this rule of customary law.[78] By the beginning

---

[74] Ethiopia is not a party to the Vienna Convention on the Law of Treaties. However, the rule embodied in Article 18 is generally considered a rule of customary international law, and was so by the second half of the 1990s.

[75] *ICRC Study*, vol. i (note 50), pp. 280–282. The study was published in 2005 and covers practice until 2003.

[76] Ibid, at p. 283.

[77] The only, somewhat curious, exception with respect to anti-personnel mines before 1998 is concerned with mines which although remotely delivered, conform fully to the standards set in the Technical Annex to the 1996 Amended Protocol II referred to in Article 6 (1) and (2). To my knowledge, such anti-personnel mines were not (or were very rarely) used in the Eritrea-Ethiopia conflict.

[78] See on the 'persistent objector' in the formation of international customary law, Charney,

of 2008, State practice confirming the rule, including the increasing number of States parties to the Ottawa Convention – 155 in addition to another 15 since 2003 – has multiplied.

b. Anti-Vehicle Mines and Booby Traps

With respect to anti-vehicle mines and the use of booby-traps, the legal situation is different. As we saw above, the regulation of the use of anti-vehicle mines is still rather limited, notwithstanding the very significant numbers of civilian casualties they cause, including those in the Eritrean-Ethiopian theatre of conflict. Remotely delivered mines other than anti-personnel mines are prohibited under Article 6 of Amended Protocol II unless they are recorded in keeping with the standards provided in the Technical Annex. The same Annex contains detailed provisions on self-destruction and self-deactivation mechanisms for such mines, as referred to in Article 6 (3). If such mines are not equipped with these mechanisms 'to the extent feasible', they are prohibited. These conditions are cumulative in Amended Protocol II, as opposed to being alternative conditions, as they are in the old Protocol II.

In view of the general awareness of the huge numbers of victims caused by the continuous use of these (often very powerful) mines, attempts have been made to improve the regulation of their use. In particular, the United States has been quite instrumental here. In 2002, a draft for a new CCW Protocol on anti-vehicle mines was tabled by the United States, very much following and explicitly referring to Amended Protocol II. So far, these efforts have not led to much success.[79] In 2006, during the Third CCW Review Conference renewed efforts led to the circulation of a rather modified version of the 2000 Draft Protocol, the so-called MOTAPM proposal.[80]

'The Persistent Objector Rule and the Development of Customary International Law', 56 (1985) *BYIL* 1; and Brownlie, *Principles of Public International Law* (Sixth edition), 2003, Oxford, p. 11. The concept has its jurisprudential origins in the ICJ judgement in the *Anglo-Norwegian Fisheries* case: *ICJ Reports 1951*, p. 131. Also most of the objecting States, in particular the United States, have taken a position in favour of a total ban on anti-personnel mines.

[79] For this original '30 parties proposal', see http://www.ccwtreaty.com/usdanishproposal.html. A reason for the lack of success of the Draft is perhaps that efforts were overtaken by successive attempts to regulate the use of 'cluster bombs', which also produce UXO. The enthusiasm to regulate the use of anti-vehicle mines seems markedly greater in the developed than in the developing world.

[80] The text of the US-proposed draft was circulated at the Third CCW Review Conference of 2006. An approach based in formulating key provisions on detectability and an effective neutralising mechanism, perhaps notably by limiting the active life of anti-vehicle mines, seems to be at the core of a future instrument in the form of another CCW Protocol. For the text submitted in September 2006 see ibid.

In view of Rule 81 of the ICRC Study referred to above, together with the prohibition on the use of indiscriminate weapons according to criterion 2 of its meaning (as expressed in Article 51 (4) (c) of the 1977 Additional Protocol I), the use of anti-vehicle mines without adequate self-deactivation and self-destruction mechanisms is already prohibited under international customary law, at least since the end of the last century. The use of such mines in the Eritrea-Ethiopia war and their continued emplacement afterwards (see *supra*) would constitute war crimes. UNMEE has reported that since 2003, new anti-vehicle mines have been laid and have caused incidents in the Temporary Security Zone (TSZ) as was referred to above. If these new mines do not have had adequate self-deactivation and destruction mechanisms, then planting them would be in violation of international humanitarian law. Emplacing new mines in the TSZ is anyway a clear violation of Article 8 of the Algiers Agreement on Cessation of Hostilities concluded by Eritrea and Ethiopia. Article 8 obliges both States to de-mine the TSZ in order to allow UN peacekeeping forces and humanitarian agencies safe access. So far, it is unknown who is responsible for the emplacement of these anti-vehicle mines.

Article 6 (1) of the 1980 Protocol prohibits specific booby-traps, in addition, generally, to booby-traps designed to cause superfluous injury or unnecessary suffering. The latter prohibition is broadened in Article 3 (3) of Amended Protocol II to 'any mine, booby-trap or other device' capable of causing such injury or suffering (as was noticed *supra* in Part III, section 1). The ICRC Study has formulated a rule of customary law (Rule 80) expressing the reasoning behind the list of booby-traps prohibited in Amended Protocol II and the old Protocol II:

> The use of booby-traps which are in any way attached to or associated with objects or persons entitled to special protection under international humanitarian law or with objects that are likely to attract civilians is prohibited.

Prohibitions to this extent are also found in many military manuals and the like, including those used by States not parties to either Protocol.[81] In addition to this, Rule 81 (see *supra*) is not less applicable to landmines as it is to booby traps. The limitations set on the use of booby traps in Amended Protocol II, particularly Article 3, paragraphs 5, 7, 8 and 11, and Article 7, reinforce such a rule.[82] The use of such booby traps constitutes a war crime under international humanitarian law. In view of the broad support in manuals and its intimate

---

[81] See *ICRC Study, vol. i* (note 50), p. 279.

[82] Ibid. Amended Protocol II is in force for 87 States, including China, France, the UK, the USA and the Russian Federation. The real question to ask is whether booby traps may actually be used in a way which conforms to Rule 81. My answer would tend to be in the negative.

link to the principle prohibiting the indiscriminate use of weapons, it appears highly probable that it was applicable by the end of the 1990s. There is a lack of evidence regarding their use by Eritrea or Ethiopia.

3. The Duty to Locate and Register

With respect to landmines, a duty to record their placement can be considered to be part of customary international law, a view not inconsistent with that of the EECC, as seen above. The 1980 Protocol (in Article 7), the Amended Protocol II (in Article 9 and the Technical Annex)[83] as well as Protocol V to the CCW (Article 4 on 'explosive ordnance and their abandonment'), all contain detailed provisions on this obligation. Article 5 (2) of the Ottawa Convention requires all Parties to make an effort to identify all areas under their jurisdiction or control in which the presence of anti-personnel mines is known or suspected. They are obliged to ensure that such areas are perimeter-marked, monitored and fenced in, to ensure the effective exclusion of civilians. The marking standards are those of Amended Protocol II. Rule 82 of the ICRC Study carefully formulates a duty under customary law. Here both booby traps and explosive ordnance are included in the same duty. Rule 82 provides:

> A party to the conflict using landmines, booby-traps and explosive ordnance must record their placement, as far as possible.

The ICRC Study argues that for landmines, Rule 82 is part of customary international law, at least valid for international armed conflict, properly expressing State practice. The most detailed duties to this extent for both landmines and booby traps are to be found in Article 9 of Amended Protocol II and in its Technical Annex. Article 9 (1) includes the duty to record 'other devices' (besides minefields, mines and booby traps):

> All information concerning minefields, mined areas, mines, booby-traps and other devices shall be recorded in accordance with the provisions of the Technical Annex.

IV. *IUS IN BELLO* AND *IUS POST BELLUM*

Whereas the (potential) rules of customary international law so far discussed typically apply *in bello*, the duty to remove and destroy and the duty to assist in

---

[83] According to Article 5 (4) of the Protocol, Parties who gain control of an area with mines or other devices, its forces '... shall, to the maximum extent feasible, maintain and, if necessary establish the protections required ... until such weapons have been cleared'.

that process are primarily *post bellum* duties, or if one wishes, duties in principle covered by rules of general international law. The four instruments discussed here, have a different character. In the Ottawa Convention, the *ius post bellum* for all practical purposes prevails. Although the Preamble of the Convention welcomes the CCW and in particular the 1996 Amended Protocol II, and bases itself on some of the core principles of international humanitarian law, the main part of the Convention focuses on disarmament; on the suffering of civilians in the *post bellum* situation; and on ways of addressing and preventing civilian casualties. The history of the Ottawa Convention is marked by attempts from the early 1990s on imposing limitations on the traffic and trade in anti-personnel mines and agreements on restrictions on their use.[84]

The Convention on Certain Conventional Weapons is a framework treaty with general provisions only. The substantive law in respect of specific weapons or weapons systems is addressed in and is the object of the Protocols annexed to the Convention. Its most important purpose may be defined as one which imposes a ban on or restricts the use of specific types of weapons that are considered to cause unnecessary or unjustifiable suffering to combatants or to affect civilians indiscriminately. In this sense, the Convention, although a UN treaty, is clearly within the realm of the Geneva instruments of humanitarian law. However, the Preamble also demonstrates that the Convention is to play an important role with respect to disarmament,[85] and that nothing prevents the extension of its reach even further, namely, beyond the *ius in bello* to the *ius post bellum*, all depending on the substance of its Protocols. And that is what has happened.

The 1980 Protocol to the CCW, one of its original three protocols, is virtually completely an instrument of international humanitarian law. Only the prohibition of certain kinds of booby traps in Article 6 can be said to belong to the realm of disarmament law, while Article 9 refers to the period following the cessation of active hostilities by putting forward some (very limited) duties for the *post bellum* period. Further, Article 8, which deals with the protection of UN forces and missions from the effects of mines and the like, seems primarily of a *post ius bellum* character.[86] Amended Protocol II extends the disarmament

---

[84] See Roberts and Guelff (note 47), p. 645. In their introduction to international humanitarian law, Kalshoven and Zegveld only briefly refer to the Ottawa Convention because it is 'essentially an inter-state disarmament instrument'. See *supra* (note 72), p. 168.

[85] See Kalshoven and Zegveld (note 72), pp. 156–157 on the nature of the Convention.

[86] Although it is left open as to whether or not the situation in which they operate is characterised by a cessation of hostilities. This, in particular, may not necessarily be the case in the matter of UN fact-finding missions (Article 8 (2)). A cessation of hostilities will, normally speaking, be in place before peacekeeping, observation or similar missions (Article 8 (1)) are sent to the field.

aspect with respect to certain booby traps and mines. But what is most striking is that the provisions applying to the *post bellum* situation have been extended very considerably: Articles 10, 11 and 12, as well as Article 9 (2) on making available records of mines and other devices after the cessation of hostilities, are all part of the *ius post bellum*.

The most remarkable instrument in this respect is the 2003 Protocol V on Explosive Remnants of War. This Protocol deals almost exclusively with 'post-conflict humanitarian problems'.[87] In Article 1 (1), the High Contracting Parties agree to comply with the obligations in the Protocol, '[i]n conformity with the Charter of the United Nations and of the rules of the international law of armed conflict applicable to them …' Only Article 4 (1) of the Protocol, which provides a duty to record, is obviously also applicable during armed conflict (see also Part III, section 3 *supra*).[88]

In terms of the law, it seems sensible to divide the *ius in bello* and the *ius post bellum*, at least as far as the actual use of ordnance and mines and other devices and the resulting ERW, are concerned. The *ius post bellum* is here just part of the 'ordinary' international law in peacetime, albeit a somewhat special part thereof, its major characteristic being the fact that international humanitarian law will still apply in a situation which is otherwise covered by the rules of general international law.[89]

---

[87] This is stressed in its (short) Preamble. Protocol V is the only Protocol to the CCW with its own Preamble.

[88] Article 5 deals with other precautions for the protection of the civilian population from the risks and effects of ERW, and Article 6 with the protection of humanitarian missions and organisations from the effects of ERW. Both provisions are applicable to the situation '*in bello*'.

[89] The scope of this paper does not allow a more profound discussion dealing with the extent humanitarian law still applies in a post-conflict situation; or what constitutes the nature of this 'third' *bellum* category, that is of *ius post bellum* (besides *ius in bello* and *ius ad bellum*) for which see, for example Stahn's challenging suggestions in 'Jus ad bellum, 'jus in bello' … 'jus post bellum'? – Rethinking the Conception of the Law of Armed Force', in 18 (2007) *EJIL* 921. The subject of the distinguishing lines between *ius post bellum* and *ius in bello* and, consequently, of the applicable law in the period following armed conflict certainly deserves examination in depth. The legal consequences of its outcome may have great practical and legal relevance as, for example, by clarifying issues such as the applicability of human rights law *versus* (or in conjunction with) humanitarian law in the post-conflict situation, or responsibility for the 'remnants' of war in a wider sense than ERW. I do not believe that the extension of humanitarian law instruments into the post-conflict setting is necessarily always a positive development, as some authors seem to think: see, for example Maresca, 'A New Protocol on Explosive Remnants of War: The History and Negotiation of Protocol V to the 1980 Convention on Certain Conventional Weapons', 86 (No. 856, 2004) *International Review of the Red Cross* 833.

1. Responsibility and the Duty to Remove and Destroy

Protocol V provides clarity on the issue of responsibility with respect to ERW. In this respect, the question of who placed the mines is secondary although not entirely unimportant. Article 3 (1) says:

> Each High Contracting Party and Party to an armed conflict shall bear the responsibilities set out in this Article with respect to all explosive remnants of war in territory under its control.

With respect to the Party who has placed the explosive ordnance, which thereafter becomes ERW, but who does not exercise control of the territory, that user shall, after the cessation of active hostilities:

> ... provide, where feasible, inter alia technical, financial, material or human resources assistance, bilaterally or through a mutually agreed third party, including inter alia through the United Nations system or other relevant organisations, to facilitate the marking and clearance, removal or destruction of such explosive remnants of war.

This division of responsibilities with respect to the alleviation of such large scale, long-term suffering produced by ERW, although perhaps rather unfair, corresponds, more or less, with a situation which is practically suitable. Under international law there does not, as yet, exist any responsibility or liability for States or companies who have made or delivered the devices. States which have fought an armed conflict on a territory no longer under their control, as for example the United Kingdom, Germany or Italy, have a long history of refusing to assume (legal) responsibility for ERW left in territories not, or no longer, under their control. For purposes of the Ottawa Convention, an approach comparable with this has been agreed. Thus, 'responsibility lies with the territorial' State alone. The latter party is responsible for the destruction of its own stockpiled anti-personnel mines; and, according to Article 5 (1), it is also obliged

> ... to destroy or ensure the destruction of all anti-personnel mines in mined areas under its jurisdiction or control, as soon as possible [etc.] ...

In Article 6 on 'International Co-operation and Assistance' and elsewhere in the Convention, States which have emplaced or have provided mines and other devices but which are no longer in control of the territory where they did so place or provide such mines, will have no special duties.

The Ottawa Convention and Protocol V in this respect seemingly depart from the approach chosen in Article 3 (2) of Amended Protocol II which says:

> Each High Contracting Party or party to a conflict is, in accordance with the provisions of this Protocol, responsible for all mines, booby traps, and other

devices employed by it and undertakes to clear, remove, destroy or maintain them as specified in Article 10 of this Protocol.

However, Article 10 has formulated this responsibility as follows. Paragraph 1 stipulates that upon the cessation of hostilities, all minefields, mined areas, etc., shall be cleared. The States which control the territories in which these devices are present bear the responsibility to undertake this action: see Article 10 (2). With respect to the responsibility of 'non-territorial' States, Article 10 (3) says:

> With respect to minefields, mined areas, mines, booby-traps and other devices laid by a party in areas over which it no longer exercises control, such party shall provide to the party in control of the area pursuant to paragraph 2 of this Article, to the extent permitted by such party, technical and material assistance necessary to fulfil such responsibility.

Hence, Amended Protocol II stipulates a rather limited 'secondary' responsibility only for the State which has employed the weapons but has no territorial control. Generally speaking, this responsibility is not different from the responsibility of such States for ERW under Article 3 of Protocol V.[90] The ICRC Study found that until the 1990s '... there was little practice indicating a requirement that those laying mines have to remove them, and generally speaking the expectation was that it was up to the State with mines on its territory to decide what to do'.[91] The following rule formulated by the ICRC Study, namely Rule 83, as an expression of customary law, is provided below:

> At the end of active hostilities, a party to the conflict which has used landmines must remove or otherwise render them harmless to civilians, or facilitate their removal.

The evidence presented is of a rather general nature and it is not very convincing as regards proving that Rule 83 constitutes customary international law. In light of the approach chosen in the international instruments here examined such a rule in this form does not seem to be in the process of emerging as customary law either.[92] The following proposition seems to be a more adequate expression of the rule in the light of the available State practice and legal opinions:

> At the end of active hostilities, a party to a conflict must remove mines, booby traps or other devices from areas under its control or otherwise render them harmless to civilians, or facilitate their removal.

---

[90] Perhaps not so surprisingly in view of the rather limited scope and application of Article 9 which deals with international co-operation in the removal of minefields, mines and booby-traps; Protocol II of 1980 does not address issues of responsibility.

[91] *ICRC Study, vol. i* (note 50), p. 286.

[92] See *ICRC Study, vol. ii* (note 53), paragraphs 360–381, pp. 190–107.

As seen above, a number of provisions in international instruments provide more specific rules in this regard, including the duty of prompt clearance of minefields referred to in Article 10 (1) of Amended Protocol II. The Ottawa Convention does not relate to the end of hostilities but, as discussed above, Article 5 (1) provides:

> Each State party undertakes to destroy or ensure the destruction of all anti-personnel mines in mines areas under its jurisdiction or control, as soon as possible but not later than ten years after the entry into force of this Convention for that State Party.

The Convention does provide the possibility of an extension of this time limit (as we saw in Part II, section 2 *supra*), and contains further rules on how precisely a State is supposed to fulfil its duty specified in Article 5, as well as the duty to destroy its stock-piled anti-personnel mines under Article 4. Article 3 (3) of Protocol V stipulates more detailed measures which the High Contracting Parties are required to undertake in order to set priorities among the areas to be cleared. As soon as feasible after the cessation of hostilities they shall:

(a) survey and assess the threat posed by ERW;
(b) assess and prioritise needs and practicability in terms of marking and clearance, removal or destruction;
(c) mark and clear, remove or destroy ERW;
(d) take steps to mobilise resources to carry out these activities.

Article 3 (4) adds: 'In conducting the above activities High Contracting Parties and parties to an armed conflict shall take into account international standards, including the International Mine Action Standards'.

2. The Duty to Assist to Make Harmless

Article 4 (2) of Protocol V provides what is one of the most important and also often one of the more difficult duties to execute, namely, to make available to the party currently in control of an area the information on used or abandoned explosive ordnance which may have become or will become explosive remnants of war. In situations where tensions have not yet completely been subsided, as in the Eritrean-Ethiopian conflict, security interests are particularly likely to come in the way of this duty. Article 4 (2) recognises 'legitimate' security interests as a valid exception.

According to the second part of paragraph 2 of Article 9 of Amended Protocol II, after the cessation of hostilities, information records of the location of mines, booby traps and other devices shall be made available to the other party or parties to the conflict and to the UN Secretary-General, subject to reciprocity. Only in cases where the armed forces of one party are still in the territory of the other can such information be withheld for reasons of security.

Article 10 (3) of Amended Protocol II does not contain a (legitimate) security interest exception. It simply requires a party with respect to areas which it no longer controls 'to provide to the party in control of the area … to the extent permitted by such party, technical and material assistance …' in order that it is able to fulfil its responsibility to clear, remove or destroy the devices present. In the original unamended Protocol II, Article 7 (3) (c), provided more generally that the parties, immediately after the cessation of active hostilities, shall 'whenever possible, by mutual agreement, provide for the release of information concerning the location of mine-fields, mines [etc.] particularly in agreements governing the cessation of hostilities'. And more directly: in cases where the forces of neither party are in the territory of the adverse party, the parties shall make available to each other and to the Secretary-General of the UN all information in their possession concerning the location of minefields. There is no security exception but the more general Article 7 (3) (c) offers ample opportunity for a party to make use of such an exception.

In April 2002, Ethiopia provided the United Nations with detailed maps of mines laid by its forces during the Border War; whereas Eritrea provided information by way of its transparency reports under Article 7 of the Ottawa Convention (see *infra*). However, there is no information on the nature and quality of the reports submitted by Eritrea to the United Nations. The Ottawa Convention does not include a security exception legitimising refusal to co-operate in its extensive and detailed Article 6 on co-operation and assistance. However, the specific provisions within Article 6 are still of such a nature that a State party can refuse to provide assistance.[93] The Convention is different in nature than the other instruments, in particular it is less directly related to armed conflict and more oriented to the *post bellum* situation (as argued *supra).*

What can Eritrea and Ethiopia expect in terms of assistance and co-operation, in the first place with respect to anti-personnel mines under the Ottawa Convention to which they are both Parties? As was mentioned in Part II, section 2, *supra*, the States parties to the Ottawa Convention have identified both Ethiopia and Eritrea, as being among the 24 States parties with significant numbers of mine survivors, and with 'the greatest responsibility to act, but also the greatest needs and expectations for assistance'.[94] An important if not essential contribution on the part of the Eritrean and Ethiopian authorities, is the transparency measures requirement which they are stipulated to carry out under Article 7.

---

[93] Paragraphs 3, 4 and 5 of Article 6 address 'Each State Party in a position to do so'.
[94] See footnote 23, *supra.*

Paragraph 1 of this article includes reporting 'to the extent possible' on 'the location of all mined areas that contain, or are suspected to contain, anti-personnel mines under its jurisdiction or control'; they are required to give as much detail as possible on their types, quantity, and the like. Article 7 (1) also requires insight in the measures taken to give immediate and effective warning to the population regarding the locations identified. Submitting these reports to the Secretary General of the United Nations is essential for progress with the massive clearing operations involved. Since 2002, Eritrea has submitted a transparency report and two required annual updates; Ethiopia, a party since 2005, has not yet sent its transparency report (see, *supra*, Part II, section 2). The pace of either State in light of the problems faced has so far perhaps not been overwhelming but co-operation has not been absent either.[95] Still this type of information is obviously essential for fulfilling part of the basic obligations under the Convention: the destruction of all anti-personnel mines under its jurisdiction. States have ten years to carry out the obligation to destroy all the mines under their jurisdiction or control (Article 5 (1)); and they have four years for the destruction of stock-piled anti-personnel mines (Article 4).[96]

Article 6 provides a set of requirements and opportunities for assistance by States Parties. Both Eritrea and Ethiopia are obliged, for example, to participate fully in the exchange of mine clearance equipment and relevant scientific and technological information and States in a position to participate shall assist them in mine clearance and related activities (Article 6 (2) and 3). According to Article 6 (3), State parties are also (strongly) encouraged to provide assistance, either bilaterally or internationally with respect to care and rehabilitation, and the social and economic rehabilitation of mine victims, etc. State Parties (and, as we have seen, both States have done so) may request assistance in the elaboration of national de-mining programmes. The forms of assistance are further elaborated in Article 6 (7) (a) to (f). With the help of some of the assistance envisaged in Article 6 (7), both Eritrea and Ethiopia have adopted such national plans, but Ethiopia's plan awaits finalisation.

Article 9 requires each State party to adapt its domestic legislation (including the imposition of penal sanctions) to prevent and suppress activity prohibited under the Convention. Article 9 does not stipulate a time limit here. Neither Eritrea nor Ethiopia has been reported as having taken or having been prepared

---

[95] Article 7 (1) states clearly that '[e]ach State Party shall report ... as soon as practicable, and in any event not later than 180 days after the entry into force of this Convention for that State Party ...'

[96] Eritrea has reported that it has no stockpiled anti-personnel mines left; there is, as yet, no official documentation available on Ethiopia's stockpiled anti-personnel mines (see Part II, sections 2 and 1 respectively *supra*).

for such measures, as of October 2007. Adhering to the requirements of the Ottawa Convention has not been without its failures and, what is more, in the case of Eritrea, it has been accompanied by considerable tension and problems. Yet, both States have generally been (very) co-operative. In that sense, they have legitimate expectations of assistance. They are certainly in need of it.

The Ottawa Convention covers only part of the problem, namely the legal aspects of the problem. Similarly, Protocol V, and to a lesser extent Amended Protocol II, address more specifically ERW problems caused by mines other than anti-personnel mines, booby traps and other devices. It would be advisable if Eritrea and Ethiopia were also to become parties to those instruments in order to be able to make full use as soon as possible of the provisions on material and financial assistance with the clearance and removal of ERW.

v. Conclusion

The discussion in these pages on the explosive remnants of war from an international legal perspective consisted of two rather different but related parts. In the main Part, that is Part III, the use of landmines, booby traps and other devices producing such ERW was analysed in the light of international humanitarian law. Here the focus was on the armed conflict between Eritrea and Ethiopia, the war, in which these weapons were used. Following a brief account of the conduct of the two States with respect to the use of mines, booby traps and the like, (an account made on the basis of available reports submitted by the United Nations, Eritrea and Ethiopia and certain NGOs), the state of the applicable rules of international humanitarian law was assessed. Landmines and the other weapons producing ERW were examined in the light of some of the 'cardinal' principles of international humanitarian law: the principle prohibiting weapons which cause unnecessary suffering or superfluous injury, and the principle prohibiting the use of indiscriminate weapons. Consistent with the ICRC Study, it was noted that State practice up to the end of the 1990s provided evidence sufficient only for an 'emerging' rule of customary law prohibiting the use of landmines and the like because of the unnecessary suffering or superfluous injury they cause. The principle prohibiting the use of indiscriminate weapons as reflecting a rule of customary humanitarian rule was identified as being applicable to anti-personnel mines by the time of the 1998–2000 Border War.

The basic argument for doing so was the criterion that the use of weapons is indiscriminate if their effects cannot be limited. The EECC also emphasised the prohibition of indiscriminate use of mines as an expression of customary law. Ethiopia has always denied the use of anti-personnel mines during the war, perhaps also in the knowledge of otherwise being in breach of the Ottawa Convention which it had signed in 1997. The EECC was convinced by way of ample evidence that Eritrea had indeed used such mines during the war. This work has argued that in doing so, Eritrea violated customary humanitarian law. The use of mines without self-deactivation or self-destruction mechanisms during the war was in violation of customary law and is in principle a war crime. Whether or not either State had used anti-vehicle mines has not been proved, but it is highly probable. Moreover, anti-vehicle mines – here their kind has not been established – have also been laid after the war, in clear breach of the 2000 Algiers Agreement on Cessation of Hostilities. The ICRC Study argues that the use of certain booby traps is prohibited in customary humanitarian law. I believe that is correct and that it was the state of the law at the end of the 1990s. No evidence has been provided regarding the use of these booby traps by either party. This work has found itself in agreement with the EECC's assessment, more precisely expressed in the ICRC Study, that there exists a duty to locate and register emplaced minefields. Here such a duty was extended to include other weapons producing ERW. Although the evidence is not conclusive, it seems likely that both States have, generally speaking, acted accordingly.

Whereas Part III is concerned with duties under the *ius in bello*, the shorter Part IV deals primarily with duties relating to the *ius post* bellum: the obligation to remove and destroy; and the duty to assist in that process are matters covered in the first place by rules of general international law and only to a minor extent by international humanitarian law. After a brief discussion regarding the nature of the three Protocols and the Ottawa Convention, the sensitive subject of the legal responsibility for explosive remnants of war was addressed. Under international law, the responsibility for ERW, in particular for clearing, removal, and the like, is engaged by the State who controls the area. On this point issue was taken with the analysis provided by the ICRC Study, and a re-formulation of the rule of customary law was suggested.

Various accounts of the 1998–2000 Eritrean Ethiopian Border War comment upon matters other than the estimates of the numbers of victims, internally displaced people or the extent of the areas of land that have become useless. The reports studied also make abundantly clear the immense difficulties which have to be overcome before the problems caused by the hundreds of thousands of explosive remnants of war are really resolved. The capacity of Eritrea and Ethiopia to address these problems on their own is clearly insufficient. Some of these problems can be resolved by way of effective assistance and co-operation between the two countries as, for example, by way of generously providing location records, but in particular by way of efficient international help and co-operation. By becoming a party to the CCW Protocols, Eritrea and Ethiopia could show more willingness to co-operate. With respect to anti-personnel mines, the Ottawa Convention provides a comprehensive (legal) framework for such assistance and co-operation. Although important contributions are still required, it is the case that Eritrea and Ethiopia are, generally speaking, co-operating in this setting. International assistance in the hazardous process of de-mining and removal of other explosive devices has therefore been provided. Furthermore, assistance in areas such as risk prevention and the improvement of medical facilities has been forthcoming. However, this help and assistance should be further broadened and speeded up; it should also become more generous. The price paid for the slow process of clearing, removal and/or destroying is counted in the inconvertible currency of many more casualties among innocent Eritrean and Ethiopian civilians.

Chapter Fourteen

International Law and the Violence of Non-State Actors

Dino Kritsiotis*

I. INTRODUCTION

Questions concerning the violence of non-State actors form an ideal topic to address in this volume that rightly honours the tremendous contributions made by Professor Colin J. Warbrick to public international law, for these have been infused with his signature concern of 'how the law works in practice',[1] of how public international law engages actual challenges on the ground and of what real goods it is able to bring to the table when all is said and done. As we undertake this exercise, it is appropriate for us to view public international law within the context of its evolving framework and ambitions, where, as Professor Warbrick has observed, '[d]evelopments in the substance of international law – human rights, environmental protection, economic law – have encouraged the view that international law, whereas it once was something mainly to do with states, now might have something to do with justice (or values), such that speculation from those values could create an agenda for the law and, in the ultimate, norms binding on persons members of the international system.'[2] This is no less true of public international law's relationship with, and its treatment of, violence it must be said, where historical insistence has been placed on separating initiations of violence (for the purposes of the *jus ad bellum*) from acts of violence occurring *within* 'war' or 'armed conflict' (in terms of the *jus in bello*).

---

* Visiting Professor of Law, University of Michigan; Reader in Public International Law, University of Nottingham.
[1] Warbrick, 'Brownlie's *Principles of Public International Law*: An Assessment', 11 (2000) *EJIL* 621, at p. 633.
[2] Ibid, at p. 627.

K.H. Kaikobad & M. Bohlander (eds.), *International Law and Power: Perspectives on Legal Order and Justice*. Essays in Honour of Colin Warbrick, pp. 343–386.

That non-State actors have assumed increased significance in the authorship and perpetration of acts of violence is now an undisputed fact of international life; we have not simply had al-Qaeda's launch of an 'act of war' on the United States on 11 September 2001,[3] but, in the summer of 2006, Israel accused Hezbollah in the Lebanon of an 'act of war',[4] and, in September 2007, it followed this action with its designation of the Gaza Strip as 'hostile territory'.[5] This is a phenomenon that is set to continue,[6] as 'the advent of catastrophic terrorism has collapsed and confused the potential destructive power of private groups and States'.[7] Yet, these developments have come at a time when the law is perhaps not as explicit as it ought to have been in respect of the *violence of non-State actors*; we shall bear witness in the analysis that follows to different degrees of appreciation of such violence, and that these differences are not just evident as between the *jus ad bellum* and *jus in bello* as broad propositions but, crucially, also *within* these respective corpuses of the law. We might also wish to connect these independent trajectories to an evolving sense of *justice* within the international system, as Professor Warbrick has intimated, but our own critical reflections of the moves in this direction suggest that the relationship is an episodic and temperamental one and, at least as far as some commentators are concerned, it is not where it ought to be: '[t]he paradoxical relationship between the status of violence and the procedures of social change', wrote Richard A. Falk in the shadow of the December 1968 Israeli operation at Beirut International Airport,

---

[3]   Seelye and Bumiller, 'Bush Labels Aerial Terrorist Attacks "Acts of War"', *New York Times*, 13 September 2001, p. A16.

[4]   McGreal, 'Capture of Soldiers Was "Act of War" Says Israel', *The Guardian* (London), 13 July 2006, p. 1. See also Norton, *Hezbollah: A Short History*, Princeton, 2007, p. 7.

[5]   Erlanger and Cooper, 'Israel Calls Gaza "Hostile" in Step to Tighten Penalties', *New York Times*, 20 September 2007, p. A12. See, further, Kershner, 'Palestinian Suicide Bombers Attack Crossing into Gaza, Wounding Israeli Soldiers', *New York Times*, 20 April 2008, p. A6; and Bonner, 'Hamas in Largest Arms Buildup Yet, Israeli Study Finds', *New York Times*, 10 April 2008, p. A8.

[6]   'After Smart Weapons, Smart Soldiers', *The Economist* (London), 27 October 2007, p. 33.

[7]   Wedgwood, 'ICJ Advisory Opinion on the Israeli Security Fence and the Limits of Self-Defense', 98 (2005) *AJIL* 52, at p. 61. Described elsewhere as 'a gargantuan appetite for violence'. See Wedgwood, 'After September 11th', 36 (2001–2002) *New England Law Review* 725. See, further, Khan, 'Private Armed Groups and World Order', 1 (1970) *NYBIL* 32, at p. 41 ('the violent acts of private groups present an all too familiar range of incidents with an international bearing') and Cockayne, 'The Global Reorganization of Legitimate Violence: Military Entrepreneurs and the Private Face of International Humanitarian Law', 88 (No. 863, 2006) *International Review of the Red Cross* 459. We should be clear that this phenomenon not only covers acts of violence, but extends to threats as well: see Devenny, 'Hezbollah's Strategic Threat to Israel', 13 (2006) *Middle East Quarterly* 31 and Cooper and Rohter, 'McCain, Iraq War and the Threat of "Al Qaeda"', *New York Times*, 19 April 2008, p. A1.

'is a central deficiency of the present structure of international legal order, especially evident at a time of emergent claims for social and political justice'.[8]

Our conceptualization of this topic – on the relationship of violence and 'non-State actors' from a public international law standpoint – might reflect a little oddly to the reader given that such actors of course come in different forms and varieties, so much so that there might be little if any analytical and practical utility in comparing, say, the actions of the United Nations (as one 'non-State actor') with those of a terrorist organization (to take another 'non-State actor'), from the broadest possible understanding of this term.[9] Yet, there is surely to be some conceptual value in distinguishing between the *State* as an actor and all other actors who are *not* States, a residual definition of the non-State actor as it were, for the law continues to put tremendous store on such a distinction (most famously reflected, perhaps, in the right of self-defence which *inheres* in the State according to Article 51 of the 1945 United Nations Charter, so that no matter who or how important or legitimate a non-State actor might be, it cannot avail itself of this right under public international law).[10] However, what proves to be the uniting denominator of the non-State actors considered in our analysis, is their commitment to, or actual use of, violence in some form: they emerge as belligerent actors of some sort – or, to take a leaf out of the 1880 *Oxford Manual on the Laws of War on Land*, they constitute members of a 'belligerent armed force'.[11] It is this characteristic above

---

[8] Falk, 'The Beirut Raid and the International Law of Retaliation', 63 (1969) *AJIL* 415, at p. 427.

[9] For an important development of this theme, consider Falco, 'The Internal Legal Order of International and Regional Organizations as a Complementary Framework for the Obligations under International Humanitarian Law: The Case of the European Union', Conference paper delivered in Jerusalem: Complementing International Humanitarian Law: Exploring the Need for Additional Norms to Govern Contemporary Conflict Situations, 2 June 2008 (on file with author).

[10] Note that in its affirmation that the 'proliferation of nuclear, chemical and biological weapons, as well as their means of delivery, constitutes a threat to international peace and security', the Security Council used non-State actors as the explicit and exclusive focus of its Resolution 1540 (2004) – and, by that term, it meant an 'individual or entity, not acting under the lawful authority of any State in conducting activities which come within the scope of this resolution'. See further U.N. Press Release SC/8076, 28 April 2004; Security Council Resolution 1673 (2006) and U.N. Press Release SC/8708, 27 April 2006.

[11] Article 3 of the *Oxford Manual on the Laws of War on Land* (Resolution adopted by the Institute of International Law, 9 September 1880); reproduced in Schindler and Toman (eds.), *The Laws of Armed Conflicts: A Collection of Conventions, Resolutions and Other Documents* (Third edition), Dordrecht, 1988, p. 36. The *Manual*, it is true, specifies in Article 1 that a State of war 'does not admit of acts of violence, save between the armed forces of belligerent States', and, in its preface, refers to 'men called upon to take up arms to defend the causes of the belligerent States'. However, some accommodation would need to have been made for

all others that shall help us pry apart the conduct of al-Qaeda from that of, say, the International Committee of the Red Cross, or, to take another example, the actions of United Nations peacekeepers as opposed to those of 'belligerents' on the field which the United Nations, acting through the Security Council, has authorized.[12]

Etching this larger canvass of considerations will serve to underscore, as it will to make us appreciate more fully, the precise occasions on which public international law has broken from its Statist rank and mentalities, and addressed questions concerning the violence of non-State actors. Where this has occurred, we shall seek to give some account of why the law – or, more accurately, States acting through the law and its institutions – has done so, and *how* it has done so. (Not all non-State actors have been treated in the same manner however, and even when the law has acknowledged the possibilities for and permissibilities of violence by non-State actors, it has done so pursuant to imperatives larger than itself: the rules of warfare are applicable to all actors regardless of their legal status, the so-called principle of the equal application of the *jus in bello*).[13] We shall

---

recognized belligerency – situations in which the armed forces of *one* belligerent State would have been involved – so that, against this eventuality, Article 3 seems more encompassing and appropriate: 'Every belligerent armed force', it provides, 'is bound to conform to the laws of war.'

[12] Institute of International Law, Resolution on Conditions of Application of Humanitarian Rules of Armed Conflict to Which United Nations Forces May Be Engaged, 54 (1971–II) *Annuaire de L'institut de droit international* 465. See, further, Saura, 'Lawful Peacekeeping: Applicability of International Humanitarian Law to United Nations Peacekeeping Operations,' 58 (2007) *Hastings LJ* 479, at p. 495. Greenwood also mentions the possibility of United Nations peacekeepers who 'become involved in fighting to such an extent that the forces become parties to the conflict'. See 'Protection of Peacekeepers: The Legal Regime', 7 (1996) *Duke JCIL* 185, at p. 189. These are to be distinguished from 'non-party U.N. peacekeepers' (at p. 190), although some forces are of 'ambiguous' status (at p. 193). The example that is given of persons 'taking no active part in the hostilities' according to common Article 3 of the 1949 Geneva Conventions is the United Nations Operation in Somalia (UNOSOM) and the Unified Task Force (UNITAF), and national forces associated with them: see Report of the Commission of Inquiry Established Pursuant to Security Council Resolution 885 (1993) to Investigate Armed Attacks on UNOSOM II Personnel Which Led to Casualties Among Them, *UNSCOR*, 49th Session, U.N. Doc. S/1994/653 (1994). Recall in this context that Richard Baxter wrote after the Second World War that 'it may be anticipated that in the future the law of war may become a body of law relating to hostilities conducted between forces under the aegis of the international community and those of a state which has violated international law in resorting to war.' See 'The Municipal and International Law Basis of Jurisdiction over War Crimes', 28 (1951) *BYIL* 382, at p. 393.

[13] Considered an 'absolute dogma' by Louise Doswald-Beck, see 'International Humanitarian Law and the Advisory Opinion of the International Court of Justice on the Legality of the Threat or Use of Nuclear Weapons', [37] (No. 316, 1997) *International Review of the Red Cross* 35, at p. 53.

engage these questions within the traditional schemata of public international law, first taking questions under the *jus in bello* and, then, the *jus ad bellum*. Admittedly, this might not seem the most logical sequence for the flow of ideas and argument, but it could be said that the *jus in bello* assumed its modern form with the 1856 Paris Declaration Respecting Maritime Law,[14] whereas the earliest impulses of a *jus ad bellum* for public international law occurred a good while later, with the 1907 Hague Convention (II) on the Limitation of Employment of Force for Recovery of Contract Debts. As these rules evolved into the 1945 United Nations Charter, we shall attempt to convey and explain their dramatic Statist design and focus, with particular attention paid to the prohibition of force, its exceptions and the concept of aggression. The conclusion of the chapter shall draw together the commonality of themes that transcends both of these corpuses of the *jus in bello* and the *jus ad bellum*, and it shall attempt to position all of these developments in the broader context of the overall function and purpose of public international law.

II. Violence and Warfare

For the most part, in their earliest incarnation, the laws of war (to give them their original and still popular designation) concerned the violence of States as executed against one another. So obvious and so common was this premise to that corpus of law that it was in scare need of articulation, let alone elaboration: the 1856 Paris Declaration made simple work of this matter when it declared that it would be applicable 'in time of war';[15] from time to time, other instruments noted 'war' as the official condition which existed between the High Contracting Parties.[16] The Paris Declaration is of further interest to us here, however, because of its testament to the long-standing practice of privateering during hostilities, of the delegation of permissible violence to privateers 'as a kind of mercenary navy at a time when war ships were few and

---

[14] (1856) 115 *CTS* 1.

[15] Ibid.

[16] See, for instance, the 1868 St. Petersburg Declaration Renouncing the Use, in Time of War, of Explosive Projectiles Under 400 Grammes Weight: Schindler and Toman (note 11), p. 102; the 1899 Hague Convention (II) with Respect to the Laws and Customs of War on Land and its Annex: Regulations concerning the Laws and Customs of War on Land (at p. 69); and the 1906 Geneva Convention for the Amelioration of the Condition of the Wounded and Sick in Armies in the Field (at p. 301).

far between'.[17] States had therefore extended their monopolistic hold on violence to private ships through letters of marque and reprisal,[18] and the institution was itself critical in terms of how such violence was then viewed as a matter of law: 'a fine line served to distinguish the unlawful (and much condemned) piratical seizure of merchant vessels from the capture of prize by privateers'.[19] This the Paris Declaration sought to change, with its 'uniform doctrine' of abolishing the practice of privateering.[20]

The sense of war as an inter-State enterprise is made even more explicit from the 1863 Instructions for the Government of Armed of the United States in the Field (otherwise known as the Lieber Code, after is author Francis Lieber (1798–1872)).[21] Article 20 of the Code provided: 'Public war is a state of armed hostility between sovereign nations or governments. It is a law and requisite of civilized existence that men live in political, continuous societies, forming organized units, called states or nations, whose constituents bear, enjoy, suffer, advance and retrograde together, in peace and in war.' Though not a multilateral convention, the Code did recognize the realities of violence in warfare of individuals, either acting on their own volition or in concert with others – as with '[m]en, or squads of men, who commit hostilities, whether by fighting, or inroads for destruction or plunder, or by raids of any kind, without commission, without being part and portion of the organized hostile army, and without sharing continuously in the war' (Article 82); Article 85 considered the position of war-rebels – or 'persons within an occupied territory who rise in arms against the occupying or conquering army, or against the authorities established by the same'. These, the Code provided, could not be prisoners-of-war and 'may suffer death, whether they rise singly, in small or large bands, and whether called upon to do so by their own, but expelled, government or not'.[22] The Code therefore frowned upon those who did not form 'part and

---

[17] Porras, 'Constructing International Law in the East Indian Seas: Property, Sovereignty, Commerce and War in Hugo Grotius' *De Iure Praedae* – The Law of Prize, or "On How to Distinguish Merchants from Pirates"', 31 (2006) *Brooklyn JIL* 741, at pp. 752–53. Such measures were not in practice confined to war: Marshall, 'Putting Privateers in Their Place: The Applicability of the Marque and Reprisal Clause to Undeclared Wars', 64 (1997) *Univ. Chicago LR* 953.

[18] Roberts and Guelff (eds.), *Documents on the Laws of War* (Third edition), Oxford, 2000, p. 47.

[19] Porras (note 17), at pp. 753–54. See also Parrillo, 'The De-Privatization of American Warfare: How the U.S. Government Used, Regulated and Ultimately Abandoned Privateering in the Nineteenth Century', 19 (2007) *Yale J.L. & Human.* 1.

[20] See Dinstein, *The Conduct of Hostilities under the Law of International Armed Conflict*, Cambridge, 2004, p. 28.

[21] General Orders No. 100, 24 April 1863: reproduced in Hartigan, *Lieber's Code and the Law of War*, Chicago, 1983, pp. 45–71.

[22] Separate, we learn, to the fate of the 'unarmed civilian', who, the Code provided, 'is to be spared in person, property, and honor as much as the exigencies of war will admit'. See Article 22.

portion of the organized hostile army'; the connection was an important one as we discover in the case of partisans ('soldiers armed and wearing the uniform of their army, but belonging to a corps which acts detached from the main body for the purpose of making inroads into the territory occupied by the enemy'),[23] who, upon capture, 'are entitled to all the privileges of prisoners of war',[24] and it was further admitted in the Code that those forming *levées en masse* could acquire prisoner-of-war status in certain defined circumstances.[25]

'Guerrilla forces' were not mentioned as such in the Lieber Code, which is a curious omission because, in November 1862, Lieber had rehearsed an extensive set of arguments on guerrilla forces in correspondence with General Henry W. Halleck after Halleck had expressed specific interest in their legal status.[26] For Lieber, confusion surrounded the definition of the guerrilla following its derivation from the Spanish 'guerra' (for war – or, better, petty war),[27] but, he thought, a viable definition could be settled upon by emphasizing the constituent elements of such forces:

> a guerrilla party means an irregular band of armed men, carrying on an irregular war, not being able, according to their character as a guerrilla party, to carry on what the law terms a regular war. The irregularity of the guerrilla party consists in its origin, for it is either self-constituted or constituted by the call of a single individual, not according to the general law of levy, conscription, or

---

[23] Article 81 – although forming 'part and portion' of the regular 'organized hostile army' did not make one's status as a prisoner-of-war irrevocable. Article 83 provided that '[s]couts, or single soldiers, if disguised in the dress of the country or in the uniform of the army hostile to their own, employed in obtaining information, if found within or lurking about the lines of the captor, are treated as spies, and suffer death.' This opened the question of the *modus operandi* of warfare, and Article 88 of the Code pulled no punches in declaring, 'The spy is punishable with death by hanging by the neck, whether or not he succeeds in obtaining the information or in conveying it to the enemy.'

[24] Article 81, Lieber Code.

[25] Ibid, Article 51: 'If the people of that portion of an invaded country which is not yet occupied by the enemy, or of the whole country, at the approach of a hostile army, rise, under a duly authorized levy, en masse to resist the invader, they are now treated as public enemies, and, if captured, are prisoners of war.' Note the delimitation of Article 52 though: 'If, however, the people of a country, or any portion of the same, already occupied by an army, rise against it, they are violators of the laws of war and are not entitled to their protection.'

[26] Lieber, 'Guerrilla Parties Considered with Reference to the Laws and Usages of War'; reproduced in Hartigan (note 21), at pp. 31–44.

[27] Or 'war carried on by detached parties, generally in the mountains': Lieber in Hartigan (note 21), at p. 31. No doubt affected by the Spanish guerrillas in the 1808–1814 Peninsular War: see Esdaile, 'The Spanish Guerrillas in the Peninsular War', 38 (1988) *History Today* 29. See also Murphy, 'Evolving Geneva Convention Paradigms in the "War on Terrorism": Applying the Core Rules to the Release of Persons Deemed "Unprivileged Combatants"', 75 (2007) *Geo. Wash. LR* 1105, at p. 1109.

volunteering; it consists in its disconnection with the army as to its pay, provision, and movements; and it is irregular as to the permanency of the band, which may be dismissed and called again together at any time.[28]

In so doing, Lieber distanced himself from General Halleck's position in *International Law; or, Rules Regulating the Intercourse of States in Peace and War* (1861), which appeared to equate guerrilla forces with partisan forces.[29] Lieber instead sided with the approach of T.D. Woolsey who, in his *Introduction to the Study of International Law* (1860), drew a distinction between 'guerrilla parties' and 'regular troops or an armed peasantry':

> The treatment which the milder modern usage prescribes for regular soldiers is extended also to militia called out by the public authority. Guerrilla parties, however, do not enjoy the full benefit of the laws of war. They are apt to fare worse than either regular troops or an armed peasantry. The reasons for this are that they are annoying and insidious; that they put on and off with ease the character of a soldier, and that they are prone themselves to treat their enemies who fall into their hands with great severity.[30]

What is crucial in this reasoning of the denial of 'the full benefit of the laws of war' for guerrilla parties is that it concentrates on the *modus operandi* – or, shall we say, the assumed *modus operandi* – of guerrilla parties; it is not so much how a guerrilla party has constituted itself as a matter of fact or of the record, but of the general perception of its conduct on the battlefield and how it behaves when it gets there ('they put on and off with ease the character of a soldier, and that they are prone themselves to treat their enemies who fall into their hands with great severity'). This emphasis marks something of a shift from the general formulation Lieber had endorsed in his response to Halleck,[31] because as he proceeded with his own assessment of the situation, it is noticeable how Lieber also set his sights on this aspect of guerrilla operations: he wrote of guerrilla parties as 'self-constituted sets of armed men in times of war, who form no integrant part of the organized army, do not stand on the regular pay-roll of the army, or are not paid at all, take up arms and lay them down at intervals, *and carry on petty*

---

[28] Lieber (note 26), at p. 33. Cf. Article 51 of the Lieber Code: *supra* (note 25).
[29] According to H.W. Halleck, 'Partisan and guerrilla troops, are bands of men self-organized and self-controlled, who carry on war against the public enemy, without being under the direct authority of the state. They have no commissions or enlistments, nor are they enrolled as any part of the military force of the state; and the state is, therefore, only indirectly responsible for their acts.' See *International Law; or, Rules Regulating the Intercourse of States in Peace and War*, San Francisco, 1861, p. 386 (§ 8).
[30] Woolsey, *Introduction to the Study of International Law*, New York, 1860, p. 299.
[31] Generally, see *supra* (note 28).

war (guerrilla) chiefly by raids, extortion, destruction, and massacre, and who cannot encumber themselves with many prisoners, and will therefore generally give no quarter'.[32]

It was not lost on Lieber that untoward conduct was not the exclusive preserve of guerrilla parties, for he did conclude that the partisan had to be 'answerable for the commission of those acts to which the law of war grants no protection, and by which the soldier forfeits being treated as a prisoner of war if captured'.[33] However, if this point was left to the finer detail of the Code, the broader principle of what to do with guerrilla parties had to wait until the 1874 Brussels Conference on the Laws and Customs of War. The Conference did not culminate in the adoption of an international convention, but its resulting declaration bore the brunt of the experiences of the 1870–1871 Franco-Prussian War,[34] and provided that '[t]he laws, rights, and duties of war apply not only to armies, but also to militia and volunteer corps' who fulfilled the following conditions: 1. that they be commanded by a person responsible for his subordinates; 2. that they have a fixed distinctive emblem recognizable at a distance; 3. that they carry arms openly; and 4. that they conduct their operations in accordance with the laws and customs of war.[35] The formulation is significant, for it rendered obsolete the rule of public international law of that time that 'only the members of authorised irregular forces enjoyed the privileges due to the members of the armed forces of belligerents, whereas members of unauthorized irregular forces were considered to be war criminals and could

---

[32] Lieber (note 26), at p. 41 (emphasis supplied). See also Mougenot, *Des pratiques de la guerre continentale durant le Premier Empire*, Paris, 1903, p. 50. Though note Lieber's consideration of 'guerrilla parties' that 'aid the main army of a belligerent': 'it will be difficult for the captor of guerrillamen to decide once whether they are regular partisans, distinctly authorized by their own government; and it would seem that we are borne out by the conduct of the most humane belligerents in recent times, and by many of the modern writers, if the rule be laid down, that guerrillamen, when captured in fair fight and open warfare, should be treated as the regular partisan is, until special crimes, such as murder, or the killing of prisoners, or the sacking of places, are proved upon them, leaving the question of self-constitution unexamined.' See *supra* (note 26), at p. 42.

[33] Lieber (note 26), at p. 41. Note also the position on scouts or single soldiers in the Lieber Code: *supra* (note 23), Article 83.

[34] Coming as it did so close on its heels with 'a new class of soldier called the *franc-tireur*' during the 1870–1871 Franco-Prussian War – 'a French deserter or civilian who took up arms to obstruct the German advance or plunder the same crops and homes needed to sustain the German army'. See Wawro, *The Franco-Prussian War: The German Conquest of France in 1870–1871*, Cambridge, 2003, p. 237. The term was normally associated with 'individual acts of violence': Baxter, 'So-Called "Unprivileged Belligerency": Spies, Guerrillas, and Saboteurs', 28 (1951) *BYIL* 323, at p. 333.

[35] Article 9 of the Declaration; for the text thereof, see Schindler and Toman (note 11), at pp. 22–34.

be shot when captured'.[36] We therefore see an attempt in the declaration to broaden the appeal and effectiveness of the laws of war through its rules on the classification of combatants, as we do with its position on *levées en masse*[37] – although it is this latter issue that proved to be a major point of discord among the States of Europe in the summer of 1874, and is often used to explain why no convention succeeded their deliberations.[38]

The first formal international coda regarding the classification of combatants arrived a generation later, with the Regulations annexed to the 1899 Hague Convention (II) with Respect to the Laws and Customs of War on Land and, then, the Regulations annexed to the 1907 Hague Convention (IV) Respecting the Laws and Customs on Land – both of which contained a fond rendering of the relevant provisions of the Brussels Declaration, including its appreciation of *levées en masse*. The conceptual framework of these instruments for distinguishing between lawful and unlawful combatants was, in turn, adopted and developed by the 1949 Geneva Convention (III) Relative to the Treatment of Prisoners of War – which itself took account of the experiences of the Second World War but, it has been said, 'the Conventions are at their weakest in delineating the various categories of persons who benefit from the protection of each'.[39] As we have come to observe with the Bush Administration's 'war on terror' after September 2001, a truer statement could not have been made in respect of Geneva Convention (III) which provides in relevant part that prisoners-of-war 'are persons belonging to one of the following categories, who have fallen into the power of the enemy':

---

[36] Oppenheim, *International Law: A Treatise* vol. ii: *War and Neutrality*, London, 1906, p. 89, §80 (emphasizing, at p. 90, that 'this rule applies only to irregulars fighting in bodies, however small') and Lauterpacht (ed.), *Oppenheim's International Law: A Treatise*, vol. ii: *Disputes, War and Neutrality* (Seventh edition), London, 1952, pp. 256–57. See further Mallison and Mallison, 'The Juridical Status of Irregular Combatants under the International Humanitarian Law of Armed Conflict', 9 (1977) *Case W. Res. JIL* 39, at p. 45. Note that the last part of Article 9 of the Brussels Declaration went on to provide: 'In countries where militia constitute the army, or form part of it, they are included under the denomination "army".'

[37] According to Article 10, 'The population of a territory which has not been occupied, who, on the approach of the enemy, spontaneously take up arms to resist the invading troops without having had time to organize themselves in accordance with Article 9 [on which see *supra* (note 35)], shall be regarded as belligerents if they respect the laws and customs of war.' See further Mallison and Jabri, 'The Juridical Characteristics of Belligerent Occupation and the Resort to Resistance by the Civilian Population: Doctrinal Development and Continuity', 42 (1974) *Geo. Wash. LR* 185.

[38] Nabulsi, *Traditions of War: Occupation, Resistance, and the Law*, Oxford, 1999, p. 8 and pp. 52–55.

[39] Baxter (note 34), at p. 327.

1. Members of the armed forces of a Party to the conflict, as well as members of militias or volunteer corps forming part of such armed forces.
2. Members of other militias and members of other volunteer corps, including those of organized resistance movements, belonging to a Party to the conflict and operating in or outside their own territory, even if this territory is occupied, provided that such militias or volunteer corps, including such organized resistance movements, fulfil the following conditions:
   (a) that of being commanded by a person responsible for his subordinates;
   (b) that of having a fixed distinctive sign recognizable at a distance;
   (c) that of carrying arms openly;
   (d) that of conducting their operations in accordance with the laws and customs of war.
3. Members of regular armed forces who profess allegiance to a government or an authority not recognized by the Detaining Power.
4. Persons who accompany the armed forces without actually being members thereof, such as civilian members of military aircraft crews, war correspondents, supply contractors, members of labour units or of services responsible for the welfare of the armed forces, provided that they have received authorization, from the armed forces which they accompany, who shall provide them for that purpose with an identity card similar to the annexed model.
5. Members of crews, including masters, pilots and apprentices, of the merchant marine and the crews of civil aircraft of the Parties to the conflict, who do not benefit by more favourable treatment under any other provisions of international law.
6. Inhabitants of a non-occupied territory, who on the approach of the enemy spontaneously take up arms to resist the invading forces, without having had time to form themselves into regular armed units, provided they carry arms openly and respect the laws and customs of war.[40]

It is perhaps striking how, in this articulation of the schemata for determining prisoner-of-war status, the State is not mentioned in terms even though its presence is much felt *via* the references that are made to 'the armed forces of a Party to the conflict' (Article 4 (A) (1)), or to 'regular armed forces' (Article 4 (A) (3)) and, simply, to 'armed forces' (Article 4 (A) (4)) or of 'Parties to the conflict' (Article 4 (A) (5)).[41] It is almost as if we are being exhorted to interpret

---

[40] Article 4 (A): 75 *UNTS* 31; *UKTS* 39 (1958), Cmd. 550; hereinafter referred to as Geneva Convention (III).

[41] Indeed, there does appear to have formed a common understanding of the term 'armed forces' at the Conference of Government Experts, since it was felt there was no reason to subject this term to greater definition by replicating the approach of the 1907 Hague Regulations (i.e. to provide that the term covers both combatants and non-combatants) – for such was the general understanding and 'almost no difficulties' had come of it during the Second World War. See de Preux (ed.), *Geneva Convention Relative to the Treatment of Prisoners of War Commentary on Geneva Convention III*, Geneva, 1960, p. 52. Note that, in the *Commentary* to the Convention, it is further provided:

Article 4 in light of common Article 2 of the Geneva Conventions, so that the notion of 'a Party to the conflict' is to be considered an abbreviation for 'a *High Contracting Party* to the conflict',[42] rather than as an allusion to those belligerent

> It is the duty of each State to take steps so that members of its armed forces can be immediately recognized as such and to see to it that they are easily distinguishable from members of the enemy armed forces or from civilians. The Convention does not provide for any reciprocal notification of uniforms or insignia, but merely assumes that such items will be well known and that there can be no room for doubt.

See ibid, p. 52. This understanding is further borne out by the *Commentary's* annotation on Article 4 (A) (3) of the Convention: 'The expression "members of regular armed forces" denotes armed forces which differ from those referred to in sub-paragraph (1) of this paragraph in one respect only: the authority to which they profess allegiance is not recognized by the adversary as a Party to the conflict. These "regular armed forces" have all the material characteristics and all the attributes of armed forces in the sense of sub-paragraph (1): they wear uniform, they have an organized hierarchy and they know and respect the laws and customs of war ... The distinguishing feature of such armed forces is simply the fact that in the view of their adversary, they are not operating or are no longer operating under the direct authority of a Party to the conflict in accordance with Article 2 of the Convention.' See de Preux (note 41), pp. 62–63.

[42] Dinstein (note 20), at p. 36 (emphasis supplied); where he writes: 'These are the regular forces of the belligerent States'. Very much the interpretation, also, of Aldrich: see 'The Taliban, al Qaeda, and the Determination of Illegal Combatants', 96 (2002) *AJIL* 891, at p. 893. Consider, further, the broader historical current of the 1907 Hague Regulations and the 1929 Geneva Convention. With its reference to '[p]ersons who accompany the armed forces without actually being members thereof, such as civilian members of military aircraft crews, war correspondents, supply contractors, members of labour units or of services responsible for the welfare of the armed forces,' Article 4 (A) (4) of Geneva Convention (III) is an attempt to elaborate on Article 3 of the Regulations of the 1907 Hague Convention (IV); and Article 4 (A) (5) of Geneva Convention (III) develops the stipulation in Article 1 (2) of the 1929 Geneva Convention concerning 'all persons belonging to the armed forces of belligerents who are captured by the enemy in the course of operations of maritime or aerial war, subject to such exceptions (derogations) as the conditions of such capture render inevitable', though no mention is made in Article 4 (A) (5) of exceptions or derogations. Consider, also, the other provisions of Geneva Convention (III) itself: not only common Article 2 of the 1949 – on which more will follow – but Article 39, which reads as a *précis* of some of the component organs of the State as then understood:

> Every prisoner of war camp shall be put under the immediate authority of a responsible commissioned officer belonging to the regular armed forces of the Detaining Power. Such officer shall have in his possession a copy of the present Convention; he shall ensure that its provisions are known to the camp staff and the guard and shall be responsible, *under the direction of his government*, for its application.

Emphasis supplied. See also Articles 56 and 66 of Geneva Convention (III). Add to this, the other Conventions adopted in August 1949 – such as the Geneva Convention (IV) Relative to the Protection of Civilian Persons in Time of War (hereinafter referred to as Geneva Convention (IV)), which defines persons protected under the Convention as 'those who, at a given moment and in any manner whatsoever, find themselves, in case of a conflict forces, or parties to the conflict, that find themselves in the thick of hostilities on the ground.[43]

All of this said, some mention should be made of how pragmatic considerations have informed and shaped our understanding of this aspect of the law, so that, in the first edition of his treatise on war and neutrality, published in 1906 on the eve of the 1907 Hague Conference, Lassa Oppenheim wrote that:

> Whenever a case arises in which a State lacking the legal qualification to make war … actually makes war, such State is a belligerent, the contention is real war, and all the rules of International Law respecting warfare apply to it. Therefore, an armed contention between the suzerain and the vassal, between a full-Sovereign State and a vassal State under the suzerainty of another State, and, lastly, between a Federal State and one or more of its members, is war in the technical sense of the Law of Nations.[44]

This was not to be taken as open season on how war was defined as a matter of public international law, however: 'It may, of course, happen that a contention arises between the armed forces of a State and a body of armed individuals, but such contention is not war … Nor is a contention with insurgents or pirates a war. And a so-called civil war need not be from the beginning nor become at all a war in the technical sense of the term according to international law.'[45] There

---

or occupation, in the hands of *a Party to the conflict or Occupying Power of which they are not nationals*' (Article 4 (1); emphasis supplied). The immediate implication of this formulation is that only States can be 'a Party to the conflict or occupying Power' since it is only States that have the capacity in international law to endow individuals with nationality – an impression that is endorsed by Article 4 (2) of Geneva Convention (IV) and by the *Commentary* to the Convention, which observes that the Convention 'remains faithful to a recognized principle of international law: it does not interfere in a State's relations with its own nationals'. See Uhler and Coursier (eds.), *Geneva Convention Relative to the Protection of Civilian Persons in Time of War Commentary on Geneva Convention IV*, Geneva, 1958, p. 46.

[43] As is done with the term 'each Party to the conflict' in common Article 3 of the Geneva Conventions: *infra* text to note 67.

[44] Oppenheim (note 36), at p. 86 (§ 75) – on account of the fact that 'the possession of armed forces makes it possible for them in fact to enter into war and to become belligerents': p. 85 (§ 75). When he wrote this passage, Oppenheim had in mind the declaration of war by Serbia and Montenegro (vassal States under Turkish suzerainty) against Turkey in July 1876; the alliance between Romania (also a vassal State of Turkey) and Russia in the latter's war with Turkey in April 1877; the second declaration of war issued by Serbia against Turkey in December 1877; and the war between Serbia – which, by then (November 1885) had become a 'full-Sovereign State' – and Bulgaria (a vassal State under Turkish suzerainty): pp. 58–59 (§ 56). An armed contention 'between a Federal State and one or more of its members' is, of course, a reference to the 1861–1865 war in the United States which was, wrote Oppenheim, 'real war': at p. 59 (§ 56).

[45] Oppenheim (note 36), at p. 58 (§ 56). Here, one of Oppenheim's points of reference was

was therefore scope for a tight rein on the potential application of the laws of war, he argued, but that this ought not to have been pursued with degrees of formalism that would have defeated the purpose and even the very idea of the laws of war. It is for this reason that we find the extension of the coverage of the laws of war to situations of 'so-called civil war', as Oppenheim put it, but this would only occur upon the recognition of belligerency *within* that war:

> Certain conditions of fact, not stigmatized as unlawful by International Law – the Law of Nations does not treat civil war as illegal – create for other States the right and the duty to grant recognition of belligerency. These conditions of fact are: the existence of a civil war accompanied by a state of general hostilities; occupation and a measure of orderly administration of a substantial part of national territory by the insurgents; observance of the rules of warfare on the part of the insurgent forces acting under a responsible authority; the practical necessity for third States to define their attitude to the civil war. Without the latter requirement recognition of belligerency might be open to abuse for the purpose of a gratuitous manifestation of sympathy with the cause of the insurgents. In the absence of these conditions recognition of belligerency constitutes illicit interference in the affairs of the States affected by civil disorders – an international wrong analogous to a premature recognition of a State or a Government. Refusal to recognise belligerent status notwithstanding the existence of these conditions must be deemed contrary to sound principle and precedent.[46]

We obtain a greater sense of this pragmatism from Article 4 of the Geneva Convention (III) – not from the run of references to regular armed forces that we have observed therein, but from the engagement it makes with non-State actors. Like the 1907 Hague Regulations, the Geneva Convention (III) accepted the notion of the *levée en masse*, and the rule pertaining to '[i]nhabitants of a non-occupied territory' is reproduced in the Convention (in Article 4 (A) (6)) from the Regulations with slight modifications.[47] It was the understanding that these inhabitants could form either through self-initiative or through the encouragement of their Government,[48] though it is important to stress that this provision qualified their actions by the temporal factor of the 'spontaneous'

---

the Jameson Raid of December 1895–January 1896 against the South African Republic. For further reference, see Longford, *Jameson's Raid: The Prelude to the Boer War*, London, 1982.

[46] Lauterpacht (note 36), at pp. 249–50 (§ 76). See Draper, 'Humanitarian Law and Internal Armed Conflicts', 13 (1983) *Georgia JICL* 253, at p. 254 and pp. 257–58.

[47] Of stylistic import.

[48] See de Preux (note 41), at p. 67 (through the radio, for instance). Writing of a belligerent which 'calls the whole population of the country to arms,' Oppenheim suggests that such an action would make the population 'a more or less irregular part of his armed forces.' See (note 36), at p. 90 (§ 81).

taking up of arms 'to resist the invading forces':[49] it 'can only be considered to exist during a very short period, i.e. during the actual invasion period'.[50] What is significant with the Convention, though, is its treatment of the *levée en masse within* occupied territories. It does so as part of its broader specification for *irregular* action in international armed conflicts, or what the Convention describes in Article 4 (A) (2) as '[m]embers of other militias and members of other volunteer corps, including those of organized resistance movements, belonging to a Party to the conflict and operating in or outside their own territory, *even if this territory is occupied*'.[51]

This might seem a puzzling formulation for the Geneva Convention (III) to make, though, given that Article 4 (A) (1) already refers to 'members of militias or volunteer corps' *that form part of regular armed forces*,[52] but it has nevertheless been argued in the literature that Article 4 (A) (2) identifies the 'condition' of 'acting on behalf of a State Party' to the armed conflict and that this condition is 'irreproachable'.[53] Others have sought to argue that Article 4 (A) (2) concerns 'independent' formations,[54] and that '[m]embers of other militias and members

---

[49] Article 2 of the 1907 Hague Regulations seemed to afford less latitude: it dealt with the inhabitants of a non-occupied territory acting 'on the approach of the enemy'. Consider Draper, 'The Status of Combatants and the Question of Guerrilla Warfare', 45 (1971) *BYIL* 173, at p. 192 ('The circumstances in which it may become operative are narrow, being those of a dire national emergency and urgency, but it may well be relied upon today, having regard to the speed and effectiveness of modern armed attacks, e.g. by troops dropped or landed from aircraft.')

[50] de Preux (note 41), at p. 68 ('If resistance continues, the authority commanding the inhabitants who have taken up arms, or the authority to which they profess allegiance, must either replace them by sending regular units, or must incorporate them in its regular forces. Otherwise, the mass levy could not survive the total occupation of the territory which it has tried in vain to defend').

[51] Emphasis supplied. Note that, more recently, in December 2004, Former UN Secretary-General Kofi Annan's High-Level Panel on Threats, Challenges and Change concluded that 'peoples under foreign occupation have a right to resistance'. See *A More Secure World: Our Shared Responsibility, Report of the Secretary-General's High Level Panel on Threats, Challenges and Change* (U.N. Doc. A/59/565) (2004).

[52] *Supra* (note 40).

[53] Dinstein (note 20), at p. 40. See also Best, *Humanity in Warfare: The Modern History of the International Law of Armed Conflicts*, London, 1980, p. 298 ('the protecting of organized resistance movements (no criteria of organization stated), belonging to a Party (i.e. to an internationally-recognizable government, even if a government in exile)'). However, note Draper who wrote: 'Such a Party must be either a State or a politically organized society which has the actual elements of statehood, but lacks recognition by its adversary.' See *supra* (note 49), at p. 195.

[54] At the instigation of the Netherlands and drawing upon the formulation of Article 1 of the 1907 Hague Regulations: see de Preux (note 41), at p. 57. See also the reference in the *Commentary* to 'organized resistance movements and members of other militias and members of other volunteer corps which are independent of the regular armed forces [and which] must belong to a Party to the conflict'.

of other volunteer corps, including those of organized resistance movements' can themselves be regarded as 'a Party to the conflict' since 'organized resistance forces can clearly "belong" to their own movement which is a party to the conflict[;] [s]uch forces cannot "belong" in the sense of subordination and control, to a State party to the conflict'.[55] Perhaps the better view of the nature of the relationship between the State and 'non-State' actor envisaged in Geneva Convention (III) is the one that is moderated by the purpose of that Convention – as well as, it must be said, the larger historical forces at work that brought us Article 4 (A) (2):

> International law has advanced considerably concerning the manner in which this relationship shall be established. The drafters of earlier instruments were unanimous in including the requirement of express authorization by the sovereign, usually in writing, and this was still the case at the time of the Franco-German war of 1870–1871. Since the Hague Conferences, however, this condition is no longer considered essential. It is essential that there should be a *de facto* relationship between the resistance organization and the party to international law which is in a state of war, but the existence of this relationship is sufficient. It may find expression merely by tacit agreement, if the operations are such as to indicate clearly for which side the resistance organization is fighting. But affiliation with a Party to the conflict may also follow an official declaration, for instance by a Government in exile, confirmed by official recognition by the High Command of the forces which are at war with the Occupying Power.[56]

The fact remains that it is not until the 1977 First Additional Protocol that we observe an undisputed dissociation of the State in the law's formal rules regarding combatant status, so that 'irregular' forces are spoken of in one and the same breath as their regular counterparts: here, '[t]he armed forces of a Party to a conflict consist of all organized armed forces, groups and units which are under a command responsible to that Party for the conduct of its subordinates, even if that Party is represented by a government or an authority not recognized by an adverse Party'.[57] Furthermore, no distinction is made (as it is in the

---

[55] See Mallison and Mallison (note 36), at p. 55 ('If they do "belong" in such a meaning, they are no longer irregular forces under Article 4 (A) (2) but are regular militias or volunteer corps under Article 4 (A) (1) [of the 1949 Geneva Convention (III)]').

[56] de Preux (note 41), at p. 57. According to Part III of the *British Manual of Military Law*, London, 1958, '[t]he first condition [for irregular combatants] ... is fulfilled if the commander of the corps is regularly or temporarily commissioned as an officer or is a person of position and authority, or if the members are provided with certificates or badges granted by the government of the State to show that they are officers or soldiers, so that there may be no doubt that they are not partisans acting on their own responsibility. State recognition, however, is not essential, and an organization may be formed spontaneously and elect its own officers'. See p. 33.

[57] 1977 First Additional Protocol, Article 43 (1): 1125 *UNTS* 3; UK Misc. 19 (1977) Cmnd. 6927.

Geneva Convention (III)) between regular and irregular combatants for the determination of their legal status. A universal standard is introduced instead: 'combatants', whether of regular or irregular kind, 'are obliged to distinguish themselves from the civilian population while they are engaged in an attack or in a military operation preparatory to an attack', according to Article 44 (3) – although 'there are situations in armed conflicts where, owing to the nature of the hostilities an armed combatant cannot so distinguish himself', and, in such cases, separate provision is made.[58]

At first blush, with its reference to '[t]he armed forces of a Party to a conflict' in Article 43,[59] the First Additional Protocol appears to repeat the formulation – and, we can presume, the problems associated with – its predecessor provision in Geneva Convention (III),[60] but the *Commentary* on the Protocol is instructive on this point. It provides that:

> A Party to a war which is not recognized as such is therefore not necessarily a State, nor even an authority representing a State. In fact, this distinction was not yet made in the texts of the Conventions, which, though they are not limited to the state of war in a legal sense, are limited, as far as international conflicts are concerned, to clashes arising between two or more contracting Parties, i.e., States. However, it is clear that Article 2, paragraph 3, of the Conventions provides the possibility for their application to a Power which is not a Party to the Conventions, 'if the latter accepts and applies the provisions thereof'. [Furthermore] it is perfectly clear that the Protocol has extended its field of application to entities which are not States ... [i]f they conform to the requirements of the present article, liberation movements fighting against colonial domination ... and resistance movements representing a pre-existing subject of international law may be 'Parties to the conflict' within the meaning of the Conventions and the Protocol.[61]

---

[58] To the extent that the combatant carries his arms openly (a) during each military engagement, and (b) during such time as he is visible to the adversary while he is engaged in a military deployment preceding the launching of an attack in which he is to participate. Mercenaries are removed from this classification system, however, by virtue of Article 47 (1) of the Protocol ('A mercenary shall not have the right to be a combatant or a prisoner of war.') Note the construction of the mercenary that emerges from the Protocol as someone who, amongst other things, 'is motivated to take part in the hostilities essentially by the desire for private gain and, in fact, is promised, *by or on behalf of a Party to the conflict*, material compensation substantially in excess of that promised or paid to combatants of similar ranks and functions in the armed forces of that Party' (Article 47 (2) (c) (emphasis supplied)). Article 47 (2) (e) stipulates that a mercenary 'is not a member of the armed forces of a Party to the conflict'; Article 47 (2) (f) provides that the mercenary 'has not been sent by a State which is not a Party to the conflict on official duty as a member of its armed forces'. See, further, Walzer, 'Mercenary Impulse', *The New Republic*, 12 March 2008, p. 20.

[59] *Supra* (note 57).

[60] *Supra* (note 40).

[61] Pilloud, Sandoz, Swinarski and Zimmermann (eds.), *Commentary on the Additional Protocols of*

The *Commentary* therefore emphasizes that, as we engage the new test for lawful and unlawful combatants in the Protocol,[62] we should be mindful of the changes that have occurred in the *definition* of an international armed conflict between Geneva Convention (III) and the 1977 First Additional Protocol. And changes these have been: whereas common Article 2 to all four Geneva Conventions of August 1949 makes the Conventions applicable 'to all cases of declared war or of any other armed conflict *which may arise between two or more of the High Contracting Parties*, even if the state of war is not recognized by one of them',[63] Article 1 (4) of the Protocol expands the definition of an international armed conflict to include 'armed conflicts in which peoples are fighting against colonial domination and alien occupation and against racist régimes in the exercise of their right of self-determination, as enshrined in the Charter of the United Nations and the Declaration on Principles of International Law concerning Friendly Relations and Co-operation among States in accordance with the Charter of the United Nations'.[64] In the words of the *Commentary* to the Protocol:

---

8 June 1977 to the Geneva Conventions of 12 August 1949, Dordrecht, 1987, pp. 506–507. It has also been noted that the removal of the qualification of 'belonging' to a Party to the conflict as contained in Article 4 (A) (2) of Geneva Convention (III) 'marks an important change in the status of guerrilla movements' for 'the terms "of a Party to a conflict" might, in certain cases, apply to the movement itself'. See Hacker, 'The Application of Prisoner-of-War Status to Guerrillas under the First Protocol Additional to the Geneva Conventions of 1949', 2 (1978–1979) *Boston Coll. ICLJ* 131, at p. 150.

[62] See accompanying text to note 58, *supra*.

[63] Emphasis supplied. Earlier (*supra* note 61), the *Commentary to the Additional Protocols* referred to a different part of common Article 2, namely common Article 2 (3): 'Although one of the Powers in conflict may not be a party to the present Convention, the Powers who are parties thereto shall remain bound by it in their mutual relations. They shall furthermore be bound by the Convention in relation to the said Power, if the latter accepts and applies the provisions thereof.'

[64] So long as there was compliance with the procedure set out in Article 96 (3) of the Protocol: 'The authority representing a people engaged against a High Contracting Party in an armed conflict of the type referred to in Article 1, paragraph 4, may undertake to apply the Conventions and this Protocol in relation to that conflict by means of a unilateral declaration addressed to the depositary. Such declaration shall, upon its receipt by the depositary, have in relation to that conflict the following effects: (a) the Conventions and this Protocol are brought into force for the said authority as a Party to the conflict with immediate effect; (b) the said authority assumes the same rights and obligations as those which have been assumed by a High Contracting Party to the Conventions and this Protocol; and (c) the Conventions and this Protocol are equally binding upon all Parties to the conflict.' It has been said that this provision 'provides a method for a nonstate party' to bring into effect for itself the provisions of the 1949 Geneva Conventions as well as those of the 1977 First Additional Protocol: see Mallison and Mallison (note 36), at p. 13.

Theoretically at least, the notion of 'Party to the conflict', within the meaning of the Protocol, is fairly wide, involving not only resistance movements representing a pre-existing subject of international law and governments in exile, but also those fighting for conflicts of 'self-determination' or 'national liberation'. Those who consider this distinction to be fundamental might fear that this could result in some confusion between international conflicts and conflicts which are not international.[65]

While this arrangement has proved a controversial innovation to the meaning of an international armed conflict,[66] it also ought to be read in the context of the revolution that occurred in common Article 3 to the Geneva Conventions in August 1949 – which conferred legal obligations upon 'each Party' to an 'armed conflict not of an international character occurring in the territory of one of the High Contracting Parties' as a matter of conventional obligation.[67] The addressees of common Article 3 need not therefore all be State actors – or actors acting on behalf of or representing the State.[68] In fact, the entire ethos and underpinning of common Article 3 suggests that the provision becomes applicable to an armed conflict at least one of whose parties is by definition *not*

---

[65] Pilloud, Sandoz, Swinarski and Zimmermann (note 61), at p. 507. This outcome of the diplomatic deliberations followed the participation of ten liberation movements in the process: the African National Congress, the Angola National Liberation Front, the Mozambique Liberation Front, the Palestine Liberation Organization, the Panafricanist Congress, the People's Movement for the Liberation of Angola, the Seychelles People's United Party, the South West African People's Organization, the Zimbabwe African National Union and the Zimbabwe African People's Union. *See* Mallison and Mallison, 'The Juridical Status of Privileged Combatants under the Geneva Protocol of 1977 Concerning International Conflicts', 42 (1978) *Law and Contemporary Problems* 4, at p. 8.

[66] Mallison and Mallison have contended: 'It must be acknowledged that it is beyond the realm of reasonableness to expect such authorities or movements to apply all of the detailed rules concerning the treatment of [prisoners-of-war] in the 1949 [Geneva] Convention [(III)], which are predicated upon the existence of governmental institutions of the captor.' See *supra* (note 65), at p. 14.

[67] On this, see Draper (note 46), at pp. 259–61.

[68] Not something that can be said of the 1977 Second Additional Protocol, designed, according to its Preamble, to 'ensure a better protection for the victims' of non-international armed conflicts but applicable, according to Article 1 (1), 'to all armed conflicts which are not covered by Article 1 of the Protocol Additional to the Geneva Conventions of 12 August 1949, and relating to the Protection of Victims of International Armed Conflicts (Protocol I) and which take place in the territory of a High Contracting Party between its armed forces and dissident armed forces or other organized armed groups which, under responsible command, exercise such control over a part of its territory as to enable them to carry out sustained and concerted military operations and to implement this Protocol'. This has been widely understood to provide a more exacting threshold for application than that of common Article 3: see Rosemary Abi-Saab, 'Humanitarian Law and Internal Conflicts: The Evolution of Legal Concern', in Delissen and Tanja (eds.), *Humanitarian Law of Armed Conflict – Challenges Ahead: Essays in Honour of Frits Kalshoven*, Dordrecht, 1991, p. 209 at p. 216 (on the 'much more restrictive approach to internal conflicts' of the Second Additional Protocol).

a State actor.[69] This becomes the defining feature that separates an armed conflict not of an international character from one that *is* of an international character – so long, of course, that the non-international armed conflict occurs on the territory of *one* of the High Contracting Parties to the Geneva Conventions. The language of this law might be confusing and open to multiple interpretations, but the function and purpose of this provision are not.

The obligations specified in common Article 3 of the 1949 Geneva Conventions do, it is true, pale in extent and significance to those elsewhere in the Geneva Conventions that are applicable in international armed conflicts, but common Article 3 does go on to provide that the Parties to the conflict to 'further endeavour to bring into force, by means of special agreements, *all or part of the other provisions of the present* Convention'.[70] While this aspect of common Article 3 is not cast in the same concrete terms as the other obligations addressed to the Parties in that provision, it does give us pause to consider whether the Geneva Conventions accept the basic premise that no reason in principle exists for precluding the plenary application of the Conventions to non-State actors – that they can indeed be bound by the full range of obligations contained in the Geneva Conventions *as a matter of fact as well as law*. We can appreciate that further evidence in this direction is supplied by the historical arrangements made for recognitions of belligerency,[71] as it is from the internationalization of certain non-armed international conflicts by virtue of Article 1 (4) of the First Additional Protocol of June 1977.[72]

Yet, as we turn to the actual *content* of the obligations applicable in non-international armed conflicts as compared to international armed conflicts, it is clear from common Article 3 why it is that the law has made the

---

[69] See Mallison and Mallison (note 36), at pp. 53–54 who write, 'In addition to the legitimate government, [common Article 3] must necessarily include the revolutionaries whose military forces are typically organized as irregular groups associated with one or more revolutionary parties'. See also Cassese, 'The Status of Rebels under the 1977 Geneva Protocol on Non-International Armed Conflicts', 30 (1981) *ICLQ* 416. Draper considers that this formulation 'appears to confer a limited persona on the government and its forces and upon the insurgent authority and dissident forces, *distinct from the individuals comprising them*'. See *supra* (note 46), at p. 268 (emphasis supplied). Common Article 3 does make a point of providing in its concluding paragraph: 'The application of the preceding provisions shall not affect the legal status of the Parties to the conflict.'

[70] Emphasis supplied. 'This is a useful provision,' writes Draper, 'well adapted to the shifting scale and intensity of a civil conflict.' See *supra* (note 46), at p. 265.

[71] To be sure, 'recognition of belligerency' could come about by the intervention of other States – as well as between the parties themselves. See generally, Lootsteen, 'The Concept of Belligerency in International Law', 166 (2000) *Military LR* 109.

[72] Moir, *The Law of Internal Armed Conflict*, Cambridge, 2002, at p. 90.

dichotomous intervention it has. Consider what it is that common Article 3 of the Conventions seeks to prescribe: violence to life and person, the taking of hostages, outrages upon personal dignity and the passing of sentences and the carrying out of executions without previous judgment. These protections are afforded to '[p]ersons taking no active part in the hostilities', but their real point of focus is on those who have set out or intend to engage in such activities as a general matter: the protections can and must also be read as *prohibitions* on those who are in positions of power or control during the course of hostilities – and ought, therefore, to be interpreted as such.[73] Taking account of inescapable realities on the ground, as well as of evolving thinking within the international law of human rights,[74] some have gone on to argue that there are therefore 'good grounds' for us 'to consider a non-governmental party to

---

[73] Sivakumaran, 'Torture in International Human Rights and International Humanitarian Law: The Actor and the Ad Hoc Tribunals', 18 (2005) *Leiden Journal of International Law* 541. See also Marshall, 'Tortute Committed by Non-State Actors: The Developing Jurisprudence from the ad hoc Tribunals', 5 (2005) *Non-State Actors & Int'l L.* 171. This is not reflective of international humanitarian law alone, but of broader acknowledgements of the capacities of non-State actors within the international system: see, in this respect, the development of the concept of crimes against humanity in Article 7 of the 1998 Rome Statute of the International Criminal Court as specified acts 'committed as part of a widespread or systematic attack directed against any civilian population, with knowledge of the attack' (Article 7 (1)), when '"attack directed against any civilian population" means a course of conduct involving the multiple commission of [specified] acts ... against any civilian population, *pursuant to or in furtherance of a State or organizational policy* to commit such attack' (Article 7 (2) (a)) (emphasis supplied). This expansion of the concept beyond the furtherance of State policy is regarded as one of the 'signal achievements' of the Statute: Meron, 'Cassese's *Tadic* and the Law of Non-International Armed Conflicts', in Vohrah, Pocar, Featherstone (eds.), *Man's Inhumanity to Man Essays on International Law in Honour of Antonio Cassese*, The Hague, 2003, p. 533, at p. 538.

[74] Drawing on the United Nations' Declaration on the Protection of All Persons from Being Subjected to Torture and Other Cruel, Inhuman or Degrading Treatment or Punishment (General Assembly Resolution 3452 (XXX), of 9 December 1975), Nigel Rodley has observed:

> The paragraph of the resolution by which the General Assembly adopted the Declaration stipulated that the Declaration was a 'guideline for all States and *other entities exercising effective power*'. I suggest that the emphasized words capture precisely the spirit of both the conceptual scope of human rights and the rationale behind the international law approach to them. It conveys the reality of the human rights equation: the individual at the mercy of a government or of another power over whose actions the government is impotent. Of course, there may be difficulty in identifying whether a particular armed opposition group should be considered as falling above or below the threshold, as being required *directly* to respect basic rights or not. The concept, however, remains in tact.

> See 'Can Armed Opposition Groups Violate Human Rights?', in Mahoney and Mahoney (eds.), *Human Rights in the Twenty First Century: A Global Challenge*, Dordrecht, 1993, p. 297, at p. 313. See, in addition to this, Moore, 'From Nation State to Failed State: International Protection from Human Rights Abuses by Non-State Agents', 31 (1999) *Columbia HRLR* 81.

non-international armed conflict as being capable of violating human rights in armed conflict'.[75] We can appreciate this further with the expanded protections of the 1977 Second Additional Protocol, and in view of the fact that this set of obligations concerns those non-international armed conflicts that have met the specific conditions articulated in that Protocol.[76]

These rules are therefore directed towards those who are belligerents and engaged in hostilities, or, for want of a better expression, persons taking an active part in hostilities (presumably as members of 'each Party' to the conflict). Their value is to distinguish between the permissible and impermissible conduct in warfare irrespective of the nature of the *actor* or *actors* concerned, as we see with the addressees of certain Security Council resolutions during recent non-international armed conflicts in Angola and Afghanistan:[77] in Security Council Resolution 864 (1993), for instance, with respect to Angola, the Council strongly condemned 'the repeated attacks carried out by UNITA [*Uniao Nacional para a Independencia Total de Angola*] against United Nations personnel working to provide humanitarian assistance and [it] reaffirm[ed] that such attacks [were] clear violations of international humanitarian law'.[78] During hostilities between the Taliban and the Northern Alliance in Afghanistan, the Security Council adopted Resolution 1193 in August 1998 in which it reaffirmed 'that all parties to the conflict are bound to comply with their obligations under international humanitarian law and in particular the Geneva Conventions of

---

[75] Rodley (note 74), at p. 312. See also Nair, 'Confronting the Violence Committed by Armed Opposition Groups', 1 (1998) *Yale HRDLJ* 1, at p. 3 and p. 6.

[76] Namely Article 1 (1) of the Second Additional Protocol, which, as Solf observes, requires the rebels 'to have sufficient state-like characteristics': see 'The Status of Combatants in Non-international Armed Conflicts under Domestic Law and Transnational Practice', 33 (1983) *American ULR* 53, at p. 63. See also Smith, 'New Protections for Victims of Non-International Armed Conflicts: the Proposed Ratification of Protocol II by the United States', 120 (1988) *Military LR* 59.

[77] Kooijmans, 'The Security Council and Non-State Entities as Parties to Conflicts', in Wellens (ed.), *International Law: Theory and Practice – Essays in Honour of Eric Suy*, The Hague, 1998, p. 333.

[78] Security Council Resolution 864 (1993), thirteenth operative paragraph. In the fourteenth operative paragraph, the Security Council noted 'statements by UNITA that it will cooperate in ensuring the unimpeded delivery of humanitarian assistance to all Angolans and *demands* that UNITA act accordingly'. Emphasis original. See Kooijmans (note 77), describing as 'remarkable' Security Council Resolutions 864 (1993) and 1127 (1997) in respect of UNITA in Angola 'since on the one hand [they are] addressed to an entity which is not a state and does not even presume to be a state, while on the other this entity is evidently held to be legally responsible for its wrongful conduct'. See p. 333. See also Bourloyannis, 'The Security Council of the United Nations and Implementation of International Humanitarian Law,' 20 (1992) *Denver JILP* 335.

12 August 1949, and that persons who commit or order the commission of grave breaches of the Conventions are individually responsible in respect of such breaches'.[79]

Hence, the rules of common Article 3 of the Geneva Conventions – and, for that matter, those of the 1977 Second Additional Protocol – provide a mechanism and an essential point of reference for political and diplomatic interaction *during* hostilities; their first and principal purpose is to have some bite as and when an armed conflict is occurring. We can venture the same observation for the lion's share of rules applicable in international armed conflicts, though these rules come with the additional significance of helping determine whether a captured combatant is to be awarded the status of a privileged belligerent or not. Such decisions are not relevant in the context of a non-international armed conflict it is clear,[80] and yet they have consumed much of the earlier focus of our analysis in respect of non-State actors and international armed conflicts.[81] Important though this has been, the turn to the *substance* of these rules – that is, to these rules as 'prohibitive law'[82] – is important because many of the rules themselves have been framed without prejudice to (or even without consideration of) the identity of the actor involved: their interest and concern is the *nature of the activity in question*. We see this logic firmly at work in the reasoning of the International Criminal Tribunal for Former Yugoslavia, when its Appeals Chamber asked in October 1995: 'Why protect civilians from belligerent violence, or ban rape, torture or the wanton destruction of hospitals … when two sovereign States are engaged in war, and yet refrain from enacting the same bans or providing the same protection when armed violence has erupted "only" within the territory of a Sovereign State?'[83] This reasoning was pursued with equal vigour on the question of the wherewithal of warfare, when the Appeals Chamber declared that 'elementary considerations of humanity and common sense make it preposterous that the use by States of weapons prohibited in armed conflicts between themselves be allowed when States try to put down

---

[79] Security Council Resolution 1193 (1998), twelfth operative paragraph – though the reference to 'grave breaches' in this context suggests that the Council might have regarded this set of hostilities as an international armed conflict. See Roberts, 'The Laws of War in the War on Terror', in Borch and Wilson (eds.), *International Law and the War on Terror*, Newport, RI, 2003, p. 175 at p. 193 and *infra*, notes 87 and 93.

[80] See further Solf (note 76), at p. 54.

[81] For the purpose of deciding which combatants must be treated as prisoners-of-war and which must also be accorded combatant immunity. See Dinstein (note 20), at p. 30 and p. 234.

[82] Baxter (note 34), at p. 324 – adopting the phrase from *United States v. List et al* (1948): 11 *Trials of War Criminals* 1230, at p. 1247, and p. 1252; 8 *War Crimes Reports* 34, at p. 66.

[83] *Prosecutor v. Tadic* (Decision on Defence Motion for Interlocutory Appeal on Jurisdiction): Case No. IT-94-1-1; 2 October 1995: 105 *ILR* 453, at p. 506, paragraph 97.

rebellion by their own nationals on their own territory. What is inhumane, and consequently proscribed, in international wars, cannot but be inhumane and inadmissible in civil strife'.[84]

Viewed from this angle, we can appreciate the other function of the Geneva Conventions and their Protocols that are distinct from their role in the classification of combatants in international armed conflicts. At one and the same time, they also underpin and chart the actual responsibilities of States under public international law,[85] and have come to set the foundations – and to very much inform – the criminal consequences that can result from certain violence in warfare.[86] We say 'inform' because separate trajectories were originally envisaged for 'war crimes' in non-international armed conflicts as opposed to international armed conflicts in the Geneva Conventions of August 1949,[87] and this dichotomization as to the *form* of an armed conflict has since shaped both the structure and the substance of Article 8 of the 1998 Rome Statute of the International Criminal Court (on 'war crimes').[88] Be this as it may, it should be clear that the concept of 'war crimes' in international armed conflicts is addressed to lawful and unlawful combatants alike, since the commission of a war crime (including so-called grave breaches) is not dependent on one's privileged (belligerent) status.[89] An unlawful combatant is therefore as liable under this regime as they would be for their participation in the armed conflict and from 'warlike acts that do not violate the laws and customs of war'.[90] Indeed, the system of criminal jurisdiction that attaches to grave breaches in the wake

---

[84] Ibid, at p. 516, paragraph 119.

[85] The Conventions emphasize the 'unilateral engagements solemnly contracted' by States in common Article 1, a provision regarded as applicable to a State's population as a whole: Kalshoven, 'The Undertaking to Respect and Ensure Respect in All Circumstances: From Tiny Seed to Ripening Fruit', 2 (1999) *Yearbook of International Humanitarian Law* 3. Cf. Article 82 of the 1929 Geneva Convention Relative to the Treatment of Prisoners of War: 'The provisions of the present Convention shall be respected by the High Contracting Parties in all circumstances'.

[86] Cf. Plattner, 'The Penal Responsibility of Violations of International Humanitarian Law Applicable in Non-international Armed Conflicts', [30] (No. 278, 1990) *International Review of the Red Cross* 409, at p. 414.

[87] Where a system of 'grave breaches' was developed for certain war crimes: see the second paragraph of common Articles 49/50/129/146 of the Geneva Conventions. Note, further, Plattner's observation that '[t]he rules establishing international individual responsibility for violations of IHL applicable in non-international armed conflicts are yet to be made . . .': ibid, at p. 419.

[88] Article 8 (2) (a) and (b) for international armed conflicts; Article 8 (2) (c) to (f) for non-international armed conflicts. See also Cassese, 'On the Current Trends towards Criminal Prosecution and Punishment of Breaches of International Humanitarian Law', 8 (1998) *EJIL* 2.

[89] Dinstein (note 20), at p. 235.

[90] Solf (note 76), at p. 57.

of the Conventions and Protocols is often equated with that for piracy, 'essentially a crime committed without the authority of any State'.[91] No identical framework exists for common Article 3 of the 1949 Geneva Conventions, of course, or in the 1977 Second Additional Protocol,[92] but this does not mean that the Geneva Conventions and the Second Additional Protocol leave the matter of the criminal consequences for actions in non-international armed conflicts untouched.[93] We might not obtain this impression from an isolated reading of common Article 3, addressed as it is to the belligerent parties involved in such armed conflicts; the Rome Statute, in contrast, is specifically predicated on the basis of the *individual*, on individual action and on individual criminal responsibility. This line of focus of the Rome Statute, on 'those responsible for international crimes',[94] allows the regulation of warfare to assume new dimensions of relevance and application in modern times, for its operating premise is a class apart from the original conceptions of warfare that valued the State against, it would seem, all other considerations.[95]

---

[91] Roxburgh, 'Submarines at the Washington Conference', 3 (1922–1923) *BYIL* 150, at p. 154.

[92] Solf (note 76), at pp. 58–59; and Plattner (note 86), at p. 414. See, though, Meron, 'International Criminalization of Internal Atrocities', 89 (1995) *AJIL* 554.

[93] With, it must be said, a view to the individual: see Plattner (note 86), at p. 416. Note that the third paragraph of common Articles 49/50/129/146 of the Geneva Conventions does provide: 'Each High Contracting Party shall take measures necessary for the suppression of *all acts contrary to provisions of the present Convention other than the grave breaches defined in the following Article* ...', a formulation that must be taken to include common Article 3 (emphasis supplied). Furthermore, Article 6, paragraph 1 of the 1977 Second Additional Protocol envisages 'the prosecution and punishment of criminal offences related to the armed conflict'. See further Georges Abi-Saab, 'Non-international Armed Conflicts' in United Nations Educational, Scientific and Cultural Organization (ed.), *The International Dimensions of Humanitarian Law*, Geneva, 1988, p. 217 at p. 231. In *Tadic*, the Appeals Chamber concluded that Article 3 of its Statute – addressing violations of the laws and customs of war – was 'a general clause covering *all violations of humanitarian law* not falling under Article 2 or covered by Articles 4 or 5, more specifically: (i) violations of the Hague law on international conflicts; (ii) infringements of provisions of the Geneva Conventions other than those classified as 'grave breaches' by those Conventions; (iii) violations of common Article 3 and other customary rules on internal conflicts; (iv) violations of agreements binding upon the parties to the conflict, considered *qua* treaty law, i.e. agreements which have not turned into customary international law': *supra* (note 83), at p. 506, paragraph 89; emphasis supplied.

[94] From the sixth preambular paragraph of the Statute. See also Cassese (note 88).

[95] Danner, 'When Courts Make Law: How International Criminal Tribunals Recast the Laws of War', 59 (2006) *Vanderbilt LR* 1.

iii. On Initiations of Violence

The historical focus of the *jus in bello* on States and State actors is repeated in respect of the *jus ad bellum*, where the cardinal prohibition of Article 2 (4) of the United Nations Charter concerns the undertaking of Member States of the United Nations to 'refrain in their international relations from the threat or use of force against the territorial integrity or political independence of any State, or in any other manner inconsistent with the Purposes of the United Nations'. We have a double sense of the significance of the State in this formulation: it is States to whom this prohibition is addressed, and the prohibition is defined by that force which is threatened or used *against the territorial integrity or political independence of any State* – so that its application to force threatened or used against a non–State actor (for example, a pirate ship located on the high seas) might be open to question.[96] What is more, we find this prohibition mirrored to a significant extent in the definition of aggression reached by the General Assembly in Resolution 3314 (XXIX) of December 1974, where aggression was regarded

---

[96] Farer, *Confronting Global Terrorism and American Neo-Conservatism: The Framework of A Liberal Grand Strategy*, Oxford, 2008, p. 76. Note, though, the provision in Article 105 of the 1982 United Nations Convention on the Law of the Sea, that '[o]n the high seas, or in any other place outside the jurisdiction of any State, every State may seize a pirate ship or aircraft, or a ship or aircraft taken by piracy and under the control of pirates, and arrest the persons and seize the property on board. The courts of the State which carried out the seizure may decide upon the penalties to be imposed, and may also determine the action to be taken with regard to the ships, aircraft or property, subject to the rights of third parties acting in good faith.' In June 2008, the Security Council adopted Resolution 1816 under Chapter VII of the United Nations Charter in which in decided that for six months from 2 June 2008, 'States cooperating with the [Transitional Federal Government (TFG) of Somalia] in the fight against piracy and armed robbery at sea off the coast of Somalia, for which advance notification has been provided by the TFG to the Secretary-General [of the United Nations], may: (a) [e]nter the territorial waters of Somalia for the purpose of repressing acts of piracy and armed robbery at sea, in a manner consistent with such action permitted on the high seas with respect to piracy under relevant international law; and (b) [u]se, within the territorial waters of Somalia, in a manner consistent with action permitted on the high seas with respect to piracy under relevant international law, all necessary means to repress acts of piracy and armed robbery.' See Guilfoyle, 'Piracy off Somalia: UN Security Council Resolution 1816 and IMO Regional Counter-Piracy Efforts', 57 (2008) *ICLQ* 690. The situation on the high seas stands to be distinguished, we must argue, from a non-State actor located on the territory of another State: see Printer, Jr., 'The Use of Force Against Non-State Actors under International Law: An Analysis of the U.S. Predator Strike in Yemen', 8 (2003) *UCLA J Int'l L. & Foreign Affairs* 331. However, we must enquire whether the consent of that other State was forthcoming for the use of force in question: Pincus, 'Missile Strike Carried out with Yemeni Cooperation – Official Says Operation Authorized under Bush Finding', *Washington Post*, 6 November 2002, p. A10. This has not been a lone episode in the United States' 'war on terror': see Cloud, 'U.S. Airstrike Aims at Qaeda Cell in Somalia', *New York Times*, 9 January 2007, p. A3 and Gettleman, 'U.S. Strikes Inside Somalia, Bombing Suspected Militant Hide-Out', *New York Times*, 9 June 2007, p. A10.

as 'the use of armed force by a State against the sovereignty, territorial integrity or political independence of another State, or in any other manner inconsistent with the Charter of the United Nations, as set out in this Definition'.[97]

To be sure, although the definition of aggression by the General Assembly makes explicit the State in its formulation, it came with an important explanatory note by the General Assembly, which provided that the term 'State' '(a) is used without prejudice to questions of recognition or to whether a State is a member of the United Nations; (b) includes the concept of a "group of States" where appropriate'.[98] This clarification was clearly entered to counter the formal rigours of the law, and to effect an identical pragmatics on those without the 'legal qualification to make war', but who nevertheless possessed the wherewithal (and, we might add, the will) to do so.[99] However, it might be argued that it is one thing to follow a functional approach to matters where we are confronted with entities awaiting or falling short of recognition as States, or where a purposeful interpretation is taken toward 'the suzerain and the vassal' as we encountered earlier.[100] It is quite another to consider these rules in terms of *other* non-State actors, those without any formal pedigree or pedagogical mooring within the international system,[101] and, in view of this realization and in the wake of 11 September 2001, there were calls to update the prohibition of force in accordance with these emerging realities.[102]

---

[97] General Assembly Resolution 3314 (XXIX), 29 *UNGAOR*, Supp. No. 31: UN Doc. A/9890 (1974), Article 1.

[98] See further Cassin, Debevoise, Kailes and Thompson, 'The Definition of Aggression', 16 (1975) *Harvard International Law Journal* 589, at p. 595.

[99] See Oppenheim (note 44), p. 86 (§ 75).

[100] Ibid.

[101] As Stone has observed, the explanatory note left unresolved the matter of 'whether and in what sense the definition [of aggression] is limited to state-to-state aggression': see 'Hopes and Loopholes in the 1974 Definition of Aggression', 71 (1977) *AJIL* 224, at p. 232.

[102] As was done by Anne-Marie Slaughter and William Burke-White, to the effect that a 'new constitutional moment' had been urged by those events – a moment that required urgent legislative attention:

> In this new constitutional moment, the world's nations must come together at the outset of a war rather than at its end. They must take account of the beginning of a new century and of a renewed tide of globalization pulling us together. Their purpose must be to complement Article 2 (4), to establish an additional constitutional principle of international peace and security for a very different world. Article 2 (4) (a) should read: 'All States and individuals shall refrain from the deliberate targeting or killing of civilians in armed conflict of any kind, for any purpose.' No State or group can justify the deliberate deaths of civilians. Conversely, States and individuals will be obligated to make every effort to protect civilian lives and to structure their diplomatic and military actions to avoid civilian casualties.

See 'An International Constitutional Moment', 43 (2002) *Harvard International Law Journal* 1, at p. 2.

To these positions, it ought to be contended that the interpretative decisions we reach on the *scope* of the prohibition of force await to be informed by the historical purposes at work behind the modern rules of the *jus ad bellum*.[103] Thus far, we have considered the rules on force in terms of the *prohibition* of force in Article 2 (4) of the United Nations Charter, but it would be an error to consider this document a 'pacifist charter' since the Charter goes on to enunciate the rules for *permissible* force under public international law.[104] The Charter makes these allowances either through the right of self-defence – of States, to be sure[105] – or through the authorization of the Security Council under the executive powers it is awarded in Chapter VII. In other words, the starting premise of Article 2 (4), as well as of its antecedent provisions in the 1907 Hague Convention (II) on the Limitation of Employment of Force for Recovery of Contract Debts and the 1928 Kellogg-Briand Pact, was that States possessed a general prerogative for force or the making of war in international relations – and that this had classically been so. Public international law regarded this as much a power as it did one of the 'natural functions' of State,[106] and its ensuing interventions are best viewed as part of a general framework of rules on the permissibilities *as well as* the impermissibilities of force that has taken the *State* as its governing, we could even contend exclusive, concern. Non-State actors did not fall within the same bracket of activity or analysis and could not therefore be treated in the same breath as States and their agents: it was not admitted that non–State actors had (or shared) this prerogative, so it made next to no sense to bring them within this particular regulatory fold or to pair them with what States could not but also what they *could* lawfully do.[107] It is for this reason that we perhaps find the prohibition of force worded the way we do.[108]

---

[103] That is, in relation to *initiations* of violence; the Slaughter and Burke-White proposal, ibid, strays into the provenance of the *jus in bello* ('in armed conflict of any kind').

[104] See in this respect Greenwood, 'International Law and the Pre-emptive Use of Force: Afghanistan, Al-Qaida, and Iraq', 4 (2003) *San Diego ILJ* 7, who writes that 'the Charter is about keeping the peace not about pacifism'. See p. 10. See also Franck, 'Terrorism and the Right of Self-Defense', 95 (2001) *AJIL* 839 on the significance of the normative context in which the Charter's prohibition of force appears.

[105] The right of self-defence *inheres* in States, at least according to the terms of Article 51 of the Charter: see text accompanying *supra* (note 10). See, however, *infra* notes 137 and 142.

[106] *See* Oppenheim (note 36), p. 84, §74.

[107] For an extended analysis of linguistic differentiations within the Charter itself, consider Canor, 'When *Jus ad Bellum* Meets *Jus in Bello*: The Occupier's Right of Self-Defence against Terrorism Stemming from Occupied Territories', 19 (2006) *Leiden Journal of International Law* 129, at p. 134.

[108] In other words, that the obligation is addressed to all *Member States* of the United Nations. See, however, Article 2 (6) of the Charter, that the United Nations 'shall ensure that states which are not Members of the United Nations act in accordance with these Principles so far

Perhaps a good impression of how public international law has taken some cognizance of the practice of non-State actors under the *jus ad bellum* arises from the International Court of Justice's definition of an armed attack in its judgment in the *Nicaragua Case* in June 1986. There, the Court proceeded with its definition after its distinguished between 'the most grave forms of the use of force (those constituting an armed attack) from other less grave forms',[109] language so reminiscent of the prohibition of force in Article 2 (4) of the Charter. Yet, as the Court unfurled its definition of an armed attack in that judgment, non-State actors made a singular appearance in the Court's itinerary of examples of what *might* constitute an armed attack under public international law: 'the sending by or on behalf of a State of armed bands, groups, irregulars or mercenaries, which carry out acts of armed force against another State of such gravity as to amount to' (*inter alia*) an actual armed attack conducted by regular forces, 'or its substantial involvement therein'.[110] Note how, as the Court made this reference, it regarded the non-State actors (here 'armed bands, groups, irregulars or mercenaries') in the context of an action that involved the *sending by or on behalf of a State*.[111] This representation was not lost on President Rosalyn Higgins in the *Legal Consequences of the Construction of a Wall in the Occupied Palestinian Territory* in July 2004, when she remarked that the Court's thinking on an 'armed attack' in its advisory opinion on that occasion had its genesis in what the Court had decided in the *Nicaragua Case* a generation earlier;[112] in its opinion in July 2004, the Court had 'recognize[d] the existence of an inherent right of self-defense in the case of armed attack *by one State against another State*'.[113]

Such approaches tend to emphasize restrictive conceptualizations of the right of self-defence, and to fashion the law at the expense of its historical purpose and intentions, and do not sit well with the practice of States: the legal appreciation of the events of 11 September 2001 under the *jus ad bellum* – readily available to

---

as may be necessary for the maintenance of international peace and security'.

[109] *Military and Paramilitary Activities in and against Nicaragua (Nicaragua v. United States)*, Merits, ICJ *Reports 1986*, p. 14, at p. 101, paragraph 191.

[110] The Court is here quoting from General Assembly Resolution 3314 (note 97), Article 3 (g).

[111] On the role of the State in the definition of mercenaries under the *jus in bello*, see sources referred to in note 58, *supra*.

[112] *Legal Consequences of the Construction of a Wall in the Occupied Palestinian Territory* (Advisory Opinion), *ICJ Reports 2004*, p. 136, at p. 215, paragraph 33.

[113] Ibid, p. 194, paragraph 139; emphasis supplied. Sean Murphy considers that this position of the Court might be regarded 'ambiguous' in the sense that it does not purport to be comprehensive, but dismisses this possibility on the grounds that 'the Court understood how its language was going to be interpreted and nevertheless chose to adopt that interpretation'. See 'Self-Defense and the Israeli Wall Advisory Opinion: An *Ipse Dixit* from the ICJ?', 99 (2005) *AJIL* 62, at p. 63.

the Court when it made its advisory opinion in July 2004 – is not that difficult to discern. Though the Security Council had not invoked the concept of an 'armed attack' in Resolution 1368 on 12 September 2001, it did so in all but name as it recognized 'the inherent right of individual or collective self-defence in accordance with the Charter;'[114] it repeated this position on 28 September 2001, with the adoption of Resolution 1373. For its part, NATO concluded that 'if it is determined that this was directed from abroad against the United States, it shall be regarded as an action covered by Article 5 of the Washington Treaty, which states that an armed attack against one or more of the Allies in Europe or North America shall be considered an attack against them all',[115] and, on 21 September 2001, the Organization of American States resolved that 'these terrorist attacks against the United States of America are attacks against all American states'.[116] With these proclamations, a steady and near-universal chorus concerning the 'armed attack' in the United States on 11 September 2001 had begun to take shape and to assert itself, notwithstanding the fact that both author and perpetrator of the armed attack (armed attacks?)[117] were one and the same non-State actor.[118] Judge Peter Kooijmans took account of these developments in the separate opinion he entered to the *Israeli Wall* advisory opinion in July 2004:

> Resolutions 1368 and 1373 [of the Security Council] recognize the inherent right of individual or collective self-defence without making any reference to an armed attack by a State … This new element is not excluded by the terms of Article 51 since this conditions the exercise of the inherent right of self-defence on a previous armed attack without saying that this armed attack must come from another State even if this has been the generally accepted interpretation for more than 50 years. The Court has regrettably by-passed this new element, the legal implications of which cannot as yet be assessed but which marks undeniably a new approach to the concept of self-defence.[119]

---

[114] Preamble, Security Council Resolution 1368 (2001). The first operative paragraph of this resolution did make reference to 'the horrifying terrorist attacks which took place on 11 September 2001'. The Security Council reaffirmed its 'unequivocal condemnation' of these attacks in the preamble of Resolution 1373 (2001), as well as 'the inherent right of individual or collective self-defence as recognized by the Charter of the United Nations as reiterated in Resolution 1368 (2001)'.

[115] Statement of the North Atlantic Council: Press Release 124, 12 September 2001.

[116] Twenty-Fourth Meeting of Consultation of Ministers of Foreign Affairs of the Organization of American States, OEA/Ser. F/II.24, RC.24/RES.1/01 (21 September 2001).

[117] Bear in mind the reference in Security Council Resolution 1368 (2001) to 'terrorist attacks': *supra* (note 114), third operative paragraph.

[118] Cf. Myjer and White, 'The Twin Towers Attack: An Unlimited Right to Self-Defence?', 7 (2002) *JCSL* 5.

[119] See *Construction of a Wall in Palestinian Territory* (note 112), at p. 230, paragraph 35. Cf. Murphy (note 113), at p. 69.

All of this said, however, it must be recalled that, in response to the events of 11 September 2001, the United States was not seeking to exercise its right of self-defense *against* a non-State actor pure and *simpliciter*: its intended action was not against a non-State actor located on the high seas or upon some anonymous tract of *terra nullius*. The United States was priming itself for action against al-Qaeda *in and against Afghanistan*, and seemed committed to the idea of making some case of 'necessity' for the application of force against another sovereign State.[120] After all, before a joint session of the United States Congress on 20 September 2001, President Bush had issued an ultimatum to the Taliban Government of Afghanistan to the following effect:

> Al Qaeda is to terror what the mafia is to crime. But its goal is not making money; its goal is remaking the world – and imposing its radical beliefs on people everywhere. This group and its leader – a person named Osama bin Laden – are linked to many other organizations in different countries, including the Egyptian Islamic Jihad and the Islamic Movement of Uzbekistan. There are thousands of these terrorists in more than 60 countries. They are recruited from their own nations and neighbourhoods and brought to camps in places like Afghanistan, where they are trained in the tactics of terror. They are sent back to their homes or sent to hide in countries around the world to plot evil and destruction.
>
> The leadership of al Qaeda has great influence in Afghanistan and supports the Taliban regime in controlling most of that country. In Afghanistan, we see al Qaeda's vision for the world ... The United States respects the people of Afghanistan – after all, we are currently its largest source of humanitarian aid – but we condemn the Taliban regime ... It is not only repressing its own people, it is threatening people everywhere by sponsoring and sheltering and supplying terrorists. By aiding and abetting murder, the Taliban regime is committing murder.
>
> And tonight, the United States of America makes the following demands on the Taliban: Deliver to United States authorities all the leaders of al Qaeda who hide in your land ... Release all foreign nationals, including American citizens, you have unjustly imprisoned. Protect foreign journalists, diplomats and aid workers in your country. Close immediately and permanently every terrorist training camp in Afghanistan, and hand over every terrorist, and every person in their support structure, to appropriate authorities ... Give the United States full access to terrorist training camps, so we can make sure they are no longer operating.
>
> These demands are not open to negotiation or discussion ... The Taliban must act, and act immediately. They will hand over the terrorists, or they will share in their fate.[121]

---

[120] Trapp, 'Back to Basics: Necessity, Proportionality, and the Right of Self-Defence Against Non-State Terrorist Actors', 56 (2007) *ICLQ* 141, at p. 146. See also Murphy (note 113), at pp. 66–67.

[121] Office of the Press Secretary to the White House, Presidential Address to A Joint Session

The language against the Government of Taliban in Afghanistan had become much more robust by the time of the initiation of Operation Enduring Freedom against Afghanistan on 7 October 2001, as is evident from the position of the United States before the Security Council. In making its official argument known to the Council concerning its right of self-defence, the United States announced that it had 'clear and compelling information that the al-Qaeda organization, which is supported by the Taliban regime in Afghanistan, had a central role in the attacks'.[122] For the United States, the extent of the Taliban's implication in the activities of al-Qaeda was manifest and could not be doubted:

> The attacks on 11 September 2001 and the ongoing threat to the United States and its nationals posed by the al-Qaeda organization have been made possible by the decision of the Taliban regime to allow parts of Afghanistan that it controls to be used by this organization as a base for operation. Despite every effort by the United States and the international community, the Taliban regime has refused to change its policy. From the territory of Afghanistan, the al-Qaeda organization continues to train and support agents of terror who attack innocent people throughout the world and target United States nationals and interests in the United States and abroad.[123]

The effect of these arguments is to make it sound as if the Taliban and the al-Qaeda organization were in some sort of partnership, or were 'two sides of the same coin' as the British Government put it,[124] but there have also been occasions where States have used force in the *absence* of any form of action or support by a State for the non-State actor.[125] We might venture the Turkish application of force against Iraq in respect of the Kurdistan Workers' Party (PKK) as a modern example,[126] but there is a much more enduring illustration of the

---

of Congress and the American People (20 September 2001) (www.whitehouse.gov/news/releases/2001/09/20010920-8.html).

[122] UN Doc. S/946 (7 October 2001).

[123] Ibid.

[124] British Government, *Responsibility for the Terrorist Atrocities in the United States, 11 September 2001*, London, 2001, paragraph 19.

[125] *See* Murphy (note 113), at p. 70. The standard which the International Court of Justice appears to have set, but has yet to explain, is one of attributability: see, in particular, its decision in *Case Concerning Armed Activities on the Territory of the Congo (Democratic Republic of the Congo v. Uganda)*, 19 December 2005, paragraph 146. See further Okowa, 'Congo's War: The Legal Dimension of a Protracted Conflict', 77 (2006) *BYIL* 203, at pp. 235–49; and Trapp (note 120), at p. 141 and p. 145. See also Barbour and Salzman, '"The Tangled Web": The Right of Self-Defense Against Non-State Actors in the *Armed Activities* Case', 40 (2008) *NYUJILP* 53.

[126] See Burke, 'Turkish Onslaught Paves Way for Major Assault on Iraq Kurds', *The Observer* (London), 24 February 2008, p. 39; Tisdall, 'Reconciliation, Sealed With A Bombing Run', *The Guardian* (London), 18 December 2007, p. 22; and also 'Warplanes Attack Rebel Hideouts Near Iraq', *The Guardian* (London), 11 October 2007, p. 24. Though, as a general pattern,

use of force *against* a State where it was found not to have taken appropriate or sufficient action to thwart the activities of non-State actors based on or operating within its territory. Here we rely on the official pronouncements of Great Britain in respect of the action it took against the *Caroline* on 29 December 1837, and to the argumentative task that had been set for it by the United States Secretary of State Daniel Webster in April 1841 – that it was for 'Her Majesty's Government to show ... a necessity of self-defence, instant, overwhelming, leaving no choice of means, and no moment for deliberation. It will be for it to show, also, that the local authorities of Canada, – even supposing the necessity of the moment authorized them to enter the territories of the United States at all, – did nothing unreasonable or excessive; since the act justified by the necessity of self-defense, must be limited by that necessity, and kept clearly within it.'[127] There, although Great Britain had entered the territory of the United States, and had famously inflicted terminal damage on the *Caroline*, the main source of its concern was not only the activities of rebel units on Navy Island but also of the private assistance directed towards these units from individuals in the United States.[128] The actions – or, to be more precise, inactions – of the United States did not go unnoticed and were invoked in the course of demonstrating the necessity for action by Great Britain. Lord Ashburton, special minister or envoy of Great Britain to the United States, in his correspondence with Secretary Webster, wrote in July 1842:

> Supposing a man standing on ground where you have no legal right to follow him has a weapon long enough to reach you, and is striking you down and endangering your life, How long are you bound to wait for the assistance of the authority having the legal power to relieve you? Or, to bring the facts more immediately home to the case, if cannon are moving and setting up in a battery which can reach you and are actually destroying life and property by their fire, If you have remonstrated for some time without effect, and see no prospect of relief, when begins your right to defend yourself, should you have no other means of doing so, than by seizing your assailant on the verge of neutral territory?[129]

---

this has not formally been announced in terms of the right of self-defence: Gray and Olleson, 'The Limits of the Law on the Use of Force: Turkey, Iraq and the Kurds', 12 (2001) *Finnish YbIL* 355.

[127] Manning, *Diplomatic Correspondence of the United States, Canadian Relations, 1784–1860* vol. iii, *1836–1848: Documents 1193–1853*, Washington DC, 1943, p. 145 (Doc. No. 1269).

[128] See Murphy who wrote: 'On its facts, the *Caroline* incident concerned self-defense *as a reaction to attacks by nonstate actors* (in that case, support by U.S. nationals for a rebellion in Canada).' *Supra* (note 113), p. 65.

[129] See Manning (note 127), at p. 767 (Doc. No. 1593).

This phenomenon of 'armed bands' operating during a formal condition of peace between two States became a general problem after the First World War it has been contended, and the relationship between the non-State actor and a State actor is open to a series of characterizations – complicity, direct organization or support, toleration, 'negligence in control of armed bands', or of an inability to exercise control over such actors.[130] While the law on State obligations in this context might have been unsettled for a while,[131] the General Assembly reacted to this issue in October 1970 with its Declaration on Principles of International Law Concerning Friendly Relations and Co-operation among States in Accordance with the Charter of the United Nations, where it concluded: that '[e]very State has the duty to refrain from organizing or encouraging the organization of irregular forces or armed bands, including mercenaries, for incursion into the territory of another State', and that '[e]very State has the duty to refrain from organizing, instigating, assisting or participating in acts of civil strife or terrorist acts in another State or acquiescing in organized activities within its territory directed towards the commission of such acts, *when the acts referred to in the present paragraph involve a threat or use of force*'.[132] These emphasized words are important, because they are testament to the General Assembly's view that non-State actors *can* indeed commit threats and acts of force,[133] and, where these have occurred, States have responded with force *and* with different legal strategies – among which we would count the right of self-defence, the right of hot pursuit,[134] and even shades of the right of self-preservation.[135]

We have thus far considered how public international law has constructed an intricate framework of rules and of values for applications of force within the international system, and how that framework, taken as a totality, has concerned

---

[130] Brownlie, 'International Law and the Activities of Armed Bands', 7 (1958) *ICLQ* 712, pp. 712–13.

[131] Writing in 1958, Brownlie observed: 'The State practice is not very coherent in its legal content, but it is submitted that at least it shows that State complicity in incursions by armed bands or toleration of activities of such bands operating from national territory is "unlawful," constitutes a breach of the legal duties of a State in its international relations, and justifies a protest and request for preventive measures either by the malefactor or by an international or regional organ for maintaining peace.' *Supra* (note 130), p. 729.

[132] General Assembly Resolution 2625 (XXV), 25 *UNGAOR*, Supp. 28, at p. 131, UN Doc. A/8028 (24 October 1970) (Emphasis supplied).

[133] See sources referred to in note 7, *supra*.

[134] As it is reported France claimed against Algeria in September 1957: see Brownlie (note 131), at p. 712.

[135] As in France's action against Algerian rebels stationed in Tunisia in September 1957: Brownlie (note 131), p. 712. See also Gray and Olleson (note 126).

itself with the State and with State action.[136] This much has been emphasized in the *exceptions* to the prohibition of force, so that (as we have indicated) the right of self-defence is *inherent* in Statehood,[137] and – were it to exist – the 'right' of humanitarian intervention would be an entitlement that resides with *States* and *not* humanitarian non-governmental organizations.[138] Yet, at the same time that public international law set out to regulate rather than to banish State violence, it enjoined a considerable history of endeavours to outlaw private violence,[139] although it is true that, as we have also seen, and for better or for worse, this consideration is not reflected in explicit terms in the prohibition of force as we have come to know it.[140] That said, if it is accepted that non–State actors can commit armed attacks as a matter of law, it is hard to conceive of how they could do so without transgressing the prohibition of force since, in the understanding of the International Court of Justice in June 1986, the defining characteristic of an armed attack is that it constitutes 'the most grave form ... of the use of force' under public international law.[141] This appreciation of the scope of the application of the prohibition of force is reinforced by the essential

---

[136] Schachter, 'The Right of States to Use Armed Force', 82 (1984) *Michigan LR* 1620.

[137] Gorlick, 'Wars of National Liberation: *Jus ad bellum*', 11 (1979) *Case W. Res. JIL* 71, at p. 73. See also Franck who has observed that '[u]nder Article 51 [of the Charter], self-defense is a right exercisable at the sole discretion *of an attacked state*.' *Supra* (note 104), p. 840; emphasis supplied. Note the interpretation, though, in the Separate Opinion of Vice-President Fouad Ammoun in *Legal Consequences for States of the Continued Presence of South Africa in Namibia (South West Africa) Notwithstanding Security Council Resolution 276 (1970)* (Advisory Opinion), *ICJ Reports 1971*, p. 16, that '[i]n law, the legitimacy of the peoples' struggle cannot be in any doubt, for it follows from the right of self-defence, *inherent in human nature*, which is confirmed by Article 51 of the United Nations Charter': p. 70; emphasis supplied. The fact that an equation is happening in this particular formulation – between the right of self-determination and the right of self-defence – is confirmed when Vice-President Ammoun immediately then asserted, 'It is also an accepted principle that self-defence may be collective; thus we see the other peoples of Africa, members of the Organization of African Unity, associated with the Namibians in their fight for freedom.' Ibid. Validation for this proposition, he felt, came in part from the claim in the Universal Declaration of Human Rights that 'it is essential, if man is not to be compelled to have recourse, as a last resort, to rebellion against tyranny and oppression, that human rights should be protected by the rule of law'. Ibid.

[138] On this matter, consider Chandler, 'The Road to Military Humanitarianism: How the Human Rights NGOs Shaped a New Humanitarian Agenda', 23 (2001) *HRQ* 678.

[139] See Khan (note 7); Porras (note 17); and Parrillo (note 19).

[140] Hence, as part of the canon of just war, the stipulation of the condition of *auctoritas principis*: McDougal and Feliciano, 'Legal Regulation of Resort to International Coercion: Aggression and Self-Defense in Policy Perspective', 68 (1959) *Yale LJ* 1057, at p. 1065.

[141] *Military and Paramilitary Activities in and against Nicaragua* (note 109), at p. 101, paragraph 191 – a formulation the Court reiterated in *Case Concerning Oil Platforms (Islamic Republic of Iran v. United States)*, *ICJ Reports 2003*, p. 161, at p. 187, paragraph 51.

denial of any exceptions for private violence within the schemata of the United
Nations Charter, and it is in fits and starts, such as in October 1970, that we
find certain suggestions – and, here, suggestions is the appropriate word – of
permissible initiations of violence undertaken by actors who were actors *other*
than States.[142]

That suggestion, as we have termed it, might now be of 'considerably reduced
practical importance',[143] but it is relevant to consider how it arose and why. It
appeared in the General Assembly's Declaration on Principles of International
Law concerning Friendly Relations and Co-operation among States in accordance with the Charter of the United Nations of October 1970, which was an
attempt to give further definition to the principles of public international law –
including that of the prohibition of force. In this sense, General Assembly Resolution 2625 (XXV) was different to Resolution 1514 (XV) of December 1960,
the General Assembly's Declaration on the Granting of Independence to Colonial Countries and Peoples, which made no mention of force but '[s]olemnly
proclaim[ed] the necessity of bringing to a speedy and unconditional end to
colonialism in all its forms and manifestations'.[144] Both Declarations thus shared
the common ground of self-determination as a principle of public international
law, however, and it is in the context of articulating this principle that Resolution 2625 (XXV) proceeded to announce: 'Every State has the duty to refrain
from any forcible action which deprives peoples referred to in the elaboration
of the principle of equal rights and self-determination of their right to self-
determination and freedom and independence.'[145] Furthermore, provided the
Resolution, '[i]n their actions against, and resistance to, such forcible action
in pursuit of their exercise of their right to self-determination, such peoples

---

[142] We shall set aside here the powers of international institutions as 'non-State actors' in the
residual sense of that term: see *supra* notes 9 and 12. John Dugard has noted the 'omission'
from the 1963 Addis Ababa Charter of the Organization of African Unity (OAU) of any
provision concerning the prohibition of force akin to that in the United Nations Charter; and
that it 'differs materially' from the 1948 Bogota Charter of the Organization of American States
(Article 18) and the North Atlantic Treaty (Article 1); that this was 'deliberate' was 'apparent
from the tenor of speeches at the Addis Ababa Conference and actions taken by the OAU in
pursuance of its purpose "to eradicate all forms of colonialism"'. See 'The Organisation of
African Unity and Colonialism: An Inquiry into the Plea of Self-Defence as a Justification for
the Use of Force in the Eradication of Colonialism', 16 (1967) *ICLQ* 157, at p. 160. Note that
in December 1961, India had made the claim of the right of self-defence following its action
in Goa: UN Doc. S/PV. 987 (18 December 1961). See further Korman, *The Right of Conquest:
The Acquisition of Territory by Force in International Law and Practice*, Oxford, 1996, pp. 267 *et seq.*
[143] Gray, *International Law and the Use of Force* (Third edition), Oxford, 2008, p. 59.
[144] General Assembly Resolution 1514 (XV), 15 *UNGAOR*, Supp. No. 16, at p. 66: UN Doc.
A/4684 (14 December 1960).
[145] *Supra* (note 132).

are entitled to seek and receive support in accordance with the purposes and principles of the Charter.'[146]

This approach of the General Assembly, it is clear, addressed *both* States *and* non-State actors in respect of the right of peoples to self-determination but, whatever else it did, the language of Resolution 2625 (XXV) avoided a 'direct statement' on force.[147] Nevertheless, the General Assembly's position in subsequent resolutions has been taken to eke out the meaning of this aspect of Resolution 2625 (XXV),[148] so that it has been read to cover instances of force: Resolution 3070 (XXVIII) of November 1973 is perhaps the most cogent example of this thinking, since the General Assembly there reaffirmed 'the legitimacy of the peoples' struggle for liberation from colonial and foreign domination and alien subjugation by all available means, *including armed struggle*'.[149] That same resolution called upon States, 'in conformity with the Charter of the United Nations and with relevant resolutions of the United Nations, to recognize the right of all peoples to self-determination and independence and to offer moral, material and any other assistance to all peoples struggling for the full exercise of their inalienable right to self-determination and independence'.[150] A year later, in its definition of aggression, the General Assembly noted that none of the acts of aggression that it had identified in Article 3 of Resolution 3314 (XXIX) 'could in any way prejudice the right to self-determination, freedom and independence, as derived from the Charter, of peoples forcibly deprived of that right and referred to in [General Assembly Resolution 2625 (XXV)] particularly peoples under colonial and racist regimes or other forms of alien domination; nor the right of these peoples to struggle to that end and to seek and receive support, in accordance with the principles of the Charter and in conformity with the above mentioned Declaration'.[151] For some, these words are 'ambiguous';[152] for others, their meaning is more than clear.[153]

---

[146] Ibid. On the background to this aspect of the Declaration, see Verwey, 'Decolonization and Ius Ad Bellum: A Case Study of the United Nations General Assembly on International Law', in Akkerman, Van Krieken and Pannenborg (eds.), *Declaration on Principles: A Quest for Universal Peace*, Leyden, 1977, p. 121.

[147] Gray (note 143), at p. 61 ('it did this in order to achieve consensus').

[148] Verwey (note 146), at p. 123.

[149] General Assembly Resolution 3070 (XXVIII), 28 *UNGAOR*, Supp. 30, at p. 78: UN Doc. A/3070 (20 November 1973), second operative paragraph; emphasis supplied. Of late, the formulation has changed to 'all available means'. See Gray (note 143), at p. 62.

[150] Ibid, third operative paragraph. See further Mallison and Mallison, 'The National Rights of the People of Palestine', 9 (1980) *J. Palestine Stud.* 119.

[151] *Supra* (note 97), Article 7.

[152] Gray (note 143), at p. 62.

[153] Gorelick (note 137), at p. 86. Though to what end this clarity obtains remains unanswered: 'these resolutions [of the General Assembly] recognize the right of revolution in unequivocal

These developments all preceded the recognition in principle of 'armed conflicts in which peoples are fighting against colonial domination and alien occupation and against regimes in the exercise of their right of self-determination' as international armed conflicts in the First Additional Protocol of June 1977,[154] a much more pronounced turn for public international law to have made with the intended *effect* that such entities engaged in an armed conflict were to be treated as States (or State actors) for all intents and purposes. The idea was to create some parity of status for these exceptional situations, so that captured personnel representing these 'peoples' in combat would be treated as prisoners-of-war and where the more onerous burdens of the 1949 Geneva Conventions and the First Additional Protocol would become applicable to the armed conflicts in which they were engaged. This arrangement has of course proved quite controversial and, even though its customary status might be in some doubt,[155] the conventional footing that has been given to the violence of non-State actors in this context contrasts with the 'ambiguous' state of affairs that we find in the *jus ad bellum*,[156] which, itself, has proved no less controversial:

terms and go a long way towards condoning the granting of military aid to "liberation movements", [but] they fall short of declaring that in international relations force may be used in the pursuance of a war of national liberation, a "just" war'. See Dugard, 'SWAPO: The *jus ad bellum* and the *jus in bello*', 93 (1976) *SALJ* 144. See also Rubino, 'Colonialism and the Use of Force by States', in Cassese (ed.), *The Current Legal Regulation of the Use of Force*, Dordrecht, 1986, p. 133 at pp. 142–43.

[154] See Wilson, *International Law and the Use of Force by National Liberation Movements*, Oxford, 1988, p. 128, and Graham, 'The 1974 Diplomatic Conference on the Law of War: A Victory for Political Causes and a Return to the "Just War" Concept of the Eleventh Century', 32 (1975) *Washington & Lee LR* 25.

[155] Murray, 'The 1977 Geneva Protocols and Conflict in Southern Africa', 33 (1984) *ICLQ* 462. See, however, the discussion of Cassese, 'Wars of National Liberation and Humanitarian Law', in Swinarski (ed.), *Studies and Essays on International Humanitarian Law and Red Cross Principles in Honour of Jean Pictet*, Dordrecht, 1984, p. 313 at pp. 320–23.

[156] So labelled by Judge Stephen M. Schwebel in his famous dissent in the *Military and Paramilitary Activities in and against Nicaragua*, where he made reference to 'an acknowledged and ambiguous *dictum* of the Court on a topic of which no trace can be found in the pleadings of the Parties'. See *supra* (note 109), at p. 351, paragraph 181. In that case, the International Court of Justice had remarked that it was 'not here concerned with the process of decolonization; this question is not in issue in the present case': p. 108, paragraph 206. Yet, for Judge Schwebel, this aside of the Court, together with the context in which the remark was delivered, left much to be desired: 'the implication, or surely a possible implication, of the juxtaposition of the Court's statements is that the Court is of the view that there is or may be not a general but a particular right of intervention provided that it is in furtherance of "the process of decolonization." That is to say, by these statements, the Court may be understood as inferentially endorsing an exception to the prohibition against intervention, in favour of the legality of intervention in the promotion of so-called "wars of liberation", or, at any rate, some such wars, while condemning intervention of another political character'. See ibid, p. 351, paragraph 179.

In contemporary international law, the right of self-determination, freedom and independence of peoples is universally recognized; the right of peoples to struggle to achieve these ends is universally accepted; but what is *not* universally recognized and what is *not* universally accepted is any right of such peoples to foreign assistance or support which constitutes intervention. That is to say, it is lawful for a foreign State or movement to give to a people struggling for self-determination moral, political and humanitarian assistance; but it is not lawful for a foreign State or movement to intervene in that struggle with force or to provide arms, supplies and other logistical support in the prosecution of armed rebellion. This is true whether the struggle is or is proclaimed to be in pursuance of the process of decolonization or against colonial domination. Moreover, what entities are susceptible of decolonization is a matter of dispute in many cases. What is a colony, and who is the colonizer, are the subjects of sharply differing views. Examples of what may be contentiously characterized – though not necessarily unreasonably characterized – as colonies may be readily assembled. But for present purposes, it is enough to point out that the lack of beauty is in the eye of the beholder.[157]

Limited though it might be, some reference has thus far been made to the question of aggression in public international law, and to the emphasis which the General Assembly put on the State in its construction of that concept in Resolution 3314 (XXIX). We might say that the General Assembly actually anchored its definition in the State, but that some accommodation was made for vicarious aggressions, that is aggressions which have as their front 'armed bands, groups, irregulars or mercenaries'.[158] To be sure, this formulation answered the prevalent practices of States of that time,[159] but, we might further add that it was a deliberate move on behalf of the General Assembly, forged as it was by 'some of the most sensitive nerves of Western and Third World states':

> So far as the *perpetrator* of aggression was concerned, Third World states, championing the right of peoples to struggle *by armed force* for self-determination, were, of course, determined that *their* use of armed force should not stigmatize *them* as aggression – that is, that 'a State' should not (for this purpose) be interpreted to include such 'a people.' So far as the *victim* of aggression was concerned, the same advocates were no less obviously resolved that 'State' should be read to include 'a people' so struggling. Western states were opposed to this latter dispensation for

---

[157] *Military and Paramilitary Activities in Nicaragua* (note 109), p. 351, paragraph 180 (Dissenting Opinion of Judge Stephen M. Schwebel). See also Cassese (note 155), at p. 315.

[158] *Supra* (note 97), Article 3 (g). See also Article 16 of the International Law Commission's Draft Code of Offences Against the Peace and Security of Mankind: 'An individual who, as leader or organizer, actively participates in or orders the planning, preparation, initiation or waging of aggression *committed by a State* shall be responsible for a crime of aggression.' See 1996 *Yearbook ILC*, vol. ii, Part Two, pp. 42–43 (emphasis supplied).

[159] See Franck, 'Who Killed Article 2 (4)?: Or Changing Norms Governing the Use of Force By States', 64 (1970) *AJIL* 809.

nonstate entities to use armed force, especially since it was proposed to extend it to any third states which chose to assist them in such armed struggles. The Soviet Union and the Soviet bloc states wished both to insist on the state-to-state requirement and to support the use of armed force in 'wars of liberation.'[160]

In consequence of these deliberations, such situations were untethered from the final definition of aggression,[161] which, as we have noted, took as its inspiration the prohibition of force contained in the United Nations Charter.[162] However, as one reads further into the Resolution, one cannot fail to be struck by the ritual extent to which the State has been invoked in the non-exhaustive 'acts' of aggression itemized in Article 3:

(a) [t]he invasion or attack by the armed forces of a State of the territory of another State, or any military occupation, however temporary, resulting from such invasion or attack, or any annexation by the use of force of the territory of another State or part thereof;

(b) [b]ombardment by the armed forces of a State against the territory of another State or the use of any weapons by a State against the territory of another State;

(c) [t]he blockade of the ports or coasts of a State by the armed forces of another State;

(d) [a]n attack by the armed forces of a State on the land, sea or air forces, or marine and air fleets of another State;

(e) [t]he use of armed forces of one State which are within the territory of another State with the agreement of the receiving State, in contravention of the conditions provided for in the agreement or any extension of their presence in such territory beyond the termination of the agreement;

(f) [t]he action of a State in allowing its territory, which it has placed at the disposal of another State, to be used by that other State for perpetrating an act of aggression against a third State;

(g) [t]he sending by or on behalf of a State of armed bands, groups, irregulars or mercenaries, which carry out acts of armed force against another State of such gravity as to amount to the acts listed above, or its substantial involvement therein.[163]

As we consider each of these actions mentioned, and recall our earlier discussion of the concept of an 'armed attack' in jurisprudence as well as practice,[164] it is not unreasonable for us to contemplate the possibilities of non-State actors as both author and perpetrator of the 'bombardment' or 'the use of any weapons' against

---

[160] Stone (note 101), p. 231.

[161] *Supra* (note 151).

[162] *Supra* (note 97).

[163] Ibid, Article 3. See further Stancu, 'Defining the Crime of Aggression or Redefining Aggression', in Politi and Nesi (eds.), *The International Criminal Court and the Crime of Aggression*, Aldershot, 2004, p. 87 at p. 88.

[164] See notes 114 to 119 and accompanying text.

'the territory of another State', as was witnessed in the summer of 2006 with Hezbollah's launch of rockets and mortar shells against Israel,[165] or of an 'attack' against 'the land, sea or air forces, or marine and air fleets of another State' of the order experienced by the U.S.S. *Cole* at the hands of al-Qaeda in October 2000.[166] We should also recall that the act of 'blockade of the ports or coasts of a State' was one of the well-known strategies of recognized belligerents in their day,[167] and the Resolution itself might be taken to speak to these (and related) capabilities of non-State actors by virtue of the acknowledgment it accords peoples seeking to realize their right to self-determination in Article 7.[168]

The critical matter to stem from Resolution 3314 (XXIX) is the desirability and sustainability of a definition of aggression that appears so tailored, and so

---

[165] See Fattah and Erlanger, 'Israel Blockades Lebanon; Wide Strikes by Hezbollah', *New York Times*, 14 July 2006, p. A1. This followed the 'bold daylight assault across the border' into Israel by Hezbollah on 12 July 2006 in which two Israeli soldiers were captured. See Myre and Erlanger, 'Clashes Spread to Lebanon as Hezbollah Raids Israel', *New York Times*, 13 July 2006, p. A1. See also McGreal (note 4). The position of the Israeli Government, however, was that this event was 'not a terror act, but an act of a sovereign state that attacked Israel without reason': ibid. On 16 July 2006, Hezbollah released its 'deadliest missile yet' on the port city of Haifa, killing eight people: see Mouawad and Erlanger, 'Israel Bombards Lebanon After Hezbollah Hits Haifa With Missile: Death Toll Rises on Fifth Day of Conflict', *New York Times*, 17 July 2006, p. A1. During these hostilities, Sheik Hassan Nasrallah warned that Tel Aviv would be bombed if the Lebanese capital of Beirut was targeted: see Oppel Jr. and Erlanger, '12 Israelis Die; Sheik Threatens to Bomb Tel Aviv', *New York Times*, 4 August 2006, p. A1. For a further assessment of Hezbollah's broader actions, see Erlanger and Shanker, 'Israel Finding A Difficult Foe in Hezbollah', *New York Times*, 26 July 2006, p. A1; Kifner and Hoge, '200 Missiles Hit Israel As Battle Rages in Lebanon', *New York Times*, 3 August 2006, p. A1; and Oppel Jr. and Myre, 'Rocket Barrage Kills 15 Israelis on Deadliest Day', *New York Times*, 7 August 2006, p. A1. The ensuing hostilities caused the displacement of approximately 500,000 people in northern Israel; some 900,000 people were evacuated from their homes in southern Lebanon: see Norton (note 4), at p. 142. This is not to deny the existence of tensions between Hezbollah and Israel prior to July 2006, on which see further Norton (note 4), at pp. 134–35.

[166] Wright, *The Looming Tower: Al-Qaeda and the Road to 9/11*, New York, 2006, pp. 319–20 – though we are aware that the Resolution addresses this matter in plural terms ('the land, sea or air forces, or marine and air *fleets* of another State'); emphasis supplied. See, however, *Case Concerning Oil Platforms* (note 141), at p. 195, paragraph 72: 'The Court does not exclude the possibility that the mining of a single military vessel might be sufficient to bring into play the "inherent right of self-defence"'. Note also the targeting of an Israeli naval vessel, the *INS Hanit*, by a Hezbollah drone aircraft packed with explosives in July 2006. See Erlanger, 'Beirut Bombed – Drone Hits Israeli Ship', *New York Times*, 15 July 2006, p. A1. Four sailors were reported missing by the Israeli Government as a result of the incident. Note, too, the weapons system of the Tamil Tigers of Sri Lanka, consisting of a fleet of ten light aircraft as well as a merchant fleet of ten ocean-going vessels: 'A War Strange As Fiction', *The Economist* (London), 9 June 2007, p. 23, at p. 24. See, further, Sengupta, 'Sri Lanka's Scars Trace Lines of War Without End', *New York Times*, 15 June 2007, p. A1.

[167] See, for instance, Woolsey, 'The Consequences of Cuban Belligerency', 5 (1896) *Yale LJ* 182.

[168] *Supra* (note 97).

beholden, to the State, when, as we have argued, that definition occurs amidst a succession of legal provisions that have sought to reduce the entitlements of States for lawful force – but, also, at one and the same time, to consolidate the stranglehold on private violence.[169] This latter feature, it is true, has been more implicit in the reckoning, but the qualification of the *act* of aggression in accordance with its *actor* is not something we see repeated in kindred mechanisms in the Charter's system of collective security (i.e. in respect of 'threat[s] to the peace' or 'breach[es] of the peace').[170] These concepts take their place alongside 'act[s] of aggression' in Article 39 of the Charter in demarcating the scope of the powers and responsibilities of the Security Council, so that it is not fully clear why non-State actors should be precluded in law from committing acts of aggression.[171] Why, for instance, can a 'threat to the peace' of a non-State actor not mutate or mature into an 'act of aggression' for the purposes of the Charter?[172] As Elizabeth Wilmshurst has remarked by way of illustration, '[t]he discussion [on aggression] does not concern individual mercenaries without State backing',[173] and it behoves us to ask *why* this is so – and, indeed, *whether* it should be so. If it is indeed the legal position that a non-State actor can devise and prosecute an 'armed attack' against a State at its own behest,[174] why should that action be denied classification as an 'act of aggression'?[175] Furthermore, we

---

[169] *Supra* notes 103–108 and accompanying text.

[170] See McDougal and Reisman, 'Rhodesia and the United Nations: The Lawfulness of International Concern', 62 (1968) *AJIL* 1, at p. 8. With its particular focus on non-State actors, the Security Council affirmed in the Preamble to Resolution 1540 (2004) 'that proliferation of nuclear, chemical and biological weapons, as well as their means of delivery, constitutes a threat to international peace and security.' See generally *supra* note 10.

[171] William Schabas has made the historical observation that '[a]ggressive war was a kind of prosecutorial magic bullet capable of ensuring the conviction of those at the very top.' See 'Origins of the Criminalization of Aggression: How Crimes Against Peace Became the "Supreme International Crime"', in Politi and Nesi (note 163), p. 17, at p. 31.

[172] Without prejudice to the status of the crime of aggression as a 'leadership crime': see Stancu (note 163), at p. 88. See also Schabas (note 171); Cooper and Rohter (note 7); and generally see note 10.

[173] Wilmshurst, 'Definition of the Crime of Aggression: State Responsibility or Individual Criminal Responsibility?', in Politi and Nesi (note 163), p. 93. Cf. the ILC Commentary to Article 16 of the Draft Code where the Commission recalled that the IMT Nuremberg Judgment included non-State actors such as 'businessmen' as capable in law of committing the crime of aggressive war: *supra* (note 158), p. 43.

[174] See *supra* (note 164).

[175] Recall that in December 2001, for example, the United States Secretary of Defence, Donald H. Rumsfeld was of the view that:

> We did not start the war; the terrorists started it when they attacked the United States, murdering more than 5,000 innocent Americans. The Taliban, an illegitimate, unelected

could ask, why is it that the individual criminal consequences for this sort of action committed by non-State actors would be any different to that for, say, crimes against humanity?[176]

IV. CONCLUDING REMARKS

Our engagement with the *jus ad bellum* and the *jus in bello* from the perspective of non-State actors has demonstrated how, over time and at separate but repeated intervals, public international law has taken cognizance of the violence of these actors with differing degrees of commitment, explicitness and even cohesion. To an appreciable extent, the *focus* of the law has been on States and on State action, but its *concerns* have been much broader in character so that we must be cautious how we read or interpret the law's silences and its omissions. These are not to be taken as drafting oversights, still less as permissions for non-State actors and their members to commit acts of violence in the international sphere,[177] and are perhaps understandable in a legal system that has historically presented itself as a system of States, a system by States, and a system *for* States. Yet, it is also the case that this system has always been a system of *public* law, with its ultimate concern of the regulation of power whatever its guise and no matter its form, creed or manifestation.[178] We see this consideration foretold in the occasional pragmatic politics of public international law,[179] in the demarcation of the *vires* of international institutions,[180] and, now, *via* the regulation of the

---

group of terrorists, started it when they invited the al Qaeda into Afghanistan and turned their country into a base from which those terrorists could strike out and kill our citizens. So let there be no doubt; responsibility for every single casualty in this war, be they innocent Afghans or innocent Americans, rests at the feet of Taliban and al Qaeda. Their leaderships are the ones that are hiding in mosques and using Afghan civilians as human shields by placing their armour and artillery in close proximity to civilians, schools, hospitals, and the like. When the Taliban issue accusations of civilian casualties, they indict themselves.

See Secretary of Defence Donald H. Rumsfeld, News Conference at the Pentagon, Washington DC (29 October 2001) (http://www.defenselink.mil/transcripts/transcript.aspx? transcriptid=2226). Against the factual claims, consider UN Press Release SG/SM 8376, 11 September 2002. See also Kaikobad, 'Crimes Against International Peace and Security, Acts of Terrorism and Other Serious Crimes: A Theory on Distinction and Overlap', 7 (2007) *Int'l Crim. LR* 187, at p. 256.

[176] See, in particular, the discussion in note 73.

[177] See, in particular, the discussion in the text that accompanies notes 102–108.

[178] Another vital and abiding interest of Professor Warbrick, as exemplified in his inaugural lecture at the University of Durham, 'The Public Law of Public International Law', in May 1998.

[179] See the discussion in note 44.

[180] See the discussion in the text accompanying notes 170 and 171.

violence of non-State actors. This regulation has not been immediate and it has met with chequered patterns of success and support. Nevertheless, at each turn of this evolution, public international law has attempted to reclaim its relevance in the real world by working towards a much greater effectiveness of the regulation of violence and it has done this with an increasing measure of the fairness and justice of its approach (as argued by Thomas M. Franck in his seminal thesis, *Fairness in International Law and Institutions*, Oxford, 1995)[181] as it has the development of international criminal law, its doctrines, processes and institutions.[182]

---

[181] See Warbrick's 'Introduction to the Symposium' on Franck's *Fairness in International Law and Institutions*, 13 (2002) *EJIL* 902.

[182] See, in particular, Cassese (note 88).

Part Three

International Order and Security

Chapter Fifteen

The 'Disordered Medley' of International Tribunals And the Coherence of International Law

David Anderson*

As a teacher, commentator, author and editor, Colin Warbrick has made significant contributions to international law and the protection of human rights at the European and global levels. It is a pleasure to mark his many achievements by contributing to this volume. Since the start of his professional career, international law has been diversified and its scope has expanded to the point that some commentators have written about its 'fragmentation'; others have pointed to a 'proliferation' of international courts and tribunals. The terms 'fragmentation' and 'proliferation' are best avoided when considering these developments. A better description of what has happened is to speak of the 'diversification and expansion' of international law.[1] This process of diversification and expansion has not been confined to substantive rules of law. It has also extended to the administration of international justice. The swelling of the ranks of the international judiciary was witnessed over a relatively short span towards the end of the twentieth century. It was the creation, in particular, of the International Tribunal for the Law of the Sea (ITLOS or Tribunal) that

---

* Former Judge of the International Tribunal for the Law of the Sea, Hamburg (1996–2005); Legal Adviser to the United Kingdom's Foreign and Commonwealth Office, London (1960–1996); and Visiting Professor University of Durham.

[1] Following the usage adopted by the International Law Commission during the course of its work on the topic. Much of the literature is reviewed in Chapter XII of the Report of the International Law Commission 2006: 'Fragmentation of International Law: Difficulties arising from the Diversification and Expansion of International Law'. This item on its agenda was initially entitled 'Risks ensuing from the Fragmentation of International Law'. The title of the agenda item was changed during the course of the work.

K.H. Kaikobad & M. Bohlander (eds.), *International Law and Power: Perspectives on Legal Order and Justice*. Essays in Honour of Colin Warbrick, pp. 389–400.

raised in some quarters doubts over the wisdom of having a standing judicial body for one part of international law.[2] This paper offers some personal views on these developments.[3]

I. The Diversification and Expansion of International Law

Over the past half-century, the rules of international law have been transformed in many ways. In the mid-20th Century, the dominant source was customary law. Custom remains important;[4] but increasingly the stress is upon conventional law. Today, legal advisers, statesmen, judges and private practitioners in international law have the benefit of the major codification conventions in carrying out their day-to-day tasks. Instruments such as the Vienna Conventions on the Law of Treaties (VCLT), on Diplomatic Relations, and on Consular Relations are most useful and very widely used by lawyers and diplomats. These Conventions, by codifying legal principles, removing doubts, filling gaps and settling doctrinal disputes in major areas of international law, represent indispensable tools of contemporary diplomacy. The Conventions were all based on the drafts of the International Law Commission (ILC). The arrangements put in place during the UN era typically involved several different stages, notably expert studies, the production of initial drafts by the ILC, discussion in the Sixth Committee, written comments by Governments, a final draft and, usually, an ad hoc Diplomatic Conference. These arrangements can be said to have been thorough and to have served the States of the world better than the previous arrangements under the League of Nations which produced only limited success at the Hague Conference in 1930. The Conventions have all brought legal certainty and stability. They are difficult to modify, although they are not immutable: the UN Convention on the Law of the Sea of 1982 replaced the Geneva Conventions of 1958 with a modern, comprehensive regime; this

---

[2] An expert analysis at the time showed that the fears were overdone: Charney, 'Is International Law Threatened by Multiple International Tribunals?', 271 (1998) *Hague Recueil des cours* 105. Subsequent experience has borne out those findings.

[3] From the perspective of a former legal adviser in the Foreign and Commonwealth Office in London and to the UK Mission to the UN in New York and of a former member of the Tribunal during its initial phase.

[4] Sometimes 'running in the background' with the UN Charter or international law-making conventions: see the *Nicaragua* case, *ICJ Reports 1986*, p. 14. The statement in Waldock (ed.), *Brierly's Law of Nations* (Sixth edition), Oxford, 1963, at page 71 that '... international law is in fact just a system of customary law, upon which has been erected, almost entirely within the last two generations, a superstructure of "conventional" or treaty-made law ...' may now need reconsideration.

remains a rare example of law reform in the UN system. At the technical level, there has also been a great increase in the range and scope of global and regional conventions providing for international cooperation and laying down international standards. Many of these instruments have been adopted under the auspices of the UN and its Specialised Agencies. Together with the Principles enshrined in the UN Charter,[5] all these Conventions form part of a diversified and expanded legal order for States and international organisations.

Over the past 50 years, observers have regularly pointed to a 'crisis' of one sort or another in international law. Sometimes international law has been found wanting, or statesmen have been found wanting, or the fault lay with the 'Cold War' or the imperatives of the movement towards decolonisation. In recent years, one such 'crisis' has been the fear of 'fragmentation'. It is true that during the UN era, international law has grown so much that it has become rather too big for many experts to follow in all its details. This talk of fragmentation may be a sign of success. At least, the recent generations of international lawyers and diplomats have produced something large enough to fragment. As with the other crises, these fears can be exaggerated.

Fragmentation should be avoided as far as possible, of course. The centre should hold. Law schools should continue to teach the fundamental elements of international law as a basis for later specialisation into specific fields. Practitioners in special fields should try to keep abreast of mainstream developments and to maintain some contact with other specialised fields. In many ways, the law of treaties holds the different treaty-based arrangements together. In particular, the approach to interpretation in the Vienna Convention plays a most important role. Cases coming before international courts and tribunals are often concerned with questions of interpretation of an international convention.

The report of the Study Group of the ILC confirms that international law is a legal system and not a random or fragmented collection of rules and principles. Instead, there exist 'meaningful relations between them'.[6] In determining the inter-relationship of two rules, the Study Group paid great attention to the VCLT, especially article 31. These findings should allay any lingering concerns over the risk of fragmentation. One hesitation on the writer's part is whether the law of the sea really amounts to a special or self-contained regime: a better view would be to retain it as an integral and important part of general international law.

---

5 As to which there exist valuable commentaries in Warbrick and Lowe (eds.), *The United Nations and the Principles of International Law Essays in Memory of Michael Akehurst*, London, 1994.
6 Report of the ILC 2006, Chapter XII, paragraphs 241 ff., especially at paragraph 251. The full Report of the Study Group in A/CN.4/L.682/Add.1 is available on the UN Website.

II. The Diversification and Expansion of International Courts and Tribunals

Turning to the growth in the number of international courts and tribunals, the first point to note is that there has been no plan. Developments have been uncoordinated. There has been diversification in the sense that specialised tribunals have been created. As a result, there is no hierarchy of courts and tribunals such as exists in most domestic legal systems: instead there exists in the memorable phrase of Sir Robert Jennings 'a disordered medley'.[7] The introduction of a formal hierarchy of courts with meaningful relations between them would require a major upheaval in international organisation, akin to that marked by the adoption of the UN Charter. As others have noted, structural reform is unlikely to occur.[8] Amendment of the ICJ's Statute of the International Court of Justice (ICJ or Court) would involve amendment of the UN Charter, something that always raises delicate political issues.

The ICJ, as the principal judicial organ of the United Nations, has in recent years played an increasingly important role in dispute settlement as cases have been submitted to it from all parts of the world. The Court has developed its jurisprudence: judgments are now replete with references to the Court's previous decisions and those of its predecessor. However, from the outset the Court was not given exclusive jurisdiction by the UN Charter.[9] Other courts and tribunal, both standing and *ad hoc*, have co-existed alongside the Court. It does not serve as a court of appeal from other courts, nor can it give Advisory Opinions or interpretations at the request of other tribunals – similar, for example, to the references by national courts of specific questions to the European Court of Justice. Proposals to create such a system have been advanced by more than one President of the ICJ. However, the proposals have not been supported by the current President, Judge Higgins, on the grounds that they hark back to a by-gone age.[10] They have been rejected by other commentators[11] as misconceived. To give only two reasons, the Statutes of these other tribunals do not contain mechanisms for seeking advisory opinions from the ICJ; and

---

[7] Jennings, 'The Judiciary and International Law', 45 (1996) *ICLQ* 1, at p. 5.

[8] Shany, *The Competing Jurisdictions of International Courts and Tribunals*, Oxford, p. 275.

[9] See Article 92; and for commentary, see Oellers-Frahm, 'Article 92 UN Charter', in Zimmermann, Tomuschat and Oellers-Frahm (eds.), *The Statute of the International Court of Justice*, Oxford, 2006, p. 139.

[10] 'Respecting the Sovereignty of States and Running a Tight Courtroom', 50 (2001) *ICLQ* 121. See also her statement at the 10th anniversary meeting of the ITLOS, September 2006 (available on the ICJ website).

[11] Including the present writer: *Modern Law of the Sea—Selected Essays*, Leiden, 2008, Chapter 33: 'The Judicial Work of the ITLOS'.

States may have deliberately chosen a tribunal other than the ICJ for settling any disputes in which they were involved. Since the ICJ's own jurisdiction is based on consent, a State's withholding of consent to that jurisdiction should be respected. The proposals have not been taken up by Governments or international conferences. Under the system of the UN Charter, States have continued to have the freedom to submit disputes to arbitration or *ad hoc* panels according to their wishes.

In the absence of a formal hierarchy, the *system* of international courts can only be described as a weak one. Partly as a result, many issues of international law, some controversial, arise for decision in national courts, especially now that judicial review of administrative decisions by governments, including decisions upon the compatibility of national law with obligations under treaties, has become more widely available in many national courts. The jurisdiction of international courts is typically confined to the settlement of 'disputes' between States: although the term 'dispute' has been given a wide definition, the range of potential parties is confined to States. This means that many non-State actors who may have a keen interest in the outcome are usually not given standing to express their views. The possibility of seeking judicial review of decisions by international bodies at the behest of either States or other interested parties has not been widely introduced into the jurisdictional and procedural provisions governing the work of international courts. The excellent study by Professor Kaikobad entitled *The International Court and Judicial Review* concluded that the Court should not be precluded from refining an important aspect of its jurisdiction.[12]

A particular source of cases in the past was the Committee charged with considering applications for review of decisions in staff cases handed down by the UN Administrative Tribunal: proposals to seek an Advisory Opinion from the ICJ were often viewed with disfavour and rejected by the UN Committee on Applications for Review of Administrative Tribunal Judgements, but three references were made such as that in the *Mortished* case.[13] The procedure for seeking review was abolished in the mid-1990s.

The contentious jurisdiction of the ICJ is confined to disputes involving States; and, although that of the ITLOS, especially its Seabed Disputes Chamber, is wider in some instances, in the main it is confined to States and bodies such as the European Union. In some contexts, judicial review by international courts and tribunals of decisions by certain kinds of international organisations,

---

[12] Kaikobad, *The International Court and Judicial Review: A Study of the Court's Powers with Respect to the Judgments of the UN and ILO Administrative Tribunals*, The Hague, 2000, at pp. 302–303.
[13] Advisory Opinion of July 1982: *ICJ Reports 1982*, p. 325.

such as the various regional fisheries management organisations,[14] could have a useful role to play, always alongside existing arrangements for dispute settlement. Judicial review may provide a useful alternative form of litigation in circumstances where a formal dispute between two States is deemed by the governments concerned to be undesirable for wider political reasons unconnected with the immediate problem. It may also provide a possibility for interested persons such as the representatives of industry or non-governmental organisations to submit written materials on matters within their areas of expertise to assist the decision-makers: such possibilities are usually absent from inter-State dispute settlement but they have now been accepted in some national courts. Perhaps developments will be seen in this area in the future.

The risk of inconsistent decisions, whether deliberate or *per incuriam*, has always existed. The recent increase in the number of international courts and tribunals has sharpened the fears of fragmented jurisprudence. The risk continues to exist, although as Professor Charney demonstrated it should not be exaggerated.[15] Reasoned judgments by international courts and tribunals are widely cited in legal literature and can exercise enormous influence: it suffices to recall that *dicta* in the *Corfu Channel*, *Norwegian Fisheries* and *Nottebohm* cases were included in the ILC's draft articles on the Law of the Sea and the Geneva Conventions of 1958.[16] Although formally speaking decisions are binding only upon the parties to a particular case, in reality some decisions have influenced the state of international law, especially in cases where findings as to the condition of customary international law have been made.

The creation of specialist tribunals composed of specialist judges is a new phenomenon. The number of special courts and tribunals with judges experienced in a particular field has grown. The ITLOS is an example: according to its Statute, one qualification for membership is "recognised competence in the field of the law of the sea."[17] Experience of having applied all aspects of the law of the sea day by day as the FCO legal adviser primarily concerned with maritime affairs in the years before 1996 proved to be valuable. Less relevant

---

[14] A future possibility mentioned in the recent Report by a study group on 'Recommended Best Practices for Regional Fisheries Management Organizations'; available from August 2007 on www.chathamhouse.org.uk.

[15] *Supra* (note 2).

[16] Even a judgment such as that in the *Lotus* case (*PCIJ Reports*, Series *A*, No. 10, Judgment No. 9 (1927), p. 4), which was taken only by the casting vote of the President, criticised by dissenting judges and then, in effect, reversed for the future by international agreements, proved to be a much-cited precedent. The decision was in effect reversed by the Brussels Convention of 1952 and now Article 108 of the UN Convention on the Law of the Sea declares the law on the matter.

[17] See Article 2.

was experience as a negotiator at the LOS Conference, but this may have been simply due to the nature of the issues raised in the cases that came before the Tribunal in its early years. Above all, experience as a litigator before the ICJ, the European Court of Human Rights[18] and *ad hoc* courts was most valuable. The business of a court is litigation. Many practical and procedural issues have to be dealt with in the course of handling cases. Previous experience of participating in cases, whether as Agent, Counsel or judge/arbitrator, is clearly most valuable, even though it is not a requirement under the Statute. The Statute also provides for the representation of the principal legal systems of the world, including therefore the common law, and for the equitable geographical distribution of seats. The former is important since the approach to legal questions does vary from one legal system to another. The latter criterion plays a more prominent role in the meetings of States Parties which elect the judges than in the work of the Tribunal itself.

Like other specialised courts, the Tribunal has to decide all manner of questions, not only questions of the law of the sea properly so-called. These other questions include also the interpretation and application of treaties, State responsibility, diplomatic protection, etc.[19] The Tribunal has to decide upon its own jurisdiction and upon questions of admissibility: such issues are not peculiar to the law of the sea. Cases often raise general issues. A judge should have a general background and experience in the whole of international law. Experience in a special field should go hand in hand with wide experience of international law as a whole – and especially international litigation. This is the best guarantee of coherence in international law and jurisprudence. As indicated above, the law of the sea remains more a part of the mainstream of international law than a 'special regime'.

The question arises whether there should be a system of appeals? The Statutes of the ICJ and the Tribunal provide only limited possibilities for requesting the revision or interpretation of a judgment. These possibilities amount to much less than an appeal against the terms of a decision. Looking at the national picture suggests that a system of appeals may play a useful role: a right of appeal is allowed in most instances in national courts. It is well known that issues are often clarified and new issues may gain in prominence as a case passes from one stage to another. In other words, cases sometimes evolve and mature during the initial hearing, in drafting the judgment, in studying its terms and again during the appellate process. A decision by a court of first instance

---

[18] Including the European Commission on Human Rights during the late 1970s.

[19] Wood, 'The International Tribunal for the Law of the Sea and General International Law', 22 (2007) *IJMCL* 351.

can alarm not only the parties, but also public opinion or the experts such as professors, commentators, political and trade bodies, NGOs, etc. However, at the international level (leaving aside the criminal courts and tribunals), there are very few systems of appeals: rare exceptions are the Grand Chamber of the European Court of Human Rights and the Dispute Settlement Procedure of the World Trade Organisation. As a result, in the majority of instances, decisions by international courts and tribunals cannot be the subject of an appeal, although it is fair to hazard the guess that some decisions would be appealed if the possibility were to be provided. But for many reasons this appears at present to be most unlikely to happen. How then can international courts and tribunals get everything right first time, knowing there can be no appeal?

Judges have a responsibility towards the parties to resolve the case in accordance with what are held to be the relevant rules of law and to act fairly and justly. If a dispute is serious enough to reach an international court, there are almost always some plausible arguments on each side. Judges rely upon the parties and their counsel to present all the relevant facts and evidence, to advance the best legal arguments in support of the rival cases, and to bring all possibly relevant previous decisions to the attention of the bench. Leaving aside international criminal courts, many cases turn on questions of law, including interpretation. International courts are not well equipped to ascertain facts where they are disputed or incomplete. Some cases arising from incidents such as the *Corfu Channel* and *Saiga (No. 2)* cases[20] are fact-specific, but the majority are not.

At the end of a hearing, the judges are usually faced with two sets of plausible arguments: they have to decide where the truth lies, which legal contentions are stronger, and how to dispose of the case in a judgment. It is inescapable that judges have to make choices, especially in the handling and disposal of cases. Sometimes it is a wise course to decide there is no need to resolve a particular question. Judges do not need these days to try to fill gaps in the law by going out of their way to decide issues, especially in the abstract. There is plenty of conventional law: some questions are best left until such time as it is necessary in a case to decide them on the basis of a set of specific facts. Judicial restraint is usually the best approach.

There is nothing pre-ordained about the outcome: reading an international tribunal's judgment in the law reports *ex post facto* may give the outside reader a false impression of certainty. Turning the clock back, this certainty did not exist

---

[20] *ICJ Reports 1949*, p. 3 and ITLOS Reports 1999, p. 10. The British Institute of International and Comparative Law has embarked upon a study of evidence before international courts and tribunals. This includes its publication of Riddell and Plant, *Evidence before the International Court of Justice*, London, 2009.

at the end of the hearing. International courts and tribunals are collegiate bodies with up to as many as 21 members who reach their decisions by majority votes at the end of a structured procedure of deliberations. This procedure, usually set out in a Resolution on Judicial Practice, gives the parties an assurance of due process behind the closed doors of the Deliberations Room. Where the majority will lie on particular issues and the disposal of the case will usually be difficult for individual judges to forecast, let alone outsiders. Judges have discretion over how to dispose of a case, how to present the argumentation or reasoning in their judgments and which previous decisions, if any, to cite. Judges have a duty to administer justice in the particular case, while keeping in mind the coherence of the legal system as a whole. Coherence is especially relevant in the deliberations of standing courts such as the ICJ and the ITLOS. These courts tend to cite their own previous decisions. This is all to the good: it helps to build up a doctrine or jurisprudence. In this perspective, courts and tribunals should not shrink from citing relevant decisions of *other* courts and tribunals. The International Tribunal for the Law of the Sea, for instance, has regularly cited decisions by the Permanent Court of International Justice, the ICJ and arbitral tribunals.[21]

Conversely, judges should be slow to differ with an earlier decision, even one that is known to have attracted criticism from learned commentators. Explicitly rejecting or criticising a decision or a part of the reasoning given by another international court or tribunal is something that is best avoided. The ILC Report on the Fragmentation of International Law (2006) noted out that conflicts in case-law diminish legal security: this makes prediction more difficult for legal advisers.[22] This is clearly true. In particular, public disagreement with rulings of the ICJ (as a standing court and the principal judicial organ of the United Nations) is hazardous: it will usually be unnecessary. The Appeals Chamber of the International Criminal Tribunal for Yugoslavia (ICTY) expressly departed in the *Tadić* case from a criterion of 'effective control' laid down by the ICJ in the *Nicaragua* case.[23] In its recent decision in the case brought by Bosnia and Herzegovina charging Serbia and Montenegro with genocide, the ICJ was invited by applicants to accept the lower criterion from *Tadić* of 'overall control'. The ICJ first pointed out that the ICTY was concerned with cases against individuals, not questions of *State* responsibility: The Court then proceeded to

---

[21] See, for example, the *Saiga* (*No. 2*) (*Merits*), Judgment, citing *The I'm Alone* and *Red Crusader* cases: 1999 *ITLOS Reports* 4, at p. 62 (paragraph 156). For a review of the practice of international courts and tribunals in referring to and adopting the practice of other international courts on issues of procedure and remedies, see Brown, *A Common Law of International Adjudication*, Oxford, 2007.

[22] ILC Report 2006 (A/61/10), Chapter XII, especially paragraphs 244–46.

[23] *Supra* (note 4), pp. 64–65, paragraph 115.

state that while it would attach importance 'to the factual and legal findings made by the ICTY in ruling on the criminal liability of the accused before it .... (t)he situation is not the same for positions adopted by the ICTY on issues of general international law which do not lie within the specific purview of its jurisdiction ...' The Court went on to examine the two criteria against the background of article 8 of the ILC's Articles on State Responsibility, adopted after *Nicaragua*, before finding that the ICTY's arguments were 'unpersuasive'. Instead, the Court in measured tones followed its own 'settled jurisprudence' in *Nicaragua*.[24]

Respect for other courts' decisions should be the guiding principle.[25] In certain instances in the past, the ICJ appears to have departed from some of its own previous decisions; however, if so, the Court has not found it appropriate to say so openly. It is often possible to distinguish a previous case on the facts, or to find that it is not relevant in the circumstances of the new case.[26] Sometimes there are distinguishing features from the nature of the case: human rights conventions, laying down standards, are different from reciprocal or purely 'contractual' treaties, for example. As was pointed out in the *Bosnia* case, international criminal courts hearing charges against individuals are different from the ICJ, which is concerned with inter-State questions. Some past decisions may distinguish themselves if they date from a by-gone era when international society and international law were different from the circumstances prevailing at the time of taking the decision. Other decisions can be 'explained' and glossed.[27] In short, courts and tribunals should guard against the risk of further fragmentation by openly disagreeing with previous decisions of other courts, unless they have no alternative course of action. Instead, they should adopt a holistic approach to international law and seek to maintain its coherence. Judges from different courts could usefully meet

---

[24] Paragraphs 403–407 of the judgment of 26 February 2007 in the *Genocide in Bosnia* case: *Bosnia and Herzegovina v. Serbia and Montenegro, ICJ Reports 2007*, at pp. 142–45.

[25] Judges Fleischhauer and Higgins, in their private capacities, have advanced this argument: for Fleischhauer, see 'The Relationship between the ICJ and the Newly Created International Tribunal for the Law of the Sea', 1 (1997) *Max Planck Yearbook of UN Law* 327; and for Higgins see *supra* (note 10).

[26] The concept of the *ratio decidendi* of an international decision has been examined by Judge Shahabuddeen: see *Precedent of the World Court, Hersch Lauterpacht Memorial Lectures*, Cambridge, 1996, Chapter 11; and by Sir R. Jennings in 'The Judiciary, International and National, and the Development of International Law', 45 (1996) *ICLQ* 1.

[27] The Court of Arbitration in the *Anglo-French Continental Shelf* case (France/UK) explained the ICJ's decision in the *North Sea Continental Shelf* cases in a way that attracted favourable comment: 54 *ILR* 6.

to discuss common problems and exchange information.[28] Judicial cooperation is preferable to judicial competition.

Another feature of the jurisprudence is the respect almost invariably shown by many different courts and tribunals for the work of the ILC, particularly where it has been cast in the form of articles of codification: the reasoning has often used the formula that 'the articles reflect customary law in many ways'. This approach has even been adopted in regard to what were no more than provisional articles, subject to further consideration by the ILC and others. This approach featured again in the recent *Genocide in Bosnia* case, this time with the added element of a direct link between the ILC's articles and the Court's jurisprudence. This relationship between the ILC, on the one hand, and international courts and tribunals, on the other, is clearly one which helps to maintain coherence in international law. Conversely, the signal departure from this approach witnessed in the North Sea Continental Shelf cases (where the ILC's draft article 72[29] and article 6 of the Convention on the Continental Shelf were both rejected as not reflecting customary law) produced two results: first, great uncertainty throughout the 1970s and 1980s in advising governments on outstanding delimitations; secondly, confrontation in the negotiations on the delimitation of the continental shelf during the Third UN Conference on the Law of the Sea. In short, it produced a degree of what may be described as fragmentation which has only recently been repaired, largely thanks to the terms of articles 74 and 83 of the UN Convention on the Law of the Sea and a consistent series of decisions by the ICJ and *ad hoc* tribunals. The situation whereby the terms of a law-making convention differ from a substantive rule of customary law divides States into two groups, those bound by the Convention and the non-parties, generally with negative consequences.

The need for international courts to adopt a holistic approach to the state of international law does not mean that the vote should be concealed from the parties and the public. Both the ICJ and the Tribunal give the vote and the names of the judges voting for and against each point in the *Dispositif*. Governments and practitioners have valid reasons to wish to know whether a decision was unanimous, divided or even the result of the President's casting vote, as in the *Lotus* case. Apart from anything else, the knowledge will affect the weight to be accorded to the decision as a precedent by commentators. Transparency, within limits, is usually a good thing. Similarly, separate concurring or dissenting

---

[28] Former President Judge Higgins of the ICJ visited the Tribunal and spoke at the ceremony marking its 10th anniversary in September 2006 (Speech available on the Court's website). Brandeis University has organised several meetings of judges from different international courts and tribunals.

[29] Based on the recommendations of a Group of Experts.

opinions should be permitted. Such opinions can play several valuable roles: for example, they may cast new light upon the terms of the majority's reasoning; they give the assurance that the arguments of both parties have been fully examined; they prevent majority decisions being taken for unexpressed or even improper reasons; and they may point the way for future developments in the law. Such opinions should be confined to stating the reasons for differing from the majority and the right to deliver a separate opinion should not be abused, e.g. by writing the equivalent of a learned article for a law journal.[30] They should also be couched in terms that maintain the secrecy of the deliberations: there are limits upon what a judge may properly state in a separate opinion. Notwithstanding the views of some European lawyers, separate opinions when used with discretion do not weaken the majority decision: on the contrary, they may even strengthen the rule of law viewed overall.

III. Concluding Remarks

Since Colin Warbrick's professional career began, international law and international tribunals have both expanded. This expansion presents a challenge to all those who are concerned with international law, whether as teachers, legal advisers, diplomats or judges. The challenge is to avoid fragmentation and to maintain coherence, against the background of diversification and expansion. The challenge will have to be met in practice within the existing UN system. The present arrangements for the codification and progressive development of international law, involving a dialogue between the ILC and Governments, could continue to be used in order to maintain legal harmony. Within the disordered medley of international courts and tribunals, a conscious effort on the part of international judges to maintain coherence may be required. Here, the best approach is that of respectful coexistence and cooperation.

---

[30] The practice of the ECHR is noteworthy for succinct separate opinions.

Chapter Sixteen

Countermeasures: Concept and Substance in the Protection of Collective Interests

Elena Katselli[*]

I. INTRODUCTION[**]

That the international legal system is unique is undisputed.[1] Attempts to draw parallels with national law have led international lawyers either to disappointment or to conclusions which weaken rather than enhance the role of international law. Criticism that international law is not 'real' law but rather 'positive morality' according to Austin, or that the international legal order is primitive, anarchical and rudimentary, are not new suggestions in the theory of international law.[2] Whilst the body of the latter has been enriched with norms regulating the behaviour of States in relations between themselves, the focus of most of these points of criticism lies upon the fact that international law lacks effective and reliable centralized mechanisms for the enforcement and implementation of such norms either in the form of compulsory judicial proceedings or by way of

[*] Ph.D. (Durham); Lecturer in Law, Newcastle Law School, Newcastle University. This chapter draws on ideas more fully developed as part of a major book entitled *The Problem of Enforcement of International Law: Countermeasures, the Non-Injured State and the Idea of International Community* to be published by Routledge-Cavendish. The author owes this work to Professor Warbrick.

[**] The author would like to thank the editors of the book for inviting her to contribute this chapter in this celebratory edition in honour of Professor Colin Warbrick. She would also like to thank Mr Ian Dawson at Newcastle Law School for his useful suggestions, and Ms Sarah Hibbin at the School of Oriental and African Studies, University of London, for her assistance.

[1] Cassese, *International Law*, Oxford, 2005, p. 3.

[2] See for instance Reisman, *Nullity and Revision: The Review and Enforcement of International Judgments and Awards*, New Haven, 1971, p. 645; and Verhoeven, '*Jus Cogens* and Reservations or "Counter-reservations" to the Jurisdiction of the International Court of Justice', in Wellens (ed.), *International Law: Theory and Practice, Essays in Honour of Eric Suy*, Boston, 1998, p. 195, at 196.

K.H. Kaikobad & M. Bohlander (eds.), *International Law and Power: Perspectives on Legal Order and Justice*. Essays in Honour of Colin Warbrick, pp. 401–429.
© 2009 Koninklijke Brill NV. Printed in the Netherlands.

other centralized coercive and executive procedures.[3] Accordingly, the implementation and enforcement of international law is, as a matter of general rule, left to individual States which subsequently gives rise to legitimate fears of abuse. However, and contrary to general perception, international law has proved to be a dynamic legal order which although not perfect – if there is, or ever will exist a legal order which is truly perfect – has managed, through the existing, even if limited, institutional routes or through unilateral coercive but non-forceful measures such as countermeasures, to ensure compliance with its norms.

In more contemporary debates, the question of enforcement of international law gains particular significance in the context of the protection of so-called collective interests which are regarded as having a fundamental character for the international community as a whole and as requiring special attention. The focus of this work lies therefore upon the enforcement of collective interests through resort to countermeasures by States not directly injured (hereinafter referred interchangeably also as solidarity measures). Nevertheless, it is important to stress at the outset that countermeasures do not constitute the only means of enforcement of international rules in general, or international rules protecting collective interests in particular. On the contrary, it is suggested that international law offers various other mechanisms of protection which, although not as effective as countermeasures, still make a significant contribution to the enforcement of international law. These mechanisms include judicial proceedings initiated before the International Court of Justice (ICJ) or other judicial bodies, inter-State complaint procedures or even individual petitions against a State which infringes its international obligations such as those provided under the International Covenant on Civil and Political Rights (ICCPR) and the European Convention of Human Rights (ECHR).[4]

The scope of the current examination has intentionally been narrowed down to the question of the implementation of solidarity measures. This is owed to two closely related reasons. First of all countermeasures, because of their nature as unilateral coercive measures, are generally regarded as constituting a very powerful 'weapon' in the hands of States, a weapon which is open to

---

[3]   The question of implementation/enforcement of international law falls within the sphere of the Law on State Responsibility which is distinguished from substantive rules of international law. For an analysis of this distinction see Ago, First Report on State Responsibility, 1969 *ILC Yearbook* vol. ii, p. 125, at p. 127, paragraph 6; also see his Fifth Report, 1976 *ILC Yearbook* vol. ii, Part One, p. 3, at p. 4, paragraph 1; and see Report of the ILC to the General Assembly on the Work of its 28th Session (State Responsibility), 1976 *ILC Yearbook* vol. ii, Part Two, p. 1, 69, at p. 71, paragraph 68.

[4]   Tams, *Enforcing Obligations* Erga Omnes *in International Law*, Cambridge, 2005, pp. 259–260. For further analysis on solidarity measures also see forthcoming book by Katselli (Routledge-Cavendish).

abuse, especially by strong States. Secondly, the question of solidarity measures, five decades after the International Law Commission (ILC) was mandated to codify the law on State responsibility, still remains open. In particular, with the finalisation of its Articles on State Responsibility in 2001 the ILC concluded that contemporary international law does not currently recognise a right to countermeasures in the protection of collective interests. However, instead of ending the discussion once and for all, the ILC left the window open for further progressive developments in this area of the law for the future. In consequence, the possibility of an emergence − if this has not already happened − of such a putative right makes the discourse over countermeasures by States not injured in their individual interests as interesting and as relevant as ever before.

It is accordingly appropriate to examine how the concept of community interests has influenced the ILC in its work on State responsibility and how the concept of solidarity measures has evolved in the theory and practice of international law.

II. PROTECTING COLLECTIVE INTERESTS IN CONTEMPORARY INTERNATIONAL LAW

1. *The Emergence of the Concept of Collective Interests*

The concept of collective interests owed to the international community as a whole has emerged and developed in an international legal system which is predominantly State-centric and whose rules still 'emanate from the free will of States' as re-affirmed in 1928 by the Permanent Court of International Justice (PCIJ) in the *Lotus case*.[5] This has caused some concern among international lawyers who have warned that the concept of collective interests has compromised the Westphalian nature of international law founded as it is on principles of sovereign equality and State consent. Professor Weil, for instance, in an influential article published in the 1980s warned that the distinction made between serious and less serious violations of international law, and between international crimes and delicts constituted concepts that could not be integrated in the current international legal system.[6] He regarded this concept as an infiltration of ideology in the neutrality of international law, a concept which has threatened the heterogeneity of the international legal order. Similar concerns are raised by Professor Koskenniemi who warns that the concept of collective interests may

---

[5] *PCIJ Reports*, Series A, No. 10 (1927), p. 4.
[6] Weil, 'Towards Relative Normativity in International Law', 77 (1983) *AJIL*, 413, at p. 442.

be but another form of imperialism where powerful States wish to impose their values upon the rest of the world.[7]

Yet, despite the voiced scepticism, the concept of interests of a fundamental nature is now well established in contemporary international law as evidenced in the literature, practice and jurisprudence of international law.[8] However, this concept is not new. Vattel was among early international lawyers who wrote about law which was not only fundamental but also 'immutable'. According to him:

> Since ... the necessary Law of Nations consists in the application of the law of nature to States – which law is immutable as being founded on the nature of things, and particularly on the nature of man – it follows, that the necessary Law of Nations is immutable. Whence as this Law is immutable, and the obligations that arise from it necessary and indispensable, nations can neither make any changes in it by their conventions, dispense with it in their own conduct, nor reciprocally release each other from the observance of it.[9]

In a similar vein, Professor Root was one of the few jurists of his period who realised, as early as in 1915, the necessity of distinguishing between wrongful acts which affect the individual interests of States as opposed to wrongful acts which affect all States of the international community.[10] Two decades later, Verdross advocated the idea that the higher interests of the international community, which allowed for no derogations, restrained the sovereignty and freedom of States.[11] In the period that followed World War II another prominent scholar, Professor Sir Hersch Lauterpacht, emphasized the fact that internationally wrongful acts can be distinguished from 'ordinary' violations, such as the infringement of a treaty, but also from violations 'amounting to a criminal act'.[12] During the same period of time, Levin identified State acts which were in contravention of the 'very foundations and essential principles of the legal order of international society',[13] whilst Jessup described breaches against the

---

[7]   Koskenniemi, 'International Law in Europe: Between Tradition and Renewal', 16 (2005) *EJIL* 118.

[8]   For the progression from pure bilateralism to community interests see Tomuschat, 'Obligations Arising for States Without or Against their Will', 241 (1993-IV) *Hague Recueil des cours* 197 and particularly at p. 213; and Simma, 'From Bilateralism to Community Interest in International Law', 250 (1994 VI) *Hague Recueil des cours* 216, at pp. 232–233.

[9]   De Vattel, *The Law of Nations or Principles of the Law of Nature*, 1834, p. lviii in Jorgensen, *The Responsibility of States for International Crimes*, Oxford, 2000, p. 86.

[10]   Root, 'The Outlook for International Law', 10 (1916) *AJIL* 1, at p. 9.

[11]   Verdross, 'Forbidden Treaties in International Law: Comments on Professor Garner's Report on the "Law of Treaties"', 31 (1937) *AJIL* 571, at pp. 571–572.

[12]   Oppenheim, *International Law A Treatise* (Sixth edition by H. Lauterpacht), London, 1947, p. 307 in Ago's Fifth Report (note 3), p. 45, paragraph 136.

[13]   In Ago's Fifth Report, p. 46, paragraph 136.

peace and order of the international community as a 'violation of the right of every nation'.[14] The growing significance of fundamental human rights and of self-determination after World War II, and the outlawing of genocide and slavery among other criminal acts, promoted the idea that such violations no longer fell within the exclusive jurisdiction of States. It was pointed out in this regard that

> [I]n the international literature of various countries and of various legal systems, ideas have moved substantially ahead. The positions which in older doctrine represented the isolated voices of certain especially forward-looking thinkers have become more and more frequent and increasingly firm, to the point that in modern works they represent a solidly established viewpoint and significantly, one which is not contested.[15]

The incorporation of the notion of peremptory norms in Article 53 of the 1969 Vienna Convention on the Law of Treaties (VCLT) further cemented in international legal thought the view that there exist higher principles in the protection of which all States have an interest. According to Article 53, peremptory norms are norms which are 'accepted and recognized by the international community of States as a whole', and 'from which no derogation is permitted and which can be modified only by a subsequent norm of general international law having the same character'.[16]

A major turning point in the concept of community interests was made by way of the *obiter dictum* of the International Court of Justice in the *Barcelona Traction* case one year after the adoption of Article 53 of the VCLT. In this famous *dictum*, the Court proclaimed that international obligations are distinguished by reference to those which are derived from the law of diplomatic immunities and those obligations which are owed to the international community as a whole (obligations *erga omnes*).[17] However, the Court said little about the scope and content of this notion, although it did give indications as to what an *erga omnes* obligation may look like: these are obligations prohibiting the commission of genocide, aggression, racial discrimination and slavery. While this list is not exhaustive, it offers some general guidelines concerning the rules which belong to this category characterised as they are by the importance of the rights they

---

[14] Jessup, *A Modern Law of Nations: An Introduction*, New York, 1948, p. 11.

[15] See Ago's Fifth Report (note 3), p. 50, paragraph 142.

[16] For analysis of the concept of *jus cogens* norms as reflected in the work of the ILC, see Greig, '"International Community" "Interdependence" and All That ... Rhetorical Correctness?', in Kreijen (ed.), *State, Sovereignty, and International Governance*, Oxford, 2002, p. 521, particularly at p. 537; Koji, 'Emerging Hierarchy in International Human Rights and Beyond: From the Perspective of Non-derogable Rights', 12 (2001) *EJIL* 917, at pp. 928–929; and Verhoeven (note 2), p. 196.

[17] *ICJ Reports 1970*, p. 3, at pp. 32–33, paragraphs 33–34.

set to protect. Nor did the Court elaborate on how these norms are formulated or discuss the kind of action which could be taken by States for the purposes of the enforcement of obligations having an *erga omnes* character. Even so, the Court made clear not only that there are community interests in international law, but also that obligations belonging to this category are owed to, and are enforced by and on behalf of the international community.[18] Hence, it appears from the ruling that the notion of *erga omnes* has a twofold effect: on the one hand, it is characterized by *universality* in that *erga omnes* obligations bind all States without exception, and on the other, by way of *solidarity* in that every State has a legal interest in their protection.[19] Judge Bedjaoui, commenting upon these developments, noted that

> It scarcely needs to be said that the face of contemporary international society is markedly altered .... Witness the proliferation of international organizations, the gradual substitution of an international law of co-operation for the traditional international law of co-existence, the emergence of the concept of 'international community' .... The resolutely positivist, voluntarist approach of international law still current at the beginning of the [twentieth] century .... has been replaced by an objective conception of international law, a law more readily seeking to reflect a collective juridical conscience and respond to the social necessities of States organised as a community.[20]

This has increased the need for having a strong organised international community and solidarity among States, the latter being described by Professor MacDonald as:

> an agreement among formal equals that will all refrain from actions that would significantly interfere with the realization of common goals and fundamental interests. Solidarity requires an understanding that every member of the community must consciously and constantly conceive of its own interests as being inextricable from the interests of the whole. No State may choose to use its power to undertake actions that might threaten the integrity of the community.[21]

It is clear from the above observations that the international legal order has progressed from one which was characterised by a restrictive bilateral approach

---

[18] Greig (note 16), p. 547. However, scholars such as Professor Weil have warned against the adoption of ill-defined notions as for example the notion of 'international community as a whole': *supra* (note 6), p. 423.

[19] Ragazzi, *The Concept of International Obligations Erga Omnes*, Oxford, 1997, p. 17; and see Tomuschat (note 8), p. 231.

[20] Declaration of President Judge Bedjaoui, *Legality of the Threat or Use of Nuclear Weapons*, Advisory Opinion, *ICJ Reports 1996*, p. 226, at p. 270.

[21] Macdonald, 'The Principle of Solidarity in Public International Law', in Dominicé, Patry and Reymond (eds.), *Etudes de droit international en l'honneur de Pierre Lalive*, Basel, 1993, p. 293; as cited in Simma (note 8), p. 238.

regarding inter-State relations to the recognition of the existence of certain fundamental principles developed to promote the common interests of the international community in its entirety. These developments could not escape examination by the ILC in its work on the codification of the law on State responsibility and it is on this that attention will focus in the next section.

2. Collective Interests in the Law on State Responsibility

One of the fundamental questions that the ILC was called to consider in its work on State responsibility was whether the content of an infringed norm and the seriousness of a given breach had any bearing on the regime of international responsibility, in other words on the legal consequences that would arise as a result of an internationally wrongful act. More specifically, the ILC, in the early stages of its work and under the guidance of the second Special Rapporteur, Mr Ago, explored the question whether violations of different internationally wrongful acts gave rise to different legal consequences on the basis of the 'degree of essentiality' that conformity with a certain norm entailed for the international community, or whether a single regime of responsibility would be applicable irrespective of the nature and seriousness of the violation or the significance of the infringed norm.[22] The emphasis was accordingly placed on the content of the infringed norm and on the significance of the rights protected by it.[23] This distinction was based on the growing recognition that international law is not just about protecting narrowly-conceived State interests, but is, fundamentally, also concerned with protecting community interests. Accordingly, it was acknowledged by the ILC that not all internationally wrongful acts bear the same gravity and that the law on State responsibility should reflect the distinction between obligations of great significance to the international community as a whole, as, for instance, the prohibition of aggression and genocide, and obligations of less general importance.[24] It was on this ground that the notion of State crimes, which dominated the discussions on State responsibility, was developed until the decision was taken by the ILC not to include this notion in the second reading of the Draft Articles on State Responsibility, the deliberations on which were finally concluded in 2001.[25]

However, the 2001 Final Articles on State Responsibility have retained a distinction between serious and less serious violations of international law as

---

[22] See Ago's Fifth Report (note 3), p. 5, paragraph 9; p. 10, paragraph 26; and p. 26, paragraph 79.
[23] The rules on State responsibility should be distinguished from primary international rules.
[24] Ago's Fifth Report (note 3), p. 26, paragraph 80.
[25] Nevertheless, the debate is far from being concluded.

reflected in Articles 40 and 41. In particular, these articles make specific provision concerning the legal consequences of serious violations of peremptory norms and impose an obligation upon all States not to render any aid or assistance to the wrongdoer, not to recognize the unlawful act, and to co-operate in order to bring to an end the unlawful situation.[26]

Most important, it was soon realized that the content of the infringed rule affected not only the content of responsibility but also States which were entitled to invoke the responsibility of the wrongdoing State in the international arena, and the means by which enforcement of such rules would be accomplished. Each of these propositions is considered in turn below.

With respect to the circle of States entitled to respond to a violation of a norm protecting fundamental interests, it has already been pointed out earlier that the concept of *erga omnes* is characterized by the fact not only that it binds all States but also that the latter possess a legal interest in its protection. Hence, the ILC decided to take into consideration the question whether such protection extended to the field of international responsibility by widening the circle of States that could make a claim in the event of a violation of obligations having an *erga omnes* character. Mr Ago, for instance, acknowledged that in such circumstances the responsibility for the infringement of these obligations does not arise only towards the State which has been the 'direct victim of the breach', but also towards all States of the international community.[27] Hence, the recognition of the existence of essential rules for the international community could not have left unaffected the determination of the subjects empowered with the right to respond to such violations of international law.[28]

Nevertheless, this has not always been the position in international law. For a long time jurists such as Bluntschli, who advocated the entitlement of all States to respond to serious violations of international law and to safeguard the international legal order, were not but in the minority.[29] Since then, however, community interests have become an integral part of international law, as evidenced, *inter alia*, by the significant consideration and weight given to this notion in the work for the codification of the law on State responsibility. While the Final Articles make a distinction between 'injured' and 'other' States in Articles 42 and 48, this is only a reflection of the view that since the infringement of a particular norm does not always affect all States or in the same manner, there must be a distinction based on whether a State claims to be entitled to

---

[26] Report of the ILC to the General Assembly on the work of its fifty-third session, 2001 *ILC Yearbook*, vol. ii, Part Two, p. 20, at p. 29, Articles 40 and 41.

[27] Ago's Fifth Report (note 3), pp. 28–29, paragraph 89.

[28] Ibid, pp. 31–32, paragraphs 99–100.

[29] See Ago's Fifth Report (note 3), p. 41, paragraph 124.

invoke the responsibility of another State either as the primary beneficiary, the right holder, or the holder of a legal interest.[30] Article 48, in particular, provides further evidence of the significance of collective interests in the law on State responsibility by entitling all States to invoke the responsibility of another State that fails to meet its obligations established either for the protection of collective interests owed to a group of States to which the invoking State belongs, or for the protection of interests owed to the international community as a whole.[31] However, the distinction drawn by Articles 42 and 48 has legal significance as only the injured State is entitled to all the remedies provided under the law on State responsibility. On the contrary, non-directly injured States that fall within the Article 48 category enjoy only limited rights in relation to action they may be entitled to against the wrongdoing State.[32]

It is therefore imperative to highlight the fact that the concept of collective interests is not characterised by an inherent or an automatic right either to initiate legal proceedings before international judicial bodies or to resort to other means of enforcement such as countermeasures.[33] This is owed to the fact that while all States have an interest in the performance of international norms generally, it does not mean that all States are entitled to take all the measures that would otherwise be available to a directly injured State. However, this is not to say that States cannot take enforcement action against violations of fundamental interests owed to the international community as a whole, but rather that such a right is not an integral part of the concept of collective interests. As observed at the beginning of this chapter, the ICJ, with its *dictum* in the *Barcelona Traction* case, and its reference to obligations *erga omnes*, is silent about the enforcement of such obligations.

The entitlement of States to invoke the responsibility of another State for violations of obligations owed *erga omnes* is closely related to the concept of

---

[30] See Crawford, 'Responsibility to the International Community as a Whole', Fourth Annual Snyder Lecture, April 2000, Bloomington School of Law, Indiana University, p. 16, available at ⟨http://www.lcil.cam.ac.uk/Media/lectures/pdf/JRC%20Snyder%20lecture.pdf⟩ (last accessed on 1 June 2009); and Scobbie, 'The Invocation of Responsibility for the Breach of "Obligations under Peremptory Norms of General International Law"', 13 (2002) *EJIL* 1201, at p. 1205.

[31] Scobbie (note 30), p. 1207.

[32] Sicilianos, 'The Classification of Obligations and the Multilateral Dimension of the Relations on International Responsibility', 13 (2002) *EJIL* 1127, at p. 1141.

[33] See de Hoogh, *Obligations Erga Omnes and International Crimes*, The Hague, 1996, pp. 25–28, particularly p. 26; Simma (note 8), p. 296; Charney, 'Third State Remedies in International Law', 10 (1989) *Michigan Journal of International Law* 57, at pp. 90–91; and Chinkin, *Third Parties in International* Law, Oxford, 1993, p. 149. Also see the ruling of the International Court of Justice in the *Case concerning East Timor (Portugal v. Australia)*, *ICJ Reports 1995*, p. 90, at p. 102, paragraph 29.

standing, a concept which is of particular significance in the law of counter-measures. It is on this principle that the relationship between the State wishing to respond to a given breach and to the legal rule which has been violated is based. According to this principle, the State has standing to make international claims either, *inter alia*, by initiating judicial proceedings or by way of countermeasures.[34] The principle of standing identifies interests that are legally protected and veils them with 'legal form' on which States may rely to enforce international law.[35] As seen above, however, standing is not always equivalent to an entitlement or a right to take action in the form of countermeasures or judicial proceedings.[36] Accordingly, the violation of collective interests does not necessarily equate to a general standing possessed by all States to resort to *this* type of action.

Within the law on State responsibility the ILC makes a substantial distinction between the rights at the disposal of an injured State with the rights of a State other than the injured. According to this distinction, an injured State is entitled to demand cessation of the wrongful act, to seek reparation and guarantees for non-repetition, and ultimately, to resort to countermeasures. A State, however, entitled to invoke the responsibility of a wrongdoing State by means of Article 48 and in response to a breach of an obligation owed to the international community as a whole, has a much narrower range of options available to it. Consequently, it is entitled to demand cessation of the wrongful act, or even to demand reparation 'in the interest of the injured State or of the beneficiaries of the obligation breached', but with no reference to a right to countermeasures.

The question of countermeasures by States other than the injured has been at the heart of the discussions of the ILC. However, due to the controversy that emerged on the matter, the ILC decided to leave the recognition of a right to third-State countermeasures to the progressive development of international law. The next section turns to an examination on how the concept of countermeasures has developed in the literature and practice of international law with specific emphasis on the right of States other than the injured to resort to solidarity measures.

---

[34] Tams (note 4), p. 26.
[35] Ibid, p. 29.
[36] Ibid, p. 39 and p. 204.

III. IMPLEMENTING COUNTERMEASURES
IN THE PROTECTION OF COLLECTIVE INTERESTS

1. *An Introduction to the Concept of Countermeasures*

In a decentralized legal system such as the international one, States become the guardians of their own rights and subsequently of international law with the power and freedom not only to create the law but also to enforce such rights when they are infringed. The rule that States whose rights have been violated possess a right to countermeasures is now well established in international law. However, problems arise concerning the right of States other than the injured as defined in Article 48 of the Final Articles to resort to countermeasures in response to violations of obligations owed to the international community as a whole. States have been reluctant to accept a right to solidarity measures for fear of abuse, and therefore, a consideration of the reasons behind such reluctance is considered essential for the purposes of the current examination.

Countermeasures have often been described as mechanisms of private justice and as 'a reflection of the imperfect structure of the international community'[37] because they constitute individual, as opposed to institutional, peaceful measures of a coercive character taken by a State against another in response to an internationally wrongful act where that response would in itself constitute a violation of international law. The effect of countermeasures is that they render the obligations provided under international norms temporarily inoperative, although the obligations do not cease to exist or to produce legal effects.[38] Insofar as countermeasures aim at restoring the legal imbalance created by the unlawful act and at inducing the wrongdoing State to comply with its international obligations, the wrongfulness of the action, and subsequently the responsibility of the State resorting to them, is precluded.[39]

It is, accordingly, clear that the importance of this area of the law lies in the fact that countermeasures can be a very powerful mechanism, a mechanism which in effect is equivalent to States taking the law into their own hands. As States are the only assessors of whether a wrongful act has been committed in the first place, subject to the powers of the Security Council to take coercive action

---

[37] Report of the ILC to the General Assembly on the Work of its 44th Session, 1992 *ILC Yearbook* vol. ii, Part Two, p. 1; p. 17, at p. 19, paragraph 122.

[38] On the procedural and substantive conditions of countermeasures see Second Report on State Responsibility by Mr. James Crawford, ILC 51st session, UN Doc. A/CN.4/498/Add. 4, 19 July, 1999, paragraphs 362–370; available at ⟨http://www.lcil.cam.ac.uk/projects/state_responsibility_document_collection.php#6⟩ (last accessed on 9 April 2008).

[39] ILC Report 2001 (note 26), pp. 325–326, paragraph 3.

necessary for the maintenance of international peace and security, it is States alone which are the assessors of whether any action which they take meets the requirements of international law. The danger then of abuse is unveiled. Whilst States bear sole responsibility for their own actions, and as a consequence of any assessment they make, the exploitation of the doctrine of countermeasures to satisfy ulterior motives is not a far fetched possibility at all. Furthermore, the *de facto* inequality of States, in terms of economic and other non-forceful power, means that weaker States will be in a disadvantageous position in comparison to stronger States in implementing countermeasures.[40]

The ILC was mindful of these realities when deliberating the circumstances under which resort to countermeasures could be justified.[41] There were, therefore, voices of disagreement among members regarding the inclusion of countermeasures in the articles on State responsibility. The ILC, however, decided not to exclude this topic from consideration. It found enough evidence in customary law supportive of a right to countermeasures as a lawful response to unlawful conduct, provided that certain limitations and restrictions were met.[42] Many States who argued in support of the right to countermeasures highlighted the fact that a certain degree of coercion was acceptable in every legal order and that countermeasures constituted the only means of enforcement of international law.[43] While today it could be disputed whether countermeasures constitute the *only* means of international enforcement, it must also be recognized that their application may well have a very strong impact upon the targeted State.

Solidarity measures, however, on the other hand constitute countermeasures taken by a State which has not been injured by a violation of its individual rights. It has, nevertheless, a legal interest in the observance of the infringed norm which, while not owed to itself individually, is established for the common interest of all States. The question of whether States other than the injured may resort to solidarity measures has not been finally settled by the ILC. In particular, Article 54 of the Final Articles relating to the right of a State other than the injured to invoke the responsibility of another State avoids the use of the term

---

[40]   Report of the ILC to the General Assembly on the Work of its 48th Session, 1996 *ILC Yearbook* vol. ii, Part Two, p. 1; p. 57, at p. 66, paragraph 1.

[41]   Arangio-Ruiz, Third Report on State responsibility, 1991 *ILC Yearbook* vol. ii, Part One, p. 1, at pp. 7–8, paragraph 4. The term 'countermeasures' was substituted for 'sanctions' following the decision of the Arbitral Tribunal in the *Case Concerning the Air Service Agreement of 27 March 1946 between the United States of America and France*, 18 *UN Reports of International Arbitral Awards* 442.

[42]   *Supra* (note 40), p. 67, paragraphs 1–4.

[43]   ILC Report to the General Assembly (note 37), pp. 20–21, paragraph 131.

'countermeasures'. Instead, the ILC, faced with the concern expressed by some States in incorporating an express right to solidarity measures, refers to the right of such States to take 'lawful measures' in response to violations of obligations owed *erga omnes*. This term has raised questions regarding its interpretation, although it appears that the ILC, by adopting this term intended not to rule out the possibility of a future development of such a right.[44] In the commentary that follows Article 54, the ILC concludes that it could not find evidence of sufficient State practice and the required *opinio juris* to prove the existence of such a right.[45]

In so doing, the ILC did not follow earlier proposals to the effect that countermeasures, in protecting general interests, should be allowed in two situations: first, whenever a State was invited to resort to such countermeasures by the State directly injured on the basis and scope of the given consent, and, secondly, in the absence of an injured State, whenever an obligation owed to the international community was infringed.[46] Although, as noted above, these proposals were not followed by the ILC, it can be seen from its commentaries to both Articles 22 and 54 of the Final Articles that it did not wish to take a definite and final position that would prejudice further developments on the matter.[47] Furthermore, Article 41 (3), which refers to the consequences that derive from serious breaches of peremptory norms, provides that such consequences are without prejudice to other consequences which may arise under international law, the implication being that international law leaves room for the possibility of a right to solidarity measures vested in non-injured States.[48]

It needs to be said that the ILC's decision not to incorporate a right to solidarity measures due to insufficient State practice has been criticized as denying protection for the most serious violations of international law.[49] While concern regarding solidarity measures as opening Pandora's box cannot be ignored, it is also essential to bear in mind the fact that a refusal to take action in genuine cases of violation leads not only to impunity, but also risks

---

[44] Pellet, 'The New Draft Articles of the International Law Commission on the Responsibility of States for Internationally Wrongful Acts: A Requiem for States' Crime?', 32 (2001) *NYIL* 55, at p. 79. However, see Alland, 'Countermeasures of General Interest', 13 (2002) *EJIL* 1221, at p. 1233.

[45] Crawford, *The International Law Commission's Articles on State Responsibility: Introduction, Text and Commentaries*, Cambridge, 2003, p. 305.

[46] Third Report on State Responsibility by Mr. James Crawford, ILC 52nd session, UN Doc. A/CN.4/507/Add.4, 4 August 2000, paragraph 413; available at ⟨http://www.lcil.cam.ac.uk/ projects/state_responsibility_document_collection.php#6⟩ (last accessed on 9 April 2008).

[47] *Supra* (note 26), p. 350, paragraph 6.

[48] Alland (note 44), p. 1232.

[49] Ibid, p. 1239.

exposure to even more violations of this nature. It is therefore imperative that the right balance be struck between the rights of States as sovereign entities on the one hand and as members of the international community as a whole on the other, so as to ensure that the latter does not stand in apathy in the face of genocide, aggression, torture, slavery and other infringements of obligations in which all States have a legal interest. It is in this context that the enforcement of fundamental interests through countermeasures gains particular significance.

2. The Legal Constraints of Countermeasures

Any discussion on the right to take countermeasures either by the injured State or by a State other than the injured must look into the limitations placed by international law for the exercise of this right. This is owed to the fact that a State committing an internationally wrongful act does not become an outlaw and, therefore, its own rights must also be safeguarded.[50] It has already been discussed above that countermeasures may become such a strong weapon in the hands of States resorting to them that the imposition of the most stringent conditions regarding their use is an essential prerequisite if they are not to become an instrument of unlawfulness.[51] It is therefore common ground that countermeasures should not be punitive in character as this would contravene the foundations of the international legal system, and in particular the principle of sovereign equality of States which is the corner stone of international law. The problem becomes even more acute in the case of solidarity measures. Professor Koskenniemi argues, for example, that the ambiguity surrounding the exact scope and content of concepts such as obligations owed *erga omnes*, serious breaches, or the fundamental interests of the international community, makes the restriction of solidarity measures imperative, especially where there is fear of a future 'automaticity' of action.[52]

The Final Articles make clear that countermeasures are exceptionally permitted in order to induce a recalcitrant State to respect its obligations arising under the law on State responsibility.[53] While countermeasures must not necessarily be of a reciprocal character, they must comply with principles of necessity and proportionality. Moreover, countermeasures must be terminated as soon as the

---

[50] Riphagen, Second Report on State Responsibility, 1981 *ILC Yearbook* vol. ii, Part One, p. 79, at p. 86, paragraph 60.

[51] Arangio-Ruiz, Third Report on State Responsibility (note 41), p. 1, at p. 18, paragraph 52.

[52] Koskenniemi, 'Solidarity Measures: State Responsibility as a New International Order?', 72 (2001) *BYIL* 337, at pp. 349–350, and p. 355.

[53] Crawford (note 45) p. 284.

aim for which they have been resorted to is accomplished whilst their effects must be as far as possible reversible.[54] Furthermore, such countermeasures may not affect the rights of a third State and must not be in contravention of essential principles of international law such as the protection of fundamental human rights or obligations arising from peremptory norms.[55] While the ILC did not incorporate a specific provision on the prohibition of measures which aim to exercise economic and political coercion impairing the territorial integrity, political independence or the freedom from foreign interference in the domestic affairs of States, the commentary to Article 50 (1) (b) of the Final Articles makes particular reference to the International Covenant on Economic, Social and Cultural Rights.[56] This leads to the conclusion that particularly burdensome countermeasures will be assessed in the light of fundamental human rights. Article 50 (2) of the Final Articles goes on to stipulate that a State resorting to countermeasures is still under a duty to fulfil its obligations under (a) any dispute settlement procedure existing between itself and the wrongdoing State that is related to the dispute in question; and (b) under diplomatic and consular law.

In the light of the above, proportionality, which, according to Professor Crawford, is the *sine qua non* of the legality of countermeasures,[57] needs to be assessed within this already narrow scope of the concept of countermeasures as analyzed above. The purpose of the proportionality principle is not only to restrict the intensity and extent of countermeasures but also to provide legal certainty and predictability against which a certain action can be assessed.[58] Furthermore, proportionality should be kept distinct from necessity since it does not always follow that an act which is necessary is also proportionate.[59] Again, not unlike countermeasures themselves, the assessment of whether a State's response meets the requirement of proportionality is left to that State. It has therefore been suggested that the principle must be more precisely formulated.[60]

Currently, Article 51 of the Final Articles provides that countermeasures, the aim of which is restricted to the exercise of coercion against the wrongdoing State in order to make it comply with its obligations under the law on State responsibility, 'must be commensurate with the injury suffered, taking

---

[54] Ibid, pp. 282–283.

[55] Ibid, p. 288.

[56] Ibid, p. 289.

[57] Report of the ILC to the General Assembly on the work of its 52nd session, 2000 *ILC Yearbook* vol. ii, Part Two, p. 1; p. 18 (State Responsibility), at p. 94, paragraph 305.

[58] Cannizzaro, 'The Role of Proportionality in the Law of International Countermeasures', 12 (2001) *EJIL* 889, at p. 890.

[59] Crawford (note 45), p. 296.

[60] *Supra* (note 57), p. 102, paragraph 333.

into account the gravity of the internationally wrongful act and the rights in question'. This definition reflects international rulings on the question of proportionality such as the ruling in the *Case Concerning the Air Services Agreement of 27 March 1946* between the United States and France,[61] and the ruling of the ICJ in the *Case Concerning the Gabcikovo-Nagymaros Project* between Hungary and Slovakia.[62]

The question of assessing proportionality becomes more interesting and indeed challenging in the context of responses taken by States in the name of general interests. The recognition of a right to solidarity measures according to which every State is entitled to resort to countermeasures against another State in response to violations of fundamental norms of the international community, raises significant issues regarding proportionality. In particular, the question arises as to whether in circumstances such as these proportionality will be assessed cumulatively. In other words, the question is whether proportionality will be judged on the basis of the totality of the responses against the recalcitrant State, or assessed on an individual basis in relation to the response adopted by each State. It may be argued that the current position, reflected as it is in Article 51 of the Final Articles, omits to take into consideration the difficulties which may arise as a result of a possible recognition of a right to solidarity measures.

In addition to the above, it has been observed that the proportionality of a response to the infringement of an obligation of a bilateral nature cannot be compared to the proportionality required for a response to a violation of an obligation *erga omnes*. Whilst in the first case the reciprocal suspension of rights may suffice, in the latter case the reaction may aim at imposing the compliance of the defaulting State with the infringed rule. Furthermore, and despite the fact that it may be employed in both cases, the coercive element of the reaction may take on a different kind of significance where a measure is taken in response to a violation of an *erga omnes* obligation.[63] It has therefore been suggested that the decision of the ILC to restrict the aim of countermeasures to coercion permits no flexibility.

According to Cannizzaro for instance, 'in a plurality of instruments and tools of self-redress'[64] in the international legal order, emphasis must be placed upon the function which each response seeks to fulfil. These responses may be normative, retributive, coercive or executive in character. It is therefore suggested that proportionality should not be conceived as a fixed notion, unchangeable and inflexible, applicable to all situations. Accordingly, the nature

---

[61] *Air Service* case (note 41).
[62] *ICJ Reports 1997*, p. 7.
[63] Cannizzarro (note 58), p. 896.
[64] Ibid, p. 889.

and function of countermeasures in each instance varies significantly. Cannizzaro hence suggests that the emphasis must be placed on the appropriateness of the aim/function of the response and the appropriateness of the adopted measures in light of the result they are intended to achieve. It is the case then that countermeasures can achieve their purpose which ultimately is the enforcement of international law provided of course that they are subjected to the most stringent conditions. Proportionality in this regard plays a significant role, and it is for this reason that the question of proportionality of solidarity measures requires further attention.

IV. SOLIDARITY MEASURES IN STATE PRACTICE

One of the difficulties with which the ILC was faced in its work on State responsibility was finding sufficient evidence to establish the right of non injured States to resort to countermeasures (that is solidarity measures) whenever a fundamental norm of international law safeguarding obligations owed to all States had been infringed. Despite its early recognition that some norms are more fundamental than others and the consequential widening of the circle of States with an interest in their protection, the issue of enforcement of such norms, particularly, through solidarity countermeasures proved to be problematic. For this reason and in view of the lack of a clear norm entitling States other than the injured to effect such measures, the ILC turned its attention to State practice and *opinio juris* in order to determine whether a customary rule had indeed developed in this regard.[65] Its conclusion to the effect that existing State practice does not support a right to solidarity measures may however be questioned. The fact is that from a survey of such practice one can conclude that a right to solidarity measures is not precluded.

Most important, however, from this author's point of view, is the fact that State practice offers more examples supporting a right to solidarity measures than those briefly referred to by the ILC in its commentary to Article 54, and it is for this reason that its research on the matter was inconclusive. It is undoubtedly true that an in-depth analysis of hard-to-find or even conflicting evidence extending over a long period of time representing equally the views and positions of both the developed and developing States may have been particularly difficult to carry out by the ILC. However, a study of this kind

---

[65] For an analysis of customary rules and particularly State practice, see Warbrick, 'The Theory of International Law: Is there an English Contribution?', in Alston, Warbrick and Carty (eds.), *Theory and International Law: An Introduction*, London, 1991, p. 55.

was necessary not least because the enforcement of norms of a fundamental character for the international community as a whole is an extremely important matter. Furthermore, although not amounting to countermeasures or solidarity measures, it is the case that many of the examples of State practice which the ILC failed to examine offered valuable evidence of economic and other kinds of coercion precluding the use of armed force in favour of the protection of collective interests. The fact is that these incidents of State practice would have assisted the ILC in identifying and evaluating the views of governments in a rapidly changing international environment. Accordingly, the ILC ought not to have excluded a more detailed survey of the matter.

While the genuine intentions behind existing State practice in relation to solidarity measures by States other than the injured are not always clear, one can deduce two logical conclusions from existing practice. States may, in the first place, intend to disregard international law, or, in the second, intend to rely on a cause that would render their conduct justifiable. While the latter may not by itself be sufficient to establish the essential *opinio juris* for the formulation of a customary norm, it may well provide evidence pointing in the direction of gradually emerging *opinio juris*. The purpose, therefore, of this section is to consider some of the distinctive features of such State action in search of evidence for the existence of a right to countermeasures in the general interest. While a detailed and thorough analysis of State practice cannot fall within the limited scope of the present examination, the intention here is to look at those incidents which were not considered by the ILC in Article 54, and which in the author's view, enhance an argument in favour of an existing right to solidarity measures.[66]

1. *The Reaction of States to Violations of Fundamental Norms*

The development of the concept of solidarity measures was very much influenced by the division of the world between Western and Communist States during the period of the Cold War. More specifically, what was considered by certain States as essential, mainly economic, action against the expansion of communism through serious violations of fundamental human rights, other States viewed as a threat and an interference in their domestic affairs. It was observed in this regard that economic sanctions were often used as a 'symbol of alliance' as opposed to an 'instrument of international order'.[67]

---

[66] For detailed analysis, see forthcoming book by author (note 4).

[67] Mayall, 'The Sanctions Problem in International Economic Relations: Reflections in the Light of Recent Experience', 60 (1984) *International Affairs* 631, at p. 633.

At the same time, States had often exercised their economic powers and discretion to coerce other States from acting or refraining from acting in a particular way. Although unfriendly in character, such action often did not infringe any specific norm of international law.[68] The US approach to the Suez Canal crisis of 1956 constitutes an example for this kind of measure. Responding to this crisis and to the aggressive policies of the United Kingdom and France against Egypt, the US conditioned the provision of loans and aid in oil supplies upon a ceasefire agreement.[69] Similarly, the US, on a number of occasions, refused military assistance to Chile, Uruguay, the Philippines, Brazil, El Salvador, Guatemala, Nicaragua, Ethiopia, Argentina and South Korea in response to serious human rights violations.[70] It is worth noting that during the presidency of Jimmy Carter respect for human rights constituted a primary consideration and condition for foreign aid and military assistance. The US Government at the time held the view that it possessed not only a 'legal right' but also responsibility under the United Nations Charter and international law to respond to human rights violations, although it must be said that US foreign policy was not always disassociated from national considerations.[71] European States followed this approach in a number of instances, particularly within the framework of regional international organizations such as the European Economic Community (EEC) and the European Union (EU). The imposition of human rights clauses in exchange of certain economic and trade benefits is now common practice of the EU, while in some specific situations, it responded to serious infringements of fundamental international norms by countermeasures even though neither the EU nor any of its Member States had suffered direct injury.

While State practice has not always been uniform in this regard, a consistent trend may be identified where States respond with determination for the purpose of enforcing fundamental principles of international law, sometimes

---

[68] Eagleton, *International Government* (Third edition), New York, 1957. Also see Picchio Forlati and Sicilianos, *Economic Sanctions in International Law*, Leiden, 2004, p. 101; and Small, 'Foreign Boycotts', 1976 *Digest of US Practice in International Law* 575, at p. 577.

[69] Bowie, *Suez 1956: International Crises and the Role of Law*, Oxford, 1974, pp. 61–65. [For a more detailed examination of the Suez crisis, see Chapter 19: 'The Road to Kandahar' by N.D. White. Eds.]

[70] Hufbauer and Clyde (eds.), *Economic Sanctions Reconsidered: History and Current Policy*, Cambridge, Mass., 1985, p. 461.

[71] Cohen, 'Human Rights Decision-Making in the Executive Branch: Some Proposals for a Co-ordinated Strategy' in Kommers and Loescher (eds.), *Human Rights and American Foreign Policy*, Notre Dame, Ind., 1979, p. 212, at p. 222. Also see *President Carter's Inaugural Address*, New York Times, 21 January 1977.

by using lawful measures and sometimes by resorting to countermeasures. The Netherlands for instance, complying with a 1968 mandatory Security Council (SC) resolution for the implementation of sanctions against Southern Rhodesia, introduced the Sanctions Bill in order to enable it conform to its international obligations. It is highlighted in the Explanatory Memorandum that the Bill purported to be used as a tool for the national implementation of international decisions, recommendations or agreements concerning the maintenance of international peace and security or the furtherance of the interests of the international legal order, including the protection from gross violations of human rights.[72] The phrase 'international accords' was interpreted by the Dutch government to include accords which, although not amounting to a decision of an international organization, were taken within the framework of such an organization, such as decisions of the Council of the European Economic Community (EEC) for common action or decisions taken under the European Political Co-operation.[73] Since the Bill did not aim to restrict the implementation of measures to those adopted under SC authorization, the pre-eminence of which against other treaty obligations is safeguarded by virtue of Article 103 of the UN Charter, and since the Bill did not specify whether or not compliance with such international decisions was to be consistent with obligations arising from other international legal instruments, it could, by inference, be argued that the Bill left room for the implementation of solidarity measures. Even though the Bill did not make explicit reference to such a right, it could be argued that it demonstrated the intention of the Netherlands to support such a right for the purpose of protecting fundamental community interests by relying on even non-legally binding decisions of international bodies such as recommendations.

With these observations in mind, attention will focus in detail on some of the incidents of State practice which despite their significance to the study of solidarity measures, were not considered by the ILC, demonstrating that yet more research is required on the matter.

a. The Greek Case (1967)

Following a military coup in Greece in 1967, there were imposed on the population a number of human rights restrictions in violation of the ECHR. Denmark, Norway and Sweden initiated proceedings against Greece before the

---

[72] *Sanctions Bill*, Bijl. Hand. II 1975/76–14006 No. 3, 8.
[73] See the Dutch position in 'The Meaning of "International Accords" in Draft Article 2 of the 1976 Sanctions Bill', 9 (1978) *NYIL* 235, at pp. 235–237; and 'Violations of the sanctions against Southern Rhodesia': excerpts of the Memorandum of Reply concerning the 1976 Sanctions Bill, 9 (1978) *NYIL* 235.

European Commission of Human Rights.[74] While these States were acting on the basis of a specific agreement entitling them to take the action they did, they were not directly affected by the situation and were only acting on the basis of a violation of the public order of Europe.[75] At the EEC level however, European States were faced with the dilemma of trying to respond to these developments and queried whether or not the suspension of the 1962 Association Agreement with Greece was an appropriate response. The European Parliament, expressing its solidarity with the Greek people, made clear that for as long as Greece infringed its obligations under the ECHR, the Association Agreement would be at stake.[76] At the same time, the EEC Commission rejected a request for a $ 10 million loan for development despite the fact that the European Investment Bank had approved it.[77] Most importantly, however, the Commission decided to carry out those parts of its Association Agreement with Greece which involved specific obligations, as for example, obligations in the areas of trade and tariffs. At the same time, the Commission decided to associate those areas which still required negotiations and which were not bound by specific legal duties with the demand for political reform in Greece.[78] However, the Commission refused to proceed with the renunciation or suspension of the Association Agreement on the basis that no legal grounds for either suspension or renunciation were provided therein.[79]

The question thus arose whether the EEC possessed the competence to proceed to such partial 'freezing' of its Agreement with Greece. The fact was that apart from a general reference in the preamble concerning the need to strengthen peace and liberty, the Agreement contained no express provision with respect to the protection and respect of human rights. It seems to be the view of some authors, however, that the EEC action was

---

[74] See Council of Europe, Directorate of Information, Doc. B (67) 37 (26.6.67). See Buergenthal, 'Proceedings Against Greece under the European Convention of Human Rights', 62 (1968) *AJIL* 441.

[75] Frowein, 'Reactions by Not Directly Affected States to Breaches of Public International Law', 248 (1994-IV) *Hague Recueil des cours* 360.

[76] Resolution sur l'asociation entre la C.E.E. et la Grece, 2 June 1967, OJ (1967) No. 10, 2058; *Compte Rendu in Extenso des Seances, Parlement Europeen, Debats*, vol. VI/67, No. 91, 11–20 (1967); Written Question No. 108 of 14 July 1967; and Reply by the Commission of the European Communities, 22 September 1967: OJ (1967) No. 243/2 of 7 October 1967; and Buergenthal (note 74), p. 448.

[77] *New York Times*, 29 September 1967, p. 14, col. 3; and Buergenthal (note 74), p. 448.

[78] Coufoudakis, 'The European Economic Community and the "Freezing" of the Greek Association, 1967–1974', 16 (1977–1978) *Journal of Common Market Studies* 114, at pp. 117–118.

[79] Ibid, p. 128.

not in violation of the obligations arising under the said Agreement.[80] Yet, the scepticism that prevailed at the time regarding the lawfulness of EEC action, which affected the rights arising from the Association Agreement, can be illustrated in the writings of Buergenthal who, commenting on the EEC hesitation to resort to more 'drastic' measures against Greece, observed that

> even if the Community should for legal reasons be unable to comply with a demand for the complete suspension of the Association Agreement, it is clear that Greece would be economically harmed by a Community policy which limited co-operation with Greece exclusively to a grudging compliance with the clearly-defined obligations of the Association Agreement and left unexecuted the wider aims of this treaty.[81]

Buergenthal went on to conclude that it would have been very difficult for the EEC to suspend the Association Agreement in its entirety in the absence of a specific provision in the Agreement entitling States to resort to such action.

However, a decade later when it was called upon to follow the US example by imposing measures against the regime of Idi Amin for genocide committed in Uganda, the EEC invoked its obligations under the Lomé Convention on the basis of which it continued its payments to the brutal regime and justified its policy by reference to 'the limited possibilities for reaction which general international law offered'.[82] The EEC distinguished the case of Uganda with the action taken in response to the dictatorship in Greece ten years earlier by pointing out that the latter was justified under the Association Agreement, which, in the preamble, made reference to human rights. This distinguished it from agreements with Third World countries where no reference to human rights was made.[83]

It can be concluded from the above that the EEC action, namely the accomplishment of the wider aims of the said Agreement, was justified on the basis of a general reference to the protection of human rights, providing significant evidence in the study of solidarity measures. This is particularly so in the absence of express rules in the Agreement allowing the non-performance of the rights provided under it in response to human rights

---

[80] Ibid, p. 121 and p. 126.
[81] Buergenthal (note 74), p. 449.
[82] Riedel and Will, 'Human Rights Clauses in External Agreements of the EC', in Alston (ed.), *The EU and Human Rights*, Oxford, 1999, p. 723.
[83] See for instance *The Central African Empire*, Written Question No. 943/77, 28 March 1978, OJ (1978) No. C 74/17.

violations. Nevertheless, even if the action taken by the EEC against Greece did not infringe specific legal obligations, the incident illustrates the determination of an international organisation such as the EEC to respond to violations of obligations of a community character. The essential point is that given its significance, the incident ought not to have been overlooked by the ILC.

b. The "Arab Oil Weapon"

Another one of the incidents not considered by the ILC when it was looking at existing State practice regarding a right to third-State countermeasures is an episode which has never been regarded in the literature as an example of solidarity measures. This is the matter of the imposition of an oil embargo by Arab States against Israel and its allies in the 1970s known as the 'Arab Oil Weapon'. Since the 1947 Arab-Israeli conflict, Arab States were involved in a number of measures against Israel with a view to inducing it to cease the occupation of Arab territories and to restore the rights of the Palestinians. Measures were also taken against States providing economic, military and other support to Israel. In 1957, for instance, Arab States refused flight and landing rights to Air France in their territories in response to the latter's financial support of the Israeli film industry.[84]

However, it was in 1973 that Arab States decided to react more strongly by reducing the production of oil. This measure was adopted not only to affect Israel and States such as the Netherlands, Portugal, South Africa and Rhodesia, but was also taken in solidarity with Egypt and Syria which were trying to regain their territories lost in the 1967 war with Israel. What makes this incident particularly interesting is the fact that, with the exception of Egypt and Syria, which were directly injured by Israel's actions, the other States implementing the 'Arab Oil Weapon' such as Iraq, Kuwait, Algeria, Bahrain, Qatar, Libya and Saudi Arabia were third parties to the dispute. It appears, therefore, that these States were acting in the interest of community principles with effect *erga omnes* such as the prohibition of the use of armed force, a category of action which would today fall within the scope of Article 48 of the Final Articles. Nonetheless, the adoption of such measures by the Arab States raises some challenging questions, in particular the question whether these States were entitled to take action against Israel and other States, and if so, which States precisely were entitled to adopt such measures and on what

---

[84] This particular measure is mentioned in Doxey, *Economic Sanctions and International Enforcement*, Oxford, 1971, pp. 21–22.

legal grounds.[85] Furthermore, it is worth looking not only at whether Israel had infringed fundamental norms of international law, but also whether other States had infringed international obligations owed to the international community as a whole which in turn could trigger countermeasures by States other than the injured.

It was argued by the relevant Arab States that their action against Israel was justified in response to its unlawful use of force against other States and its occupation of foreign territory.[86] By way of inference, it could be argued that the action directed against States other than Israel was taken in response to their provision of assistance to Israel in its commission of a breach of a fundamental norm of the international legal order such as the prohibition of the use of armed force. Accordingly, it remains to consider whether the Arab action infringed any specific international rules which would render their action a solidarity measure. In this context, it has been argued that the exercise of economic coercion by the Arab States was in breach of the UN Charter[87] and of GATT obligations giving rise to most-favoured nation treatment which prohibited discriminatory practices and the imposition of export restrictions between Member States. However, a closer examination reveals that at the time only Egypt and Kuwait were signatory parties to the GATT. Since it was directly involved and injured in the dispute with Israel, Egypt was entitled to justify its actions on the national security clause provided in GATT, and hence it was only Kuwait whose action was in contravention of treaty commitments under GATT. Nevertheless, none of the Parties involved in the dispute brought the matter before the GATT which leaves the matter inconclusive.[88] Despite this, and in the light of the above, it seems that Kuwait's action enhances the argument in favour of the existence of a right to countermeasures taken in the collective interest.

Questions were also raised as to whether the oil embargo was in contravention of specific agreements in force between the US and Iraq, Oman and Saudi Arabia respectively. With respect to the two agreements concluded with Iraq and Oman, their significance lies in the fact that their suspension could arguably be justified not only on the basis of a fundamental change of circumstances but

---

[85] See *Arab Communiqué*, Conference of Arab Oil Ministers, Kuwait, October 17, 1973 in Paust and Blaustein (eds.), *The Arab Oil Weapon*, Dobbs Ferry, 1977, p. 42.

[86] See *Arab Resolution*, Conference of Arab Oil Ministers, Kuwait, October 17, 1973, Paust and Blaustein, ibid, p. 44, at p. 45.

[87] For a counter-analysis on the legality of the Arab measures see Shihata, 'Destination Embargo of Arab Oil: Its Legality Under International Law', in Paust and Blaustein, ibid, p. 97.

[88] Neff, 'Boycott and the Law of Nations: Economic Warfare and Modern International Law in Historical Perspective', 59 (1988) BYIL 113, at p. 137, note 106.

also by reference to certain express provisions contained within these treaties. While this fact would tend to preclude it from being seen as evidence of solidarity measures, the fact is that it offers valuable knowledge with respect to the existence of *opinio juris* in support of the enforcement and protection of collective rights. Nevertheless, more attention is required to be paid in relation to the 1933 Agreement between the US and Saudi Arabia according to which the two Parties agreed to accord each other unconditional most-favoured nation treatment on the import, export and other duties and charges on commerce and navigation.[89] As the Agreement made no provision on which Saudi Arabia could rely for justifying the measures taken against the US, this seems to provide further evidence in support of solidarity measures. This conclusion is supported by the fact that Shihata, one of the jurists favouring Arab measures, justified these as attempts 'to secure an objective of the highest international order: The restoration to the lawful sovereigns of illegally occupied territories and the restoration of the rights of peoples deprived of self-determination'.[90] To this end, Shihata was of the view that such measures were required for the safeguarding of international law pointing out that

> A general and absolute prohibition on the use of economic measures for political purposes in the international sphere is still an idealist's dream. Before it hardens into a rule of international law, enforcement machinery must develop for the protection of the militarily weaker States, which may happen to have a relatively great economic power. Precluding such States from the use of their economic power in the settlement of political disputes before a general ban is imposed on armaments and in the absence of an effective collective security system could not serve the interests of international justice. It would only help the development of what President Roosevelt once described as "a one-way international law which lacks mutuality in its observance and therefore becomes an instrument of oppression".[91]

Despite the fact that neither the US nor any of the participating States expressly relied on the concept of countermeasures taken in the collective interest, there is no doubt that such action did fall within this concept and for this reason merits particular attention in future discussions on State practice supportive of solidarity measures.[92]

---

[89] *Provisional Agreement between the United States of America and the Kingdom of Saudi Arabia in Regard to Diplomatic and Consular Representation, Juridical Protection, Commerce and Navigation*, signed 7 November 1933: in Paust and Blaustein (note 85), pp. 356–357.

[90] *Supra* (note 87), p. 130.

[91] Ibid, p. 132.

[92] Ibid, p. 131, and also see Lillich, 'Economic Coercion and the International Legal Order', in Paust and Blaustein (note 85), p. 151, at p. 157.

c. US Measures Against Nicaragua (1980s)

Another example in State practice which may provide useful information regarding the enforcement of collective interests concerns the economic action taken by the US against Nicaragua in the 1980s. More specifically, in 1982 the US by internal legislation implemented a quota on the imports of sugar from Nicaragua which resulted in placing particularly heavy economic hurdles upon it. This action was taken in response to Nicaragua's subversive acts in neighbouring countries such as Honduras and Costa Rica in violation of their sovereign rights. When Nicaragua referred the case to a GATT panel, the US refused to rely on any of the exception clauses under the GATT in order to justify its decision. Instead, it stressed that the dispute could not be resolved in the context of GATT and that 'its action was fully justified in the context in which it was taken'[93] without however referring to specific legal arguments for this purpose. The GATT panel on its part accepted Nicaragua's claims.

In 1985 the US intensified its measures against Nicaragua by prohibiting all imports of goods and services from, and all exports to, Nicaragua, by suspending incoming flights of Nicaraguan air carriers and by banning the entry of Nicaraguan vessels into US ports. This time the US relied upon unusual and extraordinary threats to its national security and foreign policy resulting from Nicaragua's aggressive policies in Central America caused by the subversion of its neighbouring countries and the enhancement of its military and security ties with the USSR and Cuba. The US further decided to terminate the 1956 US-Nicaraguan Treaty of Friendship, Commerce and Navigation and Protocol on the ground that Nicaragua's activities were incompatible with normal commercial activities between the two countries.[94] When the dispute was again brought before a GATT panel, the latter was unable to consider the dispute as the US had invoked national security reasons which prevented it from examining the substance of the dispute between the two States. However, in a report issued in 1986 the panel stressed that such boycotts contravened the purposes of GATT for non-discriminatory trade practices.[95]

Most interesting, however, is the fact that when the dispute was brought before the ICJ, it failed to consider the termination of the 1956 Treaty

---

[93] GATT Basic Instruments and Selected Documents, United States – Imports of Sugar from Nicaragua, Supplement No. 31, Report of the Panel adopted on 13 March 1984, paragraph 3.11.

[94] M.K. and M.N.L., 'Economic Sanctions-Union of Soviet Socialist Republics Invasion of Afghanistan (1979) Polish Repression (1981)', 1981–1988 (III) *Cumulative Digest of International Law* 2967, at p. 2979.

[95] GATT Doc. L/6053 (1986)18.

on Friendship, Commerce and Navigation in the context of the law of countermeasures,[96] despite the fact that it had already established Nicaragua's unlawful acts such as the violation of the prohibition of armed force under Article 2, paragraph 4 of the UN Charter. Notwithstanding this, it is the author's view that the measures taken against Nicaragua in 1982 and 1985 seem to enhance an argument in favour of an existing right to countermeasures by States other than the injured and for this reason they merit closer consideration in the study of establishing a right to countermeasures taken in the community interest.

d. Measures Against Haiti (1991)

Another example of State practice causing problems of legitimacy is the action taken against Haiti in 1991 in response to the military coup which ousted the democratically elected President of the country, Jean-Bertrand Aristide. The Committee of Ministers of the African, Caribbean and Pacific Group of States (ACP) recommended, not without a degree of hesitation, that States members of the Fourth Lomé Convention suspend trade with Haiti.[97] Member States of the European Community, acting under the European Political Cooperation Treaty also imposed a trade embargo on the country. Not only was it in violation of the Lomé Agreement, this measure was taken without the authorisation of the Security Council by States other than the injured and which would qualify it as a solidarity measure under international law. While this action was criticized, it was not so much because of the fact that the embargo was in violation of specific treaty commitments. Rather, the criticism was sparked by the fact that the Lome Convention, although it made reference to human rights, it made no reference to a right to democracy, and as a consequence, it left no room for action on this ground. Nevertheless, it could be argued that this incident adds to existing State practice in support of solidarity measures as an example of action by third States in violation of their international treaty commitments and in response to violations of collective interests, provided of course that the right to democracy can be described as protecting fundamental interests of the international community as a whole.[98]

---

[96] *Military and Paramilitary Activities in and against Nicaragua, Merits, ICJ Reports 1986*, p. 14, at p. 138, paragraph 87. For a critical evaluation of the Court's judgment, see Frowein (note 75), p. 374.

[97] 1992 *Keesing's Record of World Events* 38905.

[98] Chinkin, 'The Legality of the Imposition of Sanctions by the European Union in International Law', in Evans (ed.), *Aspects of Statehood and Institutionalism in Contemporary Europe*, Dartmouth, 1996, p. 183, at p. 201.

As it can be demonstrated from the above analysis, the consideration of State practice and *opinio juris* in search of a right to solidarity measures has not been exhaustive. On the contrary, these examples illustrate that there may be much more evidence in support of such measures than the one acknowledged by the ILC in its work on State responsibility. Perhaps the controversy that this discussion provoked among States, together with the concern that such a right may lead to abuse by powerful States, resulted in the ILC's decision to postpone consideration of the matter until further developments. However, the necessity of finding a way of responding effectively to serious infringements of fundamental community interests and of coercing a recalcitrant State to cease its wrongful act shows that the debate on the enforcement of international law through solidarity measures is far from over.

v. Conclusion

The discussion in this chapter, which is by no means conclusive, has intended to highlight some of the substantive issues arising from the concept of solidarity measures which lie at the heart of the enforcement of international law. It has been demonstrated during the course of this study that countermeasures, while not the only means of enforcement of international law, undoubtedly constitute one of the most powerful executive and coercive tools against a State that infringes its obligations under international law. Yet, countermeasures constitute but evidence of the uniqueness of the international legal system which, in the absence of centralized mechanisms of implementation of international law, has developed alternative procedures to achieve this end. Accordingly, countermeasures are characterized by the fact that they entitle States to respond to a violation of an international norm with another violation but with the purpose of coercing, albeit through unilateral peaceful means, the wrongdoing State to return to legality. Since an assessment whether or not an internationally wrongful act has in fact been committed in the first place belongs to the State resorting to such countermeasures, the probability of an abusive exercise of countermeasures is particularly real. It is for this reason that some States have voiced their concern over allowing States to take the law into their own hand through the exercise of such measures. Despite this, it can safely be concluded that the right of States to resort to countermeasures in response to the violation of their rights is now well established in contemporary international law.

Difficulties arise however with respect to a general right of States to resort to countermeasures for the protection of interests owed to the international community. As it becomes apparent from the work of the ILC on the law on State responsibility, the question of solidarity measures has been the subject of much controversy. As shown above, while the ILC acknowledged at an early stage of its deliberations that in view of the varying significance of the rights protected by some norms of international law not all internationally wrongful acts bear the same degree of gravity, there was a dichotomy in the Commission regarding the question of enforcement of such fundamental interests through countermeasures by States other than the injured. The ILC, in an attempt to reach completion of a programme of work that had already taken more than five decades of continuous deliberations, adopted its Final Articles on State Responsibility in 2001, but then decided to leave the question of solidarity measures unsettled. Concluding that current State practice did not provide evidence for the existence of a customary rule permitting a right to solidarity measures, the ILC left the matter to the future development of international law.

Nevertheless, the recognition of the existence of fundamental interests owed to the international community as a whole in contemporary international legal theory and practice is beyond doubt. At the same time, in the author's view, there exists growing evidence to support a right to countermeasures taken in the collective interest. It is therefore now necessary that writers begin to turn their attention to the main legal conditions governing the law of countermeasures, including proportionality, with a view to ensuring that the entitlement of States is not open to abuse especially by the more powerful members of the international community.

Chapter Seventeen

Does the Optional Clause Still Matter?

J.G. Merrills[*]

In recent years the International Court of Justice has given several decisions which have drawn attention once again to the significance and limitations of Article 36(2) of the Court's Statute, the Optional Clause, as a basis for its jurisdiction. Colin Warbrick, as all who know him will readily testify, has throughout his career never hesitated to 'tell it like it is' and acknowledge both the value and the imperfections of international law. I therefore thought it might be appropriate in this celebration of Colin's contribution to legal scholarship to return to a topic that has interested me for the nearly 40 years of our association and review where the Optional Clause, an experiment in 'compulsory jurisdiction' inaugurated in the era of the Permanent Court of International Justice, stands at the beginning of the Twenty-First Century.

In earlier articles for the British Year Book of International Law I surveyed the declarations under Article 36(2) as they stood in 1978[1] and 1993.[2] The aim of both articles was to see whether the decline of the Optional Clause which Waldock had identified in a celebrated study in the mid-1950s[3] had continued. The conclusion of my first article was that the decline had indeed continued, but that there were also some encouraging signs. In 1993 my conclusion was more optimistic. I suggested that on the evidence of recent practice the decline had been halted and the elements of a useful system of compulsory jurisdiction had begun to take shape. The purpose of this essay will be to bring the story up to date by outlining recent developments and in the light of these to gauge whether the Optional Clause still matters.

Over the last 13 years some significant changes have occurred. A number of new declarations have been made, several existing declarations have been

---

[*] Edward Bramley Professor of Law, University of Sheffield, UK.
[1] Merrills, 'The Optional Clause Today', 50 (1979) *BYIL* 87.
[2] Merrills, 'The Optional Clause Revisited', 64 (1993) *BYIL* 197.
[3] Waldock, 'Decline of the Optional Clause', 32 (1955–1956) *BYIL* 244.

K.H. Kaikobad & M. Bohlander (eds.), *International Law and Power: Perspectives on Legal Order and Justice*. Essays in Honour of Colin Warbrick, pp. 431–454.
© 2009 Koninklijke Brill NV. Printed in the Netherlands.

modified, one State (Colombia) has withdrawn its declaration without replacing it, and the Optional Clause has been relied on in cases before the Court on various occasions. To assess these developments and consider their implications, the survey which follows is divided into three parts. The first part considers how the situation now compares with 1993 as regards the number of declarations in force and their geographical distribution. The second part then examines how the quality of States' declarations compares with the position 13 years ago, having regard to the use of limitations and reservations. Finally, as the purpose of the Optional Clause is ultimately to provide a possible basis for litigation, the third part reviews recent decisions involving Article 36(2), along with a number of cases currently before the Court.

1. The Pattern of Declarations

In 1993, when my earlier survey was published, 56 States had made declarations under the Optional Clause. Since then 12 more States have joined the system and only one, Colombia, has withdrawn its declaration. The number of declarations therefore currently stands at 67.[4] Most of those with declarations in 1993 have retained them in the same form, including five States with acceptances of the jurisdiction of the Permanent Court, which are maintained in force by Article 36(5) of the Statute. However, one other State in the latter category, Nicaragua, altered its declaration by adding a reservation to it in October 2001.[5] Eight States: Canada, Nigeria, Norway, Poland, Australia, Cyprus, the United Kingdom and Portugal have changed their acceptances by making new declarations. Poland's modification was made in 1996 to introduce some minor changes just six years after making its first declaration and the other new declarations are further discussed below.

As a result of these developments the geographical distribution of the declarations has not changed very much, but certain trends which were evident in 1993 have been maintained. Australia, New Zealand and Nauru are still the only representatives of Australasia/Oceania, and the small Asian group of five has also remained constant.[6] The American group has risen to 14 with the addition of Paraguay. Peru and Dominica (and the loss of Colombia), while the African group, which increased significantly between 1978 and 1993, has gained

---

[4]   The present study is based on the declarations listed as in force on 31 July 2006 on the Court's website, together with the recent declaration of Dominica which had not yet been added. I am grateful to the Registry of the Court for providing me with this information.

[5]   See 2002–2003 *ICJ Yearbook* 156.

[6]   Cambodia, India, Japan, Philippines and Pakistan.

a further five, namely Cameroon, Guinea, Côte d'Ivoire, Lesotho and Djibouti, and now stands at 22. There has also been a significant increase in Europe with new declarations from Georgia, Greece, Yugoslavia and Slovakia. Europe was already the largest group in 1978 (with 13 declarations) and in 1993 (with 19). With the new additions there are now therefore 23 European declarations.

The accession of new States to the system and the revision of a number of declarations has maintained a situation in which many of the current acceptances are relatively recent. Thirteen declarations have been in force for 50 years or more – the six acceptances of the Permanent Court already mentioned, together with those of Mexico (1947), Switzerland (1948), Liechtenstein (1950), Egypt (1951), Liberia (1952), Denmark (1956) and the Netherlands (1956), but sixteen declarations, very nearly one quarter of the current total, have been made since 1996. This indicates a system in which declarations are constantly being made or revised and which as a result is far from moribund. More specifically, it means that the number of declarations in force in 2006 represents over one third of the membership of the United Nations, which is a slightly higher proportion than in 1978.

The declarations from States joining the system for the first time are, of course, very welcome, and it is pleasing that since 1993 there has been only one departure. However, as at the time of the earlier survey, despite the recent acceptances, there are still many notable absences: Argentina, Brazil and Chile; all the Arab States except Egypt;[7] most Asian States, including Iran; and in Europe, Germany, France and Italy. The fact that for twenty years the United Kingdom has been the only Permanent Member of the Security Council with a declaration under Article 36(2) is also noticeable. In terms of quantity, then, the situation remains very much as it was in 1993: a respectable, but not overwhelming number of declarations have been made, which are reasonably, but not fully representative of the world as a whole.

II. The Quality of Declarations

To assess the quality of the latest declarations their terms must now be considered. In 1955, when Waldock wrote of what he termed the 'decline' of the Optional Clause, he had in mind the increasing use of reservations and limitations, which in some cases had the effect of emptying acceptances of the

---

[7] Moreover, the 1957 declaration of Egypt covers only legal disputes arising under paragraph 9(b) of Egypt's Declaration on the Suez Canal and Arrangements for its Operation of 24 April 1957, and is considered by some to fall outside the scope of Article 36(2).

Court's jurisdiction of most of their content. In 1993 I suggested that not only had this decline been arrested, but that there had also been a number of positive developments in State practice. To see whether the situation has continued to improve we must look first at the different types of restrictions and then at the overall picture.

1. *Termination and Variation of Declarations*

Reservations giving the right to terminate a declaration with immediate effect, or what in practice usually amounts to the same thing, the right to vary a declaration with immediate effect, have been a feature of a number of States' acceptances of Article 36(2) for many years.[8] These reservations disturbed Waldock because a State which can modify or withdraw its declaration at any time enjoys a significant advantage over one which cannot. The *Nottebohm* case[9] established that revoking or amending a declaration cannot take away jurisdiction once proceedings have started, but a State which has reserved this power can prevent it from ever being established by terminating or modifying its acceptance the instant litigation is threatened. By 1978, when my first survey was published, many States were using this type of reservation and, as Waldock had foreseen, it was eroding the ideal of compulsory jurisdiction. It is therefore instructive to consider recent developments.

One might perhaps expect that today all States would be using this form of reservation, particularly as the *Nicaragua* case[10] in 1984 provided a practical demonstration of the disadvantages of not reserving this power. In fact this has not yet come about, but a trend in that direction is now rather clear. Thus out of the 20 declarations made since 1993, 13 expressly reserve the right to terminate at any time,[11] two were made for an initial period of five years which has now expired and so have become instantly terminable,[12] and three say nothing at all about termination[13] and so, according to the dictum in the *Nicaragua* case, are

---

[8]   For the historical background see Oda, 'Reservations in the Declarations of Acceptance of the Optional Clause and the Period of Validity of Those Reservations: The Effect of the Schultz Letter', 59 (1988) *BYIL* 1.

[9]   *Nottebohm, Preliminary Objection, ICJ Reports 1953*, p. 111.

[10]   *Military and Paramilitary Activities in and against Nicaragua, Jurisdiction and Admissibility, Judgment, ICJ Reports 1984*, p. 392.

[11]   Australia, Canada, Côte d'Ivoire, Cyprus, Djibouti, Guinea, Lesotho, Nigeria, Peru, Portugal, Slovakia, United Kingdom and Yugoslavia.

[12]   Cameroon and Greece.

[13]   Dominica, Georgia and Paraguay.

terminable on 'reasonable' notice.[14] That leaves only two declarations, those of Poland and Norway, where a period of notice is specified.

The most striking feature of these figures is the obvious preference for instantly terminable declarations and corresponding avoidance of specified periods of notice. Here comparison with the period 1978–1993 is particularly enlightening. Six out of the 14 States making declarations for the first time in those years specified fixed periods of notice, whereas not one of the 12 new parties in the latest period does so. It is, of course, easy to see why governments tend to favour instantly terminable declarations. Canada's ability to modify its declaration in 1994, ahead of the challenge to its new fisheries policy,[15] shows the advantages of flexibility, as against being bound by a period of notice. Nevertheless the ideal of compulsory jurisdiction calls for States to commit themselves to the Court for a definitive period and so, as Waldock pointed out, declarations subject to instant termination or modification go against its spirit.

It is also interesting to note that a handful of States continue to deposit declarations with no provision dealing with termination or modification. Dominica, for example, recently made a declaration of this kind when it joined the Optional Clause in 2006. The position of States which have accepted the Court's jurisdiction in this way has produced a good deal of discussion over the years and two cases currently before the Court show that this is more than an academic issue. Colombia's right to terminate its declaration appears to have been challenged by Nicaragua in the *Territorial and Maritime Dispute*,[16] while in the *Dispute regarding Navigational and Related Rights*[17] it is Nicaragua's right to add a reservation to its declaration that has been challenged by Costa Rica. At the time of writing these cases have yet to be argued and so they are further discussed in section III below.

2. *Obligations Ratione Materiae*

Another danger apparent to Waldock was the use of far-reaching reservations as a way of excluding whole categories of disputes from the jurisdiction of the Court by reason of their subject matter. The most notorious of these was the 'automatic' or self-judging reservation on matters of domestic jurisdiction which first appeared in the United States declaration of 1946 and was then used

---

[14] For the alternative view that such declarations are terminable at any time, see Oda (note 8) at p. 18.
[15] See the text accompanying note 56 below.
[16] See the text accompanying note 67 below.
[17] See the text accompanying note 69 below.

subsequently by a number of other States.[18] Close behind in ill-repute was the bizarre 'multilateral treaties' reservation. Like the automatic reservation, this was the brain-child of the US Senate which insisted that the 1946 declaration also contained a reservation excluding disputes arising under a multilateral treaty unless all the parties affected by the decision were also parties to the case. This reservation too was copied by a number of other States, sometimes in an extended form,[19] and, like the automatic reservation, if adopted generally, had the potential to destroy the Optional Clause system.

Happily, however, my survey in 1993 revealed that none of the declarations made since 1978 included either the automatic reservation or the multilateral treaties reservation. Consequently, though still featuring in some earlier declarations, both had fallen out of favour. In the latest period, India invoked its longstanding version of the multilateral treaties reservation in the *Aerial Incident* case,[20] but only one State, Djibouti, has included it in a new declaration.[21] Likewise, though several recent declarations contain a reservation excluding matters of domestic jurisdiction, all do so in the innocuous 'objective' form. For example, Côte d'Ivoire excludes 'Disputes with regard to questions which by international law fall within the exclusive competence of Côte d'Ivoire'. Thus, with the apparent demise of the automatic reservation and the slipping away of the multilateral treaties reservation, the overall quality of declarations continues to improve.

Although the decay of the automatic reservation and the multilateral treaties reservation are welcome developments, these reservations were by no means the only threat to the efficacy of the Optional Clause as the basis of a true system of compulsory jurisdiction, even if when Waldock was writing, and for some time thereafter, they could be thought of as posing the most serious risk. That is because other reservations withholding whole categories of subject matter can also be made and are regularly employed in practice. This is not the place to review reservations dealing with obligations *ratione materiae* exhaustively,[22]

---

[18] See Merrills (note 1), at pp. 113–15; also Crawford, 'The Legal Effect of Automatic Reservations to the Jurisdiction of the International Court', 50 (1979) *BYIL* 63.

[19] The declarations of the Philippines (1972), El Salvador (1973) and India (1974) omitted the words 'affected by the decision', thereby widening the reservation considerably. For a discussion of the Court's application of this reservation in the *Nicaragua* case, see Merrills (note 2), at pp. 230–32.

[20] See the text accompanying note 60 below.

[21] However, Djibouti's version of the reservation is in its extended form ('unless all the parties to the treaty are also parties to the case before the Court'). See also note 19 above.

[22] For further discussion of reservations *ratione materiae* including some not mentioned in the text, such as the reservation concerning foreign liabilities or debts in Poland's declaration, see Merrills (note 2), at pp. 224–38.

but four such reservations which feature in recent declarations, are worth a closer look. These are the type addressed to disputes concerning territory or boundaries; those which deal with environmental or resource issues; those concerned with hostilities and the use of armed force; and finally reservations excluding the jurisdiction of the Court when some other form of peaceful settlement has been agreed.

The first is the type of reservation which covers disputes concerning territory or boundaries. In 1993 a number of States had declarations containing such reservations of varying scope, and five of the latest declarations are similar. Yugoslavia simply excludes 'territorial disputes'. Nigeria now excludes 'disputes concerning the allocation, delimitation or demarcation of territory (whether land, maritime, lacustrine or superjacent air space)', a reservation which if included in Nigeria's 1965 declaration, would have changed the outcome of the *Land and Maritime Boundary* case.[23] Djibouti's recent declaration features an even more extensive reservation of the same type. Poland's new declaration of 1996 repeats the exclusion of territorial and boundary disputes in its earlier declaration with only a minor difference of wording. However, Australia, in its new declaration of 2002, included an entirely new reservation covering disputes relating to the delimitation of maritime zones and concomitant disputes over resources. Thus the sensitivity of States to compulsory jurisdiction on territorial issues is still conspicuous in practice.

Disputes relating to environmental and resource issues are another type of reservation *ratione materiae* meriting attention. Here too five of the recent declarations raise interesting points. As noted earlier, Canada's declaration was modified in 1994 to exclude certain conservation and management issues and the Court was then required to examine this reservation in the *Fisheries Jurisdiction* case[24] in 1998. Poland's declaration was modified in 1996 to provide a general exclusion of environmental disputes, in place of the more limited exclusion in its earlier declaration. Slovakia then followed suit by including a very similar reservation covering disputes 'with regard to the protection of the environment' in its declaration in 2004. Djibouti, in the comprehensive territorial reservation already mentioned, excludes not just delimitation disputes, but all disputes concerning or relating to the territorial sea, continental shelf, exclusive fishery zone and EEZ and 'other zones of national maritime jurisdiction including for the regulation and control of marine pollution and the conduct of scientific research by foreign vessels'. This clearly would cover both environmental and resource disputes, as well as other disputes pertaining to maritime zones.

---

[23] See note 53 below.
[24] See note 56 below.

Finally in this category there is Norway's latest declaration which was modified in 1996 to incorporate by reference the exceptions to compulsory settlement contained in the 1982 Law of the Sea Convention and the 1996 Straddling Stocks Agreement,[25] along with the limitations and exceptions in Norway's declarations relating to those treaties. This change ensures that Norway's obligations with regard to adjudication are no wider under the Optional Clause than under the aforementioned agreements. As such it cannot really be regarded as objectionable. Like the reservations of Canada, Poland, Slovakia and Djibouti, however, it has the effect of putting some important issues outside the scope of compulsory jurisdiction, so further demonstrating the impact of reservations *ratione materiae*.

The exclusion of disputes relating to hostilities and armed conflict, the third type of reservation to be examined here, goes back a considerable time, but has never been particularly common. In 1993 there were eight declarations with such reservations, covering a range of different subject matter. In the period under review three States, Greece, Nigeria and Djibouti, have made declarations with this kind of reservation, again with variable scope. The reservation of Greece (which is the only reservation in its declaration of 1994), is the narrowest, covering only 'any dispute relating to defensive military action taken by the Hellenic Republic for reasons of national defence'. Nigeria, on the other hand, in its 1998 declaration, excludes 'disputes relating to or connected with facts or situations of hostilities or armed conflict whether internal or international in character'. And Djibouti has a broader exclusion covering not only facts or situations of hostilities and armed conflicts, but also 'individual or collective actions taken in self-defence, resistance to aggression, fulfilment of obligations imposed by international bodies and other similar or related acts, measures or situations in which the Republic of Djibouti is, has been or may in future be involved'.

Reviewing practice in relation to this type of reservation *ratione materiae* as it stood in 1978, I identified 'a disquieting trend away from the exclusion of disputes arising out of a particular war, towards the exclusion of disputes arising out of belligerent occupation, the use of force for United Nations purposes and in the latest declarations almost any use of force by the reserving State'.[26] This trend was less prominent in 1993 and since then does not seem to have worsened. However, it is apparent from the three declarations quoted that the practice of

---

[25] See Merrills, *International Dispute Settlement* (Fourth edition), Cambridge, 2005, pp. 187–90 and 209; and also Klein, *Dispute Settlement in the UN Convention on the Law of the Sea*, Cambridge, 2005, Chapters 3 and 4.

[26] See Merrills (note 1), at p. 122.

making reservations relating to the use of force has not disappeared. In its recent case law the Court has confirmed that in principle it is competent to deal with the legal aspects of all international disputes, including those involving the use of force.[27] Whether it is able to do so in practice, however, depends on the terms on which its jurisdiction is accepted in declarations under Article 36(2) and elsewhere, which is why the number of States making declarations with reservations relating to the use of force, and the terms in which they are framed, are worth closely monitoring.

The last type of reservation *ratione materiae* excludes from the Court's jurisdiction disputes for which some other means of peaceful settlement has been agreed. A reservation of this kind was included in the declaration made by the Netherlands as long ago as 1921 and this declaration was instrumental in establishing the principle that it is permissible to employ limitations not expressly authorised by the Statute. The reservation was soon adopted generally and by 1993 featured in well over half the declarations then in force. In the latest period it has continued to be favoured, being employed by seven of the twelve States making declarations for the first time[28] and by Nigeria and Portugal in their latest declarations. Not surprisingly, all those States which have already used this reservation have retained it in their new declarations.[29] This has, for some time, actually been the commonest Optional Clause reservation and on present evidence seems unlikely to be displaced.

As in the earlier declarations, the latest reservations show a number of differences of detail. Slovakia uses the same language as the United Kingdom and excludes disputes which the parties 'have agreed to settle by some other method of peaceful settlement'. Lesotho, on the other hand, refers to 'any dispute the solution of which the parties thereto have agreed *or shall agree* to have recourse to other means of peaceful settlement for its *final and binding decision*'.[30] The most elaborate formula in recent declarations is to be found in Peru's 2003 reservation which covers 'any dispute with regard to which the parties have agreed or shall agree to have recourse to arbitration or judicial settlement for a final and binding decision or which has been settled by some other method of peaceful settlement'. Although the thrust of all these limitations is broadly the same, the use of a broader or a narrower formulation might be important in a particular case.

---

[27] See, for example, the *Oil Platforms* case, *ICJ Reports 2003*, p. 161 and the *Armed Activities on the Territory of the Congo* case, *ICJ Reports 2005*, Judgement of 19 December 2005.

[28] Côte d'Ivoire, Djibouti, Guinea, Lesotho, Peru, Slovakia and Yugoslavia.

[29] Australia, Canada, Poland and the United Kingdom.

[30] Emphasis added.

An unusual feature of Portugal's latest declaration is that, in addition to a conventional reservation on other methods of peaceful settlement, it excludes 'any dispute with a party or parties to a treaty regarding which the jurisdiction of the International Court of Justice has, under the applicable rules, been explicitly excluded, irrespective of whether the scope of the dispute refers to the interpretation and application of the treaty provisions or to other sources of international law'. The purpose of this reservation is not entirely clear, but, like the reservations on other methods of settlement, it seems designed to discourage a State from trying to take a case to the Court when to do so would violate another commitment. This would normally be an unusual thing to do and so these types of reservation *ratione materiae* can readily be justified. Their widespread use in practice has not, however, so far generated much in the way of case law.[31]

3. *Obligations* Ratione Temporis

On the evidence considered so far, practice with regard to the Optional Clause since 1993 can be regarded as quite encouraging. Acceptances of the Court's jurisdiction unqualified by significant reservations *ratione materiae* continue to be made. Whilst commitments of uncertain duration now seem to be the norm, the desuetude of the automatic reservation and the multilateral treaties reservation has not been offset by an increase in the use of similar crippling reservations, although some of the recent declarations, as noted above, do contain significant exclusions. There are, however, other, more subtle ways of limiting commitments which can likewise restrict the powers of the Court if they are widely used. One concerns the scope of the State's obligations *ratione temporis*.

Of the twenty most recent declarations four are framed in such a way that only future disputes, that is disputes subsequent to the date of deposit of the declaration fall within the Court's jurisdiction.[32] This kind of limitation is a very significant restriction, especially when one takes into account that, like all limitations and reservations, it functions on a reciprocal basis. So, for example, Yugoslavia's inclusion of this limitation in its declaration of 26 April 1999 led the Court to conclude that it lacked jurisdiction, even, *prima facie*, to consider the provisional measures of protection requested by Yugoslavia in the *Legality of Use of Force* cases.[33]

---

[31] But see the *Certain Phosphate Lands in Nauru* case (*Nauru v. Australia*), *Preliminary Objections*, *ICJ Reports 1992*, p. 240, as discussed in Merrills (note 2) at pp. 225–27.

[32] The declarations of Canada, Paraguay, Slovakia and Yugoslavia.

[33] See note 57 below.

Naturally the effect of this type of limitation is greatest in the period immediately after the declaration and diminishes over time. However, such diminution is markedly offset when the declaration employs the so-called 'double-exclusion formula' and excludes not only disputes prior to the date of the declaration, but also disputes arising out of situations or facts prior to that date. In other words, under the double exclusion formula, for a case to fall within the jurisdiction, both the dispute and the events from which it arose must follow the critical date. This further condition, which the Court has held requires it to find the source or 'real cause' of a dispute,[34] is plainly a significant constraint on its activity. Three of the four States with declarations covering only future disputes use the double exclusion formula,[35] as do several earlier declarations.

Consideration of the other recent declarations show how wide are the variations in practice with regard to limitations *ratione temporis*. Eleven contain no limitations of this kind at all, whereas the other five employ cut-off dates ranging from 12 December 1958 (Guinea) to 25 September 1990 (Poland). Nigeria excludes 'disputes in relation to matters which arose prior to the date of Nigeria's independence …'. Portugal excludes any dispute arising before 26 April 1974 'unless it refers to territorial titles or rights or to sovereign rights or jurisdiction', an exclusion within an exclusion, and the United Kingdom, in its new declaration in 2004, moved its cut-off date forward almost 30 years from 24 October 1945, the date specified in its 1969 declaration, to 1 January 1974. Of the five declarations in this group all except Guinea's employ the double exclusion formula.

From the above figures it is evident that limitations *ratione temporis* continue to be quite popular and that the double exclusion formula, which is almost invariably utilised, is also here to stay. It is, of course, understandable that former colonies should wish to exclude disputes concerning events before independence and that other States, such as the United Kingdom, prefer not having to revisit matters of (relatively) ancient history. The real risk, it is suggested, comes not from these types of limitation, but from a move towards acceptances in which the cut-off point is the date of deposit of the declaration. For, when combined with the double exclusion formula and the effect of reciprocity, such declarations represent commitments to the Court that initially, and for some time thereafter are largely illusory. In 1993 limitations

---

[34] See *Certain Property (Liechtenstein v. Germany) Preliminary Objections, ICJ Reports 2005*, p. 6, at p. 25, paragraph 46, citing earlier rulings to the same effect.

[35] Only Paraguay does not.

ratione temporis in this more pernicious form seemed likely to become standard practice. It is therefore some comfort to see that, as yet, this deterioration has not occurred.

4. *Obligations* Ratione Personae

Another method of restricting declarations is by including a reservation to cover disputes with certain other States as defined by various criteria.[36] Canada, for example, in its declaration of 1994 maintained its reservation excluding disputes with other members of the Commonwealth and, as we shall see shortly, India's reservation to the same effect was recently examined in the *Aerial Incident* case. When the United Kingdom made its latest declaration it too retained the Commonwealth reservation, but with two changes which extend its scope. The first change is a modification of the language so as to cover disputes with the government of any country 'which is *or has been* a Member of the Commonwealth', a similar formulation to that in India's reservation. The other change relates to the time element. The corresponding reservation in the 1969 declaration covered only disputes with other Commonwealth Members 'with regard to situations or facts existing before 1 January 1969'. The new declaration omits these words with the result that all disputes with present (and former) Commonwealth States are now caught by the reservation.

Although the Commonwealth reservation survives in a number of other declarations its use is plainly declining. Much more important are reservations excluding the Court's jurisdiction if the applicant has been a party to the Optional Clause for less than 12 months, or if it has accepted the jurisdiction of the Court only in relation to or for the purposes of the dispute. This reservation was devised by the United Kingdom to guard against 'surprise' applications, or unscrupulous use of the Court, and has proved increasingly popular. By 1993 it was being regularly included in declarations under Article 36(2) and can be found in seven of the latest declarations.

Nigeria, as will be seen, was caught off-guard by a case brought by Cameroon in 1994,[37] and to prevent any repetition included the reservation in its new declaration of 1998. Australia and Portugal followed suit, adopting the same exclusion in their new declarations of 2002 and 2005 and Slovakia included it in its declaration in 2004. Poland, Cyprus and the United Kingdom, which already had the reservation, carried it over to their new declarations in 1996, 2002 and 2004 respectively. In the earlier declaration of Cyprus (1988) the

---

[36] For more detailed treatment of reservations of this type, see Merrills (note 2), at pp. 219–24.
[37] See note 53 below.

'warning period' specified was unusual because it was only six rather than 12 months. However, the 2002 declaration brings it into line with comparable arrangements. Most of the reservations in this group cover States which have accepted the Court's jurisdiction only in relation to, or for the purposes of the dispute, as well as surprise applications, although the reservations of Poland and Portugal cover only the latter. In either version this type of reservation can be regarded as a legitimate way of countering the tactical advantage which a State enjoys by staying outside the system of compulsory jurisdiction until it wishes to bring a case. It does, however, constitute a further limitation on the Court's powers and on the evidence of recent practice seems set to propagate itself further.

The last kind of reservation *ratione personae* which should be mentioned is much more specialised. In declarations accepting the jurisdiction of the Permanent Court there were several reservations designed to cover disputes in which non-recognition or other political factors pertaining to the State concerned rendered judicial settlement unpalatable. By 1993 none of those declarations was still in force, but India in its declaration of 1974 had included two reservations of this kind.[38] In the latest period two further States have made acceptances under Article 36(2) with similar qualifications. Nigeria's latest declaration contains a reservation excluding the jurisdiction of the Court over disputes with any State with which Nigeria does not have diplomatic relations, while Djibouti excludes both disputes with the governments of States with which it has no diplomatic relations, or which it does not recognise, and 'disputes with non-sovereign States or territories'. Reservations of this type tend to reflect political factors unique to the State concerned and as such will probably remain exceptional.

The various reservations *ratione personae*, along with reservations *ratione materiae* and limitations *ratione temporis*, are reminders of how far we are from a true system of compulsory jurisdiction, even in relation to the minority of States which have made declarations under Article 36(2). However, this does not contradict our provisional conclusion that the improvement in the quality of declarations which was observable in 1993 has been maintained. This may be demonstrated by standing back from the review of individual reservations for a moment in order to contemplate the changing form of declarations under Article 36(2).

All the acceptances from the era of the Permanent Court, maintained in force by Article 36(5) of the Statute, are very short. Declarations from the immediate

---

[38] Israel had also employed this reservation in its 1956 declaration, but terminated its declaration in 1985.

post-war period tend to be rather longer and between Waldock's study in 1955 and my first survey in 1978 several acceptances of unprecedented length, featuring an alarming number of reservations and conditions, were deposited.[39] As these declarations were then quite recent, there was reason to fear that the era of short and uncomplicated acceptances might be over and that declarations under Article 36(2) might become increasingly elaborate and restricted. It is clear, however, that this has not occurred. Unqualified (or virtually unqualified) declarations continue to be made;[40] most of the latest declarations are quite short and nearly all compare favourably with the worst specimens from the 1970s. The exceptions are Nigeria's 1998 declaration, which introduced numerous reservations not present in its earlier acceptance, and, more recently, Djibouti's lengthy 2005 declaration which is also heavily qualified and likewise represents a backward step.

Qualified acceptances of any kind show that States which support judicial settlement in principle, nevertheless want to limit its use in practice. Reservations are, of course, perfectly permissible and, as Judge Oda has reminded us,[41] to think of a State which employs a reservation as retracting part of an *a priori* general acceptance of the Court's jurisdiction is wholly mistaken. Nevertheless, it must be a matter of satisfaction that while most declarations are qualified in some way, two fifths of those currently in force may be regarded as positive and unequivocal acceptances of international jurisdiction. This 'hard core' of more than 30 declarations represents a higher proportion of unambiguous commitments to the Court than in 1978 and 1993, so that in general terms the position as it stood 13 years ago has continued to improve.

iii. The Court's Case Law 1993–2006

The cases which have been brought to the Court on the basis of Article 36(2) since 1993 fall into three groups: those in which the question of jurisdiction was relatively straightforward; those in which it proved more complex; and those which began only recently and have not yet been concluded. The cases in this third group merit least a glance, since besides providing further evidence of how Optional Clause declarations are being used, they also raise some interesting

---

[39] See, for example, the declarations of the Philippines (1972), El Salvador (1973) and India (1974). El Salvador's declaration lapsed in 1988.

[40] See, for example, the declarations made in the last five years by Côte d'Ivoire, Dominica, Lesotho and Peru.

[41] See Judge Oda's Dissenting Opinion in the *Nicaragua* case, *ICJ Reports 1986*, p. 14; p. 212 at p. 218: paragraph 12.

issues. However, any discussion of future cases must be rather speculative and so we shall concentrate on those cases in the first and second groups, where there is something more definite to work with.

1. *Straightforward Cases*

There are four cases in this first category: the *Jan Mayen* case (1993), the *East Timor* case (1995), the *Arrest Warrant* case (2002) and the *Armed Activities* case (2005).

The first two cases may be passed over quickly. It will be recalled that the *East Timor* case[42] between Portugal and Australia was dismissed on account of the absence of Indonesia whose legal rights and obligations were regarded by the Court as constituting the 'very subject matter' of the case. This decision was therefore an application of the principle of the *Monetary Gold* case[43] and as such sheds no particular light on the Optional Clause. In the *Jan Mayen* case,[44] on the other hand, the Court was able to determine the relevant maritime boundary between Denmark and Norway because both States had made Optional Clause declarations that were effectively unconditional.

Historically, most boundary cases have been referred to the Court by special agreements and the *Jan Mayen* case is a rare example of such a dispute being referred unilaterally, something which one of the judges criticised in his separate opinion.[45] It was pointed out earlier that Norway modified its Optional Clause declaration in 1996 to cover the exceptions to compulsory settlement contained in the 1982 Law of the Sea Convention. Since Norway has excluded delimitation disputes in its acceptance of the Convention, as it is entitled to do under Article 298, the effect of Norway's new declaration is that it would not now be possible for Denmark, or any other State, to require it to adjudicate a sea boundary dispute on the basis of its acceptance of Article 36(2).

The *Arrest Warrant* case[46] between the Democratic Republic of the Congo (DRC) and Belgium concerned a disputed exercise of extraterritorial jurisdiction by the latter and an alleged infringement of the doctrine of State immunity.

---

[42] *East Timor (Portugal v. Australia), ICJ Reports 1995*, p. 90. For comment, see Chinkin, 'Case Note', 45 (1996) *ICLQ* 712 and Bekker, 'Case Note', 90 (1996) *AJIL* 94.

[43] *Monetary Gold Removed from Rome in 1943, ICJ Reports 1954*, p. 19.

[44] *Maritime Delimitation in the Area between Greenland and Jan Mayen, ICJ Reports 1993*, p. 38. For comment, see Charney, 'Case Note', 88 (1994) *AJIL* 105 and Evans, 'Case Note', 43 (1994) *ICLQ* 697.

[45] See the Separate Opinion of Judge Oda (note 44), pp. 110–14.

[46] *Arrest Warrant of 11 April 2000 (Democratic Republic of the Congo v. Belgium), ICJ Reports 2002*, p. 3. For comment, see Wickremasinghe, 'Case Note', 52 (2003) *ICLQ* 775.

Both States had declarations under Article 36(2), which were short and uncomplicated, and so the respondent, Belgium, had little scope for challenging the Court's jurisdiction. However, points worth noting were made in both the Order responding to the DRC's request for provisional measures of protection in 2000 and the subsequent judgment on the merits. Thus in its judgment the Court rejected Belgium's argument that because the situation had changed, there was no longer a 'legal dispute' for the purposes of Article 36 (2), explaining that when determining jurisdiction, the crucial moment is when proceedings are instituted.[47] At the provisional measures stage, in contrast, where a preliminary question was whether *prima facie* jurisdiction had been established, the Court made a different point when it ruled that it could take the parties' Optional Clause declarations into account although these had not been specifically invoked by the DRC until the second round of oral argument.[48]

Belgium's declaration, though largely unqualified, excluded from the Court's jurisdiction disputes' 'in regard to which the parties have agreed or may agree to have recourse to another method of pacific settlement'. At the provisional measures stage Belgium sought to rely on this by arguing that when the DRC seised the Court, negotiations 'at the highest level' regarding the disputed arrest warrant were under way. The Court, however, found that in the absence of further details, its jurisdiction to indicate provisional measures was unaffected.[49] This was clearly correct. As indicated earlier, harmonising different methods of peaceful settlement is itself unobjectionable. For reservations with this aim to function, however, clear evidence of the parties' priorities is needed. Since there was no such evidence here, the rejection of Belgium's argument was really inevitable.

Also straightforward, at least from the standpoint of jurisdiction, was the *Armed Activities* case,[50] another case initiated by the DRC, on this occasion against one of its neighbours, Uganda. The case was one of a series brought against States which were alleged to have perpetrated acts of armed aggression on the territory of the DRC, but as Uganda was the only respondent with an Optional Clause declaration, this was the only one which was to result in a decision on the merits. Uganda's declaration, like that of the DRC had no reservations or limitations. Consequently, as in the *Arrest Warrant* case, when

---

[47] *Arrest Warrant* (note 46), paragraphs 26–28.
[48] *Arrest Warrant of 11 April 2000 (Democratic Republic of the Congo v. Belgium), Provisional Measures,* Order of 8 December 2000, *ICJ Reports 2000,* p. 182, pp. 199–200, paragraphs 62–64. For comment, see Wickremasinghe, 'Case Note', 50 (2001) *ICLQ* 670.
[49] See Order (note 48), p. 200, paragraphs 65–66.
[50] *Armed Activities on the Territory of the Congo* case (note 27). For comment, see Okowa, 'Case Note', 55 (2006) *ICLQ* 742.

the DRC applied for provisional measures of protection the Court readily concluded that the parties' acceptances provided a *prima facie* basis on which its jurisdiction might be founded.[51] It then gave its judgment on the merits in 2005, again without having to address any challenge to its jurisdiction, although an issue of admissibility involving the principle in the *Monetary Gold* case did have to be considered.[52] As the jurisdictional position was so clear, Uganda took the opportunity to make certain counter-claims, one of which was eventually upheld.

2. More Complex Cases

In the period since 1993 the Court has had to examine more complex arguments concerning its jurisdiction under the Optional Clause on four occasions. In the *Fisheries Jurisdiction* case (1998), the *Legality of Use of Force* cases (1999) and the *Aerial Incident* case (2000) the question was the familiar one of the scope and effect of reservations. In the *Land and Maritime Boundary* case (1998), on the other hand, it was the more basic question of when the jurisdictional bond created by a declaration under Article 36(2) comes into effect. Whilst none of these decisions contains any great surprises, in different ways they each accentuate key elements of the Optional Clause system.

In the *Land and Maritime Boundary* case[53] between Cameroon and Nigeria the latter wished to challenge the Court's competence, but as both States had made Optional Clause declarations that were effectively unconditional, it faced an obvious difficulty. Nigeria therefore adopted the bold course of arguing that Cameroon had abused Article 36 (2) by starting proceedings in the case less than a month after making its declaration. According to Nigeria this rendered the proceedings premature and meant that the Court lacked jurisdiction. The weakness of this argument was that in 1957, when presented with a similar argument in the *Right of Passage* case,[54] the Court had rejected it. Nigeria consequently argued that the earlier decision was 'outdated' and should be overruled, but the Court, not surprisingly, was unconvinced. Its

---

[51] *Armed Activities on the Territory of the Congo (Democratic Republic of the Congo v. Uganda), Provisional Measures*, Order of 1 July 2000, *ICJ Reports*, 2000, p. 111. For comment, see Kritsiotis, 'Case Note', 50 (2001) *ICLQ* 662.

[52] See *Armed Activities in the Congo Provisional Measures* (note 51), 196–202.

[53] *Land and Maritime Boundary between Cameroon and Nigeria (Cameroon v. Nigeria), Preliminary Objections, ICJ Reports 1998*, p. 275 and see Merrills, 'Case Note', 48 (1999) *ICLQ* 651. The Court had already ordered provisional measures of protection in 1996 on the basis of a finding of *prima facie* jurisdiction. The case was eventually decided on the merits in 2002.

[54] *Right of Passage over Indian Territory, Preliminary Objections, ICJ Reports 1957*, p. 125.

decision therefore confirms that as between States with declarations under Article 36 (2) a 'consensual bond' comes into existence as soon as a State makes a declaration. It is therefore immediately entitled to initiate proceedings against other participants in the system, except, of course, those with a protection against surprise applications.

The other point of interest in this case is that as well as disputing the Court's jurisdiction, Nigeria raised a number of objections to admissibility which were also not accepted. It is unnecessary to go into these here, but it is worth noting that some of the issues raised by Nigeria's objections, such as the need to define the scope of a dispute, or even to establish that a dispute exists, are much more likely to arise in cases under the Optional Clause, where the applicant acts unilaterally, than in cases referred under a special agreement, where such vital matters are decided consensually. It was recognition of this type of problem that had led Judge Oda to question Denmark's use of Article 36(2) in the *Jan Mayen* case and he made a similar point here, maintaining that 'Cameroon *cannot* bring unilaterally to the Court a case concerning simple demarcation of a boundary line either on land or at sea'.[55] Although the view that use of the Optional Clause in boundary cases is precluded would be unduly limiting, these cases highlight a genuine problem and show the care which must be taken with this source of jurisdiction.

In the *Fisheries Jurisdiction* case,[56] brought by Spain, Canada as respondent successfully relied on the reservation covering conservation and management issues which it had included in its new Optional Clause declaration in 1994. Thus, when the Court heard the case in 1998, it concluded that it had no jurisdiction. Given the terms of Canada's reservation, this outcome was not unexpected, but several features of the judgment are worth attention. As regards it general approach, the Court rejected Spain's submission that it was for the applicant to identify the subject of the dispute, and ruled instead that where there is disagreement, the issue of characterisation is one for the Court itself to determine. This was crucial here because Spain naturally sought to characterise the dispute in a way that took it outside the Canadian reservation.

Furthermore, when the Court came to interpret the critical reservation it stressed that declarations under Article 36(2) must be interpreted as unilateral acts (that is by taking account of the declarer's intentions), rather than in accordance with the 1969 Vienna Convention on the Law of Treaties, as though they are international agreements. It also expressly rejected Spain's argument that

---

[55] *Land and Maritime Boundary* case (note 53): Separate Opinion, paragraph 32, emphasis original.

[56] *Fisheries Jurisdiction (Spain v. Canada), Jurisdiction of the Court, ICJ Reports 1998*, 432. See also de La Fayette, Case Note, 48 (1999) *ICLQ* 664.

reservations must be interpreted consistently with legality, in other words that they cannot protect illegal acts. This is plainly correct. As the Court pointed out, the reason for making a reservation may well be to prevent adjudication in relation to actions or measures of dubious legality. It could therefore defeat their purpose to accept the Spanish argument. As noted above, the ruling in the *Fisheries Jurisdiction* case could have been anticipated. This was therefore not a case which broke new ground, but, like the *Land and Maritime Boundary* case, essentially a confirmation of basic principles.

Far more difficult problems were presented by the *Legality of Use of Force* cases which were begun in April 1999 against ten NATO States, six of which: Belgium, Canada, the Netherlands, Portugal, Spain and the United Kingdom, had Optional Clause declarations. In its order in June 1999,[57] rejecting Yugoslavia's request for provisional measures of protection, the Court found that it lacked *prima facie* jurisdiction under Article 36(2), but reached the conclusion by two different routes. As regards Spain and the United Kingdom, it held that it 'manifestly' lacked *prima facie* jurisdiction because their declarations protected them against surprise applications and Yugoslavia had begun proceedings only three days after depositing its own acceptance.[58] And in relation to the other four respondents it held that the limitation *ratione temporis* in Yugoslavia's declaration, restricting its acceptance to disputes arising after 25 April 1999, was enough to deprive it of *prima facie* jurisdiction.

The ruling on the limitation *ratione temporis* was particularly controversial, with four judges taking the view that as the bombing campaign was a series of attacks, it was implausible to maintain that no disputes arose after the critical date. As noted earlier, limitations *ratione temporis* have the potential to restrict the Court's competence severely, and on account of the reciprocity principle can easily prove counter-productive. These cases are the clearest possible demonstration of the point, as well as the problem of applying such limitations in practice. Of course, in proceedings based on Article 41 the Court's treatment of jurisdiction is only provisional and so in the normal course of events the scope of Yugoslavia's commitment would have been revisited when the Court ruled definitively on the question of its jurisdiction in 2004. In the event, however, the case went off on a different point entirely. As the parties were now agreed that Yugoslavia was not a party to the Statute

---

[57] *Legality of Use of Force, Provisional Measures*, Order of 2 June 1999, *ICJ Reports 1999*, p. 124; and see Gray, 'Case Note', 49 (2000) *ICLQ* 730. As indicated in the text, the Orders in these cases were not all identical.

[58] As regards Spain, the Court also found that it manifestly lacked jurisdiction under the 1948 Genocide Convention and accordingly removed this case from the Court's list.

in 1999, the Court held that it could not bring a case with the result that the Court lacked jurisdiction to consider its claims.[59]

The last case in this group is the *Aerial Incident* case[60] between Pakistan and India. The claim here concerned the shooting down of a Pakistani military aircraft, and the Court's jurisdiction was invoked on the basis, *inter alia* of the two States' declarations under Article 36(2). Pakistan's declaration of 1960 contained no relevant limitations.[61] However, India's declaration of 1974 contained a long list of exclusions, including the multilateral treaties reservation and another excluding disputes 'with the government of any State which is or has been a Member of the Commonwealth of Nations'. When Pakistan began proceedings in 1999, both these reservations were relied on by India.[62]

In its decision in 2000 the Court held that the Commonwealth reservation was effective to exclude its jurisdiction under the Optional Clause, and rejecting various other instruments relied on by Pakistan, dismissed the case. In reaching this conclusion the Court rejected imaginative arguments from Pakistan to the effect that the Commonwealth reservation was obsolete and being 'extra-statutory', could only be relied on in relation to States which had accepted it. Although the issue of obsolescence had been raised by Judge Ago in the *Phosphate Lands in Nauru* case,[63] neither of Pakistan's points was very convincing. Since the ruling on the Commonwealth reservation was enough to dispose of the case, the multilateral treaties reservation, which had been discussed in the pleadings, was not dealt with in the judgment.

A number of other jurisdictional issues were canvassed in argument, including the significance, if any, of the General Act of 1928 and the relation between the Optional Clause and other sources of jurisdiction. For the student of Article 36 (2), however, the main interest of this case is to be found in the Court's endorsement of States' right to make reservations and its unwillingness to find artificial ways of avoiding them. If the message of the *Land and Maritime Boundary* case is that States with unqualified declarations will be held to them, that of the *Aerial Incident* case, like the other cases in this period, is that when a State has chosen to make reservations, the Court will give them effect.

---

[59] See *Legality of Use of Force, Preliminary Objections, ICJ Reports 2004*, p. 279 etc. For comment, see Gray, 'Case Note', 54 (2005) *ICLQ* 787.

[60] *Aerial Incident of 10 August 1999 (Pakistan v. India), Jurisdiction of the Court, ICJ Reports 2000*, p. 12. For comment, see Merrills, 'Case Note', 50 (2001) *ICLQ* 657.

[61] Pakistan's declaration included the multilateral treaties reservation in its narrower form. However, since India's declaration contained the wider version, this was unimportant.

[62] India's declaration also contained a reservation relating to situations involving hostilities and armed conflicts, but this reservation was not invoked.

[63] *Certain Phosphate Lands in Nauru* (note 31): see Separate Opinion, at p. 327, paragraph 5.

3. Pending Cases

There are currently four cases before the Court in which the applicants rely wholly or in part on the parties' declarations under Article 36(2) as the basis for jurisdiction. These are: the *Ahmadio Sadio Diallo* case between the Republic of Guinea and the Democratic Republic of the Congo, the *Maritime Delimitation* case between Nicaragua and Honduras, the *Territorial and Maritime Dispute* between Nicaragua and Colombia and the *Dispute regarding Navigational and Related Rights* between Costa Rica and Nicaragua. For the sake of completeness, this section also includes a note on the *Status of a Diplomatic Envoy* case which was discontinued in 2006.

In the *Ahmadio Sadio Diallo* case,[64] which began in 1998, the respondent is the DRC and the applicant Guinea whose complaint concerns mistreatment of one of its nationals. Both States have made Optional Clause declarations, and neither contains a protection against surprise applications. Consequently, the fact that Guinea's application was made less than a month after the deposit of its declaration is not enough to provide the DRC with a jurisdictional defence. Nevertheless, a number of objections to jurisdiction and the admissibility of the application have been raised, which the Court is likely to address in 2007.

The *Maritime Delimitation* case[65] was begun by Nicaragua against Honduras in 1999 and concerns delimitation in the Caribbean Sea. Both States have made Optional Clause declarations, but the declaration made by Honduras in 1986 contains a broad reservation covering territorial and delimitation issues which seems to cover the dispute. However, both States are also parties to the 1948 Pact of Bogotá, Article 31 of which provides for the reference of disputes to the Court and contains no delimitations. In the *Border and Transborder Armed Actions* case in 1988 the Court held that although the language of Article 31 is identical to that in the Optional Clause, it constitutes a separate and independent basis of jurisdiction.[66] In its application in the present case Nicaragua invoked Article 31, as well as the parties' declarations under the Optional Clause and Honduras has raised no jurisdictional objections. A decision from the Court on the merits is therefore expected in due course.

---

[64] *Ahmadou Sadio Diallo (Republic of Guinea v. Democratic Republic of the Congo)*; proceedings in this case were instituted on 28 December 1998.

[65] *Maritime Delimitation between Nicaragua and Honduras in the Caribbean Sea (Nicaragua v. Honduras)*; proceedings in this case were instituted on 8 December 1999.

[66] *Border and Transborder Armed Actions (Nicaragua v. Honduras), Jurisdiction and Admissibility*, ICJ *Reports 1988*, p. 69.

The *Territorial and Maritime Dispute*[67] is another case brought by Nicaragua against one of its neighbours, here Colombia, and in terms of jurisdiction may be more contentious. The case concerns ownership of certain islands and keys in the Western Caribbean, together with maritime delimitation. The instruments which Nicaragua relies on as the basis of the Court's jurisdiction are, as in the case against Honduras, Article 31 of the Pact of Bogotá and the parties' declarations under Article 36(2). The latter, however, presents a difficulty as Nicaragua instituted proceedings on 6 December 2001, the day after Colombia withdrew its declaration of October 1937 without replacing it. Since Colombia's declaration contained no provision dealing with termination or modification, the question could arise whether its withdrawal was effective immediately, thereby prevent Nicaragua from relying on this basis of jurisdiction. As noted above,[68] the termination and variation of declarations with no provision to that effect is a legal conundrum on which it would be useful to have an indication of the Court's opinion. However, in view of the alternative basis of jurisdiction which is available, it seems unlikely to need discussion in this case.

The last case, in which Nicaragua appears as respondent, is in some respects rather similar, although here modification, rather than termination, of a declaration is involved. In October 2001 Nicaragua sought to limit its obligations under the Optional Clause by making a reservation to its declaration of 1929 which contains no provision on termination or modification. In January 2002 Costa Rica formally objected to this reservation, then on 26 September of the same year announced an agreement with Nicaragua in which the latter undertook 'to maintain, for a period of three years from today's date, the legal status existing on today's date with respect to its declaration of acceptance of the jurisdiction of the International Court of Justice'.[69] On 29 September 2005 Costa Rica instituted proceedings against Nicaragua in the *Dispute regarding Navigational and Related Rights*,[70] citing as the basis for the Court's jurisdiction the parties' declarations under Article 36(2), as well as Article 31 of the Pact of Bogotá and the bilateral agreement of 2002. It remains to be seen whether Nicaragua challenges the Court's jurisdiction and, if so, whether the existence of an alternative basis of jurisdiction again has the effect of avoiding the need to consider the position under the Optional Clause.

---

[67] *Territorial and Maritime Dispute (Nicaragua v. Colombia)*; proceedings in this case were instituted on 6 December 2001.

[68] See the discussion of termination and variation of declarations in Part I, section 1 above.

[69] See 2002–2003 *ICJ Yearbook* 156, note 1.

[70] See ICJ Press Release 2005/20, 3 October 2005.

Finally, to round off this account of the Court's current and recent activity, a word must be said about the *Status of a Diplomatic Envoy* case[71] which was brought by Dominica against Switzerland in 2006. Dominica's complaint was that the respondent had violated its obligations under the 1961 Vienna Convention on Diplomatic Relations and various other international instruments and rules on account of its treatment of the applicant's diplomatic envoy to the United Nations in Geneva. As the basis for the Court's jurisdiction in the case Dominica relied on the parties' respective declarations under the Optional Clause and also on the Optional Protocol to the Vienna Convention which both States had accepted. The interest of the case for our purposes lies in the fact that Dominica made its application on 26 April 2006, just over a month after depositing its declaration under Article 36(2). This is, of course, just the kind of situation that the reservation covering 'surprise' applications is designed to deal with, but as both States' declarations were unconditional, Switzerland would have had no jurisdictional defence. In the event, however, less than a month after starting the case, Dominica indicated that it wished to discontinue proceedings and so the Court made an order to that effect soon afterwards.[72]

IV. CONCLUSION

Between 1993 and 2006, as in earlier periods, a high proportion of the cases taken to Court used as a basis for the Court's jurisdiction 'treaties and conventions in force' in accordance with Article 36(1) of the Statute, rather than declarations under the Optional Clause, so providing a reminder, if one were needed, that the latter is only one method of getting a case before the Court. It follows that neither the number nor the quality of acceptances of Article 36(2) provide a wholly reliable indicator of States' readiness to employ judicial settlement. Furthermore, as regards those States which had made declarations under the Optional Clause, the significance of the commitment is likely to lie as much in the incentive it provides to try to avoid going to Court, as in the number of cases actually litigated. All that having been said, however, case law demonstrates that because a functioning system based on Article 36(2) exists, legal disputes can be referred to the Court on the basis of a general consent given in advance. The question posed at the beginning was 'does the Optional Clause still matter?' The evidence of our survey suggests that it does. Those who devised the Optional

---

[71] See ICJ Press Release 2006/16, 26 April 2006.
[72] See ICJ Press Release 2006/23, 12 June 2006.

Clause hoped for a culture shift in international affairs which obviously has yet to occur. But as States continue to make declarations under Article 36(2) and to use them, that worthy ideal retains its value.

Chapter Eighteen

Internationalized Tribunals: A Search for Their Legal Bases

Sarah Williams[*]

INTRODUCTION

In recent years a number of criminal tribunals have been established to investigate, prosecute and try individuals accused of serious violations of international human rights and international humanitarian law. These tribunals have been described as 'hybrid' or 'internationalized' courts as 'both the institutional apparatus and the applicable law consist of a blend of the international and the domestic'.[1] Six such tribunals are operational: the Special Court for Sierra Leone (SCSL); 'Regulation 64' panels in Kosovo; the Extraordinary Chambers in the Courts of Cambodia (ECCC); the War Crimes Chamber for Bosnia and Herzegovina (WCC); the Iraqi High Tribunal (IHT) and the Special Tribunal for Lebanon. The Special Panels for Serious Crimes in Timor-Leste[2] (SPSC) suspended operations in May 2005. Suggestions have been made that this model of tribunal would also be appropriate for prosecution of atrocities committed in, among others, Burundi,[3]

---

[*] Dorset Fellow of International Law, British Institute of International and Comparative Law, London; former Lecturer in Law, Department of Law, Durham University.

[1] Dickinson, 'The Promise of Hybrid Courts', 97 (2003) *AJIL* 295, at p. 295.

[2] Until independence in May 2002, the territory was known as East Timor. For convenience, all references will be to Timor-Leste.

[3] The Council has previously considered proposals for a Special Chamber to be located within the national court system of Burundi. These proposals, which appeared to have stagnated, may now be revisited following a recent Council statement and as part of the work of the Peacebuilding Commission: see Presidential Statement, 30 May 2007, S/PRST/2007/16.

K.H. Kaikobad & M. Bohlander (eds.), *International Law and Power: Perspectives on Legal Order and Justice*. Essays in Honour of Colin Warbrick, pp. 455–484.

Afghanistan,[4] Palestine and the Occupied Territories[5] and Liberia,[6] and for drug related crimes in other States.[7]

Although there is currently no accepted definition of an internationalized tribunal, there is some agreement as to their core features. In particular, the tribunal must exercise a criminal judicial function; there must be a mix of international and national elements, operating at many levels; and the tribunal must have been created as an ad hoc and temporary response to a specific situation.[8] However, it has been observed that, while common characteristics may be identified, 'the general "species" of internationalized tribunals is highly heterogeneous; the circumstances of their creation are extremely different; their degree of "internationalization" is far from uniform; the scope of their jurisdiction is varied; their modes of functioning are hardly comparable'.[9] This degree of '*ad-hocism*' makes it difficult to identify any normative framework within which to assess existing and future internationalized tribunals.

Given the growing number of such tribunals, it is now necessary to examine further the features of these tribunals so as to identify more specific categories, or sub-species. To utilise the generic term 'internationalized' or 'hybrid' potentially masks a number of significant differences between such tribunals. For instance, the tribunals may apply, and be governed by, different legal regimes. Some may have the power to compel compliance with court orders by third States and international organisations, including the power to secure the surrender of suspects, while others are restricted to requesting international cooperation utilising existing domestic arrangements as to extradition and mutual legal assistance. Tribunals may have varying relationships with the domestic legal regime. Certain tribunals may be able to override domestic and international immunities, whilst others may not. It is submitted here that the most relevant criterion upon which to base any categorization of such tribunals is the

---

[4]   See Dickinson, 'Transitional Justice in Afghanistan: The Promise of Mixed Tribunals' 31 (2003) *Denver Journal of International Law and Policy* 23; and Cassese, 'The Role of Internationalized Courts and Tribunals in the Fight Against International Criminality', in Romano, Nollkaemper and Kleffner (eds.), *Internationalized Criminal Courts: Sierra Leone, East Timor, Kosovo and Cambodia*, Oxford, 2004, p. 10.

[5]   Cassese (note 4), p. 11.

[6]   In May 2007, the Blue Ribbon Experts Group was created to establish a Liberia War Crimes Tribunal. The group, which comprises academics and practitioners, intends to develop a list of possible suspects and charges, together with a proposed statute and rules of procedure and evidence. See: 'Case hosts Blue Ribbon Experts Group to establish Liberia War Crimes Tribunal', at http://www.law.case.edu.

[7]   Cassese (note 4) p. 10 (Columbia).

[8]   Condorelli and Boutruche, 'Internationalized Criminal Courts: Are They Necessary?', in Romano (note 4), pp. 428–30.

[9]   Pellet, 'Internationalized Courts: Better than Nothing ...', in Romano (note 4), p. 437.

legal basis for the creation and operation of the tribunal. Examining the legal basis for each tribunal permits an examination of the key powers and competences of each tribunal and the applicable legal regime. It is directly relevant to the issues outlined above. Accordingly, this paper will assess the differing legal bases of the existing internationalized tribunals and the proposed LST. In its concluding section it will identify three possible sub-categories of internationalized tribunals.

I. THE SPECIAL PANELS FOR SERIOUS CRIMES IN TIMOR-LESTE AND THE 'REGULATION 64 PANELS' IN KOSOVO

1. *The UN Administration and the Creation of Internationalized Processes*

Two internationalized accountability processes have been established by the United Nations as part of a mission authorized by the Security Council (the Council) to administer a territory. In Kosovo, Resolution 1244 authorized the United Nations Interim Mission in Kosovo (UNMIK) to provide 'an interim administration for Kosovo under which the people of Kosovo can enjoy substantial autonomy within the Federal Republic of Yugoslavia'.[10] UNMIK was mandated to perform a wide range of tasks, including the performance of basic civil administrative functions, the maintenance of law and order and the protection and promotion of human rights.[11] UNMIK's first legislative act was to vest itself with 'all legislative and executive authority with respect to Kosovo, including the administration of the judiciary'.[12] Shortly after establishing UNMIK, the Council authorized a similarly extensive mission in Timor-Leste.[13] Resolution 1272 established a UN administration responsible for administering Timor-Leste during a transitional period leading to independence of the disputed territory.[14] The United Nations Transitional Administration in East Timor (UNTAET) was 'endowed with overall authority for the administration' and 'empowered to exercise all legislative and executive authority, including the administration of the judiciary'.[15] In both territories, legislative and executive authority was

---

[10] Security Council Resolution No. 1244, 10 June 1999, paragraph 10. Hereinafter referred to as SC Resolution.

[11] Ibid, paragraph 11, sections (b), (i) and (j).

[12] UNMIK Regulation 1999/1, On the Authority of the Interim Administration in Kosovo, 25 July 1999, section 1.1.

[13] SC Resolution No. 1272, 25 October 1999, paragraph 1.

[14] Ibid, preambular paragraph 3.

[15] Ibid, paragraph 1.

vested in a Special Representative of the Secretary-General (SRSG),[16] who assumed responsibility for law-making functions and promulgated a series of regulations and administrative directions on a wide range of issues.[17]

As part of their civil administration function, UNMIK and UNTAET sought to reinstate the judicial system, which had been severely affected by the conflict in each territory.[18] Both missions promulgated a series of regulations making provision for the structure of the court system and the appointment and removal of judges and prosecutors.[19] Moreover, although neither mission had a specific mandate to do so,[20] each mission considered it a moral necessity to ensure accountability for the serious violations of international human rights and international humanitarian law that had occurred in the period immediately preceding the deployment.[21] However, each mission approached this task differently. In Kosovo, the ICTY was already operational and had jurisdiction in relation to serious atrocities committed within the territory of the former Yugoslavia, including Kosovo.[22] It was envisaged that those violations not investigated or prosecuted by the ICTY would be processed within the domestic

---

[16] SC Resolution No. 1244, paragraph 6; SC Resolution No. 1272, paragraph 6 (known as the Transitional Administrator).

[17] Matters the subject of such 'legislation' included the permitted currency, ownership of real property, banking arrangements and tax and customs regimes.

[18] For further discussion of the conditions facing UNMIK/UNTAET on arrival, and efforts to re-establish the judicial system(s), see: Linton, 'Rising from the Ashes: The Creation of a Viable Criminal Justice System in East Timor', 25 (2001) *Melbourne University Law Review* 122 and Strohmeyer, 'Collapse and Reconstruction of a Judicial System: The United Nations Missions in Kosovo and East Timor', 95 (2001) *AJIL* 46.

[19] See, for example, UNMIK Regulations 5, 6 and 7 of 1999, which provided for the appointment of a public prosecutor, the structure and registration of the judiciary and prosecutorial services and for the appointment of judges. For Timor-Leste, see UNTAET Regulations 11, 15 and 16 of 2000.

[20] SC Resolution No. 1244 demanded that 'all concerned', which includes UNMIK, provide full cooperation with the ICTY: paragraph 14. There was no statement as to the need to ensure that perpetrators were brought to justice by mechanisms other than the ICTY. SC Resolution No. 1272 condemned the violence in East Timor, called for its immediate end and demanded that those responsible be brought to justice: paragraph 16. It did not specify that UNTAET was to undertake that task.

[21] See comment to this affect in Strohmeyer (note 18).

[22] The ICTY's jurisdiction is open-ended. The ICTY Prosecutor indicated in September 1999 that the ICTY would investigate and try high-level leaders alleged to have committed crimes during the conflict in Kosovo. It was, however, noted that UNMIK would have primary responsibility for investigating and prosecuting such crimes: ICTY, Statement on the Investigation and Prosecution of Crimes Committed in Kosovo, The Hague, 29 September 1999: available at www.icty.org. The ICTY has considered several charges arising from events in Kosovo: see *Prosecutor v. Milosevic*, IT-02-54, for crimes committed in Kosovo, Croatia and Bosnia; and *Prosecutor v. Milutonovic et al*, IT-05-87-T, 26 February 2009.

judicial system, to be established and operated by UNMIK. However, it became apparent that the newly re-established domestic courts were largely incapable of remaining impartial and independent when trying cases concerning violations during the conflict, or those with an ethnic dimension. Nor was it considered that the national judges and prosecutors possessed the necessary experience to conduct trials of such complexity and importance.[23] After rejecting proposals for a separate internationalized tribunal,[24] UNMIK authorized the appointment of international judges and prosecutors to sensitive cases.[25] The so-called 'Regulation 64 panels' consist of three judges, including at least two international judges.[26] The jurisdiction of the Regulation 64 panels is not restricted to proceedings arising from the conflict, but extends to any criminal proceeding where the appointment of international judges or prosecutor is 'considered necessary to ensure the independence and impartiality of the judiciary or the proper administration of justice'.[27] Moreover, international judges can be appointed at any stage of the proceedings.[28] In practice, war crimes trials have been held before Regulation 64 panels, with prosecution mostly undertaken by international prosecutors.[29]

In contrast, there was not an existing ad hoc tribunal with jurisdiction over the alleged crimes in Timor-Leste. There were calls for the Council to establish an international criminal tribunal,[30] largely due to the apparent involvement

---

[23] See: OSCE Report 2, The Development of the Kosovo Judicial System (10 June through 15 December 1999); OSCE Background Report: The treatment of minorities by the judicial system, 13 April 2000.

[24] Early plans to establish a specialized court, the Kosovo War and Ethnic Crimes Court (KWECC), were abandoned, due to budget restraints, delays and (reportedly) political concerns in various capitals. See: OSCE Review of the Criminal Justice System in Kosovo, February – July 2000, pp. 71–72; OSCE Review of the Criminal Justice System, 1 September 2000–28 February 2001, section 8.

[25] Regulation 2000/64: On Assignment of International Judges/Prosecutors and/or Change of Venue, 15 December 2000. This regulation drew on the provisions of previous regulations that had provided for the appointment of international judges and prosecutors first to Mitrovica and then to the rest of Kosovo; Regulation 2000/6: On the Appointment and Removal from Office of International Judges and International Prosecutors, 15 February 2000, as amended by Regulation 2000/34 of 29 May 2000.

[26] Regulation 2000/64 (note 25), section 2(1).

[27] Ibid, section 1.

[28] Panels cannot be designated once a trial has begun or where an appellate review panel has already commenced: ibid, section 2 (4).

[29] OSCE Report: Kosovo's War Crime Trials: A Review, September 2002, p. 11.

[30] Both the Report of the Special Rapporteurs (paragraph 74(6)) and the findings of the Commission of Inquiry (paragraph 153) recommended the creation of an international criminal tribunal. More recently, calls for an international tribunal have been renewed, see the Report to the Secretary-General of the Commission of Experts to Review the Prosecution of Serious Violations of Human Rights in Timor-Leste (then East Timor) in 1999, S/2005/458, Annex

of the Indonesian military and police in the atrocities.[31] However, in the face
of Indonesian opposition to this proposal,[32] the Council instead endorsed a
dual strategy of accountability, with prosecutions to take place within both an
Indonesian national mechanism and a serious crimes process to be created by
UNTAET.[33] Accordingly, UNTAET established a system of dedicated panels to
try individuals accused of committing serious crimes, namely the international
crimes of genocide, war crimes, crimes against humanity and torture, and the
domestic crimes of murder and sexual offences.[34] The SPSC operated within
the District Court of Dili, with each panel comprising two international judges
and one Timorese judge.[35] The SPSC were supported by a Serious Crimes
Unit (SCU) staffed almost exclusively by international personnel.[36] UNTAET's
mandate terminated on 20 May 2002 with the creation of the independent State
of Timor-Leste.[37] While legally the SPSC process was now under the purview

---

1 (summary) and Annex II (full report), in particular recommendations C and D. To date the
Council has not acted upon these recommendations.

[31] Several investigative bodies sent to Timor-Leste concluded that Indonesian military and
police had participated or facilitated the violence, and had supported or directed the abuses
perpetrated by Timorese militia. See the Report on the Joint Mission of the Special
Rapporteurs and Representatives Situation of Human Rights in East Timor, A/54/660,
10 December 1999, paragraph 72; and also see the Report of the International Commission
of Inquiry on East Timor, S/2000/59, A/54/726, January 2000, paragraphs 135–41.

[32] Indonesia's objections were set out in a letter from the Minister for Foreign Affairs of Indonesia
to the Secretary-General, 26 January 2000, S/2000/65, A/54/727.

[33] The Secretary-General had opposed the creation of an international tribunal at the expense
of domestic courts: see letter from the Secretary-General to the President of the General
Assembly, 31 January 2000; President of the Security Council and the Chairperson of the
Commission on Human Rights, A/54/726, S/2000/59. The Council endorsed this strategy
in a letter to the Secretary-General: see letter from the President of the Security Council to the
Secretary-General, 21 February 2000, S/2000/13. The Council appeared to have been swayed
by Indonesia's assurances that it was 'determined to bring these individuals to justice through
the national judicial mechanism': see letter *supra* (note 32). It is likely that the Council's
decision was influenced by the growing concerns regarding the spiralling cost, delays and
inefficiencies of the ICTY and the ICTR, a sense of donor exhaustion and perhaps tension
within the Council following the adoption of the Rome Statute the previous year.

[34] Regulation 2000/15: On the Establishment of Panels with Exclusive Jurisdiction over Serious
Criminal Offences, 6 June 2006, drawing on the provisions of Regulation 2000/11: On the
Organization of Courts in East Timor, 6 March 2000, as amended.

[35] Regulation 2000/11, section 10(3); Regulation 2000/15, section 22. Although Regulation
2000/15 provided for multiple SPSC panels, with the exception of a short period in 2001, it
was not until mid-2003 that there were enough international judges to establish more than
one panel at a time.

[36] Regulation 2000/16: On the Organization of the Public Prosecution Service in East Timor,
6 June 2000, sections 1 and 2. See also Regulation 2000/11, section 24.

[37] SC Resolution No. 1392, 31 January 2002.

of the Timorese Department of Justice, the successor mission, UNMISET,[38] included a serious crimes unit, which assumed responsibility for funding and effective control of the SCU and the SPSC process. The SPSC process operated until May 2005.[39]

2. The Legal Basis of UNMIK and UNTAET, and the Serious Crimes Processes

Although there had been precedents for the involvement of the United Nations in governance tasks,[40] the mandates of the civilian components of both UNMIK and UNTAET were considered 'unprecedented in scope and complexity'.[41] Debate ensued as to whether the Council was competent to establish missions with such wide-ranging mandates and, if so, where the legal basis for that competence lay.[42] One suggestion was that both the former Yugoslavia and Indonesia had either consented to or acquiesced in the establishment of an international territorial administration in a territory they had formerly controlled.[43] The Council hinted at the presence of consent in both Resolutions 1244[44] and 1272. However, the Council did not rely on consent alone as the basis for the territorial administration as to do so would have tied the continued operation of the missions to ongoing consent. For political reasons also, relying

---

[38] Authorized by SC Resolution No. 1410, 17 May 2002.

[39] When the mandate of UNMISET, the successor mission to UNTAET, terminated in May 2005, the SPSC could not continue to operate without the support of the UN personnel and financing, and suspended its activities. See JSMP Update, *SPSC Hands Down Final Decision*, 12 May 2005.

[40] For a detailed discussion see Stahn, 'The United Nations Transitional Administrations in Kosovo and East Timor: A First Analysis', 5 (2001) *Max Planck Year Book of United Nations Law* 105 and Wilde, 'From Danzig to East Timor and Beyond: The Role of International Territorial Administration', 95 (2001) *AJIL* 583.

[41] Matheson, 'United Nations Governance of Postconflict Societies', 95 (2001) *AJIL* 76, p. 79.

[42] Generally see Matheson (note 41); and Wilde and Stahn (note 40); further see Kirgis, 'Security Council Governance of Postconflict Societies: A Plea for Good Faith and Informed Decision Making,' 95 (2001) *AJIL* 579; Ruffert, 'The Administration of Kosovo and East Timor by the International Community', 50 (2001) *ICLQ* 613; Rothert, 'UN Intervention in East Timor', 39 (2000–2001) *Columbia Journal of Transnational Law* 257; and Kondoch, 'The United Nations Administration of East Timor', 6 (2001) *JCSL* 145.

[43] The consent of the former Yugoslavia was said to be found in the acceptance of the basic principles of the administration, as set out in Annex 2 to SC Resolution No. 1244. The consent of Indonesia (*de facto* authority) and Portugal (*de jure*) authority were to be found in the agreement providing for the popular consultation and acceptance of the general principles of the administration at a meeting in September 1999.

[44] See SC Resolution No. 1244, preambular paragraphs 9 and 10; and SC Resolution No. 1272, preambular paragraphs 2, 12 and 13.

on consent alone was unacceptable.[45] Moreover, it would not ensure that other States would recognize the authority of the missions and to cooperate so as to enable the missions to function. Thus the Council invoked its Chapter VII powers to establish both missions.[46] It now appears generally accepted that both resolutions were a valid exercise of the Council's Chapter VII powers and that Article 41 of the Charter was sufficiently wide so as to support the imposition of international territorial administration as a measure to restore or maintain international peace and security.[47] The effect of the resolutions was to suspend for the duration of the transitional period the residual powers of the former Yugoslavia in respect of Kosovo and whatever authority Indonesia had exercised in relation to Timor-Leste. During the period of administration, the UN assumed full responsibility for the administration of the territories and was effectively to act as the government of each territory. However, the UN did not become the sovereign in each case: instead sovereignty was suspended and the UN administered the territory on behalf of the local population and on behalf of the international community.[48] As peacekeeping missions established pursuant to Chapter VII, UNMIK and UNTAET were subsidiary organs of the Council under Article 29, or of the organization under Article 7. As such, the missions were subject to reporting requirements and their mandate was subject to modification or termination by the Council.

Given the context of their creation, the legal basis of the Regulation 64 panels and the SPSC during the period of territorial administration is somewhat unclear.[49] As noted above, both the Regulation 64 panels and the SPSC were established by regulations promulgated by the respective SRSG. It has been observed that such regulations have a dual character.[50] The regulations are based on, and their authority flows from, the provisions of the Charter and the Chapter VII powers of the Council. In this sense, the regulations are international instruments. However, the regulations are addressed to a specific territory and, in this other sense, constitute domestic laws of that territory. This

---

[45] The validity of the consent of the former Yugoslavia was questioned owing to its military air strikes and other measures. To rely on consent alone in East Timor would have validated Indonesia's annexation of the territory as unlawful.

[46] Both SC Resolution No. 1244 and No. 1272 state that the Council is acting under Chapter VII.

[47] This is the conclusion drawn by the majority of the commentators listed above.

[48] Yannis, 'The Concept of Suspended Sovereignty in International Law and Its Implications in International Politics', 13 (2002) *EJIL* 1037, p. 1048.

[49] The legal basis of the SPSC varied after the independence of Timor-Leste in May 2002 and the period subsequent to independence will not be considered in detail in this paper.

[50] See discussion in the following sources: Stahn (note 40); Ruffert (note 42); and Wilde, 'The Complex Role of the Legal Adviser when International Organizations Administer Territory', (2001) *ASIL Proceedings* 251.

reflects the dual functions of the SRSG and the missions themselves; at least during the transitional period they operate not only as a subsidiary organ of the Council but also as the effective government of the territory concerned.

What does this duality mean for the legal basis of the Regulation 64 panels and the SPSC? At least in theory, these internationalized tribunals may also enjoy the same duality, that is they operate both as instruments of the Council under Chapter VII and as domestic judicial processes. If the tribunals were considered 'Chapter VII' tribunals in this sense, this would suggest that they should be subject to and apply international law, could compel cooperation with their orders[51] and could override immunity both at a national and international levels.[52] However, Wilde argues that the correct method of assessing the legal basis of such a regulation potentially possessing a dual character is to consider which role the international organization is fulfilling when it promulgates the regulation and to ask whether the regulation is an exercise of international legal capacity, or a governmental act.[53] Applying this approach, it would appear from the face of the regulations in question that both SRSGs acted in their domestic capacity, and did not act to establish the Regulation 64 panels or the SPSC as international legislative acts. This would base the legal authority of these bodies in domestic law. This conclusion appears supported by the practice of the panels, which have operated as domestic tribunals. Each tribunal applies the law stipulated by the relevant regulations as the law of the territory concerned, and not as a national court applying international law. Neither the Regulation 64 panels nor the SPSC asserted any binding authority based on the Charter in order to enforce their orders or to obtain the cooperation of States, including the former Yugoslavia and Indonesia. The authority of UNMIK and UNTAET – and the courts they created – is recognized as being restricted to the territory of Kosovo and Timor-Leste respectively, although it is accepted that the missions possessed limited legal personality and the capacity to enter into agreements with States.[54] Any obligation on member States to cooperate with

---

[51] See *Prosecutor v. Blaskic*, Decision on the Admissibility of the Request for Review by the Republic of Croatia of an Interlocutory Decision of a Trial Chamber (issuance of *subpoenae duces tecum*) and Scheduling Order, 29 July 1997 (Appeal Chamber), (IT-95-14-A).

[52] *Case Concerning the Arrest Warrant of 11 April 2000 (Democratic Republic of the Congo v. Belgium)*, ICJ Reports 2002, p. 3, at pp. 25–26, paragraph 61. The ICTY has tried political and military leaders that may otherwise have enjoyed immunity: see, for example, *Prosecutor v. Slobodan Milosevic* (IT-02-54).

[53] *Supra* (note 50).

[54] For example, UNTAET negotiated a treaty with Australia concerning the exploitation of petroleum resources in the seabed between Australia and Timor-Leste in February 2000, accompanied by a memorandum of understanding to govern the application of the treaty during the transitional period. In Kosovo, UNMIK negotiated a memorandum of understanding with Interpol concerning cooperation in crime prevention and criminal

the missions does not appear to have extended to cooperating with the serious crimes process, and both UNMIK and UNTAET were forced to enter into or rely upon agreements for extradition and mutual legal assistance.[55] This was particularly evident in Timor-Leste, where from the 440 individuals indicted by the SPSC, 339 remained at large, believed to be in Indonesia.[56] To date, the Indonesian Government has not extradited a single individual to Timor-Leste to face trial. Moreover, neither Indonesia nor Serbia have recognized that these tribunals may override the immunity of State officials.

The conclusion is also supported by the action — or inaction — of the Council regarding the serious crimes process in each territory. The Council did not display any sense of 'ownership' of the SPSC or the Regulation 64 panels. Key decisions, including the creation of the processes themselves, were made within the mission hierarchy, and were not instigated by the Council. Although the processes operate within restraints set by the Council, particularly in relation to the relationship between these processes and other international courts (ICTY in Kosovo) and national courts (accountability process in Indonesia for Timor-Leste), there is not a system of reporting to the Council on serious crimes issues outside the normal mission reporting structure. This limits the possibility of obtaining Council support for enforcement of orders and issues of cooperation. Even where flaws in the system were identified, for example when the failings in the trials before the Indonesian national mechanism became apparent, the Council did not act to reinforce the serious crimes process in a territory which the UN administered under its authority. Thus it appears that the Council itself does not consider the tribunals to possess international character or to have a basis in Chapter VII of the Charter.

The conclusion that the SPSC and the Regulation 64 panels are domestic institutions is logical, particularly when one considers other actions taken by the missions. Both UNTAET and UNMIK created transitional governmental institutions and were responsible for establishing institutions to draft interim consti-

---

justice. UNMIK also negotiated two agreements with the Council of Europe concerning the application in Kosovo of the Framework Convention on the Protection of National Minorities and the European Convention for the Prevention of Torture and Inhuman and Degrading Treatment or Punishment.

[55] UNTAET negotiated a memorandum of understanding dated 6 April 2000, which allowed for the enforcement of court decisions in Indonesia and the transfer of persons from Indonesia to Timor-Leste judicial authorities. UNMIK did not rely on existing extradition and mutual legal assistance arrangements between the FRY and third States and instead negotiated several memoranda with States such as Serbia, Albania and the Federal Yugoslav Republic of Macedonia and Montenegro providing for cooperation in criminal justice matters and bilateral agreements with States to enable extradition.

[56] JSMP, Overview of the Justice Sector 2005, pp. 30–31.

tutions.[57] The transitional institutions established by the missions were staffed at least in part by international personnel.[58] There has been no suggestion that the transitional governments or institutions were international in character, or that they drew their authority from the powers of the Council under Chapter VII. Instead, all transitional institutions are considered to be domestic in nature, albeit that these institutions received significant international assistance. There is no justification for conferring upon the SPSC and the Regulation 64 panels international character and authority where other transitional institutions are national in nature. Accordingly, the legal basis of these tribunals lies in national law and the tribunals operate as national courts with international participation.

III. The Special Court for Sierra Leone

The SCSL was created in response to a request from the President of Sierra Leone to the Council in June 2000.[59] In Resolution 1315, the Council requested the Secretary-General 'to negotiate an agreement with the Government of Sierra Leone to create an independent special court consistent with this resolution'.[60] The Council made several recommendations as to the subject matter and personal jurisdiction of the proposed court,[61] and asked for recommendations from the Secretary-General on key issues.[62] The Secretary-General reported to the Council on 4 October 2000,[63] and the decision to proceed with the SCSL

---

[57] In Timor-Leste, see UNTAET Regulation 2001/2: On the Election of a Constituent Assembly to Prepare a Constitution for an Independent and Democratic East Timor, 16 March 2001; and see UNTAET Regulation 2001/21: On the Establishment of the Council of Ministers, 19 September 2001. For Kosovo, see UNMIK Regulation 2001/9: On a Constitutional Framework for Provisional Self-Government in Kosovo, 15 May 2001.

[58] UNMIK Regulation 2000/1: On the Kosovo Joint Administrative Structure, 14 January 2000, provided that each administrative department established was to be managed by two Co-heads, one a Kosovar, the other a member of UNMIK; see also UNTAET Regulation 2000/23: On the Establishment of the Cabinet of the Transitional Government of East Timor, 14 July 2000, provided for the appointment of Timorese Cabinet Officers to manage transitional administrative departments. However, all officers were appointed by and reported to the Transitional Administrator.

[59] Letter from the President of Sierra Leone to the President of the United Nations Security Council, dated 12 June 2000: Annex to Letter from the Permanent Representative of Sierra Leone to the United Nations to the President of the Security Council, 9 August 2000: S/2000/786.

[60] SC Resolution No. 1315, paragraph 1.

[61] Ibid, paragraphs 2 and 3.

[62] Ibid, paragraphs 7 and 8.

[63] Report of the Secretary-General on the Establishment of a Special Court for Sierra Leone, 4 October 2000, S/2000/915.

was 'approved' by the Council on 19 March 2002, although there is no resolution or press release documenting this approval.[64] The Agreement between
the United Nations and the Government of Sierra Leone on the Establishment
of the Special Court for Sierra Leone (the SC Agreement) was signed on 16
January 2002,[65] with the SC Agreement entering into force later in 2002.[66]
The SCSL functions in accordance with its statute, which is annexed to and
forms an integral part of the SC Agreement.[67] The SCSL is considered a hybrid
tribunal because it is staffed by both international and domestic judges, and
applies a mixture of domestic and international law.[68] It has jurisdiction for
specified crimes – crimes against humanity, violations of common Article 3 and
Additional Protocol II, other serious violations of international humanitarian
law, and crimes under Sierra Leone law[69] – committed in Sierra Leone since
30 November 1996.[70]

As noted in the Secretary-General's report, 'the Special Court, as foreseen, is
established by an Agreement between the United Nations and the Government
of Sierra Leone and is therefore a treaty-based sui generis court of mixed
jurisdiction and composition'.[71] The legal status of the SCSL is determined by
its constituent instrument and it is clear that it is the SC Agreement, and not
Resolution 1315 or other subsequent Council resolutions that established the
SCSL. Article 1 of the SC Agreement clearly states 'There is hereby established
a Special Court for Sierra Leone ...'. Moreover, the preamble to the Statute
provides 'Having been established by an Agreement between the United Nations
and the Government of Sierra Leone ...'. The Council itself has referred to
the SCSL as having been established by the SC Agreement.[72] The SCSL is

---

[64] UN Press Release, *War Crimes Court for Sierra Leone Gets Security Council Go-ahead, UN Official
says*, 20 March 2002.

[65] UN Press Release, *Sierra Leone: UN, Government Sign Historic Accord to Set up Special War Crimes
Court*, 16 January 2002.

[66] Article 21 of the SC Agreement provided that the SC Agreement would enter into force on
the day after both parties notified each other in writing that the legal requirements for entry
into force have been satisfied.

[67] Article 1(2), SC Agreement.

[68] For further discussion, see, among others: Cryer, 'A "Special" Court for Sierra Leone',
50 (2001) *ICLQ* 435; Linton, 'Cambodia, East Timor and Sierra Leone: Experiments in
International Justice', 12 (2001) *Criminal Law Forum* 185; Frulli, 'The Special Court for Sierra
Leone: Some Preliminary Comments', 11 (2000) *EJIL* 857; and McDonald, 'Sierra Leone's
Shoestring Special Court', 84 (No. 845, 2002) *International Review of the Red Cross* 121.

[69] Offences relating to the abuse of girls under the Prevention of Cruelty Act and offences
relating to the destruction of property under the Malicious Damage Act: see Article 5, SC
Statute.

[70] Article 1, SC Statute.

[71] S/2000/915, paragraph 9.

[72] See SC Resolution No. 1688, paragraph 2.

thus a treaty-based court and, in this sense, has more in common with the International Criminal Court[73] than the ICTY and the ICTR.[74] As the SCSL was established by an agreement which has effect in international law, it enjoys international character of some description and in this sense can be said to be an international – and not a national – tribunal.

However, despite the clear provisions of the SC Agreement, it has been suggested that the legal basis of the SCSL lies in the Charter, in particular under Chapter VII.[75] This assertion rests on the premise that Resolution 1315 and the involvement of the Council in its creation indicate that the SCSL was established pursuant to the powers of the Council under Chapter VII. This assertion is flawed. The Council did not establish the SCSL. Before acting under Chapter VII of the Charter, the Council must make a determination that the situation in question represents a threat to the international peace and security.[76] The Council had previously determined that the situation in Sierra Leone constituted a threat to international peace and security,[77] and this determination was reiterated in Resolution 1315.[78] Thus the jurisdictional threshold for the operation of Chapter VII of the Charter was satisfied, and it was open to the Council to utilize its powers under Article 41 to establish an international tribunal as a measure to restore international peace and security. Alternatively, the Council could have relied upon its general power for international peace and security under Article 24. However, the Council did not 'act' under Chapter VII;[79] it merely requested the Secretary-General

---

[73] The ICC was established by an international treaty, the Rome Statute of the International Criminal Court, 17 July 1998: 37 (1998) *ILM* 1002.

[74] Both the ICTY and the ICTR were established by resolutions of the Council, and in particular, see SC Resolutions Nos. 827 (1993) and 955 (2004).

[75] Defendants, the Prosecution and even the SCSL have all on one occasion or another suggested that the Council created the SCSL. For example, the SCSL has observed that '[T]he establishment of the Special Court was thus an implementation of the *determination of the Security Council* to bring those responsible for serious violations of international humanitarian law to justice': *Prosecutor v. Morris Kallon and Brima Bazzy Kamara, Decision on Challenge to Jurisdiction: Lomé Accord Amnesty*, SCSL-2004-15-AR72 (E), 13 March 2004, paragraph 11; emphasis added. However, the SCSL then affirmed that it was the SC Agreement that had established the Court: see paragraph 12.

[76] Article 39 of the Charter of the UN.

[77] Previous resolutions of the Council had determined that the situation in Sierra Leone was a threat to international peace and security: see SC Resolution Nos. 1270, 22 October 1999 and Resolution No. 1132, 8 October 1997.

[78] SC Resolution No. 1315, preamble.

[79] The Council generally states whether it is acting under Chapter VII in adopting a particular resolution: contrast SC Resolution No. 1315 with SC Resolution No. 955 and SC Resolution No. 827, the resolutions establishing the ICTY and ICTR. Both Resolution No. 955 and Resolution No. 827 include the words 'Acting under Chapter VII of the Charter of the

to negotiate an agreement with Sierra Leone. It certainly did not establish the SCSL by Resolution 1315. There is not a 'decision' of the Council with which Sierra Leone could be required to co-operate under Article 25.[80] At most, SC Resolution No. 1315 is a non-binding recommendation from the Council under Article 39.[81]

In the decision determining the immunities of the former Liberian President, Charles Taylor,[82] the SCSL determined that the issue whether immunity was to be accorded to Taylor, as Head of State of Liberia, depended upon whether the SCSL was an international criminal court within the ambit of the term 'certain international criminal courts having jurisdiction' in the International Court of Justice's decision in the *Arrest Warrant* case.[83] Determining the correct legal basis of the SCSL was essential for accurately resolving the issue of immunity. The SCSL concluded that its 'competence and jurisdiction *ratione materiae* and *ratione personae* are broadly similar to that of the ICTY and the ICTR and the ICC' and that 'there is no reason to conclude that the Special Court should be treated as anything other than an international tribunal or court, with all that implies for the question of immunity for a serving Head of State.'[84] It consequently determined that Taylor was not to be accorded immunity. This conclusion rested mainly on the involvement of the Council in the establishment of the SCSL, with the latter hinting that the true basis of its authority lay in Chapter VII.[85] It also relied on the general involvement of the international community in its creation and operation.[86]

United Nations'. The Charter does not contain a requirement that the Council specify which powers it relies upon, and the inclusion of the phrase 'Acting under Chapter VII' is a matter of custom or practice only. The absence of these words in Resolution No. 1315 creates a strong presumption that the Council was not engaging its Chapter VII powers.

[80] Article 25 of the Charter obliges member States to 'accept and carry out the *decisions* of the Security Council'; emphasis added.

[81] Article 39 of the Charter provides that 'The Security Council shall determine the existence of any threat to the peace, breach of the peace, or act of aggression and *shall make recommendations*, or decide what measures shall be taken in accordance with Articles 41 and 42, to maintain or restore international peace and security.' Emphasis added.

[82] *Prosecutor v. Charles Taylor, Decision on Immunity from Jurisdiction*, No. SCSL-03-01-I, 31 May 2004.

[83] *Supra* (note 52).

[84] In the *Taylor Immunity Decision* (note 82) the Court adopted with approval the conclusions reached by Professor Sands in his submissions as *amicus curiae*: see paragraph 41, for which submissions, see the ICC 'Guest Lecture Series of the Office of the Prosecutor', 18 November 2003.

[85] *Supra* (note 82), paragraphs 37–38.

[86] For example, the SCSL referred to the preamble of SC Resolution No. 1315 which provides in part that 'the international community will exert every effort to bring those responsible to justice'. It argued that, by inserting this provision, 'it had been made clear that the Special

As discussed above, the conclusion that, having been established by a treaty, it is 'international' in nature is correct. However, this conclusion failed to distinguish between the different methods of establishing the tribunals: the ICTY and ICTR were created by the Council and bring with their creation the 'universality' of a Chapter VII mandate.[87] In contrast, the ICC, being created by a treaty, only enjoys such 'universality' where there is a Council referral. This distinction is essential for determining the immunities to be accorded to State officials: courts created by the Council acting pursuant to Chapter VII may override the principle of sovereign immunity for officials of all States, whereas courts established by treaty may override immunity only for State parties or where there is a Council referral.[88] The SCSL needed to demonstrate that its legal basis or other circumstances enabled it to override the immunity that Taylor would otherwise have enjoyed. This could have been achieved in three ways. First, the Council could have established the SCSL by way of a Council resolution under Chapter VII of the Charter, with the resolution either expressly or impliedly waiving immunity for State officials, as, for example, by requiring third States to comply with the Tribunal's orders. Second, Liberia could have consented to the waiver of immunity contained in the Agreement. Third, it is possible that the Council – again acting under Chapter VII – could waive immunity in respect of a certain individual or in respect of all individuals and proceedings before a specified tribunal. None of these circumstances existed in the case of Taylor: the SCSL was not created by the Council, nor does it receive referrals from the Council; Liberia did not waive immunity;[89] nor did the Council override the immunity or compel third States to comply with its orders.[90] As Sierra Leone is the only State party to the SC Agreement, the

---

Court was established to fulfil an international mandate and is part of the machinery of international justice': ibid, paragraph 39.

[87] For a more detailed analysis of its decision see: Nouwen, 'The Special Court for Sierra Leone and the Immunity of Taylor: The *Arrest Warrant* Case Continued', 18 (2005) *LJIL* 645 and Deen-Racsmany, '*Prosecutor v. Taylor*: The Status of the Special Court for Sierra Leone and Its Implications for Immunity', 18 (2005) *Leiden Journal of International Law* 299. The decision is also discussed in Akande, *infra* (note 88).

[88] See Akande, 'International Law Immunities and the International Criminal Court', 98 (2004) 98 *AJIL* 407.

[89] In fact, Liberia challenged at the ICJ the issue of the indictment by the SCSL: ICJ Press Release 2003/26, 5 August 2003.

[90] The Council has had the opportunity to compel States to comply with the orders of the SCSL, but it has resisted the invitation to do so. The President of the Special Court has written to the Secretary-General asking the Secretary-General to recommend to the Security Council that it pass a resolution under Chapter VII of the Charter calling on Member States to abide by the orders of the Special Court: Special Court Press Release, 'Court President Requests UN Security Council's Chapter Seven', 11 June 2003. The Council has referred to the SCSL

only officials for whom the SCSL may override immunity are those of Sierra Leone. It was therefore not possible for the SC Agreement to have waived the immunity of Liberia, a non-party.[91]

IV. EXTRAORDINARY CHAMBERS IN THE COURTS OF CAMBODIA

The process to create the ECCC was initiated in 1997. It followed a request by the Cambodian Government to the UN for assistance to establish a tribunal to prosecute the senior leaders of the Khmer Rouge for the offences committed during the period from 1975 to 1979.[92] A group of experts, convened at the request of the General Assembly,[93] recommended establishing an ad hoc international tribunal, to be situated in the Asia-Pacific region, but not in Cambodia.[94] The Cambodian Government rejected that proposal, instead requesting UN assistance in drafting domestic legislation to establish a specialized national court with international participation.[95] Following negotiations regarding the proposed structure and functions of the tribunal, the Cambodian Government introduced the Law on the Establishment of Extraordinary Chambers in the Courts of Cambodia for the prosecution of crimes committed during the period of Democratic Kampuchea (the Special Law).[96] However, in

---

in subsequent resolutions, but has only urged, not required, States to cooperate fully with the SCSL: see SC Resolution No. 1508, 19 September 2003, paragraph 6; and ibid, No. 1537, 30 March 2004, paragraph 9. There have only been two occasions when the Council has issued binding decisions under Chapter VII in relation to the SCSL: the first was a direction to UNMIL to apprehend and secure custody of Charles Taylor upon his return to Liberia and to transfer or facilitate his transfer to the SCSL, and the second concerned his transfer to The Hague to face trial: SC Resolutions No. 1638 and No. 1688 respectively. Neither raised the question of immunity.

[91] The SCSL's suggestion that the Agreement waived immunity for all Member States (*supra* (note 82), paragraph 38) is unconvincing as the United Nations enjoys separate legal personality.

[92] Letter from the First and Second Prime Ministers of Cambodia to the Secretary-General, 21 June 1997, A/51/930, S/1997/488.

[93] GA Resolution 52/135, 12 December 1997, paragraph 16.

[94] Report of the Group of Experts for Cambodia established pursuant to General Assembly resolution 52/135, AA/53/850, paragraph 219.

[95] Letter from Hun Sen, Prime Minister of Cambodia to Thomas Hammarberg, Special Representative of the UN Secretary-General for Human Rights in Cambodia, 17 July 1999.

[96] A Memorandum of Understanding was reached in May 2000, although there is some dispute as to the intended effect of this document and the extent to which it was incorporated into the Special Law: Lynch, 'UN Warns Cambodia on War Crimes Tribunal', *Washington Post*, 3 February 2001. The Special Law was introduced in December 2000, but was referred to the Cambodian Constitutional Court for approval: 'Cambodia Set for Khmer Rouge Trials', *BBC Online*, 7 August 2001.

February 2002, after two and a half years of negotiations, the UN withdrew from the process, citing a 'lack of commitment' to the process on the part of the Cambodian Government.[97]

Negotiations for a Cambodian tribunal resumed only following a General Assembly request for the Secretary-General to conclude an agreement on the establishment of the Extraordinary Chambers.[98] During the course of negotiations, the Cambodian Government rejected the majority of amendments sought by the UN and resisted any changes to the Special Law. Consequently, the Secretary-General concluded that the only option acceptable to the Cambodian Government was for a national court with the structure and organization envisaged in the Special Law.[99] An agreement, based on the provisions of the Special Law, was finalised and initialled by both parties on 17 March 2003, approved by the General Assembly on 13 May 2003, and signed on 6 June 2003 (the ECCC Agreement).[100] The ECCC Agreement entered into force in October 2004. Preparations for the ECCC commenced in 2006, and judicial activities commenced in late 2007. Like the other internationalized tribunals, the ECCC has mixed composition and applies a combination of international and domestic law.[101] The ECCC has jurisdiction in respect of senior leaders and those most responsible for the crimes and serious violations of Cambodian laws related to crimes, international humanitarian law and custom, and international conventions recognized by Cambodia, that were committed during the period from 17 April 1975 to 6 January 1979.[102]

While the General Assembly approved the ECCC Agreement prior to its signature, Resolution 57/225B does not form the legal basis of the ECCC. The ECCC was established by domestic law, operates within the existing court structure of Cambodia and forms part of the Cambodian legal order.[103] This

---

[97] Report of the Secretary-General on Khmer Rouge Trials, 31 March 2003, UN Doc. No. A/57/769, paragraph 14.

[98] GA Resolution 57/228, 18 December 2003.

[99] Secretary-General's Report (note 97), paragraph 23.

[100] See UN Press Release, 'UN and Cambodia Reach Draft Agreement for Prosecuting Khmer Rouge Crimes', 17 March 2003; ibid, 13 May 2003; ibid, 'UN, Cambodia Sign Agreement to Prosecute Former Khmer Rouge Leaders', 6 June 2003.

[101] For further discussion see, among others: Linton (note 68), *supra*; and Williams, 'The Cambodian Extraordinary Chambers: A Dangerous Precedent for International Justice?' 53 (2003) *ICLQ* 227.

[102] Article 1 of the Special Law.

[103] The ECCC Agreement regulates the 'cooperation' between the UN and Cambodia in bringing alleged perpetrators to justice; it does not establish the courts: Article 1. Article 2(1) provides that the ECCC Agreement shall be implemented in Cambodia through the Special Law. In addition, Article 31 states that the ECCC Agreement is to apply as law within Cambodia following its ratification under internal legal provisions. It appears that the intention was con-

makes the ECCC a primarily national institution. As such, the ECCC may rely upon existing extradition and legal assistance agreements, although it will depend upon the Cambodian Government for this. Moreover, unlike the SCSL, while the ECCC is the subject of a bilateral agreement, the tribunal is not a treaty-based organ: the Special Law and not the ECCC Agreement is the constitutive instrument of the tribunal. The ECCC Agreement is only 'to regulate the cooperation' between the UN and Cambodia, and to provide 'the legal basis and the principles and modalities for such cooperation'.[104] It aims to 'guarantee' the performance of the ECCC, through specifying how the ECCC must be structured and operate in order to receive assistance from the UN. If the Cambodian Government was to change the structure and organization of the ECCC so that it failed to conform to the ECCC Agreement, then the obligation of the UN to provide assistance would cease to apply.[105] The same would occur if the Cambodian Government were to cause the ECCC to function in a manner that did not conform to the ECCC Agreement,[106] including failing to conform to international procedural standards. The Cambodian Government must consult the UN prior to any amendment to the Special Law,[107] which will provide an opportunity for input into any amendments required owing to inconsistency with the Special Law. However, as the assistance is offered under the authority of the General Assembly, it is likely that any breach would be referred to that body for determination, resulting in a political, rather than legal, determination of the situation.[108]

Immunity pursuant to international law is not likely to be an issue for the ECCC as, although jurisdiction is not restricted to Cambodian nationals, individuals likely to be a target of the ECCC's investigations are Cambodian nationals and not officials of a third State. Any immunity granted by Cambodian law could be waived or removed by further national legal provisions. In fact, while the Special Law is silent as to immunity, it is arguable that the Special Law itself has achieved this result. As a separate issue, the ECCC may have to consider the effect of amnesties granted by the Cambodian Government after the atrocities were committed. The ECCC Agreement provides that the Government shall not request an amnesty for any individual. It also provides

---

sistent with giving the ECCC Agreement equal standing with the Special Law under domestic Cambodian law. Article 2 of the Special Law provides that the courts 'shall be established'.
[104] Article 1 of the ECCC Agreement.
[105] Article 2 of the ECCC Agreement.
[106] Secretary-General's Report (note 97), paragraph 51.
[107] Article 2(3) of the ECCC Agreement.
[108] Article 29 of the ECCC Agreement provides that any dispute is to be settled by negotiation or by any other mutually agreed upon mode of settlement.

that the scope of an existing amnesty, granted in 1996, shall be considered by the ECCC. This provision is reflected in Article 40 of the Special Law. As the ECCC will be a domestic court assessing the validity of a national law amnesty, the issue of whether an international court is bound by domestic law amnesties should not arise. It is open to the ECCC to construe the existing amnesty provision strictly, arguing that the amnesty was not intended to extend to international crimes, such as those included in sections 4–8 of the Special Law. A narrow interpretation would avoid a potential difficulty for the UN, which as a matter of policy would not normally wish to be associated with a criminal tribunal that recognized amnesty for international crimes.[109]

v. War Crimes Chamber for Bosnia and Herzegovina

The WCC was created in 2005, with its establishment closely linked to the completion strategy for the ICTY.[110] The Council recognized that the transfer of cases of lesser importance from the ICTY to the courts of States of the former Yugoslavia was a measure vital to achieving the completion strategy of the ICTY. In the absence of appropriate impartial national mechanisms, the Council supported the 'expeditious establishment' and 'early functioning' of the WCC.[111] However, the Council did not act to establish the WCC beyond encouraging donations from interested States. Instead, the WCC was established within the structure of an existing national court, the federal-level State Court, by the Office of the High Representative (OHR).[112] The powers of the OHR derive from the Dayton Peace Agreement (DPA),[113] which provided for the appointment of the OHR to carry out the implementation of the civil administration aspects of the peace agreement.[114] It also provided that the OHR shall have the final authority 'regarding interpretation of this Agreement on the

---

[109] For example, the UN indicated that domestic amnesties granted in Sierra Leone would not bind the SCSL. However, the position of the UN concerning amnesties has been somewhat inconsistent: see Stahn, 'United Nations Peace-Building, Amnesties and Alternative Forms of Justice: A Change in Practice?,' 84 (No. 845, 2002) *International Review of the Red Cross* 191.

[110] The Council has determined that the ICTY should complete all trial activities by the end of 2008 and all work by the end of 2010: see SC Resolution 1593, paragraph 7. This is known as the completion strategy for the tribunal.

[111] SC Resolution No. 1503, preambular paragraph 11.

[112] Decision Imposing the Law on the State Court of BiH, 12 November 2000.

[113] The General Framework Agreement for Peace in Bosnia and Herzegovina, 14 December 1995.

[114] Article I of Annex 10.

civilian implementation of the peace settlement'.[115] The OHR has interpreted this power as authorising the promulgation of laws for the civil administration of the territory, including the judiciary. Although the Council has supported the operations of the OHR[116] and has monitored implementation of the DPA, the institution of the OHR was not established by the UN under Chapter VII or otherwise, but by the DPA itself. Thus, unlike UNMIK and UNTAET, the OHR is not a subsidiary organ of the UN.

The WCC has jurisdiction to hear cases relating to persons accused of committing war crimes.[117] This includes responsibility for the prosecution of intermediate level accused referred by the ICTY and cases of a sensitive nature involving crimes under domestic law. While the WCC is a permanent institution, the OHR has appointed to the WCC international judges,[118] prosecutors[119] and an international registrar for a transitional period of no more than five years. In terms of its applicable law, even though the WCC is to accept cases referred to it by the ICTY, the Law on Transfer makes it clear that indictments are to be issued in accordance with domestic law, both procedural and substantive.[120]

What then is the legal basis of the WCC? While it would appear that the WCC is a national court established under domestic law, the situation may not be so clear. The OHR had previously established the State Court by decision, albeit this decision was subsequently confirmed by federal and entity level legislation.[121] The creation of the State Court was considered to flow from the powers of the OHR in respect of the judiciary. The same legal basis was used

---

[115] Article V, DPA.

[116] See, for example, Resolution 1035 of 21 December 1995, authorizing the involvement of the UN in the implementation of the DPA; Resolution 1088 of 12 December 1996, reaffirming support for the DPA and calling upon all parties to comply with their obligations.

[117] Law on Amendments to the Law on the State Court of Bosnia and Herzegovina, *Official Gazette* BiH 9/04, Article 24.

[118] Panels of the WCC comprise three judges, two international and one national: Article 65(1), Law on the Court.

[119] The arrangements include the creation of the Special Department for War Crimes, established within the Prosecutor's Office of BiH. During this period, this Department is headed by an international prosecutor, and other international prosecutors have been appointed: Article 18, Law on the Prosecutor's Office of Bosnia and Herzegovina.

[120] Law on the Transfer of Cases from the ICTY to the Prosecutor's Office of BiH and the Use of Evidence Collected by ICTY in Proceedings before the Courts in BiH. For example, Article 2 provides that the indictment is to be adapted so as to meet the requirements of the BiH Criminal Procedure Code.

[121] Law on the Court of Bosnia and Herzegovina, *Official Gazette* BiH 29/00. In 2002, the jurisdiction of the State Court was expanded to include panels for Organized Crime, Economic Crime and Corruption: see the Law on Amendments to the Law on the State Court of Bosnia and Herzegovina, *Official Gazette* BiH 24/02, entering into force on 6 June 2005.

to establish the WCC, again relying upon the wide powers of the OHR under the DPA. This was achieved by an amendment to the existing law on the State Court, which was subsequently approved by the parliaments of both entities and the federal parliament.[122] Despite the support of the Council for the creation of the WCC and its connection to the ICTY completion strategy, it is clear that the Council did not establish the WCC by resolution under Chapter VII or otherwise. Whilst the Council receives information on the WCC in the reports submitted by the ICTY as part of the completion strategy, that information is focused on the number of referrals from the ICTY. Moreover, the Council takes no role in enforcing compliance with the orders of the WCC, which is left to normal domestic mechanisms and international and regional agreements.

It could be argued that the legal basis of the WCC rests upon the authority conferred on the OHR by the DPA itself, an international peace agreement. The logical extension of this argument would be that the competence to establish the WCC flowed ultimately from the Federal Republic of Bosnia and Herzegovina and the Federal Republic of Yugoslavia as two of the signatories to the DPA.[123] The DPA did not itself establish the WCC, it merely conferred a general power on the OHR which has been interpreted as encompassing the power to take action in the area of law and order. In this sense, the WCC could be said to have been established as an exercise of domestic law making capacity, albeit delegated or transferred to an international actor, the OHR. This conclusion is arguably endorsed by the actions of the local legislative authorities in confirming the national legislation that enable implementation of the decision of the OHR. Even if this 'transfer' or 'delegation' argument is implausible, and the OHR was not exercising delegated authority, it appears that the WCC is still a national body. Adopting the same 'functional duality' approach as adopted in relation to the regulations promulgated by UNMIK and UNTAET, discussed above, it is necessary to ask in what capacity was the OHR acting when establishing the WCC? The answer must surely be that he acted in his capacity as a domestic authority, following local consultation. Therefore, the WCC is also a national institution and, if issues of immunity and amnesty arise, they should be assessed as if they were raised before a domestic court.

---

[122] Law on Amendments to the Law on the State Court of Bosnia and Herzegovina, *Official Gazette* BiH 9/04.

[123] The third signatory was the Republic of Croatia. The DPA was witnessed by France, Germany, the Russian Federation, the United Kingdom, the United States and the EU Special Negotiator; however this does not indicate that those States were parties to the agreement or in any way authorized the institutions and arrangements established.

VI. IRAQI HIGH TRIBUNAL

While the IHT is generally considered to be a national criminal tribunal, it may be argued that the facts surrounding its establishment, and key factors in its design and operation, place this tribunal in the category of internationalized criminal tribunals. First, as discussed in more detail below, the IHT was established in the context of an international armed conflict[124] and a military occupation.[125] Second, the crimes within the jurisdiction of the IHT are a mixture of both international – genocide, crimes against humanity and war crimes – and domestic law crimes.[126] The applicable procedural law also comprises elements of both national and international law.[127] Third, while it is a general principle of the IHT Statute that the judges, investigative judges, prosecutors, and the Director of the Administration Department shall be Iraqi nationals,[128] there is some scope for international involvement, largely through the appointment of advisors or experts.[129]

Following the occupation of Iraq in May 2003, the United States and the United Kingdom formed the Coalition Provisional Authority (CPA), a mechanism to exercise authority in Iraq in the absence of a successor government until an internationally recognized representative government was established. The Council subsequently confirmed the creation of the CPA and recognized the obligations of the United States and the United Kingdom as occupying powers under applicable international law.[130] In order to exercise authority

---

[124] On 21 March 2003, a coalition of States, led by the United States, commenced military strikes against Iraq which led ultimately to the fall of the Hussein Government in late April.

[125] On 1 May 2003, the United States announced that major military operations had ended.

[126] The crimes forming the material or subject matter jurisdiction of the IHT are defined in Articles 11 to 14 of the IHT Statute, and are a mixture of crimes under international law and crimes under domestic law.

[127] There are several legal sources that form the applicable law of the IHT. First, there are the provisions of the IHT Statute itself, and the elements of crime and rules of procedure and evidence made pursuant to them. Secondly, there are general principles of criminal law. Depending on the date of commission of the crime, various provisions of Iraqi criminal law may also apply. The 1971 Iraqi Criminal Procedure Law apparently also applies to all crimes, regardless of the time of commission. The IHT Statute and the RPE have priority over national sources of criminal law.

[128] Article 28 of the IHT Statute.

[129] The President must appoint non-Iraqi nationals to act in an advisory capacity or as observers to the Chambers and may request assistance from the international community, including the UN, in appointing non-Iraqi exerts: Article 6(b), IHT Statute. Similarly, international advisors have been appointed to the Investigative Judges (Articles 7(n) and (o), IHT Statute) and to assist the prosecutors (Articles 8(j) and (k), IHT Statute).

[130] SC Resolution No. 1483, 22 May 2003, preambular, paragraph 13. The United States and United Kingdom notified the Council of the establishment of the CPA on 8 May 2003: letter

in Iraq, the CPA promulgated Regulation Number 1,[131] which provided that the CPA shall exercise the powers of government during a transitional administration period, and that all legislative, executive and judicial authority necessary to achieve its objectives is vested in the CPA, to be exercised by the CPA Administrator. This exercise of authority was expressly stated to be under Council resolutions, including Resolution 1483, and the laws and usages of war. To meet the request for the establishment of an interim Iraqi administration, the CPA appointed 25 Iraqis to the Governing Council of Iraq (IGC).[132] Although it was recognized as 'the principal body of the Iraqi interim administration',[133] in practice, the IGC exercised virtually no real authority in Iraq, with the CPA retaining overall authority.[134]

The legal status of the IHT is connected to the status and powers of the CPA as the occupying power and the powers of the IGC. On 10 December 2003, the CPA issued an Order authorising the IGA to establish to establish an Iraqi Special Tribunal[135] to try Iraqi nationals or residents accused of genocide, crimes against humanity, war crimes and violations of certain Iraqi laws.[136] The Order annexed the IHT Statute. Although the order noted that the provisions of the statute had been 'discussed extensively' with the IGC,[137] it has been asserted that the latter had no significant role in drafting the IHT Statute, this having been already drafted under international guidance prior to the promulgation of the Order. The delegation of authority to the IGC was subject to certain terms and conditions,[138] and the CPA Administrator reserved the right to amend

---

from the Permanent Representatives of the United Kingdom of Great Britain and Northern Ireland and the United States of America to the United Nations to the President of the Security Council, 8 May 2003, S/2003/538.

[131] CPA/REG/16 May 2003/01.

[132] CPA/REG/13 July 2002/06. The creation of the IGC was welcomed by the Security Council as 'an important step towards the formation by the people of Iraq of an internationally recognized, representative government': SC Resolution No. 1500, paragraph 1.

[133] CPA/REG/13 July 2003/06, section 1.

[134] Both Resolutions 1500 and 1511 refer to the IGC as being the 'principal body of the Iraqi interim administration', yet there is no allocation of specific powers or authority to the IGC. SC Resolution No. 1511 does call upon the CPA to 'return governing responsibilities and authorities to the people of Iraq as soon as practicable': paragraph 6.

[135] The name was subsequently changed to 'Iraqi High Tribunal'.

[136] CPA Order 48: Delegation of Authority Regarding an Iraqi Special Tribunal, CPA/ORD/10 December 2003/48.

[137] Section 1(1) of the Order.

[138] The IGC was required to promulgate the elements of crimes for the international law crimes which were consistent with applicable international law; it was required to ensure that the IHT met basic international standards of justice; prior to transition, CPA promulgations were to prevail over acts of the IGC or orders of the IHT; and non-Iraqis could be appointed as judges. See Section 2 of the Order.

that Statute – or any elements of crime or rules of procedure developed for the IHT – where required in the interest of security.[139] While the IHT was established notionally by the IGC, the authority to do so flowed from the CPA. The fact that the CPA delegated power to the IGC to enable the creation of the Tribunal suggests that the IGC did not establish the IHT as the representative body of a sovereign State, but as a body operating as a 'puppet' of the occupying powers. In this sense, the IHT is a body established by the CPA, on behalf of the occupying powers while the sovereignty of Iraq was suspended during the period of occupation.

The authority of an occupying Power to establish criminal tribunals is limited by the fourth Geneva Convention,[140] which presumes that the legal system of the occupied territory should continue.[141] Existing penal laws are to remain in force, other than where they constitute a threat to security or an obstacle to the operation of the convention. The occupying power may introduce penal provisions only where essential to fulfil its obligations under the convention, to maintain orderly government and to ensure its own security.[142] Where it has done so, the occupying powers may utilise its own military courts to enforce its own penal provisions,[143] provided those courts comply with specified procedural safeguards.[144] Such courts are intended to be of a transitional nature. While the IHT has jurisdiction in relation to offences committed during the armed conflict, its temporal jurisdiction predates the armed conflict, and permits it to try offences committed from 17 July 1968.[145] It is difficult to see how the creation of the IHT was essential for public order and security. It is therefore questionable whether the establishment of the IHT as a 'special tribunal' is within the scope of international humanitarian law.[146]

---

[139] Article 1(6) of the CPA Order 48.

[140] Geneva Convention Relative to the Protection of Civilian Persons in Time of War, 12 August 1949, 75 *UNTS* (1950) 287–417.

[141] Article 64.

[142] Article 64(2).

[143] Article 66.

[144] Article 67.

[145] Article 1, IHT Statute.

[146] Commentators have suggested that the CPA attempted to bypass the laws of occupation through establishing the IGC, a supposedly national body, but one that comprised members selected by the occupying power, did not possess any real powers of a sovereign State and lacked any democratic mandate in the absence of national elections: see Bantekas, 'The Iraqi Special Tribunal for Crimes Against Humanity', 54 (2004) *ICLQ* 237. It could be argued that the authority to establish a tribunal to examine offences committed by the previous regime was based on the text of SC Resolution No. 1483, where the Council had affirmed the need for accountability for crimes and atrocities committed by the previous regime (paragraph 11 of the preamble). Alternatively, it could also be argued that the Council did more than merely

Assuming, for present purposes, that the IHT was lawfully established by the occupying powers, this would suggest that its legal basis lies in domestic law, as the occupying power acts in place of the sovereign authorities in the occupied territory during the period of occupation. In establishing the IHT, the occupying powers were acting as a domestic actor and accordingly the former is a domestic institution, with its authority based in national, and not international, law. It should therefore have the same status as a national court when assessing issues of immunity and amnesty. This conclusion is even clearer for the period following the transfer of power from the CPA to local Iraqi authorities on 28 June 2004. As one of its last legislative acts prior to the transition, the CPA provided for the transition of laws, regulations, orders and directives issued by it.[147] It also confirmed the IHT Statute exclusively defined its jurisdiction, notwithstanding the provisions of transitional laws. This order made specific provision for the IHT,[148] deleting both the power of the Administrator to alter the statute or the elements of crime or rules of procedure and evidence developed for the Tribunal,[149] and the power of the Administrator to rescind the Order establishing it.[150] From the date of transition, the IHT was evidently a national institution, albeit operating with significant international assistance.

VII. THE SPECIAL TRIBUNAL FOR LEBANON

The STL is to investigate, prosecute and try individuals found responsible for a single event, the assassination of former Lebanese Prime Minister Hariri on 14 February 2005.[151] It is thus the first internationalized – or international – tribunal created with specific jurisdiction for terrorist offences. It will build upon the efforts of the International Independent Investigative Commission (IIIC), established by the Council in 2005 to investigate responsibility for the

---

recognise the factual situation in Iraq, and instead endorsed the status of occupation and the authority of the occupying powers. Arguably, this 'endorsement' could have provided a separate and distinct legal basis for the acts of the occupying powers. However, this appears to be a stretch of the wording of Resolution 1483.

[147] CPA/ORD/28 June 2004/100.

[148] Section 3(19).

[149] This right had been reserved in Section 1(6) of Order 48, which was deleted by Order 100.

[150] This right was set out in Section 3 of Order 48, which was partly deleted by Order 100.

[151] The LST Statute provides for it to have jurisdiction for connected attacks of a similar gravity occurring in Lebanon between 1 October 2004 and 12 December 2005, and possibly also in relation to later attacks with the consent of both the Parties and the Council: Article 1. The Secretary-General's report annexed a list of 14 other attacks, identified by the IIIC, which would satisfy the connection requirement.

incident.[152] The STL resulted from a request from the Lebanese Government for assistance in determining the nature and scope of the international assistance needed to try those responsible.[153] The preferred option was for a mixed tribunal to be established by an agreement between the UN and the Government of Lebanon,[154] and the Council requested the Secretary-General to 'negotiate an agreement with the Government of Lebanon aimed at establishing a tribunal of international character based on the highest international standards of criminal justice'.[155] The Secretary-General submitted his report on the establishment of the tribunal to the Council on 15 November 2006.[156] The Council subsequently endorsed the report and invited the Secretary-General to proceed, in cooperation with the Government of Lebanon, with the final steps for the conclusion of the agreement.[157] Attached to the report was a draft agreement (the STL Agreement) and the proposed statute. Although both parties signed the STL Agreement on 6 February 2007,[158] its terms provided that it would not enter into force until the Lebanese authorities had taken the necessary steps for it to be approved and ratified.[159]

The STL Agreement was approved by the Lebanese cabinet. However, an internal political disagreement essentially precluded ratification.[160] Diplomatic efforts were unable to resolve the deadlock,[161] and the Lebanese Prime Minister requested the Council to establish the tribunal unilaterally.[162] On 30 May 2007, the Council adopted Resolution 1757, recalling the provisions of the STL Agreement and determining that the terrorist act – the assassination of Hariri – continued to constitute a threat to international peace and security.[163] Acting

---

[152] SC Resolution No. 1595, 7 April 2005.

[153] Letter of 13 December 2005, S/2005/783.

[154] Report of the Secretary-General pursuant to paragraph 6 of SC Resolution No. 1644 (2005), 21 March 2006, S/2006/176.

[155] SC Resolution No. 1644, 29 March 2006, paragraph 1.

[156] Report of the Secretary-General on the Establishment of a Special Tribunal for Lebanon, 15 November 2006, S/2006/893.

[157] Letter from the President of the Security Council addressed to the Secretary-General, 24 November 2006, S/2006/911.

[158] UN Press Release, *Hariri Murder Tribunal Awaits Approval after UN and Lebanon Sign Deal*, 6 February 2007.

[159] Article 19 of the Agreement.

[160] The Prime Minister stated that the opposition-aligned Parliament Speaker had refused to convene a parliamentary session to ratify the statute of the LST and the agreement.

[161] Under-Secretary-General for Legal Affairs, Nicolas Michel, travelled to Lebanon in an unsuccessful to attempt to resolve the impasse: *UN News*, 'No Progress in Lebanon over Hariri Tribunal Ratification – UN Legal Chief', 2 May 2007.

[162] See S/2007/281. See also the letter from the President of Lebanon, criticizing the request from the Prime Minister: S/2007/286.

[163] SC Resolution No. 1757.

under Chapter VII, the Council decided that the STL Agreement would enter into force on 10 June 2007, unless the Government of Lebanon confirmed that it had ratified the STL Agreement prior to that date.[164] This did not occur, and on 11 June 2007, the Secretary-General announced that the UN had begun steps formally to establish the STL.[165]

If established as originally envisaged, the STL would have had a similar legal basis to that of the SCSL, that is, a treaty-based court not established pursuant to the Council's Chapter VII powers. As such, the STL Agreement would only be binding on Lebanon, and would not create obligations for non-party States. Thus there would be no obligation on States other than Lebanon to cooperate with the STL.[166] The wording of Resolution 1757 suggests that the STL Agreement still forms the legal basis of the tribunal, albeit that the entry into force of the STL Agreement was compelled by a binding decision of the Council under Chapter VII.[167] It certainly does not suggest that it was the Council itself that has established the STL.[168] Indeed, had the Government of Lebanon provided notification that all necessary domestic steps had been taken, the STL Agreement would have formed the basis of the tribunal regardless of Resolution 1757. The STL is to function in accordance with the terms of the STL Agreement, albeit subject to some variations imposed by SCR 1757. Moreover, certain Council members indicated that the use of Chapter VII 'carries no other connotation'.[169]

However, it must be concluded that, in spite of the wording of Resolution 1757, the legal basis for the STL is not the STL Agreement, but Resolution 1757 itself, which is in turn based on the binding powers of the Council pursuant to Chapter VII. In the absence of Lebanese notification, Resolution 1757 deemed the STL Agreement to have entered into force on 10 June 2007, thus overriding the condition precedent for the STL Agreement to have entered into force. The

---

[164] Operative paragraph 1(a), ibid.

[165] *UN News*, 'UN Takes Steps for the Establishment of Special Tribunal for Lebanon', 11 June 2007. For an outline of the steps taken, see the Report of the Secretary-General submitted Pursuant to Security Council Resolution 1757 (2007) of 30 May 2007, 4 September 2007, S/2007/525.

[166] Lebanon is subject to a specific obligation to cooperate with the Special Tribunal: Article 15 of the Agreement.

[167] Operative paragraph 1 of the resolution provides that the provisions of the Agreement, together with the proposed statute, would enter into force on 10 June 2007.

[168] By way of contrast, the language of SC Resolution No. 827 clearly indicated that it was the Council's resolution that established the ICTY: see operative paragraph 2, which states, *inter alia*, that the Council 'decides hereby to establish ...'. See also similar wording in operative paragraph 1 of SC Resolution No. 955 of 1994 regarding the establishment of the ICTR.

[169] UK explanation of vote: S/PV.5685. Peru emphasised that the Resolution should not be considered a precedent: see explanation of vote: ibid.

Council has, by resolution, brought into force a treaty between the UN and the Government of Lebanon, unilaterally imposing obligations to which Lebanon has not consented to be bound[170] and bypassing domestic law requirements. In order to impose a treaty obligation and to override the requirement for State consent, the Council is required to act under Chapter VII. Thus the true legal basis of the STL must lie in Chapter VII, and the STL is thus more similar to the international *ad hoc* tribunals than the SCSL.

While it is not suggested here that there is anything that would preclude the Council from establishing, in the absence of consent, a tribunal of mixed composition under Article 41,[171] what is questioned is the use of a 'treaty-based' approach to do so.[172] Those States supporting the resolution justified the imposition of the STL Agreement on the need for justice for the terrorist act, the implications of the tribunal for the peace process in Lebanon and the fact that all available political and diplomatic means had been exhausted.[173] However, the approach adopted is controversial for several reasons. First, it is not clear whether this is a legitimate exercise of the Council's Chapter VII powers. While the Council has, on occasion, applied the provisions of a multilateral treaty to a State, it has never purported to do so by way of treaty law and has instead relied upon the provisions forming part of customary international law or by incorporating the relevant provisions of a treaty into a resolution.[174] It

[170] The Lebanese Prime Minister's request to the Council to take unilateral action was controversial. His authority to do so, and therefore to provide 'consent' on behalf of Lebanon, has been a matter of dispute within Lebanon.

[171] It is questionable whether such a step would be successful on a practical level. Internationalized tribunals rely upon the cooperation of the territorial State even more so than the international tribunals, for example, the territorial State is involved in the selection and appointment of judges and personnel. If an internationalized tribunal is imposed, it is probable that there will be a lack of political will to ensure adequate cooperation with the tribunal. It also reduces the likelihood that the tribunal will contribute to reconciliation with the territorial State, as there is less local 'ownership' of the process. Of course, these concerns apply irrespective of the manner in which the tribunal has been imposed.

[172] This would also depend on the threshold requirement of a threat to international peace and security being satisfied. Note, however, the suggestion by the Russian Federation that the Council may only use its Chapter VII powers to establish a tribunal with jurisdiction for genocide, crimes against humanity and war crimes, and not for terrorism: Russian Federation explanation of vote, *supra* (note 169).

[173] SC Resolution No. 1757 was passed with ten affirmative votes (UK, US, France, Slovakia, Belgium, Italy, Peru, Panama, Ghana and Congo) and five abstentions (Russian Federation, China, South Africa, Indonesia and Qatar).

[174] For example, the Council has indicated that certain provisions of international humanitarian law apply to an armed conflict regardless of whether the States concerned are party to the relevant agreements. See Cryer, 'The Security Council and International Humanitarian Law', in Breau and Jachec-Neale (eds.), *Testing the Boundaries of International Humanitarian Law*, London, 2006, p. 245.

has not unilaterally imposed obligations concerning the establishment of a legal institution. Second, such action appears to be inconsistent with the fundamental international law principle of State consent to be bound by treaty obligations, as reflected in the Vienna Convention on the Law of Treaties. The Russian Federation, identifying 'legal shortcomings' in the resolution, noted that a treaty cannot enter into force based on the decision of only one party.[175] While it is possible that Article 103 of the UN Charter would override obligations under a specific treaty, it is doubtful whether that Article would permit the Council to override such a fundamental general principle of international law. Even accepting that it could, it is certainly questionable as to whether such a step is desirable in terms of the long term stability of international law. Third, as suggested by several members of the Council,[176] the resolution could be considered an unacceptable interference in the domestic affairs of a State, which potentially destabilised further the political situation in Lebanon and undermined the Council's own calls for respect for the territorial sovereignty and political independence of Lebanon.

Resolving the uncertainty as to whether the STL is a treaty-based court or a Chapter VII tribunal will be vital for the operation of the STL. This is particularly so given the evidence of the involvement of the intelligence and security forces of both Lebanon and Syria,[177] the likelihood that defendants, evidence and witnesses will be located outside Lebanese territory and Syria's indication that it does not intend to cooperate with the STL.[178] It also means that the STL represents another category of internationalized tribunals: tribunals of mixed composition established directly by the Council acting under Chapter VII. When faced with issues concerning immunity, it is provisionally submitted that such courts would fall within the category of certain international criminal courts in the *Arrest Warrant* case and would be able to override immunity.

---

[175] Russian Federation explanation of vote: *supra* (note 169).

[176] See explanations of vote by Qatar, Indonesia, South Africa, China and Russian Federation: S/PV.5685.

[177] The initial report of the IIIC concluded that there was evidence of Syrian involvement.

[178] Syria has denied any involvement in the assassination. The Syrian President has stated that Syria will not surrender any Syrian nationals to the STL, and will limit its cooperation: see *Jurist*, 'Syrian President Limits Cooperation with UN Hariri Tribunal', 10 May 2007; and see Ladki, 'Syria May Trouble Lebanon after UN vote: Hariri', *Washington Post*, 31 May 2007.

VIII. CONCLUSION

This paper has assessed the legal basis of six existing (or previously existing) internationalized tribunals and one proposed tribunal in order to determine whether a framework for categorising such tribunals exists. Using the criterion of legal basis, three sub-species of such tribunals may be identified. The first category is a group of mainly national courts, with varying degrees and forms of international involvement in their establishment and operation. Such assistance may be provided under the auspices of the UN, or by international organisations, associations of States, or single States. This category would include the SPSC, the Regulation 64 panels, the WCC, the ECCC and the IHT. These courts should be considered as primarily national institutions, particularly for issues of amnesties and immunities. The second category comprises such courts as are established by a treaty, usually, but not necessarily, between the UN and the government of the territorial State. Such courts tend to operate outside the 'ordinary' domestic system and outside the United Nations system. The only current example of this model is the SCSL. Courts falling within this category are international in nature, although their establishment by treaty is important when determining whether immunity applies to State officials of third States. The third category includes internationalized tribunals established by the Council using its coercive powers under Chapter VII. As discussed above, the STL is the first, and so far only, example of this type of tribunal. All tribunals established by the Council using its coercive powers should be considered truly international when issues of immunity are raised.

Chapter Nineteen

The Road to Kandahar: British Military Interventions and International Law

Nigel D. White[*]

I. Introduction

The current manifestation of international intervention in Afghanistan, the NATO-led International Security Assistance Force (ISAF), is being undertaken under the authority of the United Nations Security Council. Britain as a member of the UN and NATO has since February 2006 committed a significant number of troops to ISAF,[1] and the British force has been engaged in heavy fighting with the Taliban. Though militarily extremely problematic, the international legal basis of the operation seems straightforward since the UN Charter recognises Security Council authority as one of the exceptions to the prohibition on the use of force, along with action taken in self-defence in response to an armed attack. However, Security Council authority tends to obscure the deeper justifications and arguments of politics, of law and of justice behind each State's decision to contribute to such a dangerous operation. In tracing the history of the *jus ad bellum* and Britain's attitude towards it, this essay seeks to give a more informed account of the arguments of law and justice behind the British military contribution to the current fight against the Taliban in Afghanistan.

---

[*] Professor of International Law, University of Nottingham.
[1] In February 2006, the initial deployment was 3,400 troops. By 2007, the number of British troops in the south of Afghanistan (Helmand and Kandahar) was 4,300. This was increased in February 2007 to 7,700.

K.H. Kaikobad & M. Bohlander (eds.), *International Law and Power: Perspectives on Legal Order and Justice*. Essays in Honour of Colin Warbrick, pp. 485–511.
© 2009 Koninklijke Brill NV. Printed in the Netherlands.

II. The Just War

It will be shown that the war in Afghanistan is portrayed as a just war, not simply because it is lawful but because it is morally justified. Historically, European medieval monarchs invoked various justifications for going to war, from defence of the realm to a just war. As regards interventions outside Europe, mention ought to be made of the crusades of Richard I in the Holy Land in the twelfth century. Richard was so often fighting in the Middle East doing 'God's work' that he spent less than one year out of his nine and a half year reign in England.[2]

The 'Just War' doctrine predated Richard the Lionheart, with an elaborate, but basically procedural doctrine being found in the Roman period. According to the Roman approach, a just war was commenced in accordance with the law by approval of the college of *fetiales*, 'the view of the majority of writers being that the *fetiales* were not concerned with the intrinsic justice of the war but only with the correct observance of formalities'.[3] In the fourth century St. Augustine incorporated the just war doctrine into Christianity, giving a number of just causes of war including avenging injuries, but moreover war was just if it were one which 'God himself ordains'.[4]

Whilst Augustine in the fourth century, and much later, St. Thomas Aquinas in the thirteenth century wrote in terms of war being just only if the other party was at fault, and that the attacking sovereign intended the 'advancement of good, or the avoidance of evil',[5] the principles appeared too broad to offer any precise rules as to permissible uses of force. Indeed, they seemed to advance the appalling religious wars that regularly occurred in the medieval period, culminating in the Thirty Years War that was ended by the Peace of Westphalia of 1648.

III. Westphalian Order

The period following the Peace of Westphalia marked the emergence of modern nation States in Europe, each with 'internal' sovereignty over their own territories, and each being free 'externally' to deal with sovereign powers of other States.[6] Thus international law moved away from being dominated by the

---

[2] Schama, *A History of Britain: At the Edge of the World*, London, 2000, p. 154 and p. 157.
[3] Brownlie, *International Law and the Use of Force by States*, Oxford, 1963, p. 4.
[4] Ibid, p. 5.
[5] Ibid, p. 6.
[6] See Warbrick, 'The Principle of Sovereign Equality', in Lowe and Warbrick (eds.), *The United Nations and the Principles of International Law*, London, 1994, p. 204 at pp. 204–206.

justice discourse of the medieval period, towards a more positive international law created by the practice of sovereign European States either by formal treaty or by the formation of customary rules. As regards the freedom to wage war, Machiavelli, writing in the early part of the sixteenth century, seemed to anticipate the philosophy that was to become entrenched for the next four centuries, when he wrote that the sovereign power within a State had the absolute right to wage war whenever it was felt necessary.[7]

However, the just war doctrine did not just quietly disappear, it still competed with the emerging positivist approach. Indeed, the influence of the oft-labelled 'father' of international law, Hugo Grotius writing in the period of warfare leading up to the Peace of Westphalia, was still felt for a long period. Writing in 1625, Grotius compiled a list of just and unjust causes of war, always admitting the exception for honest belief in the justice of war.[8] Other jurists took a more State-based approach such as Gentili who stated that war was permitted in cases of necessity and expediency as well as in self-defence.[9]

The natural law-motivated theories of Aquinas and Grotius largely gave way to the positivist notions of State sovereignty and freedom to contract or otherwise deal with other sovereigns, which eventually took its purest from in a period of 'political absolutism'[10] dominant in international relations until the League of Nations' Covenant in 1919. The Just War did not completely disappear, finding limited support in State practice in arguments of humanitarian intervention. In this period, though, the task of the international lawyer changed. No longer did the jurist have so much direct influence on the development of international law. Jurists tried to capture and analyse State practice, though in so doing, by virtue of their choice and emphasis, they could still influence evolution of international law. The primary sources of international law became treaty and custom, reflecting the law's consensual nature,[11] with the writings of jurists still playing a role, but a subsidiary one.[12]

The absolute sovereignty of States removed all but limited procedural constraints on the initiation of war. Brownlie reports that in the period between the Final Act of the Congress of Vienna in 1815 and the creation of the League of Nations in 1919 State practice reflected an almost unlimited right for States

---

[7]   *The Prince*, chapter 3; (first published in 153–32; Penguin edition of 2004).

[8]   *De jure belli ac pacis libri tres*: as reproduced in *The Classics of International Law No. 3*; (translation by F.W. Kelsey), Oxford, 1925, p. 565.

[9]   *De jure belli libri tres*: as reproduced in *The Classics of International Law No. 16*; (translation by J.C. Rolfe), Oxford, 1925, pp. 17–18.

[10] Wright, *A Study of War* (Second edition), Chicago, 1967, pp. 335–338.

[11] See the *Lotus* case: *PCIJ Reports, Series A*, No. 10 (1927), p. 4.

[12] Article 38 (1) (d) of the Statute of the International Court of Justice, 1945.

to wage war.[13] Britain, being a major colonial power was not averse to using force to pursue its national interests. For example, in the nineteenth and early twentieth centuries Britain intervened militarily in Afghanistan on several occasions from its colony in India, first in 1839–1842 to re-instate a deposed ruler, again in 1879 as part of the 'great game' being played out by the Russian and British empires, and again in 1919 when the newly installed king of Afghanistan declared full independence and sympathy for those seeking independence of India.[14] Military interventions were seen as part and parcel of international relations.

Some limited restrictions on the right to go to war did emerge in the decades before 1914. Peaceful methods of settling the underlying dispute should be tried, a rule that was incorporated into the 1907 Hague Convention for the Pacific Settlement of International Disputes, and later in the Covenant of the League in 1919.[15] The machinery for the pacific settlement of disputes also developed in this period with, for example, the establishment of the Permanent Court of Arbitration in 1899.

Another, more established procedural limitation was that there had to be a declaration of war, at least for a formal 'state of war' to exist. However, this was not a real limitation for full scale armed conflict could still occur without either State being at 'war' with the other in the absence of any formal declarations. States' reasons for not declaring war were mainly internal, since going to war might attract constitutional constraints, and would also require the 'preparation of public opinion'.[16] In order to avoid these constraints, States developed a variety of 'restricted forms of coercion … reprisals, pacific blockade, and intervention to protect nationals and their property in foreign states'.[17]

It will be seen that some of these forms of use of force, or variations on them have been practiced by the UK in more recent times. It is worth outlining the doctrine of reprisals as developed in the nineteenth century, and contrasting it with the doctrine of self-defence. It must be remembered though that at this stage of the development of the *jus ad bellum* these were only two of a number of legitimate justifications for using force.

---

[13] Brownlie (note 3), pp. 22–23.

[14] Heathcote, 'The Army of British India', in Chandler (ed.), *The Oxford History of the British Army*, Oxford, 1994, pp. 374–377.

[15] Brownlie (note 3), pp. 22–23.

[16] Ibid, p. 27.

[17] Ibid, p. 28.

IV. ARMED REPRISALS

In the period prior to the establishment of the League, States developed the practice of armed reprisals usually in the form of bombardments or military expeditions, as well as other forms of gun boat diplomacy, whereby States would seek to punish wrongful acts committed against them by other States. Often these expeditions served to punish States or other entities and also to protect the intervening State's interests.

An example drawn from British history, with some parallels to the Suez Crisis of 1956, was the decision by the government of William Gladstone in 1882 to punish the new nationalist government in Egypt whose anti-European sentiment was threatening the lives and property of European nationals. The arrival of a combined French and British fleet off the port of Alexandria incited the murder of a number of Europeans. The French withdrew but the British fleet bombarded the forts of Alexandria and landed marines to protect the Europeans. With Egypt falling into a state of anarchy the British army intervened to restore order by defeating the nationalist leader and occupying Cairo.[18]

The *Naulilaa* arbitration of 1928 between Germany and Portugal provided a clearer instance of a reprisal, as well as a judicial opinion on the legal content of the doctrine. It involved a German armed reprisal from its colony in South-West Africa (now Namibia) against the Portuguese colony of Angola in 1914. The initial injury to Germany arose out of a border incident which resulted in the death of three German soldiers. The German army responded by launching a military expedition into Angola which resulted in considerable damage and loss of life. These hostilities were not formally part of the First World War since Portugal was, at the time, a neutral power. The arbitral tribunal agreed to by the parties accepted that armed reprisals could be a lawful response to a prior international wrong, but Germany had not satisfied the two conditions attaching to lawful reprisals: first that it should have made a demand for reparation that had not been met; and secondly that the armed response should be proportionate to the original wrong.[19]

V. SELF-DEFENCE

Reprisals were different to action taken in self-defence. The aim of reprisals was punitive not defensive – the aim was not to repel the border attack but to

---

[18] Muir, *British History*, London, 1936, pp. 637–639.
[19] 2 (1928) *UN Reports of International Arbitral Awards* 1012.

punish Portugal for its wrongful act at a time and in a manner of Germany's choosing. In a time of an unlimited right to wage war, there was no need to define self-defence with any great precision, though it was still used as one of a number of justifications for the use of force. Classically, the *Caroline* incident of 1837 is cited as authority for a definition of self-defence in that period.[20] In the incident, the British authorities authorized the burning of a ship while it was in a US port, the ship allegedly being used to further the armed insurrection taking place in Canada at the time.

Both the British and American governments agreed during the course of diplomatic exchanges over the incident that the British would have 'to show a necessity of self-defence, instant, overwhelming, leaving no choice of means and no moment for deliberation', in order to legitimate the action. Often cited as authority for anticipatory self-defence,[21] in other words as allowing a threatened State to strike first in expectation of an imminent attack, the phrase clearly allows for some degree of anticipation but not a great deal, and it may be doubted whether the British action actually met those requirements. Moreover as Brownlie relates 'self-defence was regarded as synonymous with self-preservation or as a particular instance of it', so that it is not possible to draw out a general doctrine of self-defence from this incident, it was simply an attempt to proscribe self-preservation in relation to the particular facts.[22]

vi. Humanitarian Intervention

To this list of justifications for using force, there must be added the development of a nineteenth century version of the just war doctrine, namely the claimed right of humanitarian intervention. Brownlie summarizes the right in the following terms:

> A state which had abused its sovereignty by brutal and excessively cruel treatment of those within its power, whether nationals or not, was regarded as having made itself liable to action by any state which was prepared to intervene.[23]

---

[20] 29 *BFSP* 1137; and 30 *BFSP* 195. See Brownlie, 'Non-Use of Force in Contemporary International Law', in Butler (ed.), *The Non-Use of Force in International Relations*, The Hague, 1989, p. 19; Waldock, 'The Regulation of the Use of Force by Individual States in International Law', 81 (1952) *Hague Recueil des cours* 455; and Bowett, *Self-Defence in International Law*, Manchester, 1958, pp. 188–189.

[21] Jennings, 'The Caroline and McLeod Cases', 32 (1938) *AJIL* 82 at p. 92; Franck, *Recourse to Force: State Action against Threats and Armed Attacks*, Oxford, 2002, p. 97; but see Dinstein, *War, Aggression and Self-Defence* (Fourth edition), Cambridge, 2005, pp. 184–185.

[22] Brownlie (note 3) p. 43.

[23] Ibid, p. 338.

He further states the weakness that has always undermined this and older versions of the just war:

> Operation of the doctrine was open to abuse since only powerful states could undertake police measures of this sort; and when military operations were justified as 'humanitarian intervention', this was only one of several characterizations offered and circumstances frequently indicated the presence of selfish motives.[24]

Within a legal regime that allowed for force, humanitarian intervention was just one of many justifications that could be put forward, but the practice of States reveals very few instances of genuine interventions on humanitarian grounds.[25] Stowell cites the British, French and Russian intervention in the revolt against Turkey by Greek insurgents fighting for independence.[26] In 1821 English and French volunteers, including Lord Byron, who lost his life in the struggle, had gone to help the Greeks in their fight. These fighters and the Greek insurgents were on the brink of total defeat at the hands of an Egyptian fleet and army when a joint British, French and Russian fleet was sent to enforce demands for Greek autonomy. The decisive naval battle at Navarino in 1827 saw the defeat of the Egyptian fleet and the path was cleared to Greek independence in 1829 under the protection of Britain, France and Russia.[27] Though there may have been some humanitarian considerations in this intervention, it seems more in support of the achievement of independence, an early instance of force being used in support of the self-determination of a people. Of course policies such as the weakening of Turkey were, more than likely, the real motivating factors in this British inspired military intervention.

VII. THE INTER-WAR PERIOD

The limited constraints on 'war' and other uses of force identified earlier in this chapter were clearly insufficient to prevent the outbreak of the First World War. The total nature of the 1914–1918 hostilities had profound effects on public and governmental thinking. The British military alone lost over 700,000 men, while over 1.6 million were wounded. The creation of a universal organisation with powers to secure international peace and security was a radical development in international relations. However, the influence of State sovereignty was too

---

[24] Ibid, pp. 338–339.
[25] Ibid, p. 340.
[26] Stowell, *Intervention in International Law*, Washington, 1921, p. 126 and p. 389: cited by Brownlie (note 3), p. 339.
[27] Muir (note 18), p. 528.

strong, both on the constitution of the organisation itself, especially in the unanimity requirement,[28] and ultimately on the willingness of States to join the League and follow its strictures.[29] The United States failed to join the League, and other powerful States were outside the League at crucial times.

The Covenant did oblige members to 'respect and preserve as against external aggression the territorial integrity and existing political independence of all Members of the League',[30] and it did emphasize the need for collective action by declaring that 'any war or threat of war … is hereby declared a matter of concern for the whole League, and the League shall take any action that may be deemed wise and effectual to safeguard the peace of nations'.[31] However, these provisions were outweighed by a series of procedures that effectively allowed war or other uses of force. One provision, for instance, obliged member States to submit their disputes to arbitration or to the Council of the League and not to 'resort to war until three months after the award by the arbitrators or the report by the Council'.[32]

While the League's Covenant and machinery was defective, the lack of a substantive and clear prohibitory norm appeared to have been remedied by the 1928 Treaty for the Renunciation of War as an Instrument of National Policy (also known as the Pact of Paris or Kellogg-Briand Pact), by which State parties condemned 'recourse to war for the solution of international controversies', and renounced war 'as an instrument of national policy'. The treaty then obligated the parties to settle their disputes by peaceful means.[33] Parallels with the norm prohibiting the use of force in the UN Charter will be seen.[34] The Pact of Paris appeared to represent international law on the use of force by 1939 in that most States were parties, including Germany, Japan and Italy, and it was used as the basis for prosecuting crimes against peace at both the Tokyo and Nuremberg trials in which the surviving war leaders of Germany and Japan were tried in the immediate aftermath of the war.[35] The Pact though was weak in that it only addressed 'war' and not 'use of force' more generally, and it lacked clarity on what was meant by 'national policy'.[36] Furthermore, it is important to note that

---

[28] Article 5 (1) of the Covenant of the League of Nations, 1919.

[29] Kennedy, *The Parliament of Man*, Toronto, 2006, p. 13.

[30] Article 10 of the Covenant of the League of Nations, 1919.

[31] Article 11 (1).

[32] Article 12 (1). See also Articles 13, 15 and 16.

[33] Articles 1 and 2.

[34] Articles 2 (3) and 2 (4) of the UN Charter, 1945.

[35] Cryer, *Prosecuting International Crimes: Selectivity and the International Criminal Law Regime*, Cambridge, 2005, pp. 36–48.

[36] See, for example, Verzijl, *International Law in Historical Perspective*, vol. viii: *Inter-State Disputes and Their Settlement*, Leiden, 1976, p. 109.

neither Covenant nor Pact contained any definition of self-defence, though this was clearly recognised as an inherent right of a sovereign State in statements accompanying the 1928 Treaty.[37]

VIII. UN ORDER

In the overview of the development of the *jus ad bellum* given above, a number of justifications for using force have emerged – the just war (including human-itarian intervention), the right of self-defence and the armed reprisal. These lacked great legal clarity especially as the right to wage war and other uses of force became increasingly recognised at least until the League of Nations. With the advent of the UN Charter it appeared that a new world order was brought in whereby threat or use of force by States against other States was prohibited,[38] except in the case of a defined right of individual and collective self-defence in response to an armed attack,[39] or in the case of a Security Council sanctioned military action in response to a threat to the peace, breach of the peace or act of aggression.[40] The scheme looked straightforward and appeared to remove the doctrines of war, just war and armed reprisal, and wider doctrines of self-preservation beyond a defined right of self-defence, from the lexicon of lawful action. In fact the only just wars were those sanctioned under the UN Charter. For example States could legitimately come to the aid of a State-victim of aggression under the right of collective self-defence, and the Security Council could authorise humanitarian intervention to stop genocide within a State if it deemed it to be a threat to the peace. However, there was no mention in the Charter of States or other international actors having the right of humanitarian intervention in another State to stop widespread violation of basic human rights. In fact that sort of unilateral action seemed to be prohibited by the ban on the use of force.

Nevertheless, the Charter rules contained a number of ambiguities, and furthermore, the advent of a treaty containing rules on the use of force did not by itself exclude different customary laws continuing or indeed developing. Article 2(4) prohibits the threat or use of force 'against the territorial integrity or political independence of any state, or in any other manner inconsistent with the purposes of the United Nations'.[41] In the *Corfu Channel Case* examined below

---

[37] Brownlie (note 3), p. 90 and pp. 235–237.
[38] Article 2 (4) of the UN Charter, 1945.
[39] Article 51 of the UN Charter, 1945.
[40] Articles 39, 42 and 53 of the UN Charter, 1945.
[41] For discussion, see Randelzhofer, 'Article 2 (4)' in Simma (ed.), *The Charter of the United Nations A Commentary* (Second edition), Oxford, 2002, pp. 117–125.

Britain made the argument that the phrase 'against the territorial integrity or political independence', permitted limited uses of force not encapsulated in the exceptions contained in the Charter.

Arguments that the final phrase in Article 2 (4), 'in any other manner inconsistent with the purposes of the United Nations' somehow allows for force undertaken in pursuit of the UN's purposes, including the protection of human rights, seems to be stretching the provision beyond recognition.[42] It does illustrate though that the 'just war' doctrine still has its advocates in the modern age, including Britain, despite the fact that as recently as 1984 the UK Foreign and Commonwealth Office stated that the 'best case that can be made in support of humanitarian intervention is that it cannot be said to be unambiguously illegal'.[43]

The British reliance on humanitarian motives in the 1990s in relation to interventions in both Northern Iraq 1991 and Kosovo 1999 represented the development of a harder edged doctrine of humanitarian intervention. In the light of this practice, in 2000 Britain was proposing guidelines on humanitarian intervention to the UN under which the international community should intervene 'when faced with an overwhelming humanitarian catastrophe, which a government has shown it is unwilling or unable to prevent or is actively promoting'. That intervention should be 'proportionate to achieving the humanitarian purpose', should be collective, and 'wherever possible' should have the authority of the Security Council.[44]

The main express exception to the ban on the use of force in the Charter is contained in Article 51 of the Charter which preserves the 'inherent' right of self-defence 'if an armed attack occurs against a Member of the United Nations, until the Security Council has taken measures necessary to maintain international peace and security'.[45]

Self-defence in this provision is limited to responding to an armed attack, which will inevitably cause problems for States wishing to try and deal with threats to them, especially given the devastating potential of (nuclear) missile attack developed during the Cold War, and the growing threat of international terrorism first emerging out of the Middle East Crisis in the mid-1960s. Should States have to wait for an attack to be able to take military force in self-defence? Bearing in mind that the *Caroline* incident of 1837 seemed to allow anticipatory action, the question is whether this is still good law after 1945.

---

[42] Dinstein (note 21), pp. 88–91.
[43] See Planning Staff, Foreign and Commonwealth Office, Foreign Policy Document 148, July 1984 in 'UK Materials on International Law', 57 (1986) *BYIL* 614, at p. 619.
[44] Secretary of State, Mr. Robin Cook, in an address to the American Bar Association meeting in London, 19 July 2000; reprinted in ibid, 71 (2000) *BYIL* 646, at pp. 647-648.
[45] See further, Randelzhofer, 'Article 51', in Simma (note 41), pp. 789–806.

If States want to take military action that is not a response to an armed attack, the Charter does not leave them without any avenues, but they must persuade the Security Council to first of all make a determination under Chapter VII of 'any threat to the peace, breach of the peace, or act of aggression'. While there is an overlap between the concept of armed attack in Article 51 and 'act of aggression' in Article 39, and between 'threat or use of force' in Article 2(4) and 'threat to the peace' and 'breach of the peace' in Article 39, practice has shown that Article 39, especially the term 'threat to the peace', is not confined to breaches or indeed potential breaches of Article 2(4), so that the Council can take action under Chapter VII to deal with threats or acts of violence within countries as well as between countries.[46] While Article 41 permits the Council to take non-forcible measures such as economic sanctions, Article 42 covers the use of military force empowering the Security Council to 'take such action by air, sea, or land forces as may be necessary to maintain or restore international peace and security'.

Members of the UN were meant to contribute troops to UN operations under agreements and under the direction of the UN's Military Staff Committee,[47] but these proved impossible to achieve in the Cold War. Instead, Britain was instrumental in the Korean War in developing a new method of fulfilling Article 42, namely the deployment of coalitions of willing volunteer States (known as Coalitions of the Willing).

IX. THE COLD WAR

The Cold War period saw frequent and flagrant violations of the prohibition on the use of force, with very little enforcement action being taken against transgressors. The executive organ's principal weakness – that of the veto belonging to each of the five permanent members (P5) – meant that it was largely inactive. The right of veto operates without limitation in relation to resolutions proposing enforcement action under Chapter VII of the UN Charter,[48] in relation to resolutions proposing peaceful methods of settling disputes under Chapter VI any parties to a dispute (including any of the permanent members) should abstain from voting.[49] While this principle was respected in the early years as shown below by the UK's abstention on the

---

[46] Frowein and Krisch, 'Article 39' in Simma (note 41), p. 723.
[47] See Articles 43–47 of the UN Charter, 1945.
[48] For an argument that there ought to be limitations, see White, 'The Will and Authority of the Security Council after Iraq', 17 (2004) *Leiden Journal of International Law* 645 at pp. 666–671.
[49] Article 27 (3) of the UN Charter.

Security Council resolution which recommended that the Corfu Channel incident of 1946 be referred to the International Court, its impact was very much reduced during the Cold War period as shown below by the British and French willingness to veto proposed resolutions in the Security Council during the Suez crisis of 1956.

The veto prevented significant enforcement action being taken by the Security Council during the Cold War period. There were limited exceptions such as the US led, UN endorsed response to the North Korean invasion of South Korea in 1950,[50] but most military interventions went unpunished. The reaction to the North Korean invasion by the Security Council was only made possible by the Soviet Union's absence from the chamber, which was rather controversially treated as a case of abstention.[51] The Korean War did involve significant British political and military involvement in the development of Coalitions of the Willing acting under Security Council authority but with command and control delegated to the volunteer States.[52] Such a system is a significant departure from the original Charter scheme, and it adds further discretion into what is already a discretionary system, but it has become established as the method of utilising Chapter VII for military enforcement purposes.[53]

The only other occasion that military force was authorised by the Security Council during the Cold War also involved the British military, in this case the Royal Navy in the Beira Patrol of 1966–1975 stationed off the coast of Mozambique to enforce the oil embargo against Southern Rhodesia.[54] In requesting Security Council authority to use force if necessary to stop the embargo from being breached, the British representative Lord Caradon stated in the Council chamber that Security Council authority was essential if the patrol was to be lawful and that without it the legitimacy of the British action would be severely undermined since 'one of the very purposes of the action we are ... taking against the illegal regime in Southern Rhodesia is to assert the rule of law and the principles of the United Nations Charter'.[55]

In contrast to the clear illegality of its intervention in the Suez Crisis of 1956 (reviewed below), the United Kingdom acted within the bounds of the UN Charter ten years later in undertaking the Beira Patrol. In so doing it helped to develop further the idea that willing States could be authorised to use force under

---

[50] SC Resolution 83, 27 June 1950.
[51] Bailey and Daws, *Procedure of the United Nations Security Council*, Oxford, 1998, p. 257.
[52] See Farrar-Hockley, *The British Part in the Korean War: vol. i: A Distant Obligation*, London (HMSO), 1990, pp. 83–84, pp. 100–102, p. 191 and p. 209.
[53] But see Warbrick, 'The Invasion of Kuwait by Iraq', 40 (1991) *ICLQ* 482 at pp. 487–488.
[54] SC Resolution 217, 20 November 1965; and SC Resolution 221, 9 April 1966.
[55] SC 1276th Meeting, 9 April 1966.

Article 42, in the absence of any earmarked UN forces as originally foreseen in the UN Charter. Despite the high sounding words of Lord Caradon, this did not mark a permanent return to the rule of law in international relations, rather on this occasion the United Kingdom's and Security Council's interests coincided sufficiently for the UK to receive authority. This was not any guarantee that when such authority was not lacking in the future that the UK would not act unilaterally in the face of the UN Charter. Though Suez might have marked the end of Britain's imperial ambitions, the late 1990s would witness a resurgence in Britain's propensity to use force to solve pressing problems.

Southern Rhodesia was deemed to be a threat to the peace by the Security Council by virtue of its denial of self-determination by the white racist regime.[56] During the Cold War, only the Korean War involved the enforcement of the prohibition on the use of force, North Korea having committed an armed aggression against the South. In many other cases, the Council was inherently incapable of enforcing the prohibition on the use of force. This was especially so in the case of superpower interventions in their respective spheres of influence – for instance by the United States in Guatemala (1954), Cuba (1961) the Dominican Republic (1965), Grenada (1983) and Panama (1989), and the Soviet Union in Hungary (1956), Czechoslovakia (1968) and Afghanistan (1979).

The UK too, being a middle ranking power still able to project its military might abroad, was not averse to acting unilaterally outside the authority of the Security Council. In the Falklands War of 1982, it exercised its unilateral right to use force in self-defence in response to the Argentine invasion of the Falklands. In that situation it did not need Security Council authority though it secured a resolution demanding Argentine forces to withdraw.[57] However, in earlier instances of uses of force the British government was not averse to acting unilaterally and not clearly within one of the exceptions contained in the UN Charter.

As early as 1946, with the UN in its infancy, and the Cold War only starting, the Royal Navy was engaged in a modern form of gun boat diplomacy off the coast of Albania in the North Corfu Channel. In response to being shelled by Albanian batteries, a squadron of four warship sailed up the Corfu Channel on 22 October. Their passage was 'intended as a warning to Albania not to flex its muscles in sight of the Royal Navy'.[58] When passing through the northern part of the channel two of the ships were struck by mines with resulting loss of life

---

[56] See further SC Resolution 232, 16 December 1966; SC Resolution 235, 29 May 1968, imposing wider mandatory sanctions on Rhodesia.

[57] SC Resolution 502, 3 April 1982.

[58] Hill, 'The Realities of Medium Power, 1946 to the Present', in Hill (ed.), *The Oxford Illustrated History of the Royal Navy*, Oxford, 1995, p. 381, at p. 383.

and injury to their crews. Three weeks later on 13 November 1946, the North Corfu Channel was swept for mines by British minesweepers and twenty-two moored mines were cut.

With encouragement from the Security Council, both States referred the dispute to the International Court of Justice, in its first contentious case.[59] Thus in the *Corfu Channel* case, the Court found that Albania was responsible for the loss of the two British ships which were lawfully sailing through the Channel on 22 October in the exercise of the right of innocent passage. However, the later minesweeping operation on 13 November had violated the sovereignty of Albania. First of all Britain argued that limited intervention was allowed to secure evidence of wrongdoing (in this case the mines) in the territory or territorial waters of another State. The Court rejected this argument in language that was rather sweeping in regarding 'the alleged right of intervention as the manifestation of a policy of force, such as has, in the past, given rise to most serious abuses and such as cannot, whatever be the defects in international organization, find a place in international law'.[60]

The Court did not mention Article 2(4) but the subliminal message was clear. Forceful interventions, no matter how limited, are not permitted, and it is no excuse to argue that the Security Council has been unable to take effective action to deal with the dispute. A strict approach to the rules prohibiting forceful action was reinforced by the Court's response to the second line of argument put forward by Sir Ian Beckett on behalf of the UK, namely that the action of 13 November 'threatened neither the territorial integrity nor the political independence of Albania. Albania suffered thereby neither territorial loss not any part of its political independence'.[61] The Court again responded in broad condemnatory terms by declaring that 'respect for territorial sovereignty is an essential foundation of international relations', and in order 'to ensure respect for international law ... the Court must declare that the action of the British navy constituted a violation of Albanian sovereignty'.[62]

What the *Corfu Channel Case* of 1949 shows is an early attempt by the British government to test the limits of the rules governing the use of force, in

---

[59] SC Resolution 22, 9 April 1947. The Soviet Union and Poland abstained and the UK did not vote. Chapter VI of the Charter empowers the Council to recommend procedures or methods for the settlement of disputes, including referring the case to the International Court of Justice: see Article 36 (3). Such resolutions are recommendatory only: see *obiter* statement in the *Corfu Channel* case *(Preliminary Objection)*, *ICJ Reports 1947–1948*, p. 15: see the Joint Separate Opinion of Judges Basdevant, Alvarez, Winiarski, Zoričić, De Visscher, A. Badawi Pasha and Krylov, at pp. 31–32.

[60] Corfu Channel case *Merits*, *ICJ Reports 1949*, p. 4, at p. 35.

[61] *ICJ Pleadings*, *Corfu Channel* case, vol. iii, pp. 295–296: cited in Brownlie (note 3), p. 266.

[62] *Supra* (note 60), p. 35.

particular by trying to establish that Article 2(4) does not contain an absolute ban on the threat or use of force, so that certain limited uses of force, not taken in self-defence, may be allowed. The Court's conclusions on the minesweeping 'Operation Retail' of 13 November make clear that Article 2(4) is to be read as protecting the sovereignty of all States from forceful interventions no matter how limited. For a country used to asserting its rights and interests by forcible means, this represented a significant early blow. It did not, however, stop it from using military means to secure its interests when in 1956 it played a leading role in the Suez Crisis.

The Suez Crisis was triggered by the nationalization of the Suez Canal Company in July 1956 by President Nasser of Egypt, who had recently come to power. Britain and France had significant holdings in the Company. As part of a co-ordinated plan by France, Britain and Israel, on 29 October 1956 Israel invaded Egypt in the area of the Suez Canal.[63] A cease-fire resolution proposed by the United States was vetoed by Britain and France in the Security Council.[64] Instead, France and Britain issued an ultimatum to Egypt and Israel demanding that they agree a cease-fire and withdraw their troops from the Suez Canal and allow French and British troops to police the area around the Canal. The ultimatum was not heeded and on 31 October French and British troops landed in the Suez Canal area.

Legal advice to the government, which was not made public at the time, was against military intervention. This was reflected in the Foreign Secretary's memorandum to the Egypt Committee of Cabinet on 20 August which read in part 'however illegal the Egyptian action in purporting to nationalize the Suez Canal Company may be, it is not, in itself as things stand at present, of such a character as would, under international law, afford a justification for armed intervention'.[65] This may explain why, when the intervention was imminent, Eden was reputed to have declared, '[L]awyers are always against our doing anything. For God's sake keep them out of it. This is a political affair.'[66] It was in the House of Lords that a full legal justification was given by the Lord Chancellor, Viscount Kilmuir, during a lengthy debate in the upper house on the British and French military action in Suez. He stated that force may only

---

[63] See generally Scott, 'Commentary on Suez: Forty Years on', 1 (1996) *Journal of Armed Conflict Law* 205.

[64] UN Doc. S/3710, 1956.

[65] CAB 134/1217, 136–137 in Marston, 'Armed Intervention in the 1956 Suez Canal Crisis: Legal Advice Tendered to the British Government', 37 (1988) *ICLQ* 773 at p. 782.

[66] On 16 October 1956 at a small meeting on ministers: see Nutting, *No End of a Lesson: The Story of Suez*, London, 1967, p. 95.

be used lawfully either with the express authority of the Security Council, or in self-defence – 'but self-defence includes a situation in which the lives of a State's national's abroad are threatened and it is necessary to intervene on that territory for their protection'. He further stretched this principle to include the protection of 'valuable and internationally important foreign property' which was in danger of 'irreparable injury'.[67]

Though there has been a significant amount of State practice before and after 1945 to support limited interventions to evacuate or rescue nationals whose lives are in serious danger in a foreign State,[68] the Suez action was designed to secure wider aims – the Canal itself and to undermine the Egyptian government. Contrary to the Lord Chancellor's opinion, the Law Officers – the Attorney General (Sir Reginald Manningham-Buller), the Solicitor General (Sir Harry Hylton-Foster) – had stated in a letter to Lord Kilmuir on 12 October that it was 'difficult if not impossible to establish that such use of force by us came within the doctrine of self-defence'. The failure of the Security Council to act did not somehow free the UK from legal obligation since the 'doctrine of self-help was condemned by the International Court in the Corfu case'.[69] Neither the Law Officers nor the Foreign Office Legal Advisers (Sir Gerald Fitzmaurice and Francis Vallat) knew about the British/French and Israeli plan, and were not consulted about the legality of the British element of that plan – Operation Musketeer. The exchange of views between these advisors and the government clearly showed that the decision was taken on grounds of policy not of law, and that none of the advisors would have supported the Lord Chancellor's view that the intervention was legal. They also criticised the Cabinet and Prime Minister for taking the action solely on the advice of the Lord Chancellor.[70]

The lack of convincing legal argument seems to have undermined support in Parliament and in the country. Kyle also considers the level of international protests to be significant, especially by the United States which viewed Suez as an unnecessary distraction from the concerns of the Cold War, in particular the Soviet repression of Hungary.[71] For the United States, the confrontations of the Cold War were far more important than the dwindling imperial ambitions of Britain and France. 'So ended Britain's last serious effort to play the Great

---

[67] HL Deb., 5th Ser., vol. 199, Cols., 1349–1350, 1 November 1956. See full argument in memorandum to the Cabinet of 29 Oct. 1956, PREM 11/1129, in Marston (note 65), p. 800.

[68] See generally Ronzitti, *Rescuing Nationals Abroad through Military Coercion and Intervention on the Grounds of Humanity*, Dordrecht, 1985.

[69] LCO 2/5760, in Marston (note 65), p. 792.

[70] Marston (note 65), pp. 803–809.

[71] Kyle, 'Britain's Slow March to Suez', in Tal (ed.), *The 1956 War: Collusion and Rivalry in the Middle East*, London, 2001, p. 95, at p. 111.

Power in the Middle East and its last effort to carry out on the ground a foreign policy in the face of US dissent'.[72]

The inability of the government to carry public opinion and world opinion led to the ignominious withdrawal of British and French troops and their replacement by the first UN peacekeeping force UNEF I authorised not by the Security Council, but by the General Assembly,[73] due to the fact that the matter had been passed from the Security Council to the Assembly under the Uniting for Peace Resolution following the British and French vetoes of early cease-fire proposals.[74]

Despite superpower and middle power interventions during the Cold War, the rule prohibiting the use of force seemed to survive intact because these interventions were still recognised as violations, and not as permissible uses of force, both by the rest of the international community, and sometimes by the violators themselves, by their attempts to argue that their actions came within the exceptions to the prohibition, or that there were in fact further exceptions to the ban on the use of force other than those allowed in the Charter.[75] For instance the Soviet Union argued that its intervention in Afghanistan in 1979 was justifiable collective defence of the country at the request of the Afghan government. The falsity of this contention was not lost on the international community when it regularly condemned the Soviet Union for its invasion at each UN session until the Soviets withdrew in 1989.[76]

The reality of the Cold War period when power often prevailed over law was shown by the comment by Dean Acheson in relation to the situating of Soviet made missiles in Cuba leading to the Cuban missile crisis of 1962:

> The power, position and prestige of the United States ha[s] been challenged by another state: and law does not deal with such questions of ultimate power – power that comes close to the sources of sovereignty.[77]

For powerful States, power and prestige were more important on occasions than any notion of the rule of law. Sir Anthony Eden's statements in the Suez crisis of

---

[72] Ibid, p. 115.

[73] GA Resolution 1001, 5 November 1956. This resolution was adopted by 57 votes to 0, with 19 abstentions (including France and Britain).

[74] UN Doc. S/3710, 1956 (US); and UN Doc. S/3713/Rev 1, 1956 (USSR).

[75] See statement of the International Court in *Case Concerning Military and Paramilitary Activities in and Against Nicaragua, Merits, ICJ Reports 1986*, p. 14 at p. 98. See also Warbrick, 'The Principle of Sovereign Equality', in Lowe and Warbrick (eds.), *The United Nations and the Principles of International Law Essays in Memory of Michael Akehurst*, London, 1994, p. 204, at p. 209.

[76] Starting with GA Resolution ES-6/2, 14 January 1980.

[77] Acheson, ' 'Remarks by the Honourable Dean Acheson' [Response to Panel]: The Cuban Quarantine – Implications for the Future', 14 (1963) *ASIL Proceedings* 14–15.

1956 show that Britain, a middle ranking military power, also saw fit on occasions to ride roughshod over the rules on the use of force. Overall though, the rule prohibiting the use of force certainly seemed to receive very robust support in 1990–1991, at the beginning of the post-Cold War period, when the aggression committed by Iraq against Kuwait was repulsed by a Coalition of States acting under a UN mandate.[78] The 'relative indelibility' of the rules on the use of force in the Charter reflects their peremptory status in international law – they are widely viewed as fundamental rules – *jus cogens* – from which no derogation is allowed and which are very difficult to modify.[79] Nevertheless, the post-Cold War period has witnessed perhaps an even more concerted effort to change the rules governing the use of force. The Cold War was largely characterised by powerful States ignoring the rules when it suited their interests, the post-Cold War period has seen powerful States trying to change the rules in their favour.

x. Post-Cold War, Post-9/11

Although the rules governing the use of force survived the intense power pressures of the Cold War, it might be questioned whether the post-Cold War period, in combination with the post-9/11 era, have led to the re-emergence of older doctrines of just war, reprisals – uses of force not recognised by the UN Charter – as well as a wider right of self-defence than recognised by Article 51.

With the defeat of Iraq in 1991, the Iraqi army was turned upon the Kurds and the Shias within Iraq who had revolted against Saddam Hussein. Unable to secure any clear authority to intervene from the Security Council,[80] Western States intervened by sending troops to northern Iraq to protect the Kurds, and then by imposing no-fly zones in the north and in the south to protect the Marsh Arabs. In defending the second of these no-fly zones in the absence of an express Security Council mandate the British Foreign Secretary Douglas Hurd stated that 'not every action that a British Government … takes has to be underwritten by a specific provision in a UN resolution provided that we comply with international law', and 'international law recognises extreme humanitarian need'.[81] This argument was developed in 1999 by the UK when

---

[78] SC Resolution 678, 29 November 1990. See generally Warbrick (note 53), and ibid, 'The Invasion of Kuwait by Iraq: Part II', 40 (1991) *ICLQ* 965.
[79] Brownlie, *Principles of Public International Law* (Sixth edition), Oxford, 2003, pp. 488–489.
[80] SC Resolution 688, 5 April 1991.
[81] For this, see Weller (ed.), *Iraq and Kuwait: The Hostilities and Their Aftermath*, Cambridge, 1993, pp. 723–724. See further Warbrick, 'The United Kingdom and the United Nations', 42 (1993) *ICLQ* 938 at pp. 944–945.

it contributed to the NATO air campaign directed at stopping the crimes being committed by Serb forces against the Albanian majority in the Serbian province of Kosovo in defiance of Security Council resolutions.[82] On the day after the NATO bombing campaign started, the Foreign Secretary, Robin Cook, stated in the House of Commons that 'we are acting on the legal principle that the action is justified to halt a humanitarian catastrophe'.[83]

Such post-Cold War, arguably post-modern, interventions which disregard the formerly strong concept of State sovereignty as evidenced in the judgment in the *Corfu Channel* case, cause problems for the rules on the use of force since they appear to be a violation of them yet in their pure 'just' form they seem necessary to prevent gross violations of human rights. In essence a fundamental norm is being breached in order to uphold other fundamental norms. Because of the problem of abuse of the just war concept in the past, and the lack of support for the doctrine of humanitarian intervention in the wider international community,[84] the conclusions on these interventions seemed to be that though they were illegal they still had moral legitimacy. This was shown clearly in the report on Kosovo of the Foreign Affairs Select Committee of 7 June 2000, which contradicts the Government's claim of legality when it stated, '[A]t the very least, the doctrine of humanitarian intervention has a tenuous basis in current customary international law, and this renders the NATO action legally questionable', but then supports the strong moral justifications for the intervention put forward by the Government by concluding 'NATO's military action, if of dubious legality in the current state of international law, was justified on moral grounds.'[85]

In contrast to older versions of the just war doctrine, the modern concept of the just war exemplified by the Kosovo campaign was conducted against the background of relatively clear rules governing the use of force, giving rise to the apparent paradox of an illegal but just war. Legal rules provide clarity and certainty but because of their general nature and application they cannot always guarantee justice. Until a clear and workable exception to the ban on the use of force allowing for collective humanitarian intervention outside the authority of the United Nations can be agreed, the way forward is to try to improve the

---

[82]   SC Resolution 1199, 28 September 1998; and SC Resolution 1203, 24 October 1999.

[83]   HC Deb., vol. 328, Col. 541, 25 March 1999.

[84]   See the resolution of 133 non-industrialised States (meeting as the G77) condemning unilateral humanitarian intervention as illegal under international law: see Declaration of the Group of 77, South Summit, Havana, Cuba, 10–14 April 2000, cited in Byers, 'The Shifting Foundations of International Law: A Decade of Forceful Measures against Iraq', 13 (2002) *EJIL* 21 at p. 28.

[85]   HC Foreign Affairs Select Committee, Fourth Report, 7 June 2000, paragraphs 124–144.

efficacy of the Security Council as well as recognise the significant subsidiary responsibility of the General Assembly.[86]

Somewhat differently, the interventions in Afghanistan in 2001 and Iraq in 2003 were attempts to expand the two recognised Charter exceptions to the ban on the use of force – the exercise of the right of self-defence (re Afghanistan) and military action taken under the authority of the Security Council (re Iraq). While the underlying concerns that are driving these types of intervention are the need to combat global terrorism and the spread of WMD, made clear in the President's National Security Strategy of 2002,[87] the 'just war' arguments underpinning the Kosovo campaign were also found in relation to the response of the US and its allies to 9/11, including the campaign in Afghanistan. This is something returned to below.

In the case of Iraq in 2003, Iraq's failure to fulfil the disarmament agenda set by the Security Council in 1991,[88] frustrated the US and the UK to the extent that they intervened ostensibly on the basis of this failure. They had no real UN authority to use force – the ingenious combination of parts of Security Council resolutions[89] to construct a legal argument by the UK is ultimately unconvincing since Security Council practice on this matter is clear – there must be a clear authorisation from the Security Council to use force and there was nothing of the kind. The United Kingdom's argument is also disingenuous in that it disregards the clear statements of the other members of the Security Council that Resolution 1441 of 8 November 2002, adopted to get the weapons inspectors back into Iraq, did not contain any explicit or implicit authority to use force against Iraq in the event of Iraqi non-cooperation without a further resolution.[90] The hints by the US and the UK that this might also be justifiable self-defence against Iraq were also far-fetched since there was no armed attack or anything like an imminent threat of one by Iraq against the US or the UK.

Furthermore, just war rhetoric was less evident and less convincing in the invasion of Iraq than either Kosovo or Afghanistan, though before the invasion President Bush did try to link the proposed action to the war on terrorism and the idea of defending the nation:

---

[86] White, 'The Legality of Bombing in the Name of Humanity', (2000) 5 *Journal of Conflict and Security Law* 27 at pp. 38–41.

[87] See White, 'Self-Defence, Security Council Authority and Iraq', in Burchill, White and Morris (eds.), *International Conflict and Security Law*, Cambridge, 2005, p. 235 at pp. 236–240.

[88] SC Resolution 687, 3 April 1991. See Warbrick (note 78), pp. 969–970.

[89] SC Resolution 678, 29 November 1990; SC Resolution 687, 3 April 1991; and SC Resolution 1441, 8 November 2002.

[90] SC 4644th Meeting, 8 November 2002.

The danger is clear. Using chemical, biological or, one day, nuclear weapons obtained with the help of Iraq, the terrorists could fulfil their stated ambitions and kill thousands or hundreds of thousands of innocent people in our country or any other.[91]

Again the rhetoric is wider than the formal rules on the use of force, where defence is only allowed in response to an armed attack, and it is wider than the customary law of self-defence said to be contained in the *Caroline* incident of 1837, which permits defensive force in response to an imminent attack. While the current consensus seems to be that the *Caroline* incident still represents (or more accurately has come to represent) good law, the doctrine of pre-emption found in American claims has not been accepted.[92]

The illegal invasion of Iraq has arguably undermined the legitimacy of the occupation and reconstruction. Though both have received Security Council authorization,[93] it must be the case that the presence of American and British forces in Iraq has been tainted by that original illegality. With credibility being further cut away by the absence of WMD in Iraq, the original illegality and lack of moral justifications for the invasion have undermined the legitimacy of the British and American occupation and continuing intervention in Iraq. The sense of moral outrage that provided impetus to the Kosovo campaign in 1999, and to the invasion of Afghanistan in 2001 reviewed next, was not present in the invasion of Iraq. The reasons for the intervention seemed technical and artificially engineered, and were not justified by humanitarian necessity despite attempts post-invasion to shift the basis to regime change. Thus while the war on Serbia was deemed to be just though illegal, the invasion of Iraq was simply illegal.

XI. THE ROAD TO KANDAHAR

It will be useful now to consider the legality and legitimacy of the intervention in Afghanistan from 2001 onwards. From the perspective of British troops in Afghanistan they seem to be in a similar position to their colleagues in Iraq – fighting extremist Muslim terrorists and insurgents to achieve security and stability in a country so that it can be built, but they are arguably in a better position, not necessarily militarily but in terms of legality and legitimacy and

---

[91] News.bbc.co.uk/I/hi/world/middle-east/2858965.stm

[92] Wilmshurst, 'The Chatham House Principles of International Law on the Use of Force in Self-Defence', 55 (2006) *ICLQ* 963.

[93] SC Resolution 1483, 22 May 2003.

this arguably also affects the sustainability of the operation. However, this is not to say that there are no problems with the legality and legitimacy of military operations in Afghanistan; it is to say that compared to Iraq there are more positives in this regard.

The events of 11 September 2001, the attacks on the US, provoked the invasion of Afghanistan on 7 October 2001. Al-Qaeda was responsible for the attacks and that terrorist group had bases in Afghanistan. Moreover, they had a close relationship with the unrecognised but effective government of Afghanistan – the Taliban. The US and the UK claimed that their military actions in Afghanistan against Al-Qaeda and the Taliban were legitimate exercises of the right of self-defence.[94] This was endorsed by the EU, NATO and significantly the Security Council.[95] Thus the action seemed to be unequivocally in accordance with international law. However, the action in Afghanistan was not a straightforward application of the right of individual or collective self-defence in a number of ways. In effect it appears to be an attempted development of the right of self-defence to allow States to respond to terrorist attacks, in particular to take action against States harbouring terrorists.[96]

First, there was no on-going armed attack against the US.[97] The attacks were over, unless the vision of 9/11 as part of a wider war on terror is accepted. If the invasion of Afghanistan were a response to the armed attack of 9/11 it appeared more punitive than defensive – more akin to a reprisal. Secondly, if the invasion of Afghanistan were anticipatory self-defence, in other words it were designed to stop more imminent attacks, then this is more akin to the *Caroline* doctrine than the UN Charter rules which formally require the occurrence of an armed attack. Thirdly, self-defence should be both necessary, in other words, leave no choice, and be proportionate. With respect to the latter, although 9/11 was stated to be the equivalent of the Japanese attack on Pearl Harbor that brought the US into the Second World War thus justifying a war against the whole country from which the attack could be said to have originated,[98] it can be argued that this is over-stating the case and that strikes against the terrorist bases would have been a

[94] See UN Docs. S/2001/946 and S/2001/947, 7 October 2001.
[95] SC Resolution 1368, 12 September 2001.
[96] Ratner, 'Ius ad bellum and ius in bello after September 11', 96 (2002) *AJIL* 906.
[97] This is not to say that an attack by a terrorist group cannot be an armed attack within the meaning of Article 51 of the UN Charter; but see the International Court's advisory opinion in *Legal Consequences of the Construction of a Wall in the Occupied Palestinian Territories, ICJ Reports 2004*, p. 136 where the Court stated: 'Article 51 thus recognizes the existence of an inherent right of self-defence in the case of an armed attack by one State against another State. However, Israel does not claim that the attacks against it are imputable to a foreign State.' See ibid, p. 194, paragraph 139.
[98] Dinstein (note 21), p. 241.

more proportionate response. Fourthly, the response seemed to make the Taliban equally responsible for the 9/11 attacks as Al-Qaeda – for harbouring the terrorists and for not giving them up. But according to 'the test generally accepted by states' is that 'the use of force by individuals constituted an armed attack only when there has been a sending by or on behalf of a State of armed bands, groups, irregulars or mercenaries which carry out acts of armed force against another State of such gravity as to amount to an act of aggression', thus justifying self-defence by the attacked State and its allies against the sending State.[99]

Despite question marks about the targeting of the Taliban and the overall proportionality of the response, world opinion seemed either to endorse the view that the action against Afghanistan which resulted in the overthrow of the government and the rout of Al Qaeda-from its strongholds, was justifiable self-defence, or was silent on that matter. Though not straightforward it seemed to be accepted as a lawful application of the right of self-defence.

Acceptance of this wider right seems to have been for some States because it was a just war in response to the atrocious targeting of thousands of innocent civilians. In the aftermath of September 11 the British Prime Minister stated that 'the world should stand together against this outrage'.[100] Further, he said, '[O]ur beliefs are opposite to theirs. We believe in reason, democracy and tolerance. These beliefs are the foundation of our civilised world. They are enduring, they have served us well, and as history has shown, we have been prepared to fight when necessary, to defend them.'[101] It is noticeable how a much wider notion of defence – defence to protect beliefs is being used here. Such moral rhetoric was also present in the Prime Minister's statements at the start of hostilities in Afghanistan. He said:

> So this military action we are undertaking is not for a just cause alone, though this cause is just. It is to protect our country, our people, our economy, our way of life. If attacked, we will respond. We will defend ourselves. We will see this struggle though to the end and to the victory that would mark the victory not of revenge but of justice over the evil of terrorism.[102]

In these statements the Prime Minister is creating a much wider vision of defence. An atrocious attack on the United States is portrayed as an attack on the civilised world, and the response is a just one aimed at protecting our way of life against an ongoing evil. Though of course this mixture of political and

---

[99] Gray, *International Law and the Use of Force* (Second edition), Oxford, 2004 at p. 165, summarising the General Assembly's 1974 Definition of Aggression, Art. 3 (g) as utilised in the *Nicaragua* case, *supra* (note 75), p. 103, at paragraph 195.

[100] HC Deb., vol. 372, Col. 605, 14 September 2001, (Blair).

[101] Ibid, Col. 606.

[102] Ibid, vol. 372, Col. 814, 8 October 2001, (Blair).

moral rhetoric is not clear evidence of *opinio juris*, it could be said to provide the political platform on which legal arguments of a wider right of defence have been put forward and apparently accepted.

While the just war arguments over Kosovo produced a conclusion that the action was illegal but moral, the just war arguments over Afghanistan seemed to help create a widened notion of self-defence and thus both a lawful and just war. The question remains whether this widened right would be acceptable on future occasions without the moral outrage that followed the attacks of 9/11. For some States, however, acceptance of the wider right may have been more a question of unwillingness to criticise in the face of the 'for us or against us' rhetoric of the President George W. Bush.[103] If that were the case it would be difficult to accept that there was a true consensus about the modification of fundamental rules of the international community governing the use of force.

While the action in Afghanistan might be stronger than Iraq in terms of legality and legitimacy, it is by no means a cast iron case. If we add in the problems already identified about the proportionality of the response and the incorrect imputation of responsibility to the Taliban as well as Al-Qaeda, this again might be a case where the moral outrage of the atrocity allowed a military response to be mounted that would not normally have been acceptable to the international community, who turned a blind eye to any legal defects in the claim of self-defence.

Despite it wider acceptance as a lawful act, it was not long before the two main allies approached the Security Council to endorse a military operation in Afghanistan. While the US continued to exercise the right of self-defence to try and defeat the remnants of Al-Qaeda and the Taliban, the Security Council endorsed the creation of ISAF to provide security to the capital.[104] Legally this puts the basis of ISAF under the other exception to the ban on the use of force – military enforcement action under UN Security Council authority.

A UK-led UN-authorized security force was established in and around Kabul to provide security to enable elections and further reconstruction. NATO in fact provides the bulk of contributing nations to this force and in April 2003 (a month after the invasion of Iraq) NATO agreed to take over command of ISAF, which it did in October 2003. In that month the Security Council authorized the expansion of security to be provided by ISAF beyond Kabul.[105] Deployment in stages 1 and 2 in the Northern and Western Provinces was achieved by September 2005.

---

[103] White (note 48), p. 664.
[104] SC Resolution 1386, 20 December 2001.
[105] SC Resolution 1510, 13 October 2003.

Stage 3 in the less secure Southern provinces (including Helmand and Kandahar) was agreed in December 2005, and ISAF took over from US troops and military/civilian Provincial Reconstruction Teams in July 2006 (this technique was adopted and adjusted by ISAF). In explaining the British deployment as part of ISAF in the lawless Helmand province in February 2006, the Defence Secretary, John Reid, made clear the link between the actions of ISAF and 9/11.

> We are in Afghanistan under a UN Mandate with the support of the world community ... to help the democratically elected government of Afghanistan extend their democratic authority and build their own security forces, and to assist them in their economic development. That is precisely why we go to the South .... It is more dangerous and difficult than the first two stages ... but ... we are there to prevent Afghanistan from being used as a training ground, a planning area and a launch platform for terrorist acts such as the one we saw in New York – the worst terrorist act in history.[106]

The continuing link to 9/11 is crucial, for although the legal basis for ISAF is different from that of the initial US/UK operation in Afghanistan, ISAF's presence builds on the initial operation. In overthrowing the Taliban in the first operation, Western troops now face them as opponents in the State-building phase, making such a job extremely difficult to achieve.[107] Stage 4 in relation to the Eastern provinces commenced in October 2006 when NATO took over from US forces there. The overall aim is to achieve security in the whole of Afghanistan which will allow for the reconstruction of the State and the strengthening of democracy.

XII. CONCLUSION

Around the turn of the twenty-first century we are seeing liberal democratic countries willing to use force in circumstances that are not readily reconcilable with the rules contained in the UN Charter. This does not simply represent a continuation of the Cold War approach of the superpowers when they tended to disingenuously state that they were operating within the bounds of international law, while at the same time putting power above the law. Rather it represents

---

[106] HC Debs., vol. 443, Cols. 2 and 3, 27 February 2006. The Defence Secretary made it clear that the ISAF deployment was separate from the continuing action against Al-Qaeda. He also observed: 'Our troops are not there to seek out and destroy the terrorists, that is being done, under Operation Enduring Freedom, by an American-led multinational coalition' (ibid, col. 12).

[107] Lamb, 'Britain Told: Do Peace Deal with Taliban', *The Sunday Times*, 26 November 2006, p. 21.

a concerted attempt by these countries to develop the recognised exceptions as well as additional exceptions to the ban on the use of force. The British government though has something of a track record of attempting to develop the law in this area. On occasions its approach is viewed as a breach of international law as in the Corfu Channel incident in 1946 and ten years later in the disastrous Suez campaign, on others it is seen as a development of the law as with the idea that the Security Council can simply authorise volunteer States to undertake military action under its authority, as shown by the Korean War and the Beira Patrol.

However, the lessons of history drawn from earlier British practice show that there are a number of significant hurdles that have to be overcome to develop a legal doctrine that is not simply a clear application of the rules contained in the UN Charter. The first is legal and found in the nature of the rules themselves. As peremptory rules or *jus cogens* these rules reflect the basic values of the international system as created in 1945. The rule prohibiting the use of force has been fought for by leaders, politicians, States and many other interest groups and individuals over the centuries. Its embodiment in the UN Charter represented the climax of that struggle and it is something that will not be given up easily. For a start world opinion must come behind any attempted change to the rules.

Public opinion also constitutes a political obstacle to the legitimacy of military operations that have a controversial pedigree. British governments will struggle, as happened in the Suez Crisis of 1956, to maintain a military campaign unless it has support within Parliament and within the country. While the government of the day might be able to win narrow votes in Parliament in the short-term, the longer-term consequences for its credibility and its electability will be serious if it continues to prosecute an unpopular war. Admittedly there is no direct correlation between the illegality of a war and its unpopularity, but it is apparent that while politicians and the public will generally support a war that is in defence of the nation, or in furtherance of clearly stated universal values, wars that fall short of these requirements will usually be unpopular.

Thus while the Security Council endorsed the occupation of Iraq after an illegal invasion in 2003, the Council authorized ISAF after an invasion which generally had more support in the international community, even though it seemed to go further than the concept of self-defence as previously understood. The greater level of legitimacy achieved in the military actions in Afghanistan, by a combination of seemingly accepted arguments of an expanded right of self-defence and widespread moral outrage following the attacks of 9/11, may mean that the commitment from Western democracies to the military deployment is more sustainable and therefore likely to be more successful than that in Iraq, where grave doubts about the initial invasion have undermined the legitimacy of the subsequent actions (despite Security Council authorization), as well as undermining domestic support for the conflict in both Britain and the United States.

While its troops may face similar problems in Iraq and Afghanistan, Britain may be able to sustain its commitment in Afghanistan in the longer term because of the continuing belief in the legal and moral bases for the initial action. However, the initial military action in Afghanistan was not without its legal problems though they seemed to be swept away. In the longer term it may be that the disproportionate nature of the response, directed at the effective government as well as the terrorists, will serve to undermine the legitimacy of the current State-building enterprise. From being a war launched to deal with the threat from Al-Qaeda, it is now a war mainly fought against the former effective government of Afghanistan. Nevertheless, while the US/UK strategy in Iraq has little credibility left, the Western approach in Afghanistan may succeed, though there is a very long way to go.

Chapter Twenty

Non Consensual Aerial Surveillance in the Airspace over the Exclusive Economic Zone for Military and Defence Purposes

Kaiyan Homi Kaikobad*

Aerial surveillance in the airspace over the exclusive economic zone of a coastal State will usually have a variety of distinguishing characteristics. In the first place, aerial surveillance can be conducted by the coastal State itself or by another State, and secondly, where it is carried out by a Party other than the coastal State, such surveillance may either be consensual or non consensual. Limited financial and technological resources may compel a coastal State to invite another to undertake such surveillance on its behalf. In the third place, aerial surveillance may be carried out for a variety of purposes. Of interest here is aerial surveillance which has as its objective the collection of defence related intelligence by military aircraft; and accordingly aerial surveillance for the control of fisheries, human trafficking, illicit drugs and the arms trade is not of interest to this study. Fourthly, while some States carry out aerial surveillance openly and as a matter of right, others do so in a clandestine manner and are not open to either denying or commenting upon the existence of such operations. Finally, aerial surveillance may be authorised, directly or otherwise, by way of a resolution of the Security Council under Chapter VII of the Charter of the United Nations, a resolution which seeks to impart formal validity to non consensual aerial surveillance by maritime States in the airspace

* Professor of International Law, Brunel University. For many years, Colin and I shared at Durham the teaching of *Current Problems of International Law*, a series of lectures and seminars we ran at the postgraduate level, and one of the topics which I introduced from time to time was concerned with the issue which forms the subject matter of this chapter. I know that he will recall this and in a sense, then, this contribution is a reminder of those halcyon days.

K.H. Kaikobad & M. Bohlander (eds.), *International Law and Power: Perspectives on Legal Order and Justice*. Essays in Honour of Colin Warbrick, pp. 513–572.
© 2009 Koninklijke Brill NV. Printed in the Netherlands.

over the economic zone of coastal States. Surveillance operations lacking such formal validity would have to be justified under other provisions of international law. This investigation is limited to a study of aerial surveillance conducted in the airspace of the exclusive economic zone of a coastal State by maritime States which is (a) non consensual in character and (b) is concerned with the surveillance of defence and military assets of the coastal State or for any other kind of military objective or both.

Aerial surveillance of the kind under consideration here does not normally attract the attention of States members of the international community but this, like many other activities, ceases to be the case if and when an international incident takes place, especially where there is loss of human life. In most cases, the crucial issue is concerned with whether or not such aerial surveillance is a lawful activity, that is, whether it is consistent with the principles of the United Nations Convention on the Law of the Sea[1] and/or international law in general. The fact that there is still some disagreement between States parties and non parties to the Convention on this issue provides an opportunity to examine the reasons for and against such legality. This study, which takes up this opportunity, is distinguished somewhat by the emphasis it places on adopting a textual approach to the matter in terms of examining the *travaux preparatoires* which, it is believed, play a central role in understanding the problem under consideration and indeed its solution. It is obvious, then, that reference must be made to the relevant provisions of the Convention, but before this is done some fundamental principles and arguments relative to overflight in general and to aerial navigation in the airspace over the exclusive economic zone of coastal States may be useful.

1. The Law Relative to Overflight in General

The fundamental principles of flight are to be found in the Chicago Convention on International Civil Aviation concluded in 1944,[2] the successor treaty to the Paris Convention for the Regulation of Air Navigation of 1919.[3] For present purposes, Articles 1 to 3 are relevant. In Article 1, contracting States recognise that every State has complete and exclusive sovereignty over the airspace above its territory, and in Article 2 the territory of a State is deemed for purposes of the Chicago Convention 'to be the land areas [of a signatory State] and territorial waters adjacent thereto which are under the sovereignty, suzerainty,

---

[1] 1833 *UNTS* 3; 21 (1982) *ILM* 1261. Hereinafter referred to as the Convention.
[2] 15 *UNTS* 295; 148 *BFSP* 38.
[3] 11 *LNTS* 173; 112 *BFSP* 781.

protection or mandate of such a State'. Article 3, paragraph (c) of the Chicago Convention provides that no State aircraft of a contracting State shall fly over the territory of another State or land thereon without authorisation by special agreement or otherwise, and that such flight or landing shall be in accordance with the terms thereof. All of these principles are recognised as being consistent with customary international law.[4]

Insofar as Article 2 of the Chicago Convention is applicable only to land territory and to the territorial waters of the coastal State, the rights given to the latter cannot apply to maritime zones falling outside those waters, and it easily follows that because the exclusive economic zone is not included in the notion of territory of the coastal State as described in Article 2, the regime established by this provision of the Chicago Convention, is not applicable to this zone of maritime territory. It is, however, also appropriate to point out that the delegates to the Chicago Conference in 1944 were not even contemplating the question whether or not to exclude or include the exclusive economic zone from the sovereignty provisions of Articles 1 and 2 insofar as the notion of this zone began to take root approximately thirty years later.

In 1944, the areas which now constitute the economic zone were universally regarded as being part of the high seas, that is, the body of water lying outside the limits of the territorial seas of coastal States over which all other States are prohibited from exercising any kind of sovereignty. It is in this part of the seas and oceans that both maritime and landlocked States are entitled to exercise all the freedoms of the high seas, including fishing, navigation and overflight. It follows that the delegates to the Chicago Conference could hardly have been seeking to ascribe or to extend territorial sovereignty or sovereign rights to such waters for purposes of restricting overflight. Thus when the Chicago Convention provided contracting States the right to fly their aircraft without prior permission over the high seas, it was doing so with respect to maritime areas which, in contemporary times, would partially be considered as lying within the exclusive economic zones of coastal States with the caveat that insofar as the zone is in principle an optional one, the high seas of a coastal State could well begin at the outer limits of the territorial sea.

---

[4] Brownlie, *Principles of International Law* (Sixth edition), Oxford, 2003, at pp. 115–116; O'Connell, *International Law* (Second edition), London, 1970, pp. 518–519; Martial, 'State Control of the Air Space over the Territorial Sea and the Contiguous Zone', 30 (1952) *Canadian Bar Review* 245, at pp. 245–247; Jennings, 'International Civil Aviation and the Law', 22 (1945) *BYIL* 191, at pp. 191–192; Hailbronner, 'Freedom of the Air and the Convention on the Law of the Air', 77 (1983) *AJIL* 490; Lauterpacht (ed.), *Oppenheim's International Law A Treatise*, vol. i, *Peace* (Eighth edition), London, 1955, pp. 523; and Goedhius, 'Problems of Public International Air Law', 81 (1952, II) *Hague Recueil des cours* 205, at p. 209 *et seq.*

The United Nations Convention on the Law of the Sea is of course also a relevant treaty. The first pertinent provision in this regard is to be found in Article 2 which deals with the territorial sea. While paragraph 1 stipulates that the sovereignty of a coastal State extends beyond its land territory and internal waters to a belt of sea adjacent to the coast, paragraph 2 provides: 'This sovereignty extends to the airspace over the territorial sea as well as to its bed and subsoil.' This in fact complements the provisions of Article 2 of the Chicago Convention.

Furthermore, Article 19, paragraph 2 lists items of activity which are considered to be prejudicial to the peace, good order or security of the coastal State and as such do not constitute innocent passage. One such act identified in paragraph 2 of Article 19 is the launching, landing or taking on board any aircraft in the territorial sea of a coastal State. Articles 38 and 39 provide rules for overflight in straits used for international navigation. Paragraph 2 of Article 38 provides that transit passage in such straits constitutes the right of navigation and overflight solely for the purpose of continuous and expeditious transit of the strait and Article 39 requires, *inter alia*, aircraft in transit passage to observe the Rules of the Air established by the International Civil Aviation Organisation.

ii. The Right of Overflight in the Exclusive Economic Zone under the Convention

Part V of the UN Convention on the Law of the Sea is of course of major significance insofar as it lays down the regime of the exclusive economic zone. It is Article 55 which establishes the regime in general terms as an area beyond and adjacent to the territorial seas, leaving it to Article 56 to stipulate that coastal States enjoy sovereign rights relative to the exploration and exploitation of the living and non-living resources of the sea. The latter article also vests coastal States with limited jurisdictional rights in respect of artificial islands, marine scientific research and the protection and preservation of the marine environment. Since Article 58 is central to this enquiry, it will be appropriate to set out paragraph 1 thereof in full:

> In the exclusive economic zone, all States, whether coastal or land-locked, enjoy, subject to the relevant provisions of the Convention, and the freedoms referred to in article 87 of navigation and overflight and of the laying of submarine cables and pipelines, and other internationally lawful uses of the sea related to these freedoms, such as those associated with the operation of ships, aircraft and submarine cables and pipelines, and compatible with the other provisions of this Convention.

On the face of it, it is very easy to interpret the text of the provision. Two kinds of rights are vested in 'all States',[5] that is the three 'basic rights' or freedoms of the high seas: (a) navigation, (b) overflight and (c) the laying of submarine cables and pipelines; and the 'related rights', that is the internationally lawful uses of the sea related to the three basic freedoms. Some scholars adopt a permissive approach to paragraph 1.[6] They advocate a relatively liberal reading of this paragraph, an interpretation which would permit, or to put it more precisely, not prohibit, aerial surveillance in the airspace over the exclusive economic zone. Other scholars, however, adopt either a more restrictive view of paragraph 1 of Article 58 or a relatively nuanced approach to the provision. Both of course rely on the simple meaning of the words used in the text.

The permissive or expansive view is based on several arguments, one of the simpler being that the text of paragraph 1 is concerned only with the activity being conducted in broad general terms in the relevant zone, and aerial navigation is one of them; and accordingly it is not concerned with *how* it is carried out. Paragraph 1 says nothing about aerial surveillance because it is simply an on-board activity taking place in the context of one of the three basic rights.

The second argument in favour of this view involves reference to the juridical nature of the exclusive economic zone.[7] The rights provided in the zone are strictly sovereign rights of a very specific kind, that is sovereign rights for the purpose of exploring and exploiting, conserving and managing the living and non-living resources of the zone. All other instances of authority and control are based in jurisdiction, and even, here the jurisdictional rights of the coastal State

---

[5] This term is used to distinguish it from the coastal State, but the phrase employed here, in keeping with other writers, is mainly 'maritime States'; or 'third States'. It is, of course, recognised that a maritime State may well be a coastal State. The Convention refers also to 'other States' in contradistinction to coastal States; see, for example, Article 56, paragraph 2 and Article 59.

[6] Refer generally to Oxman, 'The Third United Nations Conference on the Law of the Sea: The 1977 New York Session', 72 (1978) *AJIL* 57, at pp. 67–75; Kwaitkowska, *The 200-mile Exclusive Economic Zone in the New International Law of the Sea*, Dordrecht, 1989, pp. 198–215; Robertson, 'Navigation in the Exclusive Economic Zone', 24 (1984) *VJIL* 865; Hayashi, 'Military and Intelligence Gathering Activities in the EEZ: Definition of Key Terms', 29 (2005) *Marine Policy* 123; Richardson, 'Law of the Sea: Navigation and Other Traditional National Security Considerations', 19 (1982) *San Diego Law Review* 553; Clingan, 'An Overview of the Second Committee Negotiations in the Law of the Sea', 63 (1984) *Oregon Law Review* 53; Treves, 'Navigation', in Dupuy and Vignes (eds.), *A Handbook on the New Law of the Sea*, vol. ii, Dordrecht, 1991, p. 835, at pp. 903–905; and Lowe for a more cautious albeit permissive approach: 'Some Legal Problems Arising from the Use of the Seas for Military Purposes', 10 (1986) *Marine Policy* 171, at pp. 178–181; and his careful 'Rejoinder', 11 (1987) ibid, pp. 250–251.

[7] Generally, see Oxman (note 6), p. 72; Robertson (note 6), pp. 870–880; Hailbronner (note 4), pp. 505–506; and p. 509; and Scovazzi, 'The Evolution of International Law of the Sea: New Issues, New Challenges', 286 (2000) *Hague Recueil des cours* 39, at pp. 164–165. For an exhaustive study on the legal nature of the zone, see Orrego Vicuña, *The Exclusive Economic Zone Regime and Legal Nature under International Law*, Cambridge, 1989, Chapter 2.

are limited to the establishment and use of artificial islands, installations and structures, marine scientific research and the protection and preservation of the marine environment; they are also limited to 'other [miscellaneous] rights and duties provided for in the Convention', under sub-paragraph (c) of paragraph 1 of Article 56. The essence of the argument is that coastal States must keep their rights in the zone in strict perspective. Insofar as the Convention does not expressly disallow overflight and insofar as it does not grant sovereignty, as opposed to sovereign rights, to the zone, coastal States have no right, based either in sovereignty or jurisdiction to prohibit aerial surveillance in the airspace over the economic zone.

The third argument supporting the permissive interpretation emerges from the fact that during the Third United Nations Conference on the Law of the Sea, agreement on the notion, status and rights relative to the economic zone finally materialised once delegates were persuaded to accept that the characteristic elements of the high seas would be grafted on to legal nature of the zone. This, indeed, was a central element of the 'Castañeda compromise'. The relevant fact is that all kinds of military activities, manoeuvres, exercises and weapons testing are allowed on the high seas and therefore they are also allowed in the exclusive economic zones of coastal States and in the airspace thereof. It is pointed out that maritime States can rely on paragraph 1 of Article 58, which specifically refers to the high seas freedoms provided in Article 87, making it clear that the coastal States' sovereign rights cannot frustrate the exercise by maritime States of their lawful high seas freedoms in the economic zones of States, provided always that they pay due regard to the rights of the coastal State.[8] Paragraph 2 in fact goes on effectively to transplant the high seas articles contained in Part VII, that is, Articles 88 to 115, on to the economic zone. The essence of the argument, as Oxman notes, is that the freedoms preserved in the economic zone are qualitatively the same as the high seas freedoms.[9] Accordingly, since there are no restrictions on aerial surveillance in the high seas no such restrictions apply here in the exclusive economic zone or airspace thereof.

---

[8]   See Oxman (note 6), pp. 72–73; and also see ibid, 'The Regime of Warships under the United Nations Convention on the Law of the Sea', 24 (1984) *VJIL* 809, at p. 837; Robertson (note 6), pp. 877–878; and Kwaitkowska (note 6), p. 200; also see her comment: 'Military Uses in the EEZ – A Reply', 11 *Marine Policy* 249, at p. 249; Hailbronner (note 4), pp. 504–505. Further, see Sharma, 'An Indian Perspective', 29 (2005) *Marine Policy* 147, at pp. 148–149; and Boczek, 'Peacetime Military Activities in the Exclusive Economic Zone of Third Countries', 19 (1988) *ODIL* 445, at pp. 449–450.

[9]   See 'The Third United Nations Conference on the Law of the Sea', in Dupuy and Vignes (note 6), p. 163, at p. 217.

Notwithstanding the above, it could also be contended that matters are perhaps not as straightforward as they would appear to be.[10] First, there is, it seems, room for the view that the scope and extent of the three basic rights provided in the first clause of paragraph 1 of Article 58 are to be seen restrictively. More specifically, paragraph 1 does not end at the point where the high seas freedoms of navigation, overflight and the laying of submarine cables and pipelines are provided but goes on to include another category of rights in the exclusive economic zone, namely 'other internationally lawful use of the seas related to these freedoms such as those associated with the operation of ships, aircraft and submarine cables and pipelines, and compatible with the other provisions of this Convention'. The argument arising from this point will be more obvious in the light of the legislative history of this article discussed in the next section.

At this stage it is important to note the effect of the second clause of paragraph 1, and that such effect is one of restriction and limitation of the three basic rights vested by the first part of the paragraph. In other words, the rights of navigation, overflight and the laying of submarine cables and pipelines are the basic rights, and all acts other than those constituting the three basic rights must fall in or be consistent with the criteria laid out in the second part, that is they must be (i) internationally lawful use of the seas (ii) which are related to the precise right in question (iii) they must have characteristics which are consistent with activities dealing with the operation of ships and aircraft and the laying of submarine cables and pipelines; and (iv) they must also be compatible with other provisions of the Convention.[11] This would mean then that where maritime States use aircraft primarily for purposes of conducting surveillance of the coastal State from the latter's economic zone and where navigating in the airspace over

---

[10] Scholars who take a restrictive view on the matter include Subedi, *Land and Maritime Zones of Peace in International Law*, Oxford, 1996, pp. 45–51; Galindo Pohl, 'The Exclusive Economic Zone in the Light of Negotiations of the Third United Nations Conference on the Law of the Sea', in Orrego Vicuña, *The Exclusive Economic Zone A Latin American Perspective*, Boulder, 1984, p. 31, at pp. 54–55; Al Mour, 'The Legal Status of the Exclusive Economic Zone', 33 (1977) *Revue Egyptienne de droit international* 35, pp. 60–61; Tetley, 'The Chinese/US Incident at Hainan – A Confrontation of Super Powers and Civilisations', McGill University: web-site: Maritime Law/History/Chinese; Meyer, 'Comment: The Impact of the Exclusive Economic Zone on Naval Operations', 40 (1992) *Naval Law Review* 241; and O'Connell, *The International Law of the Sea*, vol. i, Oxford, 1982, pp. 577–578. Hailbronner takes a somewhat nuanced view: *supra* (note 4), pp. 503–506, as do Donnelly, "The United States-China EP-3 Incident: Reality and Realpolitik", 9 (2004) *JCSL* 25, at pp. 31–35; Attard, *The Exclusive Economic Zone in International Law*, Oxford, 1987, pp. 78–86; Van Dyke, 'The Disappearing Right to Navigational Freedom in the Exclusive Economic Zone', 29 (2005) *Marine Policy* 107; Boczek (note 8), p. 445 *et seq.*; Scovazzi (note 7), p. 162 *et seq*; and Orrego Vicuña (note 7), pp. 108–22.

[11] See generally Subedi (note 10), pp. 47–48.

the zone is effectively a means to an end, then that activity does not arguably constitute overflight in the sense in which it is used in the Convention. This aspect of the point is related to the third counter-argument discussed below. Suffice it to say here that the scholars who favour the permissive approach and argue in favour of the right to conduct military activities in the exclusive economic zones of coastal States do not seem seriously to address the fact that if their point of view were accepted as correct, the closing clauses of paragraph 1 would have no meaning or reason for their existence. As O'Connell wrote:

> [The words 'related to these freedoms such as those associated with the operation of ships, aircraft and submarine cables and pipelines' were] intended to secure for warships the same operational freedoms in the EEZ as in the residue of the high seas, but the statements that these freedoms are 'subject to the provisions' of the Draft Convention, and that the Articles which embody them are applicable to the EEZ only, 'in so far as they are not incompatible' with Part V (the EEZ), tend to suggest that the quality of the freedom exercisable in the EEZ is not necessarily that exercisable in the high seas.[12]

Nor is it easy to appreciate the essential meaning of the Castañeda compromise if in fact maritime States are to be understood as having achieved everything with no evident *quid pro quo* for coastal States. If the developing States agreed to graft the high seas regime on to the economic zone, which they did in fact, but secured nothing in return then such an arrangement is hardly a compromise; more a collective abandonment of their position. The much bandied 'compromise' is only intelligible if the famous 'cross reference to Article 87' is balanced by some other right which delegates could have accepted without giving up their positions on the matter; and this corrective comes in the shape and form of a narrowing of the three fundamental rights and related rights prescribed in paragraph 1 of Article 58.

Secondly, although much is made of the specific 'cross reference' in paragraph 1 of Article 58 to the high seas freedoms identified in Article 87, it seems that supporters of the permissive view neglect to give weight to the cross reference also to be found in Article 87 which states: 'Freedom of the high seas is exercised under the conditions laid down by this Convention and by other rules of international law.'[13] Thus whatever the type and nature of the high seas freedoms transplanted on to the economic zone regime, they would have to be exercised subject to the various relevant provisions of the Convention, and one of them would clearly be the carefully *re-formulated* and restricted high seas freedoms of navigation and overflight. Indeed, there is no escape from this logical

---

[12] *Supra* (note 10), pp. 577–578. See also Attard (note 10), pp. 78–79; and Van Dyke (note 10), p. 121. Cf. Clingan (note 6), p. 66.

[13] Reference to this argument is also made by Tetley (note 10), pp. 3–4.

deduction once reliance is placed on the cross-reference to Article 87 in Article 58, paragraph 1 and therefore this constitutes, in fact, a counter-productive argument.

Thirdly, as far as the argument from aerial surveillance as an on-board activity is concerned, it is agreed that although this is an on-board activity it cannot be seen as being merely incidental to the air navigation of the exclusive economic zone because in the circumstances thereof, it is in fact integral to it, and here the test is whether there is a symbiotic link between the two categories of cases. This is concerned with determining whether the links between the impugned activity and overflight are so integral to each other that either one would not and could not have taken place without the other. Thus in order to appreciate whether the impugned activity falls in the category of 'internationally lawful uses of the sea/airspace' related to these basic freedoms, it is not the inherent or intrinsic character of the impugned act or activity which is of sole and signal importance. There has to be a determination whether a specific incident of air navigation over the exclusive economic zone of a coastal State would not have taken place had the prospects of carrying out the impugned activity not existed; and similarly, the impugned activity would not have been carried out had the facilities of air navigation in the precise circumstances of the case not been in place or were not provided. Aerial surveillance it is clear could not have been carried out without the facilities provided by overflight and there would have been no reason for the aircraft to be in the airspace of a coastal State's economic zone but for the sake of providing this facility. The relations these two activities enjoy are in a real sense symbiotic to each other.

Fourthly, Article 58, paragraph 3 imposes the 'due regard' restriction on maritime States: that is, in exercising their rights, [maritime] States 'shall have due regard to the rights and duties of the coastal State' and shall comply with the laws and regulations adopted by it in accordance with the Convention. There is of course an equivalence here in that Article 56, paragraph 2 creates a similar 'due regard' clause for coastal States with respect to the exercise of their rights and duties, but the fact remains that any kind of military activity by a maritime State which causes *bona fide* concern regarding (a) the coastal State's sovereign and jurisdictional rights in its economic zone and (b) its lawful expectations regarding the exercise by such States of their restricted high seas freedoms pursuant to Article 58, paragraph 1 is therefore legally unacceptable. Although this can be seen in some ways as begging the question, it is at least agreed that maritime States have to be cognisant of the interests of other States.[14]

---

[14] Hayashi (note 6), pp. 132–133, at p. 132, citing the letter of the President of the US dated 7 October 1994 to the Senate transmitting the Convention for adoption by it: see the attached

The fifth response[15] has reference to the argument that the coastal State enjoys 'only' sovereign rights as opposed to sovereignty in the exclusive economic zone and accordingly all rights appertaining to that State ought not only to be restrictively interpreted. They must also have direct bearing on the juridical nature of the zone in question, that is to say they must be linked to the economic nature thereof. While this proposition is in effect beyond reproach, it may be argued that there is in fact no need to ask for a liberal interpretation; and indeed a simple, fairly textual approach, predicated on a good faith interpretation of the ordinary meaning of the words, is all that is required here. As Paolillo explained, 'to navigate or fly is not the same thing as for instance to manoeuvre, to test weapons, or to install and use detection devices. Therefore it seems excessive to derive from the freedom of navigation of warships the right to use the EEZ for military purposes'.[16] In other words, supporters of the restrictive view would seek to look at nothing more than the ordinary meaning of the words in paragraph 1. It is for this reason that there is no reason to rely on Article 59 to resolve the issue, for the position taken here is that there are no unattributed rights or jurisdiction in this situation which would bring that article into play here.[17]

'Commentary', 34 (1995) *ILM* 1396, at p. 1400, and p. 1412. Also see Van Dyke, 'Military Exclusion and Warning Zones on the High Seas', 15 (1991) *Marine Policy* 147, at p. 164; Schreiber, 'The Exclusive Economic Zone: Its Legal Nature and the Problem of Military Uses', in Orrego Vicuña (note 10), p. 123, at pp. 140–141; Kim, 'A Korean Perspective', 29 (2005) *Marine Policy* 157, at p. 159; and Subedi, who warns that the due regard provision could be a double edged sword: (note 10), pp. 45–46, note 26. Cf. Oxman (note 8), p. 838; but he also observes: 'The lawfulness of any other activity in principle does not relieve the flag state of its duty to have due regard to the rights and duties of the coastal state, which presumably covers such hypothetical concerns such as damage to resources.' See *supra* (note 6), p. 265.

[15] Tetley also makes the argument that aerial surveillance which seeks and gathers intelligence relative to the military and defence interests of the coastal State is inherently unlawful insofar as offends the principle of Article 2, paragraph 4 of the United Nations Charter; but this argument it is submitted cannot be accepted without careful consideration of the facts: see *infra*, generally, Part IV, section 1.

[16] See 'EEZ in Latin American Practice and Legislation', 26 (1995) *ODIL* 105, at p. 112. He did however conclude that the question was not conclusively settled: p. 112. More forcefully, Galindo Pohl observed: 'This is true in that navigation by warships is authorised as a result of the inclusion of the rules of the high seas, but it would seem excessive to construe this one activity as grounds for the military use of the zone, because there is a good deal of difference between navigation and naval manoeuvres, a naval presence the installation of sensing apparatus, arms testing, and so on.' See *supra* (note 10), p. 55.

[17] Cf. the position adopted by Lowe on this: *supra* (note 6), p. 179; and see Kwaitkowska who refutes the need for referring to Article 59: (note 8), p. 249. While the latter is right about the need to refer to Article 59, it is the reason why she thinks it is not necessary, is questionable; and the reason is that the rights, as stated above in the main text, have been attributed to

At this juncture, it will be useful to examine the legislative history of Article 58, paragraph 1 with a view to shedding further light on the matter. This examination, it is believed, is particularly important because although many scholars have relied on the argumentation resting upon legislative history, very few, if any, have examined it to the depth required with a view to dispelling some commonly held misunderstandings about the relevant provisions.

III. Legislative History of Article 58 of the Convention

The United Nations Convention on the Law of the Sea of 1982 was drafted and seen to fruition by the Third UN Conference on the Law of the Sea which began debating the general text and rules of the Convention at the Second Session; or, as Castañeda puts it, its first 'substantive session'[18] at Caracas between June and August 1974, grounding itself primarily on the 1958 Conventions on the territorial sea, continental shelf and the high seas. Issues concerning the exclusive economic zone came within the remit of the Second Committee of the Third Conference. When delegates to the Conference met at Caracas, they had before them at least six different sets of documentation and proposals on relevant matters, including the then controversial notion of the exclusive economic zone. Importantly, all these documents and proposals accepted the general principle that third States would continue to enjoy the freedom of navigation, overflight and the laying of submarine cables and pipelines in the exclusive economic zones of coastal States. There were, of course, a variety of approaches to the matter. One of the earlier proposals was contained in a fourteen-power draft prepared by African States. This draft was submitted to the Committee on the Peaceful Uses of the Sea-bed and the Ocean Floor. It affirmed the right of free navigation and overflight without restrictions other than those resulting from the exercise by the coastal State of its rights to economic resources. It also included the freedom of laying submarine cables and pipelines, subject to the limitations imposed by the coastal State's economic rights.[19]

---

the coastal State. Further, see Hailbronner who generally takes a circumspect view of the provision: (note 4), pp. 505.

[18] See Castañeda, 'Negotiations on the Exclusive Economic Zone at the Third United Nations Conference on the Law of the Sea', in Makarczyk (ed.), *Essays in International Law in Honour of Manfred Lachs*, The Hague, 1984, p. 605. Preparatory Committee sessions had been going on since 1971: ibid. The procedural aspects were dealt with at the first session at New York in 1973: see Ganz, 'United Nations and the Law of the Sea', 26 (1977) *ICLQ* 1, at pp. 7–10.

[19] See the draft articles on the exclusive economic zone submitted jointly by Algeria, Cameroon, Ghana, Ivory Coast, Kenya, Liberia, Madagascar, Mauritius, Senegal, Sierra Leone, Somalia,

Similarly, eighteen African States submitted to the Conference a draft which reinforced the rights and obligations of coastal States in their respective zones.[20] As such, it was, by and large, consistent with the 1973 Declaration of the Organisation of African Unity which had stipulated that the coastal State shall manage the zone's resources 'without undue interference with the other legitimate use of the sea, namely freedom of navigation, overflight and the laying of cables and pipelines'.[21] It is important to note that this Declaration thus equated the three freedoms of navigation, overflight and the laying of cables and pipelines as a species of a more general notion, namely, the 'legitimate use of the sea'. Interestingly, Nigeria submitted revised Draft Articles 3 and 5 on the exclusive economic zone; but while they confirmed the three rights or freedoms described above, the provisions in question failed to link them with other 'legitimate uses of the sea'.[22]

The draft articles submitted by the East European Group of States, including Bulgaria, the USSR and the German Democratic Republic, were similar in

---

Sudan, Tunisia and Tanzania (UN Doc. A/AC. 138/SC. II/L. 40 and Corr. 1–3), Report of the Sub-Committee II, Annex II, Appendix V, in Report of the Committee on the Peaceful Uses of the Sea-Bed and the Ocean Floor Beyond the Limits of National Jurisdiction, vol. iii, Supplement No. 21 (A/9021), United Nations, *General Assembly, Official Records, 28th Session*, Supplement No. 21 (A/9021), 1973, p. 87: see Article IV. For the working paper submitted by Norway and Australia, see UN Doc. A/AC. 138/SC. II/L.36, ibid, p. 77: Article 1 (d). Similarly, see the draft articles submitted by Uganda and Zambia: UN Doc. A/AC. 138/SC. II/L. 41, ibid, p. 89: Article 4, paragraph 5; and by China, UN Doc. A/AC. 138/SC.II /L.34, ibid, p. 71: Article 73. The Declaration of Santo Domingo of 1972, and in particular Patrimonial Sea, paragraph 5 influenced these proposals. Generally see Nandan and Rosenne, *United Nations Convention on the Law of the Sea 1982 A Commentary*, Dordrecht, 1993, vol. ii, p. 553 *et seq*. Another important primary source is the work of the UN Division for Ocean Affairs and the Law of the Sea, *The Law of the Sea Exclusive Economic Zone Legislative History of Articles 56, 58 and 59* of the United Nations Convention on the Law of the Sea, New York, 1992; hereinafter referred to as *Legislative History*. For the text of the Santo Domingo Declaration, refer to 11 (1972) *ILM* 892: UN Doc. A/AC. 138/80, 26 July 1972; and Castañeda (note 18), pp. 609–610. Earlier still is the Declaration of Santiago, 1952 which was seminal as far as the notion of the patrimonial sea was concerned, for which see Nelson, 'The Patrimonial Sea', 22 (1973) *ICLQ* 668.

[20] Draft articles on the exclusive economic zone submitted by Gambia, Ivory Coast, Kenya, Lesotho, Liberia, Libya, Madagascar, Mali, Mauritania, Morocco, Senegal, Sierra Leone, Sudan, Tunisia, Cameroon, Tanzania and Zaire: 26 August 1979: UN Doc. A/CONF. 62/C.2/L.82: in *Third United Nations Conference on the Law of the Sea, Official Records*, vol. iii, p. 240; hereinafter referred to as *UNCLOS, Official Records*. For another detailed account of the legislative history of this provision, see Galdorisi and Kaufman, 'Military Activities in the Exclusive Economic Zone: Preventing Uncertainty and Defusing Conflicts', 32 (2002) *California Western International Law Journal* 253, at p. 269 *et seq*.

[21] See the 1973 Declaration of the Organisation of African Unity on the Issues of the Law of the Sea, 19 July 1974: UN Doc. A/CONF. 62/33, in *UNCLOS, Official Records* (note 20), p. 63.

[22] See UN Doc. A/CONF. 62/C.2/C.21/Rev.1, 5 August 1974, in ibid p. 199.

nature. Draft Article 4 was designed to acknowledge the rights of the coastal State as recognized by international law, and Draft Article 6 stipulated that these rights and obligations were to be exercised in accordance with the Convention, but 'with due regard to the other legitimate uses of the high seas ...' Clearly, then, the Eastern Europe Group's draft articles were different only in terms of text and emphasis.[23] A relatively more cautious and traditionalist approach is evident from a perusal of draft Articles 7 and 8 submitted by the United States on the matter of the continental shelf and the economic zone. Draft Article 7 asserts not only the rights of freedom, navigation and overflight, but also 'other rights recognized by the general principles of international law ...' Similarly, Draft Article 8, paragraph 1 precludes 'unjustifiable interference [by coastal States] with navigation or other uses of the sea [in the economic zone] ...' Draft paragraph 2 precluded only unjustifiable interference 'in the exercise of the rights or the performance of the duties of the coastal State in the economic zone'. In terms, thus, this provision would have permitted interference with the exercise of the rights of coastal States in their economic zones, provided that it was justifiable so to do.[24]

In the light of these observations, the draft working paper submitted by Canada, Chile, Iceland, India, Indonesia, Mauritius, Mexico, New Zealand and Norway was perhaps more balanced in its approach.[25] While Article 14 asserted the freedoms of navigation and overflight for all States, whether coastal or landlocked, those freedoms were 'subject to the exercise by the coastal State of its rights within the area, as provided for in this convention'. This provision is then balanced by Draft Article 15 which stipulates that the coastal State shall exercise its rights and perform its duties in the economic zone without 'undue interference with other legitimate uses of the sea, including, subject to this convention, the laying of cables and pipelines'.[26] Thus, while this nine-power working paper sought to proclaim the rights of navigation and overflight for third States, the burden was placed on the coastal State of not unduly interfering with (i) the right of laying cables and pipelines and (ii) of carrying out other legitimate uses of the sea.

The upshot of this discussion is that despite a consensus on the three fundamental freedoms, a number of States and delegates were unsure about and uneasy with the precise scope and extent of their rights and duties as coastal States *vis-à-vis* maritime States in their respective economic zones. In particular,

---

[23] Draft articles on the economic zone submitted by Bulgaria, Byelorussian SSR, the German Democratic Republic, Poland, Ukrainian SSR, and the USSR: 5 August 1974 in ibid, p. 214.

[24] See the draft articles submitted by the United States of America for a chapter on the economic zone and the continental shelf: 8 August 1974: UN Doc. A/CONF. 62/C.2/L.47, ibid, p. 222.

[25] See the Working Paper: UN Doc. A/CONF. 62/L.4: 26 July 1974, ibid, p. 81.

[26] See ibid, pp. 82–83.

the unease was that maritime or other third States could infringe upon, or carry out activities incompatible with their rights as coastal States in their respective exclusive economic zones.[27] There were pronounced misgivings to the effect that any reference to 'other legitimate uses of the sea' was far too open-ended and wide-ranging, and accordingly it was felt that greater clarity was needed in order not to weaken the authority of the coastal State in its economic zone.

This sense of unease is clearly reflected in the debates held by the delegates in the Second Committee during the Second Session. Thus the delegate of Peru expressed concern to the effect that vessels should abstain from military activities, acts of propaganda, espionage or interference with communications when in the economic zone of coastal States. He also 'wondered what those legitimate uses [of the sea] were'.[28] Brazil, conscious of the fact that it would be impossible exhaustively to enumerate the rights and duties of both the coastal State and third States, suggested that residual competence should go to the former. Adverting to the difficulties raised by certain kinds of hypothetical activities, including the conduct of military exercises, the loading and unloading of cargo, the incidence of floating casinos and the running of television stations by third States in the economic zone of another State, Mr. Marotta Rangel maintained that none of these activities were permissible and enquired, '[W]ho should decide that they did not fall under the broad category of legitimate uses of the sea[?].'[29] Agreeing with Peru, the delegate from Pakistan declared that the notion of 'other legitimate uses of the sea' ought more clearly to be spelt out;[30] and the Khmer Rouge delegate asserted that naval manoeuvres, which might disturb the living resources of the zone, should be prohibited and that the exercise of 'other freedoms' should not be prejudicial to the interests of the coastal State.[31]

---

[27] Generally see the statements of Honduras, Portugal, Mexico, Yugoslavia, Upper Volta, (Burkina Faso), Paraguay, Congo, Mauritania, Kenya, Sri Lanka, China, El Salvador, Iceland, Tonga, Burundi, Thailand, Peru, Pakistan, Argentina, Brazil, Byelorussia, Uruguay, Khmer Republic, USSR for which refer to the 22nd to 28th Meetings: July/August 1974: Second Session, Second Committee, *Third United Nations Conference on the Law of the Sea, Official Records*, vol. ii, pp. 171–220: especially pp. 171–172, paragraph 6; p. 173, paragraph 23; p. 174, paragraph 40; p. 174, paragraph 42; p. 175, paragraph 64; p. 176, paragraph 87; p. 178, paragraph 108; p. 180, paragraph 135; p. 183, paragraphs 18 and 19; p. 186, paragraph 51; p. 187, paragraph 4; p. 188, paragraph 15; p. 189, paragraph 189; p. 190, paragraph 43; p. 191, paragraphs 56 and 70; p. 192, paragraph 78; p. 193, paragraph 88; p. 195, paragraph 5; p. 196, paragraph 21; pp. 202–203, paragraphs 6 and 7, p. 205, paragraph 205, p. 208, paragraph 78; p. 212, paragraph 15; and p. 221, paragraph 54 respectively.

[28] See 24th Meeting, Second Committee, 1 August 1974, ibid, p. 193, paragraph 88.

[29] See 26th Meeting, Second Committee, 5 August 1974, ibid, pp. 202–203, paragraphs 5 to 7.

[30] See 25th Meeting, Second Committee, 5 August 1974, ibid, p. 195, paragraph 5.

[31] See 27th Meeting, Second Committee, 5 August 1974, ibid, p. 212, paragraph 15.

The anxieties expressed by States must also be considered in the context of Provision 97 of the Second Committee's working paper prepared in order to reflect the 'main trends' emerging from the proposals made by various States either before the Committee on the Peaceful Uses of the Sea-bed or the Third Conference on the Law of the Sea.[32] This draft item, in keeping with other items in the working paper, had a list of alternative provisions, namely Formulae A, B, C and D, each of which reflected the positions adopted by States in their various proposals, excluding the Cairo Declaration and the nine-power working paper.[33] It is important to note that while all three basic rights of maritime States in the economic zone of a coastal State were reiterated therein, there was, at that stage, no attempt to clarify of what was entailed by the notion of 'other legitimate uses of the sea'. Nor, indeed, did any of the four formulations contain any reference to the general limiting clause, namely 'subject to the relevant provisions of the present convention', which is now to be found at the head of Article 58.

At the Third Session in 1975, the Second Committee further examined a variety of proposals on the matter. The text prepared by the Informal Group of Judicial Experts, also known as the Evensen Group,[34] reflected, *inter alia*, the consensus and the concern expressed by States in the previous session. Draft Article 3, paragraph 1 stipulated that subject to the relevant provisions of the present convention, all States enjoyed the freedoms of navigation, overflight and the laying of submarine cables and pipelines 'and other internationally lawful uses of the sea related to navigation and communication ...'.[35] The innovation effected was two-fold. First, it chose to abandon the criterion 'the legitimate uses of the sea' referred to in earlier proposals, in favour of a more precise standard. Accordingly, for purposes of activities in the economic zone, the use of the sea by third States would not have to be *legitimate* – a broader notion encompassing various issues other than those of formal legal validity – but *lawful* in terms of being a valid act by virtue of the rules and principles of international law.

---

[32] Appendix 1 of Annex II of the Statement of Activities of the Conference during its first and second sessions: UN Doc A/CONF. 62/L.8/Rev. 1, 17 October 1974, *UNCLOS, Official Records* (note 20), p. 93, at p. 107. For the Informal Working Papers on which these trends were based, see Papers No. 4, 9 August 1974; No. 4/Rev. 1, 24 August 1974; and No. 4/Rev. 2, 27 August 1974 in Platzöder, *Third United Nations Conference on the Law of the Sea: Documents*, New York, 1982, vol. iv, pp. 314, 332 and 354 respectively.

[33] See Appendix 1 of Annex II, *UNCLOS, Official Records* (note 20), p. 122; and Nandan and Rosenne (note 19), pp. 557–558.

[34] For the contribution made by this group, see Castañeda (note 18), pp. 611–618.

[35] See the Sixth Revised Paper, 24 April 1975, Platzöder, *Third United Nations Conference on the Law of the Sea: Documents*, New York, 1982, vol. iv, p. 209, at p. 211; Nandan and Rosenne (note 19), p. 558; and Castañeda (note 18), pp. 615–616.

Secondly, the uses of the sea in the economic zone had to be linked to the twin, core elements of navigation and communication. Paragraph 2 also provided that States 'shall have other rights and duties provided in this Convention'. The object of this clause was to reinforce the point that the rights of a coastal State in the economic zone were *sovereign* rights, and accordingly all those rights and matters over which a coastal State was unable to exercise any sovereign or jurisdictional rights by virtue of the provisions of the convention, were consequently traditional high seas rights exercisable by all States therein. It follows that by reminding coastal States that the rights in the zone were limited in scope and effect, the clause appeared in principle to strengthen the position of maritime States exercising their rights in the economic zones of coastal States.

It is interesting to contrast the Evensen text of 1975 with the approach adopted by the other two major groups, the Contact Group of 77 and the Group of Landlocked and Geographically Disadvantaged States. The two proposals submitted by the Group of 77 on the matter under scrutiny were different in three ways. First, the drafts of April and May 1975 preferred to maintain the criterion of 'legitimate uses of the sea'. Secondly, while both sets of proposals included clauses making the rights subject to provisions of the convention, the text of the Group of 77 eschewed any reference to other rights and duties of States in the zone provided in the convention. By so doing, the Group ensured that the rights of maritime States in the economic zones of coastal States would continue to remain on a relatively narrower platform.[36]

The third difference was to be found in Paragraph II of Draft Article 7 which provided that States shall have due regard to the rights and duties of the coastal State, and in particular to its security interests in the zone. In other respects, the Group's text was consistent with that of the Evensen Group proposal of April 1975. The proposals submitted by the Group of Landlocked and Geographically Disadvantaged States were similar to, as opposed to being identical with, the text proposed by the Group of 77.[37] Draft Article 3 not only reiterated the three basic freedoms in the economic zones of States, but also confirmed third States rights to the legitimate uses of the sea in the economic zones of coastal States. Similarly, the draft provision made all the rights in the economic zone subject to the provisions of the convention. There was no saving clause in favour of security interests of the coastal State.

---

[36] See the draft of 24 April and the Working Paper of May 1975 in Platzöder (note 35), p. 205, at p. 207, and p. 227, at p. 230 respectively; and Nandan and Rosenne (note 19), p. 558.
[37] See the proposals of 8 May 1975, Platzöder (note 35), p. 234, at p. 235.

When delegates adopted Article 47, paragraph 1 of the Informal Single Negotiating Text in 1975,[38] it was clear that they had come to prefer the formulation presented in Draft Article 3 of the Evensen text, but not in its entirety. The latter proposal was superior in the sense that it had clarified the criteria by which third State activities in the economic zones of coastal States could be judged, but what they lost in terms of a narrower notion of such permissible activities carried out by third States in the economic zones of coastal States by reference to the *lawfulness* as opposed to the *legitimacy* of activities, coastal States gained by a straightforward linking of such activities to navigation and communication. Importantly, although paragraph 1 did not expressly reiterate that 'States shall have other rights and duties provided for in this convention', the general sense of this clause was retained in the new paragraph 2 of draft Article 47 wherein certain high seas principles were incorporated, to wit, Draft Articles 74, 76 to 97; and Draft Articles 100 to 102. As a further precaution, reference was made to 'other pertinent rules of international law' which were made applicable to the economic zone 'in so far as they are not incompatible with the provisions of this part'. As Nandan and Rosenne observed: 'The purpose of paragraph 2 was to provide for the application of important elements of the regime of the high seas to those activities over which the coastal state was not entitled to exercise sovereign rights or exclusive jurisdiction.' This includes flag State jurisdiction, immunity of certain vessels and the rules of law relative to the slave trade.[39]

At the end of the Fourth Session in May 1976, the Conference adopted the Revised Single Negotiating Text,[40] and Draft Article 47 was renumbered as 46. While no textual changes were made to paragraph 1, paragraph 2 was streamlined. It transplanted the high seas regime on to the exclusive economic zone by reference, on the one hand, to a range of articles, namely Articles 77 to 103 (now Articles 88 to 115), making them applicable to the exclusive economic zone, and, on the other, by incorporating 'other pertinent rules of international law'.[41] In his introduction of Draft Article 46, the Chairman of the Second Committee reiterated the basic legal regime situation, that is to say,

---

[38] UN Doc. A/CONF. 62/WP.8, 7 May 1975, *Third United Nations Conference on the Law of the Sea, Official Records*, vol. iv, p. 137.

[39] Nandan and Rosenne (note 19), p. 559; and *Legislative History* (note 19), p. 90.

[40] UN Doc. A/CONF. 62/WP.8/Rev. I/Part I, 6 May 1976, *Third United Nations Conference on the Law of the Sea, Official Records*, vol. v, p. 125 at p. 151.

[41] Nandan and Rosenne (note 19), p. 560; and *Legislative History* (note 19), p. 93. It was inspired by an informal proposal submitted by the European Economic Community: *Legislative History* (note 19), p. 93.

that while all relevant rights to the resources of the economic zones belonged to the coastal State, maritime third States enjoyed the freedoms of navigation and communication therein.[42]

This, however, was not the end of the matter. Various States and groups of States continued, for different reasons, to be concerned about the scope of the 'miscellaneous' rights, that is rights other than the three basic freedoms specifically identified in Article 56, paragraph 1. Indeed, the concern was greater now that the 1975/6 Negotiating Texts had introduced a subtle restriction, namely, that all internationally lawful uses of the sea had to be related to either navigation or communication or both.

Accordingly, at the Fifth Session, held between August and September 1976, the Group of Landlocked and Geographically Disadvantaged States prepared several proposals and a working paper, Draft Article 6 of which confirmed the three basic rights of navigation, overflight and the laying of submarine cables and pipelines. While it agreed to accept the criterion 'internationally lawful uses of the sea', as adopted by Articles 47 and 46 of the two Negotiating Texts, the Landlocked and Geographically Disadvantaged Group proposed that the expression 'related to navigation and communication' be deleted, enabling, thereby, these disadvantaged States to exercise a relatively broader set of rights in the economic zones of coastal States.[43] Their cause for concern was predicated in a policy designed not only to preserve and maximise their traditional rights in international waters but also to continue to enjoy rights relating to natural resources in the economic zones of coastal States.[44] Zambia's proposal was based on similar considerations and interests.[45]

An unrelenting opponent of extensive rights in the economic zone, the Federal Republic of Germany submitted draft modifications for, *inter alia*, Article 46.[46] It attempted to modify the notion of 'other internationally lawful uses of the sea' by decoupling it from the three basic rights and then by linking it to the more general criterion of compatibility with the Charter of the United Nations and with other rules of international law. The intended effect was to make the miscellaneous rights 'freestanding', as it were, and thus as wide-ranging as possible. In other words, any use of the sea was permitted in the economic

---

[42] UN Doc. A/CONF. 62/WP.8/Rev. I/Part I, *UNCLOS, Official Records* (note 40), p. 153.

[43] See Nandan and Rosenne (note 19), p. 561. For the four sets of proposals seeking amendments to, *inter alia*, draft Article 46, see the papers of 14, 23, 25 and 26 August 1976: Platzöder (note 35), pp. 410–415.

[44] For a general view of the concern felt by this Group, see the Kampala Declaration of March 1974: UN Doc. A/CONF. 62/23, 2 May 1974, *UNCLOS, Official Records* (note 20), p. 3.

[45] Proposal of 18 August 1976: Platzöder (note 35), p. 408, at p. 409.

[46] Undated proposal: see Platzöder (note 35), p. 416.

zones of coastal States as long as it was consistent with international law and the Charter of the United Nations. The activity did not necessarily have to be connected either to navigation, overflight and/or the laying of submarine cables and pipelines. The German proposals also attempted to reinforce the fact that traditional high seas rights would be applicable in the economic zone insofar as the exercise thereof was not incompatible with the rights provided by the convention with respect to the economic zone.

A proposal identical to the German draft was submitted by Norway.[47] The European Community's informal proposal conveyed effectively the same message, namely that States must be allowed *all* internationally lawful uses of the sea in coastal States' economic zones, and not only those which were related to navigation and communication. Significantly, in the Community's draft there was no reference to validating criteria of rules of international law or the Charter.[48] On the other hand, the draft submitted by the United Arab Emirates confirmed that in addition to the three basic rights, third States enjoyed 'other generally recognized high seas uses related to navigation and communication in accordance with the principles embodied in the Charter of the United Nations and other rules of international law'.[49] Clearly, the Emirates' proposals reflected the concern that any miscellaneous rights must remain linked to the twin items of navigation and communication, seeking therefore to deny third States any *carte blanche* in the economic zones of coastal States.

At the Sixth Session in 1977, further efforts to maximise their rights in the economic zones of coastal States were made by the Group of Landlocked and Geographically Disadvantaged States. In substance, these attempts were similar to the Group's earlier proposals predicated on dissociating the miscellaneous rights, that is, the 'other internationally lawful uses of the sea', from navigation and communication.[50] Greece proposed the deletion of the words 'subject to the relevant provisions of the present Convention', the purpose of which was to reduce further the restrictive scope of draft Article 58. It thus intended to grant maritime States an unqualified right to exercise the three basic freedoms and all other internationally lawful uses of the sea.[51] The avowed intention

---

[47] Proposal of 18 July 1976: Platzöder, *Third United Nations Conference on the Law of the Sea: Documents*, New York, 1982, vol. xi, p. 566. See also the anonymous proposal of 14 September 1976: ibid (note 35), pp. 433–434.

[48] Undated proposal: Platzöder (note 35), p. 431, at p. 432.

[49] Proposal of 1 September 1976: see Platzöder (note 35), p. 433.

[50] See UN Doc. A/CONF. 62/C.2/L.97, 15 July 1977: Draft Article 8: *Third United Nations Conference on the Law of the Sea, Official Records*, vol. vii, p. 84. See also proposals of 28 June 1977: Platzöder (notes 35 and 50), p. 381 and p. 568, at pp. 383–384 and p. 569 respectively.

[51] Proposal of June 1977: Platzöder (note 35), p. 418.

of this draft amendment was, as Greece observed, 'to achieve a better balance between the rights of the coastal State and those of other States in the exclusive Economic Zone'.[52] At the same time, Germany's position on the matter remained unchanged.[53]

However, the fact is that the majority of States wished to see not less but even more restrictions, clarifications and qualifications in connection with the [miscellaneous] rights of maritime States in the economic zones of coastal States. Deliberating over these and other questions regarding the economic zone was the Castañeda-Vindenes Group. Insofar as its efforts were rewarded and its proposals accepted by the Conference as Draft Article 58 of the Informal Composite Negotiating Text, it will be appropriate to examine the Group's three drafts in order to appreciate how various considerations informed the evolution of that provision. In its first draft of 8 July 1977, the Group provided as follows:

> In the exclusive economic zone, all States, whether coastal or land-locked, enjoy, subject to the relevant provisions of the present convention, the freedoms referred to in article 76 of navigation and overflight and of the laying of submarine cables and pipelines, and other internationally lawful uses of the sea related to these freedoms or otherwise associated with navigation or communication, and compatible with the other provisions of this Convention.[54]

Three changes are noteworthy. First, the Group devised two categories of miscellaneous rights, as it were, the first of which was the 'related' rights category, already referred to above, that is, rights relative to the three basic freedoms of the high seas. The second category was an even more general omnibus class of rights, that is, a class in which fell all those rights 'otherwise associated' with navigation or communication, as opposed to being *directly related* to the three basic freedoms. In effect, this category was an omnibus class within another omnibus class of rights. Despite the difference between these two categories, the chief point of interest is that both categories were, in one way or the other, connected to the notions of navigation and communication.

Secondly, the expression 'and compatible with the other provisions of this Convention' was inserted to clarify the fact that the exercise of any of the related rights was subject to being consistent with the Convention and its provisions. It followed that any attempt to assert in the economic zone of a coastal State any high seas rights related to the three fundamental freedoms, would be disallowed

---

[52] Ibid.
[53] Undated Proposal 1977: Platzöder (note 35), p. 494.
[54] Ibid, p. 419, at p. 420.

if such an attempt were found to be in conflict with any of the other provisions of the Convention, and in particular Part V thereof, notwithstanding the fact that the rights asserted were permissible in terms of international law and the traditional rights of the high seas.

In other words, the coastal State would have a basis in law to preclude certain kinds of third State activity in its economic zone, namely activity which, although a lawful freedom of the high seas relative to navigation, overflight or the laying of submarine cables and pipelines, was inconsistent with other provisions of the Convention. Thus, the construction by maritime States of artificial islands and installations for purposes of laying submarine cables or for navigation and the like without the consent of the coastal State, although a permissible activity in the high seas, would be precluded in the economic zone of a coastal State. Such activity is inconsistent with the exclusive jurisdictional right of a coastal State to establish and use artificial islands in its economic zone as seen in Article 55, paragraph 1 (b) (i) and Article 60, paragraph 1; and the rights of a coastal State to exercise jurisdiction over, and to agree to, the delineation of the course of such submarine cables under Article 79.

The third change to Draft Article 46 constituted a reference to Draft Article 76 (now Article 87) which deals with a number of the freedoms of the high seas, but its scope was limited to the three relevant freedoms, namely navigation, overflight and the laying of submarine cables and pipelines. This partial incorporation of Article [87] ensured that the exercise of the three fundamental high seas rights in the economic zone of coastal States remained subject to the *general regime* of the economic zone as provided in draft Article 46 (now Article 58). While the second draft of 10 July repeated the clause dealing with the three basic freedoms, it also succeeded in refining the latter sections by stipulating:

> ... and other internationally lawful uses of the sea related to these freedoms or otherwise associated with the operation of ships, aircraft and submarine cables and pipelines, and compatible with the other provisions of this Convention.[55]

In this version of the draft provision, the Group attempted to narrow down the relatively wide-ranging nature of the rights devised by it in the draft submitted earlier by dispensing with the more general notions of navigation and communication, and by linking the 'associated rights' with a precise activity, that is, the operation of ships, aircraft and the laying of submarine cables and pipelines. At any rate, the third version, submitted two days later on 12 July, was worded thus:

> In the exclusive economic zone, all States, whether coastal or land-locked, enjoy, subject to the relevant provisions of the present Convention, the freedoms referred

---

[55] Ibid, p. 424, at p. 425.

to in article 76 of navigation and overflight and the laying of submarine cables and pipelines, and other internationally lawful uses of the sea related to these freedoms such as those associated with the operation of ships, aircraft and submarine cables and pipelines, and compatible with the other provisions of this Convention.[56]

It is argued by several commentators that the introduction by the US delegate of the clause exemplifying the rights in question was designed not to narrow but to broaden or to preserve the scope of the high seas rights.[57] This is to be seen in the substitution of the words 'navigation and communication' for 'the operation of ships, aircraft and submarine cables'. The Group also decided to delete the words 'or otherwise', substituting it for the phrase 'such as those'. The latter expression was preferred because it was relatively less vague than the term 'otherwise associated'. Even so, while some members of the Group were eager to be as specific as possible with respect to the extent of these 'associated' rights of maritime States, the use of the phrase 'such as' imparted an enumerative or illustrative quality to the provision: the phrase hinted at the fact that there were activities other than those identified in the provision, namely, those associated with the operation of ships, aircraft and submarine cables and pipelines which could also be carried out in the zone. They would, nevertheless, have to be related to navigation, overflight and the laying of submarine cables. In other words, despite the enumerative dimension introduced by the terms 'such as', and despite the reference to the operation of ships, the overall effect was that of restriction rather than expansion.

The Castañeda-Vindenes Group's proposals were incorporated in the 1977 Informal Composite Negotiating Text (ICNT)[58] as draft Article 58, paragraph 1, but the curtailed nature of the high seas freedoms of navigation, overflight and submarine cables and pipelines continued to be a source of concern for some States and their delegates. Hence in 1978 at the Seventh Session, the Federal Republic of Germany submitted a proposal which excluded all the descriptive text inserted by the Evensen and Castañeda texts following the words 'and other

---

[56] Ibid, p. 426; and see Nandan and Rosenne, (note 19), pp. 561–562. Oxman, who was US Representative and Deputy Chief of Delegation to the 1976 and 1977 sessions, argued, in a study of the 1976 sessions, for the 'elimination of the words "related to navigation and communication" from [Draft] Article 46 [so that it] would better reflect the actual result and reduce the possibilities for misunderstanding': see 'The Third United Nations Conference on the Law of the Sea: The 1976 New York Sessions', 71 (1977) *AJIL* 247, at p. 265. According to the Co-Chairman of the Castañeda-Vindenes Group, this text was proposed by the United States: *Legislative History* (note 19), p. 113, note 180. See also Rose, 'Naval Activity in the EEZ – Troubled Waters Ahead?', 39 (1990) *Naval Law Review* 67, at pp. 75–76, note 32.

[57] Galdorisi and Kaufman (note 20), pp. 271–273.

[58] UN Doc. A/CONF. 62 /WP.10: *Third United Nations Conference on the Law of the Sea, Official Records*, vol. viii, p. 1.

internationally lawful uses of the sea related to these freedoms'.[59] Quite clearly, Germany's aim was to enhance the scope of the three basic freedoms: maritime States would then have been able to claim unqualified and hence potentially wide-ranging rights in the exclusive economic zones of coastal States, provided always, of course, that the activities constituted internationally lawful uses of the sea.

Even so, some developing States continued to demand even more restrictions in the exclusive economic zones of coastal States. Brazil asked that an 'unambiguous provision' be added to the text of Article 58 which made it clear that military activities such as manoeuvres with the use of weapons and explosives should not be carried out in the zone without the consent of the coastal State.[60] The delegates of Congo and Somalia expressed similar views.[61] No different were the proposals of Peru the delegate of which Republic suggested that a new paragraph 2 be added to Article 58 which stipulated that foreign warships and military aircraft passing through the exclusive economic zone shall refrain from engaging in manoeuvres or using weapons without the consent of the coastal State.[62] Honduras proposed tightening up the freedoms of the high seas in the economic zones of coastal States. It proposed deleting reference to Article 87 in Draft Article 58, and, more importantly, the words 'such as'. This would have removed the illustrative/enumerative character of the associated rights and limited them strictly to the operation of ships, aircraft and the laying of submarine cables and pipelines.[63] In any event, both Peru and China argued that that more work needed to be done in order to iron out these difficulties.[64]

Despite the more liberal and expansive claims, only textual, as opposed to substantive, changes were made to the draft provisions at the time of the Eighth Session in 1979. During the Ninth Session in 1980, the Federal Republic of Germany continued to express its concern regarding the scope of the rights exercised by maritime States in the economic zones of coastal States. In the Plenary Meetings of the Conference, the German delegate sought to give a broad interpretation to these rights and stated that all 'States would continue to enjoy the high-seas rights of navigation and overflight, and all other lawful uses

---

[59] Proposal, Geneva Session, 1977, Platzöder (note 35), p. 494.
[60] See 53rd Meeting, Second Committee, 17 April 1978, *Third United Nations Conference on the Law of the Sea, Official Records*, vol. ix, p. 129, paragraphs 2, 3 and 4.
[61] Ibid, pp. 129–130, paragraphs 7 and 9 respectively.
[62] Informal Suggestion by Peru, UN Doc. C.2/ Informal Meeting/9, 27 April 1978, Platzöder, *Third United Nations Conference on the Law of the Sea: Documents*, New York, 1982, vol. v, p. 13, at p. 14; and see Nandan and Rosenne (note 19), p. 563.
[63] Refer to the Informal Suggestion by Honduras, UN Doc. C.2/Informal Meeting/28, 3 May 1978, and UN Doc. C.2/Informal Meeting/28/Corr.1, Platzöder (note 62), pp. 37–38.
[64] See 53rd Meeting (note 60), pp. 131–132, paragraphs 19 and 32, respectively.

of the sea not under such jurisdiction.'[65] This was a reference to resource-related rights and jurisdiction of the coastal State, but an interpretation not at one with paragraph 1 of Article 58. Yugoslavia, too, was troubled by possible restrictions in navigation in another State's exclusive economic zone, especially in certain kinds of international straits.[66]

In the final, that is Eleventh Session in March and September-December 1982, delegates once again raised the issue of the precise scope of the rights which third States were allowed to exercise in the economic zones of coastal States. Questions were raised not only at meetings but also by way of written communications. In the Plenary Meetings in March, both Pakistan[67] and Uruguay were animated by a policy predicated in asserting the prior interests of the coastal State in its economic zone. Uruguay insisted that the formulation of Draft Article 58 reflected attempts to accommodate various considerations and that the interpretation given to other provisions of Part V of the Convention must be in 'absolute harmony' with Articles 56 and 58. Any interpretation based on the view that the latter article did not cover all the internationally lawful uses of the sea connected with the freedoms recognised in that provision and compatible with the Convention, would give counter to the very concept of the exclusive economic zone.[68] Cape Verde's delegation referred to the freedoms of navigation and of 'international communication' given to maritime States in the economic zones of coastal States.[69] The records, however, show that both Bulgaria and Yugoslavia were inclined to adopt a more liberal position in this respect.[70]

---

[65] 135th Meeting, 25 August 1980, *Third United Nations Conference on the Law of the Sea, Official Records*, vol. xiv, p. 24, paragraph 59. See also the statement made by the Federal Republic of Germany, 10 March 1981: UN Doc. A/CONF. 62/WS/16, in ibid, p. 157, paragraphs 17 and 18. Somalia's concern, however, was that Article 58 might lead to the zone becoming part of the high seas and that, therefore, it ought to be re-worded so as to restore the juridical integrity of the doctrine in respect of that zone: 138th Meeting, 26 August 1980, ibid, p. 85, paragraph 71.

[66] See the statement made by the delegation of Yugoslavia, 2 October 1980, UN Doc. A/CONF. 62/W.S./11, ibid, p. 147.

[67] 161st Plenary Meeting, 31 March 1982, *Third United Nations Conference on the Law of the Sea, Official Records*, vol. xvi, p. 38, paragraph 100.

[68] 163rd Plenary Meeting, ibid, p. 54, paragraph 26.

[69] 188th Plenary Meeting, 7 December 1982, *Third United Nations Conference on the Law of the Sea, Official Records*, vol. xvii, p. 62, paragraph 126. See also the Brazilian delegate who repeated the views expressed earlier at the Seventh Session of the Third Conference in 1978: 187th Plenary Meeting, 7th December 1982, ibid, p. 40, paragraph 28.

[70] 186th Plenary Meeting, 6 December 1982, ibid, p. 29, paragraphs 66 and 67; and 189th Plenary Meeting, 8 December 1982, ibid, p. 68, paragraph 32, respectively. Yugoslavia made a similar statement which was annexed to a Note by the Secretariat, 18 February 1983: UN Doc. A/CONF. 62/WS/36, ibid, p. 227, at p. 236.

Nonetheless, it is of interest that in a joint letter communicated in April 1982 to the President of the Conference, Chile, Colombia, Ecuador and Peru asserted sovereignty and jurisdiction in the 200-mile economic zone, and referred to a fairer and more appropriate exploitation of the resources contained in coastal waters.[71] The delegates of Germany, Japan, France and the United States sought to contradict this assertion of sovereignty, and in identical letters to the President, they emphasised the fact that there was a fundamental balance between the rights and duties of coastal State jurisdiction.[72] In keeping with their earlier positions, these States once again asserted 'the high seas freedoms of navigation and overflight and of the laying of submarine cables and pipelines and other internationally lawful uses of the sea', but, predictably, failed to add the key concluding words which qualified and reduced the scope of these freedoms.

The provision which was finally adopted at the Montego Bay Conference in 1982 as Article 58 was substantially that which had been adopted in the Informal Composite Negotiating Text in 1977. Germany however continued to maintain its position even after the Convention had been concluded. Asserting its right of reply with regard to statements made by delegates as appended in a Note by the Secretariat in February 1983, the Federal Republic reiterated its interpretation of the limited nature of coastal States' rights in their respective economic zones, but this time it added that 'the notion of a 200-mile zone of general rights of sovereignty and jurisdiction of the coastal State cannot be sustained either in general international law or under relevant provisions of the Convention'.[73] Similar views were expressed by Italy and the United States.[74]

In terms of analysis, the following points are noteworthy. First, while the right, *inter alia*, of overflight in the economic zone of a coastal State is now embedded in the Convention, it is not only overflight alone which is guaranteed: maritime States also have the right to enjoy 'other internationally lawful uses of the sea related to these freedoms' in the economic zones of coastal States. However, and this is the second point, paragraph 1 also stipulates that these

---

[71] Letter dated 28 April 1982 to the President of the Conference, UN Doc. A/CONF. 62/L. 143: ibid, p. 249.

[72] Letters dated 24 September 1982 to the President of the Conference from Japan: UN Doc. A/CONF. 62/L.157; from Germany: UN Doc. A/CONF. 62/L.155; from the United States: UN Doc. A/CONF. 62/L.158; and from France: UN Doc. A/CONF. 62/L.159: ibid, pp. 223–224.

[73] Written Statement of 9 March 1983 in Note of the Secretariat, 25 April 1983: UN Doc. A/CONF. 62/WS/37 and ADD. 1 and 2: ibid, p. 240, at p. 241.

[74] Written Statement of 7 March 1983, ibid, pp. 241–242; and of March 1983, ibid, p. 243, at p. 244. Note that while in this letter the U.S. repeats the descriptive words 'related to these freedoms', it seeks, nevertheless, to maintain that these freedoms are quantitatively and qualitatively the same as those of the high seas.

freedoms are those which are associated with the operation of ships and aircraft, and it follows that all activity associated with air and sea navigation, as, for example, the safety of aerial navigation, weather prediction reconnaissance flights and aerial refuelling would also be included in the general right of overflight.

It was this clear restriction which, it seems, the United States of America wished to avoid. In its Declaration on the Exclusive Economic Zone, it provided a truncated understanding of the rights of maritime States.[75] Issued in 1983, the Declaration's last relevant paragraph provides an interesting modification to the words used in Article 58, paragraph 1. It states:

> Without prejudice to the sovereign rights and jurisdiction of the United States, the Exclusive Economic Zone remains an area beyond the territory and territorial sea of the United States in which all States enjoy the high seas freedom of navigation, overflight, the laying of submarine cables and pipelines and other internationally lawful uses of the sea.

By failing to add the closing clause 'such as those associated with the operation of ships, aircraft and submarine cables and pipelines', the United States purported, as a coastal State, to give, in effect, a broader range of rights to maritime States in its own economic zone but, by doing so, it also assumed broader rights for itself as a maritime State. Although it is true that for the United States these rights are based not in the Convention but in customary international law, the point of interest here is that the studied departure from the precise text of Article 58, paragraph 1 is evidence of the fact that Washington wished to escape the restrictive effect of the terms of the closing clause of that provision.

The chief merit however of drawing attention to this version of the freedoms of the economic zone lies in the fact that it nullifies the argument made by the former US delegate to the Third Conference, Mr. E. Richardson;[76] by Galdorisi and Kaufmann[77] and repeated by a number of other scholars such as Hayashi[78] and Sharma[79] that the insertion of the closing clause had the effect of broadening, as opposed to narrowing, the scope of Article 58, paragraph 1. The argument is that any kind of warship manoeuvre in the exclusive economic zone constitutes an aspect of the freedom of navigation. The point however is that a manoeuvre of this kind has less to do with navigation and more to do with military exercises,

---

[75] US President's Proclamation 5030, 10 March 1983; text in UN Division for Ocean Affairs and the Law of the Sea Office of Legal Affairs, *The Law of the Sea National Legislation and Exclusive Economic Zone*, USA, 1993, p. 392.

[76] *Supra* (note 6), pp. 572–574. Also see Oxman (note 6), p. 265.

[77] *Supra* (note 20), pp. 271–272.

[78] *Supra* (note 6), p. 128.

[79] *Supra* (note 8), p. 149.

and the development and perfection of naval strategy and to that extent it has little to do with the operation of ships *per se*. Similarly, where a military hydrograhic survey ship has for its object collecting data on, *inter alia*, the depth of water, configuration and nature of the bottom and direction and force of currents, the ultimate purpose of and motivation behind these operations is military, a fact which removes it from the scope of simple navigation and the like.[80] Despite its significance, this is not the main argument here.

Nor is what Richardson himself or the United States had *intended* to secure the main argument here. It is true of course that emphasis must be placed on what was actually *accomplished* by members of the Second Committee and on the agreed collective intention and accomplishment of the Committee: the fact is that the form of words finally agreed was seen by them as conveying a restricted scope of the traditional high seas freedoms. It is relevant that although scholars freely rely on Castañeda's article to claim such a broadening,[81] they forget also to note what he said in the same context and in the very next paragraph:

> The new provision [Richardson's compromise clause] does not imply, however, – as maritime powers pretended through earlier formulations – the adjudication in principle of residual rights in the exclusive economic zone to third States. The exemplification of the uses of the sea incorporated in the provision was restricted through its linkage to the originally envisaged freedoms as well as by their compatibility with other provisions of the Convention.[82]

Again, despite its signal importance, the argument made above is not the crux of the matter for present purposes. For the point in need of attention here is that had the Richardson initiative actually secured what it had intended to secure, namely the broadening of the scope of rights, then President Regan's Proclamation of 1983 would not have eschewed the clause which his delegate had so carefully proposed at the time of the negotiations.

Thirdly, whatever they may be, these relative or associated rights of overflight are required to be compatible with other provisions of the Convention: this means that if incompatible with the provisions of the Convention, they cannot be exercised or asserted as related rights or freedoms. Finally, the rights and duties enjoyed by all States, whether coastal or landlocked, are generally subject to the provisions of the Convention and hence the general and specific regimes established by it.

---

[80] On this, see the informative article by Bateman, 'Hydrographic Surveying in the EEZ: Differences and Overlaps with Marine Scientific Research', 29 (2005) *Marine Policy* 163.

[81] See, for example, Kwaitkowska (note 8), p. 249, note 3; Galdorisi and Kaufman (note 20), pp. 272–273; and Hayashi (note 6), p. 128.

[82] *Supra* (note 18), p. 622.

As far as the evolution of Article 58 is concerned it is easy to see that there was clear consensus amongst the majority of States that the three fundamental high seas freedoms of navigation, overflight and the laying of submarine cables ought fully in principle to be afforded to maritime States in the economic zones of coastal States. Moreover, the vast majority of States were abundantly conscious of the fact that these freedoms were vulnerable to abuse and were therefore in need of precise explication in order to obviate such abuse by the major maritime States. Accordingly, in the context of these two factors, the precise formulation of these freedoms led inevitably to a degree of curtailment and restriction of the latter. The implication is that the right of overflight in the economic zones of coastal States has to be seen as restrictively as possible. It may be added that there is little or no doubt that delegates to the Conference were not prepared to admit any addition to or expansion of the stated rights other than those carefully stipulated by the delegates in Article 58.

In the light of the above conclusions, it is possible to state that to the extent that aerial surveillance in the airspace over the economic zone of a coastal State does not strictly constitute overflight *simpliciter*; and to the extent that such surveillance does not constitute an internationally lawful use of the sea related to these freedoms such as those associated with the operation of aircraft, it would follow that aerial surveillance is not consistent with a strict reading of Article 58, paragraph 1 of the Convention. Clearly, aerial surveillance is not associated with the operation of the aircraft; it is in fact an activity which is dependent upon air navigation but is not integral to it and it does not accordingly fall within the scope of the freedoms allowed under paragraph 1 of Article 58 of the Convention. Accordingly, in terms of the question posed at the head of this section, a restrictive approach to the interpretation of the latter provision is warranted. In other words, the second part of the paragraph 1 must be seen as in fact a restrictive clause in the light of which it must be interpreted.

It would follow then that any aerial surveillance as described above would constitute a breach of the Convention. It would, however, be inappropriate to draw definitive conclusions simply on the basis of a textual interpretation of the Convention especially where other factors are also at play. The question which needs to be explored now is whether there are any other considerations and factors within or outwith the Convention which either reinforce this interpretation or which demonstrate that there is in fact no breach of the Convention. In addition to the scrutiny of some of the other relevant provisions of the Convention, this exploration will need to pay attention to certain key principles of international law. Thus, the first phase of this exploration is a discussion of certain provisions in Parts V and XVI of the Convention; and the second is a discussion of State practice.

IV. The Problem in the Light of Other
Relevant Provisions of the Convention

It will be useful to scrutinise a few provisions of the Convention with a view to discovering whether or not they have an effect or shed light on the scope of Article 58, paragraph 1. This approach is in fact a requirement of the article in question on account of the general savings clause inserted in the first half of paragraph 1 of Article 58, to wit, 'subject to the relevant provisions of this Convention'. In other words, the rights conferred on maritime States *vis-à-vis* coastal States in the economic zone have to be seen in the light of the relevant provisions of the Convention. Reference to these provisions will help to determine whether the rights given maritime States in the exclusive economic zones of coastal States are affected in any way. In this context, three provisions are of particular concern.

1. *Article 301 and the Use of Force*

One possible limitation or exception to the fundamental freedoms provided in Article 58, paragraph 1 is the set of provisions which collectively deals with the notions of use of armed force and the associated concept of peaceful purposes, namely Article 301, and Article 88 read with Article 58, paragraph 2. The gist of the query is whether the freedom of overflight conflicts with the rule which prohibits the threat or use of unlawful armed force and the obligation to reserve the high seas and the economic zone only for peaceful purposes. In other words, the investigation must focus on whether aerial surveillance effected by naval aircraft for purposes of defence-related intelligence is inconsistent with the requirement of refraining from the threat or use of armed force and of reserving the high seas for peaceful purposes. If so, the right of overflight in the airspace over the exclusive economic zone must be seen as having been being restricted to the extent of these provisions of the Convention. For ease of reference these articles are examined separately below. Article 301 of Part XVI provides as follows:

> In exercising their rights and performing their duties under the Convention, States Parties shall refrain from any threat or use of force against the territorial integrity or political independence of any State, or in any manner incompatible with principles of international law embodied in the Charter of the United Nations.

This provision, then, merely repeats a general rule found in customary international law and in Article 2, paragraph 4 of the Charter in particular, and places it in the context of activities of States carried out in the maritime sphere. While Article 301 is clearly inspired by the latter provision, the language employed in Article 301 is broader in scope than the Charter article.[83] Reference to the 'principles of international law embodied in the Charter of the United Nations' ensures that Article 51 of the Charter[84] is brought within the ambit of the clause, as are the principles of collective security and enforcement provided in Chapter VIII of the Charter; and the question for investigation here is whether aerial surveillance in the exclusive economic zones of coastal States violates this principle and constitutes an unlawful threat to the peace.

On the one hand, it appears doubtful whether aerial surveillance in the airspace over the exclusive economic zone can ordinarily be described as a threat or use of force. The gathering of information by military aircraft has an obvious element of defence and security for the subject State and the utility of such information in the event of use of such force is, in all the appropriate circumstances, a foregone conclusion. On the other hand, to equate the mere gathering of military intelligence by way of aerial surveillance with the threat or use of force is to expand this notion to unacceptable and indeed illogical limits.

Be that as it may, special attention must focus on the fact that modern electronic surveillance systems are based on highly advanced computer technology. This kind of surveillance involves 'far greater interference with the communication and defence systems of the targeted coastal State than any traditional passive intelligence gathering activities conducted from outside national territory'.[85] Surveillance operations, which involve the use of active signals intelligence, also known as SIGINT, are not only capable of intercepting naval radar, but are also capable of interfering with communications systems; they can be programmed to generate responses from the relevant installations in the coastal State.[86] It could thus be argued that SIGINT surveillance systems are relatively invasive and disruptive and that they accordingly pose a greater threat to the territorial integrity of the coastal State than the earlier more passive surveillance systems.

Nonetheless, even if it is true that in principle SIGINT operations are more invasive, it is better not to see them as being a direct threat and a consequential breach of Article 301 and Article 58, paragraph 1. The reason is that there are

---

[83] Rosenne and Sohn, *United Nations Convention on the Law of the Sea 1982 A Commentary*, Dordrecht, 1989, vol. v, p. 154.

[84] Ibid.

[85] Hayashi (note 6), p. 126; and p. 130. See in general Tetley (note 10), pp. 4–5; and Ball, 'Intelligence Collection Operations and EEZs: The Implications of New Technology', 28 (2004) *Marine Policy* 67.

[86] Electronic intelligence gathering systems and communications intelligence, also known as ELINT and COMINT, are all part of the electronic warfare and information warfare capabilities to which many States are turning and paying attention in terms of development: see Ball (note 85), *supra, passim*.

so many levels and kinds of interference and degrees of provocation in such operations that it is unrealistic to generalise in this manner. Moreover, there is a difference between electronic warfare in terms of sending 'Trojan horses' and batches of virus to targeted computer systems[87] and aerial surveillance by modern electronic means. Accordingly, SIGINT and other more invasive surveillance systems should be subjected to a case-by-case examination with a view to assessing whether or not there is a *bona fide* threat to the coastal State. The crucial point here is that if such a threat is in fact established then it will hardly matter whether the surveillance is carried out from the exclusive economic zone or from the high seas; for the primary rule of law will in fact be Article 2, paragraph 4 of the Charter with Article 301 of the Convention playing essentially a supplementary role.

If, of course, aerial surveillance constitutes a direct threat to the coastal State, as for example, where unarmed surveillance aircraft are escorted by fighter aircraft ready to fire upon any attempt to frustrate such aerial surveillance, not unlike the voyage of British naval vessels on 22 October 1946 in the *Corfu Channel* case,[88] there may be grounds for an argument that such acts conflict with the rule against the threat or use of force embodied in Article 301, and are thus excluded by Article 58, paragraph 1. However, aerial surveillance by unarmed naval aircraft does not of itself constitute a threat, either lawful or otherwise, of force. To that extent, it is relevant that the scope of Article 301 is interpreted strictly.

Nor is there anything in the drafting history of this provision to suggest that the intended scope was greater than that which actually appears from the text of the article. True it is that it had evolutionary links with Article 88,[89] which indeed has a problematic scope and is discussed presently, but the two were separated precisely because the geographical scope of the two draft articles was different. The legislative history shows that an early consensus was reached on the proposal submitted by Costa Rica in 1980;[90] and that at that time delegates were preoccupied with formulating the precise scope of application of the rule contained in the draft provision: in order to provide for a global application of this draft provision, it was proposed that all references to 'maritime zones'

---

[87] See Ball (note 85), p. 77.

[88] *ICJ Reports 1949*, p. 4. However, the Court held that there was no violation of Albanian sovereignty in the factual circumstances of the incident: pp. 30–32. On this, see Hayashi (note 6), p. 126.

[89] Nandan and Rosenne, *United Nations Convention on the Law of the Sea 1982 A Commentary*, vol. iii, Dordrecht, 1995, pp. 88–89. Cf. Rosenne and Sohn (note 83), p. 157.

[90] GP/1, 21 March 1980: see Platzöder, *Third United Nations Conference on the Law of the Sea: Documents*, vol. xii, New York, 1992, p. 297.

and 'ocean space' be deleted. The effect of this was that the prohibition of unlawful threat or use of force was extended to the performance of any right or duty under the Convention and not only in the maritime zones regulated by it.[91] There was also concern that Article 301 would have an impact on Article 19, paragraph 2, sub-paragraph (a) which provides that any activity is to be considered as being prejudicial to the peace, good order or security of the coastal State if it constitutes a threat or use of force against the sovereignty, territorial integrity or political independence of the coastal State or if it violates in any manner the principles of international law embodied in the Charter. A similar provision, namely Article 39, paragraph 1 (b) regarding transit passage was also seen as being affected.[92]

It is interesting however that sub-paragraph (c) of paragraph 2 of Article 19 was not seen as having any relevance although it is the case that it precludes any act aimed at collecting information to the prejudice of the defence or security of the coastal State in its territorial sea. Nor does the interpretive statement made by the Brazilian delegate shed great light on the matter. At the resumed Eleventh Session in 1982, Mr. Thompson-Flores stated that in his understanding of the draft provision, the rule applied particularly to rights exercised by other States in the maritime zones of States. 'In other words', he observed, 'we understand that the navigation facilities accorded third world countries within the exclusive economic zone cannot in any way be utilised for activities that imply the threat or use of force against the coastal State.'[93] Plainly, Brazil wished to equate the conduct of military activities with the notion of unlawful threat or use or force, an issue which it also raised in the context of Article 88 and the idea of peaceful purposes of the high seas. This is discussed below at the appropriate place. At this point it is relevant that Article 301 is quite clear in terms of its meaning, and accordingly it appears doubtful whether military activities *simpliciter* would constitute a breach thereof. For aerial surveillance to constitute a breach of this article, it must be shown that such activities were a definite threat to the territorial integrity or political independence of a State or against the principles of international law embodied under the Charter. That would not be easy to establish as far as traditional surveillance of military assets and capabilities is

---

[91] See generally the Reports of the President on the work of the informal plenary meeting of the Conference on general provisions: 29 March and 1 April 1980: Ninth Session, UN Doc. A/CONF. 62/L.53; and ibid, ADD. 1, 'Supplementary Report', *Third United Nations Conference on the Law of the Sea, Official Records*, vol. xiii, p. 87, at p. 89. See further Malaysia's Declaration upon ratification, 14 October 1996, paragraph 2: 33 (1997) *LOS Bulletin* 8.

[92] See Supplementary Report (note 92), p. 88.

[93] 187th Plenary Meeting, 7 December 1982, *UNCLOS, Official Records* (note 69), p. 40, paragraph 28.

concerned. While it is true that modern electronic intelligence and warfare systems are in principle capable of producing such a threat to a coastal State, it is also true that such a threat will need to be very carefully established. To that extent, then, Oxman was right when he observed that this provision would not seem to add anything to the existing obligations of States, except perhaps emphasis.[94]

2. *Article 88 and Article 58, paragraph 2: Peaceful Purposes*

Articles 88 and Article 58, paragraph 2 have relatively greater bearing on the matter. The former provision stipulates as follows:

> The high seas shall be reserved for peaceful purposes.

The latter provision states:

> Articles 88 to 115 and other pertinent rules of international law apply to the exclusive economic zone in so far as they are not incompatible with this Part.

Whether or not aerial surveillance can be admitted as a 'peaceful purpose' depends on the interpretation placed on that term. On the one hand, it is arguable that aerial surveillance is not a peaceful purpose insofar as it is a form of military or defence-related activity carried out by aircraft belonging to the armed forces of the maritime State. On the other hand, a number of States and scholars insist that the notion of peaceful purposes prohibits all *unlawful aggressive* activities; and accordingly any kind of activity carried out by the armed forces of a State on the high seas and the exclusive zone is lawful where it is not inconsistent with the terms of Article 2, paragraph 4 of the Charter. The argument is predicated on the fact that a distinction can safely be drawn between activities carried out by the armed forces which are unlawful in character and those which are not, and that Article 58, paragraph 2 and Article 88 do not refer to the latter but the former kind of activity.

Indeed, the entire legislative history of Article 88 is characterised by this dispute. Even the United Nations Sea-Bed Committee, as Nandan and Rosenne observe, had before it various documents relating to the theme of peaceful uses of the high seas.[95] In 1972, Ecuador, Peru and Panama submitted a joint working paper, draft Article 18 of which stipulated that the use of the international seas

---

[94]   *Supra* (note 8), p. 814; and also see Sharma (note 8), p. 149.

[95]   See Nandan and Rosenne (note 89), p. 88. Generally on the peaceful and military uses of economic zones, see the citations in notes 6, 8 and 10, *supra*. Generally also see Bourbonniere and Haeck, 'Military Aircraft and International Law Chicago Opus 3', 66 (2001) *Journal of Air Law and Commerce* 885; and Van Dyke (note 14), pp. 160–163.

shall be reserved for peaceful purposes.[96] Of course, it was the Third Conference in which the theme of peaceful purposes of the high seas bore fruit. Included by the Conference as one of the provisions in the 1974 Main Trends working paper[97] and adopted as draft Article 74 of the Informal Single Negotiating Text at the Third Session in 1975 with textual changes,[98] this draft provision became the focus of attention during the Fourth Session in 1976 when it was debated at length by delegates.

To the extent that these debates shed light on the essential meaning of Article 88, it will be useful to observe a few significant comments made by delegates to the Conference. The President, after recalling that the first reference to peaceful uses of ocean space and zones of peace and security were made in Resolution 2467 (XXIII) of the General Assembly in 1968, which established the Committee on the Peaceful Uses of the Sea-Bed and Ocean Floor, noted that it was clear that 'any treatment of the question of the "Peaceful Uses of the Ocean Space: zones of peace and security" could not be divorced from the international negotiations being undertaken in the field of disarmament or from other measures adopted by the United Nations to ensure that the arms race, and in particular nuclear competition, should not spread beyond the outer limit of a sea-bed zone which had been strictly defined'.[99] Peru pointed out that the mandate of the Conference was to work out, in addition to various aspects of the law of the sea, 'the activities that might affect the peace and security of States and the provisions reserving the international area of the sea-bed and high seas exclusively for peaceful purposes'.[100] Noting that the freedom of the high seas had served as a pretext for countless abuses throughout the centuries,

---

[96] See Draft Articles for Inclusion in a Convention on the Law of the Sea: Working Paper Submitted by Delegations of Ecuador, Panama and Peru (UN Doc. A/AC.138/SC.II/L.27), Report of Sub-Committee II, Annex II, Appendix V, in Report of the Committee on the Peaceful Uses of the Sea-Bed and the Ocean Floor Beyond the Limits of National Jurisdiction, vol. iii, United Nations, *General Assembly Official Records, 28th Session*, Supplement No. 21 (A/9021), 1973, p. 30, at p. 34; and further see Nandan and Rosenne (note 89), p. 88.

[97] Working Paper of the Second Committee: Statement of Activities A/CONF.62/L.8 Rev.1, 17 October 1974, *UNCLOS, Official Records*, (note 20), p. 93, at p. 130; see Provision 137, Formula C: ibid; and Nandan and Rosenne (note 89), p. 88.

[98] The term 'international sea' was substituted for the traditional 'high seas', for which see Nandan and Rosenne (note 89), p. 88; and for the text, see UN Doc. A/CONF. 62/WP.8/Part II, *UNCLOS, Official Records* (note 38), p. 152, at p. 164.

[99] 66th Plenary Meeting, 19 April 1976, Fourth Session, 1976, *UNCLOS, Official Records* (note 40), p. 54, paragraph 2.

[100] Ibid. On the ambiguity surrounding this refer to Auburn, 'The International Sea-Bed Area', 20 (1971) *ICLQ* 173, at pp. 189–190.

Mr Bakula decried the open deployment of naval forces and the installation of new military bases with all the dangers existent in the nuclear age.[101]

Mr Valencia Rodriguez of Ecuador stated in more categorical terms that the 'use of the ocean space for exclusively peaceful purposes must mean complete demilitarisation and the exclusion from it of all military activities'.[102] He added that the threat of use of force, and the establishment of military installations, fortifications, bases and facilities, as well as nuclear testing, had to be prohibited.[103] He referred to the position adopted by the 'great Powers' who sought to exempt all uses consistent with the purpose of fulfilling Charter obligations, and then argued that since disarmament questions had not achieved any success, it was appropriate to consider the problem at the Conference and to lay down clear and precise rules for the area in question.[104] Romania also made an explicit linkage of peaceful purposes with the establishment of denuclearised zones, the gradual expansion of which would eventually create a world in which relations between States would be based in mutual trust and understanding.[105]

Madagascar's delegate, Mr Rabetafika, made similar linkages, but added that he would combine the concept of the exclusive economic zone with the need of countries to defend their sovereignty and security.[106] Madagascar, he said, could not accept a situation where its sovereignty and security were subordinate to the defence interests of others, and where the rich countries used their technological superiority to weaken developing countries particularly in the political and military fields.[107] It was proposed that all preparations for violent conflict at sea should be banned and that the rule of peaceful uses should be applicable also to the superjacent airspace of all zones of peace.[108] While it generally agreed with measures aimed at strengthening international peace and security and also welcomed initiatives for establishing zones of peace and security, the Soviet Union adopted a position which would have left issues for discussions on ending the arms race to a disarmament conference.[109] In other words, while it agreed with certain developing States on the general issue of the demilitarisation

---

[101] 66th Plenary Meeting *UNCLOS, Official Records* (note 40), p. 55, paragraphs 9 and 10. Also see 67th Plenary Meeting, 23 April 1976, ibid, p. 56, at p. 63, paragraphs 87 and 88.

[102] 67th Plenary Meeting, 23 April 1976, ibid, p. 56, paragraph 2.

[103] Ibid.

[104] Ibid, paragraph 3. He also linked peaceful purposes with 'economic aggression' which involved the exploitation of cheap minerals from the deep-sea bed: ibid, paragraph 4.

[105] Ibid, p. 57, paragraph 9. See Iraq's statement, ibid, p. 59, paragraphs 42–45.

[106] Ibid, p. 57, paragraph 17.

[107] Ibid, paragraph 13.

[108] Ibid, paragraph 25.

[109] Ibid, pp. 58–59, paragraphs 35–41. For similar views, see Bulgaria, ibid, pp. 50–61, paragraphs 59–68.

of the seas, the Soviet Union did not accept that the Third UN Conference on the Law of the Sea was the appropriate forum to discuss that objective.

China's delegate, importantly, was concerned that the major powers, particularly the Soviet Union, were exploiting the freedoms of navigation, fishing and scientific research 'to send fleets speeding across every ocean to plunder the fishing resources of other countries and conduct espionage activities'.[110] He added that small and medium-sized countries were aware that in order to ensure peaceful uses of the oceans they would have 'to combat resolutely arms expansion, war preparations and maritime hegemonisation on the part of the super-Powers'.[111] He challenged the Soviet Union to pledge not to stage military manoeuvres in the economic zones of other countries and to discontinue its military espionage and spying activities carried out in the name of scientific research in the off-shore seas of other countries in order to prove that the themes of peace, *detente* and disarmament referred to by the Soviet delegate were not hypothetical or deceptive.[112] Malta expressed it views, cautiously treading as it did, between the need to consider the question of peaceful uses of the oceans under the banner of disarmament and the importance of reinforcing the need for peaceful and equitable uses and preservation of the marine environment.[113] Nonetheless, it observed that 'The major powers could therefore all subscribe to a commitment of the need for balanced military restraint in ocean space.'[114]

The United States, however, insisted that the term peaceful purposes did not preclude military activities generally; that it had consistently maintained that the conduct of military activities for peaceful purposes was in full accord with the UN Charter and international law, and that any specific limitation on military activities would require the negotiation of a detailed arms control agreement.[115] The observations made by the delegation from the United Arab Emirates was consistent with the view that peaceful uses of the ocean space precluded military activities, nuclear testing, missile experiments and the parading of maritime power.[116] The Philippine Government was in agreement with the United States on this matter,[117] despite the fact that it believed that zones of peace and security had an important role to play in promoting the prohibition of weapons of mass destruction, and that the general questions of disarmament and peace and

---

[110] Ibid, p. 60, paragraph 53.
[111] Ibid, paragraph 55.
[112] Ibid, p. 63, paragraph 90.
[113] Ibid, pp. 66–62, paragraphs 73–79.
[114] Ibid, p. 62, paragraph 62.
[115] Ibid, paragraph 81.
[116] 68th Plenary Meeting, 26 April 1976, ibid, p. 64, paragraph 4.
[117] Ibid, p. 65, paragraph 18.

security zones ought to be discussed in the context of the law of the sea.[118]

The Iranian delegate took the position that the 'non-civilian' aspects of the principle of peaceful purposes ought to be set out in detail in a more appropriate forum in order to decide whether peaceful purposes precluded offensive and aggressive activities or all military acts and manoeuvres; only a general reference was needed here in order to direct States to a new forum and to a more appropriate treaty.[119] However, he identified various principles relative to the peaceful uses of the oceans all of which involved limitations on non-civilian activities, including the rule which excluded all military installations from the economic zones of States and the principle of consent by coastal States for all foreign military activities in such zones.[120] While Pakistan spoke generally of the need for maritime nuclear disarmament and the prohibition of nuclear tests, it also referred to the duty of States to curtail their national programmes for the utilisation of ocean space for 'warlike purposes'.[121] The delegate from Pakistan added that the emplacement of installations in the economic zones of coastal States ought to be carried out only by way of consent of the latter.[122]

Somalia, too, was critical of military activities on the high seas. It did not hesitate to criticise the deployment of missile-bearing nuclear submarines on the high seas, and continued to emphasise the dangers posed by 'big-Power rivalries' and the establishment of naval bases at the cost of uprooting indigenous persons.[123] Tunisia sought to adopt a middle position by drawing out in general terms the complexities inherent in asking for the disarmament and demilitarisation of ocean spaces at the Conference.[124] Subsequently, an attempt was made to amend the proposals by adding a clause similar to the form of words inspired by, and used, in Article 2, paragraph 4 of the Charter, suggesting thereby that the use of unlawful force was prohibited on the high seas. This anonymous draft amendment, submitted in 1979 at the Eighth Resumed Session, was not accepted by the delegates.[125]

A similarly-worded attempt was made in 1980 at the Ninth Session by the delegates from Africa, Asia and Latin America,[126] and although the amendment

[118] Ibid, paragraph 16.
[119] Ibid, p. 66, paragraph 24.
[120] Ibid, paragraph 26.
[121] Ibid, p. 67, paragraphs 31–36.
[122] Ibid, paragraph 37.
[123] Ibid, p. 66, paragraphs 27–30.
[124] Ibid, p. 67, paragraphs 40–44.
[125] See Platzöder (note 35), p. 518; and Nandan and Rosenne (note 89), p. 89.
[126] See UN Doc. C.2/Informal Meeting/55, 20 March 1980, in Platzöder (note 62), p. 60; and Nandan and Rosenne (note 89), p. 89. The States making the proposal were Costa Rica, Ecuador, El Salvador, Pakistan, Peru, The Phillipines, Portugal, Senegal, Somalia and Uruguay.

was not admitted as an addition or modification to Article 88, 'it was later included as Article 301'.[127] Both attempts show that despite the division amongst States on the matter of interpretation of the term 'peaceful purposes', there was general agreement that the high seas could not be used for purposes of threat or use of any kind of unlawful armed force; but by separating the latter rule from the peaceful purposes regime, States seemed clearly to be suggesting that the notion of peaceful purposes, or demilitarisation and disarmament of the high seas and the exclusive economic zone, ought not to be conflated with the concept of threat or use of unlawful armed force.[128] The net effect of this is that the definitive Article 88 is shorn of any qualifying reference to the use of armed force or threat thereof.

It is obvious that the legislative history and subsequent events are not entirely conclusive of the matter, even if they clarify the issues and positions adopted by the States Parties to the Convention. At best, it could be argued that when States agreed to adopt this provision by way of consensus they maintained their respective positions on the matter. The majority of delegates were keen to link the idea of peaceful purposes with disarmament generally, and with the demilitarisation of the high seas. Importantly, if the developing States were unhappy with the use of military activities and exercises in the high seas, then, *a fortiori*, they would be equally, if not more, uncomfortable with such activities in their respective exclusive economic zones. It is true, of course, that the United States and other key States held out for an interpretation which would associate 'peaceful purposes' with the rule prohibiting unlawful threat or use of armed force, but this narrow interpretation was very much of a minority view.

Even so, the fact is that this minority view cannot be dismissed out of hand. This is so not only because States opponents to demilitarisation are/were the major maritime powers, especially the United States and the United Kingdom. Perhaps the main reason would be that demilitarisation and disarmament with respect to the high seas is a matter which could not have been disposed of in a one-clause article in a convention not germane to issues of demilitarisation. The fact of the matter is that any demilitarisation of the high seas can only be on the basis of elaborate rules as seen in a general multilateral treaty[129] or by way of further development and refinement of the relevant rules regarding military activities on the high seas, both *jus ad bellum* and *jus in bello*. In the

---

[127] Nandan and Rosenne (note 89), p. 90.

[128] Cf. Sharma who asserts that there was a consensus to the effect that 'peaceful purposes' did not connote the imposition of any legal obligation to use the 'oceans' only for non-military purposes: *supra* (note 8), p. 149.

[129] This indeed was the position maintained by the United States: refer to Rosenne and Sohn (note 83), pp. 89–91; and see Hayashi (note 6), p. 124.

former category lie rules of law dealing with, for example, the interception of vessels on the high seas authorised by the Security Council;[130] and with zones of international peace and cooperation. Two of these zones, located as they are in the Indian Ocean and South Atlantic,[131] deal with precisely the matters some Latin American, African and Asian States had raised during the debates at the Conference. It appears clear that if the activities prohibited by Article 88 were also those precluded in the zones of peace and security, then there was little reason to have instituted such regimes in the first place, especially the zone in the South Atlantic insofar as the constitutive resolution, namely Resolution 41/11 of 27 October 1986, was adopted by the General Assembly after the Convention was signed by plenipotentiaries in 1982.

In the *jus in bello* category are rules for example dealing with the establishment of exclusion zones, not unlike the ones maintained by the United Kingdom and the Argentina during the Falkland Islands war of 1982.[132] In sum, then, military activities on the high seas are not an uncommon phenomena; and this fact reinforces the view that great caution must be exercised before asserting that the peaceful purposes provision of the high seas applies to all kinds of military activities, both lawful and unlawful.

By the same token, it could also be argued that if the rule in Article 88 were intended only to apply to activities prohibited by law, that is, militarily aggressive activities on the high seas, than such a rule is in effect also supplied in Article 301, and there would seem to be little sense in repeating a provision already in place. However, only if a wider meaning were to be ascribed to Article 88, that is, all kinds of military activities, could it be seen as covering a matter not dealt with by Article 301, which admittedly refers to an unlawful use of force.

Be that as it may, another textual argument is based on a comparison of this text, namely Article 88 with Article 141 on the common heritage of mankind. 'The Area', it stipulates, 'shall be open to use exclusively for peaceful purposes by all States ...' The argument here is that the qualifier 'exclusively' was added to emphasise that all kinds of military activities, whether or not lawful, were

---

[130] Van Dyke (note 10), pp. 116–118.

[131] While the Indian Ocean Zone is one of Peace, the South Atlantic zone is known as the Zone of Peace and Cooperation. The Resolutions were adopted by the General Assembly: 2832 (XXVI) of 16 December 1971; and 41/11 of 22 October 1986.

[132] See generally UK Ministry of Defence, *Manual of the Law of Armed Conflict*, Oxford, 2004, p. 350; and p. 364; and Doswald-Beck (ed.), *The San Remo Manual on International Law Applied to Armed Conflict at Sea*, Cambridge, 1995, pp. 181–182. The exclusion zones established by the belligerent Parties were not without controversy: see Van Dyke (note 10), pp. 116–117.

prohibited in the deep sea bed area beyond national jurisdiction.[133] Nor is the subsequent interpretive history of any great utility. Indeed, all the familiar positions were reiterated by key States when they deposited their declarations upon ratification or signature. Thus it comes as no surprise to learn that Brazil,[134] Cape Verde,[135] India,[136] Pakistan,[137] Malaysia,[138] and Uruguay[139] asserted in their interpretive declarations their right to exclude foreign military exercises or manoeuvres, especially those involving the use of weapons or explosives without the consent of the coastal State in their respective exclusive economic zones. Similarly, national laws, which purport to prohibit foreign military activities and practices, including the 'collection of information' in the economic zone have been adopted by various States, including Iran.[140]

By contrast, the Federal Republic of Germany,[141] the Kingdom of Netherlands[142] and Italy[143] decided to assert their right to conduct military exercises in the economic zone of coastal States. Interestingly, however, Germany took the position that there was a need to balance the interests of the coastal State and the freedoms and rights of all other States.[144] A number of scholars have also sought to clarify the points raised above, and a majority of them have taken the position that the regime for peaceful purposes is intended to prohibit military activities, which are unlawful or aggressive in legal character. Nelson,[145] Oxman,[146] Churchill and Lowe,[147] Treves,[148] Boczek,[149] Francioni[150] and

---

[133] Nelson is somewhat equivocal on the matter: see 'Certain Aspects of the Legal Regime of the High Seas', in Dinstien (ed.), *International Law at a Time of Perplexity Essays in Honour of Shabtai Rosenne*, Dordrecht, 1988, p. 519, at p. 530, note 41. Cf. Nandan and Rosenne who ascribe no value to this clause apart from the harmonisation of different texts: (note 89), p. 90.

[134] Declaration of 22 December 1988: Annex II, 25 (1994) *LOS Bulletin* 11; and see Declaration upon signature: Article IV, ibid, p. 25.

[135] Declaration upon signature, 10 December 1982, Annex V, ibid, p. 26.

[136] Declaration upon ratification, 29 June 1995, paragraph (b), 29 (1995) *LOS Bulletin* 8.

[137] Declaration upon ratification, 4 February 1997, paragraph (iii), 34 (1997) *LOS Bulletin* 7.

[138] Declaration upon ratification, 14 October 1996, 33 (1997) *LOS Bulletin* 8, paragraph 3.

[139] Declaration upon signature, 10 December 1982, paragraph D, 25 (1994) *LOS Bulletin* 37.

[140] See Article 16 of the Act on the Marine Areas of Iran: 24 (1993) *LOS Bulletin* 10, at p. 14.

[141] See the Declaration upon accession, 14 October 1994, 26 (1995) *LOS Bulletin* 6, at p. 7.

[142] See the Declaration upon ratification, 28 June 1996, Annex II, paragraph 2, 32 (1996) *LOS Bulletin* 8.

[143] Declaration upon signature, 10 December 1982: third paragraph, 5 (1985) *LOS Bulletin* 15.

[144] Declaration (note 141), p. 7.

[145] *Supra* (note 133), p. 531.

[146] *Supra* (note 8), pp. 837–838.

[147] *The Law of the Sea* (Third edition), Manchester, 1999, p. 208; and p. 427.

[148] *Supra* (note 6), p. 904.

[149] *Supra* (note 8), pp. 457–458.

[150] See 'Peacetime, Military Activities and the New Law of the Sea', 18 (1985) *Cornell International Law Journal* 203, at pp. 221–225.

Hayashi[151] are among them. It appears therefore that some scholarly opinion is in favour of a right to carry out military activities on the high seas and the exclusive economic zones of coastal States, provided, of course, these activities are not otherwise inconsistent with the rule against the use or threat of force. If this is a correct reading of the law, it would appear, subject to the following, that aerial surveillance does not contravene Article 88 read with Article 58, paragraph 2 and that therefore these provisions do not in any way limit the right of overflight as provided in Article 58, paragraph 1.

Notwithstanding the above, and before final and definitive conclusions are drawn on the matter, it is important to be reminded of the fact that the rule of peaceful purposes and military activities on the high seas cannot be transplanted unchanged on to the regime of the exclusive economic zone for to do so would be to forget to apply the important closing clause of paragraph 2 of Article 58 set out above, that is, 'in so far as they are not incompatible with this Part . . .', the effect of which is to give priority to the regime of the exclusive economic zone as opposed to the high seas. In other words, it has the effect of qualifying the application of the high seas regime when it is transplanted on to the economic zone of a coastal State, and accordingly if any one or more of the freedoms provided in Articles 88 to 115 clash with the rights and obligations provided in Part V, then those stipulated in the latter will prevail. Such a qualifying clause was necessary to avoid conflicting rights. Hence, for example, the coastal State's exclusive right to establish artificial islands in its economic zone would have clashed with maritime States' high seas freedom to build such installations in the high seas and consequently also in the economic zones of a coastal State.

By virtue of this reasoning, then, the clause within paragraph 1 of Article 58 becomes relevant and operative. It will be recalled that the right of overflight in the airspace over the exclusive economic zone is restricted by the rule that all internationally lawful uses of the sea must be related to navigation, overflight and the laying of submarine cables and pipelines. The implication therefore is that even if lawful military activities are acceptable and consistent with Article 88, such activities when carried out in the exclusive economic zone of a coastal State are not lawful inasmuch as they are not directly related to the activity described as overflight. Aerial surveillance is not an activity which takes place for the sole purpose of traversing the airspace over the exclusive economic zone. Not only is it quite distinct from overflight, aerial surveillance is an activity not even *related* to it, and accordingly it is not an activity connected with the operation

---

[151] *Supra* (note 6), p. 136.

of aircraft. It is easy to see how different aerial surveillance is, say, from the provision of navigational aids and weather balloons. The conclusion therefore must be that even if the high seas freedom of military activities extends to carrying out aerial surveillance from the airspace over the high seas, the same freedom ends where the exclusive economic zone of the coastal State begins. In a word, finally in this respect, the peaceful purposes rule with respect to the high seas and the economic zones of coastal States does not reinforce or affect or enhance any supposed right to conduct military and defence related activities in the economic zones of coastal States.

3. *Article 300: Good Faith and Abuse of Right*

Article 300 is equally interesting. It provides:

> States Parties shall fulfil in good faith the obligations assumed under the Convention and they shall exercise the rights, jurisdiction and freedoms recognised therein in a manner which would not constitute an abuse of right.

The question here is whether the conduct of aerial surveillance by a State in the exclusive economic zone of a coastal State can be regarded as not being in good faith and an abuse of the right of overflight. If aerial surveillance in these circumstances constitutes the above, it will accordingly be an activity effectively precluded by Article 300. If this is so then, arguably, it would come within the ambit of the clause 'subject to the relevant principles of this Convention' and thus reinforce the view that aerial surveillance in the economic zone of coastal States is prohibited by Article 58, paragraph 1.

A brief look at these closely related doctrines will be useful. As far as the doctrine of good faith[152] is concerned, it is simply that States are under a duty to discharge their obligations in good faith as opposed to pursuing a course of action which constitutes evasion or modification of the obligation at variance with the object and purpose of the treaty or other binding arrangements. Eschewing a definition, Cheng describes the rule by reference to the incidents in which the rule is applicable, including the formation and performance of treaty obligations, the foremost obligation of which is *pacta sunt servanda*. Noting that this maxim is 'now an indispensable rule of international

---

[152] See generally Cheng, *General Principles of Law as Applied by International Courts and Tribunals*, London, 1953; Cambridge Reprint, 1994, Chapter 3; O'Connor, *Good Faith in International Law*, Aldershot, 1991; D'Amato, 'Good Faith', in Bernhardt (ed.), *Encyclopaedia of Public International Law*, vol. 7 (1984) 107; and Thirlway, 'The Law and Procedure of the International Court of Justice 1960–1989, Part One', 60 (1989) *BYIL* 3, *et seq.*

law', Cheng goes on to write that it 'is but an expression of the principle of good faith which above all signifies the keeping of faith, the pledged faith of nations as well as that of individuals'.[153] D'Amato takes the view that the law on the matter has developed in such a way that in general 'the uses to which the principle of good faith now seem to be applied include statements made publicly or in negotiations, or in the course of a judicial proceeding'.[154] Given the circumstances of the problem under study, there is no need to delve more deeply into this. It will suffice to note that if applied to the problem at hand, the analysis would be that the coastal State would be obliged to ensure that the right of overflight is not obstructed in ways which constitute an actual or effective breach of the *pacta* rule; and that the State must ensure that, as Sharma observed, it does not maintain double standards with respect to navigation and overflight.[155] At the same time, the maritime State must use the right of overflight for purposes for which it was given and that quite simply was for purposes of navigation and communication.

The doctrine of abuse of rights[156] is of relatively greater interest here. For Cheng, the 'theory' of abuse of rights 'is merely an application of [the principle of good faith] to the exercise of rights'.[157] Clearly then doctrines of good faith and abuse of rights are related. A well received rule of municipal law, especially in the civil law systems of Europe,[158] the doctrine of abuse of rights has, in the

---

[153] *Supra* (note 152), p. 113. Cf. O'Connor who works towards a definition which he provides at the end of the book: p. 124. With respect to *pacta sunt servanda*, see pp. 40–41; and p. 117 *et seq.*

[154] *Supra* (note 152), p. 109. Cf. Thirlway who has criticised this view based as it is in the judgment of the International Court of Justice, namely the *Nuclear Tests* cases: *ICJ Reports 1973*, pp. 99 and 135: see *supra* (note 152), pp. 8–17. For purposes of analysis, Thirlway develops the categories of good faith *lato sensu* and good faith *stricto sensu*.

[155] *Supra* (note 8), pp. 150–151.

[156] For literature on this, see Kiss, 'Abuse of Rights', in Bernhardt (ed.), *Encyclopaedia of Public International Law*, vol. i (1992), p. 4; Lauterpacht, *The Function of Law in the International Community*, Oxford, 1933 (Reprint, 1966), Chapter XIV; Brownlie (note 4), pp. 446–448; Fitzmaurice, 'The Law and Procedure of the International Court of Justice, 1954–1959 General Principles and Sources of International Law', 35 (1959) *BYIL* 183, at pp. 207–216; Cheng (note 152), Chapter 4, p. 121 *et seq.*; Schwarzenberger, 'Uses and Abuses of the "Abuse of Rights" in International Law', 42 (1957) *Grotius Transactions* 147; Iluyomade, 'The Scope and Content of a Complaint of Abuse of Rights in International Law', 16 *Harvard International Law Journal* 47; Oppenheim/Lauterpacht (note 4), pp. 345–347; and Paul, 'The Abuse of Rights and Bona Fides in International Law', 28 (1977) *Österreichische Zeitschrift Für Öffentliches Recht und Völkerrecht* 107.

[157] *Supra* (note 152), p. 121.

[158] See generally Paul (note 156), pp. 119–121; and Gutteridge, 'Abuse of Rights', 5 (1933–1935) *CLJ* 22, at pp. 30–42. Brownlie refers to Article 1912 of the Mexican Civil Code: (note 4), pp. 447; this has point in view of the fact that it was the Mexican delegate at the Third UN Conference who introduced a version of this article in 1978, on which see further below.

opinion of some writers, consolidated itself in the corpus of international law by virtue of its standing as a 'general principle of law recognized by civilized nations' in accordance with Article 38, paragraph 1(c) of the Statute of the International Court of Justice.[159] The basic concept is easy to appreciate. A State ought not to exercise its legitimate rights in such a manner where it impairs the enjoyment and exercise of the rights of other States or where it causes harm and injury to that State. In *U.S. Nationals in Morocco*, the International Court of Justice was concerned with the authority of the customs department in the French zone to fix the valuation of imported U.S. goods on the basis of certain criteria. 'The power', it held, 'of making the valuation rests with the Customs authorities, but it is a power which must be exercised reasonably and in good faith'.[160] *Sic utere jure tuo ut alienum non laedas.*

There are several conditions for establishing an abuse of right. In the first place, the conduct in question must be attributable to a State, an arm of government or agency representing the State.[161] This is a feature of fundamental significance and it is therefore hardly debatable. Secondly, the right to exercise a power and authority must be based in law, whether international or municipal; this is the case even if there is discretion to act. Consequently, an act must, in formal terms, be a lawful act: it is when a lawful act constitutes an exercise of a right or power which is an abuse of such a right or power, that it becomes an unlawful act, not in formal terms but in terms of essential validity. Acts which are *ab initio* void because they breach the terms of the law on the basis of which they are vested in a State are thus not included in this notion of abuse of right. As Kiss observed: 'A clear violation of an existing specific obligation cannot constitute an abuse of right, since in such a case the State which acted had no

---

Refer also to Iluyomade (note 156), pp. 55–61; and Lauterpacht (note 156), pp. 290–297; cf. Schwarzenberger (note 156), p. 148.

[159] Oppenheim/Lauterpacht (note 4), pp. 346–347; Iluyomade (note 156), p. 53; and Brownlie (note 4), pp. 447–448. See also the 1953 International Law Commission Report to the General Assembly, 1953 *Yrbk ILC*, vol. ii, p. 200, at p. 219. See also Garcia Amador, Fifth Report on State Responsibility: 1960 *Yrbk ILC*, vol. ii, p. 41, at p. 58. For a cautious approach to this principle, see Fitzmaurice (note 156), pp. 210–216; and 'The Law and Practice of the International Court of Justice, 1951–1954: General Principles and Sources of Law', 30 (1953) *BYIL* 1, at pp. 53–54. Included among the sceptics are Schwarzenberger (note 156); and Verzijl, *International Law in Historical Perspective*, vol. i: *General Subjects*, Leiden, 1968, pp. 316–320.

[160] *ICJ Reports 1952*, p. 176, at p. 212. In the *Anglo-Norwegian Fisheries* case, the Court held that Norway's delimitation in its traditional fishing areas, particularly Lopphavet, was based in the vital needs of the population attested by ancient and peaceful usage; and that the delimitation appeared to have been kept within the bounds of what was moderate and reasonable: *ICJ Reports 1951*, p. 116 at p. 142. On good faith, generally, see Schwarzenberger, 'The Fundamental Principles of International Law', 87 (1955, I) *Hague Recueil des cours* 13, at pp. 290–326.

[161] See Iluyomade (note 156), pp. 74–75.

right at all. There should thus be no confusion between abuse of rights and situations where a State acts *ultra vires*, since in the latter case it has exceeded the limits of its rights, i.e., it has no right at all.'[162]

Thirdly, and this is central to the entire notion, the act must constitute an abuse, or to put it another way, it must constitute an abusive exercise of power or right. A claim of abuse has to be addressed in terms of law and by reference to legal criteria, and they branch into two categories: subjective and objective criteria.[163] In the former category, abuse is based in considerations generally of a state of mind, and intention in particular. Thus there is an abuse of right where the right is exercised with *mala fide* intentions or an intention to cause injury or to create a deprivation of benefits accruing to the affected State without contravening the law.[164] In *Barcelona Traction*, it was Belgium's contention that Spain had abused its power by depriving ownership and control of stocks held by Belgian nationals in Barcelona Traction by facilitating the transfer of such property into the hands of a private Spanish group. The abuse was thus based in implementing its *mala fide* intentions to cause injury to Belgian nationals.[165]

Where objective criteria are relied on to establish abuse, the State claiming such conduct can be expected to demonstrate certain empirical facts and legal considerations, arising out of, or attending the exercise of that right. The emphasis here is on establishing abuse by reference to legal and factual standards and criteria, which once evidenced, would characterise that exercise as abusive. One approach is a simple showing of excess in the exercise of a lawful right: where the State acts unreasonably by accepted standards, or where it exceeds the lawful limits of or meaning of a particular right, it violates a rule of international law which obliges all States to remain within the defined or even undefined, but ascertainable limits, of that right, the result of which constitutes an abuse of right.[166]

---

[162] *Supra* (note 156), p. 5; and Iluyomade (note 156), pp. 47–49. Further, see Jiménez de Aréchaga, 'International Responsibility', in Sorensen (ed.), *Manual of Public International Law*, 1968, London, p. 533, at p. 540; and Fitzmaurice, 'The Law and Procedure of the International Court of Justice: General Principles and Substantive Law', 27 (1950) *BYIL* 1, at pp. 12–14. Cf. Verzijl who enquires 'what advantage is there in, and what reasonable ground is there for, explaining such a situation by the logical *détour* of first postulating for them a positive right to act and of then denouncing the exercise of that right to act as they do, under positive international law?'. See *supra* (note 159), p. 318. In the *Nottebohm* case, Judge Read observed in his dissent: 'Abuse of right is based on the assumption that there is a right to be abused.' See *ICJ Reports 1955*, p. 4, at p. 370.

[163] On this and related aspects, see Gutteridge (note 158), p. 25 *et seq.*

[164] On this and the notion of bad faith, see Taylor, 'The Content of the Rule against Abuse of Rights in International Law', 46 (1972–1973) *BYIL* 323, at pp. 333–336.

[165] *ICJ Reports 1970*, p. 3, at p. 17. See also Iluyomade (note 156), pp. 66–71.

[166] See Ago's Second Report on State Responsibility (1970): 1970 *Yrbk ILC*, vol. ii, p. 177, at p. 193. Further, see Iluyomade (note 156), pp. 73–74.

Finally, there must be evidence of some damage, injury or deprivation of an advantage lawfully due to a State or to private individuals whose cause it may decide to espouse against the acting State. The injury may be a direct result of the measure where it is effected for that purpose. The injury may also be caused by measures taken more generally but with a view to inflicting damage on another party, not unlike the facts in *Oscar Chinn*.[167] As Judge Read observed in his dissent in *Nottebohm*: 'The doctrine of abuse of right cannot be invoked by one unless the State which is admittedly exercising its right under international law causes damage to the State invoking the doctrine.'[168]

This brief review demonstrates that the essential idea behind the doctrine is to ensure that a right or power vested in a State is exercised in a manner which precludes the occurrence of any kind of disadvantage, seen in the widest sense of the word, to other States or private individuals, both natural and legal, claiming through them. Interestingly, however, the records of the Third Conference show that the scope of this article was determined by considerations which addressed rather broader issues. The emphasis in the formative phase was placed on precluding any kind of activity by a State which abused the rights of other States as well as its own rights. This consideration was grounded in the anxiety felt by certain developing States that the more assertive maritime States, who had actively resisted the expansive approach to maritime rights, would attempt to frustrate the latter in order to weaken the new regime.

When it was introduced by Mexico in 1978 at the Seventh Session, the provision was formulated in order to preclude the exercise of rights and jurisdiction 'in such a way that they do not unnecessarily or arbitrarily harm the rights of other States or the interests of the community as a whole'.[169] Thus, what was envisaged initially and generally accepted by delegate Parties[170] was the prohibition of any exercise of rights which prejudiced the rights of other States in an unnecessary or arbitrary fashion. In other words, the key notion, as urged by Mexico, was the occurrence of some harm to the rights of other States.

---

[167] *PCIJ Reports Series A/B*, No. 63 (1934), p. 65, on which see Iluyomade (note 156), pp. 75–76.

[168] *ICJ Reports 1955*, p. 4, at p. 370.

[169] See Mexico: draft article 1, 5 May 1978: UN Doc. A/CONF. 62/L.25 in *UNCLOS, Official Records* (note 60), p. 182.

[170] 'The idea of including in the Convention a provision on the notion of abuse of rights was accepted without objection.' This citation appears on p. 119 of the Report to the Plenary by the Chairman: Results of the Work of the Negotiating Group on Item (5) of Document UN Doc. A/CONF. 62/62: Reports of the Committees and Negotiating Groups on Negotiations at the Seventh Session Contained in a Single Document both for Purposes of Record and for the Convenience of Delegates: 19 May 1978: UN Doc. A/CONF. 62/RCNG/1 in *Third United Nations Conference on the Law of the Sea Official Records*, vol. x, p. 13, at p. 117. See the statements of Turkey, Chile and Uruguay at the 98th Meeting, 15 May 1978, *UNCLOS, Official Records* (note 60), p. 42, paragraph 17; p. 44, paragraph 42 and p. 46, paragraph 72.

Importantly, while there was almost immediate consensus with respect to this provision, delegates at the Conference were determined to 'clarify whose rights were contemplated in the proposal'.[171] Hence, the President of the Conference pointed out in this Report that the acceptance of these provisions 'was on the understanding that the article on good faith and abuse of rights was to be interpreted as meaning that the abuse of rights was in relation to those of other States', that is third or maritime or non-coastal States.[172] As Rosenne and Sohn wrote: 'This presumably means the abuse of a State's own rights to the disadvantage of another State or States.'[173] In other words, the issue was to preclude an abuse of rights by a coastal State against the rights of maritime States. Even so, the fact is that the rule also applies *vice versa*. In a very real sense then this provision complements Article 58, paragraph 3 and Article 56, paragraph 2 of the Convention and Article 2 of the 1958 Convention on the High Seas[174] which, as Brownlie points out, is declaratory of customary international law.[175]

Before an analysis of the question at hand, namely whether aerial surveillance constitutes an abuse of right, is undertaken, a prefatory *caveat* is in order, predicated as it is in the inherent difficulties which abound not only in terms of meaning and content, but also whether and to what extent the notion of abuse of rights exists as positive law separate from the principle of good faith, especially in view of the fact that a plethora of rules are normally available to provide a basis for legal obligations. It is of interest that the International Court and its predecessor tribunal were always ready to proceed with a maximum degree of caution in the application of the rule signifying a heavy burden of proof. Accordingly, Article 300, despite the fact that it effectively entrenches the doctrine in the Convention, must be viewed and applied with circumspection. It would follow that in broad general terms, any allegation of abuse of rights and breach of good faith on the part of both coastal and maritime States would have to be viewed with caution. Indeed, they would be entitled to insist that insofar as abuse is not lightly to be presumed, the burden of that allegation would weigh heavily on the State alleging an abuse of right.

In any event, the criteria identified can be employed to determine whether aerial surveillance can in general be seen as an abusive exercise of right. The

---

[171] Report of the President on the work of the informal plenary meeting of the Conference on general provisions; and supplementary Report, 29 March/April 1980: UN Doc. A/CONF. 62/L.53 and Add 1, *UNCLOS, Official Records* (note 91), p. 87.

[172] Report of the President on the work of the informal plenary meeting of the conference on general provisions, 22 August 1980: UN Doc. A/CONF. 62/ L.58, *UNCLOS, Official Records*, (note 65), p. 128, at pp. 128–129.

[173] *Supra* (note 83), p. 151.

[174] There is a *confer* reference to these articles in Nandan and Rosenne (note 83), p. 151, note 1.

[175] Brownlie, *Basic Documents in International Law* (Third edition), Oxford, 1983, p. 85.

first two criteria present no problems. The acts in question are those which are normally carried out by different branches of the armed forces of a State; and clearly there is a right of overflight vested in maritime States by an instrument of international law, that is the Convention, as well as by principles of customary international law. The third element is that of an abusive exercise of power by reference to subjective and objective criteria. As far as the former category is concerned, it is the case that while *mala fide* intentions are normally difficult to establish, they will be even more difficult to establish with respect to aerial surveillance over the economic zone because the coastal State would have to show that surveillance was being carried out primarily for the purpose of causing injury to it or to deprive it of an advantage or a benefit. The main objective of surveillance is simply to gain military intelligence which may or may not be put to a variety of uses, including its use in the event of hostilities. It must be kept in mind that the ultimate objective of such data collection is not *normally* to inflict harm on the coastal State but to have the wherewithal to protect itself in the most efficient way possible. Of course, it cannot be ruled out that a maritime State will conduct aerial surveillance for the sole and exclusive purpose of causing direct or indirect tangible harm or injury in any way technically possible, but such kind of activity is rarely undertaken. Thus the element of *mala fide* intentions has little or no role to play here.

The objective element, however, is not as straightforward as the subjective. Here the standard of conduct is external to the maritime State in terms of its intentions or good faith; the abuse lies where it can be demonstrated that the conduct was objectively speaking excessive or of such a kind as to cause a deprivation of benefits and advantages or where it was inconsistent with the purpose of vesting that right or power. The test of illicit advantage does not appear to offer a solution to this problem. Where, as it usually is, the purpose of gaining an illicit advantage is to deprive the other State of benefits vested in it by way of rights based in law, or in contractual obligations or consistent State practice, then that deprivation may be an abuse of that right, as, for example, the legitimate expectation of utilising a compromissory clause in a treaty where it is calculated to deprive that State of its right and to acquire an advantage as a consequence of that deprivation. Issues of this kind were considered by Judge Anzilotti in his Dissenting Opinion in *Electricity Company of Sofia and Bulgaria (Preliminary Objection)*[176] where Belgium claimed abuse of rights when Bulgaria denounced the Convention on the Peaceful Settlement of Disputes thereby frustrating Belgium's intention to apply to the Permanent Court of international Justice.[177]

---

[176] *PCIJ Reports Series A/B*, No. 77, (1939), p. 64.
[177] See ibid, pp. 97–99 for observations he made in his dissent.

Here, there are no advantages or benefits which a coastal State can be described as having being deprived of in an illicit or abusive way. It cannot have had any legitimate expectations regarding the protection of its military secrets or defence capabilities. The onus of protection from such activity remains firmly on the subject State, constant vigilance being the only safeguard. In any event, the acquisition of military and defence intelligence even if it is a source of disadvantage to the coastal State is not necessarily an abusive or illicit act: deprivation of a right without more cannot be regarded as an abuse where the reasons, such as they are, for such deprivation is to acquire knowledge of defence matters and to factor that knowledge in its own defence policies.

Problems arise, however, where abusive conduct is based on a misuse of the right vested in it in terms of the object and purpose of the right. That the right of overflight is first and last a right of communication is not debateable. Records of the Third Conference show that the right of overflight was viewed and referred to as an aspect of communication. As a mode of aerial communication, the right of overflight sits easily in the company of other rights of communication, namely the right or freedom of maritime navigation and the right to lay submarine cables and pipelines. While pipelines allow for the flow of resources, cables facilitate the flow of communication. Arguably, then, where overflight is used not merely to communicate between two different zones of airspace, but to gather military information of the State whose exclusive economic zone is being traversed, it could be argued that such activity constitutes using that right for purposes other that those for which it was given to States as part of the overall 'package deal' of the Third UN Conference, and to that extent it is an abuse of the right of communication because not exercised either in good faith or with due regard to reasonableness or both. In this context, Judge Alvarez's Dissenting Opinion in the advisory opinion returned by the International Court in *Competence of the General Assembly Regarding Admission to the United Nations* is relevant for he wrote:

> The question whether in given circumstances, a State is or is not bound to exercise its rights, and in what way it must exercise them, depends upon the policy of that State, and policy is influenced by public opinion. But in no case may the exercise of these rights degenerate into a misuse of right. A State may remain within the limits of its rights – for instance, a right of passage – and yet may abuse this right if it takes advantage of the passage to obtain information on the natural resources, strategic bases, justification, etc., of the State through which the passage takes place.[178]

---

[178] *ICJ Reports 1950* p. 4, at p. 15; paragraph omitted. See also more generally his Separate Opinion in the *Anglo-Norwegian Fisheries* case (note 160), at pp. 149–153, and his dissent in the *Anglo-Iranian Oil Company* case: *ICJ Reports 1952*, p. 93; at pp. 128–134, especially pp. 133–134.

Thus a coastal State may be heard to argue that the right of overflight was vested in maritime States for purposes of facilitating aerial navigation and accordingly using the right to facilitate the collection of militarily sensitive information constitutes a breach of this right and contravenes Article 300.

This finally, has to be seen in the light of the last criterion, that is, there is no abuse in law if no significant harm or injury is shown to exist. Thus, if the gathering of military intelligence by way of aerial surveillance in the economic zone of a coastal State constitutes an abuse it must be demonstrated by evidence that such aerial surveillance was the cause of significant and actual harm thereto. This is predicated on the view that the main and ultimate purpose of gathering military intelligence is normally to strengthen the military capabilities of the maritime State by gaining knowledge of those of the subject State, and to that extent, the latter could be seen as having suffered damage. The fact, however, is that matters here are not as clear-cut as stated above.

It is arguable, on the one hand, that the acquisition of military intelligence falls primarily in the category of potential, not actual, harm; that it becomes real harm only where the intelligence is actually used in armed conflict to the detriment of the coastal State, and that because armed conflict does not take place in the vast majority of cases, the intelligence gained will not be put to use against it, leaving no injury to the subject State.

Secondly, there is a degree of remoteness in the harm caused by aerial surveillance. The fact is that data received from aerial surveillance has to be processed and examined in the context of a complex grid of interlocking facts of all kinds, including geopolitical conditions, integration of intelligence from other sources, decoy operation and third party involvement. Hence, it is unrealistically simplistic to maintain that mere surveillance equates to harm caused to the injured State.

Finally, and this flows from the point made above. The situation on the ground, as it were, is ever dynamic: in most cases defence capabilities are constantly evolving and the military state of affairs is never the same for long. Given this evolving defence and military profile, any military intelligence gathered will, almost certainly, be out of date sooner or later. Accordingly, it is problematic to take the view that aerial surveillance constitutes causing positive serious, harm to the coastal State. No matter how extensive it may become over a period of time, the database is only as complete as the last processing of information. Insofar as the picture available will cease at some point to be accurate, the notion of harm in this kind of situation is not only relative, but also short-lived. On this view, then, any application of the doctrine and, more specifically Article 300, will encounter problems based on an inability of showing serious positive harm caused by aerial surveillance carried out in the airspace over the economic zone.

On the other hand, it could also be argued that military intelligence may conceivably cause harm even in the absence of armed conflict. Thus, if military intelligence is passed on to a more hostile State, that alone may constitute harm; moreover, simple possession of detailed intelligence can cause harm by removing or reducing the diplomatic alternatives possessed by the subject State. Similarly, it also becomes real and actual harm where the modern active signals intelligence systems (SIGINT) used by the maritime State are so invasive, disruptive and provocative that the coastal State could be seen as having suffered harm. Moreover, it ought not to be overlooked that there is a cumulative aspect to this as well. The point here is that where aerial surveillance is an ongoing activity, the sheer magnitude of the intelligence creates actual harm because the information is always fresh and up to date.

Perhaps the most efficient way to view the matter is to adopt a case-by-case approach to the gathering of military intelligence, with the *caveat* that it must *in principle* be accepted that mere possession in the right circumstances can be seen as actual appreciable harm, but that the evidence showing harm must conclusively be established; in other words, the bar must be set high as possible as regards proof of actual harm.

V. The Problem in the Light of State Practice

Before definitive conclusions are drawn, it is important, indeed necessary, to evaluate the situation from the point of view of State practice. The merit in taking this approach is two-fold. In the first place, subsequent State practice is important because it sheds light on how a provision has been interpreted by contracting States after the conclusion of the treaty.[179] This is consistent with Article 31, paragraph 3 (b) of the Vienna Convention on the Law of Treaties. In the second place, an assessment of State practice provides an opportunity to consider whether or not the law on the matter has changed, the point here is that a rule of law, even where it is encapsulated in a multilateral treaty provision, can, over a period of time, be modified by contracting States by practice which is at a variance with the rule settled by them in the treaty, provided, however, that this practice is general as opposed to being particular, uniform as opposed to being characterised by great inconsistencies and variations, and is followed by States

---

[179] See Scovazzi (note 7), pp. 167–168; and Valencia and Akimoto, 'Guidelines for Navigation and Overflight in the Exclusive Economic Zone', 30 (2006) *Marine Policy* 704, at p. 706; Van Dyke (note 14) pp. 165–167; and Kwiatkowski (note 6), p. 204 *et seq.*

out of sense of conviction that the said practice is consistent with, or required or sanctioned by, international law. These, of course, are the recognised criteria for the formation of international custom.

The issue to be explored here is based on two alternative assumptions. If, on the one hand, the position taken is that non consensual aerial surveillance in the airspace over the exclusive economic zone of coastal States by military aircraft belonging to maritime States is an activity which is permitted by, or is not inconsistent with, the provisions of the relevant provisions of the Convention, namely Article 58, paragraph 1, then evidence of the existence of such activity would simply reinforce the point that this interpretation was, or is, the correct one in law, provided also that such activity does not encounter protest by affected States.

If, however, as it is argued here, the Convention does not sanction such activity, then the existence of aerial surveillance in the economic zones of coastal States would tend to suggest that the law on the matter has in effect undergone modification by members of the international community, provided that the requisite conditions of customary law formation are also established. Again, the existence of objections and protests will detract from the process of custom formation insofar as it will signify a lack of uniformity. Either way, if there is evidence of State practice which has endured for a reasonably long period of time, and is uniform and general in nature and is consistent with either one of the two assumptions, it would have to be conceded that military operations of the kind under study are not in breach of international law, the difference being that the threshold of State practice will be higher for the latter assumption rests on the contention of a change as opposed to an interpretation of existent law on the matter. The bar must in these circumstances be set as high as possible because allegations of change in the law cannot rest on facts and evidence which are not established as conclusively possible.

The facts suggest that there is considerable military activity of various kinds including surveillance in the exclusive economic zones of coastal States and in the airspace above such zones, both consensual and non consensual. Hayashi has gone on record by maintaining: 'All major maritime powers have been routinely conducting such activities without protest from the coastal State concerned, unless they become excessively provocative.'[180] The State taking a leading role in such activities and operations in terms of geographical extent and frequency is the United States of America. Evidence of this comes from many sources, one of which is the log of activities of the *USNS Bowditch*, a military survey ship of the United States. It was spotted in March 2001 in the exclusive economic zone

---

[180] *Supra* (note 6), p. 130.

just thirty miles off India's Nicobar Island. India issued a protest to Washington in March 2001.[181] Similarly, in the same month and year, the surveying activities of *HMS Scott* approximately 190 nautical miles off the Indian coast near Diu became the object of protest by the Indian Defence Minister.[182]

However, it is the demarche following the incident of 28 October 2001 which is particularly relevant. This happened when a South Korean naval patrol boat, having spotted the *Bowditch* approximately twenty six miles away from its coastline, approached the vessel and requested it to state its place of registration, its mission and points of origin and destination. The *Bowditch*, however, supplied only its place of registration/nationality. Subsequently, the United States Government asserted its alleged rights to the effect that military survey activities were an internationally lawful military use of the seas related to the high seas freedom of navigation in the [exclusive economic zone] guaranteed to all nations under international law and observed:

> However, we must emphasise that our military survey operations are consistent with international law and are conducted worldwide on that basis. In this regard, the United States has conducted military surveys in more than 85 different EEZs, without notice to or consent of the coastal states.[183]

The South Korean Government, however, took the position that such operations were not lawful and lodged a protest on the argument that the *Bowditch* had conducted them without prior Korean Governmental permission.[184]

Another incident is also noteworthy. On 1 April 2001, a mid-air collision took place between a US Naval propeller aircraft, the EP-3E Orion, and a Chinese F-8 fighter jet. It ended in the death of the pilot of the Chinese aircraft when it plunged into the South China Sea. The Orion, with a crew of eleven aboard, was carrying out electronic surveillance of a top military air base on Hanan Island whilst navigating the airspace over China's exclusive economic zone.[185] Importantly, the collision revealed the fact that the United States had regularly been carrying out aerial surveillance of Chinese military assets from

---

[181] Van Dyke, 'Military Ships and Planes Operating in the Exclusive Economic Zone of Another Country', 28 (2004) *Marine Policy* 29, at p. 34.

[182] Ibid.

[183] See the entry under 'Rights and Freedoms of International Community in Navigation and Other Maritime Rights ... US Military Survey Operations in East China Sea', 2001 *Digest of United States Practice in International Law* 698, at p. 699.

[184] Ibid, p. 698. See also Kim (note 14), p. 159 who takes a nuanced view of the problem and confines legally unacceptable activity to military manoeuvres and exercises where particularly weapons and explosives are used.

[185] See Donnelly (note 10), *passim*; and Murphy, 'State Jurisdiction and Jurisdictional Immunities Aerial Incident off the Coast of China', 95 (2001) *AJIL* 630. The US aircraft landed in distress but in eventual safety on Hainan Island.

the airspace over the Chinese exclusive economic zone[186] and according to some sources, the frequency of such surveillance flights is logged at about four hundred sorties a year.[187] Importantly, while the United States insisted that the operations were consistent with the Convention,[188] the Chinese Government argued that such surveillance activity was not legally acceptable.[189] Indeed, the regular 'tracking' of US naval reconnaissance aircraft by Chinese air force jets is a manifestation of Beijing's objection to such flights in its exclusive economic zone. Further incidents of US aerial surveillance activities in June, November and December 2002, resulted in more tracking by Chinese fighter aircraft and some 'close contact incidents' with a view to expressing its dissatisfaction.[190]

There are many reports of other incidents. In 1994, aircraft aboard the US *Kitty Hawk* dropped sonar devices in order to monitor a Chinese nuclear submarine off its coast in the Yellow Sea. This eventually led to a 'stand-off' with China which the latter maintained could have led to a military conflict.[191] Sharma gives an account of China's vessels carrying out live naval exercises in Vietnam's exclusive economic zone, followed by protests issued from Hanoi.[192] Ball and Valencia and Akimoto give respective accounts of the pursuit and firing by vessels belonging to the Japanese Coastguard in December 2001 at a 'North Korean spy ship' in its exclusive economic zone, approximately 150 nautical miles off the island of Amami-Oshima.[193] Beijing, too, was destined to suffer the presence of the *Bowditch* in its exclusive economic zone twice, in March 2001, when China asked it to leave its exclusive economic zone,[194] and then again in September 2002. Its response was expressed by way of harassment by its aircraft and patrol ships[195] and the adoption of legislation which now prohibits surveying and mapping activity

---

[186] Refer to the article carried by the web-site of the Chinese Embassy in the Republic of Zimbabwe, 16 August 2004, citing the point of view published by a Chinese scholar on 15 April 2001 entitled 'U.S. Seriously Violates International Law'. See paragraph 17.

[187] Van Dyke (note 181), p. 32.

[188] See US entry entitled 'Surveillance Activities and Emergency Landing by US Aircraft on Hainan Island, People's Republic of China', 2001 *Digest of United States Practice in International Law* 703.

[189] See Ren and Cheng, 'A Chinese Perspective', 29 (2005) *Marine Policy* 139 *et seq.*; Murphy (note 185), p. 631, note 4; and Chinese Embassy article (note 186), paragraphs 4 and 5. See also Van Dyke (note 181), p. 33 and Tetley (note 10), pp. 13–14, notes 38 and 39.

[190] See Van Dyke (note 181), p. 33.

[191] Song, 'Declarations and Statements with Respect to the 1982 UNCLOS: Potential Legal Disputes between the United States and China', 36 (2005) *ODIL* 261, at p. 275.

[192] *Supra* (note 8), p. 150.

[193] See respectively Ball (note 85), p. 76; and Valencia and Akimoto (note 179), p. 704. The ship subsequently sank in the exclusive economic zone of China after fleeing the Japanese coastguard attack.

[194] See Song (note 191), p. 277.

[195] Ibid; see also Van Dyke (note 181), p. 34; and Hayashi (note 6), p. 131.

in China's exclusive economic zone without its consent.[196] Van Dyke refers to reports of seventeen distinct incidents spread over the spring and summer of 2000 when Chinese naval vessels were allegedly gathering intelligence in Japan's economic zone. It is reported that Japan issued protests for such operations.[197] Further, Van Dyke gives an account of an incident which took place along the North Korean coast in March 2003 when four North Korean fighter jets intercepted a US unmanned reconnaissance aircraft and apparently tried to force it to land. After suspending such surveillance flights, the US resumed them after a few days.[198] Finally, in this context, in March 2009, five ships of the Chinese navy harassed the USNS *Impeccable*, a submarine surveillance vessel, as a form of protest against its presence seventy-five miles off the coast of Hainan Island.

It is accepted that there are, as Hayashi noted, many [non consensual] military intelligence gathering activities [both seaborne and airborne] against which coastal States have not issued protests. Ball's incisive survey into maritime intelligence gathering has shown that at least thirteen South East Asian States and Australia have wide-ranging maritime surveillance capabilities based in various kinds of aircraft.[199] Of course, the major maritime States also have these capabilities. It is tempting to argue that many of these coastal States do not have either the political will to issue protests or, where the surveillance is surreptitious, the knowledge of, and/or the resources to discover, such operations in their 200 nautical mile zones.

Notwithstanding the strength of these arguments, they must be marginalised in favour of the essential point, namely, that incontrovertible evidence of sufficient, adequate, reasonable and sustained protest and expressed resentment of such activities by a number of leading States in the developing world demonstrates that the crucial element of uniformity in State practice is absent. When this is viewed in the light of the fact that a good number of these States have proceeded at the national and international levels in ways which show without doubt that their understanding of the law is at a variance with the interpretation espoused by, say the United States, then the absence of uniformity becomes even more conspicuous. The national legislation of a number of contracting Parties, including Brazil, Uruguay, Pakistan, Burma, Cambodia, Haiti, Maldives, Portugal, Seychelles, Guyana, Mauritius, Nigeria, Cape Verde, Viet Nam, Yemen, and India is consistent with denying or severely restricting various kinds of non consensual military activities by maritime States in the

---

[196] Van Dyke (note 181), p. 34; and Hayashi (note 6), p. 131.

[197] Van Dyke (note 181), p. 34.

[198] Van Dyke (note 10), p. 120. According to Ball, they had made preparations to shoot it down: (note 85), p. 70.

[199] *Supra* (note 85), *passim*.

economic zones of coastal States;[200] and the declarations submitted by certain States while either ratifying or signing the Convention also indicate that their interpretation of the relevant provisions does not support a permissive approach to the issue.[201] Accordingly, the question whether the law has been modified by way of State practice cannot be answered in anything but negative terms.

A similar fate befalls the first assumption mentioned above, based as it is on Article 31, paragraph 3(b) of the Vienna Convention on the Law of Treaties. It must be concluded, that given the issuance of a steady stream of protests and the existence of national and international instruments at a variance with the permissive approach to the question, subsequent State practice is reasonably lacking in uniformity to shed light in positive terms on the proposition that aerial surveillance in the airspace of the economic zones of coastal States is consistent with international law. Moreover, the proceedings of senior officials and analysts of meetings held in Bali, Tokyo, Honolulu, Shanghai, and Tokyo in 2002, 2003, 2004, 2005 and 2006 on these and other issues showed clearly that while there was agreement on related issues, the main question under consideration was not graced by consensus.[202] Nor is the contention that State practice is, by and large, inconclusive, helpful for those who adhere to the permissive approach to the question. In the circumstances of the case, an interpretation based in giving full weight to the ordinary meaning of the text of paragraph 1 of Article 58 must be preferred, and the view taken here is that both the ordinary meaning and the legislative history supports the restrictive interpretation of the relevant article.

---

[200] See generally Juda, 'The Exclusive Economic Zone: Compatibility of National Claims and the UN Convention on the Law of the Sea', 16 (1986) *ODIL* 1, at pp. 31–38; Meyer, 'The Impact of the Exclusive Economic Zone on Naval Operations', 40 (1992) *Naval Law Review* 241, at pp. 248–249; Rose (note 56), pp. 79–81; Lowe (note 6), p. 180; Kwaitkowska (note 6), pp. 208–212 and Boczek (note 8), p. 452. Cf. Paolillo who notes that but for Brazil and Guatemala, there is in South and Central America a generally faithful reproduction of Article 58: *supra* (note 16), p. 112. Further see Alexander who observes that these kinds of claims have never been explicitly condoned or forbidden in the Convention: see 'Uncertainties in the Aftermath of UNCLOS III: The Case for Navigational Freedoms', 18 (1987) *ODIL* 333, at p. 336.

[201] See text to notes 134–139.

[202] Hayashi (note 6), p. 123; and also Valencia and Akimoto (note 179), p. 705. The delegates, or 'Participants in the Dialogue', who had come in their personal capacity, agreed a draft resolution, for which see p. 708. See also Djalal, Yankov and Bergin, 'Draft Guidelines for Military and Intelligence Gathering Activities in the EEZ and their Means and Manner of Implementation and Enforcement', 29 (2005) *Marine Policy* 175.

VI. CONCLUDING REMARKS

The above study has elicited a number of matters of legal interest which can be grouped in three distinct but overlapping categories. In the first place, there are matters of substantive concern; in the second there are issues relative to treaty interpretation and in the third lie questions concerning State practice. As far as the first category is concerned, the point of concern is that non consensual aerial surveillance by aircraft belonging to, or operated by or for, the armed forces of a maritime State in the airspace over the exclusive economic zone of coastal States has nearly always been a source of disputation between States. Acts of this kind fall in the general overall class of 'military activities or purposes', the point here being that some States have long-standing immutable policies predicated on carrying out certain kinds of military activities in two of the five maritime spaces, namely the high seas and the exclusive economic zone. These activities include weapons testing, naval manoeuvres, the placing of military devices and aerial surveillance.

There are several provisions in the Convention which make it amply clear that, unlike the Chicago Convention on International Civil Aviation, the UN Convention on the Law of the Sea applies to both merchantmen and men of war, although the latter does not contain rules on the conduct of naval warfare. The Convention contains a series of rules on different aspects of military activities carried out in maritime spaces during peacetime. Importantly, there are also several provisions which provide rights and duties for aircraft. However, the activity in question here, that is aerial surveillance as set out above, is not mentioned *expressis verbis* anywhere in the Convention and accordingly the rules regarding this activity have to be ferreted out by reference to the relevant provisions in the Convention. The main question regarding aerial surveillance is a simple one, that is, whether or not the Convention allows, or does not disallow such activity in the stated circumstances. While the answer is, in one sense, simple, it is, in another, quite complex.

The position taken in this study is that aerial surveillance for military and defence purposes where conducted in the airspace over the exclusive economic zone of a coastal State without its consent is an activity which is not sanctioned by the provisions of the Convention, and in particular by Article 58, paragraph 1. This position is based in a simple reading of this provision, albeit in a restrictive light. The irony is that the complexity, such as it is, arises not *despite*, but *because* of the simplicity of the phraseology of paragraph 1 of Article 58. The fact is that the terms used are ordinary everyday words, that is, words which, because they lack legal precision, are susceptible of being interpreted in diametrically opposite ways. Some scholars thus have argued that with the right of aerial navigation comes the right also to conduct aerial surveillance insofar as it is associated with normal overflight operations. Matters are compounded by the fact that some influential maritime States are able to project their views more successfully and extensively, leaving many coastal States on the backfoot, as it were, to maintain their positions.

Given this vexed interpretation, it becomes necessary to refer to the *travaux preparatoires*; but this is not the only reason to refer to the proceedings of the Third Conference. The truth is that many scholars have relied on the studies of other scholars and this has resulted in a slightly garbled analysis of the problem. Only an independent, impartial and back-to-basics examination of the proceedings can eke out the facts. The study undertaken above has demonstrated that the matter of military activities was a serious controversy between the developing coastal (as opposed to land-locked) States and the major maritime States and that the compromise finally sealed the debate shut. A careful scrutiny of the proceedings reveals the fact that while maritime States were assured of high seas freedoms in the economic zones of coastal States, these freedoms were not identical, qualitatively speaking, with the high seas freedoms exercised by maritime States in the high seas. This, in fact, was the essence of the compromise. Although the latter part of paragraph 1 may have *intended* to broaden the scope of the article, and even on a plain reading it is not readily clear how, it was in fact a gift to the opposing group because the plain words used were favourably qualified not at one but at two levels. In a word, whatever the intention may have been of the United States, the linking of the freedoms with the qualifying terms was enough for developing States to agree to the draft provision. The history of the provision, the positions taken by the two groups and the unfolding of the debates and progress of the various drafts shows that a restricted set of high seas freedoms were actually agreed by the Second Committee and subsequently/consequently by the Plenary.

Be that as it may, this study has also shown how difficult it is not only to make the law in a multilateral conference but also to interpret it after the convention has been concluded. Of course, where issues and principles of law are not very controversial and are well accepted, as for example the traditional freedoms of the high seas, consensus will be easy and simple; but where issues are complicated by, and subject to, wide-ranging differences, participating States will manage to achieve consensus, if they achieve anything at all, by way of agreement on the lowest common denominator. One way to achieve this is to agree to an absolute minimum, and to introduce textual changes to draft provisions which satisfy all participating States and groups. Thus in many highly contentious matters of principle, the tendency will be to avoid being very specific, for the higher the levels of generalisations, the greater the chances of securing some sort of agreement. The difficulty is that the agreed form of words may succeed only in disguising inner differences, and consequently, the moment the question of interpreting or applying the provisions of a convention materialises, the dichotomies leap to the surface, showing up the shallow consensus, and in fact making the law unworkable. The essential lesson therefore is that weak consensus begets weak law which in turn begets weak compliance.

Clearly, a rule or principle of law which falls at the first hurdle is a weak rule, but it is not a weakness inherent in the law; nor does it essentially lie in the text formulated by the draftsmen of the convention. The essential weakness lies in the fact that States, driven by stubborn policies, may be unable to reconcile themselves to the rule agreed and will at an opportune moment seek to interpret the convention in ways which serve those stubborn policies by exploiting the weakest aspects of the consensus and by doing so, distorting the consensus achieved by them.

This, in some ways, is what happened with respect to Article 58. Representing starkly differing views on the precise scope of the high seas freedoms in the exclusive economic zones of coastal States, the two main groups finally managed to settle the rule by agreeing a form of words which just about reached the lowest common denominator. The formulation of words was such that they met the approval of both sides, for it was agreed by the group favouring a restrictive approach that if the three relevant high seas freedoms were to be allowed, then that would have to be at the cost of restricting them in scope and operation by including appropriate qualifying language. The difficulty was that these words were also susceptible to two opposing meanings depending upon how the provision was interpreted. This of course is not a unique situation by any means, but the difficulty was complicated by the fact that the essential compromise, or the 'real agreement', became even more difficult to elicit as it became buried in layers of a selective approach to the legislative history of the provision and variant self serving State practice magnified by the degree of influence a State or States of the group was/were able to exercise in the international community.

It is this latter point which needs finally to be addressed. State practice is a valuable tool of interpretation of a vexed treaty provision insofar as it sheds light on the 'real' meaning of the text of the provision, but here, too, the intransigence of States and their diverse policies can and usually do create problems of interpretation and application of the law. Thus where the practice and legislation of States with respect to the issue in question is, by and large, at a variance with the provision in question, then these categories can begin to weaken the law, not least because variant State practice causes confusion with respect to the true meaning of the terms used. Of course where State practice is inconsistent with the relevant provision of the treaty, even if sufficiently uniform, it can perversely be seen as a positive development in the sense that the 'real meaning' can be seen in this uniform, albeit variant, treaty interpretation. Where the legislation of States is not uniform and where State practice is characterised by Parties taking objection to such legislation and practice, then the 'real' state of affairs may become even more difficult to fathom. Thus, States will not be able to rely only on practice and legislation as an aid to interpretation. It is this lack of uniformity in practice and legislation with respect to high seas freedoms in economic zones which makes interpretation that much more difficult. This lack of uniformity also makes it more difficult conclusively to prove that a new rule of customary international law has developed in this regard, a positive fact given the difficulty of proving *opinio juris* in the practice of States. In these circumstances, then, simple reliance on the original text appears to be the optimum way forward insofar as it represents, at least, a measure of agreement on how the relevant high seas freedoms were restricted by the UN Convention on the Law of the Sea.

Index